SNAKES OF EASTERN NORTH AMERICA

Carl H. Ernst

Department of Biology
George Mason University
Fairfax, Virginia 22030

Roger W. Barbour

Morgan School of Biological Sciences
University of Kentucky
Lexington, Kentucky 40506

George Mason University Press
Fairfax, Virginia

Copyright © 1989 by

George Mason University Press

4400 University Drive
Fairfax, VA 22030

Printed in the United States of America

British Cataloging in Publication Information Available

Distributed by arrangement with
University Publishing Associates, Inc.

4720 Boston Way
Lanham, MD 20706

3 Henrietta Street
London WC2E 8LU England

Library of Congress Cataloging-in-Publication Data

Ernst, Carl H.
Snakes of eastern North America / Carl H. Ernst, Roger W. Barbour.
p.   cm.
Includes index.
1. Snakes– –United States. 2. Snakes– –Canada, Eastern. 3. Reptiles–
–United States. 4. Reptiles– –Canada, Eastern. I. Barbour, Roger
William, 1919–   . II. Title.
QL666.O6E76   1989   88–34205 CIP
597.96'097– –dc19
ISBN 0–913969–24–9

(Corrected, Second Printing)

We dedicate this book to our children and grandchildren.

TABLE OF CONTENTS

TABLE OF CONTENTS

PREFACE

In 1957, Wright and Wright published their monumental multi-volumed treatise on the snakes of North America. Since then, no other such unifying publication has appeared on the snakes of eastern North America. We recognize the need for an up-to-date book, one to identify any snake from eastern North America and summarizing the information on its life history. We have attempted to do this, and have restricted the geographic range of this book to that portion of North America in which we are most familiar with its serpents, the area east of the boundary set by the Mississippi River to its juncture with the St. Croix River and thence, northwest to the western border of Ontario.

In this volume we are chiefly concerned with the ecology and ethology of snakes. We have attempted to present as complete a life history of each species as is possible in the light of present knowledge through 1986. When a topic is not mentioned in a species account, it is unknown. We provide physical descriptions that should suffice for identification of all species and subspecies, and we give enough details of classification to show relationships within the group (order Serpentes of the class Reptilia). Although we have ignored fossil species, we do include a section on fossil history when discussing each living species. As an aid to the understanding of scientific names, there is a glossary with pronunciations. We have attempted to use the currently accepted scientific names of all species and subspecies. Where we have deviated from this, we present reasons for acceptance or rejection of names. We follow the common names established in Collins et al. (1982).

In giving dimensions, we have kept to the metric system, except where the English system has been included in a quoted passage.

The literature of snakes is enormous. It includes hundreds of specialized papers on such topics as morphology, physiology and biochemistry. Our interests, however, lie principally in natural history; we have excluded technical papers that do not have a direct bearing on the life of the snake in the wild. This is especially true when discussing venoms, on which the literature may become totally confusing to one lacking the necessary biochemical background. Our discussions of venoms are general, and the literature cited likewise. Readers deeply interested in this topic are referred to the journal *Toxicon*. In the preparation of this book, we have examined nearly 2,000 original papers on snakes and have combined our own observations with pertinent parts of them. With few exceptions, we have listed only those articles and books that have appeared since 1955; older ones can be found listed in Wright and Wright (1962).

Our experience with snakes spans more than 60 years. Ernst has studied snakes and other reptiles for 30 years. Barbour has done research on snakes and other vertebrates for over 50 years, and his experience as a wildlife photographer spans 48 years. We and our students have made several collecting trips to various habitats in the eastern United States, seeking acquaintance with species we had not previously encountered in the field, and obtaining photographs. All photographs not otherwise credited are by Barbour.

A number of persons have contributed in various ways to the publication of this book. Roger Conant, Ronald J. Crombie, J. Whitfield Gibbons, C.J. McCoy, Roy W. McDiarmid and George R. Zug gave advice and encouragement. William H. Martin, Michael V. Plummer, Addison H. Wynn and Robert T. Zappalorti supplied data, or copies of their submitted manuscripts. Jan Endlich, Evelyn M. Ernst, M. Faith Kutnicki, Barbara Miller and Jay C. Shaffer helped with photography or illustrations. Ernst's students, Christopher W. Brown, Steve T. Elfers, Dale E. Fuller, Robert E. Furey, Steve W. Gotte, Arndt F. Laemmerzahl, Jeffrey E. Lovich, John F. McBreen, and James F. Snyder helped with the field collections and studies, and the following persons supplied specimens or photographs: Ted Borg, Christopher W. Brown, Stephen D. Busack, William A. Cox, Steve T. Elfers, Dale E. Fuller, J. Whitfield Gibbons, Ronald Goellner, Steve W. Gotte, George H. Grall, Sylvia Greenwald, Michael Hadley, James H. Harding, David Hild, James M. Hill, Tom R. Johnson, Richard B. King, Arndt F. Laemmerzahl, Jeffrey E. Lovich, Barry Mansell, John R. MacGregor, Ken R. Marion, C.J. McCoy, Paul E. Moler, Gregg W. North, Earl E. Possardt, Richard A. Seigel, Jay C. Shaffer, Addison H. Wynn, and Robert T. Zappalorti. Bonnie Contos, Maud Chasteen, Evelyn Ernst, Wendy Ghannam, Cathy Kennedy, Anne O'Malley, and Mary Roper patiently typed the many drafts of the manuscript.

INTRODUCTION

Snakes are fantastic creatures that have interested humans for a very long time. A snake was featured in one of the earliest written stories, the biblical account of Adam and Eve in the Garden of Eden. In it, the snake was depicted as evil, a reputation that still persists today. This is unfortunate since these animals are very shy and try to avoid humans. It is true that some are very dangerous, but the possibility of encountering a venomous snake is extremely low unless one is actually searching for it. The chance of being bitten by a venomous snake is less than that of being struck by lightning. Although they are called by many common names (snake, serpent, ophidian, culebra, schlangen, etc.), snakes come in only one shape and everyone recognizes them regardless of size, color, pattern, or origin. They have been the objects of more interest, study, and speculation than any other single group of reptiles, and probably more than all the other groups combined.

Together with lizards, amphisbaenids, turtles, crocodilians, and the tuatara, snakes constitute the vertebrate class Reptilia. Reptiles are ectotherms that have evolved walking limbs and —distinctively—a dry, scaly skin. They arose from the class Amphibia (limbed but moist-skinned animals) during the Pennsylvania Period, toward the close of the Paleozoic Era, and by rapid adaptive radiation became the dominant animals on earth during the Mesozoic Era. One of the reptilian groups gave rise to the birds, another to the mammals.

Reptiles were the first vertebrates adapted to life in dry places. It is true that amphibians can spend considerable time on land, but their eggs must be laid in water or damp places. The reptiles overcame this limitation by evolving a specialized egg, which has a calcareous or parchment-like shell that retards the loss of moisture. The egg also has embryonic membranes—amnion, chorion, and allantois—not found in amphibian eggs, as well as a yolk sac, containing nutrients. The amnion forms a fluid-filled compartment surrounding the embryo; the watery environment has been brought indoors, so to speak.

Other developments also contributed to freeing the reptiles from the water needs of amphibians. The scaly skin has few surface glands; that is, very little fluid is lost cutaneously. The well-developed lungs enable reptiles to acquire an ample oxygen supply, and modifications of the heart—incompletely four-chambered organ in most, completely four-chambered in crocodilians—have made the circulatory system more efficient, produced higher blood pressure, and led indirectly to the development of more efficient kidneys. Other important developments include the appearance of claws on the toes, the development of a palate separating the oral and nasal passages, and the evolution of a male copulatory organ, which allows internal fertilization.

Snakes belong to the subclass Lepidosauria, which is characterized by a diapsid skull—one with two temporal openings. Together with the lizards and amphisbaenians, they are members of the order Squamata, but are placed in their own suborder, Serpentes, with approximately 2700 species. In modern squamates the skull has been further modified from the ancestral diapsid form by the loss of the ventral bar closing the lower temporal fossa, thereby leaving only one temporal opening.

As a group, snakes are widely distributed, occupying suitable habitats on all continents except Antarctica and such islands as New Zealand, Greenland, and Ireland. They are most abundant in tropical countries, and become less abundant in the temperate regions to the north and south. In eastern North America, four families (one introduced, Typhlopidae) are represented by 58 species (Table 1).

Table 1. Composition of Snake Families Occurring in Eastern North America

Family	Genera	Species	Subspecies
Typhlopidae	1	1	0
Colubridae	23	50	95
Elapidae	1	1	0
Viperidae	3	6	10
Totals	28	58	105

These interesting creatures occupy a variety of habitats. Most are terrestrial, some are fossorial, burrowing beneath the surface; some arboreal, rarely coming down from the trees. Many are semiaquatic, and some live in the ocean and seldom come ashore. The snakes discussed in this book live in habitats varying from mangrove swamps and estuaries to freshwater lakes and streams, sand dunes, grasslands, and evergreen and deciduous forests. These habitats range in altitude from sea level to near the tops of the Appalachian Mountains, and in latitude from the Florida Keys to the Northwest Territory of Canada.

Snakes originated in the Jurassic Period, probably from lizard–like ancestors. The oldest known fossil snake is *Lapparentophis defrennei* from early Cretaceous deposits in Algeria (Rage, 1984); unfortunately, it gives few clues to the origin of snakes. A brief fossil history is given for each species of eastern North American snake.

Although they have undergone considerable adaptation to different habitats, snakes all possess certain characteristics in common. They are elongate reptiles with no apparent limbs or limb girdles. A few retain vestigial pelvic girdles and small spur–like remnants of hind limbs. The sternum is absent so all ribs are floating. The ear is much reduced; the external ear opening, tympanum, columella and eustachian tube are missing. Snakes cannot hear as do humans, but may instead "feel" vibrations from the ground.

Except in a few burrowing species, the eye is covered with a fixed transparent scale beneath which the eyeball moves; snakes have no upper or lower eyelids and cannot close the eyes. When the skin is shed, the transparent scale covering the eye is also shed, leaving the new one beneath exposed.

The tongue is long, protractile, and forked; within limits the individual forks can be controlled independently. It is used solely as an organ of taste and smell in conjunction with Jacobson's organ. Jacobson's organ, also known as the vomeronasal organ, is a large olfactory structure opening directly into the mouth. When the tongue is retracted, its tips are inserted into the openings of Jacobson's organ, thus inserting chemical particles from the air. Contrary to popular belief, the tongue is not a stinger or heat sensor. The touch of a snake's tongue is so gentle that it can barely be felt.

The construction of the jaws is quite distinctive. The halves of the lower jaw are attached to each other at the chin by an elastic ligament and attached to the cranium posteriorly by a loose double joint that allows them to be moved independently in nearly any direction. The upper jaws are also loosely attached to the cranium and capable of independent movement. In addition, the body is quite distensible since the ribs are free from the sternum; consequently, snakes can swallow prey substantially larger than their usual body diameter. When swallowing a larger animal, the snake merely "walks" its mouth around the prey by moving first one half of each jaw forward, then the other; it seems to literally crawl about its prey. The epiglottis is protrusible, and can be pushed under the prey during the swallowing process so the snake can breathe. The scales on a snake's head may be enlarged (Figs. 1–3), and their arrangements and the numbers of each may be used for identification. Also, the body scales may be either keeled (carinate, with a longitudinal ridge) or smooth (lacking a ridge), and the numbers of rows of dorsal scales at various points along the body may be distinctive (Fig. 4, but see Dowling, 1951a, and Kerfoot, 1969). Beneath, the belly scales (ventrals) are usually transversely elongated, and the scales underneath the tail (subcaudals) may occur in one or two rows. The number of ventrals and subcaudals are often used to separate confusing species. Ventrals are counted from the most anterior bordered on both sides by the first row of dorsal body scales and thence posteriorly to the anal plate (Dowling, 1951b). The anal plate covering the vent is single in some snakes, but subdivided into two scales in others.

The copulatory organ of male snakes is the hemipenis which lies in a cavity in the base of the tail that opens into the cloaca. A retractor muscle is attached to the tip of the hemipenis, connecting with a series of caudal vertebrae. Everted by turgidity, the hemipenis is turned inside out to protrude from the anal vent. It is traversed by a deep groove (sulcus spermaticus) on the outer surface, along which the sperm flows. The hemipenis may be single and columnar in appearance, or bifuricate with two distinct lobes, at least near the tip. The sex organ is quite ornamented, and may be adorned with spines, calyces or hooks, which serve to anchor it within the female's cloaca. Each taxon has its own hemipenial type and ornamentation, and the organ is very important in taxonomic analysis. Wright and Wright (1957) and Dowling and Savage (1960) have analyzed and illustrated the variations in hemipenial structure in North American snakes.

Another important taxonomic character is the karyotype, the normal diploid number of chromosomes found in each body cell not producing gametes. This number may vary between genera, and between species there may be variation in the position of the centromere. In the discussion of each species there is a summary of the knowledge of its karyotype, and we refer the reader to the references listed for more detailed information.

Marx and Rabb (1972) have prepared an analysis of 50 taxonomic characters of advanced snakes, and the reader is referred to this publication for a detailed discussion of the characters mentioned above and of others too numerous for us to have included in this brief introduction.

Snake populations have been decreasing at an alarming rate in the United States in recent years.

The exact causes of the decline are unknown, but a number of circumstances are suspected.

The general deterioration of the natural environment has eliminated large populations in certain regions. Swamps and marshes have been drained and woodlands cleared for additional farmland or for the construction of highways, housing developments, shopping centers, office complexes, and the like. Rivers have been dammed and low–lying woodlands and marshy ground flooded thus eliminating shallow water and terrestrial habitats. Many water bodies have become so badly polluted that snakes can no longer live in them.

Although there is little direct proof of their harmful effects on snakes, insecticides and herbicides probably contribute to the decrease in the numbers. Large quantities of chlorinated hydrocarbons (ingredients in many pesticides) surely are stored in the body fat in late summer and fall and could well cause the death of many snakes as they use this fat during hibernation.

The automobile has a detrimental effect: thousands of snakes are killed crossing highways each year. Many drivers even go out of their way to run over them.

Overcollecting is certainly a factor. The volume of the pet trade has resulted in the removal of many adults from the populations, and the gathering of eggs and juveniles reduces the rate of replacement of those adults left to die of natural causes. With their relatively slow rate of maturation, our snakes cannot withstand heavy cropping and still maintain their populations.

If snakes are to remain a conspicuous part of our fauna, we must initiate conservation measures. Although we do not yet know enough about their biology to formulate an adequate conservation plan, certain needs are obvious. The waterways and lands harboring important populations should be protected from undue human disturbance and pollution. The trend away from the use of the dangerous residual pesticides must be continued. States must pass and enforce legislation controlling the capture of these creatures in the wild, and definitely must ban snake "roundups."

Equally important: more people must become acquainted with the many fascinating aspects of snake biology. Such awareness should make people more interested in the protection of these shy creatures. The creation of such an attitude—not only toward snakes, but also toward our dwindling wildlife resources generally—is a major purpose of this book.

Finally, we want to stress that venomous snakes are dangerous. They should never be kept at home, and are best displayed in zoos or muse-

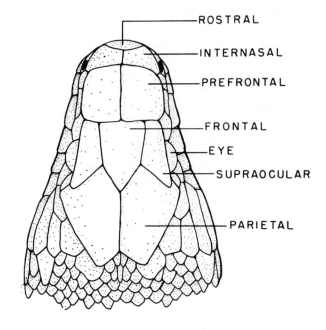

Fig. 1. Snake head, dorsal view
(M. Faith Kutnicki)

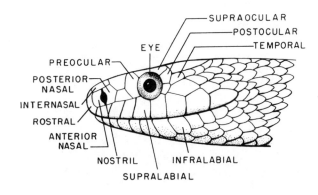

Fig. 2. Snake head, lateral view
(M. Faith Kutnicki)

MENTAL
INFRALABIALS
ANTERIOR CHIN SHIELD
POSTERIOR CHIN SHIELD
GULARS
VENTRALS

Fig. 3. Snake head, ventral view (Evelyn M. Ernst)

1
2
3
4
5
6
7
8
9
10
11
12
13
14
15
16
17

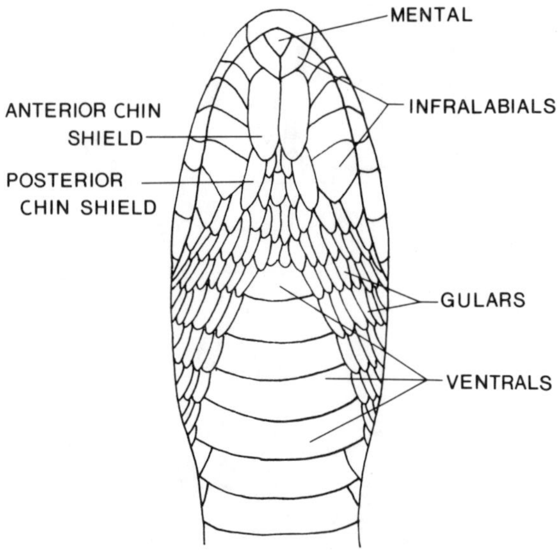

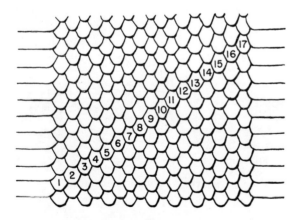

Fig. 4. Numbering snake scale rows (M. Faith Kutnicki)

ums by professional herpetologists who know how to properly and safely maintain them. If, by accident, you are bitten by a venomous snake, medical care should be sought at once. Since there is now serious doubt about the effectiveness of popular first-aid methods for snake bites, which may cause more harm than good, prompt medical treatment is the best route.

THE IDENTIFICATION OF SNAKES

The accompanying key to the snakes of eastern North America is designed to enable one to identify the animal in hand. The characters most often used are those of the head and body scalation (Figs. 1–5), color and pattern.

Within a population of snakes any character will show individual variation; the larger the sample the greater the extremes. In most cases, however, a specimen will have the character as described in the key or at least can be placed within the middle range of measurements. Still, one occasionally encounters a snake in which the character is quite different or in which the measurements fall outside the given range. For this and other reasons no key is infallible; so, after one has arrived at a name by use of the key, the animal should be compared with the photographs and the description in the species account.

Difficulties in keying are most frequent when the snake is melanistic (or sometimes, a preserved specimen). Then one should follow each alternative down to species and in each case examine that possibility by reference to the photographs and text.

If the reader still cannot identify his specimen, it is likely to be an escaped pet, a snake from west of the Mississippi River or a foreign snake. In this case, we suggest the reader take his specimen to the nearest natural history museum, zoo, or university biology department for identification.

Key To Adult Snakes From Eastern North America

1a. Ventral body scales the same size and shape as those on sides and back; eyes small, concealed beneath scales: *Ramphotyphlops braminus*, page 12.

  b. Ventral body scales transversely enlarged, wider than long; eyes visible   2

2a. Pupil an elliptical, vertical slit; a pit–like hole located between nostril and eye   3

  b. Pupil round; no hole between nostril and eye   8

3a. Scaly rattle at tip of tail   4

  b. No scaly rattle at tip of tail   7

4a. Dorsal surface of head covered with small scales   5

  b. Dorsal surface of head covered with 9 enlarged plates   6

5a. Dorsal pattern of body a series of brown or black, light bordered diamond–shaped blotches; face with two light stripes: *Crotalus adamanteus* (venomous), page 208.

  b. Dorsal pattern of body a series of brown or black chevron–shaped blotches; face without light stripes: *Crotalus horridus* (venomous), page 211.

2a

2b

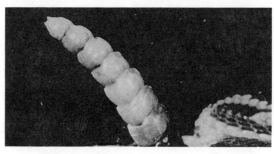

3a

4a

4b

5a

5b

6a. Prefrontal scales in broad contact with loreal scale, preocular scale does not touch the postnasal scale: *Sistrurus miliarius* (venomous), page 205.

b. Prefrontal scale not in contact with loreal scale(s), preocular scale touches the postnasal scale: *Sistrurus catenatus* (venomous), page 201.

7a. Head yellow–brown to reddish–brown, body pattern of brown dumbbell–shaped blotches on a pinkish to orange–brown ground color; loreal scale present: *Agkistrodon contortrix* (venomous), page 190.

b. Head dark brown, black or olive–brown, body pattern of dark brown or black bars on olive or brown ground color; loreal scale absent: *Agkistrodon piscivorous* (venomous), page 196.

8a. Body pattern of red, yellow, and black bands, *with the red bands separated from the black by yellow*, a pair of permanently erect fangs near front of upper jaws: *Micrurus fulvius* (venomous), page 186.

b. Body pattern not of red, yellow, and black bands, or if red, yellow, and black bands are present, the red bands are separated from the yellow by black; no permanently erect fangs near front of upper jaw 9

9a. Anal scale undivided 10

b. Anal scale divided 23

10a. Rostral scale enlarged: *Cemophora coccinea*, page 71.

b. Rostral scale not enlarged 11

11a. No loreal scale; parietal and prefrontal scales usually contact supralabials; tail short, 10% or less of total body length: *Stilosoma extenuatum*, page 103.

b. Loreal scale present; parietal and prefrontal scales do not contact supralabials; tail moderate to long, more than 15% of total body length 12

12a. Mid–body scale rows 27 or more; rostral scale completely or nearly separates the internasal scales; *Pituophis melanoleucus*, page 99.

b. Mid–body scale rows less than 27; rostral scale does not or only slightly separates the internasal scales 13

13a. Mid–body scales keeled   14

 b. Mid–body scales smooth   20

14a. A single nasal scale; 5–7 infralabials, venter with two rows of dark, halfmoon–shaped marks: *Tropidoclonion lineatum*, page 177.

 b. Two nasal scales; 8 or more infralabials, venter unmarked   15

7a

15a. Lateral light stripe occurs anteriorly on scale rows 2–4; head small, neck not distinct 16

 b. Lateral light stripe occurs anteriorly on only scale rows 2–3 or 3–4, but never involves three rows; head normal; neck distinct 17

16a. Supralabials usually 6 (rarely 7), body scale rows 17–17–17: *Thamnophis brachystoma*, page 154.

 b. Supralabials usually 7 (rarely 6), body scale rows 19–19–17: *Thamnophis butleri*, page 158.

9a

17a. Lateral light stripe occurs anteriorly on scale rows 2–3: *Thamnophis sirtalis*, page 164.

 b. Lateral light stripe occurs anteriorly on scale rows 3–4   18

18a. Tail length greater than 27% of total length; no dark bars on lips   19

 b. Tail length less than 27% of total length; dark bars on lips: *Thamnophis radix*, page 161.

9b

19a. Parietal spots usually fused, bright, and conspicuous; brown pigment of sides usually not extending onto ventral scutes, but if so, then covering less than 40% of each ventral: *Thamnophis proximus*, page 171.

 b. Parietal spots often absent, but if present, then small, rarely fused or bright; brown pigment of sides always extending onto ventral scutes and usually covering at least 40% of each ventral: *Thamnophis sauritus*, page 174.

20a. Dorsum immaculate, glossy bluish–black; chin and underside of head red; venter unmarked: *Drymarchon corais*, page 54.

 b. Dorsum usually with pattern of blotches, bars or rings, chin in black species not red; venter with some pattern of blotches or rings 21

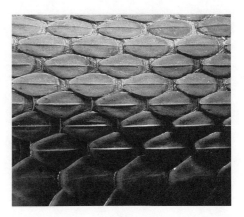

13a

13b

14a

14b

17b

21a. Dorsal ground color black; patterned with white or yellow speckles or chain–like rings: *Lampropeltis getulus*, page 90.

   b. Dorsal ground color red, brown, or tan   22

22a. Dorsal color tan to dark brown with small reddish blotches: *Lampropeltis calligaster*, page 86.

   b. Dorsal color red with a pattern of light–colored rings, or tan with a pattern of dark saddle–like blotches: *Lampropeltis triangulum*, page 94.

23a. Unpatterned head and back light, bright green; venter unmarked   24

   b. Head and back not light, bright green, pattern may be present; venter may contain a distinct pattern   25

24a. Scales keeled: *Opheodrys aestivus*, page 65.

   b. Scales smooth: *Opheodrys vernalis*, page 69.

25a. Twenty or more scale rows at mid–body   26

   b. Less than twenty mid–body scale rows   39

26a. Scales smooth or only weakly keeled   27

   b. Scales prominently keeled   29

27a. Neck stripes cross the parietals to unite on the frontal scale: *Elaphe guttata*, page 74.

   b. Stripes absent from neck   28

28a. More than 220 ventrals: *Elaphe obsoleta*, page 77.

   b. Less than 220 ventrals: *Elaphe vulpina*, page 83.

29a. Rostral scale enlarged; subocular scales present   30

   b. Rostral scale not enlarged; subocular scales absent   32

30a. Rostral scale straight; prefrontal scales touch: *Heterodon platyrhinos*, page 34.

   b. Rostral scale abruptly upturned; prefrontals separated by small scales   31

31a. Two rows of spots on side of body: *Heterodon nasicus*, page 30.

   b. One row of spots on side of body: *Heterodon simus*, page 39.

32a. Eye separated from supralabials by a series of small subocular scales   33

  b. No subocular scales present   34

33a. Venter heavily marked with brown spots: *Nerodia cyclopion*, page 108.

  b. Venter cream-colored with some small brown lateral spots near the tail: *Nerodia floridana*, page 111.

34a. Venter unmarked red or yellow: *Nerodia erythrogaster*, page 125.

  b. Venter with dark markings   35

35a. Parietal scales posteriorly divided into smaller scales; dorsal pattern consisting of 21–26 distinct blotches in adults: *Nerodia taxispilota*, page 131.

  b. Parietal scales not posteriorly subdivided; dorsal pattern, if present in adults, consists of more than 26 blotches   36

36a. Mid-body scale rows 25–31, usually 27; rhomboid-shaped dark blotches on back: *Nerodia rhombifera*, page 128.

  b. Mid-body scale rows 19–25, usually less than 25; dorsal markings, if present, not rhomboidal   37

37a. Dark stripe from eye to corner of mouth: *Nerodia fasciata* (in part), page 113.

  b. No dark stripe from eye to corner of mouth   38

38a. Venter black or dark brown to red with a median, longitudinal yellow stripe: *Nerodia fasciata* (in part), page 113.

  b. Venter unmarked cream to yellow or with either a pattern of halfmoon-shaped reddish-brown marks, or reddish-brown pigment along the transverse seams: *Nerodia sipedon*, page 118.

39a. Mid-body scale rows 13:   *Carphophis amoenus*, page 15.

  b. Mid-body scale rows more than 13   40

40a. Mid-body scale rows 19   41

  b. Mid-body scale rows 15–17   47

29a

30b

32a

43a

48a

54a

58a

58a

41a. Body scales smooth   42

  b. Body scales keeled   44

42a. Preocular scale present, no black pigment on venter: *Regina alleni*, page 134.

  b. No preocular scale, venter with black marks 45

43a. One internasal scale: *Farancia abacura*, page 24.

  b. Two internasal scales: *Farancia erytrogramma*, page 27.

44a. Infralabials 7; one preocular scale: *Clonophis kirtlandii*, page 105.

  b. Infralabials 9–11; two preocular scales   45

45a. A single dark median stripe on venter: *Regina grahamii*, page 136.

  b. Two dark longitudinal stripes or rows of halfmoons on venter   46

46a. Ventral pattern two longitudinal rows of halfmoons: *Regina rigida*, page 139.

  b. Ventral pattern two longitudinal stripes not subdivided into halfmoons: *Regina septem-vittata*, page 141.

47a. Body scales keeled   48

  b. Body scales smooth   51

48a. No preocular scale; no dorsal spots; no black spots at sides of ventrals: *Virginia striatula*, page 181.

  b. One or two preocular scales; two rows (sometimes indistinct) of dorsal spots; black spots at sides of ventrals   49

49a. Mid–body scale rows 17: *Storeria dekayi* (in part), page 146.

  b. Mid–body scale rows 15   50

50a. Venter red or pink; 6 supralabials; 2 preoculars: *Storeria occipitomaculata*, page 151.

  b. Venter cream or white; 7 supralabials; 1 preocular: *Storeria dekayi* (in part), page 146.

51a. No preocular scales: *Virginia valeriae*, page 184.

b. Preocular scales present   52

52a. Size large, total body length greater than 60 cm   53

b. Size small, total body length less than 50 cm   54

53a. Seven supralabials; frontal scale anteriorly broader than supraocular; 15 posterior body scale rows: *Coluber constrictor*, page 57.

b. Eight supralabials; frontal scale not or only slightly broader than supracular; no more than 13 posterior body scale rows: *Masticophis flagellum*, page 62.

54a. Prominent yellow or orange neck ring: *Diadophis punctatus* (in part), page 19.

b. Neck ring absent, or if present, white or cream, not yellow or orange   55

55a. Mid–body scale rows 17   56

b. Mid–body scale rows 15   58

56a. Two preocular scales; temporals 1 + 1; median, longitudinal series of dark halfmoons on venter: *Diadophis punctatus* (in part), page 19.

b. One preocular scale; temporals 1 + 2, venter lacking median halfmoons   57

57a. Venter red with black marks at sides of ventral scales: *Seminatrix pygaea*, page 144.

b. Venter yellow without black markings: *Rhadinaea flavilata*, page 41.

58a. Dark neck collar present, separated from head by lighter complete or almost complete parietal ring   59

b. Dark neck collar absent, light head pigment only occurs as a pair of small parietal spots   60

59a. Light pigment on snout; no light pigment on supralabials: *Tantilla relicta* (in part), page 51.

b. No light pigment on snout; light pigment on supralabials: *Tantilla coronata*, page 43.

60a. Postocular scale single; prairie regions of Midwest: *Tantilla gracilis*, page 46.

b. Two postocular scales; Florida   61

61a. Tail length 18–22% of total body length, males 20–22%, females 18–20%; 41–48 subcaudals in females; hemipenis with two basal hooks: *Tantilla oolitica*, page 49.

b. Tail length 19–30% of total body length, males 28–30%, females 18–29%; 46–60 subcaudals in females; hemipenis with one basal hook: *Tantilla relicta* (in part), page 51.

TYPHLOPIDAE

Blind Snakes

TYPHLOPIDAE
Blind Snakes

About 200 species of small, worm–like burrowing snakes belong to this mostly tropical family. The family range includes southern Europe, southern Asia, Africa, Australia, tropical America, North America, and many oceanic islands.

Typhlopids have solidly fused skulls with a coronoid bone, but lack ectopterygoid, supratemporal and circumorbital bones. The prefrontal bone contacts the nasal bone; the maxilla is only loosely attached to the cranium and lies transverse to the axis of the skull. The maxilla has only a few teeth, while the reduced mandible contains none; no teeth occur on any palatal bone. The hyoid is Y–shaped. Vestiges of a pelvic girdle remain in the form of pubic, ischial, and illiac elements, with traces of pubic and ischial symphyses, or a single elongated bone on each side. The left lung is usually absent, but a tracheal lung is present. The left reproductive tract is absent from females. The head is covered with enlarged plate–like scales; the nasal and prefrontal scales are fused. The smooth body scales are uniform in size and shape. The eyes are small and concealed beneath scales, and there is no visible neck. A spine–like scale adorns the tip of the tail. Reproduction is mostly oviparous, but at least one species is ovoviviparous.

One introduced species has become established in Dade County, Florida.

RAMPHOTYPHLOPS BRAMINUS
(Daudin, 1803) Brahminy Blind Snake

Recognition: A small (possibly to 20 cm), thin brown to black, blunt–headed snake resembling a worm. The snout is rounded with lateral nostrils, the lower jaw countersunk, the eyes barely visible, and the head and body blend together obscuring the neck. The tail ends in a spine. There are 291–348 rows of smooth scales from the occiput to the vent, and from 8–11 rows on the tail. Circling the body at the mid–point is a series of 18–20 scales. On the head is a large rostral scale, about 1/3 as wide as the head, sepa-rated from the nostrils by an almost vertical suture. Up to 5 teeth may occur on the maxilla.

Karyotype: The karyotype is 3n = 42; this snake appears to be a triploid species, as other typhlopids have either 32 or 34 chromosomes (Wynn et al., 1987).

Distribution: This is the most widely distributed terrestrial reptile in the world due to its accidental introduction in soil of potted plants and in soil used as ship ballast. It now occurs in southern Asia from Arabia to Japan, the Malay Archipelago, the Philippines, Madagascar, southern Africa, Mexico, and on many islands in the Indian and Pacific oceans, including Hawaii. In the continental United States it is known only from Dade County, Florida (Wilson and Porras, 1983) where it has been introduced in the pots of imported tropical plants.

Geographic Variation: Wall (1921) recognized three varieties, but the subspecific status of the Florida population has not been established.

Confusing Species: All other snakes in southern Florida have prominent eyes and transversely enlarged ventral scutes.

Habitat: This small burrower prefers the loose soil of mesic habitats, particularly that of flower beds. It also is commonly found in the decaying wood of logs and stumps, and under rocks or moist leaves on the ground. Presumably it needs a moderately moist habitat to balance water loss through its skin.

At times it appears in unusual situations. Several writers have commented on its emergence through floor cracks in Asian homes, and Minton (1966) reported that some, particularly the young, have been found in the gutter in the most exclusive shopping district of Karachi, Pakistan, on the second floor of a shop on the same street, a hospital ward, and the bathroom of a modern apartment. Wall (1921) commented that this small snake was certainly the species that invaded the water supply in Calcutta, India, many individuals finding their way into the distribution pipes. Could you not visualize the shock and consternation this would cause if it occurred today in the tourist and wealthy sections of Miami?

Daniel (1983) reported another potential problem with this small snake. In India it is popularly believed to enter the ear of persons sleeping on the ground. There may be some truth to this, as captives we have had regularly entered crevices or holes to hide.

Behavior: Little is known of the habits of *R. braminus*. It is a predominantly nocturnal burrowing species, that comes to the surface at night, particularly after rains.

Reproduction: It is generally believed that *R. braminus* is an all female, parthenogenetic species; however, Wall (1921) and List (1958) have both reported finding males, but possibly these may have been wrongly sexed or misidentified as to species. Nussbaum (1980) felt that the reports of males, in addition to taxonomic and distributional considerations, indicate that *R. braminus*, as now recognized, may be a complex of unisexual and bisexual species.

Nussbaum (1980) reported that in the Seychelles Archipelago *R. braminus* 111 mm in total length or longer possessed enlarged yolky follicles, so maturity probably occurs at this size. Wall (1921) found that gravid females in India were at least 152 mm in length. Dissections by Nussbaum revealed that the ovarian eggs were arranged linearly and normally were graded in size with the anterior-most eggs the largest. He thought that this arrangement probably indicated that not all eggs with yolk are laid simultaneously, and that counts of enlarged follicles in preserved specimens are not good estimates of clutch size. As further evidence of this, he described a preserved specimen with three shelled oviducal eggs which were apparently ready to be laid, and a fourth ovarian egg which had yolk but was only half the size of those in the oviduct. Nussbaum found that the number of enlarged ovarian eggs per specimen with eggs ranged from 2–6 (x = 4.8).

Clutch size ranges from 2–8 eggs with 3–6 probably more common. The eggs are elongated (12–17 x 3–4 mm) with a leathery shell. A survey of the literature shows that *R. braminus* oviposits through most of the year and possibly breeds continuously. Cagle (1946) reported that two of three eggs laid 21 April hatched 29 May, and that the third egg contained a completely developed dead snake. The two hatchlings measured 62 mm and 53 mm in total length. These lengths agree with those of the smallest young, 61 and 68 mm, collected by Minton (1966).

Food And Feeding: Because of their small heads and mouths *R. braminus* are restricted to eating prey with small diameters, predominantly such insects as ants, termites, small beetles, and various soft-bodied larvae. Annandale (1907) observed a captive devour the excretia of caterpillars. It is also possible that small earthworms may be eaten.

Predators And Defense: Undoubtedly, birds and other snakes prey heavily on *R. braminus*.

These small creatures are inoffensive when handled. They do not bite, but may excrete musk and prick your fingers with the tip of their tail. When first discovered they try to escape, often frantically thrashing their bodies back and forth in a manner reminiscent of movements in nematodes.

Populations: In the tropics this small snake often is locally quite common. Wall (1921) found large aggregations in rotten wood, and reported that in Sri Lanka one of his subalterns collected about 100 in his house in a month.

Map

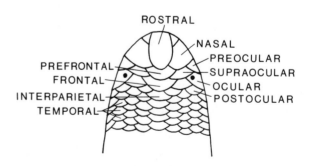

Fig. 5. Head scalation of *Ramphotyphlops braminus* (Evelyn M. Ernst)

COLUBRIDAE

Colubrid Snakes

This, the largest family of living snakes, contains over 300 genera and more than 1,400 species. The family is represented on all continents except Antarctica, as well as on many islands. More persons in eastern North America have experience with colubrids than with other types of snakes.

The United States has about 94 species in 39 genera. East of the Mississippi River there are 23 genera and 50 species. Most are small to medium–sized, but the black rat snake, *Elaphe obsoleta obsoleta*, and the indigo snake, *Drymarchon corais couperi*, may reach lengths of 270 cm.

The family is characterized by having no postfrontal, coronoid, or pelvic bones. The hyoid is Y–shaped with two superficially–placed parallel arms. The horizontal, stationary, elongated maxilla articulates with the anterior frontal bone by a lateral process. Usually premaxillary teeth are absent, but teeth occur on the maxilla, palatine, pterygoid and dentary. No anterior hollow fangs occur on the maxilla, but some posterior teeth may be enlarged with (opisthoglyphous) or without (aglyphous) grooves. The supralabial gland may produce a venomous secretion. The left lung is vestigial or absent, and the hemipenis is variable.

The dorsal surface of the head usually has, anteriorly to posteriorly, the following enlarged scales: a rostral, an internasal, 2 prefrontals, a single large frontal, 2 supraoculars, and 2 elongated parietals. Laterally are a single or divided nasal scale, a loreal (absent in some), 1 or more preoculars, 1 or more postoculars, 2 or more temporals and several supralabials. In a few genera (*Nerodia*, *Heterodon*), some species have completed the ring of scales around the eye by adding subocular scales between the orbit and supralabials. On the lower jaw is a mental scale usually separated from the anterior of two pairs of chin shields by 1 or more of the several pairs of infralabial scales. Occasionally additional scales may be inserted between the head scales. On the back and sides of the body are usually overlapping, keeled or smooth scales. The ventral body scales are horizontally expanded plates extending from side to side.

Reproduction in colubrids may be oviparous, ovoviviparous, or viviparous.

The colubrids of eastern North America are members of four subfamilies (see Underwood, 1967; Dowling, 1975; Dowling and Savage, 1960; and Meylan, 1982):

1. Xenodontinae. The posterior body vertebrae of these snakes, either lack hypapophyses or, if present, they are flat and broad. The spinose hemipenis usually has a capitate, calyculate apical region, and a bifurcated, centrifugal (bilobed) sulcus spermaticus. Most members have two enlarged, posterior (sometimes opisthoglyphous), maxillary teeth. Body scales row reduction is usually paravertebral (*Carphophis*, *Diadophis*, *Farancia*, *Heterodon*, *Rhadinaea*, *Tantilla*).

2. Colubrinae. Snakes without hypapophyses, or with narrow, elongated hypapophyses on their posterior body vertebrae. The hemipenis is usually spinose near the base and calyculate near the tip; there is no capitation or apical disk, and the single sulcus spermaticus is asymmetrical in those which are bilobed (extending into only one lobe). A few have enlarged (sometimes opisthoglyphous) posterior maxillary teeth. Body scale row reduction is usually mid–lateral or vertebral (*Coluber*, *Drymarchon*, *Masticophis*, *Opheodrys*).

Snakes of this subfamily differ from those of the closely related Lampropeltinae in having vertebrae with moderately to well developed epizygapophyseal spines, the accessory process longer than the prezygapophyseal width, the accessory process anterolaterally directed, and the centra length/neural arch width usually greater than 1.36.

3. Lampropeltinae. Snakes resembling the Colubrinae, but differing in having vertebrae with the epizygapophyseal spines absent or only weakly developed, the accessory process shorter than the prezygapophyseal width, the accessory process laterally directed, and the centra length/neural arch width usually less than 1.27 (*Cemophora*, *Elaphe*, *Lampropeltis*, *Pituophis*, and *Stilosoma*).

4. Natricinae (sometimes considered a separate family, see Underwood, 1967). All body vertebrae have elongated, recurved hypapophyses. The symmetrical spiny hemipenis has two or more basal hooks, lacks calyces or an apical disk, but has a single or bifurcated, centripetal sulcus spermaticus. The maxillary teeth become gradually longer toward the rear; the posterior–most may be greatly enlarged, usually aglyphous and separated from the anterior teeth by a diastema. Body scale row reduction is usually mid–lateral or sub–lateral (*Clonophis*, *Nerodia*, *Regina*, *Seminatrix*, *Storeria*, *Thamnophis*, *Tropidoclonion*, *Virginia*).

CARPHOPHIS AMOENUS

Worm Snake

CARPHOPHIS AMOENUS (Say, 1825)
Worm Snake

Recognition: A small (to 37.5 cm), cylindrical, unpatterned snake with a gray or tan to dark brown back, a pinkish venter, a pointed head, and small eyes. The pinkish ventral coloration extends dorsally onto 1 to 3 lateral scale rows. The tail is short and ends in a blunt spine–like scale. The body scales usually occur in 13 rows and are smooth, pitless, and opalescent; the anal plate is divided. Laterally on the head are a nasal, a loreal, a postocular, 1 + 1–2 temporals, 5 supralabials and 5–6 infralabials. No gulars occur between the posterior chin shields. The single hemipenis has a forked sulcus spermaticus, a calyculate crown, numerous small spines along the shaft, and 3 large basal spines. Each maxilla has 9–12 small teeth.

Males have 106–138 ventrals, 28–41 subcaudals, and tails 16.5–20.5% as long as the total body length; females have 112–150 ventrals, 21–33 subcaudals, and tails 11–16% of the total body length. Adult males have ridges on the body scales dorsal to the anal plate (Blanchard, 1931).

Karyotype: Unknown.

Fossil Record: Pleistocene remains of *C. amoenus* are known from the Irvingtonian of Maryland and the Rancholabrean of Arkansas, Florida, Georgia, Missouri, Pennsylvania, Tennessee, and Virginia (Holman, 1981). The Florida fossil sites are well south of the present known range of *C. amoenus*.

Distribution: *C. amoenus* ranges from southern New England, adjacent New York, southeastern and southcentral Pennsylvania and West Virginia west to southern Iowa and southeastern Nebraska and south to South Carolina, northern Georgia, Alabama, Mississippi and southeastern Louisiana.

Geographic Variation: There are three subspecies. *Carphophis amoenus amoenus* (Say, 1825), the eastern worm snake, has the internasals and prefrontals usually separated, 2 posttemporal scutes, and the light ventral coloration extending only onto 1 or 2 lateral scale rows. It is found from southwestern Massachusetts south to South Carolina, northern Georgia and central Alabama. *C. a. helenae* (Kennicott, 1859), the midwest worm snake, usually has each internasal fused with the corresponding prefrontal scale, 2 posttemporal scales, and the light ventral coloration extending onto 1 or 2 lateral scale rows. It ranges from southern Ohio west to southern Illinois, and south to the Gulf Coast in Mississippi and southeastern Louisiana. *C. a. vermis* (Kennicott, 1859), the western worm snake, usually has the internasals and prefrontals separated, 1 posttemporal scale, and the light ventral coloration extending to the 3rd lateral scale row. It occurs from southern Iowa and southeastern Nebraska south to northwestern Louisiana and adjacent Texas. Isolated colonies are also found in westcentral Illinois, Grant County, Wisconsin, and northcentral Louisiana.

Clark (1968) proposed that *C. a. vermis* be elevated to specific status based on the absence of fusion of the internasal and prefrontal scales, single posttemporal scale, ventral scale count, and extent of ventral coloration on the lateral scale rows. He concluded the Mississippi River formed an effective barrier to gene flow between *C. a. vermis* and its eastern relative *C. a. helenae*. However, Rossman (1973) reported that intergrade specimens, *C. a. helenae* x *a. vermis*, occur in northeastern Louisiana, and Sajdak (1978) has discovered *C. a. vermis* east of the Mississippi River in southwestern Wisconsin. Zones of intergradation between *C. a. amoenus* and *C. a. helenae* occur in Ohio, West Virginia and eastern Kentucky (Smith, 1948; Barbour, 1960; Pauley, 1973).

Confusing Species: Snakes of the genera *Virginia* and *Storeria* have keeled body scales.

Habitat: Worm snakes prefer moist, rocky woodlands. Clark (1967b, 1969) found that in Kansas *C. amoenus* was most often associated with soil moisture levels of 21–30%, but occurred at levels of 11–80%. Similarly, Elick and Sealander (1972) reported that this snake occurred in soil moisture levels of 16–42% in Arkansas. It apparently requires a moderate level of soil moisture to offset evaporative water loss through its skin. Those studied by Elick and Sealander lost 2.3–6.7 mg of water per g of body weight per hour through the skin and respiratory passages when subjected to dessication. In nature, these small snakes soon disappear from recently cleared areas, apparently because of the increased heating and drying of the soil.

Behavior: We have collected individual worm snakes from March to October, and this annual cycle agrees with those dates of appearance in Wright and Wright (1957). Most activity is in the

CARPHOPHIS AMOENUS

Worm Snake

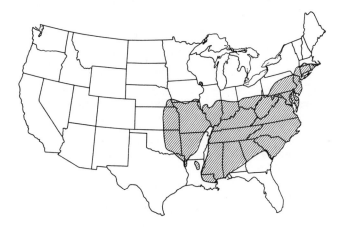

Map

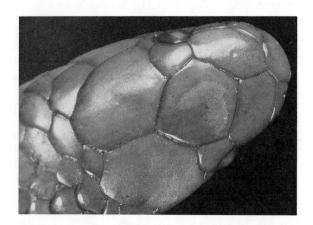

Fig. 6. The internasals and prefrontals are united into a pair of large shields in *Carphophis amoenus helenae*.

spring, especially from late April to early June. The hot weather then seems to drive them underground or to shelter in rotting logs, stumps or under rocks where they estivate until late August when there is a second lesser peak of activity.

Hibernation occurs underground. Neill (1948a) reported that in Georgia they overwinter beneath rocks in small tunnels about 360–720 cm beneath the surface. Grizzell (1949) found a *Carphophis* about 720 cm deep in the soil in February.

Although generally thought to be nocturnal, Barbour et al. (1969) found no movements occurred between midnight and 0300 hr. Activity increased rapidly to a high of 55% between 1500 and 1800 hr, and then declined toward midnight; 29% of the movements ceased between 0700 and 0900 hr and 58% between 2100 and 2400 hr.

Fitch (1956) recorded the body temperatures of 20 *Carphophis* from Kansas. Excluding one very low body temperature, these averaged 26.4 C (19.0–31.7); the average and maximum body temperatures were lower than any other reptile he studied. Fitch found one dormant snake beneath a rock on 29 March when light snow was falling and the air temperature was –3 C; it had a body temperature of only 3.5 C (the same as the soil around it) and could hardly move. Cloacal temperatures of 42 Kansas worm snakes taken by Clark (1970a) averaged 18.3 C (9.9–23.8); the corresponding substrate temperatures averaged 17.5 C (9.6–25.5). In the laboratory, when given a choice of temperatures in a gradient, *Carphophis* chose an average temperature of 23 C (14.4–30.8) (Clark, 1967b).

Body heat, and cutaneous moisture loss are probably the controlling factors of habitat selection and activity patterns in this small snake. To escape overheating or dessication, *Carphophis* has adopted a fossorial life style. It has several morphological characters that facilitate burrowing in the soil: a narrow head, cylindrical body, small eyes, smooth scales, and a relatively short tail. Clark (1970a) has described the burrowing behavior.

Both Fitch (1958) and Clark (1970a) reported data on movements of *C. a. vermis* in Kansas based on recaptures. A more thorough study was conducted by Barbour et al. (1969) on radio-isotope tagged *C. a. amoenus* in Kentucky. Each of 10 snakes was located 46–89 times. Home ranges were calculated using the minimum area method and averaged 253 m² (23–486). The longest movement during a 24 hr period was 45 m (in 14.5 hr). Most periods of movement were less than 12 hrs long, and periods of inactivity ranged from a few minutes to over 14 days. Although individual snakes returned to certain places within their home ranges several times, when snakes were displaced 150–800 m from where captured, they exhibited no homing ability.

Reproduction: Most male *C. a. vermis* are mature at a snout–vent length of 216 mm (Clark, 1970a). The smallest male with sperm found by Clark was 177 mm. Clark also dissected a series of male *C. a. amoenus* and *C. a. helenae*; 90% of the mature *amoenus* had snout–vent lengths of 170 mm or more, and 90% of the mature *helenae* were 178 mm or more. Clark found that most males had developed ridges on the dorsal body scales near the anus by snout–vent lengths of at least 147 mm in *helenae*, 159 mm in *amoenus*, and 170 mm in *vermis*.

Aldridge and Metter (1973) observed the seasonal changes in the testes of *Carphophis*. During the winter a sertoli syncytium is prevalent within the seminiferous tubules. During spring, summer, and fall each meiotic stage becomes prevalent within the tubule with sperm being most common in the fall, having been formed from mid–July to mid–September. Sperm is stored in the vas deferens throughout the year.

All female *C. a. vermis* are sexually mature at a snout–vent length of 250 mm, and some may reach maturity at 240 mm (Clark, 1970a). Small follicles 1 or 2 mm in length are present in the ovaries throughout the year. After oviposition in June some of these begin to enlarge, and by the fall have reached 7 mm in length having grown about 0.3 mm per week (Aldridge and Metter, 1973). No growth occurs during the winter, but after the snakes emerge from hibernation in April the follicles grow rapidly to about 19 mm in length, a growth rate of 1.5 mm per week while vitellogenesis occurs. Ovulation is in late May. In Kentucky, the follicles of *C. a. amoenus* increase in length from about 5 to 15 mm between March and May, and mean clutch length at ovulation was 23.9 mm (Barbour, 1960). Clark (1970a, b) has reported that the number of eggs produced and the weight of each clutch increases with the age and size of the female.

Mating and courtship behavior have not been recorded, but, from the incidence of sperm in the reproductive tracts of adult females, Clark (1970a) thought that most mating occurs in September and October, with a second lesser copulatory period in April and early May. Apparently, females store the sperm over winter.

Nesting occurs in June and early July, almost always in the morning, and several hours may pass before all the eggs in a clutch are laid (Clark, 1970a). Typical nesting sites are depressions under rocks, inside rotting logs or stumps, old

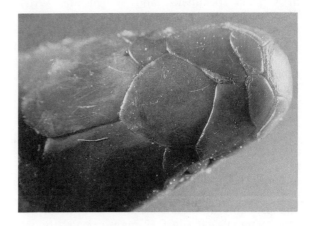

Fig. 7. The internasals and prefrontals are separate in *Carphophis amoenus amoenus* and *C. a. vermis*.

sawdust piles, and possibly ground squirrel burrows.

A clutch may consist of 1 (Anderson, 1965) to 8 (Wright and Wright, 1957) eggs, but 2–5 eggs seem most common. The eggs are cream or pale white to translucent, thin–shelled, and elongated (14–29 x 6.5–11 mm). They normally hatch in August or September. Depending on the temperature, the incubation period may extend 18–60 days, but is probably about 50 days in nature (Clark, 1970a).

The young are more sharply two–toned than adults, having very reddish–pink venters. They are 75–124 mm in total length and weigh 0.7–1.1 g at hatching.

Growth And Longevity: Clark (1970a) estimated the following growth rates in snout–vent length for *C. a. vermis* in Kansas: males—hatchlings (112–124 mm), 0.185 mm/day; 1st year (125–179), 0.266 mm/day, 2nd year (180–215 mm), 0.172 mm/day; 3rd year (216–235 mm), 0.094 mm/day; and 4th year (236–247 mm), 0.054 mm/day; females—hatchlings (117–135 mm), 0.277 mm/day; 1st year (136–196 mm), 0.296 mm/day; 2nd year (197–249 mm), 0.256 mm/day; 3rd year (250–273 mm), 0.113 mm/day; and 4th year (274–285 mm), 0.054 mm/day.

CARPHOPHIS AMOENUS

Worm Snake

Clark (1970a) thought that some individuals in his natural population exceeded 4 years in age.

Food And Feeding: *Carphophis* is almost entirely an earthworm predator, and most dietary studies have found this to be the exclusive food (Barbour, 1950a, 1960; Hamilton and Pollack, 1956; Bush, 1959; Minton, 1972; Brown 1979a). However, Uhler et al. (1939) found fly larvae (Tabanidae) in Virginia specimens, and Wright and Wright (1957) also list slugs and snails as prey items. Clark (1970a) found the remains of a salamander (*Eurycea*) in one, and Hurter (in Clark, 1970a) reported that a captive ate a small ringneck snake (*Diadophis punctatus*). The small mouth and head of *Carphophis* limit it to soft–bodied, narrow, elongated prey.

Predators And Defense: Predatory snakes, such as kingsnakes, milk snakes, racers, copperheads, and possibly ringneck snakes are the major natural enemies of worm snakes, but toads, opossums, and barn owls also occasionally eat them. It is possible that moles and shrews may attack them, and probably other nocturnal birds and carnivorous mammals eat a few. Humans remain, though, the most destructive force with their habitat destruction and indiscriminate use of pesticides. Ernst (1962) reported the death of *Carphophis* which had eaten chlordane poisoned insects.

Carphophis amoenus is a very shy, mild mannered creature that seldom, if ever, bites. Instead, when handled, it will twist and thrash about, try to crawl between your fingers, probe your hand with is pointed tail, and emit a rather pungent musk.

Populations: This small snake may exist in large numbers where the habitat is suitable. Clark (1970a) found densities of 60–120 *Carphophis* per hectare at his study site in Kansas, and Ernst and his students collected 108 individuals from beneath rocks in 100 m along a hillside overlooking the Kentucky River in one hour on an April afternoon. The sex ratio of the 926 individuals collected by Clark (1970a) did not differ significantly from 1:1. Of 913 *Carphophis* aged by Clark, 6.6% were hatchlings, 19.4% 1st year snakes, 18.2% 2nd year, 21.6% 3rd year, 13.4% 4th year, and 20.9% older than 4 years.

DIADOPHIS PUNCTATUS

Ringneck Snake

DIADOPHIS PUNCTATUS (Linnaeus, 1766) Ringneck Snake

Recognition: A small (to 70.6 cm), plain greenish–gray, blue–gray, or black snake with a cream or yellow neck band. The neck band may be incomplete in some individuals, and is totally absent in one eastern race. The venter is yellow to orange or reddish–orange, and may be variously spotted or lack spots (see **Geographic Variation**). There are 13–17 anterior rows of body scales, 14–17 rows at mid–body and 13–15 rows just anterior to the anal vent. The body scales are smooth but with an apical pit; the anal plate is divided. Males have 126–169 ventrals and 33–65 subcaudals, females have 134–185 ventrals and 30–61 subcaudals. Head scalation is that of a typical colubrid snake; there are a loreal, 2(1–3) preoculars, 2(1) postoculars, 1 + 1(2) temporals, 6–8 supralabials, and 6–8 infralabials on each side of the head. The single hemipenis has its head slightly constricted at the base and shallowly bilobate, the sulcus spermaticus only distally forked and the shaft covered with spines (see Fitch, 1975, for an illustration). Each maxillary has 12–21 teeth; those anterior are slender and erect, the 2 most posterior teeth are longer, thicker and directed backward, and separated from the anterior teeth by a diastema.

Males have a tail length 17–22% that of the total body length; females 15–18% of the total body length. Some adult males have ridges on the body scales near the anal vent (Blanchard, 1931, 1942).

Karyotype: Chromosomes total 36, with 16 macrochromosomes and 20 microchromosomes (Bury et al., 1970).

Fossil Record: Pleistocene fossils of this snake have been found in Irvingtonian deposits in Maryland, and Rancholabrean deposits from Florida, Georgia, Missouri, New Mexico, Pennsylvania, Tennessee, and Texas (Holman, 1981). Hemphillian fossils from Florida have been assigned to the species *D. elinorae* (Auffenberg, 1963; Meylan, 1982).

Distribution: *D. punctatus* ranges in the East from Nova Scotia and New Brunswick through southern Canada to Lake Superior and south to the Florida Keys, Arizona, New Mexico, and Texas, and from Nayarit to Veracruz in Mexico. Western subspecies are found from central and southern Washington to Baja, Mexico, with scattered populations in Idaho, Nevada, and Utah.

Geographic Variation: There are 12 subspecies of *Diadophis punctatus* (some of the western races may represent a separate species), but only 5 occur within the range of this book, and the above description is a composite of these. *Diadophis punctatus punctatus* (Linnaeus, 1766), the southern ringneck snake, ranges from southeastern Virginia south through peninsular Florida and southwest to southeastern Alabama. It has a single, median row of black half–moon shaped spots on the venter, usually 8 supralabials, as many as 170 ventrals, and an incomplete neck ring. *D. p. edwardsii* (Merrem, 1820), the northern ringneck snake, is found from New Brunswick and Nova Scotia, southern Quebec, Ontario, Michigan, Wisconsin and northeastern Minnesota, south to Virginia, western North Carolina, northern Georgia and northeastern Alabama. It usually has no black spots on the venter, 8 supralabials, as many as 170 ventrals, and a complete neck ring. *D. p. arnyi* (Kennicott, 1859), the prairie ringneck snake, is found from southeastern Minnesota and southeastern South Dakota south to southcentral Texas; although most of the range is west of the Mississippi River, it also occurs in southwestern Wisconsin and the length of western Illinois. This race has scattered black spots on the venter, usually 7 supralabials, up to 185 ventrals, the neck ring occasionally broken, and the dark head pigment extending across the angle of the jaw and slightly forward on the lower jaw. *D. p. stictogenys* Cope, 1860, the Mississippi ringneck snake, occurs from southern Illinois south in the Mississippi Valley to western Alabama, Mississippi, Louisiana, and eastern Texas. It has an irregularly spotted venter with the spots often clumped along the midline, usually 7 supralabials, less than 145 ventrals, and a narrow, often interrupted, neck ring. *D. p. acricus* Paulson, 1966, the Key ringneck snake, is known only from Big Pine Key, Florida. It has a pale green head, a single median row of black half–moons on the venter, 8 supralabials, less than 140 ventrals, and no neck ring. There are broad zones of intergradation where the ranges of the subspecies meet (Barbour, 1950a; Martof, 1955; Johnson and Webb, 1964; Paul, 1967; Blem and Roeding, 1983).

DIADOPHIS PUNCTATUS

Ringneck Snake

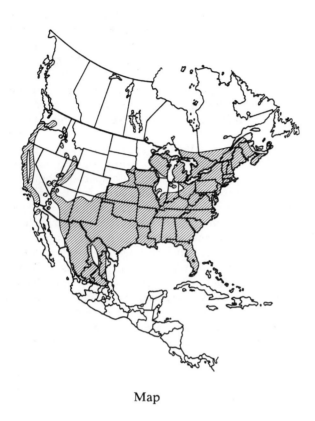

Map

Fig. 8. *Diadophis punctatus punctatus* has a medial row of dark spots on its venter (Carl H. Ernst)

Confusing Species: *Storeria dekayi* and *S. occipitomaculata* have keeled body scales and lack spots on their venters.

Habitat: In the East, *D. punctatus* is a woodland species, rarely found more than a few meters from the woods, but in the prairie areas of the Midwest it has become an ecotonal species, occurring both in the patches of woods along streams and in the shrubland between these woods and the prairie. Since it is quite secretive, it requires rocks, logs, stumps, fallen bark or human debris under which to hide. Also, its habitats are usually moist, at least in the spring and fall, and it seems to require moist soil to balance evaporative water loss from its body (Myers, 1965; Clark, 1967), for it becomes subterranean and estivates during the hot, dry periods in summer. It occasionally can be found in moist caves. The ringneck is quite sociable, and in proper habitat aggregations are often found under rocks or within rotting logs; in such places, we have found as many as 10 at one time.

Behavior: Over most of its eastern range, *D. punctatus* has a yearly activity period extending from late March through October or early November. It is most active in the spring, with a second lesser active period in September and October, and from mid–July through August is seldom seen. Fitch (1975) estimated the season of activity averaged 213 days at his Kansas study site. Farther south it may be active all year. Myers (1965) collected them in every month in Florida, but at reduced rates in the summer. We have found them extremely abundant during March and April in Florida. In some populations spring and fall migrations occur from and to hibernacula (Blanchard et al., 1979).

Most daily activity occurs at night (Blanchard, 1942; Blanchard et al., 1979), but, if weather conditions are right, some daylight activity does occur, especially during the breeding season.

Ringneck snakes occasionally bask, but most often warm their bodies through contact with sun–warmed surfaces. Fitch (1975) recorded body temperatures of 11.7 – 34.4 C (x = 26.1) for 129 ringnecks found beneath surface objects. In 109 of these, the body temperature exceeded air temperature. For 37 snakes found in the open, body temperatures averaged 26.6 C (18.2 – 33.3), an average of 3.7 C above the air temperature. A basking snake was 30.3 C, while the air was 16.3 C. Most ringnecks found active on the surface were 25–27 C or 29–31 C. Both digestion and water loss increase with an increase in ambient temperature (Buikema and Armitage, 1969; Henderson, 1970).

Hibernacula include mammal burrows, old wells, stone walls, brush piles, rotting logs and stumps, sawdust piles, gravel banks, and rock out croppings. Often several individuals of *D. punctatus* may be found at one site. Winter temperatures in hibernacula in Kansas 30–80 cm beneath the surface are usually 0–10 C.

In a study of movements in a Kansas population, Fitch (1975) found that nearly 25% of the movements were of less than 10 m, 33% were 10–70 m, 22% were 70–140 m, and the remaining longer movements were up to 1700 m. The movements up to 70 m probably represented normal movements within the home range. Fitch thought that habitual return to a favorite spot within the home range occurred, even after long intervals of time. Home ranges were often elongated, with maximum axes of about 140 m, and seemed to be progressively altered through time.

Diodophis has some climbing ability. Myers (1965) found them several centimeters above ground on the trunks of cabbage palms in Florida, and McCauley (1945) reported ringneck snakes in Maryland 180 cm above ground in an old snag.

Reproduction: Myers (1965) found that in Florida, some male *D. punctatus* had enlarged kidney tubules, and sperm in the vas deferens at a total body length of about 180 mm in their second spring. Once a length of 200 mm was reached, all males were mature. The testes were smallest in the winter and spring. Spermatogenesis was initiated in the spring and cellular proliferation was greatest in summer. Mature sperm released from the testes in late summer and fall are stored in the vas deferens throughout most of the year. In Kansas, Fitch (1975) found active sperm in 98% of the males in April, 95% in May, 91% in September, and 93% in October. Fitch reported that sperm can survive for relatively long periods in vascularized pouches in the female's oviducts, but probably survive only a few days in the cloaca.

In Florida, female ringneck snakes mature by their 2nd spring (Myers, 1965), but in Kansas they mature in their 3rd spring at a snout–vent length of about 235 mm (Fitch, 1975). Young Florida females in their first fall had ovarian follicles 1.0 mm in diameter (Myers, 1965). The follicles had increased to 1.5 – 2.0 mm in diameter by the first spring. In mature females the largest ovarian follicles increased from about 3 mm in April to nearly 24 mm eggs in the oviducts in July. Ovulation occurs in June in Kansas (Fitch, 1975). Female *D. punctatus* apparently reproduce annually.

Although this species is normally oviparous, Peterson (1956) has reported a case of ovoviviparity in a female from Florida that gave birth to 6 living young after apparently having retained the eggs within her oviducts. In newly laid eggs, embryos of *Diadophis* are somewhat more

Fig. 9. *Diadophis punctatus arnyi* has many scattered dark spots on its venter (Steve W. Gotte)

advanced than those of many other species of oviparous snakes (Fitch, 1975).

Apparently pheromones released from the skin are responsible for aggregating individuals of *D. punctatus* (Noble and Clausen, 1936; Dundee and Miller, 1968). Most aggregations occur in the spring and fall, and mating apparently may occur at either time (Fitch, 1975). In Kansas, active sperm were found in about 6% of the females in April, 20% in May, 16% in June, 8% in September and 2.5% in October (Fitch, 1975). Fitch observed courtship and copulation.

Active courtship was observed on 24 September 1959 at 4 p.m. The female involved was in the process of sloughing and was crawling slowly through the surface litter in open woodland, partly exposed. The slough had peeled back for about half the length of her body. A male was beside her, facing in the opposite direction. For several minutes that the snakes were watched, the male alternately lay passive or made jerky animated courtship movements, obviously stimulated by scent emanating from the moist, newly-exposed skin. The snakes moved out of sight beneath leaf litter, and when it seemed that they should not reappear, leaves were gently brushed aside exposing the pair to view. Meanwhile another male had joined them and both males pressed against the female but the anterior ends of all three snakes were concealed. Posterior ends of the two males were momentarily intertwined and were apart

DIADOPHIS PUNCTATUS

Ringneck Snake

from the female. There was no evident rivalry between the males as each pursued its courtship, but confusion and delay resulted from the presence of the extra male. Soon the snakes again moved out of sight and could not be relocated.

Copulation was observed at approximately 5 p.m. on 7 May 1974. The pair of snakes was found in damp soil beneath a heavy decaying plank. They did not separate when exposed by turning of the plank nor for about 20 minutes subsequently that they were kept under observation. The female was nervous and active, darting out her tongue almost continually, shifting position frequently, and sometimes crawling a short distance, dragging the relatively passive male after her. From time to time the snakes coiled together in a fairly compact mass, the male often pressing his snout against the female's side. After a few minutes' gap in the observations, the snakes were found to have disappeared and could not be relocated.

In the North, egg laying occurs in June or early July, but Iverson (1978) reported an oviposition on 14 September in Florida from which the eggs hatched 22 October. Typical nesting sites are under rocks, leafpiles, or fallen bark, in rotting logs and stumps, sawdust piles, or in the walls of animal burrows. Preferred sites may be used by several females at the same time; Blanchard (1942) found 48 and 55 eggs in two nests, and Gilhen (1970) 47 in another.

Two to 10 eggs may be laid in one clutch (Myers, 1965), but 3–4 eggs are more common. Larger females lay more eggs (Barbour, 1950a) and during dry years, smaller clutches are produced (Seigel and Fitch, 1985). The white eggs have a rough, but thin leathery shell and are elongate, 16–43 x 6–12.7 mm. Normal eggs weighed by Fitch (1975) averaged 0.89 g (0.58–1.35). Hatching usually occurs in late August or September, after an incubation period of 46–60 days (Blanchard, 1926). The process of hatching takes several hours (15–27) (Blanchard, 1926).

Hatchling ringneck snakes are usually 85–115 mm long, although Groves (1978) reported two were 136 and 148 mm.

Growth: Blanchard et al. (1979) reported the following estimated lengths for Michigan ringneck snakes: females, 1st year, to 200 mm (60% increase in length); 2nd year, to 245 mm (23% increase); 3rd year, to 290 mm (18% increase); 4th year, to 340 mm (17% increase); and 5th year, to 390 mm (15% increase); males, 1st year, to 210 mm (68% increase); 2nd year, to 260 mm (24% increase); 3rd year, to 280 mm (8% increase); and 4th year, to 310 mm (11% increase). Fitch (1975) found similar growth rates in his Kansas snakes.

Although the maximum life span of *D. punctatus* is unknown, both Fitch (1975) and Blanchard et al. (1979) had individuals live for more than 10 years during their studies.

Food And Feeding: Earthworms, salamanders (*Plethodon, Eurycea, Desmognathus*) and small insects are the most frequently eaten prey (Surface, 1906; Blanchard, 1942; Barbour, 1950a; Hamilton and Pollack, 1956; Bush, 1959; Myers, 1965; Fitch, 1975; Brown, 1979a, b), but slugs and grubs (Ernst, 1962), salamander eggs (Barbour, 1950a), small frogs (*Gastrophryne*, juvenile *Rana pipiens*; Myers, 1965), lizards (*Eumeces, Scincella, Ophisaurus*; Myers, 1965; Fitch, 1975) and small snakes (*Opheodrys, Storeria*; Blanchard, 1942) have also been found in the stomachs of ringneck snakes. It is interesting that, whereas other authors inevitably mention earthworms as food, Uhler et al. (1939) reported that food items by volume found in Virginia ringnecks consisted of 80% salamanders, 15% ants, and 5% miscellaneous insects and arthropods.

Digestion increases with a rise in temperature, and Henderson (1970) found that when *Diadophis* was maintained at 35 C, the first defecation after feeding occurred in 7 hours, but only after 15–30 hours when maintained at 24–33 hours. Fitch (1975) thought the average ringneck snake feeds about once every 8 days and that half of that period is required to digest and assimilate the meal.

Earthworms are usually grabbed in the mouth and held there as the snake works to one end of the worm and then begins swallowing. Salamanders are also treated in this way, but may also be held tight in the mouth until they stop struggling and then are swallowed. This same behavior is evident when *D. punctatus* captures a small lizard or snake. Myers (1965) has postulated that the enlarged posterior maxillary teeth are used to inject saliva into prey and that this snake may be mildly venomous. Gehlbach (1974) has reported that *D. p. arnyi* may chew snakes before swallowing them, and that bitten snakes become immobile in 40–375 minutes. Shaw and Campbell (1974) reported that one person bitten felt a burning sensation, but Henderson (1970) was bitten several times without experiencing any discomfort. There seem to be behavioral differences between the southwestern snake and lizard–eating populations (Gehlbach, 1974) and those from the more northern prairie and eastern worm–eating populations (Myers, 1965; Henderson, 1970; Fitch, 1975).

Predators And Defense: This small snake has many natural predators. Snake–eating serpents, such as coral snakes, copperheads, racers, kingsnakes and milk snakes take their toll, and bull frogs, predatory hawks, owls, and small mammals eat a few. Barber (in Myers, 1965) reported an attack on a ringneck snake by a carabid beetle larva, and Ernst (1962) saw a trout eat a swimming *D. punctatus*. However, in recent years most have died as a result of habitat destruction by humans. Ernst (1962) has also reported that some Maryland *D. punctatus* died from insecticide poisoning.

When first handled, *D. punctatus* tries to escape by vigorous squirming or crawling between the fingers while releasing a strong musk. Occasional ringnecks may pretend to be dead (Gehlbach, 1970), and others may tuck the head beneath their coils while rolling the tail into a tight coil and displaying the bright yellow or orangish-red venter of the tail in a flash display (David, 1948; Smith, 1975). Whether this latter behavior is to startle a predator, or to direct its attack toward the less crucial tail, is not known.

Populations: Fitch (1975) and Blanchard et al. (1979), have conducted long-term ecological studies of *D. punctatus* in Kansas and Michigan. At two sites in Kansas, Fitch (1975) estimated the populations contained 2700-7000 and 4500-10400 snakes, for densities of 700-1800 and 775-1800 snakes per hectare. At the Michigan study site, the population size was estimated to be 77-150 snakes (Blanchard et al., 1979), and since many ringnecks were never recaptured, it was thought that at any time a large proportion of the snakes were transients. These transients were generally shorter in length than the native ringnecks. The juvenile to adult ratio of ringnecks collected in Michigan was 1:8, which may indicate how secretive the young are rather than a greater juvenile mortality rate; in fact, Fitch (1975) and Blanchard et al. (1979) thought the mortality rate was rather constant throughout life, a 21-29% reduction in each age or size class. In Kansas, the sex ratio varied drastically with the season, but was skewed toward males. Myers (1965) found a 1:1 adult sex ratio in Florida, but in juveniles the ratio favored males. Females were predominant in a population in Nova Scotia (Gilhen, 1970).

Remarks: Gehlbach (1974) thought that perhaps the enlarged posterior, maxillary teeth of eastern and southwestern *D. punctatus* are ancestral, an adaptation for holding earthworms and slippery amphibians, and preadaptive to the behavioral employment of venom. This evolution would be of great advantage to those southwestern populations which feed more on lizards and snakes.

FARANCIA ABACURA

Mud Snake

FARANCIA ABACURA (Holbrook, 1836)
Mud Snake

Recognition: A thick–bodied (to 206 cm) black and red snake with a terminal tail spine. Dorsally, the glossy body is bluish–gray to black, often with a metallic sheen. The dark pigment on the sides is interrupted by a series of salmon–pink to red bars, and the venter has alternating reddish and black transverse bars. The lips, chin, and throat are yellowish with a black spot on each scale. The wedge–shaped head is almost as wide as the neck. The pitless, smooth scales (some near the anus may be keeled) usually occur in 19 (18–21) rows with no reduction along the body. The anal plate usually is divided. Lateral head scalation includes a loreal, 2 postoculars, 2 + 2 temporals, 7 (6–8) supralabials (the 3rd and 4th enter the orbit), and 8 (7–10) infralabials. The bifurcate hemipenis has dentate calyces and numerous spines. There are two enlarged teeth at the rear of each maxilla.

The smaller males (to 110 cm) have 168–180 ventrals, 44–55 subcaudals and a tail 14–18% of the total body length; the larger females (to 206 cm) have 185–208 ventrals, 31–43 subcaudals and a tail 8–14% of the total body length. Males have distinct keels on the dorsal body scales in the anal region; these are absent from the dorsal scales of females.

Karyotype: Unknown.

Fossil Record: Meylan (1982) found a maxilla and 5 thoracic vertebrae in Pleistocene (Irvingtonian) deposits in Citrus County, Florida.

Distribution: *F. abacura* ranges from southeastern Virginia south to the tip of Florida, west to eastern Texas and southeastern Oklahoma, and north along the Mississippi River to southeastern Iowa, southern Illinois, and southwestern Indiana.

Geographic Variation: Two subspecies are recognized. *Farancia abacura abacura* (Holbrook, 1836), the eastern mud snake, ranges from southeastern Virginia southward through peninsular Florida and west to the Florida panhandle and eastern Alabama. It has 53 or more triangular–shaped red bars along the sides of its body, the distal red bars on its tail frequently uniting medially, and 3–4 median scale rows separating the light bars on the neck. *F. a. reinwardti* (Schlegel, 1837), the western mud snake, ranges from eastern Alabama westward to eastern Texas and southeastern Oklahoma and northward along the Mississippi Valley to southern Illinois and southwestern Indiana. It has 52 or fewer rounded red bars along the side of the body, the distal red bars unite medially only at the tail tip, and 8–9 median scale rows separate the light bars on the neck. The two subspecies intergrade in eastern Alabama and the panhandle of Florida.

Confusing Species: Rainbow snakes, *Farancia erytrogramma*, have 2 internasal scales, and 3 longitudinal red stripes on their backs. The *Nerodia* all have heavily keeled dorsal scales, and *Seminatrix pygaea* does not have broad black bars crossing its red venter.

Habitat: The mud snake inhabits shallow, mud–bottomed waterways with slow current, including cyprus swamps, marshes, bogs, creeks, and sloughs. It also is tolerant of brackish water and often occurs in bays or tidal creeks.

Behavior: In the north it is forced to hibernate during the colder months, but in the southern parts of its range, *F. abacura* may be active for most of the year; we have collected foraging individuals in February and early March in southern Florida.

Mud snakes in Georgia leave the water in late fall and burrow deeply in the pulpy wood of decaying pine stumps on hills or banks overlooking the water (Neill, 1948a). Meade (1935a) reported that a captive stopped feeding in late October and attempted to dig into the ground whenever possible. Meade allowed the snake to hibernate under dirt in a wooden box placed in a hole in the ground on 4 November. A pan of water was provided and the snake occasionally drank from this, as it had lost only about 3 grams of weight when weighed after emergence on 6 March. Scudder (1972) found a 24 cm juvenile in the burrow of a mole cricket at Gainesville, Florida, so possibly the young escape extremes of heat and cold in small animal burrows.

F. abacura is chiefly nocturnal, especially in the summer, hiding in burrows or in aquatic vegetation during the day. In the spring there is some diurnal activity, at least in Florida where Ernst has collected several during the morning in March. Mud snakes studied by Jacob and McDonald (1976) exhibited slowed heart rates during diving, and showed some evidence that the heart rate depends on how excited is the snake.

Reproduction: Mating has been observed in June (Anderson, 1965) and July (Meade, 1937). The mating reported by Meade occurred on 11 July.

The paired captive snakes were first observed at 0700 hr in the water but moved out soon afterward and coupled the rest of the day. During much of this time the female was in a loose coil with the male in a fairly straight line at right angles to the posterior part of her body.

Female *F. abacura* construct a nest burrow and tend the eggs after they are laid, usually lying in a loose coil about them (Meade, 1937, 1940, 1945; Reynolds and Solberg, 1942; Reimer, 1957; Hahn and Wilson, 1966). A female observed by Meade (1935b) began the color changes associated with ecdysis the day after ovipositing, and refused all food until it shed two weeks later. Nesting extends from April to September, and 4–104 (Van Hyning, 1931; Kennedy, 1959), elliptical (30–35 x 19.5–25 mm), smooth, white eggs are laid at one time. Incubation lasts 60–80 days and the young emerge from July to October. Wright and Wright (1957) reported receiving an egg on 10 April which had hatched enroute from Alabama, perhaps this egg had overwintered from the previous autumn. The young are 180–234 mm long when hatched, and usually shed their skins soon after.

Longevity: A female *F. abacura* survived 18 years, 10 days at the Philadelphia Zoo (Bowler, 1977).

Food And Feeding: The aquatic salamanders, amphiumas and sirens, are the preferred foods of adult *F. abacura*, although freshwater eels, various adult frogs, tadpoles, aquatic salamanders, and occasionally fish are consumed. The young apparently feed on tadpoles, small salamanders, and frogs. Many captives refuse all food except amphiumas or sirens and starve if these prey are not available.

Mud snakes have enlarged teeth at the rear of their upper jaws which probably give them a more firm grip on their large, slippery amphibian prey. Taub (1967) found a Duvernoy's gland with numerous mucous cells in one *F. abacura* but none in another, so it is not known whether mud snakes use venom to subdue their prey.

Predators And Defense: Large wading birds, carnivorous mammals, various snake–eating serpents, and alligators probably take their share of mud snakes, especially the young.

When disturbed *F. abacura* often tuck their heads beneath their coils, curl the red and black tail and display it prominently. Such a flash of color has been thought to be a warning display by Davis (1948). Davis also reported that his snake, if further disturbed, would turn over on its back and remain quiet, displaying its red and black belly. When handled, newly caught individuals some times jab the hands with their tail spine, but do not penetrate the skin.

Map

Fig. 10. *Farancia abacura abacura* (Steve W. Gotte).

FARANCIA ABACURA

Mud Snake

Populations: *F. abacura* may occur in great numbers at some sites. Hellman and Telford (1956) collected 478 young snakes on a 2.7 km stretch of road fill in Alachua County, Florida following torrential rains from an October hurricane.

The number of males and females in two broods of *F. a. reinwardti* reported by Hahn and Wilson (1966) were 10 and 10 and 26 and 18, respectively.

Remarks: The genus *Farancia* may represent a lineage independent of those of other neotropical and North American xenodontines (Cadle, 1984). In a study of skull morphology Cundall and Rossman (1984) found the skulls of both subspecies of *F. abacura* to be significantly separated in multivariate space. In fact, separation of these subspecies required little more information than the separation of *F. erytrogramma* from either, and Wright and Wright (1957) reported an apparent hybrid *abacura* x *erytrogramma* from Florida.

FARANCIA ERYTROGRAMMA

Rainbow Snake

FARANCIA ERYTROGRAMMA
(Palisot de Beauvois, in Sonnini and Latreille, 1801) Rainbow Snake

Recognition: This is one of the most attractive of our native snakes (to 168 cm). It is iridescent black to violet or violet–blue with 3 reddish longitudinal stripes; the large head scales often have red edges. The supralabials, infralabials, chin, and throat are lemon–yellow; the centers of each supralabial, mental scale, chin shields, and the anterior infralabials are usually violet. The venter is red to reddish–yellow with 2 rows of anterior black spots at the sides of the ventral scales; and a shorter mid–ventral row of black spots. The wedge–shaped head is about as wide as the neck. The pitless, smooth body scales (some near the anus may be keeled) usually occur in 21 anterior rows, 19 at mid–body (the 4th row is lost at the level of the 8th–14th ventrals), and 18 near the anus (the reduction occurs at the level of the 5th to 7th ventrals anterior to the vent). The anal plate usually is divided, but is single in some Virginia specimens (Richmond, 1954a). Head scales are like those of *F. abacura*, except there are usually 7 (6–10) infralabials. The tail ends in a sharp spine–like scale. Cope (1900) described the hemipenis as bifurcate with each apex having a moderate number of slightly serrate calyces, and numerous spines. Two enlarged teeth occur posteriorly on the maxilla.

Males have 155–162 ventrals and 44–49 subcaudals; females 170–182 ventrals and 35–42 subcaudals; in males the tail is 15.8–17.6% of the total body length, while that of the female is only 12.7–15.3% (Richmond, 1954).

Karyotype: Unknown

Fossil Record: Pleistocene or Recent fossils of *Farancia* from Florida have been found at Vero Beach, St. Lucie County (Wisconsin; Hay, 1917; Weigel, 1962); Orange Lake, Marion County (Illinoian; Holman, 1959); Reddick, Marion County (Illinoian; Auffenberg, 1963), and Seminole, Pinellas County (Brattstrom, 1953). Auffenberg (1963), Neill (1964) and Holman (1981) considered these vertebrae to be difficult, if not impossible, to assign to either *F. abacura* or *F. erytrogramma*.

Distribution: *F. erytrogramma* is found from southern Maryland (Charles County) southward to central Florida (Lake and Pinellas counties) with an isolated population in Glades County, Florida, and westward to central Mississippi and southeastern Louisiana.

Geographic Variation: Two subspecies are recognized, the latter of these is poorly known. *Farancia erytrogramma erytrogramma* (Palisot de Beauvois, in Sonnini and Latreille, 1801), the rainbow snake, ranges from Charles County, Maryland south along the Atlantic Coast to Lake and Pinellas counties, Florida, and west through the Gulf states to southeastern Louisiana. It has red or pink ventrals with the black pigment restricted to a lateral row and a short mid–ventral row of spots, black spotted subcaudals with the red pigment not restricted to the borders of the spots, no black pigment on the first dorsal scale row, scale row 2 less than 25% black, scale row 3 less than 75% black, and no black encroaching on the lateral red stripe. *Farancia e. seminola* Neill, 1964, the South Florida rainbow snake, is known from only a few specimens taken in the vicinity of Fisheating Creek and Lake Okeechobee, Glades County, Florida. It has much black pigment on the ventrals behind the throat, the black subcaudal spots with narrow red borders, the scales on dorsal rows 1 and 2 less than 50% black, those of row 3 all black, and black pigment encroaching on the red lateral stripe.

Confusing Species: Both the mud snake, *Farancia abacura*, and black swamp snake, *Seminatrix pygaea*, have plain black backs.

Habitat: This secretive snake prefers coastal plain waterways (rivers, creeks, swamps, tidal and freshwater marshes, lakes) surrounded by sandy soil.

Behavior: A burrower, it is often plowed up in sandy fields near waterways. It is nocturnal and remains hidden beneath the soil, under logs or in old stumps during the daylight hours. Neill (1964) reported that in Florida, rainbow snakes usually live in the roots of bald cypress trees growing in about 60 cm of water, and that shortly after dark they slowly stretch upward until the eyes and nostrils are above water while their tails remain coiled among the roots. Man–made structures are also used for retreats (docks, log or stone piles); we once took several from the pilings of a boat ramp in North Carolina. Neill (1964) found that in Florida these snakes do not emerge completely until 2100–2130 hr, and then forage along the bottom of the waterway until about 2330 hr when they return to their retreats.

In Florida, rainbow snakes are active in every month with low activity in March and October and greater activity in June, possibly due to increased movements of gravid females. March activity probably represents mating and foraging after the partial inactivity of winter, while the October activity may represent increased foraging to build up winter fat supplies (Neill, 1964).

As a result of drift–fence sampling in South Carolina, Gibbons et al. (1977) suggested the following hypotheses for seasonal activity of immature rainbow snakes: 1. After hatching in the fall *F. erytrogramma* remain in the soil in the vicinity of the nest, overwintering on land. 2. In March and April they move overland to an aquatic area. 3. If the aquatic habitat is "suitable," the individual remains at the site. 4. If the aquatic habitat becomes undesirable in some feature, individuals may emigrate, moving overland to seek another aquatic site in the vicinity and, perhaps, even remaining on land in a fossorial state for extended periods of time. Migrations may be made at any warm period of the year. 5. Such an opportunistic approach would permit individuals to utilize the most suitable habitat in an area. This strategy should have high selective value on the southeastern coastal plain where many aquatic habitats have unpredictable, fluctuating water levels from year to year.

Rainbow snakes caught by Gibbons et al. (1977) in March and early April characteristically were associated with warm periods (night temperature over 10 C) following 2 or more days of cooler weather, and captures were often made on the day prior to or following rainfall, but they thought temperature was the more influential variable.

In Florida higher winter water temperatures may allow *F. erytrogramma* to be active for more extensive periods; farther north thermoregulatory basking or hibernation may be necessary. However, even in Virginia they may be active in every month; Richmond (1945) observed a hawk eating one on the ice of a marsh in February.

Reproduction: The courtship and mating acts of *F. erytrogramma* have not been described. Nests are dug in sandy soil to depths of 20–25 cm (Neill, 1964). A nest measured by Richmond (1945) was 10 cm deep, 20 cm long and 15 cm wide. N. Fry (in Wright and Wright, 1957) reported the female may make a burrow in the sandy soil 30 cm or more wide, and that she may remain with the eggs, although, this has not been verified. The nesting period extends from early

Map

Fig. 11. Venter of *Farancia erytrogramma erytrogramma* (Carl H. Ernst).

June to mid–August, and 20–52 cream–colored, leathery eggs (37–40 x 22–29 mm) comprise a clutch. Incubation takes 75–80 days, and the young usually hatch from September to November. The 20–26 cm young use their caruncle (egg tooth) to slit open the eggshell, and after emergence may remain in the nest for some time. They usually shed within two weeks after hatching, often before leaving the nest.

Growth: Richmond (1954a) suggested that juveniles of both sexes grow about 24 mm during their first five months, and Rothman (1961) had a captive that grew 90 mm in nine months.

Food And Feeding: Adults feed primarily on freshwater eels (*Anguilla rostrata*). Wild juveniles eat tadpoles, and Rothman (1961) had captive juveniles that consumed live salamanders (*Plethodon cinereus, Eurycea bislineata, Desmognathus* sp.) and small leopard frogs (*Rana pipiens*), but they would not accept dead food.

It is not known if *F. erytrogramma* uses venom to overcome its prey, but it has enlarged posterior maxillary teeth and a mixed Duvernoy's gland containing mucous cells (Taub, 1967).

Predators And Defense: Richmond (1945) three times observed hawks feed on *F. erytrogramma*, and Neill (1964) reported an indigo snake (*Drymarchon corais couperi*) disgorged an adult rainbow snake. Ernst found a juvenile in the stomach of a bullfrog.

Captive rainbow snakes often develop skin ulcers which are probably of fungal or bacterial origin, and Richmond (1945) found heavy infestations of nematode worms.

Farancia erytrogramma never bite when handled; however, when first captured wild individuals may press the tail spine into their captor's hand, resulting in a prickling sensation.

Populations: Because of their secretive habits rainbow snakes give a false impression of being rare. In fact, they can occur in dense populations; Mount (1975) collected 8 within 30 m.

Remarks: Rainbow snakes usually are very poor captives, refusing food and eventually starving to death. We urge this be taken into consideration when they are caught.

HETERODON NASICUS

Western Hognose Snake

HERTERODON NASICUS (Baird and Girard, 1853)
Western Hognose Snake

Recognition: A thick-bodied, medium-sized snake (to 89.5 cm) with a sharply upturned rostrum bearing a dorsal keel, and a mostly black venter. The ground color is buffy gray, brown or olive, and a series of about 35 to 40 dark brown blotches occurs on the back. There are two longitudinal rows of smaller dark brown blotches along each side of the body, and the tail is ringed with dark bands. A dark v-shaped mark with the apex on the parietal scales occurs behind the eyes, and a transverse dark bar between the eyes extends downward behind the eyes to the corner of the mouth. The keeled body scales are pitted, and occur in 23 rows anteriorly and at mid-body, and 19 rows near the anal vent. The anal plate is divided. Eight to 28 azygous scales lie between the internasals and prefrontals, and there is a complete ring of ocular scales around the eye. Laterally, there are 2 nasal scales, 2 or more loreal scales, 4 (2–5) + 5(3–7) temporals, 7–8 supralabials, and 10–12(9–13) infralabials. Each maxilla usually has ten teeth; a diastema separates the enlarged posterior tooth from those anterior to it, and the maxilla can rotate to elevate these rear teeth (Kroll, 1976). The bilobed hemipenis has a bifurcate sulcus spermaticus, a spiny base, and calyces distally (see Platt, 1969, for a more complete description).

Males have 125–139 ventrals, 34–50 subcaudals, and tails 13–19% as long as the total body length; females have 134–156 ventrals, 26–41 subcaudals, and tails 12–14% of the total body length.

Karyotype: The karyotype is 2n = 36; 16 macrochromosomes, 20 microchromosomes, sex determination, ZZ males, ZW females (Baker et al., 1972).

Fossil Record: Fossil *H. nasicus* are known only from the Pleistocene (Blancan of Kansas; Irvington of Texas; Rancholabrean of Kansas, New Mexico, Oklahoma, and Texas; Holman, 1981).

Distribution: *H. nasicus* ranges from western Minnesota and southwestern Manitoba, west to southern Saskatchewan and southeastern Alberta and south through the Great Plains to northern Zacatecas and San Luis Potosi in Mexico. Isolated colonies also occur in east–central Minnesota, western Illinois, northwestern and southeastern Missouri, and eastern Texas.

Geographic Variation: Three subspecies have been described (Edgren, 1952), but only two occur east of the Mississippi River in Illinois. *Heterodon nasicus nasicus*, Baird and Girard, 1853, the plains hognose snake, is described above. It occurs in intergrade populations with *H. n. gloydi* in central and west–central Illinois (Smith and Smith, 1962). Its main range is from southwestern Manitoba to southeastern Alberta, south to Oklahoma, the panhandle of Texas and eastern New Mexico. *Heterodon n. gloydi* Edgren, 1952, the dusty hognose snake, is similar to *H. n. nasicus*, but usually has less than 32 obscure dorsal blotches in males and less than 37 in females. Besides occurring in intergrade populations in Illinois, it also is found in a pure colony in southwestern Illinois and southeastern Missouri, but its main range is from southeastern Kansas through most of eastern and central Texas.

Confusing Species: *H. platyrhinos* usually has the underside of its tail a lighter color than its belly, the pointed rostral scale not sharply upturned, and few if any azygous scales. *H. simus* has the underside of its tail similar in color to the body, but lacks black pigment, and has only one row of lateral spots. *Sistrurus miliarius* has a rattle, a facial pit, and vertical pupils.

Habitat: The western hognose snake is a prairie or savannah species. It prefers to live in areas with well drained sandy soils, into which it burrows for concealment and out of which it can easily dig its major prey, toads, lizards, and reptile eggs (Platt, 1969).

Behavior: Surprisingly we know relatively little about this fairly common snake. Most data have been anecdotal, but Platt (1969) has published a rather thorough review, and we have drawn heavily from it.

In Alberta, at the northern extent of its range, *H. nasicus* has been found as early as 10 May and as late as 20 September, an annual activity period of 133 days (Pendlebury, 1976). In the more southern populations, it is probably active from April through October. In Kansas, Platt (1969) found western hognose snakes from 24 April to 31

October. Wright and Wright (1957) report activity from January to October. They may become inactive for short periods during the summer when the air temperatures are high. Males are most active early in the season, particularly during the mating season; females are most active in the last half of July, after the egg–laying period.

H. nasicus apparently overwinters underground or in mammal burrows (Smith, 1961), but there is little information available on hibernation. Since there are no recorded mass autumn movements, hibernation probably takes place individually within the home range.

Daily activity is diurnal. Platt (1969) occasionally saw them at dusk, but never found any active after dark either in the field or in an outdoor pen. The nights are spent in temporary burrows the snakes dig in loose soil with their upturned snouts (Edgren, 1955; Platt, 1969). The rostrum is more upturned and larger than that of *H. platyrhinos* and forms a better scooping surface. The dorsal scooping edge is rounded giving a broad edge for dorsal thrusts, as well as lateral thrusts (Platt, 1969). They seldom take shelter under rocks or logs.

Platt (1969) reported that the cloacal temperatures of active *H. nasicus* were 21.4–36.2 C (ground surface temperatures, 17.6–36.0 C). The usual activity range was 27–35 C. A snake in a trap with a cloacal temperature of 13.7 C was sluggish, but others were first able to make avoidance movements at 4 C and were first able to right themselves at 5.6 C.

The mean distance between points of capture of individual male *H. nasicus* at two Kansas sites were 79 and 207 m, and of females, 93 and 255 m (Platt, 1969). A movement of 408 m between 26 April and 12 May, and one of 378 m between 2 August and 20 October were made by males in the spring and autumn breeding seasons at one of the sites. Males that moved 777 m between 18 June and 20 July and 602 m between 17 October and 28 June at Platt's other study site probably shifted their home ranges. The longest recorded movement was that of a female which crawled approximately 1.6 km between 9 August and 12 June of the next year.

Reproduction: Females may possibly mature at a snout–vent length of only 310 mm. The smallest female that Platt (1969) found to be definitely gravid was 366 mm, but another 312 mm in snout–vent length appeared gravid, but later resorbed its eggs. Platt felt that most females mature at a snout–vent length of 350–400 mm, at 20–22 months of age.

Map

Fig. 12. *Heterodon nasicus nasicus* (Carl H. Ernst).

HETERODON NASICUS

Western Hognose Snake

In the spring, immature females examined by Platt (1969), contained 7–15 ova that were 1–3 mm in length. In the late summer preceding sexual maturity, some of these ova had enlarged to 3–5 mm in length. Approximately 50% of these enlarged ova matured the following spring. The maturing ova enlarged rapidly in the spring. Females seem to have an annual reproductive cycle.

Platt (1969) found motile sperm in 3 of 7 males with snout–vent lengths less than 300 mm, from 13 of 23 males 300–349 mm long, and from 43 of 48 males 350 mm or longer. Most initiated spermatogenesis at 9 months in their first spring and were mature when one year old. Those collected in May had spermatogonia common, although some primary spermatocytes were present. Spermatogenic activity reached its peak in July and early August. Primary spermatocytes and early spermatids were common in early July, and by late July spermatids of all stages were present. Some mature sperm were in the tubules in July, and by September sperm were common in the ducts.

The principal mating period is in the spring, but copulation may also occur in the fall. Platt (1969) felt that since *H. nasicus* does not hibernate in groups, the males probably wander widely and seek out the more sedentary females in the first few weeks after emergence from hibernation. They possible follow odor trails to the females. The courtship and mating acts have not been described.

H. nasicus is oviparous, normally laying its eggs in July, although there are nesting records in the literature extending from 3 June in Texas (Werler, 1951), to 28 August in Illinois (Smith, 1961). Nests are excavated in sandy or other loose soil to a depth of 10 cm; at times eggs may be laid one after another in a tunnel instead of in a cluster in a depression (Platt, 1969). Iverson (1975) gave the following notes on embryos and hatching.

> After 40 days, the first of several developing eggs was opened. It contained a viable 14 cm male embryo. A 43–day egg yielded a live 16 cm female embryo, a 47–day egg a 16.5 female, and a 50–day egg a 15 cm female...
>
> During the morning of August 30 (52 days incubation) hatching began. Two days were required for all hatchlings to complete the hatching process. However, only 10–15 hours were required for each individual snake.

The elliptical eggs are white or cream, have smooth leathery shells, and are 22.0–42.0 x 14.5–25.0 mm. A clutch may contain 2 (Sabath and Worthington, 1959) to 24 (Wright and Wright, 1957) eggs, but 8–12 eggs are most common. The incubation period is 50–60 days, and the young hatch from early August to late September. Munro (1949c) observed the hatching of a clutch of 11 eggs. Most required 40–60 hours to leave the egg after making the first slit. The quickest emergence took 30 hours. Hatchlings are 170–195 mm in total length.

Growth And Longevity: Platt (1969) reported the following probable growth rates for male western hognose snakes in Kansas: 9 months old, 179–255 mm in snout–vent length (20.6 mm increase per month); those 21 months, 282–326 mm, (18.6 mm/month); 33 months, 330–356 mm (6.3 mm/month); and 45 months, 360–377 mm (4.8/month). Similarly, females 9 months old were 206–296 mm (29.3 mm growth per month); 21 months, 312–398 mm (22.9 mm/ month); 33 months, 418–451 mm (16.6 mm/ month); and 45 months 471–490 mm (7.7 mm/ month).

The longevity record for *H. nasicus* is 9 years, 2 months, 7 days (Bowler, 1977).

Food And Feeding: *H. nasicus* is not as dependent on amphibian prey as are its more eastern relatives, *H. platyrhinos* and *H. simus*. Captives have eaten toads, frogs, lizards, snakes, birds, shrews and mice (Munro, 1949a; Edgren 1955; Swenson, 1950; Wright and Wright, 1957, Platt, 1969). Natural prey includes toads (*Bufo*) spadefoots (*Scaphiopis*), leopard frogs (*Rana*), tadpoles (*Rana*), tiger salamanders (*Ambystoma tigrinum*), lizards (*Cnemidophorus, Eumeces, Sceloporus, Uta, Crotaphytus*), lizard eggs (*Eumeces*), snakes (*Thamnophis, Coluber*), snake eggs, turtles (*Kinosternon flavescens*), turtle eggs (*Emydoidea, Terrapene, Chelydra*), birds (meadowlark, grasshopper sparrow), birds' eggs (ringneck pheasant or quail), mice (*Peromyscus, Microtus, Perognathus, Reithrodontomys*) and insect fragments (Breckenridge, 1944; Diener, 1957a; Wright and Wright, 1957, Gehlbach and Collette, 1959; Platt, 1969; Pendlebury, 1976, Barten, 1980; Murphy and Dloogatch, 1980). A summary of prey by Platt (1969) indicates that amphibians are taken 13–57% of the time, reptiles 17–48%, mammals 5–33%, and birds 1–14%. C. B. Perkins (in Edgren, 1955) stated that *H. nasicus* from areas where toads are common refuse frogs, while those from areas where frogs are abundant refuse toads.

Odor and sight are the senses used to detect prey. When the prey is sighted, *H. nasicus* does not strike but instead crawls quickly toward the prey, attempting to seize the animal with wide open mouth, often attempting to hold the animal down with a coil of its body (Platt, 1969). Buried prey, such as reptile eggs, toads or spadefoots, is dug out with the upturned snout.

The saliva of *H. nasicus* is toxic to its prey (Weaver, 1965; Kroll, 1976; McKinistry, 1978). The enlarged posterior maxillary teeth are used as fangs, and several cranial adaptations are used to subdue prey (Kapus, 1964, Kroll, 1976). Kroll (1976) reported that the maxillae articulate freely with the prefrontal bones; anteroventral movement of ectopterygoid is produced by constriction of the protractor pterygoideus muscle and is transmitted to a ventrodorsal rotation of the maxillae around the prefrontal bones. This rotation elevates the rear teeth which inject the venom, then hold and manipulate the prey during swallowing. The superior labial gland, which produces the venom, consists of two parts: a dorsal seromucous venom gland and a ventral mucous supralabial gland. These two glands are morphologically distinct. The venom gland connects with the enlarged rear teeth via a duct.

The bite of *H. nasicus* has caused painful envenomation in humans (Bragg, 1960; Morris, 1985). Symptoms experienced by Morris (1985) included discoloration and swelling of the bitten finger and adjacent hand, and slight continuous bleeding from the wounds. Care should be taken when these snakes are handled.

Predators And Defense: There are few records of predation on *H. nasicus*; Swainson's hawk, ferruginous hawks, *Buteo* hawks, crows, coyotes, and eastern hognose snakes (Platt, 1969; Blair and Schitoskey, 1982). Surely other carnivorous mammals and serpent–eating snakes also prey on them. Greene and Oliver (1965) saw a western massasauga eat a road–killed *H. nasicus*, and Iverson (1975) reported a case of attempted cannibalism.

Like other *Heterodon*, *H. nasicus* has a stereotyped defensive display. If it cannot escape when disturbed, it spreads its neck and hisses loudly while occasionally striking with mouth closed. If this does not drive away its adversary, it will then contort its body, writhe about, vomit up food, and finally roll over on its back and play dead with tongue extended and blood seeping from the mouth. At times its writhing may become so violent that it bites itself (Kroll, 1977).

Populations: Platt (1969) calculated that the sizes of his two study populations were 57 and 121 *H. nasicus*, for densities of 2.8 and 6.0 snakes per hectare, respectively. At one of the sites, snakes older than 2 years composed 88% of the population (1st year, 12%; 2nd year, 30%, 3rd year, 26%, 4th year and older, 32%). The size structure of this population was as follows: less than 360 mm snout–vent length, 21%, 360–399 mm, 19%; 400–439, 13%; 440–489 mm, 26%; and over 489 mm, 21%. Platt (1969) thought the primary sex ratio is probably 1:1.

HETERODON PLATYRHINOS

Eastern Hognose Snake

HETERODON PLATYRHINOS
(Latreille, 1801)
Eastern Hognose Snake

Recognition: A thick–bodied, medium–sized snake (to 115.6 cm) with an unkeeled, only slightly upturned rostrum, that has the underside of the tail lighter in color than the rest of the venter. The ground color is either gray, light pinkish–brown, yellow, olive or black. There are usually 20–30 pale transverse bars separating rows of dark spots along the sides and back, but some individuals are entirely olive or black. A dark v–shaped mark, with the apex on the parietal scales, occurs behind the eyes, and a transverse dark bar between the eyes extends downward behind the eyes to the corner of the mouth. The keeled and pitted body scales occur in 25(21–27) rows anteriorly and at mid–body, and 19(16–21) rows near the anus. Usually only one (0–2) azygous scale lies between the internasals and prefrontal scales, and there is a complete ring of ocular scales around the eye. Laterally there are 2 nasal scales, 1(2–4) loreal, 3–4 + 4–5 temporals, 7–8 supralabials and 10–11(9–14) infralabials. Each maxilla has 11–13 teeth; a diastema separates the enlarged posterior tooth from those anterior to it. The maxilla can rotate to elevate the rear teeth (Kroll, 1976). The hemipenis is similar to that of *H. nasicus*.

Males have 112–141 ventrals, 30–60 subcaudals, and tails 17–22% as long as the total body length; females have 126–154 ventrals, 34–52 subcaudals, and tails 12–17% that of the total body length. Edgren (1951, 1958) found that males have 90–109 ventrals anterior to the unbilical scar, while females have 101–120.

Karyotype: Edgren (1953b) reported *H. platyrhinos* has 40–44 diploid chromosomes, but Baker et al. (1972) reported the karyotype was similar to that of *H. nasicus*, with 36 chromosomes.

Fossils: Fossils of *H. platyrhinos* are known from the upper Pliocene of Kansas and Texas (Hol-

man, 1979), and from the Pleistocene Blancan of Kansas and Nebraska, Irvingtonian of Florida, Georgia and Maryland, and Rancholabrean of Florida, Georgia, Kansas, Missouri, Tennessee, and Texas (Holman, 1981; Meylan, 1982).

Distribution: *H. platyrhinos* ranges from southern New Hampshire and southwestern Ontario west to Minnesota and southern South Dakota, and south to Florida and Texas (Conant, 1975; Blem, 1981a)

Geographic Variation: No subspecies are currently recognized. The form *H. platyrhinos browni* Stejneger, 1903a from southern Florida, which was diagnosed as lacking azygous scales, is within the normal variation of *H. platyrhinos* (Duellman and Schwartz, 1958).

Confusing Species: Both *H. nasicus* and *H. simus* have sharply upturned snouts and 3 or more azygous scales. *H. nasicus* has much black pigment on the venter, and *H. simus* has the underside of its tail the same color as the rest of the venter. *Sistrurus miliarius* has a rattle, a facial pit, and elliptical pupils.

Habitat: The habitat varies from wooded hillsides to grassy and cultivated fields. Areas with sandy or sandy–loam soils are essential. We have most often encountered them along the edge of woodlands or on roads passing through woodlands, and on sandy barrier beaches in tidal areas. In such places, Rodgers (1985) has even seen them swimming in the breakers. Although we have taken them from under logs in wooded habitats, they are usually found on the open ground prowling for prey. Funderberg and Lee (1968) have also found them in pocket gopher mounds in Florida.

Behavior: *H. platyrhinos* is one of the last snakes to enter hibernation and one of the first to become active again in the spring (Neill, 1948a; Guidry, 1953). They are most active from April to early November, and particularly from May to July, but active *H. platyrhinos* have also been found from December through March (Neill, 1948a; Guidry, 1953; Wright and Wright, 1957; Platt, 1969; Jones, 1976a). Normally they hibernate individually under rocks, in rotting logs or stumps, under trash piles, in mammal burrows, or in burrows in the soil that they dig themselves (Neill, 1948a; Anderson, 1965; Platt, 1969). Arndt (1980) observed an individual bury itself to a depth of 58 cm in sandy soil to hibernate. Later, when he recorded the cloacal temperature of this snake, it had a body temperature of 9.2 C while the sand temperatures was 8.5 C. Lee (1968b) has found an eastern hognose snake hibernating with several individuals of four species of snakes and seven species of amphibians in and above a small spring in Maryland. Estivation probably also occurs during the hottest weather. Daily activity is almost strictly in the morning hours (Platt, 1969; Scott, 1986).

Platt (1969) reported that the voluntary minimum and maximum temperatures of *H. platyrhinos* from Kansas were 22 C and 34 C, respectively, and Jones (1976a) reported a similiar temperature range for active individuals in Maryland. Kitchell (1969) found that *H. platyrhinos* presented a thermal gradient chose temperatures from 22.4–37.4 C. Platt (1969) discovered that at a body temperature of 5.6 C they could still crawl slowly, spread their necks and hiss.

Little is known of the movements of this snake. Stickel and Cope (1947) reported one was recaptured only 30 m from the original capture point after 5.5 months. *H. platyrhinos* recaptured by Platt (1969) at two Kansas sites had moved mean distances of 208 m and 290 m, respectively; these distances indicate a larger home range than that of *H. nasicus*. Platt's longest movements were 783 m and 858 m by males during the breeding season. Distances moved between captures by *H. platyrhinos* in Virginia ranged from 40 to 760 m (x = 390 m) (Scott, 1986).

When not foraging, *H. platyrhinos* usually burrows into loose soil. It bends its head downward in such a way as to apply the broad dorsal surface and pointed snout to the soil and then moves the head back and forth laterally while pushing into the soil. The flattened dorsal surface of the head may be used to bring soil to the surface. *H. platyrhinos* is not restricted to dry land, but has been seen swimming in both fresh and brackish water on several occasions (Vance, 1981; Rodgers, 1985). Munyer (1967) has observed it perform its characteristic death feigning behavior while in water.

Reproduction: Platt (1969) reported that female *H. platyrhinos* mature at 21 months of age at about 550 mm snout–vent length. His smallest mature female was 500 mm. Females contain large yolked eggs and weigh the most in April and May, and probably reproduce annually.

The male spermatogenic cycle is similar to that of *H. nasicus* (Platt, 1969). Males are probably sexually mature at snout–vent lengths of 450–500 mm (Ernst, personal observation), and this length is reached in 1.5–2.0 years (Platt, 1969).

Mating occurs in the spring. The earliest date copulation has been observed was 28 March in Texas (Guidry, 1953), but over most of the range the main breeding period is from mid–April through May. Since *H. platyrhinos* hibernates individually, the males must expend much energy

Map

Fig. 13. *Heterodon platyrhinos.*

seeking the females, and so are most active during the spring. Nichols (1982) described two instances of mating behavior:

> The male approached the female about three quarters of the way down her body and contacted her side with his rostrum. After contact, he advanced anteriorly along her laterally, nudging her with his rostrum as he moved. When he reached her neck, his body was parallel with that of the female. He continued to nudge her with his rostrum, looped his tail over hers and attempted to push a loop of his tail underneath. The undulations of the tail moved anteriorly until his entire body was undulating against the female's body. The female usually remained still but occasionally advanced. During most observations, the female moved away shortly before the male's tail search and copulatory attempt, but in one instance he was observed forcing his tail under hers, and the undulations of his body became more rapid causing the female to move quickly away...

> The male approached about three quarters of the way down the body of the female on the right side making tongue-flicks at a rate of about one per second. After contact with his rostrum, he moved anteriorly along the female's dorsum with his head pressed against her body. He made short tongue-flicks at a rate of about two-three per second and sudden jerking movements described as forward-jerking in rat snakes by Gillingham (1979). During his advance, the female occasionally moved forward with the male partially draped over her body. The male began to undulate his tail over the tail of the female and shortly thereafter these undulations moved anteriorly in waves described as caudocephalic waves in rat snakes by Gillingham (1979). He then forced a loop of his tail under the female's tail and began to rapidly move it back and forth.

> Intromission was accomplished with the left hemipenis. The male was lying alongside the female with his head pressed against the back of her neck. The female periodically moved forward; the male's body moved apart from hers during coitus. Copulation lasted about five hours, after which the female was removed.

The penial spines and calyces help anchor the base of the hemipenis in the female's cloaca in such a way that the distal portion remains in position despite movement of the snakes (Edgren, 1953a).

The eggs are laid from late May to mid-August, with most oviposition occurring in June and early July. The earliest and latest dates in the literature are 27 May (Kennedy, 1961) and 28 August (Smith, 1961). Most nests are depressions in loose soil or under rocks (Edgren, 1955). Kennedy (1961) has described the egg-laying behavior:

> The body of the snake was in an acute U form. The tail was extended anterior to the head with the base of the tail almost touching the head. Slow contractions were discernible

Fig. 14. A juvenile *Heterodon platyrhinos*.

Fig. 15. *Heterodon platyrhinos* feigning death.

from anterior to posterior as the eggs passed through the oviducts. Just before the egg was to be expelled, the tail was slowly elevated and the cloacal region was greatly distended. The posterior wall of the cloaca was visible as it circumscribed the egg... After most of the eggs had been laid the tail of the snake was drawn posteriorly so that the body was roughly J–shaped. None of the eggs were deposited on top of each other.

The eggs appeared at intervals of approximately 23 minutes. Hahn (in Edgren, 1955) found a female coiled around eggs, and, although this has been interpreted as a possible case of brooding (Edgren, 1955), it is more likely she had just finished laying these eggs and had not yet crawled away.

The incubation period is only known from clutches laid in captivity, 31–88 days, but most records are for 50–65 days (Platt, 1969). In nature, hatchlings are most often found in August or early September, but Clark (1949) reported that eggs in a natural nest in Louisiana hatched 4–12 July.

The hatching of a clutch of 12 eggs observed by Platt (1969) took 55.5 hours. The mean time between the appearance of the first slit in the egg and the snake leaving the egg was 27.5 hours (15–44.5).

The eggs are cream–colored, elliptical (21–39 x 13–28.5 mm, 7–12 g), and have thin parchment–like shells. Clutches vary from 4 (Cagle, 1942) to 61 (Platt, 1969) with 15–25 eggs most common. Larger females lay larger clutches.

Hatchlings are 168–250 mm in total length and more brightly patterned than the adults. They display the typical defense behavior.

Growth And Longevity: Platt (1969) estimated the following probable growth rates for *H. platyrhinos* in Kansas: males–9 months old, 269–383 mm snout–vent length (426 mm/month); 21 months, 454–521 mm (33.9 mm/month); 33 months, 540–553 mm (11.1 mm/month); and 45 months, 580–597 mm (8.1 mm/month); females –9 months, 240–385 (43.2 mm/month); 21 months, 555–567 mm (45 mm/month); 33 months, 630 mm (12.3/month); 45 months, 685 mm (9.6 mm/month). His largest female grew from 685 mm to 748 mm in less than a year, a growth rate of 10.2 mm per month.

The longevity record for *H. platyrhinos* is 7 years, 8 days (Lardie, 1978).

Food And Feeding: Wright and Wright (1957), Edgren (1955), Hamilton and Pollack (1956) and Platt (1969) have summarized the prey taken by eastern hognose snakes. Amphibians (toads, spadefoots, treefrogs, salamanders, newts), reptiles (lizards, lizard eggs, small snakes, hatchling turtles), and insects (some secondarily ingested with amphibians) are the primary foods; but fish, birds, mammals (mice and chipmunks), earthworms, isopods, centipedes, spiders, and snails are sometimes eaten. Uhler et al. (1939) reported that in Virginia the major foods taken by volume were toads (40%), frogs (30%), salamanders (11%), and small mammals (19%). In Kansas, amphibians occurred in 58% of the stomachs examined by Platt (1969), and insects in 35%. The capacity for food is quite large; Anderson (1965) reported a 61 cm *H. platyrhinos* once ate 7 medium–sized toads.

In captivity, *H. platyrhinos* seldom accepts any food but amphibians; however, some can be induced to eat mice if these are first rubbed with a toad's skin.

Smith (1976) calculated an assimilation efficiency (ingestion egestion/ingestion x 100) for *H. platyrhinos* of 73.7% for toads.

Snakes of the genus *Heterodon* seem well adapted for feeding on toads. Their large mouths, mobile maxillae, and elongated posterior maxillary teeth are ideal for holding and deflating struggling, inflated toads, and their saliva has venomous properties (McKinistry, 1978). The resistance to the powerful digitaloid and epinephrine–containing skin secretions of toads is inherent (Huheey, 1958). In *Heterodon* the adrenal glands are enlarged, even at hatching (Spaur and Smith, 1971), and Smith and White (1955) thought this an adaptation to bufophagy, as the extent of toad–eating seems to be directly correlated to adrenal size in xenodontine snakes and also in the small rattlesnakes, *Sistrurus*.

The saliva of *H. platyrhinos* can cause a burning pain, discoloration, swelling, and bleeding from the puncture wounds (McAlister, 1963; Grogan, 1974a), so care should be taken when handling these snakes.

Predators And Defense: Platt (1969) listed the following as documented predators of *H. platyrhinos*: kingsnakes, racers, coachwhips, black rat snakes, cottonmouths, red–tailed hawks, and barred owls. Owens (1949b) reported that a captive tarantula ate a hatchling. Surely other ophiophagous snakes, birds of prey, and small carnivorous mammals occasionally feed on this snake, particularly on the juveniles.

Humans have the distinction of being the worst enemy of hognose snakes. Many are killed because they appear ferocious, and many others die on our highways, but the constant destruction of natural habitat is the worst thing humans can do to a wild species.

Ferguson (1963) reported an apparent death of *H. platyrhinos* by heptochlor poisoning, and

HETERODON PLATYRHINOS

Eastern Hognose Snake

Brisbin et al. (1974) found *H. platyrhinos* with elevated radiocesium levels at the AEC Savannah River Plant. So, they may also be poisoned by human activities.

Like other *Heterodon*, *H. platyrhinos* has a stereotyped bluffing and death feigning display (Edgren and Edgren, 1955; Platt, 1969; Sexton, 1979). It may even experience bradycardia during this behavior. (McDonald, 1974).

Populations: Platt (1969) calculated the population sizes at his two study sites in Kansas were 10 and 43 *H. platyrhinos*, for densities of 0.5 and 2.1 snakes per hectare, respectively. At one of these sites, snakes younger than 2 years comprised 69% of the population (hatchlings, 28%; 1st year, 41%; 2nd year, 19%; 3rd year and older, 12%). The size structure of this population was as follows: less than 560 mm snout–vent length, 61%; 560–609 mm, 23%; 610–724 mm, 12%; 725 mm or more, 4%.

The sex ratio at hatching is 1:1 and this may carry through to adulthood (Platt, 1969), but Platt (1969) caught 87 males to 38 females (2.29:1) at one of his study sites.

Remarks: Platt (1985) has pointed out that the oldest available name for the eastern hognose snake, as proposed by Latreille (1801), was spelled *platirhinos*, and since there is no evidence this was a spelling error, the proper binomial for this species is *Heterodon platirhinos*. We believe that to adopt this spelling now would cause confusion, and feel that the name *platyrhinos* should be retained because of its common use for many years.

HETERODON SIMUS

Southern Hognose Snake

HETERODON SIMUS (Linnaeus, 1766)
Southern Hognose Snake

Recognition: A short (to 61 cm), stout, light brown, blotched snake with a sharply upturned, keeled rostrum. The dorsum is gray–brown to tan with three longitudinal rows of dark brown blotches outlined anteriorly and posteriorly with black; usually the larger mid–dorsal blotches alternate with smaller lateral blotches. There is a dark brown or black stripe on each side of the neck, and a short dark stripe may occur from the rear of the eye to the corner of the mouth. A dark transverse bar often occurs on the snout in front of the eyes. The venter is white, cream, or pinkish–brown with faint brownish pigment posteriorly. The body scales are keeled with pits, and usually occur in 25 rows anteriorly and at mid–body, and 21 rows posteriorly. The anal plate is divided. Dorsally, on the head behind the rostral scale are 3 or more azygous scales separating the 2 internasals. Pertinent head scalation includes a loreal, a complete ring of oculars, 3–4 + 4–5 temporals, 6–8 supralabials, and 9–12 infralabials. The bilobed hemipenis has a bifurcated sulcus spermaticus. The proximal end bears very small spines while those on the medial portions are long and the distal lobes are covered with papilla–like calyces. The 6–11 anterior maxillary teeth are separated from the 2 enlarged, ungrooved, posterior teeth by a diastema.

Males have shorter bodies with 122 or fewer ventrals, and longer tails with up to 44 subcaudals; females have 134 or fewer ventrals and 35 or less subcaudals.

Karyotype: Unknown.

Fossil Record: Pleistocene (Rancholabrean) remains of *H. simus* have been found at Williston, Levy County, near Haille, Alachua County, and near Reddick, Marion County, Florida (Holman, 1959; Auffenberg, 1963).

Distribution: *H. simus* occurs from southeastern North Carolina south to Pinellas, Polk and Brevard counties, Florida and west to southern Mississippi.

Geographic Variation: Unknown.

Confusing Species: *Heterodon platyrhinos* has the underside of the tail lighter than the belly, and a relatively straight rostral scale. The pygmy rattlesnake, *Sistrurus miliarius* has a tail rattle, a pit between the nostril and eye, and a vertical pupil.

Habitat: This small burrower prefers the sandy soils occurring in xeric communities, such as sandhills, pine and wire grass flatwoods, or long–leaf pine–turkey oak habitats.

Behavior: *H. simus* displays the same stereotypic pattern of bluffing and death–feigning that occurs in the other two species of *Heterodon* (Van Duyn, 1937; Myers and Arata, 1961), and like them is also diurnal or crepuscular.

Reproduction: Neill (1951) found a captive female mating simultaneously with two males of the same species on 23 May. One male had inserted his right hemipenis, the other its left. While the copulation occurred, a third male tried to get in on the act; he crawled over the three snakes with his tail upraised, and made a few ineffectual attempts to participate before finally moving away. The female then crawled away, dragging the two males with her. She left a trail of blood which Neill thought resulted from the males lacerating

Map

Southern Hognose Snake

each other with their hemipenial spines. In the same paper, Neill reported an interspecific mating between a large female *H. simus* and a smaller male *H. platyrhinos* that occurred on 29 May. The coitus lasted about 3 hours, but possibly would have taken longer since the pair was disturbed. Afterwards the female's cloaca was swollen and bloody, and she died 3 days later, possibly from injuries sustained during the abnormal copulation.

Price and Carr (1943) reported that a captive Florida female laid 6 eggs (2 each day) on 20–22 October. The yellowish–brown, almond–shaped eggs were 25–30 x 11–14 mm, and weighed 2.1–2.5 g. Edgren (1955) found 10 eggs in a female from Georgia, and Ashton and Ashton (1981) noted a female laid 9 round white eggs in mid–July. Saul (1968) reported that a possible hybrid *H. platyrhinos* x *H. simus* from Duval County, Florida laid 18 infertile eggs on 31 May; however, judging by the large size of this clutch, the snake was probably a *platyrhinos*. Neonates resemble the adults in pattern and coloration.

Food And Feeding: Toads (*Bufo* sp.) and spadefoots (*Scaphiopus holbrooki*) are the primary prey of *H. simus* (Deckert, 1918; Goin, 1947; Ashton and Ashton, 1981), but tree frogs (Ashton and Ashton, 1981), lizards (Van Duyn, 1957) and small mammals (Martof et al., 1980) are also eaten.

The upturned rostral scale may be used to dig out buried spadefoots and toads; Goin (1947) watched a southern hognose snake use this scale as a "shovel" to excavate a half–grown *Scaphiopus* that was 115 mm underground.

Toads, spadefoots, and frogs that inflate themselves when seized, apparently are deflated by puncturing with the enlarged posterior maxillary teeth (Ashton and Ashton, 1981).

There is some question as to the toxicity of the saliva of *H. simus*. It has parotid glands (Kapus, 1964), but their secretions have not been tested. It has enlarged posterior maxillary teeth that could possibly inject saliva. Perhaps the saliva is only toxic to amphibians.

Remarks: Neill (1963b) suggested that the blotched pattern of *H. simus* is perhaps mimetic of the venomous pigmy rattlesnake, *Sistrurus miliarius*.

This species is known occasionally to hybridize with *H. platyrhinos* (Edgren, 1952; Saul, 1968).

Our knowledge of the ecology and behavior of this snake is inadequate; a good natural history study is needed.

Fig. 16. *Heterodon simus* (Carl H. Ernst).

Fig. 17. A juvenile *Heterodon simus* playing dead (Sylvia Greenwald, courtesy J. Whitfield Gibbons).

RHADINAEA FLAVILATA
Pine Woods Snake

RHADINAEA FLAVILATA (Cope, 1871)
Pine Woods Snake

Recognition: This docile, slender snake (to 40.3 cm) is yellowish–brown to reddish–brown dorsally, lighter laterally, and white, cream, or yellowish–green ventrally; a mid–dorsal, diffused stripe is present on some. A dark brown stripe runs posteriorly from the nose through the orbit to the corner of the mouth. The chin and lips are white, cream, or yellow with varying amounts of dark flecking. The tail ends in a terminal spine. The body scales are smooth, pitless, and in 18(17–19) rows on the neck and 17 rows posterior to the neck; the anal plate is divided. Laterally on the head are a grooved nasal scale, a loreal, 1 preocular, 2 postoculars (occasionally also suboculars resulting from transverse division of the labials), 3 (1 + 2) temporals, usually 7(7–8) supralabials, and 7–10 (usually 9) infralabials. There are 112–139 ventrals and 59–83 pairs of subcaudals with no sexual dimorphism. The single hemipenis is clavate with a smooth base, the middle spiny with the largest spines toward the surface opposite the bifurcated sulcus spermaticus, and the distal end with calyces which are papilla–like apically and spiny basally (Myers, 1967). There are 14–15 anterior maxillary teeth, gradually lengthening posteriorly, separated by a short diastema from two enlarged, ungrooved teeth.

Females attain greater snout–vent lengths than males, but have shorter tails (27–32% of total length), and less than 50% of females have anal ridges (keel–like ridges on the dorsal body scales of the anal region, Myers, 1967). Males have longer tails (28–36% of total length), and mature individuals possess anal ridges.

Karyotype: Unknown.

Fossil Record: Florida Pleistocene (Irvingtonian and Rancholabrean) remains of *R. flavilata* have been found in Citrus and Levy counties (Holman, 1981; Meylan, 1982).

Distribution: *R. flavilata* ranges from Carteret and Dare counties, North Carolina southward along the coastal plain through peninsular Florida to Glades and Palm Beach counties, and westward along the Gulf Coast to the Mississippi River.

Most localities are less than either 30 m elevation or 120 km from the coast (Myers, 1967).

Geographic Variation: No subspecies are recognized; however, Myers (1967) reported clinal changes in the number of dark marks on the labials (greatest north, least south), occurrence of a mid–dorsal stripe (greatest north, least south), and number of ventrals (decreasing slightly from south to north). Also the number of supralabials and infralabials vary more in peninsular Florida than elsewhere in the range.

Confusing Species: No other small, basically unpatterned snake within its range has a dark stripe through the eye.

Habitat: This secretive, burrowing snake usually lives in low coastal plain flatwoods characterized by poorly drained soils on which slash and long–leaf pines predominate (Myers, 1967). Such a habitat is dependent on occasional fires to preserve its successional stage. A few individuals have been taken in Florida hardwood hammocks adjacent to pine flatwoods, and some occur on coastal islands off North Carolina and Florida where the habitat is dry woodlands or marsh. Within these habitats, *Rhadinaea* spends most of its time under logs, leaves and other ground debris, buried in sandy soil, or under the loose bark of pine trees.

Behavior: *Rhadinaea* has been collected in every month, but more than twice as many have been captured in April, followed by March and then May. Spring is obviously its season of greatest activity (Myers, 1967). When forced to hibernate, they enter rotting logs, stumps, and animal burrows or crawl below the frost line in the sandy soil. During dry weather, Neill (in Myers, 1967) found them in crayfish burrows.

Reproduction: Mating probably occurs in the spring; Brode and Allison (1958) thought possibly as early as mid–February in Mississippi when several males were found near a female. Based on the presence of anal scale ridges, males over 25 cm in total length were arbitrarily considered to be adults and those under 20 cm juveniles by Myers (1967).

Myers (1967) reported that the largest ovarian follicles in a February adult female were 4 mm in diameter, in late April the ovarian follicles of two females were 12 x 4, 13 x 4, and 15 x 4 mm; and 6 x 4, 15 x 5, and 16 x 5 mm, respectively. A third late April female had two oviducal eggs, 26 x 6 and 28 x 6 mm; and on 25 May a female had three oviducal eggs, 25 x 7, 27 x 7, and 27 x 7 mm. Funderburg (1958) also found a North Carolina gravid female on 11 May, which laid four 13 x 5 eggs in a non–adherent cluster on 4 June. Telford (in Myers, 1967) reported a 20.7 cm Florida female laid four 20 x 4 mm eggs on 19 July and another 38.1 cm Florida female laid four 18 x 5 mm eggs on 6 July. A 4 July female collected by Myers (1967) had two oval (probably ovarian), 14 x 4 and 16 x 5 mm, eggs. Allen

RHADINAEA FLAVILATA
Pine Woods Snake

(1939) mentioned a Florida female that laid three eggs averaging 23 x 8 mm on 19 August. Apparently two to four eggs comprise the normal clutch; most clutches are deposited in rotting wood.

The eggs are white to yellow in color, and Funderberg (1958) described the leathery surface as granular to the naked eye, but with distinct, irregular, wavy longitudinal ridges when observed under a binocular microscope.

The young hatch in September (Allen, 1939) and are approximately 140 mm long (Martof et al., 1980). Allen (1939) reported that young *Rhadinaea*, several days old when discovered, averaged 167 mm in total length and 41 mm in tail length.

Food And Feeding: Natural foods include frogs, salamanders, lizards, and possibly small snakes. Malnate (1939) found the remains of small frogs (likely *Hyla*) and the tail of a *Scincella laterale*, and Myers (1967) found an unidentified frog (*Gastrophryne* or *Rana*), a tree frog (*Hyla*), a cricket frog (*Acris gryllus*) and the tail of *Scincella laterale* in the digestive tracts they examined. Brode and Allison (1958) observed *R. flavilata* feeding on *Acris gryllus*.

Rhadinaea seizes its prey along the body, moves it to the rear of its mouth where it embeds its elongated, posterior, maxillary teeth and chews; the snake then lies quietly until the prey is immobilized by its venom (Malnate, 1939; Neill, 1954a; Willard, 1967: McKinistry, 1978). Neill (1954a) reported that seldom is prey held for less than 45 minutes; usually a frog will be held for 70–80 minutes, and a large active frog or lizard may be retained for 2–3 hours.

The venom is apparently produced in a serous–mucous Duvernoy's gland (Taub, 1967), and is mild and of no danger to humans.

Predators And Defense: *Rhadinaea* is probably eaten by ophiophagous snakes, such as *Micrurus fulvius* and *Lampropeltis getulus*, and by nocturnal predatory mammals.

Populations: Little is known of the population dynamics of this secretive snake. Allen (1939) found them very common in a limited area near Burbank, Marion County, Florida where he collected 21 on 28 March, and in about 30 days a farmer collected 80.

The sex ratio for a combined sample from Alachua and Marion counties, Florida examined by Myers (1967) was 25 males (37%) and 43 females (63%), but the combined ratio for specimens examined from all states by Myers was 93 males to 92 females, or 1:1.

Myers (1967, 1974) suggested that *R. flavilata* or an ancestor migrated into the southeastern United States via a coastal route from the west, as other *Rhadinaea* are from Mexico and Central America.

Map

Fig. 18. *Rhadinaea flavilata* is rear–fanged (Barry Mansell).

TANTILLA CORONATA

Southeastern Crowned Snake

TANTILLA CORONATA (Baird and Girard, 1853)
Southeastern Crowned Snake

Recognition: The unpatterned body (to 33 cm) is tan to pinkish–brown or dark brown dorsally, gradually blending laterally into the pinkish–white to cream–colored venter. The pointed to slightly rounded head does not have a countersunk lower jaw. The head pattern consists of a dark brown or black crown followed by a light white to cream-colored band 2 (1–3) scales wide which separates the dark cap from a dark brown or black collar usually less than 3(2–6) scales wide at the midline. A pale postocular blotch is present on each side of the head. The body scales are smooth with no pits, and they occur in 15 rows with no reduction at any point along the body; the anal plate is divided. Lateral head scalation consists of 2 nasal scales, a single preocular, 2 postoculars, 2 temporals, usually 7 supralabials, and 6 infralabials. The mental scale may touch the anterior chin shields. The hemipenis bears two basal hooks; the larger adjacent to the basal third of the sulcus spermaticus, and the smaller along the middle third of the organ. On each maxilla are 13–17 (usually 15) teeth separated by a diastema from an enlarged posterior fang.

Females are slightly longer (maximum snout-vent length 21.7 cm to 19 cm for males; Telford, 1982), have more ventrals (usually 138–143 to 131–135 for males; Telford, 1966), but fewer subcaudals (usually 42–45 to 46–47 for males; Telford, 1966). Males have longer tails; usually 20–21% (17–23) of the total body length to 18–19% (15–21) in females (Telford, 1966).

Karyotype: Cole and Hardy (1981) found the diploid chromosome number to be 36; 16 macrochromosomes (pairs 1,3 and 4 are metacentric, 2,5 and 7 are submetacentric, pair 8 is subtelocentric, and pair 6 is telocentric), and 20 microchromosomes.

Fossil Record: Fossils from northcentral Florida reported as *T. coronata* by Auffenberg (1963) may be *T. relicta*.

Distribution: *T. coronata* ranges southward from the Delmarva Penninsula, southcentral Virginia, and southern Indiana to southern Georgia, the panhandle of Florida, and the Gulf Coast of Alabama, Mississippi and southeastern Louisiana. It is not found west of the Mississippi River.

Geographic Variation: Telford (1966) has shown that the forms *T. c. wagneri* (Jan, 1862) and *T. c. mitrifer* Schwartz, 1953 are not valid. *T. c. wagneri* is really *T. relicta*, and there is insufficient variation from other *T. coronata* to recognize *T. c. mitrifer*.

Confusing Species: *Tantilla relicta* may lack a neck collar, but if one is present, there is also either a light blotch on the snout or a lack of light pigment on the supralabials. The brown snake, *Storeria dekayi*, and redbelly snake, *S. occipitomaculata*, have keeled scales. Ringneck snakes, *Diadophis punctatus*, have a pattern of black spots on their brightly colored venters, and earth snakes, *Virginia*, lack a neck collar.

Habitat: *T. coronata* is a secretive burrower that may be found in a variety of habitats ranging from mesic Appalachian forests to the wet borders of marshes, swamps, and the banks of rivers. It has been taken at elevations to 600 m in the southern Appalachians, almost always under stones, moist logs, or within rotting stumps.

Semlitsch et al. (1981) studied the habitat preferences of *T. coronata* by comparing drift fence captures in pine stands to those from the mesic areas around two Carolina Bays at the U.S. Department of Energy's Savannah River Plant near Aiken, South Carolina. They found that the pine and mesic areas were not utilized differently. However, within these various habitats, drift fences in more xeric conditions were more productive. They concluded that a xeric micro–habitat with sufficient rocks, logs, or rotting stumps that provide cover appears more important for utilization of an area than either the predominant vegetation or macrohabitat.

Behavior: We caught an active *T. coronata* on 16 March, 1969 at Osewitchee Springs, Wilcox County, Georgia. Other active *T. coronata* have been found as early as 27 March in South Carolina (Semlitsch et al., 1981) and 29 March in Indiana (Minton, 1949a), and as late in fall as 28 October in North Carolina (Brimley, 1941–42) and 6 November in South Carolina (Semlitsch et al., 1981). Drift fences with pitfall traps in South Carolina showed that regular captures of *T. coronata* began after a rise in mean maximum and

TANTILLA CORONATA

Southeastern Crowned Snake

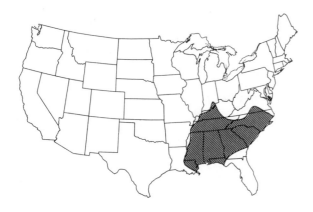

Map

minimum air temperatures above 20 and 10 C, respectively, and that it was most active during July and August (Semlitsch et al., 1981). Rainfall did not seem to affect activity.

Most activity seems to be at night. During the day these snakes hide beneath objects or remain underground. Captives also display nocturnal tendencies.

The colder months are presumably spent in hibernation, although there are only two records of this. Allen (1932) found several inactive specimens in winter below the surface of the ground or inside pine stumps, and Huheey and Stupka (1967) reported five were found in the ground at depths of 5 to 30 cm between 18 February and 26 March at Gatlinburg, Tennessee.

Reproduction: Telford (1966) reported that the smallest mature male in his sample from throughout the range had a snout–vent length of 135 mm while the smallest female was 153 mm. In South Carolina, sexual maturity in females was attained at a snout–vent length of about 145 mm (Aldridge and Semlitsch, 1982). Semlitsch et al. (1981) thought hatchlings matured during their second year (approximately 12 months old) because a distinct distribution of subadults (121–151 mm snout–vent length) did not appear in their spring, summer or fall samples. However, they point out that it is also possible that juveniles are subterra-

nean and do not travel extensively above ground until mature.

Female *T. coronata* have a complete, functional, right oviduct, but the left is reduced; both ovaries are present and normally developed (Clark, 1970c). In South Carolina, vitellogenesis begins in the spring and ovulation occurs from early May to mid–July; spermatogenesis begins in May, peaking in July, spermiation begins in late June with sperm being stored in the vas deferens (Aldridge and Semlitsch, 1982). The diameter of the sexual segment of the kidney increases significantly after early August, and its peak size corresponds to the peak activity period of these snakes (Aldridge and Semlitsch, 1982). This is interesting, since the only observed matings in this species took place in April and early May; these Georgia mated pairs were intertwined beneath a scrap of bark at the base of a rotting tree stump (Neill, 1951).

Nesting occurs in June and July. Neill and Boyles (1957) dissected a gravid Alabama female on 25 May which contained three shelled eggs, and Minton (1949a) reported an Indiana female appeared to contain 2 or 3 elongated eggs on 30 May. Semlitsch et al. (1981) collected four females, each with shelled eggs, on 11 June (3 eggs), 16 June (3 eggs), and 18 July (1 and 2 eggs) in South Carolina.

In addition to shelled eggs, Neill and Boyles (1957) also found smaller, spherical eggs, and concluded *T. coronata* may mature 8 to 12 ova, but produce only three young per year. It is possible that the 1 and 2 shelled eggs found in gravid July females by Semlitsch et al. (1981) may represent second smaller clutches.

The eggs are white with a leathery shell. Although usually elongated (21.3–23.7 x 5.0–5.6 mm; Neill and Boyle, 1957), those found by Neill (1951) were more nearly oval. Neill (1951) described the only reported nest as a cup–shaped depression beneath two overlapping bark fragments in a small mass of wood pulp and rotting bark near the base of an old stump. The nest seemed in an ideal location; it was shielded from rain and drainage from the stump, was exposed to sunlight in the morning and evening, but was shaded at mid–day.

Young southeastern crowned snakes resemble the adults in coloration and head pattern. The smallest juvenile measured by Telford (1966) had a snout–vent length of 78 mm; the smallest male measured by Minton (1949) was 76 mm and the smallest female 80 mm.

Food And Feeding: Prey eaten by wild and captive *T. coronata* includes earthworms, centipedes, spiders and termites. Although this species has venom glands and a pair of enlarged grooved teeth at the rear of its upper jaw, the efficiency of it venom apparatus is questionable. It has been presumed that the venom is used to subdue its invertebrate prey, but Minton (1949) forcibly made a *T. coronata* bite an earthworm, with seemingly no effect on the worm.

Predators: This species is known to have been eaten by the snakes *Micrurus fulvius*, *Stilosoma extenuatum*, *Lampropeltis getulus*, and *Lampropeltis triangulum elapsoides*, and by the lizard *Ophisaurus ventralis*. It is probably also eaten by a variety of birds and carnivorous mammals.

Populations: *T. coronata*, although often locally common, appears to be rather rare due to its secretive nature. Being largely nocturnal and spending the daylight hours undercover, it is seldom encountered. Drift fence sampling in South Carolina has showed that a good population occurs at the Savannah River Plant (Semlitsch et al., 1981), and Brode and Allison (1958) collected 10 individuals from stumps on less than five hectares in Harrison County, Mississippi. Neill (1951) reported it was unusually common on certain wooded hillsides bordering a small stream on the northwestern outskirts of Augusta, Georgia.

Of the 54 *T. coronata* collected by Semlitsch et al. (1981), only two (3.7%) were juveniles; a juvenile/adult ratio of 1/27. However, it was thought that juveniles probably move less than adults and may have remained underground until mature. Most of the South Carolina individuals ranged in snout–vent length from 160–250 mm, and were sexually mature. The sex ratio was 2:1 (36 males, 18 females). This ratio may reflect differential mortality, but it is more likely an indication of sampling bias toward the more active males (Semlitsch et al., 1981).

TANTILLA GRACILIS

Flathead Snake

TANTILLA GRACILIS (Baird and Girard, 1853)
Flathead Snake

Recognition: A small (to 24.4 cm) snake with an unpatterned tan to gray–brown or reddish–brown body, a salmon pink to orange venter, and a head only slightly darker brown than the body. Posteriorly, the dark cap is dorsomedially concave. The pointed head has a countersunk lower jaw. The body scales are smooth and pitless and usually occur in 15 rows along the entire body (some reduction may occur in the preanal scale rows); the anal plate is divided. Lateral head scalation includes a nasal scale divided below the naris, 1 preocular, 2 postoculars, 2 temporals, 6–7 supralabials, and 6 (5–7) infralabials. The hemipenis bears two basal hooks; a large one adjacent to the basal third of the sulcus spermaticus, and another of similar size on the opposite side of the organ. Several smaller spines are present along the mid–section. Ten to 14 teeth occur on each maxilla anterior to the enlarged, grooved posterior fang; a diastema separates the fang from the other teeth.

Females grow longer (to 244 mm) than males (to 215 mm), but males have longer tails (21–53 mm, 21–27% of total body length) than females (16–50 mm, 17–22%) (Hardy and Cole, 1968). Females have 122–138 ventrals and 33–53 subcaudals, males have 106–131 ventrals and 43–58 subcaudals.

Karyotype: Unknown.

Distribution: *T. gracilis* ranges from southwestern Illinois (Union, Randolph, Monroe, and probably St. Clair counties; Neill, 1951; Smith, 1961; Moll, 1962) southwestward through southern Missouri and eastern Kansas to southern Texas. Isolated populations also occur in northcentral Missouri, the panhandle of Texas, and in Coahuila, Mexico (Conant, 1975).

Geographic Variation: No subspecies are currently recognized; Dowling (1957) and Hardy and Cole (1968) have shown that recognition of *Tantilla gracilis hallowelli* Cope, 1860 is unsupportable.

Confusing Species: *Tantilla coronata* has a very dark headcap separated by a lighter band across the back of the head from a very dark neck band. *T. nigriceps*, of the Great Plains, has 7 supralabials and a dark headcap which is convex posteriorly. The earth snakes, *Virginia striatula* and *V. valeriae*; the brown snake, *Storeia dekayi*, and the redbelly snake, *S. occipitomaculata*, have at least weakly keeled body scales. The ground snake, *Sonora episcopa*, has a loreal scale and a cream to white venter.

Habitat: This semifossorial species lives under rocks, logs, or other moist debris in oak–hickory or mixed deciduous–pine woodlands and brushy slopes often situated in limestone areas. On the Great Plains, it may inhabit grasslands. It was thought to prefer loose sandy soils, but Clark (1967) found that it had no soil preferences and did not seem to be an extensive burrower. Most deep burrowing probably occurs in the summer when surface soils become dry. Jackson and Reno (1975) reported that the free margins of the dorsal, lateral, and ventral body scales of *T. gracilis* are of uniform length and presumably aid in limited burrowing activity.

Behavior: Most specimens have been found in the spring and fall. March 8 is the earliest record (Wright and Wright, 1957) while some Oklahoma *T. gracilis* have been active in November (Force, 1935). Their relative scarcity in summer may be due to warmer and less moist soil conditions, as many summer captures have been after rains. Where they spend the summer is unknown, but probably they occasionally use small animal burrows and ant mounds. Hibernation occurs during the colder months, when these small snakes retreat underground or into animal burrows. Clark (1967) recorded body temperatures of 10 *T. gracilis* in the laboratory as 19.6–27.5 C (x = 23.85).

Smith (1956) thought them probably nocturnal, and Force (1935) reported that one of their favorite foods is the meadow maggot or leatherjacket, a nocturnal insect.

Reproduction: Force (1935) considered female *T. gracilis* to begin maturing sexually at 12.5 cm at 1–1.5 years of age; females 12.5–15.5 cm contained noticably developed ova 1–2 mm in length, those below 12.5 cm in body length had only microscopic ova. Females 18.5 cm (1.5–2.5 years old) or longer were definitely mature. Mature females have a complete, functional, right oviduct, but the left is reduced to a vestige (Clark, 1970c); both ovaries are present.

Force (1935) thought males to be mature at 17.4 cm (1.5–2.5 years old); in those 15.5–17.5 cm in length there was a gradual change from a flabby, white immature testis to a firm, elongate, yellowish, apparently mature testis. Males 18.5 cm long were definitely mature.

Oklahoma males contained well–developed 5–9 mm testes during May, and presumably this is the mating period (Force, 1935). Prior to May the testes were much smaller. Courtship and mating have not been described, but males may find mates by following pheromone trails laid down by females (Gehlbach et al., 1972).

Eggs are deposited in June and the first half of July; Force (1935) reported that captives always laid their eggs at night. Normally 2–3 eggs are laid, but clutches of 1 or 4 occasionally occur. The white to cream–colored eggs are elongate or ir-regularly shaped (13–26 x 4–6.5 mm) with smooth shells, and a distinctly visible germinal disc. Anderson (1965) found two clutches, one of two eggs and another of three eggs, in barely moist sand between two layers of limestone, and Collins (1974) reported that eggs are laid in a nest be-neath a rock. The eggs usually hatch in Septem-ber, but Wright and Wright (1957) reported that one young *T. gracilis* emerged in July. The only incubation periods in the literature are 83 and 84 days for eggs laid by captives (Force, 1935). Hatchlings are 77–96 mm in total body length.

Growth And Longevity: Force (1935) reported the following size/age relationships by sex for Oklahoma *T. gracilis*: females 90–125 mm (year-ling), 125–185 (1–1.5 years), and 185–230 (1.5–2.5 years); males 85–125 mm (yearling), 125–175 (1.–1.5 years), and 175–205 (1.5–2.5 years). Longevity is unknown.

Food And Feeding: Centipedes, sowbugs, soft-bodied insect larvae, spiders and slugs are eaten. Gehlbach et al. (1972) found that captive *T. gracilis* followed pheromone trails left by army ants and termites, and concluded that the snakes use olfaction to detect prey.

The two enlarged teeth on the rear of the maxillae contain shallow lateral grooves, as is the case of such teeth in other *Tantilla*, and Smith (1956) pointed out that teeth having such grooves are more properly called pleuroglyph than opis-thoglyph. These teeth are probably used to subdue softbodied prey. Small venom glands are present, but the effectiveness of their secretions is ques-tionable. Anderson (1965) macerated the head tissues of several *T. gracilis* and rubbed these into cuts in the skin of humans and laboratory mice with no adverse results; however, the venom may

Map

Fig. 19. Venter of *Tantilla gracilis* (Steve W. Gotte).

be specialized for invertebrates. In any case, *T. gracilis*, which is normally inoffensive, does not present a danger to humans.

Predators And Defense: Collins (1974) listed birds, small mammals, lizards and snakes as predators of *T. gracilis*. More specific observations include predation by a leopard frog (Burt and Hoyle, 1935) and a coral snake, *Micrurus fulvius* (Fisher, 1973). When held, these small snakes do not bite, but instead spray musk and thrash about.

Populations: Little is known of the population structure of this small snake, although they may be common in some areas. Of the 411 *T. gracilis* from Oklahoma collected and dissected by Force (1935), 245 were males and 176 females, a 1.39:1 sex ratio. The sex ratio of 246 *T. gracilis* from the vicinity of Winfield, Cowley County, Kansas examined by Hardy and Cole (1968) was 139 males to 107 females, 1.30:1.

TANTILLA OOLITICA

Rim Rock Crowned Snake

TANTILLA OOLITICA (Telford, 1966)
Rim Rock Crowned Snake

Recognition: This very rare, small snake (to 29.2 cm) is most closely related to *Tantilla coronata* with which it shares similarities in morphology, scalation, and hemipenial adornment. It is tan to light brown dorsally with a pinkish-white to cream-colored venter, the nape and rounded head dark brown to black, and the snout tan. On the unpatterned body, the darker dorsal coloration extends ventrally to about the level of the third scale row, below which it gradually lightens to the pale ventral coloration. A light-colored, sometimes broken, neck band may occur on the postparietal and posterior temporal scales in some individuals, and a pale postocular blotch is usually present on each side of the head. As in other *Tantilla*, the body scales are smooth and pitless, and the anal plate is divided. Lateral head scalation consists of a preocular, 2 postoculars, 2 temporals, 6–7 supralabials, and 5–6 infralabials. The mental scale may touch the chin shields. There are 15 scale rows along the entire body, 135–146 ventrals, and 41–63 subcaudals. The hemipenis has two similar-sized basal hooks, one along the basal third of the sulcus spermaticus and another along the middle third of the organ. The maxilla contains 13–15 separated by a diastema from the enlarged posterior fang.

Although less than 15 specimens of *T. oolitica* are known, several points of sexual dimorphism are evident. Females reach a greater length than males, 24.6 cm to the 17.1 cm maximum snout-vent length of males (Telford, 1980a). Males have slightly longer tails, 20.8–22.4% of the total body length to the 19.1–19.6% of females, with a greater number of subcaudals, 51–63 to the 41–48

of females (Telford, 1966; Porras and Wilson, 1979).

Karyotype And Fossil Record: Unknown.

Distribution: *T. oolitica* is known from metropolitan Dade County, and Key Largo and Grassy Key in Monroe County, Florida.

Geographic Variation: Variation occurs in the extent of development of the pale neck band. The band is lacking in mainland specimens, but occurs in varying degrees on those from the Keys. Porras and Wilson (1970) also pointed out the *T. oolitica* from Grassy Key have shorter relative tail lengths (17.9–18.1% to 19.1–19.6%) and fewer subcaudals (41–44 to 45–48) than other known specimens; however, once again, we caution that few specimens have been collected. In fact, *T. oolitica* may be the most rare of all North American snakes.

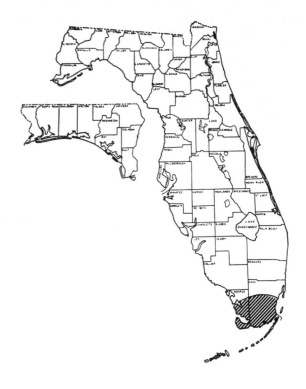

Map

Confusing Species: Within its range, the only other *Tantilla* is the smaller *T. relicta pamlica* (to 21.6 cm) which has only one basal hook on its hemipenis, a longer tail in females (over 20% of total body length), fewer ventrals (115–129), a broad light neck band; and some white flecks on its snout. *Storeria dekayi victa* is larger (to 48.3 cm), has two pale neck bands, a dorsal pattern of two rows of faint dark spots, and keeled body scales.

TANTILLA OOLITICA

Rim Rock Crowned Snake

Habitat: Tropical hardwood hammocks in shallow sand soils over oolitic limestone formations were probably the ancestral habitat; there this small burrowing snake hid in stumps and under logs, rocks and fallen palmetto leaves. In developed habitats it has been found under boards, logs and trash in vacant lots and pastures. Porras and Wilson (1979) thought that eroded cavities in the limestone substratum probably provide refugia. With the rapid urbanization of southeastern Florida, the natural habitat of *T. oolitica* is disappearing, and its future is in jepoardy. Populations occurring in natural areas must be located and their habitat preserved from future development, otherwise this small snake faces extinction.

Remarks: Almost nothing is known of the life history of this secretive, semifossorial snake. It has been taken in September, February, April and June, and Porras and Wilson (1970) thought it likely *T. oolitica* emerges principally from its hiding places during and after rains, since two of the specimens they reported were collected after rains. Its feeding habits are unknown, but it may eat centipedes, insects, and other small invertebrates. Porras and Wilson (1979) suggested that the scorpion *Centruroides gracilis*, which is abundant where the snake occurs, may be a natural predator.

TANTILLA RELICTA

Florida Crowned Snake

TANTILLA RELICTA (Telford, 1966)
Florida Crowned Snake

Recognition: The unpatterned body of this small snake (to 24.1 cm) is tan to reddish–brown dorsally, gradually becoming lighter along the sides and blending with the pinkish–white to cream-colored venter. The pointed to slightly rounded head has a pattern that varies from completely dark brown or black to having a prominent whitish to cream-colored neck band dividing the darker pigmented areas into a separate headcap and a separate neck collar; the dark neck collar is over 1–9 scales long (x = 4.4; Telford, 1980b). A pale postocular blotch is usually present on each side of the head, and it may connect with the neck band. The body scales are smooth with no pits, and occur in 15 rows with no reduction at any point along the body; the anal plate is divided. Laterally on the head are a single preocular, 2 postoculars, 2 temporals, 6–7 supralabials, and 6 infralabials. The mental scale may touch the anterior chin shields. The hemipenis bears a single basal hook along the proximal third of the organ. Each maxilla has 13–15 teeth separated by a diastema from the enlarged posterior fang.

Females are slightly longer than males, 19.4 to 19.0 cm maximum snout–vent length (Telford, 1980b), and have more ventrals, 119–142 to 115–135 (Telford, 1966). Males usually have longer tails, 28.7–29.7% of total length to 18.5–29.1% in females, with a greater number of subcaudals, 44–67 to 40–60 in females (Telford, 1966).

Literature descriptions of *Tantilla coronata wagneri* (Jan, 1862) from peninsular Florida by Blanchard (1938), Carr (1940) and Wright and Wright (1957) are based on *T. relicta*.

Fossil Record: Auffenberg (1963) reported fossil *Tantilla* from middle or late Pleistocene deposits in northcentral Florida which may be *T. relicta*.

Distribution: *T. relicta* is restricted to peninsular Florida where it ranges in the north from Lafayette and Suwannee counties east to possibly Duvall County and the St. Johns River, southward to Sarasota and Charlotte counties in the west and Highlands County in the center, and from Cape Canaveral to Palm Beach County in the east.

Geographic Variation: Three subspecies are recognized, based largely on head patterns, and appear to be ecologically separated by their habitat preferences. *Tantilla relicta relicta* Telford, 1966, the peninsula crowned snake, occurs from Lake George, Marion County southward along the central ridge of Florida to Polk and Highlands counties. It has also been reported from the Florida west coast on Seahorse Key, Levy County, and in Pinellas, Sarasota and Charlotte counties (Telford, 1966). This subspecies intergrades with *T. r. neilli* in the vicinity of Lake George, Marion County and around the former Suwannee Straits (Telford, 1980b). *T. r. relicta* has a light neck band in most individuals (87%, Telford, 1966) followed by a dark collar which is 1–5, usually 4, scales wide at the dorsal midline, a pointed head with a countersunk lower jaw, 117 to 134 ventrals, 40–59 subcaudals, and the tail length 18–24% of the total body length. *T. r. neilli* Telford, 1966, the Florida crowned snake, ranges in northcentral peninsular Florida from Lafayette, Suwannee, Columbia, and possibly Duval counties southward to the Hillsborough River and northern Polk County, and eastward to the St. Johns River. It lacks a light neck band, but has a narrowly rounded head on which the lower jaw is not countersunk, 123–142 ventrals, 46–67 subcaudals, and a relatively long tail, 19–29% of the total body length. *T. r. pamlica* Telford, 1966, the coastal dunes crowned snake, is found along the Florida east coast from Cape Canaveral southward to Palm Beach County. This race with a pointed head and countersunk lower jaw has a broad light neckband, and, in over 60% of the individuals, there is an absence of dark pigment on the parietal, supraocular, and temporal regions (Telford, 1966); there is also extensive light pigment on the snout. The dark neck collar is 2–5, usually 3, scales wide at the dorsal midline. It has 115–129 ventrals, 45–51 subcaudals and a tail length 20–24% of the total body length. Christman (1980) reported that ventral and subcaudal counts tend to decrease clinally to the south in the various subspecies.

Telford (1980b) recommended that the southern population at Archbold Biological Sta-

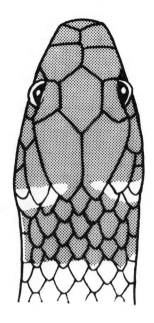 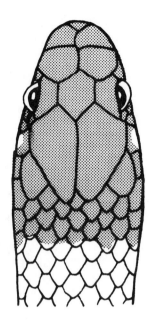 

RELICTA   NEILLI   PAMLICA

Fig. 20. Head patterns of the subspecies of *Tantilla relicta* (Evelyn M. Ernst).

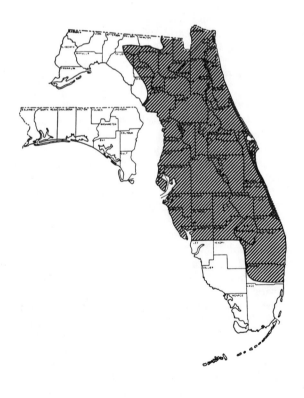

Map

tion, Lake Placid, Highland County be critically examined, since specimens from there have 6 supralabials, a condition rarely found in other *T. relicta* populations.

Confusing Species: The larger *Tantilla oolitica* (to 29.2 cm) lacks a light neck band, and has 135–146 ventrals, and 41–63 subcaudals. *Tantilla coronata* lacks light pigment on the snout, has a dark neck collar usually only 3 or less scales wide, 123–147 ventrals, 34–53 subcaudals, and a tail length of only 15.9–23.0% of the total body length. Both *T. oolitica* and *T. coronata* have two basal hooks on their hemipenis. *Storeria dekayi* and *S. occipitomaculata* have keeled body scales, and *Diadophis punctatus punctatus* has a ventral pattern consisting of a central row of black half-moons.

Habitat: Like other *Tantilla* this species is a burrower, hiding beneath rocks, logs or other prone objects. The three subspecies seem to prefer different habitats. *T. r. relicta* is strictly fossorial and prefers scrub woodlands, while *T. r. neilli* is semi-fossorial and is found in sandhills and mesic hammocks; where these subspecies are allopatric, *relicta* may occur in sandhills, suggesting it is prevented from living elsewhere by competing *neilli*. *T. r. pamlica* lives in isolated coastal dunes and scrub woodlands. In scrub habitats *T. relicta* is most often found in the early successional stages, thus it depends on periodic disturbance, such as fire, or clear–cutting, to remove the matted understory or pine canopy (Campbell and Christman, in Scott, 1982). Funderburg and Lee (1968) reported that *T. relicta* (as *T. coronata wagneri*) may take up permanent residence in the mounds of Florida pocket gophers. In 12 months Mushinsky (1984) collected 150 *T. relicta* in pitfall traps on approximately 20 hectares of sandhill habitat.

Telford (1966) suggested that the banded head pattern gives more protection from avian predators by breaking up the head outline, allowing *T. r. relicta* and *T. r. pamlica* to inhabit white sand areas, while the darker head of *T. r. neilli* would be at less disadvantage in areas of thick vegetation. This may account for some of the ecological separation noted between the three races.

Wilson and Porras (1983) reported that the habitat of *T. r. pamlica* in southeastern Florida has been reduced by increasing urban and agricultural development.

Remarks: Little is known of the natural history of this small snake. Telford (1966) thought it a "submerged basker" since his captives laid beneath the surface of the sand with just the head above ground. Annually, *T. relicta* is active from late February to early December with peak activity ocurring in late March and early April and again in late September and October (Smith, in Scott, 1982). Smith (in Scott, 1982) reported that they were completely fossorial, living under surface litter, and specialized in feeding on tenebrionid larvae. This species is known to be eaten by other snakes (*Stilosoma extenuatum*, *Lampropeltis getulus*, *Micrurus fulvius*), and probably various birds and mammals are also predators.

All *Tantilla* are oviparous, but the eggs of *T. relicta* have not been described. Juveniles resemble the adults in pattern and coloration, but have large heads in proportion to body length; the smallest juvenile examined by Telford (1966) had a snout–vent length of 77 mm. The smallest mature male he examined had a snout–vent length of 120 mm, while the smallest mature female was 124 mm.

DRYMARCHON CORAIS

Indigo Snake

DRYMARCHON CORAIS (Boie, 1827)
Indigo Snake

Recognition: A large (to 263 cm), shiny, bluish-black, stout snake with reddish to brownish-orange pigment on the chin and sides of the head. The scales are smooth, with two apical pits. They occur in 17 rows anterior and at midbody, and usually 14 (13–16) rows posteriorly. On the side of head are a nasal, a loreal, a preocular, 2 postoculars, usually 2 + 2 temporals, 8 (7–9) supralabials (the 3rd from the last is small and does not touch the postocular or temporal scales), and, on the lower jaw, usually 8 (7–10) infralabials. There are 182–195 ventrals and 64–70 subcaudals with no sexual dimorphism; the anal plate is not divided. The bilobed hemipenis is naked at the base, has a band of small spines medially, and numerous fringed calyces distally. There are 17–18 aglyphous teeth on each maxilla.

A low, inconspicuous keel, requiring very close inspection to detect, is located near the anterior edge of the dorsal body scales on some individuals. These keeled scales start at about 25–33% of the total body length behind the head to the area of vent. Layne and Steiner (1984) reported that 17 of 36 males from Florida had these keels while none were found in 35 Florida females. They found that the presence of the keels was clearly related to male size and maturity, as the frequency of occurrence increased with size over 140 cm, and was apparently associated with reproductive status.

Mount (1975) reported that females from Alabama have more prominent reddish or cream-colored pigment about the chin, throat and cheeks than do males; however, Moulis (1976) found the opposite to be true in males from Georgia.

Karyotype: The diploid number of chromosomes is 36; the 20 macrochromosomes include 12 metacentrics and submetacentrics, and 2 acrocentrics; there are 14 microchromosomes. Sex determination is ZW (Z metacentric; W acrocentric) (Becak et al., 1973).

Fossil Record: The indigo snake is only known from several Pleistocene Rancholabrean sites in Florida (Holman, 1981).

Distribution: *D. corais* has a disjunct range. The distribution of *D. c. couperi* is described below. The other subspecies range from southern Texas southward along the Atlantic versant of Mexico and southward from Sonora, Mexico on the Pacific versant to southern Brazil and northern Argentina east of the Andes, and to northwestern Peru in the west. The species is also known from Trinidad and Tobago islands.

Geographic Variation: Eight subspecies are recognized (see McCranie, 1980a for a review), but only one occurs east of the Mississippi River; *Drymarchon corais couperi* (Holbrook, 1842), the eastern indigo snake. It occurs from southeastern Georgia south to the Florida Keys and westward along the Gulf coastal plain to Mobile Bay.

Confusing Species: Other black snakes east of the Mississippi River have either noticeably keeled scales, whitish or tan chins, or a divided anal plate.

Habitat: Over much of its range, the indigo snake prefers high dry areas adjacent to water (pine barrens, oak forest, palmetto flats), but in southern Florida it can be found along canals or wet fields, and possibly into mangrove thickets. In Georgia, 78% of sightings were in dwarf oak forest (longleaf pine–turkey oak) or planted slash pine–dwarf oak forest (Diemer and Speake, 1983). When gopher tortoise burrows are present, they are heavily used as retreats, and Lawler (1977) reported that in areas of southern Florida where tortoises do not dig burrows, crab holes are instead used.

Bogert and Cowles (1947) studied moisture loss in a small *Drymarchon* (368.5 g) by placing it in a thermal chamber and allowing its body temperature to rise from 26.9 to 37.5 C within two hours. When they removed the snake after 9.5 hours, it was abnormally sluggish and died within 7 hours. It had lost moisture to the extent of 46.2 g (12.5%) at a mean rate of nearly 5 g (1.3%) per hour. Another 1247.4 g indigo snake was placed in the chamber for more than 5 hours before it died. It had lost 211 g (16.9%) of water. These studies indicate a rapid desiccation rate, and may explain why the snake spends so much time underground in humid animal burrows. Bogert and Cowles also placed a 114.5 cm individual in direct sunlight and after 10 minutes, when its cloacal temperature reached 42.2 C, its movements became uncoordinated. The snake was removed from the sunlight and it recovered; however, it is apparent that its temperature approached its critical thermal maximum.

Behavior: Indigo snakes are diurnal and may be active in all months during mild years, but they often become inactive during very warm summers and may be forced to hibernate during cold winters, especially in Georgia. Sites selected for both are usually animal burrows. Over a nine year period (1966–1975) Moulis (1976) found them most active in Georgia in April, when he thought they mated. He observed only one snake (in January) from October to March, and none during June and July.

Reproduction: Little is known of the reproductive habits of wild *Drymarchon*. Moulis (1976) thought that mating occurs in April in Georgia, but all reported courtship sequences in captives have occurred between 30 October and 20 January (Tinkle, 1951; Groves, 1960, Beardsley and Barten, 1983; Stirnberg and Broer, 1984), and since most egg laying seems to occur in May (Carson, 1945; LeBuff, 1953; Groves, 1960, Iverson, 1978; Beardsley and Barten, 1983), a fall and winter breeding season is probably more normal.

Gillingham and Chambers (1980) gave the best analysis of courtship (based in part on behavior patterns described in Gillingham, 1979): Phase I.—The tactile chase–phase began when the male initiated courtship activities, and ended at the first copulatory attempt (approximately 12 minutes). The male approached the female and touched his snout to her body and then placed his head on her back. At times he had to pursue her or move with her while maintaining his chin on her back. He then mounted the female by crawling onto her back. This was followed by several behavioral patterns: 1) writhe–bump, a rhythmic sliding, twisting and turning movement with local dorsoventral trunk movements; 2) nudging, pushing the snout forcibly against the female's body resulting in moving her body along the substrate; 3) dorsal-pin, making a u–shaped curve with the neck and using it to pin the female's anterior trunk to the substrate (usually exhibited when the female began to crawl forward); 4) neck–curl, the mounted male slid his head and neck under the female's neck, passed to the opposite side of her body and lifted her upwards, and then curled his neck posteriorly cradling the female's anterior body on his back (at times the female responded with a neck–curl in the opposite direction). Phase II.—The tactile–alignment phase began with the first tail–search copulatory attempt and ended at hemipenial intromission (about 8.5 minutes). Some caudocephalic waves occurred during this phase. Phase III.—Begins with intromission of a hemipenis as the female opened her vent, and ended with hemipenial withdrawal approximately

Map

193 minutes later. Beardsley and Barten (1983) observed a copulation which lasted over 4 hours.

Gillingham and Chambers (1980) observed no biting by either sex, nor did Beardsley and Barten (1983) see biting during the matings they witnessed. This leads us to believe that the behaviors reported by Tinkle (1951) and Waide and Thomas (1984) were more aggressive than amorous.

Female *Drymarchon* are capable of storing viable sperm for a considerable period. A female purchased from a dealer and housed alone laid a clutch of 5 eggs, one of which contained an embryo, after 4 years and 4 months (Carson, 1945).

Natural nests are unknown, but it is suspected that the eggs are laid in the underground burrows of pocket gophers (*Geomys pinetis*) or gopher tortoises (*Gopherus polyphemus*).

Three to 12 eggs comprise a typical clutch, and Moulis (1976) reported that females under 152 cm, possibly in their first breeding season, lay fewer than 6 eggs; those longer than 152 cm lay 9-12 eggs. Larger females probably also lay larger eggs. The eggs are elongate (54–100 mm x 27–45 mm) with cream-colored leathery shells bearing calcified patches. Hatching takes place in August in 73–102 days. Hatchling total lengths reported in the literature vary from 340 to 485 mm, but Neill (1951) found some over 600 mm long with

DRYMARCHON CORAIS

Indigo Snake

still prominent yolk scars. Hatchlings differ from adults in having faint cross–bands or light anterior speckling.

Growth And Longevity: Moulis (1976) presented growth data for captive indigo snakes from Georgia. One, 40.6 cm at hatching, grew to 104.1 cm in one year, and reached 146 cm in its third year. Two other hatchlings grew 19.1 and 16.2 cm in about a year. *Drymarchon c. couperi* is relatively long–lived (25 years, 11 months in captivity; Bowler, 1977) and is the largest known snake in the eastern United States (Conant, 1975).

Food And Feeding: *Drymarchon* seems to prefer reptilian prey. It feeds on a variety of snakes (including venomous species), lizards, small turtles and turtle eggs (Carson, 1945; Babis, 1949; Wright and Wright, 1957; Mount, 1975; Moulis, 1976; Ashton and Ashton, 1981). Ashton and Ashton (1981) reported that rat snakes are a favorite food. In addition to reptiles, other foods such as frogs, toads, ground nesting birds, and small mammals are eaten, and in at least some tropical populations fish are consumed (Wehekind, 1955). Neill and Allen (1956) found a number of beetles in the stomachs of an indigo snake, but thought these were secondarily ingested, possibly having been previously eaten by frogs.

Snakes, including venomous species, are seized by the head and chewed vigorously until immobilized (Keegan, 1944; Moulis, 1976). *Drymachon* crawls along the side of the snake until reaching its head and then quickly seizes the head, often in such a way as to prevent the other snake's jaws from opening. After the head is almost pulverized, the snake is quickly swallowed head first. Waide and Thomas (1984) observed aggressive behavior between two *Drymachon c. melanurus* in Campeche, Mexico. This has been interpreted as a possible example of male combat, but may have been an attempt by one snake to eat the other since biting was involved. Similarly, the aggressive behavior of a snake toward a female in captivity, which included biting, observed by Tinkle (1951) may also have been an attempted predation.

Moulis (1976) reported that when pit vipers bite indigo snakes, reactions to the venom do occur, but that the indigos usually survive.

Predators And Defense: Young indigo snakes are probably preyed on by ophiophagous snakes (*Lampropeltis*, *Micrurus*), birds of prey, and carnivorous mammals, but large adults have few natural enemies. Neill (in Moulis, 1976) saw an alligator feeding on an adult indigo snake, but humans are their worst enemies, with their automobiles, commercial collecting, and habitat destruc-

tion. One of the worst problems is the gassing of gopher tortoise burrows by pouring gasoline into the burrow. This is known to kill indigo and other snakes that may have retreated there (Speake and Mount, 1973).

When first disturbed *Drymarchon* often shakes its tail, and Neill (1960) reported that in the South American subspecies *D. c. corais* the tail and posterior part of the body are deep yellow while the rest of the snake is black. When approached, the snake raises the bright tail in the air and waves it about. *D. c. couperi* also may vertically flatten its neck and make threatening gestures, but seldom bites if handled.

Remarks: Monroe and Monroe (1968) found that *Drymarchon* has a pattern of undulating lines on the surface of the skin, formed by the junction of rows of cells that acts as a two–dimensional optical diffraction grating to produce the iridescence common to this snake. Also, Baden et al. (1966) reported that in indigo snakes the melanocytes in the dermis have fine, dendrite–like processes that extend through the basement membrane into the first layer of the epidermis.

Considering the size of this prominent snake, very little is known of its life history in the wild. Most of our knowledge on feeding and reproduction has been learned from captives. It is possible we may never be able to learn much of its wild behavior as *Drymarchon c. couperi* is threatened or endangered over most of its range. It would be a great loss if this magnificent creature should become extinct.

COLUBER CONSTRICTOR

Racer

COLUBER CONSTRICTOR
(Linnaeus, 1758)
Racer

Recognition: Adults are large (to 185 cm), almost uniformly shiny black to bluish snakes with smooth scales and irrascible tempers. The chin and throat may be white, gray, or brownish, and the venter is yellow to gray. Juveniles are patterned with a distinct mid–dorsal row of dark gray, brown, or reddish–brown blotches and a series of small dark spots on the sides and venter, on a grayish ground color. All traces of these blotches and spots fade with age and finally disappear completely when the snake reaches 70–80 cm in length. The body scales occur in 17 rows at mid–body and 15 rows near the anus; the anal plate is divided. On each side of the head are 2 nasals, a loreal, 2 preoculars, 2 postoculars, 2 + 2 + 2 temporals, 7(8) supralabials, and 8(9–10) infralabials. Males have 167–193 ventrals and 78–120 subcaudals; females have 151–184 ventrals and 70–99 subcaudals. The cylindrical hemipenis is widest basally, has an undivided sulcus spermaticus, and contains only 3 large hooked spines on the smooth basal portion. Distally to these spines is a zone of small recurved spines. Each maxillary contains 14–16 small recurved teeth.

Males have tails 23–27% as long as the total body length; the female tail is 19–24% as long as the total body length.

Karyotype: The karyotype is 2n = 36; 16 macrochromosomes, 20 microchromosomes, sex determination is ZZ/ZW (Baker et al., 1972).

Fossil Record: Fossils of *C. constrictor* date from the lower Pliocene of Nebraska, middle Pliocene of Oklahoma, and upper Pliocene of Kansas and Texas (Holman, 1979), and from the Blancan (Kansas, Nebraska), Irvingtonian (Florida, Kansas, Texas), and Rancholabrean (California, Florida, Georgia, Missouri, Tennessee, Texas) of the Pleistocene (Holman, 1981; Meylan, 1982).

Distribution: *C. constrictor* ranges from southern Maine, central New York, and southwestern Ontario, west to southern British Columbia and south to the Florida Keys, Gulf of Mexico, southwestern Belize and northern Guatemala in the east, and to northern Baja California and Chiapas, Mexico in the west (Wilson, 1978).

Geographic Variation: Eleven subspecies are recognized (Wilson, 1978), but only seven occur east of the Mississippi River. *Coluber constrictor constrictor* Linnaeus, 1758, the northern black racer, is shiny black dorsally and ventrally, has little white on the supralabials, and has the enlarged hemipenial spine less than 2.5 times as large as the adjacent proximal spines. It ranges from southern Maine and central New York south to northern Georgia and Alabama. *C. c. foxii* (Baird and Girard, 1853), the blue racer, is pale bluish gray or bluish green dorsally, and white to cream ventrally. It is found from Michigan, Wisconsin and Minnesota south to Ohio, Indiana, and Illinois. *C. c. priapus* Dunn and Wood, 1939, the southern black racer, is essentially like the nominate race, but has the enlarged hemipenial spine at least 3 times larger than the adjacent proximal spines. It ranges from southern Indiana and Illinois and southeastern North Carolina to central Florida, the Gulf Coast of Alabama and Mississippi, and to southern Arkansas. It also occurs on some of the Florida Keys. *C. c. paludicola* Auffenberg and Babbitt, 1953, the everglades racer, is bluish–gray, greenish–gray, or brownish–gray dorsally, white to light blue ventrally, and has a reddish iris and more than 99 subcaudals. It is found in southern Florida. *C. c. helvigularis* Auffenberg, 1955, the brownchin racer, occurs only in the lower Chipola and Appalachicola River valleys in Georgia and Florida. It is a black snake with pale brown labials, chin and throat. *C. c. latrunculus* Wilson, 1970b, the blackmask racer, is gray dorsally, grayish–blue ventrally, and has a black postocular stripe. It occurs in southeastern Louisiana and adjacent Mississippi. In addition to these six subspecies, individuals resembling a seventh, *C. c. flaviventris* Say, 1823, the eastern yellowbelly racer, are found in Illinois (Smith, 1961). This racer is pale bluish–gray or bluish–green dorsally and yellowish ventrally.

Confusing Species: *Elaphe obsoleta* has keeled body scales. *Masticophis flagellum* has 13 scale rows near the anal vent, reddish pigment on the tail, and lighter dorsal pigment posteriorly. *Drymarchon corais* has red or orange pigment on the labials, chin and throat and an undivided anal plate. Melanistic individuals of *Thamnophis* have keeled body scales and undivided anal plates.

Map

Fig. 21. *Coluber constrictor priapus*
(Christopher W. Brown).

Habitat: This snake occurs in a variety of open to dry habitats in the east, but most have some water available; deciduous woodlands, shrub grasslands, prairies, old fields, swamp and marsh borders. Bogert and Cowles (1947) reported that a *C. c. priapus* placed in a thermal–drying chamber died after a 25% reduction of initial body weight through evaporative water loss.

Behavior: The agile racer is a diurnal snake, and can often be seen in woodlands or old fields quickly crawling along with its head raised off the ground. Most daily activity is in the morning hours. Nights and dark or rainy days are spent in some shelter.

Over most of its eastern range it is active from late March to late October, but in Florida and along the Gulf Coast it may be active in every month, especially during warm years. Even in the north, warm winter days may bring some individuals out of hibernation (Conant, 1938; Robinson et al., 1974). However, most hibernate in winter. Mammal burrows, caves, rock crevices, gravel banks, old stone walls, cisterns and wells, rotting logs and stumps are most commonly used as hibernacula, and often these are shared with other species such as *Elaphe obsoleta*, *Pituophis melanoleucus*, *Thamnophis sirtalis*, *Agkistrodon contortrix*, and *Crotalus horridus*. Emergence from hibernation is gradual, and usually involves several days of basking at the site before full activity is resumed (Cohen, 1948a).

C. constrictor is often active at warmer air temperatures than other snakes. We have seen them prowling on summer days when the air was 32 C or warmer, and no other terrestrial snakes were evident. Bogert and Cowles (1947) reported the critical thermal maximum for *C. c. priapus* from Florida was 43–45 C. However, they seem to prefer air temperatures of 22–30 C (Fitch, 1950; 1963a; Ernst, personal observations). Kitchell (1969) reported that *C. constrictor* on a thermal gradient chose temperatures of 22.4–37.4 C. Cloacal temperatures of active racers usually are 25–38 C (Ernst, personal observations). The critical thermal minimum for *C. constrictor* must be near 3 C (Robinson et al., 1974).

Racers are fond of basking, and can often be seen stretched out on the branches of some shrub or on a log. Activity is not restricted to the ground as this snake is a good climber. Basking on the branches of low trees seems to be very common in the hammocks of the Florida Everglades.

This serpent occupies a rather large home range. Fitch (1963a) reported that in Kansas, males had average home ranges of about 10.5 hectares, while that of females was about 9.7 hectares. Fitch found that many racers made movements of 600–1200 m, and that some shifted their home ranges. The longest movement he recorded was 1225 m, after a lapse of four seasons. Kansas *C. constrictor* equipped with radio transmitters averaged movements of only 10 m/day (0–454 m/day) (Fitch and Shirer, 1971). In Maryland, Stickel and Cope (1947) recorded racer movements of 91 m to 1.8 km in one day to two years. Many long distance movements may be associated with migrations to or from hibernacula. During the summer, some racers remain close to specific retreats in which they apparently sleep each night (Ernst, personal observation).

Reproduction: In Kansas, males mature sexually and first produce sperm in August and September when they are little more than a year old, but do not mate until the next spring (Fitch, 1963a). Upon emergence from hibernation, the seminiferous tubules are filled with sertoli syncytium, but contain few germ cells. Spermatogonia proliferate in May and June, and by the first half of July primary spermatocytes are dominant in the tubules. The first spermatozoa are present in early August, and by late October spermiogenesis is essentially completed and mature sperm are in the vas deferens and epididymides.

Some female *C. constrictor* become sexually mature in their second year (Fitch, 1963a). Vitellogenesis occurs in the spring after the female emerges from hibernation. The eggs enlarge rapidly and are usually ovulated in late May. Collard and Leathem (1967) found a biphased pattern in ovarian weight; it was greater in March and June than in April and July. Reproduction appears to be annual, and the clutch size increases with the age and body length of the female.

Mating usually occurs in the spring (12 April to 25 June; Anderson, 1965; Lillywhite, 1985), but Wright and Wright (1957) reported one of their students once saw a ball of racers in the fall in New York that may have been an attempted mating. Males follow scent trails to find females (Lillywhite, 1985), and several males may court the same female. Fitch (1963a) gave the following summary of courtship and mating in the racer.

> A courting male lies on or alongside a receptive female, with spasmodic rippling abdominal movements, and with his vent adpressed to hers. At intervals in the courtship period the female moves swiftly for a few feet or a few yards shifting to a new spot, and during her activity the male strives to maintain contact with her. From time to time the male leaves the female briefly and courses rapidly around her in a devious route. Courtship is consummated when the female raises her tail in acceptance of the male and intromission is effected. During coitus, which lasts for periods of minutes, the female moves forward slowly, dragging the passive male, tail-first behind her.

Fig. 22. *Coluber constrictor paludicola* is found in the Florida Everglades (Steve W. Gotte).

Fig. 23. *Coluber constrictor flaviventris* has a yellow venter, and is found in Illinois (Steve W. Gotte).

Fig. 24. A juvenile *Coluber c. constrictor;* note the enlarged preocular scale.

Fig. 25. Venter of a juvenile *Coluber c. paludicola* (Steve W. Gotte).

Over most of the East, *C. constrictor* lays its eggs from early June to early August, but in Florida, *C. c. priapus* may nest as early as March or April (Gillingham, 1976; Iverson, 1978). Mammal burrows, rotting logs and stumps, and old sawdust piles are favorite nesting sites. While individual nesting is most common, some females nest communally at the same site year after year (Foley, 1971; Swain and Smith, 1978).

Two to 31 eggs are laid in each clutch (Fitch, 1963a), but probably 9–12 eggs are most common. The white, elliptical eggs have leathery shells with granular surfaces. The shell lacks a calcareous layer, but the outer surface is dotted with isolated calcareous patches (Packard et al., 1982). Total calcium in embryos rises rapidly during the last half of incubation as embryos increase in size. Most calcium is drawn from the yolk, but hatchlings contain more calcium than was present in the yolk at oviposition. This extra calcium apparently comes from the eggshell (Packard et al., 1984). When first laid, the eggs are 27–39 mm x 14–23 mm. Incubation takes 43–65 days with about 50 days being most common. The young snakes hatch as early as June in Florida, but usually from late July to September, elsewhere. They are about 270–290 mm in total length (215–355 mm), and, although the young of each subspecies differ somewhat, each has a dorsal pattern of dark gray, tan or reddish brown blotches on a lighter gray or brown ground color, and some have numerous small spots on the venter. With age, this pattern is replaced by the dark adult coloration.

Growth And Longevity: Fitch (1963a) reported the following observed ranges in snout–vent length per age for *C. constrictor* from Kansas: 2 years—males 560–674 mm, females 580–738 mm; 3 years—males 648–755 mm, females 730–880 mm; 4 years—males 725–809 mm, females 791–920 mm; 5 years—males 743–855 mm, females 833–1088 mm; 6 years—males 765–883, females 892–1020; 7 years—males 788–900 mm, females 919–1050 mm; 7+ years—males 740–890, females 930–1085 mm.

Food And Feeding: A literature survey of the prey taken by the eastern subspecies of *C. constrictor* shows it has a catholic appetite, eating many different animals, apparently opportunistically as they become available. Fitch (1963a) has given the most complete summary of prey taken by the racer, and we have drawn heavily on this account, but have also supplemented his list of foods with reports published since it appeared. Prey eaten by eastern *C. constrictor* include: small snails; spiders; insects—grasshoppers, crickets, mole crickets, cicadas, various beetles, true bugs, ichneumonid wasps, moths and their caterpillars; amphibians–anurans (15 species; *Bufo, Hyla,*

Acris, Pseudacris, Rana), salamanders (*Desmognathus*); reptiles—small turtles (*Kinosternon, Chrysemys, Terrapene*), lizards and their eggs (9 species; *Ophisaurus, Cnemidophorus, Eumeces, Scincella, Anolis, Crotophytus, Sceloporus*); snakes (20 species; *Carphophis, Coluber, Diadophis, Elaphe, Farancia, Heterodon, Lampropeltis, Masticophis, Nerodia, Opheodrys, Pituophis, Storeria, Tantilla, Thamnophis, Virginia,* and *Agkistrodon*); birds—nestlings and eggs of various species; mammals—moles (*Scalopus*), shrews (*Blarina, Cryptotis*), mice (10 species; *Clethrionomys, Microtus, Mus, Peromyscus, Reithrodontomys, Synaptomys*), rats (*Neotoma, Oryzomys, Rattus, Sigmodon*), squirrels (*Glaucomys, Tamias*), rabbits (*Sylvilagus*), and weasels (*Mustela*). It is truly cannibalistic, and often feeds on young of its own species. One of the strangest reports is that of *C. c. priapus* swallowing fish eggs as they emerged from an effluent pipe at a hatchery (Cook and Aldrige, 1984). There are also several reports of racers swallowing their shed skins (Mattlin, 1946; Munro, 1949a; Brown, 1979a).

Several studies have commented on the percentage of occurrence of various prey items in racer stomachs. In Virginia, Uhler et al. (1939) found the following foods by volume; snakes 26%, birds 18%, shrews 12%, caterpillars and moths 10%, frogs 9%, moles and lizards 6%, squirrels 5%, and other insects and arthropods 5%. Hamilton and Pollack (1956) recorded the food percentages by occurrence in Georgia racers; lizards 65%, snakes 28%, amphibians 9%, mammals 3.5%, and insects 1.7%. In Illinois, Klimstra (1959c) recorded the following percentages of occurrence; insects 48%, mammals 43.5%, birds 16.5%, amphibians 13%, and reptiles 12%. In Kansas, Fitch (1963a) found insects in 77% of the stomachs he examined, mammals in 15% and snakes in 5%; and in North Carolina, Brown (1979a) found that reptiles, mammals and insects comprised 80% of the prey items. Both Klimstra (1959c) and Fitch (1963a) have noted seasonal shifts in food preferences and volume, apparently reflecting the availability of various prey in different seasons.

Contrary to its specific name, the racer is not a constricting snake. When prey is detected, the snake rapidly crawls after it and seizes it with its mouth. Small animals are eaten alive, but larger ones may be pressed to the ground with the body and then chewed until dead. Many of the insects and mammals it commonly eats are economically undesirable, so this snake should be regarded as beneficial to the farmer.

Predators And Defense: The natural enemies of *C. constrictor* are probably many, although only a few instances of actual predation have been recorded. Many young racers fall prey to other ophiophagous snakes (*Micrurus fulvius, Crotalus horridus, Agkistrodon contortrix, Elaphe obsoleta, Lampropeltis calligaster, L. getulus*) and they are known to frequently eat their own species (Fitch, 1963a; Jackson, 1971). Fitch (1963a) found the remains of a racer in a slender glass lizard, *Ophisaurus attenuatus*. Hawks (broad–winged, marsh, red–shouldered, red–tailed, sparrow), barn owls, crows, and roadrunners also attack them, and foxes, opossums, raccoons, and skunks probably also eat them. Owens (1949) reported his captive tarantula ate hatchling racers. However, humans are the most destructive animal to racers. The automobile, pesticides, and widespread habitat destruction have drastically reduced the numbers of racers in many states.

When first discovered, *C. constrictor* usually tries to flee, relying on its speed to elude the pursuer. It can achieve a speed of at least 5.6 km/hr (Mosauer, 1932). If trapped, it quickly coils, vibrates its tail, strikes and bites viciously. Generally, this snake has a rotten disposition. When handled, if it cannot bite, it will defecate and spray musk all over you. They usually remain high strung and nervous, and make poor captives. Many refuse to eat anything but their keepers' hands. They may also be occasionally agressive and deliberately attack in the wild. Barbour recalls one Kentucky episode where a large racer approached his grandfather and wrapped itself about his lower leg before it was killed, and Ernst has been attacked in the wild by an irate, previously unseen racer in Virginia.

If aggression does not drive off an enemy, apparently some individuals will then play dead; Lynch (1978) relates how a *C. c. flaviventris* in Saskatchewan feigned death.

Populations: Where there is still suitable habitat and abundant prey, *C. constrictor* may occur in rather large populations. Fitch (1963a) thought the population he studied in Kansas had a summer density of about 2–7 adults per hectare, and at a northern Virginia wildlife refuge preliminary observations by Ernst indicate the presence of 1–3 adults per hectare in summer. In Florida, Telford (1952) has seen as many as 19 in one hour.

Fitch (1963a) reported the sex ratio at hatching is approximately 1:1, but in later life females make up about 60% of the adults. The composition by age groups of the adult racers captured in Kansas by Fitch was as follows: 2 year olds, 41.5%; 3 years, 17.8%; 4 years, 12.6%; 5 years, 9.5%; 6 years, 6.1%; 7 years, 4.3%; 8 years, 2.7%; 9 years, 2.4%; 10 years, 1.2%, and over 10 years old, 1.9%. In late summer during the hatching period, hatchlings may comprise nearly 50% of the population, yearlings a little less than 25%, and adults a little more than 25%.

MASTICOPHIS FLAGELLUM

Coachwhip

MASTICOPHIS FLAGELLUM
(Shaw, 1802)
Coachwhip

Recognition: *Masticophis flagellum* is a long (to 260 cm) snake with the scales on the tail arranged in such a pattern as to suggest a braided whip. Anteriorly, it is dark brown or black on the head and forepart of the body with the dark pigment gradually fading until the tail is much lighter. Coloration of the venter is like that of the back. Some lighter colored individuals may retain the juvenile pattern and have the dark pigment reduced to narrow crossbands over the back, while some other coachwhips may be totally dark brown or black. The body scales are smooth with two apical pits and occur in 17 rows at mid–body and 13(12) near the vent; the anal plate is divided. Laterally on the head are 2 nasals, 1(2–3) loreal, 2(3) preoculars, 2(1–3) postoculars, 2 + 3 temporals, 8 (7–9) supralabials, and 10(8–13) infralabials. Ortenburger (1928) described the hemipenis as only slightly bilobed with a single sulcus spermaticus, 40–60 spines in 2–3 rows, 3 large basal spines (one much larger than the other two), and 10–13 rows of deep calyces. On each maxilla are 18–20 short teeth.

Males have 188–212 ventrals and 94–122 subcaudals; females 186–208 ventrals and 91–123 subcaudals; tail length/total body length ratios are 22–27.5% and 21.7–30% for males and females, respectively (Wilson, 1970a).

Karyotype: There are 36 chromosomes; 16 macrochromosomes, 20 microchromosomes; sex determination is ZZ/ZW (Baker et al., 1972).

Fossil Record: Pleistocene coachwhip remains have been found in Blancan deposits in Arizona and Texas, Irvingtonian deposits in Florida and Arkansas, and Rancholabrean sites in California, Florida, Nevada, New Mexico, and Virginia (Wilson, 1973b; Holman, 1981; Meylan, 1982).

Distribution: *M. flagellum* is found from southeastern North Carolina, westward to Nebraska and eastern Colorado, New Mexico, Arizona, southwestern Utah and Nevada and southern California, and southward through peninsular Florida, and eastern and central Mexico to Veracruz, Queretaro, Durango and Sinaloa, and through Baja California (Wilson, 1973b).

Geographic Variation: Seven valid subspecies exist (Wilson, 1970; 1973b), but only one, *Masticophis flagellum flagellum* (Shaw, 1802), the eastern coachwhip, occurs in eastern North America. It ranges from southeastern North Carolina west to eastern Nebraska, and south through peninsular Florida and the Gulf Coast to eastern Texas. Isolated records are known from southeastern Tennessee and Barren and Edmonson counties, Kentucky, although this latter population may be extinct.

Confusing Species: Racers (*Coluber*) have 15 body scale rows just anterior to the anal vent, and no reddish pigment on the sides of the tail. Melanistic garter and ribbon snakes (*Thamnophis*) have keeled body scales.

Habitat: *M. flagellum* is basically a grassland, savannah or scrubland dweller. It is a rapid crawler, and in such habitats can quickly elude a human chasing it. Many a herpetologist has tried to catch one in such situations only to have the snake disappear down a hole at the last second.

This snake is also a very capable climber, and can often be seen in shrubs or trees stalking birds and their nestlings.

Behavior: *M. flagellum* seems to be strictly diurnal. Seasonally, it may first appear in March, but most often in April or early May. As long as the autumn is warm it may continue to forage into late October. In Florida, it may be active in the winter, but may retreat into animal burrows to escape the severe summer heat. Little is known of its hibernating behavior. Neill (1948a) reported that in Georgia it overwintered in tunnels formed by the decay of pine roots on dry hillsides. In Kansas, they hibernate in deep crevices on rocky hillsides or in small mammal burrows on the open prairie (Collins, 1974). Cowles (1941) found one hibernating in the desert that had a body temperature of 17 C.

Bogert and Cowles (1947) found two *M. flagellum* from Florida to be extremely resistant to dessication. One which weighed 536 g when placed in a thermal chamber at 38 C for over 46 hours, lost only 0.14% of its body weight per hour. The second snake (655 g) had lost only 11.3% of its initial body weight after 99.5 hours in the same chamber. Field body temperatures of two western subspecies recorded by Brattstrom (1965) ranged between 24 and 37 C, and Bogert and Cowles (1947) reported a field temperature of 32.6 C for *M. f. flagellum* They also calculated its critical thermal maximum to be 42.4 C. Ruben (1983) found that *M. flagellum* exhibits great stamina and high rates of oxygen consumption when active.

Reproduction: Adults are probably mature at a total body length of 70–90 cm, but there has been no study conducted of the sexual cycles and maturity in this snake. Mating apparently occurs soon after emergence from hibernation; Minton (1959) reported a 30 April copulation.

The eggs are laid in the summer from early June to the beginning of August (Clark, 1949; Guidry, 1953; Wright and Wright, 1957; Carpenter, 1958). The average number of eggs per clutch for 16 clutches of *M. f. flagellum* reported in the literature was 12.3 with a range of 4 (Collins, 1974) to 24 (Wright and Wright, 1957). The eggs are elongate (31.8–49.5 x 15.4–26.3 mm), with coarse leathery shells covered with rugose granulations. They are laid in loose soil, in animal burrows, or in the rotting wood of old stumps or logs. Incubation takes 45–79 days (Perkins, 1952; Guidry, 1953), usually from late July to early September.

Newly hatched young are 300–360 mm in total length. Dorsally they are reddish–brown to olive–brown with a series of narrow to broad dark tranverse bands beginning on the neck and continuing to varying distances along the body. A double row of reddish spots occurs on the venter.

Food And Feeding: Prey naturally taken include insects (Hamilton and Pollack, 1956; Carpenter, 1958); lizards, snakes (including smaller *Masticophis*; Guidry, 1953), small turtles (Hamilton and Pollack, 1956); both adult and nestling birds, rats, mice, shrews and bats (Collins, 1974). Of 30 stomachs examined by Clark (1949), 18 contained mammals and 12 birds. Hamilton and Pollack (1956) reported the following percentages of occurrence and volume (in parentheses) for foods of 45 *M. flagellum*: lizards, 68.9 (63.4); mammals, 17.8 (14.7); snakes, 8.9 (8.9); insects, 8.9 (8.3); birds, 2.2 (2.2); and a turtle, 2.2 (2.2).

M. flagellum is an active forager, crawling about, often with its head and neck well off the ground, until it finds a scent trail, or flushes some small animal. Then it rapidly crawls after the prey, seizes it and quickly swallows it. Being long and slender, *M. flagellum* can follow prey into narrow burrows, and probably captures many lizards and small mammals underground. Hunting is not restricted to ground level or subterranean burrows, as coachwhips often climb high into trees to raid bird's nests. In this respect, they remind one of rat snakes (*Elaphe obsoleta*).

Predators And Defense: Natural enemies include carnivorous mammals, hawks, roadrunners, and

Map

Fig. 26. Venter of a juvenile *Masticophis f. flagellum* (Carl H. Ernst).

other snakes. The automobile takes a high toll every year, and indiscriminate use of insecticides probably kills many (Herald, 1949).

When first discovered in the open *M. flagellum* quickly crawls away if possible; if not, it will turn, strike and bite viciously, often aiming for the face. They also spray musk and fecal matter about when disturbed.

Gehlbach (1970) and Smith (1975) have each reported that some *M. flagellum* will play dead; cocking the head ventral or lateral, salivating, rotating the eyes ventral until the sclera are well exposed, opening the mouth, and partially extending the tongue.

There is a folk tale which states that a large coachwhip will wrap its forebody around a human's leg and then lash its antagonist with its whip-like tail. This is utterly unfounded.

Remarks: As can be seen above, we know very little about the natural history of this locally common species. This is unfortunate since its habitat is being rapidly degraded or destroyed, and the coachwhip could disappear from some areas before we come to know it well. Obviously ecological studies are needed.

M. flagellum is such a nervous snake that it does poorly when restrained in captivity. We have had no success keeping them as most refuse to eat, and we do not recommend them as captives. In all fairness, however, we must compliment the Pittsburgh Zoo which kept a male alive 16 years, 7 months, and 21 days (Bowler, 1977).

OPHEODRYS AESTIVUS

Rough Green Snake

OPHEODRYS AESTIVUS (Linnaeus, 1766)
Rough Green Snake

Recognition: *Opheodrys aestivus* (to 116 cm) is unpatterned green, and its body scales are keeled. The supralabials and lower portion of the head are light yellow; the venter is white, cream, yellow or greenish–yellow. The body scales occur in 17 rows at mid–body, and the anal plate is divided. Laterally on the head are a nasal, a loreal, 1 preocular, 2 postoculars 1 + 2 temporals, usually 7 supralabials, and 7–8 infralabials. The ventrals number 148–166 and the subcaudals 110–148; males appear to have approximately 3 fewer ventrals and 7 more subcaudals than do females (Grobman, 1984). The hemipenis has numerous fringed calyces, and 20–25 recurved teeth occur on each maxilla.

Karyotype: Unknown.

Fossils: Pleistocene remains have been found in Rancholabrean deposits in Florida and Texas (Holman, 1981).

Distribution: *O. aestivus* ranges from southern New Jersey south through peninsular Florida, and west to eastern Kansas, central Texas, and Tamaulipas and Nuevo Leon in northeastern Mexico.

Geographic Variation: Four subspecies have been described. *Opheodrys aestivus aestivus* (Linnaeus, 1766), the eastern rough green snake, ranges from southern New Jersey south to northern Florida and westward to southern Illinois and eastern Texas. It has 151 or more ventrals in males and 155 or more in females, 128 or more caudals in males and 122 or more in females, and no keels on the body scales of the 3rd dorsal row (opposite the 7th ventral). *O. a. majalis* (Baird and Girard, 1853), the western rough green snake, ranges southwest from Madison and St. Clair counties, Illinois, through Iowa, western Missouri, and eastern Oklahoma to central Texas

and northeastern Mexico. It has at least 155 ventrals in both sexes; 127 or fewer caudals in males, 121 or fewer in females; and no keels on the body scales of the 3rd dorsal row (opposite the 7th ventral). *O. a. carinatus* Grobman, 1984, the Florida rough green snake, occurs in the southern half of peninsular Florida. It has at least 155 ventrals in both sexes; 128 or more caudals in males, 122 or more in females; and the body scales of the 3rd dorsal row are keeled. *O. a. conanti* Grobman, 1984, the barrier islands rough green snake, is found only on Assateague, Parramore, Revel, and Smith Islands, Virginia. It is characterized by as many as 154 ventrals in both sexes; 127 or fewer caudals in males, 121 or fewer in females; and keeled scales on the 3rd dorsal row.

Confusing Species: The only other bright green snake in the eastern United States is *Opheodrys vernalis,* which has smooth body scales, and usually 15 mid–body scale rows. *Nerodia floridana* is stocky, has dark bars on its lips, 9 or more infralabials, and a patterned venter.

Habitat: *O. aestivus* is most frequently found in or near moist habitats, particularly marsh or lake borders, moist meadows, or along waterways in woodlands. Although not aquatic, it has been frequently observed in water or in habitats reached only by crossing water (Duellman, 1949; Richmond, 1952). It is a good climber, being found much more frequently above the ground than its congenor, *O. vernalis.* At night, it most often sleeps in bushes and shrubs. Plummer (1981b) studied perch variables in a population of *O. aestivus* from Arkansas, and found 88% of night perches and 86% of day perches were within 3 m from water. These perches were usually not over 3 m above ground (75% night, 71% day), 10 mm in diameter or less (99% night, 83% day), distally on the branch (87% night, 63% day), and at less than a 60 degree angle (92% night, 88% day). Despite preferring low perches, this snake has been observed in trees at heights over 5 m (Plummer, 1981b).

Arboreal perching among transpiring leaves may retard moisture loss. Dove et al. (1982) reported mean rates of cutaneous water loss of 0.18 and 0.39 mg cm² hr for adults and hatchlings respectively, and Baeyens and Roundtree (1983) found a water loss rate of 0.21 mg cm² hr for adults. *O. aestivus* seems to be less arboreal during the spring and fall, possibly because of the reduced numbers of leaves at those times. McComb and Noble (1981) found an *O. aestivus* in a tree cavity 10.6 m high; such a retreat would give protection from both predators and desiccation.

There is little sexual dimorphism in relative tail length, indicating an adaptation for arboreality in body proportions (Goldsmith, 1984).

OPHEODRYS AESTIVUS

Rough Green Snake

Map

Behavior: Morris (1982) reported that in southern Illinois the rough green snake is active from March to November, with adults being most active from April to July, and again in September and October. In southern Indiana, Minton (1972) found it to be among the last snakes to appear in spring with few being seen before May; however, his latest autumn record was 17 November. Some overwinter in rotten stumps or logs, possibly ant hills may be used as hibernacula, as in *O. vernalis*.

O. aestivus seems to be strictly diurnal. In Arkansas, Plummer (1981b) found them to be active most of the day; activity began soon after first light and terminated 30 minutes to an hour before dark. Nights were spent on some perch.

Plummer (1981b) found that their home ranges were restricted in size, especially within a season. Most movement was parallel to the shoreline of a lake at the vegetation edge. For 38 snakes captured at least 4 times a season the mean length of the activity range was 62 m; for 17 males, 56 m (15–102), and for 21 females, 68 m (21–247). The greatest horizontal distance moved in one day was 60 m; and for 75 snakes captured at least twice in each of at least two seasons the interseasonal shifts in location of the activity range averaged 45 m (0.5–420).

Reproduction: Sexual maturity is attained by female *O. aestivus* from Louisiana at a snout-vent length of about 350 mm. The smallest female with convoluted oviducts, ovulation scars and ovarian follicles of at least 3 mm measured by Tinkle (1960) was 355 mm, and no specimen larger than 396 mm was immature. Tinkle thought that the age at sexual maturity was probably one or two years. Plummer (1984) also found that in Arkansas most females mature between 360–400 mm snout-vent length; the smallest mature female he found was 335 mm. Males also probably mature in their second year.

Tinkle (1960) reported that the maximum size of the testes in young of the year was 0.8 mm in greatest diameter and 5.5 mm in greatest length. The largest testis of an adult male was 4.0 mm wide and 22.0 mm long. The testes become progressively longer, wider and more cylindrical as the male grows. Tinkle also found that the right testis were slightly longer than the left and positioned anterior to it.

Plummer (1984) found 1–5 mm follicles present in ovaries throughout the sampling period. Follicles 1–3 mm proliferate in post reproductive females in July and August and increase to a maximum 5 mm by October. Females collected both in September and February had two sets of follicles, 1–3 mm and 3–5 mm, indicating little activity occurs over winter. Vitellogenesis resumed in the spring and rapid yolking and enlargement to 15–25 mm occurred in May, with oviducal eggs present from late May to early July. Morris (1982) found essentially the same ovarian cycle in females from Illinois.

In Illinois, the left and right ovaries or oviducts contained an equal number of secondary vitellogenetic follicles or ova (Morris, 1982), but in Arkansas the right ovaries contained a mean 3.6 enlarged follicles while the left only a mean 2.6 (Plummer, 1984). Plummer (1984) found apparent extrauterine transfer of ova in 60% of the post–ovulatory females he examined.

Plummer (1983, 1984) reported that the amount of body fat is negatively correlated with reproductive activity in female *O. aestivus*. It is greatest in early spring and late fall and least in June; the significant reduction occurring during vitellogenesis. Plummer (1983) made comparisons between reproductive output following a climatically normal year, followed by an extemely hot, dry year when stored body fat was reduced by approximately 70%. He found no significant differences in any reproductive parameter between the two years, and suggested that spring foraging success provided the energy needed for vitellogenesis despite reduced fat supplies.

Mating occurs in the spring. Plummer (1984) found sperm present in most mature females in spring but did not detect any in other parts of the year. He did not find sperm in any female less than 350 mm snout–vent length. However, Morris (1982) found males from Illinois to be very active during September, and thought this to be the result of an autumnal increase in sexual activity. Richmond (1956) has observed a September copulation in Virginia. Anderson (1965) and Morris (1982) thought April and May the likely spring mating period, and McCauley (1945) observed a captive male *O. aestivus* try to copulate with a female *O. vernalis* on 18 May.

Courtship has not been described, and the only description of the mating act is that given by Richmond (1956):

> I noticed two of these snakes in a pecan tree. When first noticed, they were approximately 20 feet from where we were and 10 feet above ground. Even though the snakes were crawling rapidly in an intricate pattern I could see definitely that they were in copula. The terminal twigs of the pecan had dense foliage and the snakes were rapidly weaving in and out of the leaves, occasionally crossing to other twigs. At intervals they would pause, or crawl slowly, then suddenly go into the fast swirling motion that first attracted my attention. Although their movement was fast, the total distance moved in 15 to 20 minutes was only 3 feet. After a period of being motionless, the male left and climbed higher in the tree. The female remained coiled in the sun on the lower branch. The female was much larger than the male and almost olive drab in color. The male was small, slender and very bright green. The snakes were observed from approximately 3:30 P.M. to 4:00 P.M. The day was warm and sunny and the snakes were in full sun on the west side of the tree.

Oviposition occurs in June and July. Natural nest sites include rotten logs and stumps, and cavities in moss and beneath flat rocks. While most seem to nest alone, Palmer and Braswell (1976) reported a communal clutch of 74 eggs laid in rock wool insulation inside a metal refrigeration panel in North Carolina, and Plummer (1981a) has forced female *O. aestivus* to lay communally in the laboratory.

A typical clutch consists of 2–14 eggs, but 4–6 eggs are probably most common. Larger females produce both larger eggs and clutches. The adherent eggs are elongate (17–37 x 7–12 mm) with thin leathery shells. Plummer (1984) examined 77 females and found no evidence that more than a single clutch is produced each season, but Conant (1951) reported that 3 additional eggs were found in a female from Ohio that had previously laid 4 eggs. Perhaps these 3 eggs represented a second clutch. Ashton and Ashton (1981) reported that some Florida females may carry eggs over the winter and lay them in early spring.

Of 180 eggs laid and incubated in Plummer's laboratory (1984), 161 (89.4%) were fertile, and 145 (90%) of the fertile eggs hatched; incubation periods were 36–43 days. Hatching occurs in nature during late August and September. The young are 179–211 mm in total length and paler green than are adults.

External incubation may alter the composition of the eggshell in *O. aestivus* and *O. vernalis*. At oviposition *Opheodrys* eggs contained 28–40% calcium and 33% protein (*vernalis*), but after incubation these levels were reduced to 17–41% and 15.4% (a 53.8% decrease), respectively (Cox et al., 1984).

Growth: Morris (1982) examined growth data from *O. aestivus* in Illinois, and found four snout-vent size classes. Hatchlings had a maximum growth of 26 mm, while the greatest growth in the 1st season following hatching was 141 mm. During the 2nd season the growth slowed so that the maximum increase was 67 mm. There was much overlap in growth between 3rd year and older snakes, so maximum growth after 3 years could not be calculated. There is some geographical variation in body length, with southern Florida *O. aestivus* achieving the greatest lengths (Plummer, 1987).

Food And Feeding: Caterpillars, grasshoppers, crickets and spiders constitute the major diet (Van Hyning, 1932; Hamilton and Pollack, 1956; Bush, 1959; Minton, 1972; Plummer, 1981b).

Plummer (1981b) observed that foraging often entailed searching leaves and small branches as the snake very slowly moved distally on a limb, and Minton (1972) has seen these snakes stalk insects with an almost imperceptible gliding movement until the prey could be seized with a quick strike. Goldsmith (1986) observed that these snakes used visual cues exclusively for detecting moving insects, and were unable to detect motionless insects. Once the insect was seen, the initial phase of approach was rapid and sporadic, while the final approach was slow and deliberate. Neither tongue flicking or lateral head movement occurred during the approach. When within 3 cm of the insect, the snakes formed a series of anterior sigmoid body curves, then straightened out, propelling the head toward the insect. The mean distance of 78 strikes in Goldsmith's captive snakes was 1.64 cm, and the strikes were usually directed toward the head or thorax of the insect. The insects were usually swallowed head first and were manipulated by unilateral jaw movements.

Predators And Defense: Snake–eating serpents, such as kingsnakes and coral snakes, and predatory mammals (skunks, weasels, raccoons, foxes, coyotes) are probably the greatest predators on rough green snakes, but birds and fish may also take their toll. Tomkins (1965) reported an incidence of a swallow–tailed kite having an *O. aes-*

tivus wrapped around its wing, apparently the result of an attack on the snake, and Guthrie (1932) reported the Mississippi kite eats this snake. Clark (1949) saw an alligator gar attack a swimming *O. aestivus*.

In the daylight, the green coloration of *O. aestivus* makes it extremely hard to distinguish the snake against a leafy background, and it usually "freezes" when first discovered. If touched it will attempt to flee, and if further disturbed may widely gape its mouth displaying the dark lining. They rarely bite if handled, but may void the contents of their cloaca and musk glands.

Due to its insect–eating habits, the rough green snake may be reduced in numbers in those areas where insecticides are widely applied.

Populations: Tinkle (1960) found that juvenile males and females made up 22 and 16%, respectively of a population in Louisiana; a 0.48/1 juvenile to adult ratio. He also found that 30% of the snakes were less than 25 cm snout–vent length. For the 132 dissected specimens in which the sex could definitely be determined, there were 63 females (47.7%) and 69 males (53.3%), a 1:1 sex ratio. Plummer (1984) found a 1:1 sex ratio in 141 hatchlings he sexed, but also found (1985) that the sex ratio varied monthly in his Arkansas population, favoring males in the early season (60–80%) and females in mid–season (60–80%). The density of Plummer's (1985) population was approximately 430/ha.

OPHEODRYS VERNALIS

Smooth Green Snake

OPHEODRYS VERNALIS (Harlan, 1827)
Smooth Green Snake

Recognition: This is an unpatterned green snake (to 66 cm) with smooth body scales. The supralabials are yellowish and the venter white to cream–colored. The body scales occur in 15 rows at mid–body; the anal plate is divided. The head scalation is like that of *O. aestivus* except for 6–7 supralabials and 7–8 infralabials. The hemipenis has numerous fringed calyces. Each maxilla bears 15–18 teeth.

Males have 116–145 ventrals and 74–96 subcaudals, while females have 121–154 ventrals and 60–84 subcaudals.

Karyotype: Unknown.

Fossil Record: Pleistocene remains are known from Citrus County, Florida (Irvingtonian), Alleghany County, Maryland (Irvingtonian) and Monroe County, Indiana (Rancholabrean) (Holman, 1977; Holman and Richards, 1981; Meylan, 1982).

Distribution: *O. vernalis* is found from Nova Scotia and Manitoba westward to southeastern Saskatchewan and southward to the Smoky Mountains of North Carolina, Texas, New Mexico, and Chihuahua, Mexico.

Geographic Variation: Two subspecies are recognized. *Opheodrys vernalis vernalis* (Harlan, 1827), the eastern smooth green snake, ranges from Nova Scotia westward to northern Wisconsin, Minnesota and Manitoba, and southeast to the Smoky Mountains of Tennessee and North Carolina. It is greenish in color, usually has 7 supralabials, and less than 130 ventrals in males and 139 or fewer in females. *Opheodrys v. blanchardi* Grobman, 1941, the western smooth green snake, ranges from southern Manitoba and Saskatchewan southward to northwestern Indiana, northern Illinois, Missouri and northeastern Kansas. It is also found in the Black Hills of South Dakota and adjacent Wyoming, southeastern Idaho and adjacent Utah, and from southern Wyoming to New Mexico; scattered populations also occur in Texas and Chihuahua, Mexico. This race is light brown dorsally, usually has 6 supralabials, and 131 or more ventrals in males and 140 or more in females.

Confusing Species: The only other greenish–colored snakes in eastern North America have keeled body scales.

Habitat: *O. vernalis* lives in a variety of mesic habitats such as wet prairies, meadows, bog and marsh borders, and open woodlands. Although predominantly ground dwellers, they occasionally climb into low bushes and shrubs.

Behavior: *O. vernalis* is active from mid–April to October; their shortest period of activity is in the north where they may be abroad only from late May to September.

The colder months are spent in hibernation underground. In Pennsylvania they have been uncovered from a gravel bank (Lachner, 1942), and elsewhere ant mounds seem to be preferred hibernacula where they have been found buried at depths greater than 15 cm (Criddle, 1937; Carpenter, 1953a; Lang, 1969; Young, 1973). Criddle (1937) reported that in an ant mound in Manitoba that contained water at a depth of 145 cm some smooth green snakes were partly submerged with their heads pointed upward, and that most of the large adults were at the lowest levels of the mound, while the majority of the smaller *O. vernalis* were nearest the surface. Such mounds are popular overwintering sites for snakes, and several species may hibernate simultaneously.

Brattstrom (1965) found that the body temperatures of 5 active *O. vernalis* ranged from 18–31.2 C (x = 25.6), and Seibert and Hagen (1947) reported they were most active when air temperatures were 21–30 C. Kroll et al. (1973) found that the maximum metabolically produced heat by an *O. vernalis* was 3.0 C, and that this heat production was related to the snake's diurnal activity cycle, as its body temperature decreased at night. After eating a frog its body temperature dropped rapidly, then increased slightly and leveled off. The maximum difference observed between the snake's body temperature and that of the air during the interval was + 1.2 C.

Reproduction: Mating occurs in May (Collins 1974), and August (Dymond and Fry, 1932). Stille (1954) showed that when temperatures during May were above 18 C *O. vernalis* failed to reproduce.

The nesting period ranges from June to September, depending on the latitude; in the south–

OPHEODRYS VERNALIS

Smooth Green Snake

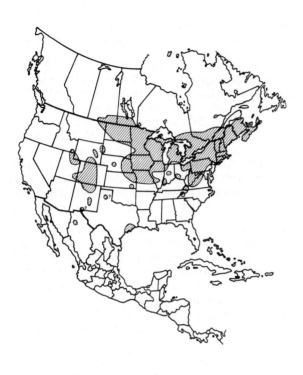

Map

ern portions of the range the eggs are laid in June and July, while in Michigan and southern Canada nesting occurs from late July to early September. Females in the northern populations probably incubate the eggs internally by basking before actual oviposition, and possibly some eggs overwinter before hatching. Nest sites vary from mounds of rotting vegetation, sawdust piles, and rotten logs to the shallow underground burrows of rodents.

Blanchard (1932) mentioned that it is fairly common for *O. vernalis* to lay their eggs in two or more clutches. Individual clutches contain 3–13 eggs, with 4–6 being most common. However, several female *O. vernalis* may share a single nest site. Several communal nests containing up to 31 eggs have been discovered (Cook, 1964; Fowler, 1966; Gordon and Cook, 1980; Lawson, 1983), and Gregory (1975a) and Gordon and Cook (1980) found aggregations of gravid female *O. vernalis* that were near the time of laying.

The eggs are loosely adhered and elongate (19–34 x 8–18 mm) with blunt ends and thin white shells. The young (83–154 mm) emerge in August or September after incubation periods of 4–23 days, and resemble the adults in color, but are slightly more grayish.

Food And Feeding: *O. vernalis* feeds almost exclusively on arthropods; spiders, centipedes, millipedes and especially insects (moth larvae, crick-

ets, beetles). Wright and Wright (1957) also listed slugs, snails and salamanders as prey. Newly hatched young apparently do not feed for several weeks until they have used all of the yolk material absorbed from the egg and have shed their skins (LeBuff, 1951).

Predators And Defense: Neill (1948b) reported that a black widow spider preyed on *O. vernalis*, and ophiophagous snakes, birds (domestic chickens), and mammals all take their toll of this species.

Generally inoffensive when handled, *O. vernalis* may void the contents of its cloaca and musk glands on the handler, and Schlauch (1975) reported they may occasionally gape and feign striking, but not bite.

Populations: Seibert (1950) estimated a population of smooth green snakes in the Chicago area to be 237 with a density of approximately 185 per hectare.

Of 32 *O. vernalis* collected in Manitoba by Gregory (1977a), 19 (59%) were males and 13 (41%) were females.

Remarks: *Opheodrys vernalis* is a useful species that feeds on some harmful insects, and is probably most common in areas where insects abound. The common use today of insecticides in such areas may have a detrimental effect on its population. Minton (1972) collected two individuals from a section of northern Indiana that had been heavily sprayed; one was barely alive and the other appeared normal but died two weeks later.

CEMOPHORA COCCINEA

Scarlet Snake

CEMOPHORA COCCINEA
(Blumenbach, 1788)
Scarlet Snake

Recognition: *Cemophora coccinea* is a small to medium sized (to 82.3 cm), red, black and yellow (or cream) snake with a projecting rounded snout. The back is patterned banded with transverse red saddles bordered by black, between which are yellow or cream–colored rings. The head is red, with a dark transverse bar at or behind the eyes. The venter is immaculate white or cream. The head is barely broader than the neck, and the tail is rather short. The body scales are smooth with two apical pits and usually in 19 rows throughout; the anal plate is undivided. The rostral scale is enlarged and projects beyond the lower jaw. On the side of the head are a divided nasal, a loreal, 1–2 preoculars, 2 postoculars, 1 + 2 temporals, 6–7 supralabials (2nd and 3rd enter the orbit if 6 supralabials, 3rd and 4th if 7), and 7 (6–9) infralabials. There are 149–195 ventrals and 31–50 pairs of subcaudals. The bilobed hemipenis is naked proximally but spinose distally; the apex is calyculate. The single sulcus spermaticus extends onto the lateral lobe, and the area between the lobes is naked. Nine to 10 teeth occur on the maxilla; the last pair are elongated and blade-like.

Males seem to reach a greater length (82.3 cm) than females (65 cm) (Wright and Wright, 1957). Females have slightly longer bodies and, thus, more ventrals, x = 170.3, than do males, x = 165.8; while the longer tailed (14.8% of total body length) males have more subcaudals, x = 41.7, than the short–tailed (13.8%) females, x = 40.4.

Karyotype: Unknown.

Fossil Record: Meylan (1982) found vertebrae of *Cemophora* in early Pleistocene (Irvingtonian) deposits in Citrus County, Florida.

Distribution: *C. coccinea* ranges from the Delmarva Peninsula south through Florida, and west to Missouri, eastern Oklahoma and eastern Texas to Jim Hogg County along the Gulf Coast (Williams, 1985).

Geographic Variation: Three subspecies are recognized, but only two occur east of the Mississippi River. *Cemophora coccinea coccinea* (Blumenbach, 1788), the Florida scarlet snake, is restricted to peninsular Florida from Citrus, Lake and Volusia counties southward. In this race the first black band behind the eyes does not touch the parietal scales (usually separated by 2 scale lengths), and there are usually 7 supralabials. *C. c. copei* Jan, 1863, the northern scarlet snake, ranges from New Jersey, Delaware and eastern Maryland south to northern peninsular Florida and west through Virginia and southern Tennessee to Oklahoma and eastern Texas. There are also several records from Kentucky, central Missouri, and one from southwestern Illinois (Williams, 1985). Scarlet snakes from Levy, Alachua and Marion counties, Florida were considered to be intergrades by Williams and Wilson (1967).

Confusing Species: The coral snake, *Micrurus fulvius*, has a black face, and its red and yellow bands are in contact. The scarlet kingsnake, *Lampropeltis triangulum elapsoides*, has black on its venter.

Habitat: This semifossorial species most often occurs in pine, hardwood, or mixed woodlands in sandy soil in the South, but also in rocky or loamy soils in the northern part of its range. Usually it is found under leaf litter, rocks, logs, or in stumps; but we have taken several from under old wooden ties along abandoned railway lines, especially in Florida.

Burrowing is achieved by thrusting the head right and left until the head and neck are concealed, then the snake forces its snout deeper into the soil and lifts the soil upward until completely concealed (Wilson, 1951).

Behavior: In the northern part of its range, *C. coccinea* becomes active in April or May and remains so well into autumn. A study in South Carolina using drift fences and pitfall traps indicated these snakes were active above ground during five months of the year, May to September (Nelson and Gibbons, 1972). It is possible that during mild years scarlet snakes are active in all months in Florida, but Nelson and Gibbons (1972) found no strong correlation between their activity and temperature, nor did rainfall seem to influence them. Hibernation is spent in underground burrows or in hollow logs or stumps.

Daytime is usually spent hiding, but as darkness approaches these snakes emerge and forage

CEMOPHORA COCCINEA

Scarlet Snake

Map

Fig. 27. *Cemophora coccinea copei*
(William A. Cox).

through the night, and even into the early morning hours (Neill, 1957; Palmer and Tregembo, 1970; Nelson and Gibbons, 1972).

Minimal distances moved between successive captures in South Carolina varied from 1 to 600 m with no apparent relationship to snake size or time of year (Nelson and Gibbons, 1972). Four individuals traveled a minimum of 15 meters per day.

Reproduction: Little is known of the reproductive habits of *Cemophora*. Eggs apparently are laid underground; the only natural nests that have been found were under humus in a pine woods (Woolcott, 1959) and beneath pine straw and humus covering the red clay of a south-facing embankment (Trauth, 1982a). Nesting dates range from 23 June (Ditmars, 1931a) to 24 August (Palmer and Tregembo, 1970). This long nesting season has prompted Fitch (1970) to suggest that *C. coccinea* may lay more than one clutch per season. Clutch size ranges from 2 (Martof et al., 1980) to 9 (Herman, 1983), and the average number of eggs in the 9 reported clutches was 5.8. The white eggs are very elongated (26.0–39.0 x 9.2–19.0 mm), weigh 2.9–6.0 g, and may adhere in clusters. The young apparently hatch in September after an incubation period of about 70–80 days, and are 130–185 mm in total length. In a clutch of 7 young sexed by Braswell and Palmer (1984), 5 males were 168–183 mm in total length, weighed 3.3–3.6 g and had tail lengths of 25.0–28.5 mm (14.9–16.2% of total body length), while 2 females were 174 and 179 mm, weighed 3.1 and 3.4 g and had 24.0 and 25.5 mm tails (14.0–14.7% of total body length). The yellow pigment between the dorsal saddles of adults usually is lacking in hatchlings as these areas are whitish; a general darkening of pigmentation occurs with age (Neill, 1950a).

Food And Feeding: There are several reports of egg-eating by this species; including eggs of turtles (Dickson, 1948; Neill, 1951), lizards (Brown, 1979a), and snakes (Ditmars, 1936; Minton and Bechtel, 1958; Palmer and Tregembo, 1970; Brown, 1979a). Dickson (1948) reported the snakes actually enter large eggs to drink the contents; however, Minton and Bechtel (1958) thought that the teeth were used to slit the egg shell, but that the snakes did not enter the egg. Palmer and Tregembo (1970) several times observed *C. coccinea* feed on large eggs and never saw them enter one. Instead the snake seized the egg at one end and began chewing. Its jaws extended forward until the enlarged posterior maxillary teeth apparently pierced the shell. The snake then looped part of its body over the egg and often wedged it against the cage wall; a combination of vigorous chewing and depressing the body then forced out the egg's contents. Small eggs are apparently swallowed whole (Brown, 1979a).

In addition to reptile eggs, other prey reported taken include insects (Hamilton and Pollack, 1956), small frogs (Brode and Allison, 1958), small lizards (Ditmars, 1936; Hamilton and Pollack, 1956), small snakes (Ditmars, 1936), and the young of wild mice (Ditmars, 1936). Several times sand or detritus has been found in the digestive tract of scarlet snakes suggesting earthworm predation, but no setae have been found (Hamilton and Pollack, 1956; Brown, 1979a).

Live prey is apparently constricted; Willard (1977) reported that constricting *Cemophora* makes irregular somewhat overlapping coils with no consistent lateral surface against the prey item.

Predators And Defense: Brown (1979a) found a *Cemophora* that was in the process of being swallowed by a southern toad, *Bufo terrestris*, and surely ophiophagous snakes and carnivorous mammals prey on this snake. Guthrie (1932) related a case of apparent predation by a loggerhead shrike. Interestingly, Ditmars (1936) reported that they eat their own eggs in captivity; perhaps this also occurs in nature.

When first discovered a scarlet snake may try to conceal its head by tucking it under one of its coils; it may also elevate its tail at the same time, presumably directing the predator away from its head. When handled these snakes seldom, if ever, bite.

Populations: The size structure of the 62 *Cemophora* collected by Nelson and Gibbons (1972) at the Savannah River Plant ranged from 11 to 51 cm snout–vent length, with most falling between 21 and 40 cm.

Remarks: *Cemophora* seems related to the colubrid genera *Lampropeltis*, *Rhinocheilus*, *Stilosoma*, *Arizona*, and *Pituophis* (Underwood, 1966; Williams and Wilson, 1967); of these, certain members of the *L. triangulum* group seem to be its closest relatives. Auffenberg's (1963) extinct Miocene genus *Pseudocemophora* has features in common with both *Cemophora and Lampropeltis*, and may be ancestral to both.

Fig. 28. Scarlet snakes are shove–nosed (Ted Borg, courtesy of J. Whitfield Gibbons).

ELAPHE GUTTATA

Corn Snake

ELAPHE GUTTATA (Linnaeus, 1766)
Corn Snake

Recognition: The corn snake is a gray snake (to 183 cm) with black–bordered orange or red dorsal blotches and spots, black spots on the lips, and large black squared–blotches on a white venter. A prominent black–bordered, spear–shaped blotch extends forward from the neck between the eyes, and another black–bordered stripe extends backward from the eye past the corner of the mouth and onto the neck. The underside of the tail is usually dark striped. The pitted body scales are keeled and usually occur in 25 (23–27) rows anteriorly, 27 (25–29) at mid–body, and 19 (19–23) at the anal vent (Thomas and Dixon, 1976, discuss scale row reductions). The anal plate is divided. Ventrals total 205–244, subcaudals 47–84; there is no sexual dimorphism. Diagnostic lateral head scalation includes a loreal, 1 preocular, 2 postoculars, 2 + 3 temporals, 8 (6–9) supralabials, and 11(12) infralabials. The fringed hemipenis has a single sulcus spermaticus and numerous calyces. About 9–12 smooth, equal–sized teeth occur on each maxilla.

Males have tails 13–20% as long as the total body length; the female tail is 12–20% as long.

Karyotype: There are 36 chromosomes; 16 macrochromosomes (12 submetacentric, 2 acrocentric, 2 subtelocentic) and 20 microchromosomes; sex determination is ZZ/ZW (Baker et al., 1971; 1972).

Fossil Record: Remains of *E. guttata* are known from the upper Pliocene of Texas (Holman, 1979), and Irvingtonian (Florida) and Rancholabrean (Arkansas, Florida, New Mexico, Texas, Virginia) of the Pleistocene (Holman, 1981; Meylan, 1982).

Distribution: *E. guttata* can be found from southern New Jersey, southwestern Illinois and southern Nebraska south to the Florida Keys and San Luis Potosi and northern Veracruz in Mexico. Isolated populations also occur in Kentucky, western Colorado and adjacent Utah.

Geographic Variation: Two subspecies are currently recognized. *Elaphe guttata guttata* (Linnaeus, 1766), the corn snake, has its 40 or fewer dorsal red or orange blotches boldly outlined in black. It occupies the eastern portion of the species range from southern New Jersey to the Florida Keys and Louisiana. Isolated colonies also occur in Kentucky. *E. g. emoryi* (Baird and Girard, 1853), the Great Plains rat snake, has 39 or more dark gray to reddish–brown blotches which are only narrowly bordered with black. It ranges from southwestern Illinois to southeastern Colorado and New Mexico, and south to San Luis Potosi and Veracruz in Mexico. There is also a disjunct population in western Colorado and eastern Utah.

Formerly the reddish–colored corn snakes of the Lower Florida Keys were designated by the name *rosacea* (Cope, 1888), but Duellman and Schwartz (1958), Mitchell (1977), and Christman (1980) have shown that this population represents the end of a clinal variation in the number of ventrals, subcaudals and body blotches. Accordingly, *rosacea* has been synonymized with *E. g. guttata*.

Confusing Species: Milk and kingsnakes (*Lampropeltis*) have smooth body scales and undivided anal plates. *Elaphe obsoleta* has no spear–shaped mark on its head. *Pituophis melanoleucus* has an undivided anal plate. *Agkistrodon contortrix* has no pattern on its head, a pit between the nostril and eye, and a vertical pupil.

Habitat: This terrestrial snake is most often found in brush fields, pine barrens, open deciduous woodlands, canyons, rocky ledges, caves, or around trash dumps and old buildings. It is a good climber and is often above ground in trees or bushes. Those on the Florida Keys sometimes climb about in the mangrove thickets. *E. guttata* is also a good swimmer, and can be occasionally seen swimming across small streams.

Behavior: In Kentucky it emerges from hibernation in late March or April and remains active to at least October. Hibernacula include rodent burrows, old stumps, hollow logs, caves, rock crevices, and old stone walls and building foundations. Farther south *E. guttata* probably has a longer annual activity period, and in southern Florida it may remain active all year.

It is usually considered to be a nocturnal snake, but most we have caught were found in the morning or late afternoon. Ernst once caught one in Florida in the early afternoon of a very hot day in August. Unfortunately, nothing has been reported on the thermal ecology of this species.

Male *E. guttata* often perform dominance combat dances (especially when a new male is introduced into their cage). This usually first involves a series of short, jerky, spasmotic, forward movements and can end with the dominant, usually larger, male pinning the body of the other male to the ground. Shaw (1951) has also observed this behavior in relation to both sexual and feeding activity.

Reproduction: Golder (1981) and Bechtel and Bechtel (1958) have reported that captive female *E. guttata* attained sexual maturity at 16 and 18 months of age, respectively. The Bechtels' females were 53–74 cm (x = 63.5) when first observed copulating; all laid fertile eggs. Bechtel and Bechtel (1958) also reported that males were sexually mature when about 18 months old.

Little is known of the sexual cycles of this snake. Iverson (1975) collected three females on 13 May in Nebraska. Two had enlarged follicles, while the third had 6 large follicles in her right ovary and 4 in the left. Presumably, ovulation would have occurred in late May.

Mating usually takes place in the spring from March to May (MacMahon, 1957; Bechtel and Bechtel, 1958), but in Florida winter copulation may occur (Ashton and Ashton, 1981). The following description is from MacMahon (1957).

Map

> The male placed his ventral surface along the dorsal surface of the female with his head near hers. As she moved about the cage, her forward movement seemed to excite him. Although her movements were quick and deliberate, he maintained his position. He moved his body into numerous undulating curves that followed the contour of her body. At the same time, his lower sides twitched along their full length. Ripples in this region were numerous and fast and, along with a jerky movement of the entire body, seemed to form the preliminary courtship.

> The male moved his body forward along the back of the female, and as he did so she became more active. He moved his tail posteriorly along the lower one–fourth of her body. With a sudden jerk, his tail entwined hers and the hemipenis was inserted. After union was effected, the male again aligned his body with that of the female. The hindquarters of both snakes, from slightly anterior to the anus to the tip of the tail, were occasionally elevated and then slowly lowered ... Copulation occurred again in the morning and afternoon of the second day, lasting fourteen and nine minutes, respectively. Each of the three observed meetings was less vigorous than the preceding one.

Gillingham (1979) has presented a detailed analysis of the courtship and mating behavior of the eastern North American species of *Elaphe*, and we refer the reader to this paper for additional information.

Fig. 29. A juvenile *Elaphe guttata guttata*.

Corn Snake

The gestation period between copulation and oviposition has been reported as 35–68 days (Bechtel and Bechtel, 1958; Holman, 1960). The eggs are normally laid in late May or June, but some females may nest in early May or early July. Favorite nest sites are mammal burrows, sawdust piles, and rotting stumps and logs. The white, elongated eggs (35–61 x 15–26 mm) have very tough leathery shells. This toughness prevents some hatchlings from emerging, and, at least in captivity, an alarming number of eggs do not hatch, even though they contain fully formed young. The eggs are somewhat adherent, and reported clutch sizes range from 3 eggs (Bechtel and Bechtel, 1958) to 30 eggs (Muir, 1981). Probably 10–15 eggs are more common.

Incubation may take from 51–83 days, and hatching occurs from late July into early September, with most young emerging in August. Hatchlings are more red than the adults, and 290–370 mm in total length.

Female *E. guttata* have the potential for laying more than one clutch of eggs each year. This has occurred several times in captivity; Golder (1981) reported a female laid two clutches 99 days apart, and Tryon (1984) reported another female laid a second clutch 43 days after she had first oviposited.

E. guttata is known to have hybridized with *E. obsoleta* in captivity (Bechtel and Mountain, 1960).

Longevity: An *E. guttata* survived 21 years and 9 months at the Philadelphia Zoo (Bowler, 1977).

Food And Feeding: *E. guttata* seems to prefer warm–blooded prey, such as mammals and birds and their eggs, but will also eat lizards, snakes, small frogs and some insects. Mammal prey eaten includes mice (*Microtus, Peromyscus, Mus*), rats (*Oryzomys, Sigmodon*), shrews (*Cryptotis*), moles (*Scalopus*), and bats (*Tadarida*). Birds as large as juvenile quail may be consumed (Ditmars, 1936). In captivity they may be cannibalistic, eating smaller individuals of their own species (Ippoliti, 1980; Polis and Myers, 1985).

In a study of the foods eaten by 36 Georgia corn snakes, Hamilton and Pollack (1956) found that mammals made up 59% by occurrence and 45% by volume.

E. guttata is a voracious feeder, and Smith (1976) found it had an assimilation efficiency (ingestion–egestion/ingestion x 100) of 88.9% when fed on laboratory mice. Small animals may be swallowed alive, but most prey are constricted. In captivity, constriction is not always entirely within the coils, as corn snakes may pin prey against the floor or walls of the cage with their bodies. Perhaps they also do this in rodent burrows. Smith and Watson (1972) have shown that movement and proximity of mice appeared to be more important than color conspicuousness in selection of prey.

Predators And Defense: Natural predators include many mammals (coyotes, foxes, bobcats, skunks, weasels, raccoons, oppossums), hawks, owls and other snakes (coral snakes, kingsnakes, and, at least in captivity, their own species). We once had a corn snake that "turned the tables" and ate a similar–sized kingsnake housed in the same cage.

Humans kill some corn snakes when they mistake them for copperheads, and automobiles and habitat destruction have thinned some populations. Another problem, since the snake makes a pretty and hardy captive, is overcollection for the pet trade. Fortunately, corn snakes readily breed in captivity, and now many of those offered for sale are from captive parents.

Wild corn snakes can be worthy opponents. They vibrate their tails and strike with amazing speed. Ernst once had the embarrassing problem of trying to board an AMTRAK train in Florida with a corn snake he had just caught in the parking lot firmly biting his pantleg!

Populations: Fitch (1977) estimated that *E. guttata* occurred at a density of less than one per 100 hectares on the University of Kansas Natural History Reservation.

Remarks: *E. guttata* frequently occurs in various albinistic stages. The genetics and distribution of these color phases and other mutant patterns have been the subject of several studies (Groves, 1967; Bechtel and Bechtel, 1978; Bechtel, 1980; Wagner, 1982).

Although *E. guttata* may be common in some areas, there is very little known of its behavior and ecology. Most data published have been from casual observations or laboratory studies. A thorough field study would be very helpful.

ELAPHE OBSOLETA

Rat Snake

ELAPHE OBSOLETA (Say, 1823)
Rat Snake

Recognition: This common species is one of the largest snakes in North America, having a record total body length of 256.5 cm. It is also quite variable in color and pattern (see **Geographic Variation**), making a composite description difficult. Ground color varies from gray to olive–gray, black, yellow or orange, and the dorsum may have a pattern of dark blotches or two dark longitudinal stripes. Some races become more melanistic with age, but still retain some light pigment between the body scales. There is always a dark stripe extending from the eye to the corner of the mouth, and a transverse dark bar may occur between the eyes. The lip scales may contain dark bars. The underside of the tail is not striped and the dark markings on the ventral scales are small and often indistinct. The chin and throat are unpatterned. The body scales are pitted, weakly keeled, and occur in 25(23–27) rows anteriorly, 23–27(23–29) medially, and 19(17–21) rows near the vent. The anal plate is usually divided or semi-divided. Pertinent lateral head scalation includes a divided nasal, a loreal, 1 preocular, 2–3 postoculars, 2 + 3–4 temporals, 8(7–9) supralabials, and 11–12(13–14) infralabials. Males have 221–243 ventrals and 70–101 subcaudals; females have 226–252 ventrals and 63–92 subcaudals. Sides of body are straight, not rounded as in some other black snakes, giving a cross–sectional profile like that of a loaf of bread. The head is anteriorly truncated (squared off) not rounded, and is widest behind the eyes near the corner of the mouth, giving it a distinct oblong appearance. The hemipenis has a single sulcus spermaticus, and numerous fringes and calyces. The 12–14 maxillary teeth are ungrooved and of equal length.

Males have tails 16–19% as long as the total body length, while the female tail is 14–18%.

Karyotype: Becak and Becak (1969) and Trinco and Smith (1971) reported a male *E. o. obsoleta* had only 35 chromosomes, but the normal diploid chromosome complement is 36 (8 pairs of macrochromosomes, 10 pairs of microchromosomes; Baker et al, 1972). The 5 largest pairs are submetacentric; the 6th largest pair acrocentric, and the remaining 2 pairs are submetacentric and subtelocentric, respectively (Chang et al., 1971; Baker et al., 1971). Sex determination is ZZ/ZW; the submetacentric Z is smaller than the 3 largest pairs of autosomes, and the W is smaller than the Z and nearly metacentric. This same pattern occurs in *E. guttata* (Baker et al., 1971).

Fossil Record: Fossils of *E. obsoleta* are known from the upper Pliocene of Kansas and Texas (Holman, 1979), and Pleistocene of Florida (Irvingtonian, Rancholabrean) and Kansas (Blancan, Irvingtonian, Rancholabrean) (Holman, 1981; Meylan, 1982).

Distribution: *E. obsoleta* ranges from southwestern New England and southeastern Ontario west to southwestern Wisconsin and south to the Florida Keys, the Gulf Coast and Coahuila, Nuevo Leon, and Tamaulipas in Mexico.

Geographic Variation: Five subspecies are recognized and all occur east of the Mississippi River. *Elaphe obsoleta obsoleta* (Say, 1823), the black rat snake, is found from Connecticut, western Massachusetts, southern Vermont and eastern Ontario west to southwestern Wisconsin, central Iowa, and southeastern Nebraska and south to Georgia, eastern Alabama, Arkansas and northeastern Texas. Adults are black, but with some indications of blotches and light pigment (white, yellow, orange or red) on the skin between the scales, and a white to yellow venter bearing a faded gray or brown pattern of blotches or a black checkerboard pattern. *E. o. quadrivittata* (Holbrook, 1836), the yellow rat snake, occurs along the Atlantic Coastal Plain from southeastern North Carolina south to Lee, Charlotte, Glades, Okeechobee and St. Lucie counties, Florida. It is yellow to grayish or greenish–yellow with 4 dark longitudinal stripes, and a black tongue. *E. o. lindheimeri* (Baird and Girard, 1853), the Texas rat snake, ranges from the Pearl River in southern Mississippi and Louisiana west to central Texas. It is gray or yellow with a dorsal pattern of auburn, brown, or bluish–black blotches, and often a black head. *E. o. spiloides* (Dumeril, Bibron, and Dumeril, 1854), the gray rat snake, ranges southward in the Mississippi Valley from extreme southwestern Indiana and southern Illinois to southern Georgia and the Gulf Coast of the Florida panhandle, Alabama, and Mississippi. It is gray or light brown with a pattern of brown or dark gray blotches. *E. o. rossalleni* Neill, 1949b, the Everglades rat snake, is restricted to southern

ELAPHE OBSOLETA

Rat Snake

Map

Florida from Levy to Martin counties southward to the Keys. It is bright orange, orangish–yellow, or orangish–brown with 4 faint gray longitudinal stripes and a red tongue.

Several other color or pattern phases are known, but are not currently recognized as subspecies. In southern North Carolina where the subspecies *obsoleta* and *quadrivittata* intergrade they produce the "greenish rat snake" which is olive to greenish–yellow with 4 dark stripes. In northwestern peninsular Florida where the ranges of *E. o. quadrivittata* and *E. o. spiloides* meet, intergradation produces the "Gulf hammock rat snake" (formerly recognized as the subspecies *E. o. williamsi*, Barbour and Carr, 1940) which is whitish or gray with both dark blotches and 4 dark longitudinal stripes. The rat snake population of extreme southern peninsular Florida and the Keys has been recognized in the past as *E. o. deckerti* Brady, 1932, the Key rat snake, but is not now considered valid. It is light brown or orange with both 4 dark stripes and dark spots, and a black tongue. For discussions on these variations, see Dowling, 1952; Neill, 1954; Duellman and Schwartz, 1958; and Christman, 1980.

Since the juveniles of all subspecies and the adults of the western races are blotched, Christman (1980) theorized the blotched pattern to be the ancestral condition, and that *E. o. lindheimeri* most clearly matched it. He also thought that geographic variation in most of Florida has led to the development of the striped pattern seen in *quadrivittata* and *rossalleni* and in the eastern parts of the United States to the solid-colored snake known as *E. o. obsoleta*. Populations from extreme southern Florida have probably diverged less from the ancestral condition, and still retain the darker pigmentation and blotched phenotype. More recent geographic variation on the Florida peninsula has led to the reduction in ground color dark pigment along the coasts and in the Everglades region. The development of the striped phenotype in peninsular Florida was probably expedited by a reduction in gene flow brought about by the isolation of parts of Florida during periods of higher sea level. Populations in the Gulf Hammock region (*E. o. williamsi*) probably represent hybrids from a subsequent contact between mainland blotched and peninsular striped forms. The fact that all combinations of striped and blotched phenotypes can be found in the Gulf Hammock region today suggests a pattern of recombinants such as would be observed when isolated populations come secondarily into contact.

Fig. 30. A juvenile *Elaphe obsoleta obsoleta*.

Confusing Species: Adult racers (*Coluber*), coachwhips (*Masticophis*), indigo snakes (*Drymarchon*), milk and kingsnakes (*Lampropel-*

tis) have either smooth body scales or single anal plates, or both. Garter snakes (*Thamnophis*) have undivided anal plates. Fox snakes (*Elaphe vulpina*) have 216 or less ventral scutes; this is especially important to remember when comparing juveniles. Juvenile racers (*Coluber*) and coachwhips (*Masticophis*) are also very similarly patterned to those of *E. obsoleta*, but the former two species always have a small preocular scale wedged between the supralabials.

Habitat: *E. obsoleta* lives in a variety of woodland or shrub habitats; including deciduous forests, scrub pine woods, mixed palmetto–pine woods, swamp and marsh borders, bayous, and mangrove thickets. It often is common about abandoned or partially demolished buildings where rodents are abundant. Weatherhead and Charland (1985) found that Ontario rat snakes showed a preference for fields or the ecotone between fields and deciduous forests during the bird breeding season.

Behavior: In the northern part of its range, *E. obsoleta* emerges from hibernation in late March or April and remains active until late October or early November. Most activity occurs from late April through June. Farther south it may become active in late February or March, and Clarke (1949) collected at least one in each week of the year in Louisiana. He reported that on warm days throughout the entire winter rat snakes could be found on sunny wooded hillsides. They may also be active all year in southern Florida.

Where the winters are cold, rat snakes hibernate in rock crevices, caves, hollow logs, stumps, mammal burrows, old buildings, stone walls, old cisterns or wells, or under large rocks. They may actually hibernate under water when in the cisterns or wells (Owens, 1949a). Those overwintering in caves are quite active and may change position several times during the winter, apparently while seeking more favorable temperatures (Sexton and Hunt, 1980). Often they share their hibernaculum with other species, such as *Coluber constrictor*, *Agkistrodon contortrix* or *Crotalus horridus*. During extremely hot summer weather in Florida, rat snakes may be forced to estivate.

E. obsoleta is chiefly diurnal, but may become crepuscular during the summer. Air temperatures of 15–30 C seem to be preferred by active rat snakes. Fitch (1956) recorded 53 body temperatures from Kansas rat snakes found in the open; these ranged from 18.2–38.0 C, but 73% were in the range of 24–31 C. Landreth (1972) found rat snakes become very active at 10 C, and could survive temperatures near 0 C for 2 hours. Kroll et al. (1973) studied the thermogenic cycle of *E. obsoleta* in the laboratory and found its heat production was associated with light–dark cycles;

Fig. 31. *Elaphe obsoleta quadrivittata* (Christopher W. Brown).

Fig. 32. Intergrade *Elaphe o. obsoleta x E. o. quadrivittata* are greenish in color (Carl H. Ernst).

ELAPHE OBSOLETA

Rat Snake

Fig. 33. Hatching *Elaphe obsoleta obsoleta* (Steve W. Gotte).

minimum heat was produced during the mid–day, and also during the night. They thought the latter heat production associated with crepuscular feeding.

Jacob and McDonald (1975) studied the relationship between heartbeat and body temperatures in unrestrained *E. obsoleta*. At 18 C the heart beat per minute was 11, while at 30 C the heartbeat was 83.3 beats per minute. The rate of heartbeat generally increased with increased body temperature, but several snakes experienced arythmic periods of varying lengths.

The extent of the home range of *E. obsoleta* has been studied in Kansas and Maryland populations. Fitch (1963b) reported that in Kansas the average distance moved from a hibernaculum was 384–403 m for 8 males and 362 m for 7 females. For 6 males the average distance between successive rock ledge locations for the same snake was 532 m, but for 6 females was only 217 m. In 81 instances, recaptured rat snakes were recorded at successive capture points away from hibernacula. The average distance was 202 m; and most were in the range 0–421 m, but there were three long movements–683, 683, 975 m. Fitch thought these longer movements represented shifts in the home range or occasional wanderings. The average distance moved per day by snakes equipped with radio transmitters was 44.7 m (0–260) (Fitch and Shirer, 1971). The home ranges in Kansas were

approximately 10–12 hectares. In Maryland, Stickel and Cope (1947), recorded movements of 40–536 m between captures 3 days to 2 years apart. Stickel et al. (1980) found that established home ranges were kept for many years, perhaps for life, and found no evidence of shifts or changes in range of any major extent among 38 males and 28 females. Travels recorded for individual snakes were 0–1333 m. The diameter of the home ranges in males averaged at least 600 m and in females at least 500 m.

Movement in *E. obsoleta* is not restricted to the "terra firma." Rat snakes are accomplished climbers (Jackson, 1976), and are often seen stretched out on the limbs of trees or hanging partially out of tree holes 10–15 m above the ground as they hunt for birds' nests or squirrels. They frequently return to the same tree (Stickel et al., 1980). This may pose a problem at sites where nest boxes are used for bird or squirrel propagation (McComb and Noble, 1981).

E. obsoleta is also a good swimmer, and dives into water when disturbed, or purposely swims across small water bodies when prowling. Baeyens et al. (1978, 1980) found they can survive submerged for over an hour. In fact, rat snakes had the same survival rate in these tests as the aquatic snake *Nerodia rhombifera*. *E. obsoleta* had a greater lung volume and larger and more numerous alveoli than *N. rhombifera*.

Male *E. obsoleta* have on several occasions been observed to participate in dominance combat dances (Rigley, 1971; Stickel et al., 1980; Gillingham, 1980; Mitchell, 1981). Two such episodes have been described by Stickel et al. (1980):

> Male *Elaphe* were observed in combat under a large willow oak on the headquarters lawn on 22 May 1951 and again on 12 June 1952. One of the same snakes was involved in both years.
>
> The 1951 episode occurred at 1315 on a warm sultry day after a warm night. One snake had about 40% of its length spirally twisted about the posterior body and tail of the other, and anteriorly tried to keep its head in a superior position and force the other to the ground. The second jerked the front of its body as if to throw off the first, and tried to get its head and neck on top. This sequence was repeated several times. Once the aggressor deliberately bit the other across the back. This had no apparent effect and the interactions continued. The aggressor loosened his coils and left after the pair had been observed for about 3 minutes. One snake was 1475 mm long and the other was 1555 mm. It was not possible to determine which of the two was the aggressor.
>
> The 1952 episode was observed for 45 minutes at 1255–1340 on a bright dry relatively cool day 23 C, after an unusually cool night 10 C. The two snakes behaved very similarly to those observed in 1951, although there was

no biting. The head and neck contest, posterior parts intertwined went on repetitiously. All the while, the more passive snake kept moving forward intermittently, so that the two progressed at perhaps 30 cm per min. Occasionally it straightened abruptly or jerked its body sideward, thereby usually loosening the restraining coils of the other.

Then the aggressor regained his position anteriorly and coiled his whole body spirally around the other, and both writhed slowly, their whole lengths intertwined. Soon the twining loosened anteriorly and became tighter posteriorly, and the snakes resumed their head and neck contest. Two or three times, they drew their foreparts away from one another and turned their heads inward, facing one another and thus forming something of a lyre pattern anteriorly. Most of the time, however, the one continued his efforts to force the other's head to the ground, and the other in turn, attempted to throw off the coils. The snakes paid no attention to the observer who was 4.5 m away. They finally broke and moved into the hollow base of the tree where they were captured.

Gillingham (1980) has analyzed combat behavior in rat snakes and described seven motor patterns involved: touch mount, dorsal pin, hover, push-bridge, avoid, head raise, and no response, and we refer the reader to his paper.

Reproduction: Females in Kansas generally first reproduce late in their fourth year when at least 87 cm in snout-vent length (Fitch, 1963b; 1981). In Maryland females reach maturity at a total length of 110 cm during their fourth year (Stickel et al., 1980). Males are also probably mature in their fourth year at a snout-vent length greater than 80 cm (Fitch, 1981).

Details of the sexual cycles of *E. obsoleta* have not been reported; however, Callard and Leathem (1967) found that ovarian weights were comparable in May and July, but that oviductal weight was significantly greater in July. Mating usually occurs in the period between mid-April and mid-June, but Fitch (1965b) found abundant active sperm in a female's cloaca on 14 October. Courtship and mating may be more successful in rat snakes that have first hibernated (Gillingham and Carpenter, 1978). Kennedy (1978) has described a typical mating:

> At 1500 on 7 May 1970, *E. o. quadrivittata* was observed during courtship and copulation ...

> The snakes were observed mating in sandy soil beneath scrub oak on Blackbeard Island, Georgia. The ambient temperature was 26° C. The male approached from the rear, crawled along the dorsal surface of the female, and grasped her 10 cm from the head. The male then positioned himself along the side of the female and slowly began to contract and undulate his entire body and vibrate his tail. During this activity, the male and female were in constant contact. After 5 minutes of this activity, the male forced his tail

> under that of the female and brought their vents in direct contact. At this time, the hemipenis was inserted. As the snakes lay side by side with their vents facing, the male continued to contract slowly and to vibrate his tail. After 3 minutes, the hemipenis was withdrawn and the female released. Although both pairs of snakes were observed from within 1-2 meters, neither seemed aware of my presence during or immediately after courtship and copulation. From the time when the male grasped the female until release, the female remained motionless. After release, bloody marks were visible where the male had grasped the female ...

After a gestation period of 37-51 days the female lays her eggs in such places as hollow logs or stumps, manure piles, piles of rotting vegetation, sawdust piles, or beneath rocks. Several females may oviposite at the same site (Lynch, 1966). Nesting may occur from mid-May through July with females from more southern populations laying earliest. Usually only one clutch of eggs is laid each year, but Cohen (1978) has reported that a female *E. o. quadrivittata* laid two clutches of 13 and 10 eggs, respectivly, 59 days apart. Occasionally twins may be produced in one egg (Shuette, 1978).

Clutches may contain 5-44 eggs (Fitch, 1970), but 10-14 are most common. The elongated, white eggs have leathery shells with granulated surfaces, are 35-55 mm in length, 16-30 mm in width, and weigh 9-15 g.

Hatching usually takes place in late July to mid-September, after an incubation period of 60-75 days, but has been observed in the wild as late as 20 October (Sexton et al., 1976). Hatching success in Ernst's laboratory has ranged from 50-100%. The hatchlings are blotched and resemble the adults in coloration, except for those of *E. o. obsoleta* which are gray in contrast to the black adults. Hatchlings are 290-368 mm in total length (Fitch, 1965b).

Growth And Longevity: Growth is rapid at first, but declines once maturity is reached. Ford (1974) showed that there is a decrease in the rate of length increase but no corresponding change in the rate of increase in weight with accumulated food consumption. Stickel et al. (1980) reported that in Maryland growth in males slowed conspicuously near 134 cm at about 6-8 years; growth of females slowed near 125 cm at an estimated mean age of 6.6 years. Rat snakes in Kansas, although shorter, followed the same general growth pattern (Fitch, 1963b). In Kansas, yearling rat snakes were 50-65 cm in snout-vent length. Snakes to 90 cm had an average gain in mm/month/snake of 35.8; those to 110 cm, 31.8; those 114-135 cm, 5.7 mm; and those 137-145 cm, 3.2 (Fitch, 1963b).

The maximum in longevity for wild rat snakes recorded by Stickel et al. (1980) during their

Maryland long–term study was 20.6 years for a male and 15.1 years for a female. In Kansas, Fitch (1963b) thought the largest rat snakes captured were near or more than 20 years old. The longevity record for a captive is 20 years, 1 month, 23 days (Bowler, 1972).

Food And Feeding: *E. obsoleta* prefers to eat mammals and birds. Surface (1906) found that mammals comprised 47% and birds and their eggs 32% of food items in Pennsylvania. In 100 rat snakes from Louisiana, Clark (1949) found 78 mammals and 17 birds. Barbour (1950a) found that 47% of prey in Kentucky was mammalian and 53% birds. In Kansas, Fitch (1963b) recorded 66% mammals and 23% birds (most in June) as prey, and in North Carolina Brown (1979a) recorded 59% mammalian and 37% bird foods. Uhler et al. (1939) examined the stomach contents of 85 rat snakes from Virginia, and found the major food items by volume were mice 32%, birds 31%, chipmunks and squirrels 15%, rabbits 9%, and shrews 4%.

A list of all the prey species taken by *E. obsoleta* is beyond the scope of this book; however, the following summary should suffice: mammals—shrews (*Cryptotis, Blarina*), moles (*Condylura*), bats (*Eptesicus, Myotis, Tadarida*), weasels (*Mustela*), rabbits (*Sylvilagus*), squirrels (*Glaucomys, Sciurus, Tamias, Tamiasciurus*), mice (*Microtus, Mus, Peromyscus, Reithrodontomys, Zapus*), rats (*Neotoma, Oryzomys, Rattus, Sigmodon*); birds—nestlings, fleglings and adults of over 25 species (taken both on the ground and in trees), and the eggs of several wild and domestic species; reptiles—lizards (*Anolis, Cnemidophorus, Eumeces, Sceloporus, Scincella*), lizard eggs (Kennedy, 1964), snakes (*Elaphe, Storeria, Thammophis*), snake eggs (Brown, 1979a); amphibians—frogs (*Acris, Hyla, Rana*); invertebrates—snails, beetles, caterpillars.

There are several records of unique feeding episodes. Holt (1919) reported that an *E. obsoleta* had swallowed a smooth, oval stone that had served as a nest egg in a poultry house, and that another rat snake had swallowed a china nest egg. Two accounts of autophagy (trying to swallow oneself) are also in the literature (Mitchell et al., 1982; Morris, 1984). In both cases the juvenile snake had seized and attempted to swallow its own tail.

Large prey is seized in the mouth and quickly constricted in the snake's coils. Several animals may be constricted simultaneously; Ernst had a 213 cm *E. o. obsoleta* that regularly constricted three large laboratory rats at one time. Small and helpless animals are swallowed alive. Eggs are swallowed whole and then broken in the esophagus, the shells may be either disgorged or, more often, swallowed. From our experience, most food is found either by sight or smell. Campbell (1970) reported that naive hatchlings will respond to prey extracts, particularly those of frogs (*Hyla*), a favorite food of juveniles.

Although they may occasionally enter poultry houses and eat the eggs and fledglings, rat snakes are of positive economic importance. They are highly efficient rodent–catchers, and consume many destructive mice and rats about farms each year. Some farmers recognize their value, and when we both taught at the University of Kentucky several local farmers would come to us each year for excess rat snakes which they then placed in their barns and corn cribs.

Predators And Defense: Adult rat snakes have few enemies other than humans with their automobiles and habitat destruction. However, the juveniles may be preyed upon by other snakes (coachwhips, indigo, milk, king, coral, and copperheads), alligators, various large hawks and owls, wood ibis, egrets, herons, roadrunners, bobcats, domestic cats and dogs, foxes, otters, opposums, raccoons, skunks and weasels.

When prevented from fleeing, *E. obsoleta* will coil and strike, and large individuals can deliver severe bites. If handled, they spray a strong musk.

Populations: Rat snakes may be locally common in the right habitat if rodents are abundant. Fitch (1963b) reported an average density of about one *E. obsoleta* per hectare at his Kansas study site, or 166 individuals in 182 hectares. In a smaller population in Maryland, Stickel et al. (1980) reported that 24 snakes occupied an area equivalent to 103 hectares, a density of 0.23 per hectare.

In Maryland, the sex ratio at hatching was 1:1, but at lengths of 90–130 cm more females were captured, suggesting a higher mortality rate in males (Stickel et al., 1980).

Remarks: There are several reports of hybridization between *E. obsoleta* and *E. guttata* in captivity (Lederer, 1950; Mertens, 1950; Bechtel and Mountain, 1960; Broer, 1978), and Bechtel and Bechtel (1985) have studied the genetics of color mutations in *E. obsoleta*.

In the Appalachian Mountains the common name of "pilot black snake" is often applied to *E. obsoleta*. According to many residents, the snake is supposed to lead copperheads and rattlesnakes away from danger, thus acting as their "pilot." The belief has no basis in fact. In central Kentucky and adjacent Indiana, this species is thought to milk cows, hence the common name of "cowsucker." Again, there is no truth in this belief.

ELAPHE VULPINA

Fox Snake

ELAPHE VULPINA (Baird and Girard, 1853)
Fox Snake

Recognition: This is the least known of North American *Elaphe*. It is a yellowish brown snake (to 179.1 cm) with a dorsal series of large dark brown to black rectangular–shaped blotches and a yellow, heavily black spotted venter. There are also a series of smaller dark blotches along the sides of the body, and a dark stripe extending diagonally backward from the orbit past the corner of the mouth. Dorsally, the head of adults is usually plain yellow to reddish–brown. The keeled body scales occur in 23–27 rows anteriorly, 23 rows at mid-body, and 21 rows near the tail. The anal plate is divided. Laterally on the head are a preocular (rarely 2), 2 postoculars, 2–3 + 3–4 temporals, 8(7–9) supralabials and 11(9–12) infralabials. The fringed hemipenis has numerous calyces and an undivided sulcus spermaticus. Sixteen to 17 teeth occur on each maxilla.

Males have 190–212 ventrals, 52–71 subcaudals, and tails 13–19% of their total body length; females have 198–216 ventrals, 45–60 subcaudals, and tails 12–17% of their total body length.

Karyotype: Unknown.

Fossil Record: Remains of *E. vulpina* have been found in upper Pliocene deposits in Idaho, Texas, and Nebraska (Holman, 1979, 1982), and at numerous Pleistocene sites (Blancan: Kansas, Nebraska; Irvingtonian: Maryland, South Dakota; Rancholabrean: Arkansas, Missouri; Holman, 1981).

Distribution: As below under **Geographic Variation**.

Geographic Variation: Two subspecies have been described. *Elaphe vulpina vulpina* (Baird and Girard, 1853), the western fox snake, has 32–52 (x = 41) dorsal body blotches. It occurs from the northern peninsula of Michigan and northwestern Indiana westward through southern South Dakota and eastern Nebraska. *E. v. gloydi* Conant, 1940, the eastern fox snake, has fewer, larger dorsal body blotches, 28–43 (x = 35). This subspecies is found in southern Ontario, eastern Michigan, and northcentral Ohio around lakes Huron and Erie.

Confusing Species: Milk and kingsnakes (*Lampropeltis*) have smooth body scales and undivided anal plates. *Pituophis melanoleucus* has an undivided anal plate, a pointed snout, and strongly keeled body scales. *Elaphe obsoleta* has 219 or more ventrals, and *Elaphe guttata* has a spear–shaped mid–dorsal head mark.

Habitat: In contrast to its frequent climbing, woodland dwelling relative, *E. obsoleta*, this species seldom climbs and seems to be the least arboreal of the North American species of *Elaphe*. It is an inhabitant of open grasslands, scrub areas, hedge rows, and marsh borders.

Behavior: *E. vulpina* is diurnally active from mid– or late April to October (Conant, 1951), with the peak of activity occurring in May and early June (Conant, 1951; Minton, 1972; Smith, 1961). Smith (1961) collected an active *E. vulpina* on 4 December. They are most often found prowling along rodent runways or marsh borders especially during the morning (0600–1100 hr) and evening (1600–2000 hr), or basking at the base of shrubs. While most activity is at ground level, Smith (1961) and Brown and Brown (1975) cited examples of occasional climbing in this snake. Smith reported that they are sometimes found nearly 2 m above ground under the bark of dead trees or stumps, and Brown and Brown observed one exploring a bird nest on a barn rafter about 10 m above ground.

Little is known of the thermal ecology of this snake. Dill (1972) implanted thermal transmitters in an *E. vulpina* and found no statistical difference between overall anterior and posterior body temperatures, but during the diurnal warming period the anterior temperature was significantly less (p < 0.05) than the posterior temperature.

The winter is spent underground in some crevice or animal burrow. It is possible that those living about marshes may use muskrat lodges or burrows as hibernacula. Several fox snakes may aggregate at suitable overwintering sites. Smith (1961) found 16 in March in an old well, and Zaremba (1978) found a colony of hibernating *E. vulpina* in late April in a concrete cistern where six of the snakes were submerged in approximately 0.9 m of water.

ELAPHE VULPINA

Fox Snake

Map

Reproduction: Mating occurs in June and early July. Gillingham (1974) published the most detailed description of courtship in *E. vulpina*:

> The courtship and mating behavior can be divided into three phases: chasing, tactile and mounting, and biting and intromission.
>
> The chasing phase always seemed to be initiated by the male. Prior to chasing, the male usually appeared restless and moved randomly while the female remained in a resting position. Occasionally the male, while moving would make contact with the female. Such contact consisted of tongue-flicking starting from any section of her body and gradually reaching her head. The female responded by rapidly moving away, which stimulated the male to chase her. During the chasing phase the male followed the female at a distance of 15–20 cm. The period of chasing ranged from 6–40 min...
>
> The chasing phase ended when the female appeared receptive, allowing the male to approach and contact the middle of her body. This initiated the tactile and mounting phase. When the female stopped moving the male invariably moved forward along her side rapidly flicking his tongue and then gently nudged her at midbody...
>
> At this point the male began forward jerking motions with the whole or part of his body. Each jerk consisted of two opposite motions: first, the dorsal part of his body was thrown forward 1–2 cm; and second, the ventral part was thrown backward the same distance repeatedly. The frequency of these motions varied from 80–100/min.
>
> Immediately after the male began jerking movements, the female responded with the same jerking movements. When both the male and the female started the jerking movements, the male slowly lifted his head from the lateral midpoint position to the female's dorsum.
>
> While both were still exhibiting jerking movements the male began moving anteriorly with his head closely adpressed to the dorsum of the female.
>
> When the male reached a point halfway between the female's midbody and head, he began to twitch his tail from side to side, slowly at first but becoming very rapid within 5–10 seconds. With the onset of this lateral tail-twitching he began to pull the posterior portion of his body forward into several S-shaped curves, while moving laterally progressively closer to the female. When any of these S-shaped curves made contact with the female, such curves were lifted 5–8 cm off the ground and placed on top of her... This continued until the male had completely mounted her. Mounting was completed when the male lifted the posterior third of his body and placed it on top of the identical portion of the female's body. When this occurred, both snakes began to twist their tails around each other rapidly until they were intertwined tightly. The intertwining marked the end of the male's tail twitching and initiated a back and forth rubbing movement of the posterior third of his body against that of the female until the ventral surface of both snakes became juxtaposed.
>
> The rubbing of the male's body against the female's continued until intromission took place. While the male was assuming the mounting position, the female maintained her previous jerking motions and, in some instances, began to shorten the posterior portion of her body and from S-shaped curves corresponding to those of the male. The period of mounting varied from 4–12 min...
>
> While the pair was juxtaposed, rubbing of the male against the female continued and finally his head reached a position just behind hers. During this time intromission took place and rubbing movements ceased. This was confirmed in several instances when the pair was separated and the hemipenis found to be fully inserted into the cloaca. Actual hemipenis eversion was never observed due to the closeness of their bodies.
>
> After intromission had taken place, the male grasped the female behind the head with his mouth and held her for the remainder of coitus... This was observed on 11 different occasions. However, on three other occasions the biting took place before intromission occurred.
>
> Coitus periods ranged from 10–40 min... During mating the jerking motions of the pair either continued or were confined to a slight twiching of the tails.
>
> Copulation was terminated when either the male or the female tried to separate from the

other; however, they remained connected by the hemipenis for 3–15 min... Following coital separation the females would immediately move into a resting position similar to that which was assumed before copulation had taken place. The male, on the other hand, would move about for approximately a minute before assuming a resting position.

The eggs are laid about 30 days after copulation (Zehr, 1969), usually in late June or July, in the soil, hollow logs, rotting stumps, sawdust piles, under logs, and possibly mammal burrows. Several females may lay at the same site. Clutches contain 7–29 eggs (Wright and Wright, 1957), but 15–20 eggs are most common. The elongated, leathery shelled eggs are 29–58.5 x 14.5–30 mm and several may adhere together. Incubation periods in the literature range from 35 (Minton, 1972) to 78 days (Wright and Wright, 1957), but average about 50 days. Hatching occurs from mid–August to early October (Wright and Wright, 1957); the young are 230–310 mm in total length, weigh 8–13 g, and have dark markings on the dorsal surface of their heads.

Food And Feeding: Most prey is detected by actively searching, but some fox snakes may lie beside rodent runways and ambush their prey, grabbing them in their mouths and quickly constricting them. Mammal prey includes mice, rats, ground squirrels, and young rabbits; birds and their eggs and nestlings are also eaten. Adults may consume eggs as large as those of ducks (Wheeler 1984). Young *E. vulpina* may also eat earthworms and insects. A captive ate a smooth green snake (Markezich, 1962).

Predators And Defense: Natural enemies probably include carnivorous mammals, hawks, and serpent–eating snakes, but humans with their automobiles, habitat destruction, and pet trade are probably responsible for large declines in many local populations.

Evans and Roecker (1951) reported the apparent destruction of fox snake eggs by prairie deer mice that shared the same cover for nesting.

Adult *E. vulpina* seldom bite if disturbed; instead they vigorously shake their tails and, if handled, may spray musk. The young, however, may strike and bite.

The plain–colored yellow or red head of adults and their habit of vibrating the tail has led to many being mistaken for venomous copperheads or rattlesnakes.

Remarks: Bowler (1977) has reported a captive longevity of 7 years, 5 months and 18 days for a female *E. v. gloydi.*

LAMPROPELTIS CALLIGASTER

Prairie Kingsnake

LAMPROPELTIS CALLIGASTER
(Harlan, 1827)
Prairie Kingsnake

Recognition: This snake (to 107 cm) is shiny, gray to brown with a dorsal pattern of brown to red, dark bordered blotches and a cream to yellow venter with square to mottled brown blotches. Two alternating rows of dark spots (which may be fused) occur on each side of the body. Some individuals may be very dark so the dorsal pattern is obscured or forms a striped pattern. There is a dark stripe extending backward from the eye to the corner of the mouth, another dark stripe extending downward from the eye onto the supralabials, and a horizontal dark bar across the head just in front of the eyes. The smooth body scales occur in 25 rows anteriorly, 27 rows at midbody, and 20 rows posteriorly; the anal plate is not divided. Important head scalation includes a loreal, 1 preocular, 2 postoculars, 2 + 3 + 4 temporals, 7(8) supralabials, and 8–9(10–11) infralabials. The bilobed hemipenis has a single sulcus spermaticus which runs to the tip of the longest lobe and ends in a smooth area at the tip of the shortest lobe. Calyces are present, which are larger on the longer lobe, and there are a few fringes and short, stout spines. The base of the hemipenis is smooth. The maxilla usually contains 12–15 teeth.

Males usually have longer tails (12–15% of total body length), 170–215 ventrals and 37–57 subcaudals; females have tails 10–13% of total body length, 186–219 ventrals, and 31–52 subcaudals.

Karyotype: There are 36 chromosomes; 16 macrochromosomes, 20 microchromosomes; the 4th pair of macrochromosomes is submetacentric and heteromorphic (ZW) in females (Baker et al., 1972).

Fossil Record: Fossil remains of *L. calligaster* have been found in the following Pleistocene deposits: Blancan, Kansas; Rancholabrean, Arkansas, Kansas, Pennsylvania, and Texas (Holman, 1981).

Distribution: *L. calligaster* ranges from Maryland, central Kentucky, western Indiana, Illinois and southern Iowa, southward to central Florida and along the Gulf Coast to eastern Texas.

Geographic Variation: Two subspecies have been described. *Lampropeltis calligaster calligaster* (Harlan, 1827), the prairie kingsnake, is found from western Indiana and western Kentucky to southern Iowa and southeastern Nebraska southward to the Gulf Coast in central Louisiana and eastern Texas. It has about 60 brown dorsal blotches, a yellow venter with square brown blotches, 25–27 mid–body scale rows, and 9–10(8) infralabials. *L. c. rhombomaculata* (Holbrook, 1840), the mole kingsnake, ranges from Maryland's western shore west to central Tennessee and south to central Florida and eastern Louisiana. It has about 55 reddish, well separated, dorsal blotches, a white to cream venter with square, rounded or mottled brown blotches, 23(21) mid–body scale rows, and 8(9)infralabials.

Intergradation between the two subspecies was reported from Tennessee, western Alabama, and Mississippi by Blanchard (1921), and Smith (1956) reported a gradient in the number of dorsal blotches in Illinois, where the number of blotches is reduced as one progresses southward.

Confusing Species: Rat snakes (*Elaphe*) have keeled body scales and divided anal plates. Milk snakes, *Lampropeltis triangulum*, have red, black–bordered, blotches or rings and black blotches on the venter.

Habitat: *L. calligaster* lives in a variety of habitats, including old fields, marsh borders, thickets, second–cut woodlands, and even urban lots.

Behavior: In the northern part of its range, *L. calligaster* is most active from April to early November, but warm temperatures may bring them out to bask during the winter months or in early spring. The duration of annual activity is lengthened in the south, and in northern Florida and along the Gulf Coast they may be active most of the year, especially when the winter is mild. Little is known of its hibernating behavior. Smith (1961) reported they occasionally use road embankments as winter retreats, and Fitch (1978) reported a rock ledge hibernaculum in a woodland. Surely, animal burrows are also used.

During the spring and fall this snake can be found prowling during the early morning hours, but with the onset of warm summer weather it shifts its daily activity to twilight and night, becoming mostly nocturnal. The daylight hours are usually spent in some underground retreat or under logs or rocks.

The thermal relationships and movements of *L. calligaster* have not been seriously studied; it is such a secretive animal that it is seldom seen. The only body temperatures recorded for wild individuals were reported by Fitch (1956), 30.4 and 33.0 C.

Stickel and Cope (1947) reported that one individual had moved 183 m in six weeks. Fitch (1978) equipped two adult *L. calligaster* with radio transmitters and recorded their day–to–day movements. The male made successive daily movements of 11, 18.5, 7, 15, and 4.5 m; while the female's daily movements were 12, 22, 21, 0, 0, 4.5, 29, 12, 0, 0.6, 0, 0, 0, 0.5, 0, 20, 3, 0, 0, and 0.8 m. An additional 25 marked prairie kingsnakes were recaptured after intervals of from nine days to 46 months, but none was recaptured more than five times. For 35 distances recorded by Fitch between successive capture points, the average was 232 m (18.3–764). After exclusion of the exceptionally long 764 m movement, the remaining 23 records of males formed a graduated series averaging 265 m (18–482 m), whereas the females moved an average of 169 m (52–348 m). This suggested a greater activity range for males, and if these movements are taken as representing the radii of circular home ranges, those of males averaged 22 ha and those of females about 9 ha.

A combat dance between two wild male prairie kingsnakes has been recorded by Moehn (1967).

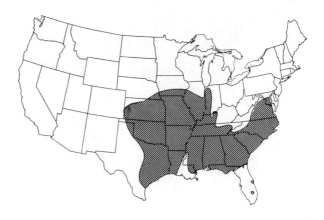

Map

> On 5 May 1966, I observed combat behavior in the field between two male prairie kingsnakes, *Lampropeltis c. calligaster* (Harlan). The observations were made at Nevada, Missouri, on a recreational area owned by Cottey College. The snakes were first noticed in an open grassy area at 9:15 a.m. and were watched until 9:45 a.m., when they were captured.
>
> When first observed, the two snakes were completely intertwined except for their heads, necks, and anterior parts of their bodies. The neck of each snake was formed into a loop and it appeared that each snake attemped to throw the other by pushing the loop against the neck of its opponent. Because they were so closely intertwined, it was impossible to determine whether one of the snakes acted as an aggressor. The two snakes were horizontal on the ground and with one exception their heads were no more than two or three inches above the surface of the ground. The exception occurred when the anterior end of one snake flopped up into the air some six or eight inches, presumably due to muscular contractions in its attempt to throw the other snake. The posterior parts of the two snakes were closely intertwined throughout the dance. It appeared that each snake attemped to tighten its coils around the other. In some instances they rolled completely over as a unit ...

Fig. 34. Hatching *Lampropeltis calligaster rhombomaculata* (Steve W. Gotte).

LAMPROPELTIS CALLIGASTER

Prairie Kingsnake

Reproduction: Fitch (1978) felt that sexual maturity is probably attained in the third year in most individuals, which breed at an age of 32 months after emerging from their second hibernation. The smallest male with mature sperm had a 64 cm snout–vent length, and males larger than 70 cm usually had sperm. Females shorter than 70 cm lacked the prominent thickening of the cloacal wall which indicates the approach of sexual maturity (Fitch, 1960a), but a 65 cm female produced a clutch of very small eggs.

Mating occurs in the spring soon after emergence from hibernation. Tryon and Carl (1980) recorded the following observation on copulation.

> Female ecdysis occurred on 18 April. On two occasions during the next seven days, she was seen lying on, and parallel to, the male's body. Although the male remained motionless, the female moved her cloacal region dorsally and dorsolaterally along the male's cloacal and tail regions. She exhibited occasional anterior jerking and tongue flicking. This behavior lasted 5–10 min., at which point she crawled slowly from the male and moved around the enclosure.

> Although male courtship was not noted, the pair was observed *in copulo* at 1430 h and 1500 h, 26 and 27 April, respectively. The male's body was lying loosely on and parallel to the female's. Initially, his head rested on her nape, but moved during later observations. On both occasions, the only movement was intermittent waving and pulsating of the male's tail, which was turned laterally and held in a horizontal plane on, or as much as 2.5 cm above, the substrate; the female's tail was held vertically ... Tongue flicking, body jerking and biting were not noted. Observed copulatory durations were greater than two hours. Reproductive behavior was not seen after 27 April.

> In 1979, the pair was observed *in copulo* on 21 April at 1545 hours. At this time, the male was lying in a superior position with a biting hold on the female dorsolaterally at the fifth anterior body blotch. This hold continued for at least one hour when observations were discontinued. The only movement was that of the tails as described above.

The eggs are laid in the summer, usually from late June to mid–July (Ernst et al., 1985), underground in mammal burrows or in the loose soil of recently plowed fields. Clark (1954) has described the oviposition.

> 9:00 a.m.–When observations were started, six eggs had already been deposited, three others, could be seen as bulges in the body. The female was lying in a circular position with head beneath the loose pile of eggs. The tail was lying on top of the pile of eggs.

> 9:10 a.m.—The position of the snake was unchanged. One of the unlaid eggs had moved nearer to the anal opening. Periodic contractions were occurring in the anal region. These were short spasms in which the

> tail, slightly arched, was raised and lowered a little. The egg moved only slightly during each contraction. The anal plate was pushed down and the opening to the cloaca was enlarged.

> 9:16 a.m.—The contractions were still occurring. The tip of the egg was now visible.

> 9:17 a.m.—The egg was extruded, except for the tip. No movement was noted as the egg emerged. The tail seemed to slide over to the left as the egg was laid.

> 9:26 a.m.—Two eggs were still within the body, and the next egg had not yet approached the anus. The body was tightly compressed now, and both the sides and the top of the vertebral column stood out in sharp relief for a distance of about five inches (127 mm) anterior to the last egg contained in the body.

> 9:50 a.m.—The next egg had moved into position and the anal plate had extended. The same muscular contractions as described before had taken place for two minutes. The periods between contractions were timed and found to have no set pattern. Some periods were of only three seconds duration, whereas others were as much as fifteen or twenty seconds in duration.

> 9:52 a.m.—The egg was now out. Still the female had not changed position. The only movements observed so far were the contractions just before the egg was extruded. The tail did not seem to move into position for the next egg voluntarily; the emergence of the egg forced the tail to one side or the other, and there the next egg was deposited.

> 10:44 a.m.—The last egg had moved into position and the contractions had begun.

> 10:52 a.m.—The tail was raised slightly and the contractions were rhythmic, but irregular in intensity.

> 10:53 a.m.—The tip of the egg was visible.

> 10:54 a.m.—The egg began to emerge.

> 10:56 a.m.—The egg had emerged, except for the tip. The tail was lying on top of the egg.

> 10:58 a.m.—The tail was still on top of the egg, but the egg was free of the body.

Ernst et al. (1985) and Carpenter (1985) have summarized egg and hatchling data for the two subspecies; clutch size in *L. c. calligaster* is 7–21 eggs, while that of *L. c. rhombomaculata* is 5–16 eggs. Generally, clutch size increases with female body length. The eggs of *calligaster* are larger (34–50 x 16.5–28 mm) than those of *rhombomaculata* (25.3–43 x 14–23.2 mm). The length of the incubation period in captivity is 45–78 days and the hatching rate is 56–100%. Tryon (1984) reported that a captive female *L. c. calligaster* mated twice during one year resulting in two different clutches.

In nature, hatching occurs in August or September. The hatchlings are more brightly patterned than adults, and are 244–305 mm in total length in *calligaster* and 193–236 mm in *rhombomaculata*.

Growth And Longevity: Fitch (1978) believed one–year–old *L. c. calligaster* to be 41.7–59.6 cm in snout–vent length, approximately twice the length of hatchlings. These snakes must have grown about 41 mm per active month. Two–year olds were 63.5–71.3 cm, having grown 23 mm per active month.

An individual of this species lived 12 years, 5 months and 18 days at the Oklahoma City Zoo (Rundquist, 1981).

Food And Feeding: Our experience with the prairie kingsnake indicates it is an active hunter of small rodents, often pursuing them into their burrows, but other observers have reported they may ambush prey (Seigel and Fitch, 1984). Prey are subdued by constriction.

Klimstra (1959b) studied the food preferences of 124 *L. calligaster* in southern Illinois, and found that mammals were the most frequent prey (79.8% of stomachs) followed by frogs, birds and insects (15.3%). Surprisingly, lizards and snakes were only found in 8% of the snakes. A survey of the literature provided the following list of food items: mammals—moles, shrews, mice, rats, gophers, ground squirrels, small rabbits; ground nesting birds and their eggs; reptiles—skinks, racerunners, fence lizards; frogs and toads; various insects; and small fishes (Wright and Wright, 1957; Klimstra, 1959b; Fitch, 1978). Adults seem to favor mammals and reptiles while young prairie kingsnakes eat amphibians, small snakes, lizards and insects.

Predators And Defense: Natural enemies of this snake include kingsnakes (*L. getulus*), owls, hawks, opossums, adult ground squirrels, skunks, raccoons, and foxes (Knable, 1970; Minton, 1972; Brown, 1979a; Linzey and Clifford, 1981; Black, 1983b). Humans also kill many individuals with their automobiles and habitat destruction.

Although most remain quietly coiled or try to flee when disturbed, some may be quite vicious, shaking their tails, striking and biting, and spraying musk and cloacal contents. Usually, they calm down, and tolerate handling thereafter, but they are often indifferent feeders and may make poor captives.

Populations: Fitch (1978) trapped *L. calligaster* during 1961 in Kansas and caught 10 in a continuous block of approximately 32 ha of grassland, and 13 others on 4 separate grassland areas of about 32 ha combined. This suggests a minimum density of one snake per 2.6 ha (0.38 per ha), but many present were probably not captured. In 30 years (1948–1977), 166 prairie kingsnakes were captured by Fitch, suggesting a density of 0.55 per

ha, but their secretive nature must still be considered.

Of 25 specimens from Alabama for which Mount (1975) recorded the sex, 19 were males. Tryon and Carl (1980) reported a hatchling sex ratio of 11 males to 6 females from a clutch of 17 eggs, and Ernst et al. (1985) reported a male to female ratio of 4:5 for nine hatchlings.

LAMPROPELTIS GETULUS

Common Kingsnake

LAMPROPELTIS GETULUS
(Linnaeus, 1766)
Common Kingsnake

Recognition: Common kingsnakes are glossy black or dark brown snakes (to 208 cm) with white or yellowish spots on the smooth doubly pitted body scales, and an individual anal plate. The size and patterns of the light spots vary considerably (see **Geographic Variation**), but there are always dark bars on the lips. The venter is usually patterned with a mixture of cream or yellow and black. The body scales occur in 21–23 rows anteriorly, 21 rows at mid–body and 17–19 near the vent. Males have 199–238 ventrals and 40–58 subcaudals, females 199–223 ventrals and 30–48 subcaudals. The nasal scale is divided; other pertinent lateral head scales include a loreal, 1 preocular; 2(3) postoculars, 2 + 3 temporals, 7(6–8) supralabials, and 9(8–11) infralabials. The bilobed hemipenis has calyces near the tips and small spines on the lower half; the sulcus spermaticus is single and extends toward the longer lobe. There are 12–16 ungrooved maxillary teeth.

Males have tail lengths 12–15% of the total body length. The tail of females is 10–13% of the total body length.

Karyotype: The diploid chromosome number is 36 (16 macrochromosomes, 20 microchromosomes); sex determination is ZZ/ZW (Bury et al., 1970; Baker et al., 1972).

Fossil Record: Fossil remains of *L. getulus* have been found in Pleistocene deposits from the Blancan of Kansas, Irvingtonian of Florida and Texas, and the Rancholabrean of Arizona, California, Florida, Georgia, Kansas, Nevada, New Mexico, Tennessee, and Texas (Holman, 1981; Meylan, 1982).

Distribution: *L. getulus* is one of the few snakes that ranges from the Atlantic Coast to the Pacific Coast in North America. Its northern limits are New Jersey and Maryland (there is an old record from Pennsylvania) to southern Illinois in the East, southern Iowa and Nebraska in the central states, and southwestern Oregon, northern California, and central Nevada in the West. It ranges southward to Sinaloa, San Luis Potosi, and Tamaulipas on the Mexican mainland, and through Baja California.

Geographic Variation: Eight subspecies of *L. getulus* are recognized, but only five occur in eastern North America. *Lampropeltis getulus getulus* (Linnaeus, 1766), the eastern kingsnake, ranges from southern New Jersey to southern Florida and adjacent Alabama east of the Appalachian Mountains. It is black with a bright chain–like pattern of narrow white to yellow cross bands. *L. g. niger* (Yarrow, 1882), the black kingsnake, is found generally west of the Appalachian Mountains and east of the Mississippi River, from West Virginia and southern Ohio to southeastern Illinois and south to central Alabama. It is black with the chain–like pattern absent, incomplete, or only faintly present in the form of a series of small white or yellow spots. *L. g. holbrooki* Stejneger, 1903b, the speckled kingsnake, occurs from southwestern Illinois and Iowa southward to central Alabama and the Gulf Coast at Mobile Bay to eastern Texas. It is dark brown or black with each scale having a white or yellow spot producing a "salt and pepper" pattern. *L. g. floridana* Blanchard, 1919, the Florida kingsnake, occurs on peninsular Florida from Pinellas and Hillsborough counties south to western Dade County, with a second disjunct population in Duval and Baker counties in northeastern Florida. It is pale cream to pale yellow with each dorsal scale brown at the tip, and faint indications of light crossbands (especially on the neck). *L. g. sticticeps* Barbour and Engels, 1942, the Outer Banks kingsnake, is known only from the coastal islands of North Carolina from Cape Hatteras to Cape Lookout. It is brown with small white spots on the dark areas between the chain–like bands.

Where the ranges of these races meet, large zones of intergradation occur, which in several localities produce distinctly marked individuals. In southern Georgia and northern Florida, intergradation between *L. g. getulus* and *L. g. floridana* produces the "blotched kingsnake" with broad dark blotches between very broad light crossbands. On peninsular Florida, intergradation between these same subspecies produces the "peninsula kingsnake," a form with a variable pattern of numerous small dark blotches. Where the races *getulus, holbrooki* and *niger* interbreed, the offspring have a variable pattern of light speckles and chain–links. In southern Florida, another color phase of *L. g. floridana* occurs which is white to cream, with little or no blotching, the dorsal scales tipped in black, and the venter with faint gray blotches. In the past, this form has been recognized as a separate race, *L. g. brooksi.* Christman (1980) has speculated that the kingsnakes in peninsular Florida, and especially southern peninsular Florida, have remained relatively unchanged with respect to dorsal color pattern and number of mid–body scale rows while populations to the north have differentiated.

The validity of the race *sticticeps* has been questioned by Blaney (1979a), but upheld by Lazell and Musick (1981). The confusion occurs from intergradation with *L. g. getulus* in the area about Cape Hatteras, but individuals from the more southern barrier islands are very distinct and easily separated from *L. g. getulus*. Thus, we continue to recognize this race as valid.

Dessauer and Pough (1975) performed electrophoretic analyses of blood proteins on six subspecies of *L. getulus*. Their molecular data indicated that *L. getulus* is a single species, but that east–west differences are greater than had been realized from morphological characters. The eastern races *getulus*, *niger*, *holbrooki* and *floridana* form a natural group (*sticticeps* was not tested).

Confusing Species: Snakes of the genera *Elaphe* and *Pituophis* have keeled body scales, and the *Elaphe* have divided anal plates. *Coluber constrictor* lacks alternating light and dark lip bars and has a divided anal plate.

Habitat: The habitat varies with the subspecies, but most eastern populations are found in dry pine or deciduous woodlands. Those living in Florida and along the Gulf Coast sometimes enter marshes and occur along swamp margins, and some Florida populations and *L. g. sticticeps* may be found about brackish water.

Behavior: *L. getulus* normally has an annual activity period extending from late March or early April to October or early November. They hibernate during the winter in caves (Orda, 1968), rock crevices, mammal burrows, hollow logs, and old stumps. In southern Florida, they may be active in every month. During the summer, they are predominantly nocturnal, but in the cooler days of spring and fall may be found prowling in the daytime.

Brattstrom (1965) reported that the critical thermal minimum and maximum for this snake were –2 and 42 C, respectively, and that the minimum and maximum voluntary temperatures of 18 *L. getulus* he measured were 15.1 and 31.4 C. His 17 active kingsnakes had an average body temperature of 28.1 C (18.0–31.4). The body temperature of 13 active kingsnakes from Georgia taken by Bothner (1973) averaged 28.7 C (23.0–33.5). Studies on Arizona kingsnakes by Sullivan (1981) indicated the body temperature of kingsnakes was highly correlated with that of the substrate.

The extent of the home range and normal movements of *L. getulus* have not been studied. However, Stickel and Cope (1947) did report that

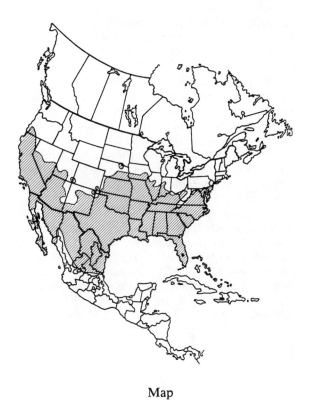

Map

Fig. 35. A female snake *Lampropeltis getulus sticticeps* (Carl H. Ernst).

one kingsnake moved over 100 m before being recaptured 1.8 years later.

L. getulus is not restricted to land or to ground level. Ernst has seen one swimming in a Florida swamp, and on another occasion found one in a tree hole 2 m above ground. Minton (1972) observed one in a mass of honeysuckle about 1.5 m above the ground raiding a cardinal's nest.

Male *L. getulus*, like those of many other snakes, sometimes engage in combat behavior. Carpenter and Gillingham (1977) analyzed a videotape of the interactions between two male *L. g. holbrooki*. Along with almost continuous contact, specific actions included forward jerks (a slight rapid forward integumentary movement with return in the trunk region), jerk–crawls (a rapid jerk forward as the snake crawled, which moved the trunk forward slightly), body–bridging (raising a portion of the trunk vertically or obliquely up to 5 or 6 cm), lying on, crawling over, entwining, hovering (one snake raised its head and anterior trunk region above the head and trunk of the other; the hovering snake then moved back and forth), and topping (from the hovering position, the snake lowered his anterior trunk region or head onto the head and neck region of the other snake, or one snake crawls on and back and forth over the head and anterior trunk of the other). After one male achieved dominance over the other, the losing snake became submissive, broke contact with the dominant male, retreated, and finally showed negative behavior by lying in a prone position with head flat on the substrate or in a coil with the head flat inside or next to the coil, and showed little response.

Reproduction: The attainment of sexual maturity has not been studied in *L. getulus*, but Tryon (1984) reported that a female *L. g. holbrooki* hatched 29 June 1978 laid eggs on 30 April 1981, and Lewke (1979) reported that two kingsnakes that hatched 16 August 1970 first attempted copulation on 15 May 1973 (the male was 112 cm long and the female was 115 cm)

Courtship and mating occur in the spring, as early as 18 March in Florida (Knepton, 1951), but usually in April or May farther north. Lewke (1979) gave the following description of the mating act:

> The male's body was superior to the female's, and caudocephalic waves passed over his body. The tail–search copulatory attempt was then observed. The male's tail undulated more rapidly than his body and got lower and lower on the tail of the female until a loop of the male's tail allowed a ventral–to–ventral position to be obtained. The male then slid his tail forward until both cloacal openings were juxtaposed. At this time the male rapidly everted one hemipenis toward the cloaca of the female. The female remained passive

Fig. 36. *Lampropeltis getulus floridana* (Carl H. Ernst).

Fig. 37. Intergrade *Lampropeltis g. getulus* x *L. g. floridana* are blotched (Carl H. Ernst).

during this and subsequent copulatory attempts of the male. By 1400 I had observed 15 eversions of a hemipenis (always the one on the right side) without one successful penetration. During this half hour of observation, the male did not bite the female.

At 1500 after an unavoidable absence of an hour, I found the two snakes copulating. The male held the female's neck firmly in his mouth ... and continued to do so for the 2 h of continuous copulation that I observed.

During copulation the male continued the same rhythmic undulations of his body as seen earlier, but at what appeared to be a much slower pace. Periodic pumping movements were made by the male in the cloacal region, presumably to aid sperm transmission. During these pumping movements, the pre-cloacal region of the female would swell noticeably, and small amounts of a milk-colored liquid (semen, I assume) would seep from around the site of intromission.

Van Hyning (1931), McCauley (1945), and Kennedy (1978) had previously published brief descriptions of copulation in this species.

It is possible that a female may mate with more than one male during the breeding season and then produce a single litter containing offspring from these different males (Zweifel and Dessauer, 1983). Females may also produce more than one clutch per season as a result of more than one mating (Tryon, 1984). The gestation period between copulation and oviposition is about 60–80 days.

The eggs are deposited as early as May in Florida (Knepton, 1951; Iverson, 1978), but farther north most eggs are laid in late June or July. Typical nesting sites are rotting logs or stumps, sawdust piles, and mammal burrows. The elongated eggs are 28–60 mm x 17–24 mm, and have parchment–like shells. Some may have constricted nipple–like points at one end, and clusters of 7–8 eggs may adhere together. Clutches produced by females of the eastern subspecies contained 3 (Minton, 1972; Mount, 1975) to 24 eggs (Mount, 1975), but the average number of eggs in a clutch was 10.8. When laid, the eggs weigh 9–14 g.

The incubation period ranges from 49–81 days, depending on the incubation temperature. Hatching may occur as early as mid–July in Florida, but most northern clutches hatch in August or early September.

Hatchlings resemble the adults in coloration and pattern, having total body lengths of 202–300 mm, and weights of 5–12 g when they emerge.

Growth And Longevity: Nothing has been reported on the rate of growth in the wild, but in captivity hatchlings may nearly double their lengths in one year.

The longevity record for kingsnakes from eastern North America is 21 years, 5 months, 2 days by a male *L. g. getulus* at the John Ball Zoo, Grand Rapids, Michigan (Bowler, 1977).

Food And Feeding: *L. getulus* seems to prefer reptilian prey. It is known to feed on a great number of snake species, including members of the venomous genera *Micrurus*, *Agkistrodon*, *Sistrurus* and *Crotalus*, to whose venom it shows a certain amount of immunity. It will not hesitate to eat smaller members of its own species. Lizards (*Ophisaurus*, *Scincella*, *Eumeces*, *Cnemidophorus*, *Sceloporus*) are frequently eaten (46% incidence, Hamilton and Pollack, 1956), and small turtles are also consumed. Kingsnakes readily dig up and eat the eggs of other snakes, lizards and turtles. Turtle nests may be searched out and then dug up by pushing the head sideways into the soil (Posey, 1973; Knight and Loraine, 1986). Frequently, turtle eggs may pass unharmed through the snake, and if incubated, may later hatch (Forks, 1979; Knight and Loraine, 1986).

In addition to reptiles, homiothermic prey such as nestling and fledgling birds, mice (*Mus*, *Microtus*, *Peromyscus*), and rats (*Sigmodon*, *Rattus*) are taken. Adult birds may be taken as carrion (Brown, 1979a).

Young kingsnakes probably eat small snakes, lizards, frogs, salamanders, and insects. Weldon et al. (1984) reported that cotton swabs containing snake extracts elicited a tongue flick and feeding response in 60% of newborn *L. getulus* tested.

Prey is located by its odor (Williams and Brisbin, 1978; Brock and Myers, 1979), or by sight (person. observ.). *L. getulus* can distinguish between the odors of colubrid and crotalid prey (Weldon et al., 1984). *L. getulus* is a constrictor, and large prey is seized by the mouth and quickly immobilized by the snake's coils. Snakes are often grabbed by the head and chewed and twisted. Small prey may be swallowed directly.

Predators And Defense: The young may be eaten by larger snakes, even of their own species, but hawks, raccoons, skunks, and opossums are probably the most serious predators on adults.

Humans have a detrimental effect on kingsnake populations. Not only are many killed on our roads, by habitat destruction, or the use of pesticides, but many others are taken from the wild for the pet trade.

When cornered, *L. getulus* will put up quite a fight; hissing, striking and biting viciously, and spraying a rather pungent musk on its tormentor. This musk may serve as an alarm substance to other kingsnakes in the area (Brisbin, 1968).

Remarks: Although *L. getulus* is not a rare snake and may be locally common, surprisingly little is known of its life history. A good ecological study is needed.

LAMPROPELTIS TRIANGULUM

Milk Snake

LAMPROPELTIS TRIANGULUM
(Lacepede, 1788)
Milk Snake

Recognition: This is a small to medium–sized (to 132 cm) snake varying in color from grayish–brown, olive–brown, reddish–brown, or red with a series of white or yellow and black rings on the body (see **Geographic Variation**). The head is only slightly pointed. The dorsal head pattern is also variable in the eastern subspecies, and ranges from plain red to mostly black, or has a light V or Y–shaped blotch near the back of the head. The supralabials may bear black bars. The venter may be white with rectangular black blotches or have the dorsal light and dark rings continue across. The body scales are smooth with two apical pits and occur in 17–23 rows anteriorly and at mid–body, and 15–19 rows near the anus; the anal plate is not divided. Ventrals total 152–215 and subcaudals 31–55, with no apparent sexual dimorphism. Pertinent lateral head scalation includes divided nasal scales, 1(0–2) loreal, 1(0–2) preocular, 2(1–3) postoculars, 1 + 2–3 temporals, 7(6–9) supralabials, and 8–9(7–11) infralabials. The hemipenis is bilobed with a single sulcus spermaticus extending onto the left lobe, is proximally naked, and has spines medially which gradually merge distally with papillate calyces and a naked apex (Williams, 1978). Maxillary teeth from 11 to 15, with the two most posterior largest.

Males have tails 12–17% as long as the total body length; females, 11–16% as long.

Karyotype: Unknown, but presumably the diploid chromosome number is 36 as in other *Lampropeltis*.

Fossil Record: Fossils of *L. triangulum* have been identified in deposits from the middle Pliocene of Oklahoma, upper Pliocene of Texas, and the Blancan (Kansas), Irvingtonian (Florida, Kansas, Maryland) and Rancholabrean (Arkansas, Florida, Georgia, Kansas, Missouri, Pennsylvania, Tennessee, Texas, Virginia) of the Pleistocene

(Holman, 1979, 1981; Meylan, 1982). Blanchard (1921) suggested the Southwest as the center of origin for *L. triangulum* with a pre–Pleistocene radiation from the Southwest to the Southeast. Current fossil evidence supports this view.

Distribution: *L. triangulum* is one of the most widely distributed of all North American snakes (Williams, 1978). It ranges from 48° N latitude in Canada to nearly 4° S latitude in Ecuador, a distance of almost 5800 km; the greatest longitudinal range in the United States is almost 3000 km.

Geographic Variation: Twenty–three subspecies are recognized by Williams (1978), but only four occur in eastern North America. *Lampropeltis triangulum triangulum* (Lacepede, 1788), the eastern milk snake, ranges from southern Maine, Quebec and Ontario west to Minnesota and northeastern Iowa and south to North Carolina, Tennessee and Kentucky. It has grayish–brown, olive–brown or reddish–brown, black–bordered dorsal blotches, a V or Y–shaped light mark on the nape, a white venter with a black checkerboard pattern, and 21 mid–body scale rows. It is a much larger snake, and is usually 100 cm or more in length while the other three eastern races seldom reach 70 cm in length. *L. t. elapsoides* (Holbrook, 1838), the scarlet kingsnake, is found from southeastern Virginia and southwestern Kentucky southward east of the Mississippi River through peninsular Florida and to the Gulf Coast. It is a coral snake mimic with a red head, alternating red, black and yellow rings, circling the body, and 19 or 17 scale rows at mid–body. *L. t. amaura* Cope, 1860, the Louisiana milk snake, ranges from southeastern Louisiana and adjacent southwestern Mississippi west to southwestern Arkansas, southeastern Oklahoma, and central Texas. It has a black head with a lighter snout, the body with alternating broad red and narrower black and white to cream–colored rings which extend onto the venter. There are usually 21 mid–body scale rows. This race is found east of the Mississippi River only as intergrades with *L. t. elapsoides* or *L. t. syspila* (Williams, 1978). *L. t. syspila* (Cope, 1888), the red milk snake, has a range extending from southeastern North Dakota and adjacent Iowa and Nebraska east to Illinois and southwestern Indiana and south to eastern Oklahoma and Mississippi. It is an orangish–red snake with broad dorsal blotches separated by white bands, few lateral blotches, a light collar, a black checkerboard ventral pattern, and usually 21 mid–body scale rows.

Formerly, specimens intergrade between *L. t. triangulum* and *L. t. elapsoides* found on the Atlantic Coastal Plain were assigned to the taxon *L. t. temporalis* (Cope, 1893), known as the coastal plain milk snake, but this form is no longer considered valid (Williams, 1978). Specimens resulting from such a cross are very attractive, having orangish–red blotches alternating with narrow black–bordered cream–colored bands, and with a black–bordered complete band or separate blotch on the nape. It is highly prized in the pet trade.

Confusing Species: *Elaphe guttata* has a divided anal plate and a spear–shaped mid–dorsal head mark. The water snakes (*Nerodia*) have keeled scales and divided anal plates. Young racers, *Coluber constrictor*, have divided anal plates. The copperhead, *Agkistrodon contortrix*, has a reddish, unmarked head, dumbbell–shaped dorsal blotches, elliptical pupils, and a pit between the nostril and eye. The scarlet snake, *Cemophora coccinea*, has an immaculate cream–colored venter. The coral snake, *Micrurus fulvius*, has a black snout and red bands touching yellow bands.

Habitat: In eastern North America, *L. triangulum* can be found in a variety of habitats ranging from deciduous and pine woodlands to rocky hillsides, brushy fields, bogs, marsh and swamp borders, and river bottoms. The milk snake is a secretive species, seldom seen in the open, and it is most frequently discovered hiding under logs, rocks or the bark of old stumps. It is often common in the debris around abandoned buildings or about farm outbuildings where rodents are abundant.

Behavior: Because of its secretive nature, we know less about the behavior and ecology of *L. triangulum* than many other snakes. Over most of its range, the milk snake is active from late March or April to October or early November, but in peninsular Florida it may be active all year if the winter is mild. Vogt (1981) reported that they are most active in May and September in Wisconsin, and that they remain basking near their hibernacula in early spring before dispersing to summer feeding ranges. Hibernacula include old wells and cisterns, stone walls, gravel and dirt banks, mammal burrows, rock crevices, hollow logs, rotting stumps, and the crumbling foundations of old buildings.

It is mostly nocturnal. The only ones we have found during the day have been undercover, but others have found them active rarely during the day. In Illinois, Dyrkacz (1977) found most milk snakes were undercover either early in the morning (0700–0900 hrs), or late in the afternoon (1800–2000 hrs), but did find one active during the middle hours at 1000.

Body temperatures of five *L. triangulum* from Kansas recorded by Fitch (1956) averaged 26.2 C (22.3–31.7). Body temperatures recorded from Wisconsin milk snakes by Henderson et al. (1980) ranged from near 13 to almost 30 C.

Map

Fig. 38. A juvenile *Lampropeltis triangulum triangulum*.

Aerial basking is not common; Fitch and Fleet (1970) observed that in Kansas *L. triangulum* does not ordinarily bask in direct sunlight, but obtains body heat by contacting the underside of sun–warmed objects.

In the spring and fall milk snakes are often found in more upland situations than during the summer months; presumably they migrate to and from hibernacula. The same shelter may be used frequently. Fitch and Fleet (1970) found a hatchling at the same place three additional times, the last about 9 months from the first, and another juvenile beneath the same shelter twice. Six Kansas milk snakes made movements of 76–396 m (x = 254), six of the movements were within 244–293 m (Fitch and Fleet, 1970). If 254 m represented a typical home range radius of these snakes, then a home range of 20 hectares is indicated.

Shaw (1951) has described the male combat behavior in the western subspecies *L. t. annulata*.

> In all instances the combat behavior followed immediately after the snakes had been fed or while one of them was still feeding. In the first two 'dances' witnessed there was no biting of one male by another, nor were any courtship motions observed; combat behavior appeared to be caused by a search for additional food on the part of the aggressive male. The second case of combat witnessed in these snakes lasted about 15 minutes and was terminated by the non–aggressive male which fled from the aggressor. The non–aggressive male was repeatedly re–approached by the aggressive male but steadfastly refused to be re–engaged in combat. A short while later the aggressive male suddenly spied the movements of his own tail and immediately seized it and succeeded in swallowing two or three inches of it before finally letting go. On April 30, 1951, while being fed, these snakes were observed in combat, for a third time this spring. The somewhat larger male had already finished feeding, but the smaller male still was holding his mouse by the head. The larger male was crawling over the smaller male's back and was being nudged in an attempt by the smaller male to rid himself of this annoyance. Both snakes had flexed their necks and were following through with the usual twisting of their bodies. The larger male was making what appeared to be courting motions over the back of the smaller male, jerky undulations of his body with his chin pressed firmly against the back of the smaller male. The larger male showed no interest in attempting to eat the mouse the smaller male was still holding in his mouth. The aggressive male bit the smaller male twice during the observations, but whether such biting represented an attempt to secure the neck or head–biting hold of the courtship pattern is unknown. On two occasions the smaller male made four or five typical constricting loops about the body of the larger male; these were not the 'twisted rope' loops of combat behavior. These activities were observed for about

Fig. 39. *Lampropeltis triangulum syspila* (Carl H. Ernst).

Fig. 40. *Lampropeltis triangulum elapsoides* has a rounded snout (Ted Borg, courtesy of J. Whitfield Gibbons).

30 minutes and were terminated when the smaller male finally released his hold on the mouse and fled from the larger male. The aggressive male showed no interest in the mouse that had been released by the other snake.

Reproduction: The smallest female *L. t. syspila* that laid eggs during Fitch and Fleet's (1970) study was 48 cm in snout–vent length, so maturity is first attained near this length. The sexual cycles have not been studied, but Kansas females contained enlarged oviducal eggs from the latter half of May to 17 June and oviposition occurred from the middle of June to early July (Fitch and Fleet, 1970).

The mating season extends from mid–April to early June, but most copulation occurs in May. Herman (1979) described the mating act in *L. t. elapsoides.*

> Copulation was already in progress when observed on 27 April 1971 at 0115. Intromission and coitus were similar to that observed by Gillingham, et al. (1977) ...
>
> The male was observed pressing the female down mid-dorsally with four body loops. The female's venter rested upon the substratum with her tail slightly raised. The male's tail was in a ventrolateral position and under the female's tail without encircling it. The male rubbed his chin lightly along the female's neck for 3.5 minutes; tongue flicks occurred at 4–6 second intervals for 2 minutes. After ca. 30 minutes, the male relaxed, moved slightly forward, and retracted his hemipenis. The snakes slowly crawled away from each other with their tails raised to 40–45° angle from the substratum. The tails were lowered slowly, after 2 minutes, as they crawled about the cage.

Gillingham et al. (1977) have published a detailed analysis of courtship and copulation in the Mexican subspecies *L. t. sinaloae.*

The gestation period is about 30–40 days. The nesting season normally extends from late May to early July, but Groves and Assetto (1976) reported a female *L. t. elapsoides* from Florida laid 5 eggs on 8 October, and captives have laid eggs as early as 7 March (Tryon, 1984). Clutch size for the species varies from 3 (Barten, 1981) to 24 (Wright and Wright, 1957) eggs. The number of eggs laid is in direct correlation to the female's body length; females of the smaller eastern races *amaura, elapsoides* and *syspila* lay fewer eggs (4–9) than do females of the largest race, *triangulum.* Apparently, at least some females have the potential for laying more than one clutch per season (Tryon, 1984).

In the wild, the eggs are laid in rotting logs and stumps, piles of decaying vegetation, under rocks, sawdust piles or mammal burrows, and several females may oviposit at the same site (Henderson et al., 1980). The eggs have parchment-like, slightly granular shells, are 21–35 mm x 11–15 mm, and weigh about 4.5 g each. They often adhere in batches of 6–10 eggs. Egg size is proportional to female length.

Incubation takes 50–70 days, and most young hatch in August or September. Dyrkacz (1977) reported that of 80 eggs from Illinois *L. t. triangulum,* 79(99%) were fertile and that 57(72%) hatched. Hatchlings of the tricolored races are colored and patterned like the adults, but those of *L. t. triangulum* often have deeper reddish–brown blotches than do the adults. Hatchlings are 190–255 mm in total length, and about 2.5–3.5 g each.

Growth And Longevity: *L. t. triangulum* from Illinois grew from an average of 248 mm in total length at hatching to an average of 260 mm in one month (Dyrkacz, 1977). The two smallest milk snakes from Indiana examined by Minton (1972) were 209 and 232 mm in total length and probably 9–10 months old.

In Kansas, Fitch and Fleet (1970) found that first–year *L. t. syspila* ranged from 198–268 mm (x = 237) in snout–vent length; hatchlings had grown an average of about 30 mm or 15% over their original length in about two months. Second–year young were 296–397 mm (x = 360) in snout–vent length, and third–year snakes were usually over 400 mm but less than 500 mm.

A female *L. t. triangulum,* adult when caught, lived an additional 21 years, 4 months and 14 days at the Philadelphia Zoo, and a wild caught *L. t. amaura* lived 20 years, 7 months in the collection of George P. Meade (Bowler, 1977). Fitch and Fleet (1970) thought the largest wild adults in their study were 6–10 years old.

Food And Feeding: The milk snake's head and jaws are small and the body is narrow, so it must eat relatively slender prey. Mammals (mice—*Microtus, Mus, Peromyscus, Napaeozapus, Zapus;* shrews—*Blarina, Cryptotus*); birds and their eggs; reptiles (lizards and their eggs—*Anolis, Sceloporus, Eumeces, Scincella;* snakes and their eggs—*Agkistrodon, Carphophis, Crotalus, Diadophis, Lampropeltis, Nerodia, Opheodrys, Regina, Storeria, Thamnophis, Virginia*), small frogs, small fish, earthworms, slugs, and insects are eaten (Williams, 1978). Brown (1979b) reported that 59% of the mammals taken were young. Mammals made up 79% of the food volume and 68% of all items in those milk snakes examined by Brown (1979b); birds comprised 12.7% of food volume (19% frequency) and reptiles 8.1% of food volume (12.4% frequency). Uhler et al. (1939) found mice 42%, snakes 26%, songbirds and their eggs 16%, insects 11%, and shrews 5% by volume in Virginia milk snakes. Kamb (1978) reported that captive *L. t. syspila* twice ingested formerly regurgitated mice, and Skehan (1960) caught a *L. t. triangulum* that regurgitated a partially digested juvenile milk snake, so they may be cannibalistic.

Milk snakes are constrictors. They seize prey in their mouths and quickly wrap it in coils of the body, slowly squeezing until it has suffocated.

Predators And Defense: The only three authentic reports of predation on wild *L. triangulum* were the case of cannibalism mentioned above, that of a bullfrog that had eaten two *L. t. amaura* (Hensley, 1962), and an attack by a brown thrasher (Flanigan, 1971). However, predatory mammals (raccoons, coyotes, foxes, skunks, opossums) and hawks and owls probably take a few. Many die each year on our highways or through destruction of their habitats, and the more colorful subspecies are in demand in the pet trade.

When excited, milk snakes vibrate their tails, strike, retain hold, and chew. Some may spray musk and cloacal contents, and others may hide their heads beneath their coils. Tri–colored individuals may be particularly pugnacious, and often remain so when kept in captivity. The eastern red, black and yellow races form a mimicry complex with the venomous eastern coral snake, *Micrurus fulvius*.

Populations: Dyrkacz (1977) studied *L. t. triangulum* at two quarries in McHenry County, Illinois. Both quarries were approximately 5000 m² in area. At the first quarry 36 adults, 2 juveniles and 5 hatchlings were found, and at the second 14 adults and 2 hatchlings were collected, giving population densities of 86 and 32 milk snakes, respectively, for the two quarries. Guidry (1953) once collected 18 *L. t. amaura* on a single afternoon in an area of approximately 1.6 km² in Newton County, Texas.

The only sex ratio datum available is for a clutch of five hatchling *L. t. syspila* which contained four males and one female (Fitch and Fleet, 1970).

Remarks: A folktale explains the common name "milk" snake. Since this snake is often found around barns and farm outbuildings, where it undoubtedly has been seeking mice, the mistaken idea has arisen that it sucks milk from cow's udders. This is entirely false. The snake probably has little ability to suck fluids, and besides, what cow would stand still for having its teats grasped by a mouth with so many sharp teeth!

PITUOPHIS MELANOLEUCUS

Pine Snake

PITUOPHIS MELANOLEUCUS
(Daudin, 1803)
Pine Snake

Recognition: Bull snakes are large (to 254 cm) white, tan or black serpents with an enlarged, elongated rostral plate, dark bars on the supralabials, a dark bar extending from the eye downward onto the supralabials, another dark bar extending diagonally downward from the eye to the corner of the mouth, and four prefrontal scales. This is a quite variable snake, and the coloration and patterns of the eastern subspecies are discussed under **Geographic Variation**. The body scales are keeled and contain apical pits. They occur in 25–31 rows anteriorly, 27–37 rows at midbody, and 19–27 rows near the anal vent. The anal plate is not divided. The rostral plate partially divides the internasals. The nasal scale is divided, and on each side of the head are a loreal, 1–2(3) preoculars, 2–6 postoculars, several temporals, 6–9 supralabials, and 10–15 infralabials. There are 194–233 ventrals; males have 44–63 subcaudals, females 29–57. The hemipenis is subcylindrical and slightly bilobed with a single sulcus spermaticus. Both the base and terminus are spinose. The spines at the base are generally small, those in the middle larger and recurved, and those spines at the distal terminus small (see Stull, 1940; and Cliburn, 1975 for illustrations). Each maxilla contains 16–17 teeth.

Males have tails 11–14% as long as the total body length; females have tails only 10–12% of the total body length.

Karyotype: The karyotype consists of 36 chromosomes; 16 macrochromosomes, 20 microchromosomes (Bury et al., 1970; Trinco and Smith, 1971; Baker et al., 1972).

Fossil Record: Fossils of this species are known from the upper Pliocene of Kansas (Holman, 1979); and Blancan (Kansas), Irvingtonian (Florida) and Rancholabrean (Arkansas, Arizona, California, Florida, Illinois, Kansas, Missouri, Nevada, New Mexico, Oklahoma, Texas) of the Pleistocene (Holman, 1981; Meylan, 1982).

Distribution: *P. melanoleucus* ranges from Illinois, Wisconsin, southern Minnesota, southeastern Saskatchewan, southeastern Alberta, and southcentral British Columbia, south through Baja California and to southern Sinaloa and Veracruz in Mexico, and from western Virginia and southeastern North Carolina to southern Florida, Alabama and Mississippi. Isolated populations also occur in New Jersey, northwestern and southwestern Indiana, northwestern Minnesota, eastern Texas, and adjacent west–central Louisiana (Conant, 1975; Stebbins, 1985).

Geographic Variation: As many as 15 subspecies of *Pituophis melanoleucus* may exist (Samuel S. Sweet, person. comm.), but only four occur east of the Mississippi River. The above description is a composite of the four eastern races. *Pituophis melanoleucus melanoleucus* (Daudin, 1803), the northern pine snake, can be found from the pine barrens of southern New Jersey, coastal plain of southern North Carolina and South Carolina, and the mountains of western Virginia west to Alabama, Tennessee and southern Kentucky. It is a large, white to pinkish–cream snake with black body blotches anteriorly, and brown blotches posteriorly. *P. m. sayi* (Schlegel, 1837), the bullsnake, occurs from northwestern and southwestern Indiana, Illinois, Wisconsin and southern Minnesota west to southern Saskatchewan and Alberta and southwest to southern and western Texas and adjacent Mexico. It is a large, yellow to tan snake with reddish–brown body blotches. *P. m. mugitus* Barbour, 1921, the Florida pine snake, is found from southwestern South Carolina, west to Mobile Bay and south on peninsular Florida to Charlotte, Palm Beach and Dade counties. It is tan to gray–brown or rusty–brown with a faded, indistinct, blotched pattern. *P. m. lodingi* Blanchard, 1924b, the black pine snake, is only found in southwestern Alabama and adjacent southeastern Mississippi. It is a nearly or totally black or dark brown snake with a reddish snout and labials.

Confusing Species: Rat snakes (*Elaphe*) and kingsnakes (*Lampropeltis*) have only two prefrontal scales, and *Elaphe* has a divided anal plate. Whipsnakes (*Masticophis*), racers (*Coluber*), and indigo snakes (*Drymarchon*) have smooth body scales.

Habitat: In the East, *P. melanoleucus* is usually found in areas with sandy soil and scrub pines and various other shrubs; in the Midwest it inhabits grasslands with clumps of vegetation and sandy soil.

Behavior: This snake is usually diurnal, although a few may be active at twilight. Northern popu–

PITUOPHIS MELANOLEUCUS

Pine Snake

Map

Fig. 41. *Pituophis melanoleucus lodingi.*

lations are active from late March or April to October or early November (Wright and Wright, 1957; Collins, 1974). Occasionally, an individual snake will be active in winter (McDowell, 1951; Parks, 1973). In Florida, *P. m. mugitus* may be active in every month.

The winters are spent in hibernation in mammal burrows. Schroder (1950) excavated an Indiana hibernaculum situated on the north rim of a large dune riddled with abandoned mammal burrows. It contained 5 *P. melanoleucus* and 7 *Coluber constrictor* in two chambers 91 and 107 cm below the surface. Air temperature in the chambers was less than 9 C. Fitch (1958) reported that one female was caught near the same ledge in October for three successive years, and had evidently returned there each year to hibernate.

Probably, *P. melanoleucus* also utilizes such shelters to escape the more intense heat of summer, but little is known of the thermal ecology of this snake. Fitch (1956) recorded the body temperatures of eight active individuals from Kansas that averaged 28 C (19.5–32.4), and Collins (1974) stated it was active at air temperatures above 16 C. In New Jersey, active pine snakes had cloacal temperatures of 22–34 C (Zappalorti et al., 1983). It will bask in the mornings to raise its body temperature, and Brattstrom (1965) has reported that the threshold of normal locomotion in laboratory tests was about 18 C for juveniles. He also reported the thermal activity range was 16.4–34.6 C, and that the critical thermal minimum and maximum were –3.0 and 40.5 C, respectively.

Parks (1973) found a bullsnake crawling along a Kansas road on 21 February when the air temperature was only 4 C, and Landreth (1972) reported that bullsnakes first started to awake from cold narcosis at 8 C. Landreth subjected several bullsnakes to –4 C temperatures for two hours and their body temperatures remained near 0 C. All survived, but required several weeks for complete recovery.

P. melanoleucus is an accomplished burrower, and may simply dig itself into the ground to escape uncomfortable temperatures. Their pointed snout and enlarged rostral scale are quite effective for tunneling in loose soil. Carpenter (1982) reported that the digging sequence is stereotyped. Spading actions by the snout are followed by scooping a load of soil in a head/neck flexure, moving posterior, and dumping the soil away from the burrow at varying distances. He estimated that a burrowing bullsnake could move up to 3400 cm³ of soil in an hour. Carpenter thought this behavior important for digging retreats or nests, and for excavating rodents, especially pocket gophers, to which the snakes responded positively to the soil from their characteristic mounds. Burrowing may help snakes avoid excessive evaporative water loss during dry weather, but Prange and Schmidt–Nielson (1969) have found that the skin of this species is relatively impermeable. Knight (1986) has reported that the skulls of the eastern races of *P. melanoleucus*, including *P. m. sayi*, differ in structure (particularly the nasal/premaxilla articulation) from those of the western races. Possibly, this indicates a difference in excavating ability or behavior.

Although usually found on the ground, individual *P. melanoleucus* may ascend into low bushes or even climb trees. (Bullock, 1981).

In the East, *P. melanoleucus* does not seem to have a particularly extensive home range for such a large snake. Fitch (1958) reported movements between captures of 94, 128, and 823 m. Imler (1945) recaptured 11 bullsnakes that had moved less than 100 m, and another which had moved 2.4 km. The average distance crawled per day for radio–equipped bullsnakes in Kansas was 142 m (Fitch and Shirer, 1971).

Males of the various subspecies of *P. melanoleucus* are known to engage in dominance combat bouts, as also occur in other colubrid and viperid snakes. Rather than discuss this behavior, we refer the reader to the long and graphic descriptions of male combat in three subspecies as reported by Shaw (1951).

Reproduction: The sexual cycle of male *P. melanoleucus* was studied by Goldberg and Parker (1975). Testes are regressed in April and May; recrudescence begins in June. Spermiogenesis occurs in late summer and early autumn. The sperm then passes to the epididymis and vas deferens where it is stored over winter until the spring breeding season. The diameters of interstitial cell nuclei are of maximum size during the autumn and spring, and of minimum size in the summer. The body length and age of maturity in male and female *P. melanoleucus* have not been reported, but females appear to have an annual breeding cycle (Fitch, 1970; Zappalorti et al., 1983).

The mating period extends from April to early June over most of the range, but Ashton and Ashton (1981) thought that in Florida breeding possibly occurs in the winter. During courtship the male crawls beside and over the female until he eventually rests almost entirely on top of her. While doing this he exhibits jerking body movements. The female usually remains passive except for elevating and waving her tail. Just prior to copulation the male may seize the female with his mouth, biting her head or neck. He curls his tail beneath hers until their cloacal openings meet and then inserts his hemipenis. Copulation may last over an hour (Collins, 1974).

The eggs are laid in June or July in burrows excavated by the female in loose soil, beneath large rocks or logs, or possibly in small mammal burrows. Nests may be 25–30 cm deep. Burger and Zappalorti (1986) studied nest site selection in New Jersey. All nests were in large clearings with less than 10% tree cover in pitch pine–scrub oak uplands. Nests were in soft sand in open, unvegetated sections of clearings. Sixteen snakes nested solitarily, 8 nested communally in double clutches, 3 snakes laid in one nest, and 4 laid in another nest. There were few differences between solitary and communal nests, except that more solitary nests were in sedge rather than in grass in areas with greater tree cover and closer to roads. The nests were 90–305 cm (x 187.6) in length, and the chambers were about 14 cm wide. The eggs were about 15 cm below the surface.

The eggs are elliptical with a rough, leathery shell, and often adherent. A survey of egg measurements in the literature gave the following dimensions: length, 46.3–94.7 mm (x = 55); width, 21.7–44.7 mm (x = 40), and weight, 20.3–133 g (x = 64 g). However, some of these eggs had been developing for some time, while others were newly laid. Mehrtens (1952) and Zappalorti et al. (1983) have reported that the eggs increase in width and weight during incubation, and that while some increase in length, others may actually shrink. Clutches may contain 3–24 eggs (Wright and Wright, 1957; Zappalorti et al., 1983), but since females often nest communally, perhaps the higher number represents more than one clutch. Thirty–five New Jersey clutches contained 3–14 eggs with an average of 8–9 eggs (Zappalorti et al., 1983).

Incubation normally takes 50–100 days, but probably 70–75 days are most common. The young emerge in August and September at total body lengths of 222–256 mm. They are dull in color at first, but brighten after shedding their skins.

Growth And Longevity: In a study of bullsnake growth in Kansas, Platt (1984) found that those in their first year grew at a mean rate of 56.5 mm/30 days, a mean relative growth rate of 9.4%; those in their second year grew 26.9 mm/30 days (3.1%); third–year snakes, 12.2 mm/30 days (1.2%); and those over three years, 6.0 mm/30 days (0.5%). Some snakes grew to 110 cm snout-vent length in four years. Variations in relative growth occurred from year to year, probably due to meteorological factors and prey availability. Peabody (1958) examined the growth zones in the squamosal and ectopterygoid bones of Kansas

PITUOPHIS MELANOLEUCUS

Pine Snake

bullsnakes, and found them excellent indicators of age and of the droughts in Kansas.

The longest-lived *P. melanoleucus* was 22 years, 5 months, and 1 day old (Bowler, 1977).

Food And Feeding: A variety of small mammals form the chief foods of *P. melanoleucus*; a survey of the literature reveals it eats various mice and rats, ground squirrels, tree squirrels, pocket gophers and rabbits (Hamilton and Pollack, 1956, Wright and Wright, 1957; Minton, 1972). Its value as a rodent eater is well known to farmers. Hisaw and Gloyd (1926) estimated the monetary value of an adult bullsnake as $3.75 per year in rodents; imagine the inflated value over 60 years later.

It also eats small birds and their eggs, lizards, small snakes, snake eggs, and insects. Wellstead (1981) observed a possible attempted cannibalism in *P. m. sayi*. Linzey and Clifford (1981) reported that when a large egg is eaten, it is swallowed for a short distance and then the strong neck muscles break the shell. The liquid contents are swallowed, and the shell may be disgorged or swallowed.

P. melanoleucus is an active forager, and prey is found either by olfaction (Dyrkacz and Corn, 1974; Chiszar et al., 1980) or sight. It is seized in the mouth and quickly constricted in the snake's coils. Small prey may be merely pinned on the ground or against the wall of a burrow, but larger dangerous prey is more often completely wrapped in the snake's coils. The snake does not always win these battles, and some prey, especially the larger ones, may escape. In fact, *P. melanoleucus* may occasionally be killed by large ground squirrels (Haywood and Harris, 1972).

Predators And Defense: The predators of *P. melanoleucus* have not been documented, but probably large carnivorous birds and mammals, and ophiophagous snakes eat some. Automobiles, habitat destruction, and pesticides are more serious concerns than natural predators.

When disturbed, *P. melanoleucus* throws itself into a coil, vibrates the tail rapidly, and strikes repeatedly and viciously, all while uttering a series of hisses that are audible for some distance. Although the display is largely bluff, some individuals will inflict serious bites, Ernst was once severely bitten by a *P. m. lodingi*. The epiglottis is enlarged and keeled in *Pituophis*, and may help to amplify the hiss (Martin and Huey, 1971; Saiff, 1975).

Sweet (1985) has shown that western North American races of *P. melanoleucus* share aspects of coloration, pattern, and defense behavior with the sympatric rattlesnake *Crotalus viridis*, and some populations seem to be good mimics of that rattlesnake.

Populations: Gutzke et al. (1985) reported that the secondary sex ratios obtained for adult and hatchling bullsnakes from Nebraska were significantly different than 1:1. Adults and hatchlings had proportions of male:male + female of 0.67 each. They attributed this to the fact that females typically disperse less distance from hibernacula than do males, and so are more likely to compete for local resources with other females more genetically similar to themselves than do males. Thus, clutches with sex ratios skewed toward males would be expected to have inter-sibling competition.

STILOSOMA EXTENUATUM

Short-tailed Snake

STILOSOMA EXTENUATUM
Brown, 1890
Short-tailed Snake

Recognition: This very slender snake (to 65 cm) has a tail usually no longer than 10% of its total body length. The body is usually gray with dark brown or black lateral and dorsal blotches, and many have orange or reddish pigment separating the dorsal blotches. The short, blunt head is black dorsally, and has a black postocular stripe. There are many black speckles on the chin. The eyes are small, and a distinct neck is lacking. The venter is gray with numerous dark brown or black blotches. The body scales are smooth, pitless, and usually occur in 19 rows; the anal plate is undivided. The rostral scale is prominent and the internasals and prefrontals may fuse. Laterally there are a single nasal scute, 1 preocular, 2 postoculars, 2 temporals (the anterior separated from the postoculars by the parietal scale), usually 6 supralabials, and 5–8 infralabials. The hemipenis has only a few apical calyces (Cope, 1895; Wright and Wright, 1957). Each maxilla has 10–11 small, ungrooved teeth.

Females have 256–277 ventrals and 33–45 subcaudals; males 223–261 ventrals and 38–48 subcaudals. Females also have significantly longer tails (9.5–14.1% of the total body length) than males (8.8–12.1%) (Highton, 1956).

Karyotype: Unknown.

Fossil Record: A mid–Pliocene fossil from Alachua County, Florida named *Stilosoma vetustum* by Auffenberg (1963) may be of this species, and another Pleistocene vertebra from Alachua County seems to be *S. extenuatum*. Meylan (1982) had found vertebrae of *S. extenuatum* in early Pleistocene deposits (Irvingtonian) from Citrus County, Florida.

Distribution: North and Central peninsular Florida west of the St. Johns River from Suwannee and Columbia counties southward to Highland County.

Geographic Variation: No subspecies are recognized; see Highton (1956, 1979) and Woolfenden (1962) for discussions of variation.

Confusing Species: No other Florida snake has such a short tail.

Habitat: This is a fossorial, xeric adapted, upland snake occurring most frequently in the sandy soils of long leaf pine–turkey oak woods or occasionally in xeric oak hammocks. Campbell and Christman (1982) reported that they are more abundant in early successional stages in pine scrub than in the advanced stages with a full pine canopy, dense evergreen shrub layer, and matted ground cover. The short–tailed snake's principal food, *Tantilla relicta*, is also plentiful in such habitats.

Behavior: The habits of this snake are poorly known, and few specimens reside in museum collections. Apparently it spends most of its life burrowed beneath sandy soil. Woolfenden (1962) reported that they enter the sand by pressing the nose against it and moving the head up and down. Once buried they use lateral undulations of the body to move through the sand.

Specimens have been taken between 25 January (Carr, 1934) and 19 November (Highton, 1956); however, *Stilosoma* is probably active all year, weather permitting. Ashton and Ashton (1981) reported they are sometimes found in late fall under objects or leaf litter. On a daily basis, most activity is nocturnal.

Reproduction: *Stilosoma* is apparently oviparous (Wright and Wright, 1957), but the eggs have not been described. Most likely they are laid in underground burrows. Juvenile museum specimens resemble the adults in pattern and coloration.

Food And Feeding: *Stilosoma* is predominantly a snake eater, and its chief prey seems to be *Tantilla relicta*. Ditmars (1939) reported his captives ate brown snakes, *Storeria dekayi*, but refused small lizards and newborn mice, and in feeding trials conducted by Mushinsky (1984) a *Stilosoma* ingested *Tantilla relicta* but avoided five lizards and three other Florida snake species. In contrast, Allen and Neill (1953) reported it eats lizards as well as snakes, and Ashton and Ashton (1981) stated captives will occasionally devour ground skinks.

Prey may be constricted first if active and struggling, or may be seized near the head and quickly swallowed if small and weak. Mushinsky (1984) has shown that its constricting ability is limited, may take considerable time (over two

STILOSOMA EXTENUATUM

Short–tailed Snake

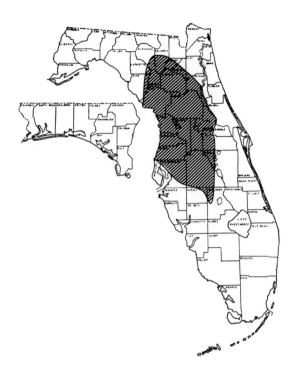

Map

hours), and that the *Tantilla* may escape. *Stilosoma* used the anterior third of its body to wrap three coils around the *Tantilla* and then stretched it between the coils and its more anterior bite. It then worked its mouth anteriorly as the *Tantilla* was pulled posteriorly by the coils. This is very similar to the boid–pattern of constriction described by Greene and Burghardt (1978).

Predators And Defense: Short–tailed snakes have been found in the stomachs of coral snakes, *Micrurus fulvius*. *Stilosoma* are very nervous when first caught, thrashing around, vibrating their tails and often biting viciously.

Remarks: The status of *S. extenuatum* has not been determined adequately. Some consider it threatened, but it may be more common than its secretive habits reveal.

Fig. 42. *Stilosoma extenuatum* is usually underground.

CLONOPHIS KIRTLANDII

Kirtland's Snake

CLONOPHIS KIRTLANDII (Kennicott, 1856)
Kirtland's Snake

Recognition: This poorly known species is a small (to 62.2 cm), stout snake with a red venter bearing a row of black rounded spots on each side. The back and sides are gray–brown to reddish–brown with four alternating, longitudinal rows of black or dark brown, rounded blotches which may be lighter posteriorly, or indistinct in some individuals. The head is olive, brown or black, and may contain some light mottling; the dark pigment extends ventrally onto the most posterior supralabial, other labials, chin and throat are cream to yellow. In appearance, the head is barely wider than the neck. The body scales are keeled, overlapping, and each bears two faint apical pits (which may be absent). There are usually 19 (17–21) scale rows anteriorly and 17 at mid–body where the fourth lateral row on each side is dropped between ventrals 71–96. A further reduction in scale rows to 14–16 may occur just anterior to the anus. The anal plate is divided. Laterally on the head are a loreal, 1(2) preocular, 2(1–3) postoculars, 1 + 2 temporals, 6(4–7) supralabials, and 7(6–9) infralabials. The hemipenis is distally bilobed with smooth saccular tips, and a simple sulcus spermaticus that ends in the depression between the lobes. Most of the surface of the lobes is covered with small spines, but two at the base are large and hooked and the apical surface is nude. There are 19–21 maxillary teeth; those most posterior are slightly enlarged.

Adult females have total body lengths to 62.2 cm, short tails (19–24% of total body length), 123–137 ventrals, and 44–61 pairs of subcaudals; males grow to 33 cm, have longer tails (22–28% of total body length), 121–135 ventrals, and 56–69 pairs of subcaudals.

Karyotype: Unknown.

Distribution: Kirtland's snake ranges from central western Pennsylvania westward through Ohio, Indiana, southern Michigan, northcentral Kentucky and central Illinois to southeastern Wisconsin and northeastern Missouri.

Geographic Variation: No subspecies are recognized.

Confusing Species: *Regina septemvittata* has a yellowish or cream–colored belly with 4 longitudinal dark stripes. *Storeria occipitomaculata* has no dark spots at the sides of its belly.

Habitat: Although not as aquatic as many North American natricine species, *Clonophis* seems to require open damp habitats such as the edges of marshes, creeks and canals, wet pastures and fields. Minton (1972) reported that in Indiana they are usually found in open grassy areas with few trees, clay soil that is quite dry in summer, some water (a sluggish creek, pond or ditch), and earthworms. Some of the best known populations are from metropolitan areas, such as Toledo and Cincinnati (Conant, 1951), Cook County, Illinois (Smith, 1961), Indianapolis (Minton, 1972) and Louisville (Barbour, 1971). Minton (1972) captured one individual three times in one year at virtually the same spot, indicating these snakes have favorite refuges within their home ranges.

Behavior: Although they have been collected in all months of the year, *Clonophis* are most active in the spring, April and May, and fall, October (Conant, 1938, 1943b; Minton, 1972). In Toledo, Ohio, 43% of those caught were taken in April and 18% in May (Conant, 1943b). Conant (1943b) found males more numerous in the spring, but the majority caught in July and August were females. Most *Clonophis* emerge from hibernation in late March or April and enter hibernation in late October or early November. Some, at least, spend the winter buried in the soil (Conant, 1943b). Many also use crayfish burrows for hibernation, estivation, and cover.

Most activity is at night, especially during the summer; the days are spent under some sheltering debris, such as a log, pile of leaves, or rock.

Reproduction: Mating pairs have been found on 1 May in Indiana (Minton, 1972), and 10 and 14 May in Illinois (Smith, 1961). Minton (1972) reported the snakes were tightly intertwined and remained together after being placed in the collecting bag. Females 36 to 47 cm produced young in Ohio (Conant, 1951), and females probably become sexually mature at a total length of about 30 cm, while the shorter males may attain maturity at about 23 cm total length.

CLONOPHIS KIRTLANDII

Kirtland's Snake

Map

Fig. 43. Venter of *Clonophis kirtlandii.*

Nothing is known of the sexual cycles in this species, but gestating females have been found in July and August (Conant, 1943b).

Dates of parturition in this viviparous snake extend from 30 July (Minton, 1972) to 24 September (Conant, 1943b), with 4 (Conant, 1943b) to 15 (Tucker, 1976) young comprising a litter. It is not known whether females produce more than one litter a year. Tucker (1976) observed the birth of 7 of 15 young from a 48.5 cm female. The first five were born at approximately two minute intervals. Three left their chorions within one minute of birth, but two failed to break out of their chorions on their first attempts but were successful on their second attempt after a 12 minute quiescent period. The births of the last two young were protracted, taking about five minutes each. All shed their skins within 24 hours. During parturition the female remained unconcealed and crawled slowly about the cage; as each fetus was slowly pushed toward the vent, a distinct bulge was visible at the posterior end of the the female's body.

New born young are 110–168 mm in total length, and weigh 1.2–1.4 g. A plot of data on young per litter and embryo counts from females of known size taken from Conant (1943b) and Tucker (1976) suggests a positive correlation. Minton (1972) described the young as being much darker than the adults, and having indistinct dorsal blotches and deeper red venters.

Growth: Minton (1972) found that a wild *Clonophis* which measured 175 mm on 16 August had grown to 215 mm by 6 June of the following year. Another measured 195 mm when captured on 12 April, 250 mm when recaptured on 23 June, and 350 mm on 22 September of the same year.

Food And Feeding: In the wild, *Clonophis* are known to eat earthworms and slugs (Conant, 1943b; Minton, 1972); earthworms, slugs, chopped fish and the sympatric terrestrial leech, *Haemopsis terrestris,* have been eaten by captives (Conant, 1943b; Minton, 1972; Tucker, 1977). However, neither Conant (1943b) nor Tucker (1977) could induce captives to eat small frogs, toads or salamanders.

Predators And Defense: A black kingsnake, *Lampropeltis g. niger,* found in Indiana, had eaten a *Clonophis* (Minton, 1972). Probably predatory mammals and some birds also eat this snake. When first discovered, *Clonophis* often flattens its body and becomes rigid. If further disturbed it may strike, bite, and chew if handled.

Populations: Kirtland's snake may be very common in some areas; Minton (1972) found 19 in two mild days following rain along a 0.6 km section of an Indianapolis street.

The sex ratios of the 264 *C. kirtlandii* examined by Conant (1943b) were 1:1 in 84 new–born young (42 of each sex) and 0.86:1 (84 males, 96 females) in the adults.

Remarks: Rossman (1963a) studied the osteology of this species and recognized it as a separate genus. His studies also suggested a possible relationship to the genus *Storeria*; Varkey (1979) also found that *Clonophis* shared several cranial muscle characters with *Storeria*. However, Rossman et al. (1982) found *Clonophis* to be most similar to *Tropidoclonion* in relative size and placement of their internal organs.

Clonophis kirtlandii is a typical snake of the Prairie Peninsula where it has survived as a relict (Conant, 1943b). With the increasing loss of natural prairie, and the destruction of habitat due to the spread of our cities, this snake is in danger of extirpation over much of its range. Barbour remembers when they were much more common in Kentucky than at present.

NERODIA CYCLOPION

Green Water Snake

NERODIA CYCLOPION (Dumeril, Bibron, and Dumeril, 1854)
Green Water Snake

Recognition: This heavy-bodied olive to brown water snake (to 127 cm) has much dark spotting on the posterior venter, and a series of subocular scales between the eye and the supralabials. Faint dark transverse bars cross the back, and grayish spots or half-moons occur on the cream to yellow venter. The keeled, doubly pitted body scales are in 25-33 rows anteriorly and 19-21 rows near the vent; there are 136-148 ventral scutes. The anal plate is divided. On each side of the head are a divided nasal, a loreal, 1-2 preoculars, 1-2 suboculars, 2 postoculars, 1 + 2-3 temporals, 7-9 (usually 8) supralabials, and 9-13 infralabials. The hemipenis has an undivided sulcus spermaticus, numerous spicules, only a few spines, and enlarged basal hooks. Twenty or 21 teeth occur on the maxilla; the posterior are elongate.

Females grow larger and heavier than males, have 57-75 subcaudals, and tail lengths 20-25% of the total body length. Males have 64-78 subcaudals and tails 22-26% of total body length.

Karyotype: The karyotype is composed of 18 pairs of diploid macrochromosomes; pairs 1-3 and 5-6 are submetacentric, pair 4 is metacentric (Eberle, 1972).

Distribution: The range of *N. cyclopion* extends southward from extreme southwestern Illinois through the Mississippi Valley to the Gulf Coast, then west to southeastern Texas and east to Mobile Bay, Alabama.

Geographic Variation: *Nerodia floridana* was originally described as a subspecies of *N. cyclopion* (Goff, 1936); however, because the geographic ranges of these two snakes are essentially allopatric, and they differ in both habitat and food preferences, as well as having basic differences in scalation and ventral patterns, we feel that they should be treated as separate species. This arrangement is also used by Lawson (1982). Cooper (1977) has reported an apparent hybrid from Baldwin County, Alabama where the ranges of the two snakes meet.

Confusing Species: *Nerodia floridana* has the ventral pattern only near the vent and on the tail; all other *Nerodia* lack subocular scales. *Agkistrodon piscivorus* has light facial markings, facial pits, elliptical pupils, an undivided anal plate, and a single row of subcaudals.

Habitat: It prefers quiet waters in wooded habitats such as tree-lined swamps, shallow lakes, marshes, sloughs, oxbows, bayous, and sluggish streams. Along the Gulf Coast it enters brackish zones (Guidry, 1953).

Behavior: Mushinsky et al. (1980) found *N. cyclopion* to be the only *Nerodia* active in all months of the year in a swamp-bayou system in southern Louisiana. In more northerly localities they are forced to hibernate during the winter and are probably only active from late March or April to October or early November. In Illinois, they leave the water in September and October to overwinter in adjacent bluffs, returning in the spring (Garton et al., 1970). They probably also utilize rodent bank burrows, muskrat and beaver lodges, and such sites as earth or rock dams as hibernacula.

The green water snake is most active during the day in the spring and fall, spending much time basking on emergent objects or along the bank. We have not seen them in low bushes, but they use such sites to bask in the cold months (November-March) (Mushinsky et al., 1980). Summer foraging usually occurs in the early morning or at night but in the spring and fall most hunting is diurnal.

Mushinsky et al. (1980) found that in Louisiana *N. cyclopion* make seasonal adjustments of their daily activity periods and arboreal tendencies to maintain a fairly uniform body temperature. Average yearly cloacal temperatures over a three year period ranged from 26.1-28.9 C.

Reproduction: Mating occurs in April. Meade (1934a) reported that in his captives mating invariably occurred out of the water, but Kofron (1979a) observed wild *N. cyclopion* mating in the water. Females probably exude pheromones which attract males, and several males may court one female. Courtship apparently occurs in the water. Tinkle and Liner (1955) saw 9 *N. cyclopion* swimming back and forth, occasionally nudging one another, in a Louisiana slough. The snakes were oblivious to the presence of humans, and were easily approached and captured. They did not sex the snakes, but thought on the basis of body size that they were all males; however, females may have been involved. Carpenter and Ferguson (1977) reported that during courtship *N. cyclopion* may sway the head and anterior neck region forward and backward in a raised position, and that the male prods or nudges the female with his head. Meade (1934a) stated that during mating the female lies in a rather extended position with the male above in sinuous curves. Coupling may continue for several hours. Kofron (1979a) found a mated pair swirling around in the shallow water of a tidal pool. The female left the pool dragging the joined male. She was killed and the joined pair were placed in a cloth sack; 75 minutes later the male was still attached to her. Kofron thought that the male was unable to disengage his spined hemipenis from the female's cloaca.

The smallest mature female of 31 from Louisiana examined by Kofron (1979a) was 63.7 cm snout–vent length. The largest ovarian follicle in this specimen was 9.7 mm; follicles in other females collected in April were 10.3–39.7 mm. During January and February females had 10–20 mm follicles. Vitellogenesis began in late March, and during April and May, follicles were 20–46 mm in diameter. Embryos were first found in late May and early June. By 25 July, one female was postpartum, containing 11 corpora lutea. Kofron found evidence of transcoelomic migration of ova in one female. Ovulation occurred from late April through June and the young were born from late July through September; Kofron reported the gestation period to be 3 months or less and that the female reproductive cycle occurs annually. Barbour (1971) thought that the gestation period in Kentucky was about 4 months; possibly cooler temperatures there somewhat retard development.

Placentation occurs in *N. cyclopion*, and Conway and Fleming (1960) reported the placental transmission of ions from mother to young.

Litters consist of 9–19 young; larger females seem to produce more young (Kofron, 1979a). Newly born young are usually 250–270 mm in total length.

Growth: Tinkle (1959) reported a pregnant 75 cm female grew to 76.5 cm snout–vent length between 10 April and 6 June.

Food And Feeding: Fish seem to be the preferred food. Clark (1949) found only fish in the 8 stomachs he examined. Mushinsky and Hebrard (1977a) reported that fish made up 98.4% and amphibians only 1.6% of the total volume of food in their 83 specimens, and 94% of the identifiable food remains from stomachs examined by Kofron (1978) were fish (crayfish 3%, amphibians 2%).

Map

Fig. 44. *Nerodia cyclopion.*

Green Water Snake

Some of the fish identified by Kofron were tidal species. Adult frogs and toads, and tadpoles are occasionally eaten, and Garton et al. (1970) and Kofron (1978) found a siren and an amphiuma in stomachs.

We have seen *N. cyclopion* actively pursue and capture small fishes and suspect that this is their normal feeding behavior. Evans (1942) reported that this snake will swim through the water with its mouth open while foraging, but we have not observed such behavior. They will eat fish carrion, and in this way help clean up waterways.

Although green water snakes eat fish throughout their lives, with maturity and increased body size they change portions of their diet to include more centrarchid fish.

Predators And Defense: Adults are preyed on by cottonmouths, alligators, and possibly by large aquatic birds (anhingas, herons, cormorants), and carnivorous mammals, but humans are the worst enemy, destroying many each year in the mistaken belief that they are cottonmouths. The young fall prey to all classes of vertebrates.

The several individuals of *N. cyclopion* we have handled all had nasty dispositions and would bite at the least provocation. They also frequently sprayed musk and cloacal contents. Tongue flicking occurs during defensive behavior, and Scudder and Burghardt (1983) reported a tongue–flick rate significantly higher in this snake than that of *N. rhombifera* and *N. fasciata* during trials; *N. cyclopion* was significantly more reactive, and males were more aggressive than females.

Populations: Mushinsky and Hebrard (1977b) reported that of 478 snakes in their Louisiana 3 km study area, *N. cyclopion* was the most abundant (32.2%), and that they were especially abundant during the summer months. However, in northeastern Arkansas *N. cyclopion* only comprised 0.8% (4) of the 477 *Nerodia* collected by Hanebrink and Byrd (1986). They attributed its rareness to marginal habitat and the presence of the cottonmouth, *Agkistrodon piscivorus*, a major predator.

The sex ratio of a litter born in Illinois was 8 males and 4 females, and another female carried 8 male and 6 female embryos (Garton et al., 1970).

Remarks: North American water snakes that belong to the genus *Nerodia* were formerly assigned to the genus *Natrix*, along with certain Old World snakes. Rossman and Eberle (1977) demonstrated major differences in the blood proteins, chromosomes, scalation, cranial morphology and hemipenes of the New and Old World species. They reserve the name *Natrix* for the European species while proposing the names *Sinonatrix* and *Afronatrix* for the Asian and African genera. *Nerodia* Baird and Girard, 1853 was revived for the North American snakes.

NERODIA FLORIDANA

Florida Green Water Snake

NERODIA FLORIDANA (Goff, 1936)
Florida Green Water Snake

Recognition: It is similar to *Nerodia cyclopion* in having the eye separated from the supralabials by a series of subocular scales. However, *N. floridana* has a plain whitish to cream–colored venter, except near the vent and under the tail where spots or half–moon shaped marks occur. It is a large snake (to 188 cm), with a brownish to olive–green dorsum and up to 57 lateral bars. Body scale rows occur in 29–33 rows, anteriorly, but only 21–23 near the vent. There are 7–8 supralabials, 11–14 infralabials, 130–142 ventrals, and 63–84 subcaudals; the anal plate is divided. Each maxilla has 20–21 teeth.

Males have tails 25–30% of the total body length; females have tails 20–23% of the total body length.

Karyotype: Presumably 18 diploid pairs of chromosomes in the same proportions and arrangements as those in *N. cyclopion*.

Fossils: Pleistocene, (Rancholabrean) remains have been found in Florida (Auffenberg, 1963).

Distribution: *N. floridana* ranges from southern South Carolina southward through peninsular Florida and west through southern Georgia and the panhandle of Florida to Baldwin County, Alabama.

Geographic Variation: Unknown.

Confusing Species: *Nerodia cyclopion* has a heavily spotted venter; all other *Nerodia* lack subocular scales. Cottonmouths, *Agkistrodon piscivorus*, have light facial markings, facial pits, vertical–slit pupils, an undivided anal plate, and a single row of subcaudals.

Habitat: *N. floridana* is a denizen of the quiet waters in lakes, ponds, swamps, and sloughs. It occasionally enters brackish waters, and also uses muskrat lodges as dens.

Behavior: Surprisingly, little of its behavior has reached literature. Active individuals have been seen in Florida in all months, but even there it may be forced to become dormant during severe cold weather and farther north it hibernates during the winter.

It spends much of the daylight hours basking, most foraging is done either nocturnally, at twilight, or during the morning.

Reproduction: Courtship and mating occur in the spring; however, there is no published description. Seven to 101 young are born in the summer, during June to early August (Telford, 1948; Wright and Wright, 1956). Betz (1963) observed the birth process: "The young were delivered approximately 2.5 minutes apart. . . most of the young were delivered with the chorioallantoic membranes intact and had managed to free themselves within 10 minutes after birth. They repeatedly opened their mouths widely in an apparent attempt to clear glotal openings of amniotic fluid, after which they began to breathe immediately." The average total body length of 204 newborn young was 247 mm (Conant and Downs, 1940; Duellman and Schwartz, 1958; Betz, 1963). Betz (1963) showed there is a positive correlation between body length or weight of the female and the number, length or weight of the young.

Van Hyning (1931) reported that two female *N. floridana*, which gave birth in captivity, devoured a large number of their young; however, such behavior is probably rare in nature.

Food And Feeding: Frogs and fish are the preferred prey, but Ashton and Ashton (1981) reported that in the wild they also eat salamanders, tadpoles, small turtles, and invertebrates. Van Hyning (1932) examined 75 stomachs of *N. floridana*, and found 66% of the food consisted of frogs, which were found in 10 stomachs. Fish were found in 4 snakes (26% of the bulk), and one stomach contained a salamander (8% of the bulk).

Predators And Defense: Adults are eaten by alligators and cottonmouths, and the young are preyed on by a variety of large fish, snakes, alligators, predatory birds, and mammals. The greatest losses, however, come from humans who destroy the habitat or kill them outright. In the past, the indiscriminate use of insecticides probably resulted in the deaths of many individuals. Herald (1949) reported that captives sprayed directly with DDT developed paralysis and died within 4 days, and that several *N. floridana* died after their pond was sprayed.

NERODIA FLORIDANA

Florida Green Water Snake

Map

One should be wary when handling these snakes. They are large, vile tempered, have long teeth, and do not hesitate to bite. The resulting wounds may be deep and painful slashes. They also frequently defecate or spray musk on their captor; generally speaking, they are rather obnoxious.

NERODIA FASCIATA

Southern Water Snake

NERODIA FASCIATA (Linnaeus, 1766)
Southern Water Snake

Recognition: This is one of the most variable of North American snakes; much variation occurs even within individual subspecies (see **Geographic Variation**). It is a medium–sized snake (to 159 cm) with a body color ranging from gray, olive, or black to yellow or brick red; body pattern may be nonexistent or consist of light or dark transverse bars, or of longitudinal stripes. The supralabials usually have dark bars, and a dark stripe may extend from the eye to the corner of the mouth. The yellow venter is variously marked with dark spotting, half–moons, or longitudinal stripes. To make matters worse, older individuals become progressively more melanistic. The body scales are doubly pitted, strongly keeled, and occur in 21–23 rows anteriorly, 21–27 rows at midbody, and 17–19 rows near the anus; the anal plate is divided. Pertinent lateral head scalation includes a loreal, 1(2) preocular, 2(3) postoculars, 8(7–9) supralabials, and 10(9–11) infralabials. There are 110–143 ventrals with no sexual dimorphism; subcaudals total 50–88 in males and 52–76 in females. The hemipenis has few spines, but many spicules and several enlarged basal hooks; the sulcus spermaticus is single and undivided. Each maxilla has 22–23 teeth.

Males have tails 24–32% of the total body length, females 19–28%.

Karyotype: *N. fasciata* has a diploid chromosome number of 36, consisting of 18 pairs of macrochromosomes (pairs 1–3, 5, 6 submetacentric, pair 4 metacentric). Sex determination is ZZ/ZW, both Z and W are submetacentric (Eberle, 1972; Kilpatrick and Zimmerman, 1973).

Fossil Record: Holman (1981) lists *N. fasciata* as having been identified from the Pleistocene (Rancholabrean).

Distribution: *N. fasciata* ranges from Albermarle Sound, North Carolina south on the Atlan-

tic coastal plain to the Florida Keys and northern Cuba, west along the Gulf Coast to southern Texas, and south from southern Illinois to the Gulf Coast and southern Oklahoma and central Texas.

Geographic Variation: Six subspecies are known. *Nerodia fasciata fasciata* (Linnaeus, 1766), the banded water snake, ranges southward mostly on the coastal plain, from Albemarle Sound, North Carolina to northern Florida and west to Mobile Bay, Alabama. It has dark, often black–bordered, dorsal transverse bands, a dark stripe extending backward from the eye to the corner of the mouth, and dark rectangular–shaped spots along the sides of the venter. *N. f. clarki* (Baird and Girard, 1853), the Gulf salt marsh snake, ranges along the Gulf Coast from Citrus County, Florida west to southern Texas. It is distinguished by its two dark brown and two tan or yellow longitudinal stripes on each side of the body, and a belly pattern of a medial row of white or yellow spots on a reddish–brown to brown ground color (some individuals may have an additional row of small light spots on each side). *N. f. compressicauda* Kennicott, 1860, the mangrove salt marsh snake, occurs along the coast of Florida from Palm Beach County west to Hernando County, on the Florida Keys, and on the northern coast of Cuba. It is quite diverse in both general coloration and pattern. The ground color ranges from gray, olive or black to yellowish–red; and some individuals are unpatterned while others may have dark dorsal spots to transverse bands. *N. f. taeniata* (Cope, 1895), the Atlantic salt marsh snake, is only found along the Atlantic Coast of Florida from Volusia County south to Martin County. It has dark lateral stripes on the anterior portion of its body, dark blotches posteriorly, and a single medial row of light spots on the venter. *N. f. pictiventris* (Cope, 1895), the Florida water snake, ranges from southeastern Georgia south through peninsular Florida to Dade and Monroe counties. It has dark tranverse dorsal bands, dark lateral spots between the bands, a dark stripe from the eye to the corner of the mouth, and wavy reddish–brown transverse lines on the venter. *N. f. confluens* (Blanchard, 1923a), the broad–banded water snake, occurs from southern Illinois, adjacent Kentucky and southeastern Missouri south in the Mississippi Valley to the Gulf Coast in Mississippi and Louisiana, and west through eastern and central Arkansas to southeastern Oklahoma and central Texas. It has the dark transverse dorsal bands so wide that only 11–17 occur on the body (other *Nerodia* have 19 or more bands), a dark stripe from the eye to the corner of the mouth, and large rectangular reddish–brown spots on the sides of the venter.

Southern Water Snake

The taxonomic history of these subspecies has been confusing. They have previously been considered as, at first, separate individual species, later as subspecies of *Nerodia sipedon* (Clay, 1938), and at present as subspecies of *N. fasciata*. Some certainly resemble *N. sipedon*, but others are so divergent as to almost defy proper placement. In 1963, Conant presented evidence for separating *N. f. fasciata*, *N. f. confluens* and *N. f. pictiventris* from *N. sipedon*, and this has generally been accepted, although Schwaner and Mount (1976) and Blaney and Blaney (1979) reported evidence of conspecificity in Alabama, Mississippi and southeastern Louisiana. Conant (1963) also tentatively included the forms *clarki*, *compressicauda* and *taeniata* in *N. fasciata*, pending additional study, which has not occurred. Adding to the confusion is the fact that the thermal environment may affect the development of meristic characters in embryos (Osgood, 1978) of the freshwater forms, while the degree of salinity possibly may also affect pattern development.

Dunson (1979) has relegated *N. f. taeniata* to the synonymy of *N. f. compressicauda* because neither coloration nor scale characters could be used unequivocally as diagnostic characters where their ranges meet. A survey of salt marsh snakes from Brevard and Indian River counties by Hebrard and Lee (1981) also showed characters of both forms present, thus supporting Dunson.

Given the uncertain taxonmic validity of some forms of *N. fasciata*, and its supposed hybridization with *N. sipedon* at several localities, we feel a complete study of the status and relationships of all color and pattern forms across the range is desired.

Confusing Species: *Nerodia sipedon* usually lacks the dark stripe from the eye to the corner of the mouth, has dark transverse dorsal bands only on the anterior portion of the body, and has reddish–brown half–moons on the venter. Cottonmouths, *Agkistrodon piscivorus*, have elliptical pupils, a pit between the nostril and eye, and a single row of subcaudals. Snakes of the genus *Regina* have no more than 19 scale rows on the bodies. Garter and ribbon snakes, *Thamnophis*, have an undivided anal plate and only one light stripe on each side of the body.

Habitat: The subspecies of *N. fasciata* can be divided into two groups in regard to their salinity preferences. The races *fasciata*, *confluens* and *pictiventris*, while they may spend some time in brackish habitats, are primarily freshwater snakes over most of their ranges. Conversely, *clarki*, *compressicauda*, and *taeniata* are salt marsh snakes that apparently require at least brackish waters but may occasionally enter freshwater. The freshwater races can be found in the shallow

Map

Fig. 45. *Nerodia fasciata compressicauda* (Barry Mansell).

parts of rivers, streams, lakes, swamps, marshes, ponds, sloughs, and oxbows; they also frequently inhabit the burrows of crayfish and muskrats. The salt–loving forms occupy salt marshes, mangrove swamps and estuaries.

Pettus (1958, 1963) studied the water relations of *N. f. clarki* and *N. f. confluens*, and found that individuals of both subspecies preferred freshwater to sea water when only given a choice between the two. He concluded that *clarki* maintains water balance through utilization of preformed water from the body of its prey plus water derived from oxidative metabolism. Also, *clarki* will not drink sea water, whereas *confluens* will and consequently dies. Since the skin of both is relatively impermeable, and their kidney structure is similar, Pettus felt that because *confluens* will drink the water it is restricted to freshwater habitats, while the undrinking *clarki* can occupy salt marshes.

Similarly, Zug and Dunson (1979) found that *N. f. pictiventris* and *N. f. compressicauda* also preferred freshwater to sea water. At 15% sea water, *compressicauda* still preferred freshwater, but *pictiventris* showed a slight preference for the sea water. At 10% sea water, *compressicauda* again preferred freshwater, but *pictiventris* showed no preference for either salinity. Previously, Dunson (1978) had found that when *pictiventris* was placed in sea water, it lost weight but gained sodium (probably by drinking) and died. When kept in air (at 30 C) pumped at 300 ml/min, *compressicauda* lost weight; individuals weighing initially 55, 69, and 152 g, respectively, lost 0.55, 0.35, and 0.21% mass/day (Dunson, 1982). Dunson (1980) conducted experiments to determine the relation of sodium and water balance to survival in *N. f. clarki*, *N. f. compressicauda* and *N. f. pictiventris*. When placed in sea water, *pictiventris* had a higher body water influx and efflux, a higher body sodium influx, and its skin was more permeable to water and sodium than either that of *clarki* or *compressicauda*. The high influx of sodium was probably caused by the drinking of the sea water. The distinction between the freshwater race and the two brackish water races is more physiological than previously believed. Dunson also found that intergrades between *pictiventris* and *compressicauda* had sea water tolerances like that of *compressicauda*. Dunson concluded that *clarki* and *compressicauda* are in the process of evolving into true marine species.

Behavior: In our experience in Florida and North Carolina, *N. fasciata* is mostly nocturnal; in fact, some of the salt marsh forms can seldom be found during the day (Swanson, 1948). Daylight hours are spent under cover or in basking either

Fig. 46. Venter of *Nerodia fasciata pictiventris* (Christopher W. Brown).

on the banks or on branches overhanging the water. They begin foraging as darkness approaches, and can often be found crossing roads at night. Osgood (1970) has reported a similar daily cycle. In contrast to our observations, Mushinsky and Hebrard (1977b) found that in Louisiana they were mostly diurnal, but became nocturnal in September (possibly in response to other water snakes becoming more diurnal at that time of year).

The salt marsh individuals may be active in every month, especially those from Florida. However, the freshwater races seem more affected by cold temperatures, and may become dormant over the winter. In Kentucky, they emerge from hibernation in March or April and become dormant in late October or November. Tinkle (1959) reported that they became active in late February in a Louisiana swamp, and disappeared in early December, and Mushinsky and Hebrard (1977b) found a similar annual cycle in their Louisiana *N. fasciata*.

N. fasciata has been found hibernating beneath logs or rocks in swampy areas in Georgia (Neill, 1948a), and Kofron (1978) reported that during cold weather they could be collected from under debris which was always near water. However, most probably spend the winter underwater or in crayfish or muskrat burrows.

In a telemetric study, Osgood (1970) showed that the body temperature of *N. fasciata* remained close to that of the water but varied during the day, depending upon the amount of direct sunlight on the holding cage. When at 1400 hrs the snake left the water to bask, its body temperature increased to 26–29 C. In the field, Osgood found the general pattern of body temperature in gravid females was one of warming in the morning when the sun appeared, then maintenance of a body temperature at about 26–31 C as long as possible in the afternoon. When the air temperature fell lower than that of the water, the snakes slid back into the water, thus slowing the drop in their body temperature. The minimum and maximum body temperatures recorded in the field for active *N. fasciata* by Osgood were 21.5 and 32.0 C, respectively. Semlitsch (1979) has reported that the rate of ecdysis is increased at higher temperatures.

Only a few observations on the movements of *N. fasciata* have been published. Tinkle (1959) found a dead individual in the same quadrat in which it had been marked four days earlier, and Phillips (1939) recovered an *N. f. compressicauda* a year later about 0.47 km from where it had been released. Holman and Hill (1961) observed a mass unidirectional south–southwest movement in 107 of 108 *N. f. pictiventris* across a Florida road between 1945 and 2215 hrs, 2 June 1961, and 21 of 22 individuals on 3 June between 2017 and 2110 hrs. They felt these movements were associated with a general drought in the area.

N. fasciata is a good swimmer and is capable of remaining underwater for extended periods of time. Jacob and McDonald (1976) recorded a maximum period of voluntary submergence of 24 minutes. They also found that *N. fasciata* exhibited classic bradycardia when allowed to submerge voluntarily, supressing the heart rate from an average of 33.2 beats/minute when surfaced to an average of only 6.77 beats/minute when submerged. Belkin (1968) studied the ability to tolerate the lack of oxygen by *N. fasciata*, and found its tolerance less than that of two turtles.

Reproduction: The smallest sexually mature female and male *N. f. confluens* from Louisiana examined by Tinkle (1959) were 58 and 52 cm in snout–vent length. In South Carolina, female *N. f. fasciata* contained enlarged follicles at snout–vent lengths of 45 cm or more (Semlitsch and Gibbons, 1982). A 41.5 cm male was immature.

Little has been published on the sexual cycles of this snake. Tinkle (1959) reported that a female dissected on 10 April had 11 preovulatory follicles greater than 12 mm in length, and another examined on 24 April contained 27 follicles greater than 16 mm in length. He recorded the first pregnant females on 1 May, and by 27 June embryos had scales and color patterns. A male dissected by Tinkle on 6 June had active sperm in its testes.

The breeding season may vary with locality and subspecies. Swanson (1948) thought the mating season in *N. f. compressicauda* living near Key West, Florida was between 24 January and 22 February, and Ashton and Ashton (1981) felt that the overall mating season for *N. fasciata* in Florida may extend from autumn to early spring. Meade (1934a) observed mating in *N. f. confluens* in April, and Anderson (1965) observed two males of this race attempt to mate with the same female at Reelfoot Lake, Tennessee, on 16 April.

Swanson (1948) reported the following courtship and mating behavior in *N. f. compressicauda*:

> ..the male approached a female and followed her body with his snout until his head covered hers. His head, and often parts of his body, would twitch in erratic little jerks, whether or not he was in contact with the female. When actually in contact, this jerking motion had the effect of a rubbing motion. After such preliminary activity, the remaining effort was made by the tail and the posterior portion of the body. At this stage, the heads were sometimes far apart, and the anterior portions of the bodies often not even parallel. The male thrust a U–shaped loop of the tail beneath the posterior portion of the female in an apparent effort to locate the cloaca. The bodies of the snakes were always in a normal position insomuch as the dorsal surfaces of both were always uppermost, with the exception of a very small part of the posterior part of the male that was being used in an exploratory effort to locate the female's cloaca.

Tinkle and Liner (1955) and Tinkle (1959) observed aggregate swimming bouts that may have been associated with reproduction. The snakes appeared to be males, and they swam back and forth across ponds, coming at frequent intervals to the shoreline with continual tongue flicking. At times one snake would approach another, hesitate briefly beside it, and then move away in a diagonal course to continue swimming. The snakes were unwary and easily approached, displaying curiosity to disturbances. Copulation observed by Meade (1934a) had the female laying in a rather extended position with the male above in sinuous curves.

The young develop in the female and are nourished through a placenta. The gestation period is about four months (Meade, 1934a). Osgood (1970) reported the embryos cannot tolerate constant temperatures outside the 21–30 C range for the entire gestation period. Short periods beyond those mentioned probably can be tolerated, except during critical periods of development.

Birth usually occurs in the summer from mid-July to mid-September, but Guidry (1953) reported a brood of 22 born on 20 October and Iverson (1978) reported another of 14 was born on 23 November. There is apparently a direct correlation between the body length of the female and the potential number of offspring she can produce at one time (Tinkle, 1959; Semlitsch and Gibbons, 1982). A survey of 35 broods in the literature gave a range of 2–57 young with an average brood size of 18–19 young. The larger freshwater subspecies may produce from 30 to over 50 young, while the shorter salt marsh races have usually less than 20 young per brood.

The young are colored and patterned like the adults, but the patterns are usually more pronounced. Total body length varies from 140 to 255 mm, but again there is a correlation of the neonate body length to that of the mother. The smaller salt marsh subspecies often have young shorter than 200 mm, while those of the larger freshwater races are usually longer than 200 mm.

Food And Feeding: The shorter salt marsh snakes feed on small fish (*Fundulus, Poecilia*) and small crabs. In the United States they have little chance to capture frogs, but Neill (1965) found a Cuban *N. f. compressicauda* which disgorged a small bullfrog. The larger freshwater subspecies take a greater variety of prey: fish (*Anguilla, Dorosoma, Elassoma, Esox, Fundulus, Gambusia, Heterandria, Ictalurus, Lepomis, Lucania, Micropterus, Notemigonus, Poecilia*); frogs and toads (*Acris, Bufo, Gastrophryne, Hyla, Pseudacris, Rana*), salamanders (*Desmognathus, Necturus, Notophthalmus, Siren*), tadpoles, small snakes and turtles, birds, worms and crayfish. Clark (1949) found 60 fish, 85 frogs, and 5 birds in the stomachs of *N. f. confluens* from Louisiana. In two other food studies on this subspecies in Louisiana, Mushinsky and Hebrard (1977a) found the following percentages of total food volume: 71.5% large fish, 13.6% frogs, 6.3% small fish, 4.9% tadpoles, 3.3% toads, and 0.3% crayfish; and Kofron (1978) recorded 10 frogs (including 2 tadpoles) from 9 snakes, and 22 fish from another snake. In Georgia, Camp et al. (1980) found fish, frogs, toads, tadpoles, and sirens in stomachs of *N. f. fasciata*. Mushinsky et al. (1982) reported that in Louisiana the major prey of *N. fasciata* changes from fish to frogs as the snakes exceed a snout–vent length of 50 cm.

Prey is located by both sight and olfaction. These snakes actively prowl about while foraging, often probing crevices and vegetation with their heads. When food is located, it is quickly seized and swallowed alive. Brown (1979a) has observed them eating dead frogs off a highway on a rainy June night in North Carolina.

Mushinsky and Lotz (1980) presented prey extracts to *N. fasciata* to test its chemoreceptive responses. Neonates gave a strong response to fish extract that remained unchanged by early dietary restrictions for their first six months. After that, their responses were more variable and could be altered by recent feeding experience, but there was a highly significant increase in responsiveness to frog extracts.

Predators And Defense: Little has been published regarding the various predators of *N. fasciata*. Cottonmouths eat them, and surely other ophiophagous snakes must take some. Birds of prey, large wading birds, predatory mammals, and large fish probably also eat them. Ernst has seen a great blue heron and an alligator eat small *N. fasciata* in Florida. Many are killed crossing highways adjacent to their waterbodies, and the draining of these waterways also causes much mortality.

When disturbed these snakes coil, flatten themselves, strike, bite visciously, and spray a pungent musk. Large individuals may deliver deep scratches, but they are not generally thought to be venomous. However, Klynstra (1959) was bitten by a large female and received a painful arm and swollen lymph nodes (possibly from a secondary bacterial infection?).

Populations: Of 477 *Nerodia* collected by Hanebrink and Byrd (1986) in northeastern Arkansas, 134 (28%) were *N. f. confluens*. It was only surpassed in the survey by *N. rhombifera* (236 individuals, 49.5%).

Sabath and Worthington (1959) found a sex ratio of 5 males to 7 females in a brood of 12 embryos.

NERODIA SIPEDON

Northern Water Snake

NERODIA SIPEDON (Linnaeus, 1758)
Northern Water Snake

Recognition: This is another extremely variable water snake. It is heavy bodied (to 144 cm), and usually tan to gray with wide brown, or reddish–brown crossbands alternating with dark squarish blotches along the sides. Its supralabials contain dark bars, and the cream to yellow venter has a pattern of reddish–brown half–moons. There is usually no dark stripe from the orbit to the corner of the mouth. Older individuals often have the dorsal and ventral patterns obscured, and may become totally brown. Also, non–banded individuals occur in several populations. The body scales are strongly keeled and doubly pitted; they occur in 21–23 rows anteriorly and at mid–body and 17–19 rows near the anus. The anal plate is divided. Lateral head scalation includes a loreal, 1(2) preoculars, 2–3 postoculars, 8(7–9) supralabials and 10(9–11) infralabials. There are 123–155 ventrals with no sexual dimorphism; males have 66–84 subcaudals, females 42–77. The hemipenis is similar to that described for *N. fasciata*. Each maxilla has 23–25 teeth.

Males have tails 23.5–29% as long as the total body length, females have tails only 20.5–25% as long.

Karyotype: *N. sipedon* has 36 macrochromosomes (28 submetacentric and 6 subtelocentric autosomes); sex determination is ZZ/ZW, each Z and W is submetacentric (Eberle, 1972; Kilpatrick and Zimmerman, 1973).

Fossil Record: Pleistocene fossils of *N. sipedon* are known from the Blancan of Kansas and Nebraska, the Irvingtonian of Kansas, Maryland and South Dakota, and the Rancholabrean of Georgia, Kansas, Missouri, Pennsylvania and Tennessee (Holman, 1981, 1986; Rogers, 1982).

Distribution: *N. sipedon* ranges from extreme southern Quebec, Maine, and southern Ontario south to the Carolinas, central Georgia, the Gulf Coast from the Florida Panhandle west to eastern Louisiana, and eastern Colorado, Oklahoma, and central Arkansas.

Geographical Variation: Four subspecies have been described. *Nerodia sipedon sipedon* (Linnaeus 1758), the northern water snake, occurs from extreme southern Quebec, coastal Maine, and southern Ontario south to northern South Carolina, Georgia and Alabama, and west to Nebraska, Kansas, eastern Colorado and northeastern Oklahoma. It has dark crossbands on the neck and forepart of the body, the dark marks wider than the light spaces between them, dark brown or reddish–brown half–moons on the venter, and the dark pattern continuing to the tip on the underside of the tail. *N. s. pleuralis* (Cope, 1892b) the midland water snake, ranges from the southern portions of Indiana, Illinois and Missouri west to eastern Oklahoma, and south to the Gulf Coast from eastern Louisiana to Escambia County, Florida, and east to Georgia and South Carolina. It has the dark markings smaller than the light spaces between them, and a double row of half–moons on the venter. Some individuals have the dark crossbands the entire length of the body. *N. s. insularum* (Conant and Clay, 1937), the Lake Erie water snake, only lives on the islands of the Put–in–Bay Archipelago, Lake Erie. It is a pale gray to olive, usually patternless snake with a cream–colored venter. If a dorsal pattern is present it is similar to that of *N. s. sipedon*, but often faded. *N. s. williamengelsi* (Conant and Lazell, 1973), the Carolina salt marsh snake, is only found on the Outer Banks of North Carolina and the adjacent mainland coasts of Pamilico and Core Sounds. It is almost completely black dorsally, and the ventral half–moons posterior to the 50th ventral are solid black.

Cliburn (1961a) doubted the validity of *N. s. insularum* due to the variation in the occurrence of body bands in the population. While many individuals totally lack any dorsal pattern, others are banded or contain faint traces of bands. Cliburn thought *insularum* only an incipient subspecies at best. However, more than 75% of the snakes in this population are readily distinguishable from *N. s. sipedon* (Conant and Clay, 1963), and there is ample evidence that the patternless or weakly patterned individuals are being favored by natural selection since banded individuals are more heavily predated by birds (Camin et al., 1954; Camin and Ehrlich, 1958; Ehrlich and Camin, 1960; Beatson, 1976; Pough, 1976). We feel that *N. s. insularum* should continue to be recognized as valid.

N. sipedon hybridizes with *N. fasciata* at several scattered areas within its range, but we believe these forms still represent valid species (see discussion under *N. fasciata*). Dessauer and Fox (1958) have found significant variation between the plasma protein patterns of *N. sipedon* from Pennsylvania and *N. fasciata* from Louisiana.

Confusing Species: *Nerodia fasciata* has a dark stripe from the eye to the corner of the mouth and crossbands along its entire length. *N. erythrogaster* has no dorsal pattern and a plain–colored venter with dark pigment only at the edges of the scutes. *Agkistrodon piscivorus* has an elliptical pupil (rounded in *Nerodia*), a pit between the nostril and eye, and a single row of scales on the underside of the tail.

Habitat: This snake can be found in any freshwater body within its range; as long as there is abundant food and cover it is satisfied. It has been taken from lakes, ponds, swamps, marshes, sloughs, oxbows, rivers, creeks, and brooks, with bottoms varying from rock or gravel to sand or mud. The race *N. s. williamengelsi* is even a salt marsh and brackish water inhabitant closely associated with the plants *Spartina* and *Juncus* (Conant and Lazell, 1973).

Behavior: Next to the garter snake, *Thamnophis sirtalis*, *N. sipedon* has the greatest literature of North American snakes. Both its behavior and ecology have been well documented.

In the North, *N. sipedon* usually emerges from hibernation in April (occasionally March) and remains active until October (occasionally early November), but in the southern parts of its range it may be sporadically active over the winter.

It is diurnal during the spring and fall, but in the summer months most foraging is done from twilight to about midnight (Diener, 1957b; Brown, 1958). Swanson (1952) has pointed out that while unquestionably nocturnal in many localities, they are decidedly diurnal in the trout streams in Pennsylvania where the water may be too cold for night activity. Fitch (1956) reported that the average body temperature of four active *N. sipedon* from Kansas was 24.5 C (16–29.5). Brattstrom (1965) recorded a temperature of 26.4 C for another individual, and Collins (1974) reported a preferred optimal temperature of near 24 C for Kansas *N. sipedon*. When given a choice of environmental temperatures in a thermal gradient, *N. sipedon* normally selected 20.8–34.7 C (x = 28.0), but chose gradients of 22.2–31.6 C (x = 28.8) after feeding and 17.2–20.4 C (x = 18.7) while undergoing ecdysis (Kitchell, 1969). Carpenter (1953a) recorded a cloacal temperature of 7 C for hibernating northern water snakes in Michigan, and Brattstrom (1965) reported a questionable critical thermal minimum of –2 C for this species.

Map

Fig. 47. *Nerodia sipedon pleuralis.*

Fig. 48. *Nerodia sipedon insularum,* unpatterned phase (Richard B. King).

Fig. 49. *Nerodia sipedon insularum,* patterned phase (Richard B. King).

When forced to hibernate, *N. sipedon* normally uses such sites as earthen dams, stone causeways, flood walls, levees, ant mounds, crayfish burrows, muskrat and beaver bank burrows and lodges, and meadow vole tunnels near its summer feeding range, but some apparently move to more upland rock crevices, hollow logs or stumps. Breckenridge (1944) found 35 *N. sipedon* in the fall moving toward hills overlooking the water.

Although *N. s. williamengelsi* habitually lives in salt marshes and at some other sites individuals of *N. sipedon* may occasionally enter brackish water, this snake does require much fresh water. When compared to various marine or estuarine races of *N. fasciata, N. sipedon* had a greater rate of water influx (Dunson, 1980). It is interesting that Bennett and Licht (1975) found that aberrant scaleless *N. sipedon* had about the same rate of pulmocutaneus and cutaneus water loss as normally scaled individuals. They concluded that reptilian scales and their associated features (thick keratin layers, superficial dermal layer) cannot be considered adaptations for curtailment of integumentary water loss.

Except for possible migrations to or from hibernacula (Breckenridge, 1944), *N. sipedon* are rather sedentary animals. Stickel and Cope (1947) recaptured an individual 2 years later only 116 m away, and Fitch (1958) recaptured four Kansas snakes which had moved maximum distances of 30 and 179 m. One juvenile was recaptured three times within a 4.6 m radius. Fitch and Shirer (1971) put radio transmitters on several *N. sipedon* and followed their movements. The snakes moved an average of 3.7 m per day. One male was found 15 times in 23 days within a space of 9 m along a pond edge, and another male remained at one site for all but one of 13 straight days. A gravid female was located 24 times in 35 days, with an 8–day interruption while she gave birth in the laboratory. She made one shift of 21 m, two of 10.5 m, and one of 9 m, but otherwise stayed in the same place or made shifts of no more than 4.5 m. Another gravid female made only short movements of 1.2–7.5 m in four days.

Fraker (1970) studied the home range and homing ability of *N. sipedon* at an Indiana fish hatchery. Those marked in the ponds tended to stay in one pond; 61% of the recaptures in small ponds were in the same pond as the previous capture, and 80% in large ponds. If an adjacent pond was included, 81% of those from small ponds were recaptured in either the original or the adjacent pond, and for large ponds this figure rose to 98%. *N. sipedon* living in a nearby stream were recaptured less often. Fraker displaced some snakes short distances (0.12 km) and long distances (0.31 km) both upstream and downstream, and about 20% of the snakes returned home. However, only larger snakes returned from 0.31 km, while shorter snakes could home from 0.12 km. Fraker thought odors may have aided the snakes' orientation, but Newcomer et al. (1974) have shown that *N. sipedon* is capable of sun compass orientation.

The water snake is a good swimmer, and is often seen crossing water with only its head above the surface. It is capable of foraging underwater and can remain submerged for long periods if disturbed. Ferguson and Thornton (1984) found it can remain underwater for over 65 minutes with no signs of stress. During this time period the snake's heart rate fell to 9% (5 beats/min) of its rest rate.

Reproduction: In Michigan, female *N. sipedon* become sexually mature at an age of 24 months and a snout–vent length of 475–630 mm (Feaver, 1976), in Missouri they mature in 2–3 years at a snout–vent length of 570–680 mm (Bauman and Metter, 1977), and on the Lake Erie Islands at 3 years and about 590 mm snout–vent length (King, 1986).

Males reach maturity when 21–24 months old at snout–vent lengths of 370–450 mm in Michigan (Feaver, 1976), and about 430 mm on Lake Erie (King, 1986).

Bauman and Metter (1977) studied the reproductive cycle of females from Missouri. Follicular growth was minimal throughout the year except for a short period prior to ovulation in which explosive growth and yolking occurred; follicular weight increased from about 0.2 g to almost 4 g between mid–May and late June. The first pregnant females were found on 22 June by Bauman and Metter; at Lake Erie, King (1986) recorded apparent pregnant females on 3 June. Aldridge (1982) found that the number of previtellogenic follicles is approximately three times larger than the number of vitellogenic follicles or embryos present. Follicles less than 5 mm in length do not appear to have a seasonal growth pattern, but larger follicles undergo marked seasonal changes. Those greater than 5 mm are absent during gestation, begin to appear after parturition, and reach a maximum length of 9 mm by hibernation. When vitellogenesis occurs in the spring, all follicles greater than 5 mm become yolked and are either ovulated or become atretic. Langlois (1924) reported that in Michigan the embryos increased in length from about 75 mm to 180 mm between 10 July and 21 August. The embryos are nourished through a placenta (Conway and Fleming, 1960). Birth usually occurs in late August or September after a gestation period of about 58 days (Bauman

Fig. 50. *Nerodia sipedon williamengelsi* (Christopher W. Brown).

and Metter, 1977). Only one litter is produced a year, and the females apparently reproduce annually. There is no evidence of sperm storage by female *N. sipedon*.

Males have a postnuptial–type reproductive cycle, where the sperm is produced after the breeding season and stored over the winter for use the following spring (Bauman and Metter, 1977, Weil and Aldridge, 1981). Upon emergence from hibernation, the seminiferous tubules are filled with sertoli elements and the remaining sperm and germinal elements that were not released the preceding fall (Bauman and Metter, 1977). During mid–April, spermatogonial proliferation begins, and many cells transform into primary spermatocytes and move to the center of the tubule. By early May primary spermotocytes are predominant, but some secondary spermatocytes begin to appear. The first spermatids appear during early June and by mid–July mature sperm are present. As the sperm mature, they move out of the testes and are ultimately stored in the vas deferens. The testis contains sperm and spermatids until early October, when Sertoli cells again fill the lumen of the tubules. The rate of spermatogenesis increases with increased environmental temperatures (Weil and Aldridge, 1979). The diameters of the seminiferous tubules increase from a minimum upon emergence from hibernation to a maximum during

Northern Water Snake

July and August, the peak of spermatogenesis, and then begin to regress during September and October until they once again reach a minimum size in December (Bauman and Metter, 1977). Correspondingly, seasonal plasma androgen levels are highest in the spring at the time of mating, decrease in mid–summer, and increase again in late summer and fall during maximum spermiogenesis (Weil and Aldridge, 1981).

The breeding season extends through May to mid–June. Courtship and mating take place during the daylight hours and may last over 2 hours. Males probably recognize females by the pheromones they release (Scudder et al., 1980), and several males may court a single female. Mushinsky (1979) has published the following account of mating in *N. sipedon*.

> The three snakes, presumably two males and one female, were lying side by side and were rapidly and vigorously rubbing against one another. Most contact was made in the anterior region and only the posterior 1/4 of the body. The two males appeared to have a total body length of 75–85 cm and the large female was about 90–100 cm total body length. Both males were pressing their chins along the dorsum of the female. At 1030 h another male of approximately the same size swam across the creek (south to north) and approached the others, which were on land. When the third male slowly raised its head out of the water it flicked its tongue rapidly. It continued to exit the water and crawled onto land where it slowly began to join the other three mating snakes.
>
> The next 10 minutes of activity were not observed as I left the area to get a pair of binoculars. At 1042 all three males were observed in the process of courtship. Each individual was chin pressing with the anterior portion of the body and rapidly coiling and probing at the cloaca of the female with the posterior end. The twisting and writhing caused this cylindrical quartet of snakes to slowly creep along the grassy shore and their heads were gradually disappearing under some ragweed plants. One individual was copulating with the female but all were very active.
>
> At 1045 the snake that had been lying under the ragweed was pushed into the water by the four snakes that were mating. It turned and swam back to shore and crawled over the other four snakes. This fifth snake (presumed to be a male) circled the mating group and then joined in the mating activities. By this time the anterior 1/3 of the snakes were obscured from vision by the small ragweed plants. About 2 minutes after the last snake joined the mating group, the entire group slid down the gently sloping shoreline into the water. This did not disturb the snakes which maintained parallel orientation to each other as they all turned and came back to shore. For the next 2 or 3 minutes the snakes were 3/4 submerged in the shallow water along the shore. The anterior 1/4 of the female was out of the water and extended onto the land. It was at that time that I could see the full size of the snakes; the female was thick bodied and healthy looking. All four males were of comparable size and the abundant pattern variation that existed was very evident on their wet scales.
>
> A sixth *Nerodia sipedon* approached the mating group by land. It moved to within 1 m of the mating group and stopped, after much tongue flicking and raising and lowering of the head it turned and crawled back to its original point of entry and disappeared. The sex of this snake could not be determined.
>
> The water was very clear and it was apparent that one snake was copulating with the female, presumably the same individual that was involved on land. Their bodies were postured parallel to each other with only the posterior 1/4 of the male wrapped around the female. The anterior chin pressing was less intense but the tails of all the males were still probing rapidly, at 1055 the three escorting males drew apart a short distance (10 cm) and the copulating pair changed position. The female began to swim very slowly toward the waterfall, and as she turned away from the shore the male positioned himself completely upon her back. She turned, faced across the creek, and stopped swimming. They stayed very still at a right angle to the shoreline with the tip of the female's tail just on shore. The male was completely out of the water, riding on the back of his mating partner. After 2 motionless minutes the pair began to move their heads and the male unwrapped his tail from around the female and moved away from her. She immediately started swimming slowly westward, toward the waterfall. The mated male joined the three escort males and all four remained in the water along the shore. After a few minutes 2 male snakes swam under the bridge that I was standing on and were not seen again. One snake went upstream while the other swam across the creek to a pile of logs and debris. The one that went upstream was observed to cross the creek just below the waterfall and circle back to the bridge. It joined the other snake in the log pile and both were seen crawling into a rock wall along the south bank of the creek. The female continued to swim toward the waterfall and once there crossed the creek. She slowly vanished into a stonewall along the southern bank of the creek. The entire observation period lasted for nearly 40 minutes ... During my observation I noticed wave–like contractions that appeared to originate in the anterior third of the body and proceed posteriorly. There were no sudden or spasmodic jerks but rather a deliberate pumping or milking action. Also, the copulating pair remained parallel to each other throughout the event. As the act was terminated the male body slowly slid off the back of the female and the two snakes parted.

The young are usually born from mid–August to late September, but Dunn (1915) and Bleakney (1958b) reported litters born on 12 and 16 October. There are numerous published reports of litter size (see Wright and Wright, 1957). These show the number of young per litter to range from 4 to 99 (Slevin, 1951), but most include between 20–50 young with the average nearer to 20. Fitch (1985) showed that females from more northern populations seem to produce more young per litter than do southern females. Also, litter size tends to increase with increased female body length (Bauman and Metter, 1977; King, 1986).

The newborn young are typically 140–240 mm in total length, and more brightly patterned than the adults. Neonates may weigh about 5 g.

Growth And Longevity: Early growth of *N. sipedon* may be rapid, but the growth rate slows with age. Raney and Roecker (1947) found that New York *N. sipedon* collected in their first fall and early the following spring were mostly 200–250 mm long, while those one year old were 350–400 mm. These lengths represented an annual growth rate for juveniles of slightly greater than 50%. In Missouri, juvenile 1–year–old males averaged 430 mm snout–vent length as compared to 190 mm when born (Bauman and Metter, 1975).

King (1986) determined seasonal growth rates of young of the year *N. s. insularum*. Growth rates estimated from differences in mean snout–vent lengths between 20–day time intervals were 0.002, 0.034, 0.083, 0.128, 0.256, and 0.066 cm/day going from spring to fall with the highest rate of growth occurring between late July and mid–August. The growth rate was 6.09 cm/day over the entire 160–day period. The annual growth rate of these young snakes was estimated to be 0.033 cm/day, a value 2–3 times that obtained for older juveniles and adults. Juvenile and adult males had a mean annual growth rate of 0.012 cm/day (maximum 0.053), while juvenile and adult females grew at an average annual rate of 0.014 cm/day (maximum 0.058). Female *N. s. insularum* grew to much longer body lengths (59–144 cm snout–vent length) than did males (43–125 cm) (King, 1986).

Adult *N. s. sipedon* can sustain maximum activity at 25 C for 42 minutes while neonates are exhausted in 5 minutes. The increased endurance of the larger snakes is paralleled by an ontogenetic increase in blood oxygen capacity and a decrease in blood oxygen affinity (Pough, 1978).

The longevity record for *N. sipedon* is 7 years, 4 months, and 7 days (Bowler, 1977).

Food And Feeding: *N. sipedon* dines mainly on fish, over 30 species are preyed on (*Campostoma, Carassius, Catostomus, Chrosomus, Cottus, Cyprinus, Dorosoma, Esox, Etheostoma, Fundulus, Gambusia, Hypentelium, Ictalurus,* *Lepomis, Lota, Micropterus, Morone, Moxostoma, Nocomis, Notemigonus, Notropus, Noturus, Perca, Percina, Percopsis, Petromyzon, Pimepheles, Pomoxis, Rhinichthys, Salmo, Semotilus, Umbra*). Other prey taken includes frogs and toads (*Acris, Bufo, Hyla, Rana, Scaphiopus*), tadpoles, salamanders (*Ambystoma, Desmognathus, Eurycea, Necturus, Notophthalmus, Plethodon, Pseudotriton, Siren*), snakes (*Nerodia sipedon*), lizards (*Sceloporus undulatus*; in captivity, Conant and Bailey, 1936), mammals (*Microtus, Sorex*), earthworms, leeches, slugs, snails, insects, millipedes, spiders, and crayfish (Surface, 1906; Uhler et al., 1939; McCauley, 1945; Raney and Roecker, 1947; Barbour, 1950a; Conant, 1951; Hamilton, 1951; Diener, 1957a, Wright and Wright, 1957; Brown, 1958, 1979a,b; Bush, 1959; Laughlin, 1959; Langlois, 1964; Anderson, 1965; Zelnick, 1966; Minton, 1972; Bauman and Metter, 1975; Camp et al., 1980; Collins, 1980; Kats, 1986; King, 1986). In the studies listed, fish comprised 50–96% of the food volume and 56–90% by frequency of occurrence, amphibians 4–52% by volume and 17% by occurrence. While it does take some game and pan fish, most species eaten are rough fish, and many may have been taken as carrion.

Most foraging occurs from 1800–2400 hrs, but easily captured prey will not be passed up in the daytime. *N. sipedon* is an active hunter. We have often seen them crawling about in shallow water exploring and probing with their snouts every little crevice or place where prey could be hidden. They may also swim about after fish with their mouths opened wide. When the prey is seized, it is usually worked about in the mouth until it can be most easily swallowed (head first for fish and frogs). Large prey, especially if caught in deep water, is brought to more shallow water or onto the bank before being swallowed. Porter and Czaplicki (1977) reported that *N. sipedon* that have had experience in capturing cryptic prey may adopt a specific searching image whereby prey that are colored similarly to the background are more readily captured than are more conspicuous prey. Dix (1968) has shown that food preferences are innate, but that geographic variation in food preferences is not clearcut.

Prey is detected by either sight (Czaplicki and Porter, 1974; Drummond, 1979, 1983, 1985) or odor (Burghardt, 1968; Gove and Burghardt, 1975), but when both are integrated the capture rate is increased (Drummond, 1979). Juvenile *N. sipedon* may be imprinted early with the odors of their main prey species, and this feeding experience may result in chemical food preferences later in life (Dunbar, 1979).

NERODIA SIPEDON

Northern Water Snake

N. sipedon is not considered venomous. A study of the enzymatic constitution of its saliva by Hegeman (1961) showed the saliva contained only 16.5% protein, and had little proteolytic or hemolytic ability, but that it did contain 7.4 units of cholinesterase, a neurotoxic factor, but which was not like that of elapid snakes.

Predators And Defense: As with other snakes, the natural enemies of *N. sipedon*, especially of the young, are numerous: minks, skunks, otters, red–tailed hawks, red–shouldered hawks, marsh hawks, turkey vultures, herons, egrets, American bitterns, clapper rails, herring gulls, cottonmouths, kingsnakes, racers, larger water snakes, snapping turtles, alligators, bullfrogs, bass, pickerel, pike, and catfish. Conant and Lazell (1973) even suggested that crabs may be predators. Human predation is also a major problem.

Anyone who has worked with *N. sipedon* knows it is particularly vile tempered. When first disturbed, they will try to escape, usually by diving into the water, but if prevented from crawling away they will flatten their bodies, strike, bite (often retaining hold and chewing), and spray a horrendous musk. They do not always tame in captivity.

Populations: *N. sipedon* may reside in rather dense populations where other water snakes are rare. Conant (1951) reported the capture of 395 *N. s. insularum* in one day at Middle Island, Ontario; less than 50 of these were juveniles. More recently King (1986) has estimated the average population density of *N. s. insularum* to be 90.5 (22–381) adults/km of lake shore. Beatson (1976) captured 197 snakes in 6.4 km in Kansas, and estimated this to be 75–90% of the entire population; the density was 4–41 juvenile and adults/km of stream.

However, where there is competition from other larger species of *Nerodia*, *N. sipedon* populations are often reduced. Hanebrink and Byrd (1986) collected 477 specimens of five species of *Nerodia* in northeastern Arkansas; only 12(2.5%) of these were *N. sipedon pleuralis*.

During his study of *N. s. insularum*, King (1986) captured 728 males and 643 females, a 1.13:1 sex ratio. Slevin (1951) reported a litter of 99 *N. sipedon* contained 42 males and 56 females (one individual unsexed), a 0.75:1 sex ratio, and Bleakney (1958b) reported a litter of 32 from Ontario had 16 males and 14 females (2 malformed young unsexed), a 1.14:1 sex ratio. So, the normal male to female ratio of *N. sipedon* probably does not vary significantly from 1:1.

Remarks: While *N. sipedon* is not a serious economic threat to the fishing industry in our native waterways, it can create serious economic problems when present in fish hatcheries. At Ozark Fisheries, Inc., a goldfish hatchery in Camden County, Missouri, a bounty was placed on *N. sipedon* (Bauman and Metter, 1975). In 1973, 6328 *N. sipedon* were killed. Bauman and Metter (1975) estimate these snakes would have consumed over 8656 kg of goldfish in a year, at $10.00/kg commercial value. At this value the snakes would have consumed $86,560 worth of fish in 1973. The bounty of 15 cents per snake paid for the 4958 turned in amounted to only $743.70. It is obvious that this resulted in a substantial economic savings for the hatchery. We do not condone indiscriminate killing of these snakes, but in cases such as this it may be necessary to at least trap the snakes and release them elsewhere.

NERODIA ERYTHROGASTER

Plainbelly Water Snake

NERODIA ERYTHROGASTER
(Forster, 1771)
Plainbelly Water Snake

Recognition: This water snake (to 157.5 cm) has a uniformly brown to greenish–gray back (or with faint cross bars), a yellow, orange, or red unpatterned venter, and dark bars on its light–colored lips. The keeled, doubly pitted body scales occur in 19–23 rows anteriorly, but only 16–17 near the vent; the anal plate is usually divided (single in about 10% of individuals). There are 147–158 ventrals with no sexual dimorphism. On each side of the head are a preocular, 3 postoculars, and a single anterior temporal scale; normally there are 8 supralabials and 10–11 infralabials. Twenty–two to 27 teeth occur on each maxilla.

Adult males are shorter than females, have 75–81 subcaudals, and tail lengths 23–26% of their total body length; females have 64–70 subcaudals, and tails 19–22% of total body length.

Karyotype: The diploid chromosome number is 36; Eberle (1972) and Kilpatrick and Zimmerman (1973) found the normal chromosome complement only to be composed of macrochromosomes, but Baker et al. (1972) reported there were 32 macrochromosomes and 4 microchromosomes. Kilpatrick and Zimmerman (1973) classified the autosomal complement as 8 large submetacentric chromosomes, 6 medium-sized submetacentric chromosomes, 6 small subtelocentric chromosomes, and 14 small metacentric chromosomes. Sex determination is ZZ/ZW; the Z is submetacentric while the W is subtelocentric.

Fossil Record: Fossil *N. erythrogaster* are known from the upper Pliocene (Blancan) of the Beck Ranch local fauna, Texas (Rodgers, 1976), and the Pleistocene (Irvingtonian) of Citrus County, Florida (Meylan, 1982).

Distribution: *N. erythrogaster* ranges from southern Delaware, southcentral Michigan, and southeastern Iowa southward to northern Florida, Texas, southeastern New Mexico in the United States, and to eastern Durango and Zacatecas in Mexico.

Geographic Variation: Six subspecies are recognized, but only three occur in eastern North America. *Nerodia erythrogaster erythrogaster* (Forster, 1771), the redbelly water snake, ranges from the Delmarva Peninsula south to northern Florida, and west to southeastern Alabama. It has a plain red to orangish–red venter, a brown to brownish–gray dorsum (often with some green on the sides), and usually no parietal spots or post–parietal streak on the head. *N. e. flavigaster* (Conant, 1949), the yellowbelly water snake, is found from southeastern Iowa south to eastern Texas, and southeast to northcentral Georgia. This subspecies is olive–gray dorsally, yellow ventrally (sometimes with faint grayish markings), and occasionally has parietal spots or a post–parietal streak. *N. e. neglecta* (Conant, 1949), the copperbelly water snake, occupies a disjunct northern range in southcentral Michigan and adjacent Illinois and Indiana, southwestern Indiana, southern Illinois, and western Kentucky and adjacent Tennessee. There are also isolated colonies in westcentral Ohio and southcentral Indiana. Dorsally, it is gray to olive or brown with at least faint dark blotches, the venter is yellow to orange with some of the dorsal pigment invading along the sides, and there are almost always parietal spots and a post–parietal streak. A blending of characters may occur where the subspecific ranges meet.

Confusing Species: Other *Nerodia* have strongly patterned venters, and *Clonophis kirtlandii* has two rows of dark ventral spots.

Habitat: *N. erythrogaster* seems to prefer slow moving waterways with mud bottoms, abundant emergent vegetation, and brushy shorelines situated in bottom woodlands. A survey of the literature shows it has been taken from bayous, swampy woodlands, lowland swamps, cypress swamps, river bottoms, rivers, streams, sloughs, ditches, lakes and mill ponds. Cool, moist areas seem to be a requirement, and often its waterways are quite tannic.

They may occasionally wander far from permanent water, especially through moist woodland. Neill and Allen (1954) have noted that captives may develop algal growth on their scales. This is probably due to their confinement and inability to bask in natural sunlight.

Behavior: *Nerodia erythrogaster* are usually first active in April, but warm spells may temporarily bring them out in March. They remain active until

NERODIA ERYTHROGASTER

Plainbelly Water Snake

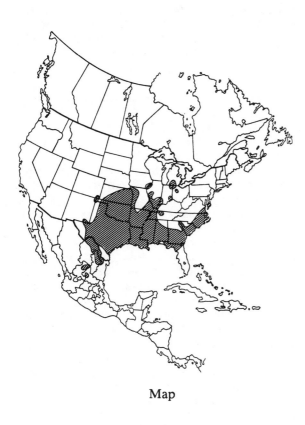

Map

Fig. 51. A juvenile *Nerodia erythrogaster erythrogaster.*

October or November, depending on the warmth of the autumn, and in the southern portion of the range they may be intermittently active throughout the winter (Guidry, 1953; Kofron, 1979a). When forced to hibernate, they do so in rock piles, muskrat and beaver burrows, earth and rock dams, and hollow logs and stumps along the bank. They are predominantly nocturnal (Mushinsky et al., 1980), but may forage during the early morning hours. Most of the daytime is spent either basking on the bank, in overhanging branches, or on partially submerged logs, or submerged, and they are capable of remaining underwater for over an hour (Baeyens et al., 1980).

Mushinsky et al. (1980) recorded the body temperatures of 51 *N. erythrogaster* and found that most ranged between 24 and 29 C, and that the yearly average cloacal temperatures for 1976–1978 were 25.8, 25.7, and 28.0 C, respectively.

Reproduction: The smallest mature Louisiana female found by Kofron (1979a) was 73.4 cm; presumably males mature at a shorter length. The earliest evidence of vitellogenesis found by Kofron was on 26 April. Prior to this the follicles had been 5–10 mm in diameter, but during April and May they enlarged to over 35 mm. Ovulation occurred during late May and June.

Mating has been observed from April to June (Conant, 1951; Wright and Wright, 1957), but courtship behavior has not been described.

N. erythrogaster is viviparous. The young are usually born from August to October, but Kofron (1979a) found a juvenile of newborn length which still had an umbilical remnant on 10 April in Louisiana and felt this evidence of a spring parturition. Female *N. erythrogaster* may store active sperm for almost two years after mating (Conant, 1965). Broods of 5–37 young are produced (Fitch, 1970; Minton, 1972), but 10–20 are most common. Often a series of stillborn young or unfertilized eggs is also passed at the time of birth (Laposha et al., 1985), and Minton (1972) thought this evidence that the reproductive cycle is not as well adapted to a northern climate as that of *N. sipedon.*

The young are more strongly patterned, both dorsally and ventrally, than are adults, having pronounced dorsal blotches and dark pigment on the ventrals. New born young are 190–283 mm in total length. If they escape their enemies, young *N. erythrogaster* may live a relatively long life (to almost 9 years, Bowler, 1977).

Food And Feeding: Our experience with this snake in the wild indicates it is mostly a fish eater; Barbour has even seen them congregate about a spillway from an impoundment to feed on the fish washed over the dam. However, tadpoles, adult frogs and toads, ambystomid salamanders, and sirens are also taken in large quantity. Minton (1972) thought the preponderance of amphibians in the diet of *N. erythrogaster* at some localities may reflect the snake's choice of temporary waters where fish are uncommon, but Mushinsky and Hebrard (1977a) reported that at their Louisiana site 67.4% of the total food volume was frogs or tadpoles. Clark (1949) and Ashton and Ashton (1981) listed crayfish and aquatic invertebrates as food items.

Their catholic appetite is reflected in studies of food preferences of newborn by Mushinsky and Lotz (1980). They exposed *N. erythrogaster* to skin extracts of prey frequently ingested in southern Louisiana (various fish, frogs, and toads), and found that while the newborn did not respond preferentially to any of the prey extracts, a significant response rate was established by two months of age that persisted for several months regardless of dietary restrictions. These snakes then subsequently shifted their preference to frog extract at eight months of age, and Mushinsky and Lotz thought this may reflect a maturational process.

Most *N. erythrogaster* we have seen feeding, actively sought and pursued their prey; however, Gillingham and Rush (1974) observed these snakes with their tails anchored to rocks, their heads facing into the current, and their mouths gaping. Evans (1942) has also reported "open mouthed" foraging by *N. erythrogaster*.

Predators And Defense: This species has a variety of natural enemies: large fish, snapping turtles, ophiophagous snakes (cottonmouths, kingsnakes, coral snakes), large aquatic birds, red–shouldered hawks, otters, minks, and raccoons. Humans, however, cause the most loss of life by habitat destruction, driving over them on highways, shooting, and poisoning with insecticides.

Like other large *Nerodia*, *erythrogaster* has a nasty disposition. When cornered or handled, they flatten their bodies and strike viciously, and their bites can be severe. They also indulge in the disagreeable practice of smearing musk and fecal matter on those who handle them. However, if given a chance, they will try to escape. Usually this is accomplished by diving into the nearest water and swimming to the bottom where they can remain for considerable time (see Jacob and McDonald, 1976; or Baeyens et al., 1980 for duration capabilities and diving physiology).

Populations: Ninety–one (19%) of the 477 *Nerodia* taken by Hanebrink and Byrd (1986) in northeastern Arkansas were this species.

Fig. 52. A juvenile *Nerodia erythrogaster flavigaster*.

NERODIA RHOMBIFERA

Diamondback Water Snake

NERODIA RHOMBIFERA
(Hallowell, 1852)
Diamondback Water Snake

Recognition: The diamondback water snake is heavy–bodied (to 160 cm), and has a pattern of square to diamond–shaped, dark bordered light areas on its back. The dark lines of the border are connected, forming a chain–like pattern. The lips are usually yellow with dark bars. Dark gray or black (brown) half–moons occur on the yellow venter. The keeled, doubly pitted body scales are in 21–28 (usually 25) rows anteriorly, 25–31 (usually 27) rows at mid–body, and 21–26 rows near the vent; the anal plate is divided. Lateral head scalation includes 1 (rarely 2) preoculars, usually 3(2–4) postoculars, 8(7–11) supralabials, and 10–13 infralabials. Each maxilla contains 23–24 teeth.

Male *N. rhombifera* have conspicuous projecting tubercles on their chins. Males are also shorter, have 141–152 ventrals and 68–84 subcaudals; the longer females have 132–146 ventrals and 56–72 subcaudals. Male tail length is 24–27% of total body length, that of the female only 19–23.5%.

Karyotype: The diploid chromosome number is 2n = 36. Eberle (1972) found all 18 pairs to consist of macrochromosomes (pairs 1–3, and 5–6 are submetacentric, pair 4 is metacentric), but Baker et al. (1972) reported 17 pairs of macrochromosomes and one pair of microchromosomes.

Distribution: *N. rhombifera* may be found from southwestern Indiana, southern Illinois, and southeastern Iowa west to eastern Kansas, and south to central Alabama and the Gulf Coast in Mississippi, Louisiana and Texas through the Atlantic versant of Mexico to Tabasco and southwestern Campeche.

Geographic Variation: Three subspecies are recognized (McAllister, 1985), but only one, *N. rhombifera rhombifera* (Hallowell, 1852), described above, occurs in the United States.

Confusing Species: Cottonmouths have a facial pit, an undivided anal plate and only one row of subcaudals.

Habitat: The diamondback water snake can be found in a variety of slow flowing and permanent water bodies, such as lakes, ponds, swamps, marshes, sloughs, oxbows, bayous, and streams, and we have even taken them from the bank of the Mississippi River. At some sites algal mats may be present, and Neill and Allen (1954) have reported that these snakes may become covered with algae in captivity, but their habit of basking probably prevents algal buildup on the skin in nature.

Behavior: In the southern portions of its range *N. rhombifera rhombifera* may be active most of the year, especially when the winters are warm, but to the north it must hibernate. Rossman (1960) found them active from February to September in southern Illinois, Mushinsky et al. (1980) reported activity from February to November in Louisiana, and Wright and Wright (1957) gave the annual activity period as late March to late September. In Kentucky they are usually active by mid–April and continue activity until late September or early October. Winter hibernation is spent in muskrat or beaver lodges or bank burrows, or possibly in the mud bottom of some swamp.

Most foraging and other activity is nocturnal (Cagle, 1937; Rossman, 1960; Mushinsky and Hebrard, 1977b), but occasionally they prowl during the day, especially in the spring and fall. Summer daytime activity usually consists of basking on the bank, logs, or on branches overhanging the water. It is apparently more arboreal during the summer months (Mushinsky et al., 1980).

Brattstrom (1965) reported that the body temperatures of 6 *N. rhombifera* averaged 26.9 C (25.8–29.8). Most of the 343 body temperatures taken by Mushinsky et al. (1980) were in the 24–29 C range, and the average cloacal temperatures for three consecutive years were 26.8, 27.5, and 28.5 C. Jacobson and Whitford (1970) reported that the critical thermal maxima were 40 and 41 C for *N. rhombifera* acclimated to 15 and 30 C, respectively. Gratz and Hutchison (1977) found that this snake exhibited significant daily cycles of oxygen consumption when acclimated at 15 and 35 C, but not at 25 C. They further reported that there was a high dependence on anaerobiosis at all temperatures, and thought this may be an adaptation to the snake's semiaquatic habits.

Reproduction: In Kentucky, mating occurs in mid–April soon after emergence from hibernation. Meade (1934a) previously reported early April matings in captives from Louisiana. Ernst observed a mating pair in a shallow pool in a western Kentucky swamp. They were entwined with the male assuming a more dorsal position. The male did not rub his chin tubercles on the female, but frequently touched her nape with his tongue. Studies by Betz (1963b, c; 1966) indicate that females produce young annually.

Betz (1963b) found that females from Missouri mature at an age of 2.5 years. Females over 90 cm are mature; Kofron (1979a) found a mature 68.8 cm female from Louisiana but reported that 10 larger females (74.8–87.9 cm) were immature. Blanchard (1931) reported that almost all males 80 cm in length have developed chin tubercles and knobbed anal keels, and are probably sexually mature. Blanchard thought the males first breed at 2.5 years of age.

The earliest evidence of vitellogenesis found by Kofron (1979a) was on 2 April. Ovulation occurs from early May through the 3rd week of July in Louisiana (Kofron, 1979a), but only from 15 May until 15 June in Missouri (Betz, 1963b, 1966). Females are noticeably pregnant by late June, and in Louisiana the young are born from early August through the 3rd week of October (Kofron, 1979a). However, Kennedy (1964) reported a Texas female gave birth on 3 November, and Gloyd (1928) noted an 8 November parturition in a Kansas captive.

Steward and Castillo (1984) reported that recently ovulated eggs of *N. rhombifera* contain 41–48% water, 46–56% organic matter, and 3–5% inorganic salts. Total protein is higher in the yolk than total lipid. Steward and Castillo also found evidence of placental transfer of certain mineral ions; newborn young contained more sodium and potassium than the recently ovulated eggs.

Broods range from 8 (Wright and Wright, 1957) to 62 young (Guidry, 1953), but 17–25 is probably more normal. Cagle (1937) reported a direct correlation between the number of young born and the length of the female. He also observed that female *N. rhombifera* apparently often contain more embryos than are eventually born. Neonates are about 245–270 mm in total length and have more pronounced patterns than adults.

Food And Feeding: Fish is the preferred food (Cagle, 1937; Clark, 1949; Sisk and McCoy, 1963; Bowers, 1966; Hess and Klimstra, 1975; Mushinsky and Hebrard, 1977a; Kofron, 1978), but frogs also comprise a large part of the diet. Bowers (1966) reported fish comprised 50% and anurans 44.6% of the total volume of his entire

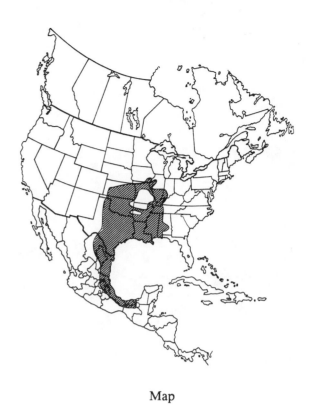

Map

Fig. 53. Venter of *Nerodia rhombifera rhombifera.*

by Evans were swimming with open mouths. Kofron and Dixon (1980) observed that *N. rhombifera* feeding in shallow water trapped fish in their coils before seizing them with their mouths.

Predators And Defense: The young are preyed upon by large fish, bullfrogs, snapping turtles, other water snakes, wading birds and carnivorous mammals. Natural predators of adults include cottonmouths, alligators, large gars, and probably otters.

Humans are by far the worst enemy. Many *N. rhombifera* are killed because they are mistaken for venomous cottonmouths, and many others are destroyed on our roads. Habitat destruction has also taken a heavy toll in recent years. Fortunately, the indiscriminate use of insecticides has slowed and this may save many individuals; death of *N. rhombifera* by DDT and heptachlor poisoning has been documented by Boyd et al. (1963) and Ferguson (1963).

Disturbed diamondback water snakes drop or crawl quickly into the water, dive to the bottom, and swim away. They are capable of remaining underwater for over an hour (Baeyens et al., 1978). If handled, these snakes, like other large *Nerodia*, bite viciously and spray musk.

Populations: Diamondback water snakes comprised 49.5% (236 individuals) of 477 specimens of *Nerodia* from northeastern Arkansas examined by Hanebrink and Byrd (1986).

Remarks: Cliburn (1956) studied the relationship of *N. rhombifera* to *N. taxispilota* and concluded that typical *rhombifera* grade into *taxispilota* in both the number of scale rows and dorsal color pattern, but that no intergradation was shown in the patterns of the anterior temporal scales. Cliburn felt the two snakes only represented subspecies of a single species: *N. taxispilota taxispilota* and *N. t. rhombifera*. However, in a more recent study, Mount and Schwaner (1970) found no evidence of intergradation, and we feel it is best these two snakes be treated as separate species.

Fig. 54. A juvenile *Nerodia rhombifera rhombifera*.

sample; Mushinsky and Hebrard (1977a) reported 95.2% of the total volume of food in their study was fish. Among the fish commonly eaten are catfish, and Kofron (1978) found two *N. rhombifera* with catfish spines projecting through their skin, but despite the puncture wounds both snakes were active and appeared otherwise healthy. Most fish captured are rather slow swimming species, and probably many fish are taken as carrion. Turtles and crayfish also are eaten occasionally (Cagle, 1937; Sisk and McCoy, 1963).

There is a gradual ontogenetic shift in the diet of *N. rhombifera* from small fish species to larger ones (Mushinsky et al., 1982; Plummer and Goy, 1984). Snakes longer than 80 cm snout–vent length shift entirely to large fish.

Prey species are located both by olfaction and sight. Czaplicki (1975) showed that the prey–attack response could be elicited by fish extracts, but Czaplicki and Porter (1974) reported that contrast of the fish with their background was a major factor in selection, while size, activity and proximity were of little or no importance.

Evans (1942) and Gillingham and Rush (1974) have described a peculiar open–mouthed feeding behavior in this snake. Gillingham and Rush reported the snakes were facing into the current with their mouths open and their tails anchored to rocks, but the *N. rhombifera* observed

NERODIA TAXISPILOTA

Brown Water Snake

NERODIA TAXISPILOTA
(Holbrook, 1838)
Brown Water Snake

Recognition: This is a large (to 175.3 cm) brown, thick–bodied water snake with a dorsal pattern of three longitudinal rows of alternating, square, dark–brown blotches. These blotches may be only slightly darker than the chocolate–brown ground color; especially in older individuals. The triangular shaped head is plain brown with some dark bars on the lips; the chin and lower lips may be lighter in color. The venter is cream to light brown with a pattern of dark spots or half–moons. The body scales are strongly keeled and doubly pitted, occurring in 27–33 (rarely 25) rows at mid–body; the anal plate is divided. Head scalation is typical of *Nerodia*; the parietals are shortened and subdivided posteriorly into several small scales. Supralabials total 8–10, infralabials 10–13. The hemipenes are greatly expanded apically with a simple straight sulcus spermaticus and a very extensive nude apical area (McCranie, 1983). Twenty–one teeth are on each maxilla.

Adult females reach significantly larger sizes than do males. Males have 132–152 ventrals and 70–85 subcaudals; females have 128–137 ventrals and 62–74 subcaudals.

Karyotype: Each body cell has 36 macrochromosomes; pairs 1–3, 5 and 6 are submetacentric, pair 4 is metacentric (Eberle, 1972).

Fossil Record: Pleistocene (Rancholabrean) fossils have been found in Florida (Weigel, 1962, Auffenberg, 1963).

Distribution: *N. taxispilota* ranges southward from southeastern Virginia along the coastal plain to southern Florida, and westward to eastern Baldwin County, Alabama. It is also known from the piedmont of North and South Carolina, Georgia and Alabama.

Geographic Variation: No subspecies are recognized.

Confusing Species: Cottonmouths, *Agkistrodon piscivorus*, lack dorsal dark blotches and have a facial pit between the eye and nostril. *Nerodia cyclopion* and *N. floridana* lack the heavy dark ventral markings and have subocular scales between the eye and supralabials. *Nerodia fasciata* usually has a dark stripe from the eye to the posterior corner of the mouth.

Habitat: This is a species of open rivers, lakes and cypress swamps, and, while often abundant along such shores, it is rarely found in small creeks or weedy sloughs. Near the mouths of rivers it may occur in waters influenced by the tides; Ernst has caught them in such places in Virginia and North Carolina. *N. taxispilota* is arboreal, and can often be seen basking on branches overhanging the water.

The brown water snake is highly adapted to an aquatic existence. Its skin is very permeable, and it will lose much water through evaporation from the skin if deprived of water. Prange and Schmidt–Nielsen (1969) reported that in tests the total evaporation of *N. taxispilota* was 3.3 times greater than that of the terrestrial inhabitant, *Pituophis melanoleucus affinis*.

This snake is capable of remaining submerged for considerable lengths of time (just ask those who have chased one into the water and waited for it to come back to the surface). Irvine and Prange (1976) reported that during such dives breath holding is more important than anaerobic mechanisms. Also, its hemoglobin has a very high oxygen affinity (Sullivan, 1967).

Behavior: Little is known about many of the behavioral aspects of this diurnal animal. Most daylight activity is spent either foraging or basking. Annually, it may be active in all months in Florida during warm winters, but at more northern sites it may be forced to hibernate. Neill (1948a) thought that those from Georgia overwintered in cavities or burrows near the waters edge, since a rise in water level brought them out in numbers regardless of the temperature. Ernst has also seen this along the James River in Virginia.

Osgood (1970) used radio telemetry to measure body (stomach) temperatures of 4 unrestrained *N. taxispilota* in an outdoor cage. Three were gravid females, the other a male. The general pattern of body temperature in gravid females was to leave the water and warm in the morning when the sun appeared, then to maintain the body temperature at about 26–31 C as long as possible into the afternoon. When the air temperature finally fell below that of the water, the snakes en-

NERODIA TAXISPILOTA

Brown Water Snake

Map

Fig. 55. The head of *Nerodia taxispilota,*
like that of several other species of
Nerodia, is triangular-shaped
(William A. Cox).

tered the water and slowed the drop in their body
temperatures. The snakes were active during this
period, and this was when most long–range movements would have occurred. The extremes in
body temperature reached by the three females
were 21 and 36 C, and for the male 20 and 37 C.
In a study in South Carolina, Semlitsch (1979)
found that at warm temperatures *N. taxispilota*
consumed more food (although they did not grow
faster) and shed their skins more often.

Reproduction: White et al. (1982) found that the
smallest mature male from Virginia was 50.3 cm
in snout–vent length, and that 83% of the mature
males were in the 50–80 cm range. Constrastingly,
the smallest mature female was 72.5 cm in snout-
vent length, and most mature females were in the
80–90 cm range. However, Mitchell and Zug
(1984) found three Virginia males with 46.3–48.8
cm snout–vent lengths possessed developing
sperm in their testes, and thought males 46–51 cm
were in their first reproductive season.

Spermatogenesis begins in April and terminates in November in Virginia (Mitchell and Zug,
1984). Recrudescence reaches a peak in midsummer, and spermiogenesis occurs principally
from September through November. The seminiferous tubules increase in diameter with spermatogenic activity, and sperm that passes from the
testis is stored in the epididymides. Testes are
small during April–June, largest in August, and
then decrease in size from September to November (White et al., 1982).

Females reproduce annually (Semlitsch and
Gibbons, 1978; White et al., 1982). In Virginia,
vitellogenesis occurs from April to early June,
ovulation in late June and parturition in September (White et al., 1982). Litter size increases with
increasing female body length (Semlitsch and Gibbons, 1978; White et al., 1982). White et al
(1982) reported that the mean total clutch size is
33.9, but that only a mean of 28 reach full–term.
Semlitsch and Gibbons (1978) found that the ab-
solute amount of body tissue partitioned into reproduction increased with body size, but the proportion did not. Most resources were partitioned
into the developing eggs during the summer, and
total lipid content of the eggs increased. At the
same time, a decline of 2.2% in female body fat
occurred between May and July.

Mating usually occurs in the spring (March–
May); however, Ashton and Ashton (1981) reported it occurs from mid– to late summer in
Florida. Mating usually takes place on the ground
or in the water, but these snakes may also copulate above ground while suspended from
branches. Devine (1975) reported the presence of
copulatory plugs in the cloacae of recently mated
N. taxispilota.

Ten to 58 young are born on shore in summer or fall (June–November; Wright and Wright, 1957). The 175–270 mm newborn are lighter brown in ground color, making the pattern of dorsal blotches stand out.

Food And Feeding: *N. taxispilota* is predominately a fish eater (Richmond, 1944; Hamilton and Pollack, 1956; Laughlin, 1959; Collins, 1980; Camp et al., 1980); Camp et al. (1980) found 15 species of identifiable fish during their study of its food habits. Frogs may also occasionally be taken (Wright and Wright, 1957), although captives we have had refused everything but fish.

Predators And Defense: Natural predators include cottonmouths, alligators, large fish, wading birds, and carnivorous mammals. However, humans are by far the worst enemy. Each year fisherman slaughter these snakes indiscriminately because they either believe they are venomous, or that they compete for game or pan fish.

When first caught large individuals are formidable opponents and can inflict deep lacerations when they bite. They also share with other *Nerodia* the obnoxious habit of spraying musk and fecal matter. When kept for awhile in captivity, they often become tame, but do not always do well.

Populations: Duellman and Schwartz (1958) reported that a Florida litter of 16 was composed of 9 males and 7 females, and White et al. (1982) found the sex ratio over a three-year collecting period in Virginia was 70 males to 54 females (1.2:1). They reported a 1:1 sex ratio in the spring and summer, but a 2.5:1 ratio in the fall. If only mature individuals were considered, the proportion of males to females increased from 1.4:1 in spring to 1.9:1 in the fall.

Fig. 56. A juvenile *Nerodia taxispilota* (Jay C. Shaffer).

REGINA ALLENI

Striped Crayfish Snake

REGINA ALLENI (Garman, 1874)
Striped Crayfish Snake

Recognition: This shiny, brown snake (to 65.4 cm) has inconspicuous dark dorsal stripes and a broad yellow stripe along its lower sides. The venter is usually immaculate pinkish to yellow or orange, but may have a mid-ventral row of dark spots. The body scales are smooth (or occasionally slightly keeled), usually pitless, and occur in 19 rows at mid-body (sometimes reduced to 17 near the anus). The anal plate is divided. On the short head, the two nasal scales are in contact behind the rostral, and laterally there are a single internasal scale, 1 preocular, 3 postoculars, 8(7-9) supralabials, and 11(10) infralabials. The single or slightly bilobed hemipenis has 2 enlarged basal hooks, many rows of small spines, and an undivided sulcus spermaticus. The 26-29 short, stout teeth on the maxilla have chisel-like tips (Rossman, 1963a).

Females are larger (to 65.4 cm), have 120-133 ventrals, and 53-61 subcaudals. The smaller males (to 60 cm) have 110-124 ventrals and 59-69 subcaudals. Males also have keeled ridges on the dorsal body scales near the anus (Blanchard, 1931).

Karyotype: *Regina alleni* has a karyotype of 18 pairs of macrochromosomes (Eberle, 1972; Kilpatrick and Zimmerman, 1973).

Fossil Record: Pleistocene remains have been found in Rancholabrean deposits in Florida (Auffenberg, 1963).

Distribution: *R. alleni* is found from southern Georgia southward through peninsular Florida.

Geographic Variation: No subspecies are currently recognized. Duellman and Schwartz (1958) reported that the race, *lineapiatus* (Auffenberg, 1950), characterized by having ventral spots, is only the terminal population of a continuous north-south cline showing an increase in spotting toward the south.

Confusing Species: *Regina rigida* has a double row of half-moon shaped spots on its venter, and the garter and ribbon snakes, *Thamnophis*, have keeled body scales and a single anal plate.

Habitat: This shy, very aquatic snake prefers slow moving and standing waterways with soft bottoms, such as swamps, marshes, bogs, lakes, ponds, sluggish streams and sloughs, where it often hides within aquatic vegetation, especially mats of water hyacinths. It may enter brackish coastal waters (Neill, 1958).

Behavior: Except during very cold periods, *R. alleni* is active in every month. Most activity, either basking or feeding, is diurnal (Godley, 1980), but in the warmest months nocturnal foraging also occurs. Feeding during the day when water temperatures are highest probably maximizes its pursuit and capture success, and higher body temperatures may help in the digestion of hard-bodied prey. Godley (1980) found *R. alleni* with food in their stomachs at mean water temperatures of 15.5-27.4 C.

Terrestrial activity is often limited to basking on the bank, but after warm rains *R. alleni* crawl about on land. At such times, many are killed while crossing roads adjacent to their waterways.

Reproduction: The mating period is unknown, but possibly is in spring (Ashton and Ashton, 1981); the courtship and mating acts have not been described.

R. alleni is apparently viviparous, as living young are produced. Literature reports of the actual size of broods at birth range from 4-12 (Neill, 1951; Duellman and Schwartz, 1958; Ashton and Ashton, 1981), but apparently more ova are fertilized than young born. Telford (1952) found 15 embryos, about 50 mm long, in a 50.8 cm female, and Tschambers (1950) reported a 65.4 cm female contained 34, 19-mm embryos (confirmed by Neill, 1951). The only date of birth in the literature is 28 June, when a 37.2 cm female produced 4 young, and another 41.5 cm female had 8 young (Duellman and Schwartz, 1958). Ashton and Ashton (1981) reported that the young are born between May and September. The brood of 8 young reported by Duellman and Schwartz consisted of 2 males 170 mm and 178 mm long and 6 females which averaged 168 mm in total length.

Food And Feeding: Juvenile *R. alleni* (120-200 mm snout-vent length) feed primarily on dragonfly nymphs, but may switch seasonally to abundant palaemonid shrimp and astacid crayfish. Between 200 and 300 mm snout-vent length, a major dietary shift occurs and crayfish slowly replace the insects and shrimp as the primary prey (Godley, 1980).

Adults feed predominantly on crayfish (Van Hyning, 1932; Franz, 1977; Godley, 1980; Ashton and Ashton, 1981), but other prey may occasionally be taken. Although Franz (1977) reported that captive striped crayfish snakes refused many of the same potential prey, Van Hyning (1932) previously found dwarf sirens (14% of the bulk) and frogs (13%) in addition to crayfish (73%) in the stomachs of 9 wild caught individuals.

Godley (1980) found that in most seasons juveniles consumed more but smaller prey than adults; however, since they fed on insects that were higher in protein but lower in ash content than the crayfish eaten by adults, their energetic intake per gram body mass was generally higher.

R. alleni capture crayfish in "rat snake" fashion by immobilizing them with their body coils (Franz, 1977). They do not constrict the crayfish, but instead just hold them while they are swallowed. Ingestion is abdomen first, and takes 4–5 minutes. Franz (1977) observed that foraging behavior of captives consisted of crawling and probing about the bottom in "exploratory" patterns.

Predators And Defense: Godley (1982) noted that the following animals prey on *R. alleni*: crayfish (on juveniles and newborn young), greater sirens, kingsnakes, cottonmouths, great blue herons, great egrets, river otters, and raccoons. Alligators probably also eat them. Godley (1982) used tail loss as an indication of the rate of predation on *R. alleni*, and found that 10.2% of the snakes studied had lost part of their tail.

R. alleni seldom if ever bite; however, Godley (1982) observed an unusual "gape and sway" behavior when the snakes were handled. When grasped firmly near mid–body some of the snakes rigidly arched their back, opened their mouth nearly 180 degrees exposing the white interior, and swayed their heads and necks laterally. Usually the mouth was closed after a few lateral oscillations of the head. Godley thought this behavior to be a "flash display" used to startle predators or to mimic more noxious (*Nerodia*) or venomous (*Agkistrodon*) water snakes that do bite. He has also observed *R. alleni* occasionally coiling into a ball, concealing the head beneath a coil, and laterally flattening the body. It will also discharge fecal matter and cloacal gland secretions.

Populations: In the Florida slough in which he studied *R. alleni*, Godley (1980) found a density of 1289 snakes per hectare of water hyacinth habitat. He calculated the mean biomass to be 30.79 kg of *R. alleni* per hectare of hyacinths. The density patterns varied seasonally; low in summer, increasing in fall and winter, decreasing in spring.

Remarks: Relationships within *Regina* and those to other closely related genera have been studied by Nakamura and Smith (1960), Smith and Huheey (1960), and Rossman (1963a). Smith and Huheey (1960) revived the genus *Regina* for the species *grahamii*, *rigida*, and *septemvittata*, but also included *Clonophis kirtlandii*. At that time, *R. alleni* was relegated to the genus *Liodytes*. Rossman (1963a) removed *kirtlandii* from *Regina* and placed it in the long neglected genus *Clonophis*. He also showed that *alleni* is most closely related to the three *Regina*, and that it should be included in that genus. This arrangement has been generally accepted, but Price (1983) questioned the inclusion of *alleni* in *Regina*, showing the surface of the dorsal scales of *grahamii* and *septemvittata*, as shown in electron micrographs, have a canaliculate pattern, while those of *alleni* and *rigida* have a plicate pattern. On this basis, he resurrected the name *Liodytes* for *alleni* and *rigida*, and, because *grahamii* and *septemvittata* had similar scale surface patterns to *Nerodia*, supported inclusion of these two species in *Nerodia*. This soon invoked a response from Rossman (1985), who listed in detail the numerous characters shared by *alleni*, *grahamii*, *rigida*, and *septemvittata*, and, on the basis of this latter paper, we have retained these four species in the genus *Regina*.

Map

REGINA GRAHAMII

Graham's Crayfish Snake

REGINA GRAHAMII (Baird and Girard, 1853)
Graham's Crayfish Snake

Recognition: An olive-brown to dark-brown striped snake (to 119 cm), it has a yellow to buff-colored venter which may possess a row of black spots down the center. On each side there is a broad, cream to yellow, stripe on scale rows 1-3, and there is also a black-bordered, light brown mid-dorsal stripe. A wavy, narrow black line separates the body scales from the ventrals. The chin and throat are yellowish. Body scales are keeled, pitted (the first scale row may be smooth), and usually occur in 20-19-17 rows from anterior to posterior; the anal plate is divided. On each side of the head are 2-3 postoculars, 1 + 1-3 temporals, 7-8 supralabials, and 8-11 infralabials. Each maxilla has 25-28 teeth; the posterior-most are slightly enlarged.

Males have 162-175 ventrals, 60-67 subcaudals, and tails 17.5-20.5% of the total body length; females have 155-169 ventrals, 51-64 subcaudals and tails 16-20% of total length.

Karyotype: Each body cell has 36 macrochromosomes (Eberle, 1972; Kilpatrick and Zimmerman, 1973). Kilpatrick and Zimmerman (1973) found that the autosomal complement is composed of 4 pairs of large submetacentric chromosomes, 3 pairs of medium-sized submetacentrics, 5 pairs of small metacentrics, and 5 pairs of small to medium-sized subtelocentric chromosomes. Sex determination is ZZ/ZW; the Z chromosome is a large submetacentric and the W is a medium-sized subtelocentric.

Fossil Record: Remains have been found in Pleistocene (Blancan) deposits in Kansas (Holman, 1981).

Distribution: Northcentral Illinois, central Iowa and southeastern Nebraska southward, west of the Mississippi River to the Gulf Coast of Louisiana and eastern Texas. It is absent from Ozark-Ouachita highlands, but is present east of the Mississippi River in northwestern Mississippi.

Geographic Variation: No subspecies are recognized, but individuals from Iowa are darker dorsally, lacking the median light stripe.

Confusing Species: *Regina septemvittata* has four dark longitudinal stripes on its venter. Both the garter snakes, *Thamnophis*, and lined snakes, *Tropidoclonion*, have an undivided anal plate. The lined snake also has two longitudinal rows of half-moons on its venter; the venter of the garter snakes lacks dark marks.

Habitat: *R. grahamii* is usually found about sluggish water bodies such as slow moving streams, marshes, swamps, ponds, sloughs, roadside ditches and rice fields. These waterways have soft bottoms, an abundance of aquatic emergent vegetation such as cattails, rocks and logs along the bank for hiding places, and abundant crayfish burrows in which to hide and hibernate. Brode (in Neill, 1958) also found them in brackish marshes.

The burrowing habit is apparently well developed. Kofron and Dixon (1980) observed a captive *R. grahamii* excavate burrows both underwater and in soil on several occasions. The resulting burrow was usually a chamber beneath water level into which the snake withdrew its entire body. Breathing was accomplished by extending only the nostrils and eyes above the water for short periods of time. Duration between breathing bouts ranged from 5 to 46 minutes.

Behavior: *R. grahamii* can be found above ground from February to November in the South, but probably mid-April to late September or early October in the North.

In the spring and fall, this timid snake is more active during the daylight hours; but as the daily temperatures rise in summer, it does most of its foraging at night. During the daytime in summer, it spends much time basking along the banks or in the bushes overhanging the water. Mushinsky et al. (1980) reported that most body temperatures of the 27 *R. grahamii* they caught fell between 22 and 27 C and the average temperature of the 12 males was 26.1 C and that of the 15 females, 25.7 C; from 1976-1978 the average yearly cloacal temperatures were 26.2, 25.8, and 28.4 C. Their body temperatures were closely related to the air and water temperatures recorded at the same time.

Little is known of the daily movements of *R. grahamii*. Hall (1969) recaptured 3 of 14 marked snakes in Kansas. One, recaptured after three days, was still in the same pond, and two others, recaptured after 8-9 weeks, were taken in ponds adjacent to that of their first capture. None had moved more than 100 meters.

Reproduction: Females reach sexual maturity at snout–vent lengths of about 60 cm (Hall, 1969; Kofron, 1979a). Hall (1969) reported that all non–gravid females were in the 50–60 cm size range, and the shortest mature female measured by Kofron (1979a) was 60 cm. Hall (1969) found a 42.2 cm female carrying eggs, but thought she was stunted in growth and a year older than most females her size. Females probably can first breed during their third spring, but Hall felt that many females do not mate their first year of adulthood.

Kofron (1979a) determined that females in Louisiana ovulate from the end of April through the third week of June. The first evidence of vitellogenesis was on 16 March, but by 20 June females contained embryos. Females reproduce annually.

Hall (1969) found the smallest males containing sperm were 32–40 cm in snout–vent length, indicating maturity is attained during the first summer after birth. However, he felt that mating probably does not ordinarily occur before the second spring. Sperm were present throughout the annual activity period (9 April to 1 October).

Mating occurs in the water during April and May and several males may attempt to mate with a single female (Wright and Wright, 1957; Anderson, 1965) while pushing and prodding her body with their heads and stroking her neck with their tongues (Ernst, person. observ.).

Dissection of gravid females in Kansas by Hall (1969) revealed that the viviparity involves more than retention of eggs. In females with enlarged ovarian eggs, the oviductal walls were thickened and folded. The eggs lacked a shell and those in the oviducts had their chorionic membranes in intimate contact with the distended oviduct. Hall calculated that the dry weight of the eggs increased during June and July, indicating placental transmission.

Six to 39 young are born from late July through September; but a normal brood probably consists of 16–20. There is a positive correlation between female body length and the number of young per clutch (Hall, 1969). Newborn young are 153–238 mm in total length.

Food And Feeding: Crayfish are the preferred food (Wright and Wright, 1957; Laughlin, 1959; Hall, 1969; Young, 1977; Mushinsky and Hebrard, 1977a; Godley et al., 1984); however, fish (Strecker, 1927; Clark, 1949; Liner, 1954), and small frogs (Strecker, 1927; Anderson, 1965) are also eaten. Strecker (1927) reported that in a small lagoon where crayfish were abundant *R. grahamii* fed almost entirely on them, but that in a stream where crayfish were scarce the snakes

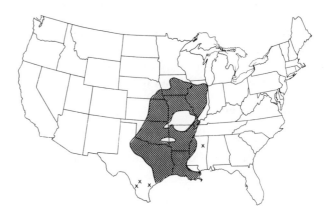

Map

Fig. 57. Venter of *Regina grahamii* (Earl E. Possardt).

fed on minnows and cricket frogs. Liner (1954) observed them feeding on fish trapped in a pond.

During foraging, *R. grahamii* prowls about searching for crayfish and when they are found quickly seizes and devours them. As expected, younger, smaller snakes feed on shorter crayfish than adults (Godley et al., 1984). Crayfish that have recently molted are more easily digested. Burghardt (1968) studied the chemical preference of newborn *R. grahamii* and found they responded only to crayfish extracts, and most strongly to extracts from newly molted crayfish.

Predators And Defense: Ophiophagous snakes, such as cottonmouths, large wading birds, hawks, and predatory mammals are natural predators, but humans, which drain more habitat each year, are the principal enemy.

R. grahamii are shy and retiring in disposition, and seldom, if ever, bite when handled, but they will spray musk, urine and fecal matter on their handler.

Populations: Populations may be dense where crayfish are abundant. Hall (1969) found a sex ratio not differing significantly from 1:1 (75 males, 66 females) in his Kansas population. He also found a 1:1 sex ratio (44 males, 43 females) in 87 unborn snakes. Similarly, in Louisiana, Mushinsky et al. (1980) found a 1:1 adult sex ratio (12 males, 15 females).

Remarks: A good long-term ecological study of this species is very much needed.

REGINA RIGIDA

Glossy Crayfish Snake

REGINA RIGIDA (Say, 1825)
Glossy Crayfish Snake

Recognition: This shiny brown to olive-brown snake (to 79.7 cm) has 2 faint brown or blue to black longitudinal stripes on its dorsum. The venter is light green to yellow with 2 longitudinal rows of black half-moon or triangular-shaped black spots; the labials and chin are yellow. The keeled (except row 1), pitted body scales occur in 19 rows anteriorly, but are reduced to 17 rows posteriorly; the anal plate is divided. On each side of the head are a semidivided nasal, 2(1) preoculars, 2(3) postoculars, 1 + 2(3) temporals, 7(6-8) supralabials, and 10-11 infralabials. The hemipenis is similar to that of *R. alleni*, but the spine adjacent to the basal hook is slightly smaller than the hook (Rossman, 1963a). Each maxilla contains 20-24 rounded, chisel-like, teeth (Rossman, 1963a).

Ventral counts (124-144) overlap between the sexes, but males have 57-71 subcaudals and females 50-64. Females are larger than males.

Karyotype: As described for *R. alleni*.

Distribution: *R. rigida* is found from the vicinity of Lake Mattamuskeet, North Carolina southward along the Atlantic Coastal Plain to northern Florida, and westward to southeastern Oklahoma and eastern Texas. The population reported from New Kent County, Virginia by Richmond (1940) is thought to be extinct. The area has been heavily developed, and collecting trips by Ernst and his students have failed to locate this snake.

Geographic Variation: Huheey (1959) proposed three subspecies. *R. rigida rigida* (Say, 1825), the glossy crayfish snake, occurs along the Atlantic Coastal Plain from Washington and Tyrrell counties, North Carolina southward to Citrus and Volusia counties, Florida. It has 2 preoculars on each side, dark pigment along the edges of the lateral throat scales, no more than 62 subcaudals in males and 54 or less in females. *R. r. sinicola* (Huheey, 1959), the Gulf crayfish snake, ranges from central Florida and the Florida panhandle west to southeastern Oklahoma and eastern Texas. It has 2 preoculars on each side, no dark pigment along the edges of the lateral throat scales, at least 63 subcaudals in males and 55 or more in females. *R. r. deltae* (Huheey, 1959), the delta crayfish snake, occurs only in the Mississippi River delta in Louisiana and adjacent Mississippi. It has only 1 preocular on each side, no dusky pigment on the lateral throat scales, at least 58 subcaudals in males, and no more than 58 in females. Intergradation between the subspecies *rigida* and *sinicola* occurs from southcentral Georgia to Apalachee Bay, Florida, and between *deltae* and *sinicola* in southcentral Louisiana (Huheey, 1959).

Confusing Species: *R. septemvittata* has 4 longitudinal rows of dark ventral spots; *R. grahamii* and *R. alleni* have immaculate venters or with only a single row of dark spots, and yellow dorsal or lateral stripes. *Thamnophis* and *Tropidoclonion* have light dorsal stripes and undivided anal plates.

Habitat: Lowland waterways, such as swamps, marshes, sphagnum bogs, lakes, ponds, sloughs and small streams are the usual habitats. It also occurs in brackish tidal areas at the mouth of the St. Johns River, Florida (Neill, 1958).

Behavior: *R. rigida* is a secretive snake, seldom seen on land except after rains. Activity may be nocturnal; during the day they can occasionally be found under logs, stones or plant debris at the water's edge. Wright and Wright (1957) gave the annual activity period as 5 March to 28 October, but they may be active in all months along the Gulf states and in northern Florida, especially during years with warm winters.

Reproduction: Ashton and Ashton (1981) thought mating in Florida probably occurs in April and May, and Kofron (1979a) reported that in Louisiana ovulation occurs in May or early June, so spring mating is indicated.

Like other *Regina*, this species is viviparous. The earliest evidence of vitellogenesis found in Louisiana by Kofron (1979a) was on 29 March; this specimen had follicles 12 mm long. In January and February the largest follicles were about 6 mm in length, by May some females had follicles 20 mm long. The smallest mature female dissected by Kofron had a snout-vent length of 51.5 cm.

The young are usually born in August or September with total body lengths of 155-188 mm. They resemble the adults in coloration and pattern, but have more pinkish venters. Newborn young total 8 (Abercrombie, 1973) to 16 (Ashton and Ashton, 1981), but embryo counts give a brood range of 8 (Mount, 1975) to 14 (Huheey, 1959). The average brood size of all reported newborn and embryos is 10.1 young. A plot of number of young or embryos versus female body size for those few cases in which these data are available indicates a positive correlation.

Food And Feeding: Adults feed predominantly on crayfish (Huheey, 1959; Huheey and Palmer, 1962; Kofron, 1978), but fish (Strecker, 1926; Clark, 1949), sirens (Strecker, 1926), frogs—*Acris, Gastrophryne, Rana* (Clark, 1949; Hamilton and Pollack, 1956) are also consumed. Juveniles, apparently have diet preferences similar to the young of *R. alleni*, eating dragonfly nymphs and other aquatic insect larvae (Brown, 1978; Martof et al., 1980; Ashton and Ashton, 1981).

Predators And Defense: The only recorded cases of predation on *R. rigida* involve a kingsnake (Viosca, 1926) and a bullfrog (Hensley, 1962). The Viosca account is of interest.

> On April 29, 1925, while on an auto trip out Gentilly Road in company with Dr. E. N. Transeau of Ohio State University, we witnessed, about 12 miles east of New Orleans, the following mute evidence of a snake tragedy to be added to the toll of the automobile. We had passed what appeared to be two snake carcasses lying parallel at the edge of the road. Upon stopping to investigate, it was found that they were in an advanced state of decomposition, but the teeth of the smaller, a water snake, (*Natrix rigida*), were imbedded firmly in the neck of the larger, a king snake, (*Lampropeltis getulus holbrooki*). Closer inspection showed about three inches of the tail of another water snake of the same species protruding from the mouth of the king snake. It was during the height of the breeding season, and the evidence seems to indicate that the water snake will defend his mate. The trio was crushed by automobiles during the struggle, and even death did not them part.

Map

Probably other aquatic feeding predators, such as alligators, cottonmouths and other large watersnakes, turtles, wading birds, minks, raccoons, and otters, also prey on *R. rigida*.

When approached they invariably dive into the water and hide under bottom debris, but if trapped on land they will flatten their heads, bite, and spray musk and cloacal fluids.

Remarks: So little is known of the biology of this snake that a good behavioral and ecological study is strongly needed.

Fig. 58. *Regina rigida sinicola*
(William A. Cox).

REGINA SEPTEMVITTATA

Queen Snake

REGINA SEPTEMVITTATA (Say, 1825)
Queen Snake

Recognition: The queen snake is a slender, medium-sized (to 92.1 cm), brownish to olive serpent with a yellow stripe on each side flanking 3 narrow dark dorsal stripes, and having 4 brown stripes on the yellowish venter. The labials, chin, and throat are cream to yellow. The keeled body scales occur in 19 rows anteriorly, but may be reduced to 17 rows posteriorly; the anal plate is divided. Head scalation is similar to that of other *Regina*; there are 2(1) preoculars and 2 (occasionally 1 or 3) postoculars on each side, 7(6–8) pairs of supralabials and 9(8–11) pairs of infralabials. The hemipenis is single (weakly bilobed in some), and has one enlarged basal hook, many rows of small spines, and a single, undivided sulcus spermaticus. The maxillary teeth are short and stout, but pointed; normally there are 23–27 on each maxilla.

Females have 118–154 ventrals, 54–87 subcaudals, and tails 19–30% as long as the total body length; males have 127–158 ventrals, 65–89 subcaudals, and tails 23–34% as long as the total body length.

Karyotype: As described for *R. grahamii*.

Distribution: *R. septemvittata* ranges from southeastern Pennsylvania, western New York, and southwestern Ontario west to southeastern Wisconsin and adjacent northeastern Illinois, and southward to Alabama. There is also an isolated population in the interior highlands of Arkansas and Missouri.

Geographic Variation: No subspecies are now recognized. The population from Baldwin County, Alabama, named *mabila* by Neill (1963a), has been shown not to differ significantly from other populations of *R. septemvittata* in Alabama by Spangler and Mount (1969).

Confusing Species: Other *Regina* have no more than 2 ventral stripes; *Thamnophis* have undivided anal scutes.

Habitat: The queen snake lives in clean, unpolluted brooks, streams, or marshes in open areas or woodlands. Crayfish must be present. Stokes and Dunson (1982) found that *R. septemvittata* has the most permeable skin of any snake, and this probably restricts it to at least the near vicinity of water. Unfortunately, water pollution (and possibly acid rain) has reduced crayfish populations in many parts of the range, and this, along with habitat drainage, has consequently eliminated the snake from many areas where it once was common.

Behavior: Our field experience in Kentucky, Pennsylvania, and Virginia indicates that the queen snake is predominately diurnal. This daily pattern is supported by similar observations of Wood (1949) in Ohio and Branson and Baker (1974) in Kentucky. Most foraging occurs in the morning, followed by a period of mid–day basking in branches overhanging the water or on the adjacent bank. On very hot days, it retreats under stones, logs, or other debris on the shore, and other favorite retreats are muskrat bank burrows and earth and stone dams. Often several may be found basking together or in the same retreat.

Activity may occur throughout the year in the south, but at a reduced rate during cold weather. In the north, this snake may be first seen in March during warm spells, but more often it first emerges in April. It may enter hibernation as early as October, or as late as November during warm autumns, and aggregations may occur prior to entering hibernacula (Wood, 1944, 1949; Neill, 1948a). We have found these snakes hibernating in muskrat burrows, and crayfish burrows are probably used. Earth and stone dams or causeways are also used as hibernacula. Even in the north they may occasionally emerge to bask on warm winter days (Reinert, 1975), and Conant (1951) once found one lying on the ice on the surface of a creek.

Branson and Baker (1974) recorded the body temperatures of 116 *R. septemvittata* that were partially or completely submerged in water; their temperatures were 0.2–6.2 C above that of the water. Of the 89 queen snakes found out of water, 60 (67.4%) had body temperatures lower than the air temperature. The highest recorded body temperature was 30.4 C, the lowest 12.2 C; the mean cloacal temperature for all snakes was 25.6 C. Branson and Baker found the critical thermal maxima for adults varied from 43.4 to 44.5 C, whereas that of juveniles was 39.5–41.5 C.

REGINA SEPTEMVITTATA

Queen Snake

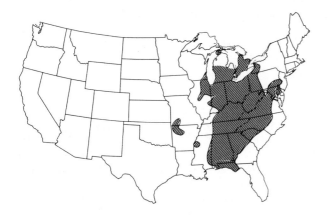

Map

Home ranges of queen snakes are relatively small. Of 13 recaptures by Branson and Baker (1974), the straight–line distances from point of release to point of recapture were 3–137 m (x = 22.6 m). Newcomer et al. (1974) studied orientation in this species and discovered it possesses the ability to use the sun for Y–axis orientation toward a particular shore line.

Reproduction: Females may mature late in their second year, but generally do not reproduce until their third year. The shortest mature female examined by Branson and Baker (1974) was 34.4 cm in total length; this is less than the 37.5 cm total length reported by Wood and Duellman (1950). Branson and Baker (1974) found that males also mature in their second year.

Minton (1972) observed a pair of queen snakes in an apparent copulatory attempt on 28 May, and McCauley (1945) and Ashton and Ashton (1981) thought that mating occurs in the spring, possibly as late as June. However, Branson and Baker (1974) reported mating probably occurs both in spring and fall. Spermatogenesis begins in late spring and peaks during the summer. Spermeation begins in mid–July and the sperm are subsequently stored in the ductus deferens (Minesky and Aldridge, 1982).

The only description of courtship in any species of *Regina* is that for *R. septemvittata* by Ford (1982b).

> In most regards, male queen snakes showed courtship behavior closely paralleling other natricines. The male approached and tongue flicked the female repeatedly. The male mounted the female and proceeded to move forward until aligned on her dorsum. At this time the male queen snakes began a behavior different from other colubrids. They proceeded to 'bounce' dorsoventrally on the female. This movement was vertical oscillation of the first 6 to 20 cm of the neck. It did not involve any lateral sliding of the body but in other regards did appear to be similar to the writhe–bump seen by Gillingham in *Elaphe* (1979). Each bounce lasted 0.05 seconds and the bounce rate alternated between 60 to 70/min. up to 91 to 115/min. The slower rate involved higher dorsoventral movement ... The faster rate occurred with oscillations in which the male did not lose contact with the female's dorsum. After a variable period of this behavior, the males would begin the tail-search copulatory attempts. As the typical natricine caudalcephalic waves were absent this suggests the vertical oscillations substitute for this reproductive cue.

The queen snake is viviparous, and the chorionic membrane lies in intimate contact with the female's distended oviduct during embryonic development. Both become richly supplied with a fine network of blood vessels (Branson and Baker, 1974).

Young queen snakes are born from late July to late September at total body lengths of 175–208 mm. Literature reports of brood size range from 5 (Dunn, 1915) to 31 (Ashton and Ashton, 1981), but the usual brood consists of 10–12 young. Branson and Baker (1974) described the birth process, which requires 1.5–2.5 minutes with a lapse of 4 minutes to 1 hour between births.

Growth: Raney and Roecker (1947) and Branson and Baker (1974) reported average increases of 79% and 75% in length for yearling *R. septemvittata*. Wood and Duellman (1950) reported a 50% increase during the second year, and diminishing growth rates in subsequent years; Branson and Baker (1974) noted a growth rate of 44.8% in the second year.

A wild caught adult male *R. septemvittata* survived 19 years, 3 months and 17 days at the Racine Zoo, Wisconsin (Bowler, 1977).

Food And Feeding: Our experience with wild and captive *R. septemvittata* strongly suggests that it eats almost nothing but crayfish. These observations agree with those of Raney and Roecker (1947), Wood (1949), Conant (1951), Judd (1955), Adler and Tilley (1960), Minton (1972) and Branson and Baker (1974). Of 44 stomachs containing food examined by Raney and Roecker

(1947), crayfish made up 99.2% of the total volume of the food items, and in the 110 stomachs containing food dissected by Branson and Baker (1974), 98.6% of that food consisted of crayfish. Other prey reported taken in the wild include small fish (Wood, 1949; Conant, 1951; Adler and Tilley, 1960; Branson and Baker, 1974); toads (Surface, 1906), dragonfly nymphs (Raney and Roecker, 1947), and snails (Adler and Tilley, 1960). Wright and Wright (1957) also reported that "froglets" and newts are eaten, and McCauley (1945) found the head of an ant in one stomach, but thought it probably the stomach contents of some frog or fish the snake had eaten.

Ernst has seen queen snakes forage among rocks in a small Pennsylvania stream, and on several occasions has observed them disturb crayfish from their hiding places, seize them by the tail and proceed to swallow them tail first. All of the crayfish were small and appeared to have just molted. Crayfish carrion may also be consumed (Wood, 1949), and odor may play an important role in prey hunting. Burghardt (1968) tested the response of newborn queen snakes to water extracts of several small animals, but they only responded to those of crayfish (especially those that had recently molted).

Predators And Defense: Minton (1972) saw a fish seize a small queen snake but subsequently release it, and he had a report of another taken from the stomach of a great blue heron. Branson and Baker (1974) observed juvenile queen snakes attacked by crayfish, and found young snakes in the gut of a hellbender. Raccoons and otters probably also take a few (Linzey and Clifford, 1981), and the larger *Nerodia* are also potential predators. During hibernation, crayfish and mice may attack dormant individuals (Wood, 1949; Branson and Baker, 1974).

Despite the number of queen snakes that may fall to natural predators each year, humans cause the most destruction. The results of habitat destruction and pollution have been commented on above. In addition, humans may directly prey upon these harmless snakes. Ernst observed the disappearance of about 100 individuals from a rock dam in Pennsylvania; apparently all were shot by local teenage boys.

When first handled, *R. septemvittata* squirm violently and spray their captors with musk and feces, but they seldom, if ever, bite.

Populations: *Regina septemvittata* may be very common at suitable sites with crayfish. Branson and Baker (1974) found densities of 35 per 192 m and 62 per 237 m at two sites in a Kentucky stream, and Wood (1949) reported collecting 125 queen snakes within 92 m in a stream in Ohio.

Of 229 queen snakes examined by Branson and Baker (1974) during their study in Kentucky, 113 were males and 116 were females, essentially a 1:1 sex ratio. Similarly, the sex ratio of the 128 young born in captivity during their study was 65 males to 63 females.

Remarks: It is our experience that most *R. septemvittata* do poorly in captivity, and we suggest they not be kept as pets.

SEMINATRIX PYGAEA

Black Swamp Snake

SEMINATRIX PYGAEA (Cope, 1871)
Black Swamp Snake

Recognition: This is a small snake (to 65.4 cm) with an immaculate, shiny, black back and a red venter with black bars or triangular blotches at the anterior edge of each scute. Some buff to greenish–yellow pigment may occur on the lips, and the chin may have brownish pigment. The 17 rows of body scales are smooth and poreless, but those of the lower–most rows on each side have a pale longitudinal line resembling a keel. A scanning electron microscope study has shown the surface of the body scales to have prominent sharp spines (Price, 1982). The anal plate is divided. Lateral head scalation includes a loreal, 1 preocular, 2 postoculars, 1 + 2 temporals, 8(6–9) supralabials, and 9 infralabials. There are 112–134 ventral scutes with no sexual dimorphism, but males have 40–56 subcaudals while females have only 35–49. The spiny unforked hemipenis has a single sulcus spermaticus with inconspicuous lips. Papillae are absent, but there are indistinct groups of enlarged spines near the base and 2 lateral basal hooks. The 19–21 maxillary teeth become slightly longer toward the rear of the jaw.

Karyotype: Unknown

Distribution: *Seminatrix* ranges from northeastern North Carolina (Albermarle Sound) southward along the coastal plain through peninsular Florida, and west into the panhandle of Florida and adjacent southern Alabama.

Geographic Variation: Three subspecies occur within its range. *Seminatrix pygaea pygaea* (Cope, 1871), the north Florida swamp snake, ranges from the Savannah River south to Pasco, Lake and Orange counties Florida, and west to Santa Rosa County, Florida and Covington County, Alabama. It has an immaculate red belly or with a pair of black bars at the sides of each of the 118–128 ventrals. *S. p. paludis* Dowling, 1950, the Carolina swamp snake, is found from Albemarle Sound southward along the Atlantic Coastal Plain to the Savannah River in South Carolina. It has a pair of black bars at the sides of each of the 127 or more ventrals. *S. p. cyclas* Dowling, 1950, the south Florida swamp snake, inhabits southern peninsular Florida. This race has a short triangular–shaped black blotch at the anterior edge of the 117 or fewer ventrals.

Confusing Species: *Storeria occipitomaculata* and the various species of *Nerodia* have keeled body scales. *Farancia abacura* has a terminal tail spine and red pigment on its labials.

Habitat: *Seminatrix* is highly aquatic and can be found inhabiting many types of water bodies within its range: cyprus swamps, marshes, lakes, ponds, slow flowing streams and rivers, sloughs and canals. It is tolerant of brackish water and has been found in salt marshes in South Carolina, Georgia and Florida (Neill, 1958), and we have taken it from tidal waters in Hyde County, North Carolina. Within its aquatic home it prefers to burrow in mats of aquatic vegetation, such as *Eichhornia*, *Nuphar*, *Pontederia* or *Sagittaria*. One of the best methods of collecting these snakes is to rake out mats of floating vegetation, such as water hyacinths (*Eichhornia crassipes*). On land, it seldom crawls far from water, and is most often found beneath logs or vegetable debris.

Behavior: *Seminatrix* is probably active all year in Florida, but farther north it hibernates and is

Map

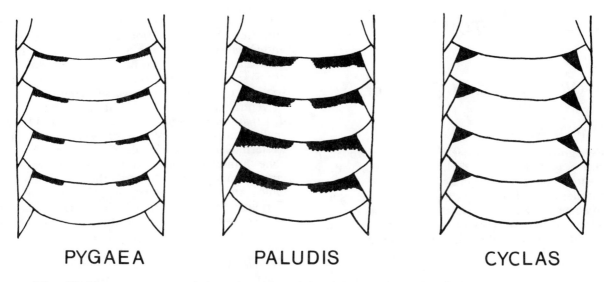

PYGAEA   PALUDIS   CYCLAS

Fig. 59. Venter patterns of the subspecies of *Seminatrix pygaea* (Evelyn M. Ernst).

active from late March to late October or early November. In winter it buries itself in mud, sphagnum, or vegetable debris; Carr (1940) found them buried as deep as 60 cm, and Scudder (1972) has taken them from the burrows of mole crickets. *Seminatrix* is very secretive and mostly nocturnal, although Ernst has collected them on land in the early morning and on roads during daytime rains. Dowling (1950) reported that during extended periods of cold weather, they may leave the water and seek shelter under debris on the banks. Warm rainy nights also stimulate them to move overland. *Seminatrix* seldom, if ever, basks as do other aquatic snakes.

Reproduction: Courtship and mating have not been described, but the ovoviviparous *S. pygaea* probably mate in the spring or early summer. Dowling (1950) thought the increased activity of these snakes in spring may indicate the breeding season.

Dowling (1950) examined the ovaries and oviducts of a series of females from Alachua County, Florida, and found small eggs (1–4 mm) throughout the year. Only those females less than 18 cm long lacked such eggs and were probably immature, although a 15 cm female did contain visible eggs. The largest female with undeveloped eggs was 35.5 cm, and the smallest with enlarged eggs was 24 cm. Females collected in the spring showed some ovicular growth. In April, the eggs were about 5 mm long; in May, nearly 10 mm, but without visible embryos; and in June, 12–16 mm with embryos. A single female taken in July contained 7 well–developed young which would probably have been born in early August.

The 2–14 young are born during the period of August to October; the usual litter size is 5 or 6, and Dowling (1950) found no correlation between female body length and litter size. Newborn young are 95–150 mm in total length; they shed their skins almost immediately, probably in the water amongst aquatic vegetation.

Growth: Dowling (1950) reported that the only character to vary with age, other than size was the relationship of tail length to body length. The probable tail length of a *Seminatrix* of any size could be obtained by the equation 0.287 x body length—0.588 in males, and 0.204 x body length + 2.979 in females.

Food And Feeding: In nature, most feeding is probably done under water at night, although captives have shown they can swallow food when out of the water. Worms (oligochaetes, leeches), small fish, tadpoles, small frogs and salamanders probably are natural foods; captives we have kept fed readily on earthworms and guppies.

Predators: Large fish, such as large–mouthed bass, ophiophagous snakes, and wading birds are the chief predators.

Remarks: Biochemical studies have shown that *Seminatrix* is most closely related to the natricine genera *Natrix*, *Nerodia*, *Regina*, *Sinonatrix*, *Storeria*, *Thamnophis* and *Tropidoclonion* (Dessauer, 1967; Schwaner and Dessauer, 1982).

STORERIA DEKAYI

Brown Snake

STORERIA DEKAYI (Holbrook, 1836)
Brown Snake

Recognition: *Storeria dekayi* is a small (to 52.7 cm) grayish–brown to dark brown snake with a cream to pink venter and a variable pattern of two parallel rows of dark brown spots on the dorsum. In some individuals the dark dorsal spots may be joined by narrow transverse bars; and in most individuals the mid–dorsum is lighter in color than the sides. Usually either a dark temporal stripe or dark blotches on the supralabials, or both, are present. One or two longitudinal rows of small dark spots may occur along the sides of the ventral scales. The pitless, keeled scales occur in 15 or 17 rows, usually with no reduction along the body; there are 112–149 ventrals with no sexual dimorphism, and the anal plate is divided. Normally there are a preocular, 7(6–8) supralabials and 7(5–9) infralabials on each side of the head; no loreal scale is present. The individual hemipenis is not distally expanded and may be shallowly forked (in *S. d. victa*). It is rather spinose, and has a straight sulcus spermaticus. Each maxilla has 15 teeth, with the most posterior shorter than those anterior to them.

Males have 46–73 subcaudals, while females have 36–66 subcaudals. The male tail is 23–26% of the total body length; that of females, 17–23%.

Karyotype: The diploid chromosome number is 2n = 36 macrochromosomes; sex determination is ZZ/ZW (Hardy, 1971).

Fossil Record: Pleistocene remains of *Storeria dekayi* have been found in Rancholabrean deposits in Florida and Texas, and other fossils, identified only to the genus *Storeria*, have been found at an Irvingtonian site in Kansas and at Rancholabrean sites in Kansas, Missouri, Pennsylvania, and Virginia (Holman, 1981; Christman, 1982).

Distribution: *S. dekayi* can be found from southern Maine, Quebec and Ontario west to Wisconsin and Minnesota, and southward through Florida in the East, to the Gulf of Mexico in the Midwest, and to Veracruz and northeastern Oaxaca,

Mexico in the West. There is also a tropical subspecies which ranges from eastern Chiapas, Mexico to central Honduras.

Geographic Variation: Christman (1982) recognizes eight subspecies, five of which range east of the Mississippi River. *Storeria dekayi dekayi* (Holbrook, 1836), the northern brown snake, occurs from southern Maine and southern Quebec and Ontario southward to South Carolina. It has a dark diagonal or vertical bar on the anterior temporal scale, the two longitudinal rows of dark spots on the body not transversely connected, and its ventrals plus subcaudals total less than 175. *S. d. wrightorum* Trapido, 1944, the midland brown snake, ranges from Wisconsin southward to the western Carolinas and the Gulf Coast. A wide zone of intergradation with the nominate race occurs from southern Canada through Michigan, Ohio and the western Applachians to the Carolinas. *S. d. wrightorum* has dark transverse bars connecting the two longitudinal rows of dark spots on the dorsum. *S. d. victa* Hay, 1892, the Florida brown snake, is found from southeastern Georgia southward through peninsular Florida, except along the Suwannee River Valley. It has a broad light band across the back of the head, dark pigment on the supralabials below the eye, two rows of small dark spots on each side of the venter, and 15 mid–body scale rows (the other five races have 17 rows). *S. d. texana* Trapido, 1944, the Texas brown snake, ranges from Minnesota and Wisconsin southwestward to Texas and northeastern Mexico; a zone of intergradation between it and *S. d. wrightorum* extends along the eastern edge of its range from Wisconsin southward in the Mississippi Valley. This subspecies has no pigment on the anterior temporal scale, a large dark occipital blotch, and dark pigment on the supralabials below the eyes. *S. d. limnetes* Anderson, 1961, the marsh brown snake, ranges from Colorado County, Texas eastward along the Gulf Coast to Pensacola, Florida. It has a dark horizontal bar on the anterior temporal scale, but lacks dark pigment on the supralabials.

Confusing Species: *Storeria occipitomaculata* has a red venter. The earth snakes (*Virginia*) have a long horizontal loreal scale. Worm snakes (*Carphophis*) have smooth body scales.

Habitat: This small common snake can be found in nearly all terrestrial and marshland habitats within its range; it may occur in dense colonies and frequently inhabits urban areas. As long as there is an abundance of materials under which to hide and a ready supply of earthworms, it may flourish.

Behavior: Brown snakes become active soon after the ground begins to thaw in late March or April. At that time they can often be found basking, sometimes above ground, during the daylight hours, or prowling for worms. Over most of the range they remain active until late October or November, but warm spells often bring them out even in winter. Ernst has collected a specimen on 19 December following an unseasonally warm day in northern Virginia, and Conant (1951) collected this snake in every month. When the weather is severely cold, these small serpents retreat to some shelter beneath the frost line and hibernate. Hibernacula include stone walls, ant hills, old wells, rock crevices, logs, and rodent burrows, and usually face south. *S. dekayi* may also enter buildings during its search for a winter den. Often several will hibernate together; Clausen (1936b) removed over 200 from four hibernacula on Long Island. They may also aggregate with other species during the winter. In the northern parts of the range, mortality from freezing may be great (Bailey, 1948), but in the South, especially Florida, they may remain active all year.

During the early spring and in the fall most activity is diurnal, especially in the late morning, but during the summer they become active in early evening and presumably are mostly nocturnal. Temperatures of active wild *S. dekayi* have ranged from 23.8 to 27.0 C (Fitch, 1956; Brattstrom, 1965). Clausen (1936a) has shown that oxygen consumption and metabolism in *S. dekayi* increase with rising temperatures.

Although the home ranges of most *S. dekayi* are probably small (less than 60 m; Freedman and Catling, 1979), some individuals may travel rather long distances for such a small snake. Freedman and Catling (1979) reported that in 30 days a 31 cm male traveled 374 m and a 39 cm female crawled 226 m. Noble and Clausen (1936) found some of their marked snakes moved about 1.2 km.

Reproduction: Kofron (1979b) studied the reproductive cycle of female *S. dekayi* from Louisiana, and found the smallest mature female to be 170 mm in snout–vent length, a size probably reached during the second year. He also reported that females reproduce annually.

Vitellogenesis of ovarian follicles proceeds rapidly during the spring. In late winter or early spring the follicles are 3.1–6.0 mm in diameter, but by April they have enlarged to 6.1–12.0 mm (Kofron, 1979b). Ovulation usually occurs in late March or April, but Kofron found evidence of a July ovulation in one female. He also found that transcoelomic migration of ova to the opposite oviduct had occurred in 7 of 17 females containing young. The gestation period in Louisiana was about 2.5 months, with the first young born on 11 June, but most births occurred during late June

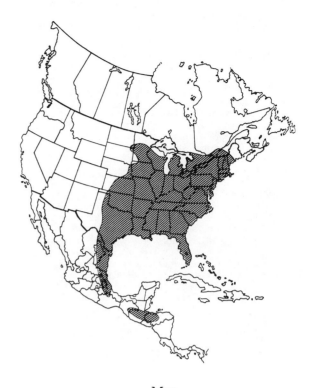

Map

Fig. 60. *Storeria dekayi dekayi* (Christopher W. Brown).

and July. Clark (1949) found Louisiana females near parturition from mid–July to mid–August. In Florida, Iverson (1978) reported that female brown snakes contained enlarged follicles in March, enlarged ovarian eggs or embryos in May, and nearly full–term young in June; parturition occurred in July or August. Iverson also found partially to nearly full–term embryos in September.

Spring mating in northern populations has been observed in the laboratory or in the field from late March through May (Clausen, 1936b; Conant, 1951; Ernst, person. observ.), and Ashton and Ashton (1981) reported that mating occurs from early spring through early summer in Florida. Trapido (1940) found that a female from Canada that had been collected in late August and sent to him in early October contained abundant sperm in the oviducts when dissected on 6 December. This suggests an August mating, but Fox (1956) reported that female *S. dekayi* can store viable sperm for up to four months.

Noble (1937) has given the following detailed description of the courtship and mating of this species.

> During April, 1932, I had more than 50 adults under observation and from April 12 to 22 some courtship activity occurred nearly every day. Courtship could be stimulated during this period by temperature change. Leaving the snakes in an ice–box at 7° C. and then moving the cages to a well–illuminated room at approximately 25° C. seldom failed to induce some response. Thus, on April 22, after the snakes had been left over night in the ice–box, five pairs were observed courting at one time. *Storeria* is generally assumed to be nocturnal. Both adults and immatures prowl about their cages at night but also during the day. All the courtship in our series occurred during the daytime and usually in the morning after 9 o'clock. Although cages with courting snakes were left in the warm rooms throughout the night and observed at intervals until 9 P.M., no courtships were recorded ... During the breeding season a rising temperature tends to induce courtship and, since this is more apt to occur in the morning hours in a state of nature, courtship presumably occurs at that time.

> Courtship occurs in early spring when numbers of individuals are found together near the entrance of hibernation dens. All of the specimens which courted in the laboratory had recently been collected near some holes which were known to harbor numbers of hibernating *S. dekayi* during at least two winters...

> The first sign of courtship is disclosed by the male which twitches the tip of his tail nervously but slowly from side to side. The movement is much slower than the tail vibrations many snakes practice when frightened. The male flickers his tongue rapidly in several directions and moves away toward other active snakes. The male soon singles out an individ-

Fig. 61. *Storeria dekayi wrightorum.*

Fig. 62. Venter of *Storeria dekayi victa* (Steve W. Gotte).

ual which later cloacal examination reveals to be a female and attempts to run his chin along her back. In moving forward along her back he flickers his tongue first on one side of the mid-line of her back and then on the other. In doing this he turns his head slightly from side to side and often brings his tongue in contact with her skin. The female is usually approached from the side and as she almost invariably moves away from the advances of the male, the bodies of the two snakes soon come to be parallel. If two or three males begin to court the same female there is always considerable jockeying for the dorsal position. Such rivalry frequently puts the female to flight and as she glides rapidly away the males follow neck to neck like so many hounds on a hot trail. The first to make contact with the female slides rapidly along to bring his chin in contact with her neck, that is, with the skin on the dorsal surface of her body immediately behind the occiput. There is never any hesitation in the region of the cloaca, and if a male slides too far forward onto the occipital shield he soon works back to the neck.

Although the males are usually smaller than the females, there is considerable variation. Several of our courting males were as large or larger than the females they pursued. Nevertheless, the males have little difficulty in rapidly identifying sex. If a female is quickly removed from the cage when being followed by two males, the latter start flickering their tongues at one another but make no attempt to court. Again, when two or more males are courting the same female one may be crowded out from immediate contact with the body of the female. Such a male frequently persists and may run his chin along the back of another male but will never continue courting one of his own sex.

Although the males recognize sex within a few moments there is never any antagonism among them. In endeavoring to secure a position on the back of a female they may crowd a rival off but their movements against one of their own sex are never more violent than toward an inanimate obstruction. In following the trail of a rapidly disappearing female a male makes no attempt to drive his rivals away. These observations repeated many times lead to the conclusion that while the female sex attracts, the male sex does not repel the sexually active male...

As soon as the male has reached a position approximately a centimeter behind the occiput of the female he attempts to encircle the female with the posterior part of his body. While the head and neck of the male come to lie above the female the greater part of his body usually falls to one side or the other. If the middle section of the male's body changes to lie on one side, the region immediately anterior to his cloaca is thrown across the back of the female and the section including the cloaca bent under her body in the form of a sharp turn or wedge. A firm grip on the female's tail is secured by one or more twists of the male's tail. Then as the cloacal section of the male's body is pried under the

cloacal region of the female, the male's body begins to writhe. These violent lateral movements are soon replaced by a series of caudocephalic waves of the body which may begin simultaneously in two different parts of the male and run rapidly forward. The waves may begin near the center of the tail and, closely resembling a series of antiperistaltic ripples, run the full length of the body to the head. The male endeavors to keep his chin on the neck of the female, even when these caudocephalic waves are again replaced by more violent movements. Both the body waves and the writhing serve the purpose of tapping many parts of the females's body. As the movements continue the wedge-like turn of the male's body lifts the cloacal region of the female two or three centimeters from the ground. The base of the hemipenis on the side in contact with the female's body is slightly protruded and the prominence brought close to the cloacal slit of the female ... Within five minutes after being placed in the observation cage, one male inserted his right hemipenis into the cloaca of the female. He then no longer made an effort to keep his chin on her dorsum but allowed himself to be dragged about the cage by the female, which continued her progress about the cage ... As soon as the male had become attached by his hemipenis to the moving body of the female, his cloacal region and tail began to jerk spasmodically. Each movement of these regions was essentially a forward thrust. There were two or three rapid thrusts followed by a pause of two seconds. These movements were continued even when the male had been dragged about until his head pointed in the opposite direction from that of the female and his cloacal region was bent sharply back on itself. The thrusts were readily distinguished from the caudocephalic waves of courtship both in their tempo and in the fact that they did not extend anterior to the cloaca.

The female's cloaca was greatly distended by the single hemipenis of the male and the cloacal lips at the point of juncture were wet with lymph and a little blood... 24 minutes after beginning the copulation, the male gained his freedom... The spines on the hemipenis do not help a male maintain his position in struggles with rival males but rather they insure the continuing of copulation by males which otherwise would be rubbed off by their active partners.

Pheromones are apparently released by female *S. dekayi*, and these trails may lead the male to his potential mate. Ernst once took an April female and rubbed her cloaca on a linoleum floor, leaving an intricate twisting pathway. When three male *S. dekayi* were individually released at the end of this trail, they quickly followed it through all its turns.

The gestation period ranges from 105 to 113 days (Clausen, 1936b, Fitch, 1970), and the young are born from late July through early September, with August the usual month. However, Ashton and Ashton (1981) reported that in Florida some young are born in the spring. Females may give birth to 3 (Wright and Wright, 1957) to 41 (Morris, 1974b) young; the average number of young in 62 litters in the literature was 14.0 (Fitch, 1970).

During explusion of the babies the female elevates her tail and then muscular contractions, which can be seen along her body wall, force the young through the cloacal orifice. The young are born at about 1 minute intervals (Morris, 1974a, b). Ernst had a *S. d. victa* give birth to a young in his hand as we attempted to pose her for photographing for this book. The young are covered with a transparent membrane which is soon ruptured; they are 74–117 mm in total length, dark brown, and have a light occipital collar. Burghardt (1983) has found that the tendency to aggregate with conspecifics is strongly developed in newborn *S. dekayi*.

Growth And Longevity: Minton (1972) reported that Indiana young entering hibernation for the first time were 140–225 mm, and by the fall of their second year had grown to 280–305 mm and were probably sexually mature. He also reported that a male captured on 9 October, 1948 grew to 290 mm by 28 March 1950, and to 320 mm by 9 September 1950. Longevity is unknown.

Food And Feeding: Earthworms and slugs are the favorite foods, but there are literature records of *S. dekayi* eating sow bugs, various small insects, spiders, small fish, amphibian eggs and small frogs (Surface, 1906; McCauley, 1945; Wright and Wright, 1957; Barbour, 1971; Mount, 1975). *S. dekayi* feeds mostly in the early evening and at night. They actively search for their prey and apparently depend highly on olfaction for locating it (Burghardt, 1967). Ernst has observed them capture worms many times. When the worm is located, the snake rapidly crawls to it, seizes it along the body, and then begins to work to the closest end. Once the end of the worm is reached, the snake quickly swallows it.

Predators And Defense: The list of predators of this small snake is long. They are commonly eaten by other snakes, especially racers and kingsnakes; in fact the subspecies *S. d. victa* was first described from a specimen found in the digestive tract of an eastern coral snake. Toads may eat young *S. dekayi* (Linzey and Clifford, 1981), and raccoons, skunks, weasels, and opossums readily devour them. Birds (Virginia rail, robin, loggerhead shrike) are also their enemies (Guthrie, 1932; Netting, 1969; Browning, 1973); Ernst has found brown snake remains in a red–shouldered hawk nest. Neill (1948b) has even reported an apparent attack by a black widow spider.

S. dekayi is one of the most inoffensive snakes. When handled they only rarely attempt to bite (Ernst has had one coil and strike at him), but instead thrash around and spray musk and cloacal fluids. Liner (1977) has reported a case of death feigning (letisimulation) in an *S. d. limnetes*. When touched it writhed, became kinked, and rolled onto its back presenting a dead, desiccated appearance.

Populations: Freedman and Catling (1978) studied a population of *S. dekayi* in an abandoned quarry site in southwestern Ontario. They estimated the population size by using four different methods and found a range of 471–610, with a mean for the four methods of 545. This yielded a density close to 70 snakes/hectare. The male/female ratio for 96 adults they examined was 0.365:1.

In 1960 Ernst examined the site of an abandoned "shanty town" outside Lancaster, Pennsylvania. Beneath the litter of sheet metal, tar paper and cardboard he found 603 *S. dekayi* in slightly over two hectares. The ratio of adult males to females was 197:219.

Sabath and Worthington (1959) reported the following sex ratios for three litters: 5:5, 5:7, and 4:4.

STORERIA OCCIPITOMACULATA

Redbelly Snake

STORERIA OCCIPITOMACULATA
(Storer, 1839)
Redbelly Snake

Recognition: *Storeria occipitomaculata* is a small (to 40.6 cm) light brown to dark brown, olive-black or grayish snake with a reddish venter and 3 small light blotches on the nape. There may be a light mid–dorsal stripe or indications of other dark dorsal longitudinal stripes. Also, the venter may be yellow to orange instead of red, the light nape spots may fuse to form a complete ring or any one of them may be missing, and there is usually a light spot on the 5th labial scale. The pitless, keeled scales occur in 15 rows at mid–body (occasionally 16 or 17 rows anteriorly); there are 110–133 ventrals with no sexual dimorphism, and the anal plate is divided. It differs from *S. dekayi* in having 2(3) preocular scales. Usually there are no loreal scales, 6(5–7) supralabials and 7(6–8) infralabials. The individual hemipenis is short with a flattened distal end that has five spines at its edge. These five spines become larger near the base, but enlarged basal spines are absent. The sulcus spermaticus begins medially, runs around the rear to the side, and then to the tip in a relatively straight path. Fourteen or 15 teeth of equal length occur on each maxilla.

Males have 42–63 subcaudals and tails 21–27% (x = 24–25) of the total body length; females have 35–54 subcaudals, and tails 17–25% (x = 21–22) of total body length.

Karyotype: *S. occipitomaculata* has 36 macrochromosomes; sex determination is ZZ/ZW (Hardy, 1971).

Distribution: *S. occipitomaculata* may be found from Nova Scotia west to southeastern Saskatchewan, and south to central Florida and the Gulf Coast to eastern Texas. There are also relict populations in the Black Hills of South Dakota and adjacent Wyoming, and in northeastern Mexico (Neuvo Leon, San Luis Potosi, Hidalgo).

Geographic Variation: Four subspecies are known, but only two occur in eastern North America. The following ranges and characters are based on a study by Rossman and Erwin (1980). *Storeria occipitomaculata occipitomaculata* (Storer, 1839), the northern redbelly snake, ranges from Nova Scotia westward to southeastern Saskatchewan and south to the Carolinas, Georgia, Tennessee, Arkansas and northeastern Oklahoma. It has a pinkish to red venter, the light neck marks usually separated from the venter, tail length relative to total body length of less than 25% in males and 22% in females, and less than 49 subcaudals in males and 42 in females. *S. o. obscura* Trapido, 1944, the Florida redbelly snake, ranges from central Florida north to Georgia and the Carolinas, and west along the Gulf Coastal Plain to eastern Texas. It has a yellow, orange or tan venter, the lateral neck blotches extending to the venter, relative tail lengths of over 25% in males and 22% in females, and more than 53 subcaudals in males and 45 in females. Intergradation occurs in southeastern Oklahoma, western Tennessee, northern Alabama, Georgia, and on the coastal plain and piedmont of the Carolinas.

Confusing Species: *Storeria dekayi* and the earth snakes, *Virginia*, have cream–colored venters. *Seminatrix pygaea* has smooth body scales, and *Clonophis kirtlandii* has two longitudinal rows of black spots on its venter.

Habitat: The redbelly snake lives predominantly in moist woodlands where it usually hides under rocks or logs, or within rotted stumps. It often shares its hiding place with *Carphophis amoenus*, *Diadophis punctatus*, *Storeria dekayi*, or *Virginia valeriae*. However, it is by no means restricted to woodlands and may also be occasionally found in open fields, bogs, or along the border of marshes or swamps. It sometimes climbs into low shrubs (Smith, 1961), but most activity is at ground level.

Behavior: In the north, *S. occipitomaculata* may first appear in March during warm springs, but more often they do not emerge from hibernation until April, and in Manitoba not until May (Gregory, 1977a). Bider (1968) found that in Quebec they were most active during the second week of August. They remain active until October or November when cold temperatures force hibernation. Winter mortality may be high (Bailey, 1948). The winter is spent in soil or gravel (Lachner, 1942; Wright and Wright, 1957), in ant mounds (Criddle, 1937; Lang, 1969), in rock crevices (Bothner, 1963), or under bark (Neill, 1948a). In the south they may be active in all months (Semlitsch and Moran, 1984).

During the summer months, these small snakes are nocturnal or crepuscular. In Quebec,

Map

Fig. 63. *Storeria occipitomaculata occipitomaculata.*

Bider (1968) found them to be active from 2200–2400 hrs in June, 2200–2300 hrs in July, and in August at 1000–1100 and 1300–1400 hrs. In the spring and fall they are more diurnal. Semlitsch and Moran (1984) found that in South Carolina when air temperature increased and a nearby waterbody began to dry, redbelly snake activity increased. Body temperatures of two *S. occipitomaculata* caught by Brattstrom (1965) were 24.3 and 28.2 C, respectively, and he calculated the critical thermal maximum to be 37.8 C.

Redbelly snakes may move considerable distances in a short period of time. Blanchard (1937) recaptured a female that had moved about 400 m in 24 hours, but another was recaptured after 7 days only 30 m from the site of first capture. Semlitsch and Moran (1984) thought that in South Carolina these snakes occupied small home ranges.

Reproduction: Dissections of redbelly snakes from South Carolina by Semlitsch and Moran (1984) showed those 94–110 mm in snout–vent length were immature. The shortest female with enlarged follicles was 126 mm, and the smallest male with enlarged testes was 118 mm. Both sexes probably mature by the end of their first full year of growth, but first reproduction in South Carolina probably occurs the following spring or summer at 2 years of age. Blanchard (1937) also concluded that *S. occipitomaculata* from Michigan bred in their second year.

In South Carolina, females apparently reproduce annually, as all those larger than 126 mm snout–vent length contained enlarged vitellogenic ovarian follicles (Semlitsch and Moran, 1984). Follicles were largest in May (5.5 mm), and two females examined on 9 and 17 July were parturient. Semlitsch and Moran (1984) reported that their females contained an average of 9 (2–15) enlarged follicles, and that the number of follicles increased significantly with female size.

Trapido (1940) dissected male redbelly snakes in the fall, and each had mature sperm in their vas deferens. He also found active sperm in the oviducts of females dissected in October. Apparently the sperm may remain viable for some time after copulation.

Mating may occur during the spring, summer, or fall (Wright and Wright, 1957). Ernst has seen them copulate in late May in Minnesota, while Gregory (1977a) found a female in Manitoba that contained a copulatory plug in her cloaca on 22 August, and Trapido (1940) reported a 6 September mating.

In South Carolina, birth may occur as early as June and continues through August (Semlitsch and Moran, 1984), but in the more northern part of the range the young are probably born from late July to early September. Carr (1940) reported a female *S. o. obscura* from Florida contained 8 large but incompletely developed embryos on 17 April which possibly would have been born in May. Gregory (1975a) and Gordon and Cook (1980) have found aggregations of gravid females in Canada.

The young are born singly and are enclosed in a thin membrane which is soon ruptured. Many are stillborn, and as much as 30 minutes may elapse between births (Nelson, 1969). Cohen (1948b) reported a female from Maryland gave birth to 2 living young and then had 3 dead young 12 days later, and Nelson (1969) reported a female took three days to pass her 15 young.

Most broods contain 4–9 young (Blanchard, 1937), but a female may give birth to as few as 1 or as many as 21 young (Wright and Wright, 1957). Nelson (1969) reported that 6 females from Minnesota had an average of 15 young per brood, with the largest brood containing 20 young. Newborn young are of similar color and pattern to adults and 70–110 mm in total length.

Growth And Longevity: Blanchard (1937) thought that Michigan redbelly snakes collected in mid–summer and measuring approximately 170–210 mm in total length were about one year old. In South Carolina, juveniles grew from about 61 to about 90 mm in snout–vent length by winter and then reached 110 mm by the following summer at one year of age (Semlitsch and Moran, 1984).

The longevity record for this snake is 2 years, 2 months (Bowler, 1977).

Food And Feeding: Slugs seem to be the preferred diet (Barbour, 1950a; Hamilton and Pollack, 1956; Brown, 1979a,b), but other small invertebrates, such as earthworms, beetle larvae, snails, and isopods are also eaten. Linzey and Clifford (1981) reported they may eat "tiny frogs," and Ashton and Ashton (1981) thought that salamanders occasionally are prey.

Predators And Defense: This small snake is prey for many other animals. Knapik and Hodgson (1986) took one from the stomach of a large-mouth bass, Conant (1951) reported predation by a red–tailed hawk, and Blatchley (in Minton, 1972) retrieved one from a chicken. Various snakes (milk snakes, kingsnakes, black racers, coral snakes) also take their share. Small mammals may also feed on them; Wistrand (1972) saw a thirteen–lined ground squirrel eat one. There are also records of this snake being devoured in captivity by various animals: a spider (Swanson, 1952), a fence lizard (*Sceloporus undulatus*;

Busack, 1960), a gray treefrog (*Hyla versicolor*; Puckette, 1962), and a marbled salamander (*Ambystoma opacum*; Linzey and Clifford, 1981).

When first approached *S. occipitomaculata* usually flattens its head and body, and, if handled, will curl its upper lips to expose the maxillary teeth while pushing these teeth outward. This results in a startling "grin," and Axtell (in Wright and Wright, 1957) noted it may press the side of the head against its captor in such a way that these teeth may snag in the skin. If further disturbed it will spray musk. Jordon (1970) has reported this species plays dead by rolling onto its back and becoming rigid and contorted.

Populations: In their South Carolina study, Semlitsch and Moran (1984) found relative small populations at the 3 sites sampled; they captured only 113 at Rainbow Bay during 4 years, and 39 at Bullfrog Pond in 2 years, and 24 at Sun Bay in almost 4 years. They marked 61 from September 1980 to September 1981, and, of those marked, only 3% were recaptured at Rainbow Bay (1 of 34), 9% at Sun Bay (1 of 11), and 13% at Bullfrog Pond (2 of 16) during the remainder of the study. This limited number of recaptures did not warrant calculation of population size using a mark–recapture index. Similarly, Blanchard (1937) recaptured only 2 of 157 marked *S. occipitomaculata* during his study in Michigan.

Although the populations from South Carolina and Michigan mentioned above seem small, large populations may occur. Lang (1969) captured and marked over 1500 redbelly snakes on a 24 ha grassy section in the woodland near Itasca State Park, Minnesota.

In Michigan, Blanchard (1937) caught 16 male and 9 female juveniles in 12 years. He also recorded the sex of 61 newborn, 28 males and 33 females, for a combined juvenile sex ratio of 44 males and 42 females, essentially 1:1. During this same period he collected 39 adult males and 71 adult females, a 0.55:1 ratio. The sex ratio of 81 adult redbelly snakes from South Carolina dissected by Semlitsch and Moran (1984) was approximately 1:1 (44 males and 37 females).

THAMNOPHIS BRACHYSTOMA

Shorthead Garter Snake

THAMNOPHIS BRACHYSTOMA
(Cope, 1892a)
Shorthead Garter Snake

Recognition: The body (to 55.9 cm) is olive–gray to light brown or black with a pale orange or yellow dorsal stripe and a lateral buff–colored to yellow stripe on each side. The dorsal stripe may be indistinct. The lateral stripes are two scale rows wide; usually occurring anteriorly on rows 2 and 3, but occasionally on the lower half of row 4. Normally, there is no longitudinal series of black spots between the dorsal and lateral stripes. The venter is olive–gray to light gray or tan with some brighter pigment at the sides of the ventral scutes. The head is as broad or only slightly broader than the indistinct neck, giving the head a very short appearance. Dorsally, it is olive–gray to light brown with an orange or yellow parietal spot; dark seams separate the supralabials. Ventrally, the head is salmon pink, yellowish or cream–colored. The body scales are keeled, pitless, and usually occur in 17 rows throughout (76% of 155 Pennsylvania snakes examined by Barton, 1956), or 17–19–17 (11%), or 17–17–15 (8%). The anal plate is not divided. On the side of the head are a loreal, 1 preocular (occasionally 2), 2 or 3 postoculars, 2 temporals, 6(7–9) supralabials, and 7–8(9) infralabials. There are 131–146 ventrals with no sexual dimorphism. The hemipenis has not been described. Each maxilla has about 17 teeth, those in the rear are slightly enlarged.

Males have 57–75 subcaudals, and tails approximately 25% as long as the total body length. Females have 51–64 subcaudals, and tails only about 22% as long as the body.

Karyotype And Geographic Variation: Unknown.

Distribution: The shorthead garter snake occurs mainly in the unglaciated portions of the upper Allegheny River drainage from southern Chautau-qua, Cattaraugus, and Allegheny counties, New York south to eastern Mercer, Venango, Clarian, and Jefferson counties, Pennsylvania at elevations of 270 to over 700 meters (Bothner, 1976; Price, 1978). Colonies have also been established at Pittsburgh, Allegheny County, and in Butler and Erie counties, Pennsylvania (McCoy, 1982), and an old, unverified record exists for Horsehead, Schemung County, New York in the Susquehanna River drainage (Wright and Wright, 1957). It is thought to have survived the Wisconsin glaciation in essentially the same area it now occupies (Netting, in Conant, 1950).

Confusing Species: In *Thamnophis sirtalis* there is often a longitudinal series of black spots located between the dorsal and lateral stripes; also the lateral stripes never touch scale row 4. *Thamnophis butleri* normally has 19 mid–body scale rows, and its head is distinct from the neck.

Habitat: *T. brachystoma* is most often found under stones, logs, or boards in meadows, old fields, or along marsh borders where the ground cover is predominantly low herbs. Apparently, deep woodlands are avoided. The introduced colonies in Allegheny, Butler, and Erie counties are all in urban settings.

Behavior: Klingener (1957) conducted a mark–recapture study of 14 *T. brachystoma* in Crawford County, Pennsylvania, and recovered five (35.7%) at the site of capture, a sheet of corrugated galvanized iron. He concluded the snakes were using the metal sheet as a home site or refuge, and Asplund (1963) reported it very common to find from 4–12 specimens of both sexes coiled together under one piece of cover.

Asplund (1963) took cloacal temperatures from 128 *T. brachystoma*, most of which were under cover, and found the mean body temperature to be 30 C. The body temperatures of two active snakes were 31.8 C (late afternoon, 26 June) and 29.2 C (1430 hr, 16 July). Asplund thought the temperatures of active individuals indicated an adaptation to a relatively cool climate, and that thermal activity levels might have a great bearing on this snake's distribution.

Winter is apparently spent in an underground hiberaculum beneath the frost line. Such a site was excavated in Cattaraugus County, New York during March 1962 by Bothner (1963). It was on a west–facing bluff with a 45 degree slope in loam soil having accumulations of shale and sandstone at an altitude of approximately 147 m. The opening was situated between two loose pieces of shale in a well–weathered outcropping. In three days, Bothner found 13 *T. brachystoma* (9 females, 4 males) buried at depths of 43–114 cm and soil temperatures of 2.8–3.3 C. Most were situated alone, but two pairs of intertwined males and females were found, perhaps in preparation for mating. Bothner (in Pisani, 1967) thought that the males emerge from hiberation before the females.

During the warmer months these snakes frequently bask.

Reproduction: Males mature at a total length of about 28 cm and females at approximately 33 cm, both in their second year (Pisani and Bothner, 1970).

The male sexual cycle is similar to that of *T. sirtalis*. Spermatogenic activity is clearly under way by the time of spring emergence in April and mature sperm occur in the Sertoli cells by late July–early August, when the testes reach maximum size. Sperm pass into the lumen of the seminiferous tubules from mid–August through September, and then rapidly pass into the epididymides and vas deferens, where they apparently overwinter (Pisani and Bothner, 1970).

In females, ovarian follicles 4–5 mm in diameter grow rapidly during the spring and reach a size of 6–7 mm by ovulation in May or June, depending on the temperatures of the preceding spring (Pisani and Bothner, 1970).

Mating begins in April just after emergence from hibernation, and the sperm is stored in seminal receptacles in the female's oviduct until ovulation. All of the mature females examined by Pisani and Bothner (1970) during April had motile sperm in their cloaca, but no sperm was found in females examined during the fall.

Pisani (1967) observed two pairs of courting and mating *T. brachystoma* on 17 April 1966 in Cattaraugus County, New York.

> At 1:00 p.m. EST, a specimen of *T. brachystoma* was seen crawling rapidly across the leaf litter with a smaller specimen in close pursuit... later capture of these two individuals showed the former to be a female and the latter a male. During pursuit, the male's chin and labial regions were continually rubbed along the female's dorsum, and continual attempts were made by the male to align his body with hers. The female paused occasionally, at which times the male would attempt to insert his anal region beneath hers. This behavior seemed to prompt the female to move off again... the male would immediately resume pursuit. As the pair moved past other males resting in the area, these would immediately show interest in the female and join the chase. They ceased to follow, however, after traveling, about three to four feet. Attraction in these cases seemed to be visual, as the active pair passed the resting males at a distance of six to twelve inches. These 'secondary' males were entirely ignored by the pair.
>
> On several occasions, the male was seen to fall behind the female. When this occurred, he apparently kept track of her route via vis-

Map

ual means, the tongue rarely being employed, though olfaction could conceivably play a role...

The chase was observed for a total distance of about 30 feet, this being traversed by the animals in approximately three minutes, including pauses. The snakes were moving when sighted, and the distance previously traveled is unknown. At the end of this distance, the pair started to move beneath the shale fragments, at which time they were captured for positive sex identification. At no time did they show any sign of returning in the direction from which they had come, but rather proceeded in a roughly linear, downhill direction...

At 1:13 p.m., another pair was observed lying among the leaves. At this point, a fall inactivated the author's watch, so that subsequent activity could be precisely timed. The female, again the larger of the two (s–v 320 mm), remained relatively quiescent throughout, her head and part of her neck elevated above the leaves. The two lay side by side, their bodies in contact the entire length. The head and part of the neck of the male lay along the female's back, his snout about one-fourth of the female's total length posterior to hers. Those regions of the male's body immediately anterior and posterior to his vent were draped in single loops over the female's back, the remainder of their tails being tightly entwined.... The male *T. brachystoma* was observed to make a rapid, spasmodic series of pre-coital courtship movements every thirty to seventy-five seconds, pressing his anal region tightly against the fe-

THAMNOPHIS BRACHYSTOMA

Shorthead Garter Snake

male's lifting it up. No cooperation was observed on the part of the female...

The above behavior persisted for about ten minutes, at which time the male succeeded in inserting his left hemipenis into the female's cloaca. A series of caudocephalic waves was then initiated in the male, and continued for roughly two minutes. After a brief pause, rhythmic waves were observed to now progress cephalocaudally in the male, terminating in a brief contraction of his anal region, presumably to expel sperm from his hemipenis. These waves continued at regular intervals of ten to twenty seconds for the remainder of the time that the two were in union. Their bodies were now untwined, but still in close proximity. After about twenty minutes had elapsed, the female waved her head and neck (as yet still elevated) laterally several times, then lowered her head and crawled beneath some shaded leaves out of the direct sunlight (temperature in direct sunlight 86° F., beneath leaves 65° F). The male was dragged after her. Leaves were removed from about the anal regions of the animals so that observation could continue, and this action failed to disturb them. Behavior of the animals was not observed to differ from that described prior to their move, save that they were now in contact only at their anal regions and the female's head was no longer elevated.

When approximately fifteen to twenty minutes more had elapsed, the female started to move into dense cover, the male still dragging behind. He made no attempt to crawl with her, but lay quietly, the cephalocaudal waves still in progress. At this point, the pair was captured and the female saved for future data on gestation period. Unfortunately, the male was accidentally lost, but measured approximately 260 mm, in s–v length.

On 13 May at approximately 1130 hr, Ernst found a mating "ball" of 10 *T. brachystoma* (7 males, 3 females) under a flat rock in Forest County, Pennsylvania.

Pisani and Bothner (1970) concluded that female *T. brachystoma* probably have a biennial reproductive cycle, as 25% of the mature females examined between May and September showed no signs of ovulation that year (no enlargement of mature ovarian follicles, no embryos, no recent corpora lutea). They thought this possibly an adaptation to a habitat where short, cool summers are common.

Most young are born in August; Pisani and Bothner (1970) recorded parturition on days 2–9, Swanson (1952) on 5, 15–17, and 19–20, and Ernst had litters born in his laboratory on 14 and 20 August (Ernst and Gotte, 1986). However, Stewart (1961) reported a gravid female contained 9 near–term young on 25 July and Swanson (1952) reported the birth of a litter on 10 September. Swanson's litters averaged 8.6 young (5–14), Ernst and Gotte's (1986) 6.5 (5–8), and

Pisani and Bothner (1970) calculated the mean reproductive potential of their females as 7.2 young per litter, average: 2.4 (1–4) embryos in left oviduct, 4.8 (2–8) in right. The male:female ratio among Pisani and Bothner's prenatal and neonate *T. brachystoma* was 1.5:1. The largest females produced the greatest number of young in both Swanson's and Ernst and Gotte's samples.

The young resemble the adults in pattern, but are somewhat darker in ground color at first. The mean total body length of Ernst and Gotte's (1986) young was 136.6 mm (118–145), while Swanson's (1952) young were 125–158 mm long. Barton (1956) reported that in three litters produced in the laboratory and preserved at once, 12 males averaged 146.4 mm in total length and 15 females, 146 mm.

Growth And Longevity: Barton (1956) studied the size of 194 *T. brachystoma* and concluded that neonates approximately double their length during the first year of life, that they reach mature size at the end of the second year, and then only increase in length slowly throughout their remaining lives. Individuals have lived for more than three years in Ernst's laboratory.

Food And Feeding: *T. brachystoma* seems to be strictly an earthworm eater, no other animals have been found in its digestive tract (Asplund, 1963; Wozniak and Bothner, 1966). Wozniak and Bothner (1966) found that 25% of the garter snakes they examined contained earthworm remains, and Asplund (1963) reported that 55% of those he examined had eaten earthworms. Asplund found that an average earthworm meal comprised 4.75% (0.7–13.9) of the snake's weight. Richmond (in Klingener, 1957) suggested that *T. brachystoma* also feeds on isopods and slugs, and Asplund thought slugs or small salamanders might be eaten. Captives readily feed on earthworms, which they seize along the body and then work their mouths to one end of the earthworm and quickly swallow it.

Predators And Defense: Swanson (1952) felt that small mammals and possibly birds prey on *T. brachystoma*. Certainly, the automobile has killed many from colonies adjacent to roads. When approached they either remain quietly coiled or try to flee. When first handled they thrash about and spray musk, but never bite.

Populations: Asplund (1963) studied two Pennsylvania populations of *T. brachystoma* and found the colonies were large (555–1290, and 218–418 snakes, respectively), and that individuals moved freely in and out of each study area. Densities of colonies seem high, but due to its gregarious nature a false impression of abundance may be given.

Pisani and Bothner (1970) found a 1.4:1 adult male to female ratio, but Wozniak and Bothner (1966) reported a 0.6:1 ratio. Swanson (1952) found the sexes to be about equally represented in his study.

Remarks: That *T. brachystoma* and Butler's garter snake, *T. butleri*, are closely related is of little doubt. Barton (1956) thought that before the Wisconsin glaciation *brachystoma* and *butleri* were members of a single species occupying a continuous geographical range, but the glacier's advance forced the main body of the species to retreat ahead of it to a point south of its terminal moraine, meanwhile leaving the segment of the population which has become *brachystoma* isolated in its high plateau locale. Due to pressures, competitive or climatic, *butleri* later migrated northward and has come to occupy primarily glaciated territory. Since *brachystoma* has remained virtually stationary during and since the Wisconsin glaciation, it likely is morphologically nearer the pre–glacial stock, whereas *butleri* has possibly evolved slightly more to fit the new demands of its glacier–modified habitat. The belief that *butleri* and *brachystoma* were once a single species is supported by the fact that most *butleri*-like *brachystoma* are those from the southern and southwestern borders of the present range, the area presumably last in contact with *butleri*. Typical *butleri* characteristics (namely, scale rows 19 at mid–body, 7 supralabials, lateral stripes invading the fourth scale row) are possessed by more than twice as many specimens from this area as those from the remainder of the range. While this finding must at present be regarded as tentative due to incomplete sampling, the fact that one third of the southwestern *brachystoma* show one or more of these *butleri* characters is strongly suggestive, and were the two forms in geographical contact, it is possible that this section would be regarded as an area of intergradation.

THAMNOPHIS BUTLERI

Butler's Garter Snake

THAMNOPHIS BUTLERI (Cope, 1889)
Butler's Garter Snake

Recognition: This small snake (to 69.4 cm) is black to olive–brown with distinct, yellow to orange longitudinal stripes. The lateral stripes occur on the 2nd and 3rd scale rows, and, at least anteriorly, on the ventral half of row 4; black spots may occur between the dorsal and lateral stripes. On the greenish–yellow belly, the sides of the ventral scutes are brownish, and there is a streak of black pigment along the lateral portions of the ventral seams. The olive to black head is small, and only slightly broader than the neck. A small yellow spot occurs on each parietal, and the upper labials may be tinged with orange; the chin and throat are yellow. The body scales are keeled, pitless, and usually occur in 19–21 rows anteriorly and at mid–body, but only 17 rows near the anus; the anal plate is not divided. Distinctive head scales are the loreal, 1 (occasionally 2) preoculars, 2–3 postoculars, 2 temporals, 6–7 supralabials, and 6–7 infralabials. There are 130–154 ventrals with no sexual dimorphism. The hemipenis has not been described. Seventeen teeth occur on the maxilla, those most posterior are slightly enlarged.

Males have 60–72 subcaudals, females 49–64; there is only a slight difference in tail length between the sexes.

Karyotype: Oguma and Makino (1932) reported that the diploid chromosome number of a male was 36.

Distribution: *T. butleri* ranges from northcentral Ohio west to northcental Indiana, and northward through eastern Michigan and southwestern Ontario. An isolated population occurs in southeastern Wisconsin.

Geographic Variation: No subspecies are recognized.

Confusing Species: *Thamnophis sirtalis* has its lateral stripes only on scale rows 2 and 3; *T. radix* has its lateral stripes on rows 3 and 4; and *T. brachystoma* usually has only 17 mid–body scale rows.

Habitat: Wet open areas, such as mesic prairies, pastures, fields in parks, marsh borders, sides of canals, and vacant city lots are favored. *T. butleri* is one of the few reptiles to have benefited from urbanization, and large populations can often be found in cities (Minton, 1968; Vogt, 1981).

Behavior: The normal annual activity cycle extends from March to November. In Ohio, Conant (1951) collected *T. butleri* in every month except December with a decided activity peak in April, when over 10 times as many were taken as in any other month, and a minor peak in October.

Butler's garter snakes often are active during the morning hours, and we have also observed them foraging during the early evening; in the summer almost all activity is crepuscular. These snakes sometimes travel over broad areas while searching for food. Carpenter (1952a) reported an adult in Michigan moved a minimum distance of 121 m in 2 hours; the average distance moved during his study for over 200 days between captures was 120 m, and for less than 200 days, 115 m. In over 200 days, females moved an average distance of 111 m, while males moved 125 m. For recaptures less than 200 days apart, females moved an average of 161 m, males 98 m. Carpenter never found *T. butleri* in the woods, and felt woodlands probably act as a natural barrier to their dispersal. The maximum distance between any two points of capture was 305 m and the maximum width 17 m, indicating a rather long, narrow home range. However, he found many individuals at distances of 30 m from the margin of the marsh and thought this distance was perhaps more indicative of the home range width.

In Ontario, Freedman and Catling (1979) found that 50% of their recaptures of *T. butleri* were at distances less than 50 m from the initial point of capture; however, a 31 cm male crawled 433 m and a 47 cm gravid female 517 m in 70 days. Minimum home ranges for three Ontario *T. butleri* were 50, 50, and 600 m², respectively. Freedman and Catling also noticed a tendency for *T. butleri* to avoid crossing roads.

Carpenter (1956) took the cloacal temperature of 54 Butler's garter snakes and found them to average 26.1 C (12.4 – 34.0); mean environmental temperatures measured at the same time were: air, 20.9 C (7.0–29.0); ground surface, 24.2 C (7.0–36.0); and soil (depth 25 mm), 19.3 C (7.0 –32.0). More than 70% of the cloacal tem-

Diadophis punctatus edwardsi, Northern Ringneck Snake

Ramphotyphlops braminus, Brahminy Blind Snake (Carl H. Ernst)

Farancia abacura reinwardti, Western Mud Snake

Carphophis amoenus amoenus, Eastern Worm Snake

Farancia erytrogramma erytrogramma, Rainbow Snake
(Christopher W. Brown)

Heterodon platyrhinos, Eastern Hognose Snake (Ernst)

Heterodon platyrhinos, Eastern Hognose Snake

Heterodon simus, Southern Hognose Snake (Ernst)

Tantilla coronata, Southeastern Crowned Snake

Heterodon nasicus nasicus, Plains Hognose Snake (Ernst)

Tantilla gracilis, Flathead Snake (Steve W. Gotte)

Rhadinaea flavilata, Pine Woods Snake (Barry Mansell)

Tantilla oolitica, Rim Rock Crowned Snake (Mansell)

Drymarchon corais couperi, Eastern Indigo Snake (Dale E. Fuller)

Tantilla relicta neilli, Central Florida Crowned Snake (Mansell)

Coluber constrictor constrictor, Northern Black Racer

Opheodrys vernalis vernalis, Eastern Smooth Green Snake (James H. Harding)

Masticophis flagellum flagellum, Eastern Coachwhip

Cemophora coccinea coccinea, Florida Scarlet Snake

Opheodrys aestivus, Rough Green Snake

Elaphe obsolete rossalleni, Everglades Rat Snake

Elaphe guttata guttata, Corn Snake

Elaphe vulpina gloydi, Eastern Fox Snake

Elaphe obsoleta obsoleta, Black Rat Snake

Lampropeltis calligaster rhombomaculata, Mole Kingsnake (Brown)

Lampropeltis getulus getulus, Eastern King snake (Ernst)

Lampropeltis getulus holbrooki, Speckled Kingsnake

Lampropeltis triangulum triangulum, Eastern Milk Snake

Pituophis melanoleucus sayi, Bullsnake

Lampropeltis triangulum elapsoides, Scarlet Kingsnake

Stilosoma extenuatum, Short–tailed Snake

Pituophis melanoleucus melanoleucus, Northern Pine Snake
(Brown)

Clonophis kirtlandii, Kirtland's Snake

Nerodia cyclopion, Green Water Snake

Nerodia floridana, Florida Green Water Snake

Nerodia fasciata fasciata, Banded Water Snake

Nerodia sipedon sipedon, Northern Water Snake

Nerodia rhombifera rhombifera, Diamondback Water Snake

Nerodia erythrogaster flavigaster, Yellow belly Water Snake

Nerodia taxispilota, Brown Water Snake (Ernst)

Regina rigida rigida, Glossy Crayfish Snake (Mansell)

Regina alleni, Striped Crayfish Snake

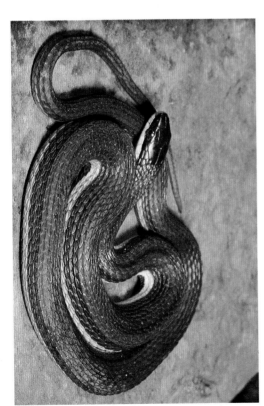

Regina septemvittata, Queen Snake

Regina grahamii, Graham's Crayfish Snake (Earl E. Possardt)

Seminatrix pygaea paludis, Carolina Swamp Snake

Storeria occipitomaculata occipitomaculata, Northern Redbelly Snake

Storeria dekayi victa, Florida Brown Snake

Thamnophis brachystoma, Shorthead Garter Snake

Thamnophis sirtalis sirtalis, Eastern Garter Snake

Thamnophis butleri, Butler's Garter Snake

Thamnophis proximus proximus, Western Ribbon Snake

Thamnophis radix radix, Eastern Plains Garter Snake

Virginia striatula, Rough Earth Snake (William A. Cox)

Virginia valeriae elegans, Western Earth Snake

Thamnophis sauritus sauritus, Eastern Ribbon Snake

Thamnophis lineatum annectans, Central Lined Snake (Steve W. Gotte)

Micrurus fulvius fulvius, Eastern Coral Snake (Robert T. Zappalorti)

Agkistrodon piscivorus piscivorus, Eastern Cottonmouth (Ernst)

Agkistrodon contortrix mokeson, Northern Copperhead

Sistrurus catenatus catenatus, Eastern Massasauga (Zappalorti)

Crotalus adamanteus, Eastern Diamondback Rattlesnake

Sistrurus miliarius barbouri, Dusky Pigmy Rattlesnake

Crotalus horridus horridus, Timber Rattlesnake

Sistrurus miliarius streckeri, Western Pigmy Rattlesnake

peratures were between 20 and 30 C. During cold and hot weather respectively, cloacal temperatures were above and below the immediate environmental temperatures. The cloacal temperatures were most closely correlated with the temperature at the ground surface. *T. butleri* exhibited behavioral thermoregulation; basking in cool weather, seeking shelter in hot weather. In Michigan, they hibernated about 150 days with emergence occurring from late March to late May (Carpenter, 1952a, 1953a); ant mounds and meadow vole tunnels were used as hibernacula. In the ant mounds, *T. butleri* was found at depths of 35–68 cm.

Reproduction: Females attain sexual maturity at a snout–vent length of about 340 mm during their second spring, while a male of this species 321 mm in snout–vent length was observed courting a larger female. This length is also within the range of those in their second spring (Carpenter, 1952b). Smith (1946) noted that mature males develop tubercles on their mental scale, chin shields and anterior labials.

During late March and April, breeding activities begin immediately after hibernation. The males actively seek females by following their pheromone trails (Ford, 1982a). At times this leads several males to one female. Finneran (1949) observed four males closely intertwined about a female and a sixth smaller *T. butleri* of unknown sex, and later another male joined the aggregation.

During courtship, a male endeavors to achieve a dorsal position in relation to the female. He then rubs his chin along her back as he slowly crawls forward until reaching her neck. He also frequently touches her back with his tongue, probably smelling pheromones secreted through her skin. When his chin finally rests on her neck, several loops of his body lie across her back. Before his cloaca is pushed under the female, the region immediately anterior to the cloaca is thrown across her back and his cloacal region, bent, and forced under her body from the side opposite to that on which the most posterior portion of his body lies. The body and tail are then thrown into a series of rhythmic caudocephalic waves. These waves may occur at a frequency of less than a second, and hemipenial insertion usually occurs within a few minutes after the beginning of these waves. After coitus is achieved, no further rhythmical tail thrusts occur (Noble, 1937). Noble (1937) observed that in one mating, there occurred a rhythmical pulsation of the sides of the female's body immediately anterior to the cloaca (one beat approximately every three seconds), and he thought this due to the movements of the

Map

male's hemipenis. One copulation observed by Noble lasted 40 minutes.

The anterior cloaca of recently mated females contains a copulatory plug which blocks the oviducal openings (Devine, 1977). This plug is apparently formed by the copulating male after ejaculation. Devine (1977) interpreted this as a form of intrasexual competition in which the successfully copulating male makes the female temporarily unavailable to other males, and reduces the likelihood of multiple inseminations. Apparently males recognize those females with plugs and treat them as if they were unavailable. In any given year, about 67% of the females become pregnant (Carpenter 1952a).

The 4–20, 125–185 mm young are usually born in August and early September. Ford and Killebrew (1983) reported that the length and mass of newborn *T. butleri* are positively correlated with the length and mass of the female but negatively correlated with clutch size.

Growth And Longevity: Carpenter (1952b) studied growth in a marked population of *T. butleri* from Michigan. He estimated the annual growth period was the five months from May through September (153 days), and found a steady decrease in growth rate as the snake became larger. Females 20–24 cm in initial snout–vent length grew 1.15 cm (7.0%) per month; those 30–34 cm,

THAMNOPHIS BUTLERI

Butler's Garter Snake

1.24 cm (3.6%) per month; and those 40–44 cm, 0.2 cm (0.5%) per month. Males 20–24 cm long grew 1.9 cm (8.9%), those 25–29 cm, 2.9 cm (10.8%); males 30–34 cm, 0.8 cm (2.5%); and those 35–39 cm, 0.2 cm (0.5%).

Natural longevity is unknown, but probably is longer than the 2 years, 3 days reported for an individual at the Philadelphia Zoo by Bowler (1977).

Food And Feeding: *T. butleri* is predominantly a worm eater (Ruthven, 1908, Conant, 1951, Carpenter, 1952a; Catling and Freedman, 1980b). Carpenter (1952a) reported that 83% of his food records were for earthworms and 10% for leeches, while Catling and Freedman (1980b) reported that 96% of the prey items regurgitated consisted of earthworms. The eating of earthwoms seems instinctive. Burghardt (1967, 1969) found that inexperienced young responded to extracts of fish, earthworms, slugs, and amphibians, but were most interested in earthworms and showed little interest in slug extract. Occasionally, however, small frogs are also eaten (Ruthven, 1908); Test (1958) reported a young *T. butleri* from Michigan regurgitated an adult spring peeper, *Hyla crucifer*, and a Canadian individual regurgitated a chorus frog, *Pseudacris triseriata* (Catling and Freedman, 1980b). Captives readily take earthworms, guppies, and small frogs (*Acris, Pseudacris, Hyla*).

Predators And Defense: Since *T. butleri* is a small snake, its natural enemies are probably numerous. Vogt (1981) thought that birds, milk snakes, and carnivorous mammals, including domestic cats, probably prey on it, and Carpenter (1952a) suggested crayfish may kill and devour them. Probably any carnivore larger than *T. butleri* will attack it on occasion.

When first encountered, *T. butleri* does not bite; instead it attempts to flee by vigorously throwing its body into a series of whipping, sideways motions. If handled it will expel musk from cloacal glands, and its tail may break off, but not as frequently as in *T. sirtalis* or *T. sauritus* (Willis et al., 1982).

Populations: In his study in Michigan, Carpenter (1952a) found *T. butleri* comprised only 13% of the three speices of *Thamnophis* collected in three years, and 15% of those caught were neonates or less than one year old. His combined population estimate for the three years was only 111 individuals. In Ontario, Freedman and Catling (1978) estimated the population size for their 40–ha study area to be 900; 23 per hectare. Most individuals were over 30 cm in total body length and relatively few juveniles were caught. The male to female ratio in Ontario was not significantly different from 1:1.

Remarks: That *T. butleri* is a separate species from *T. brachystoma* has been well documented (Smith, 1945; Conant, 1950; Barton, 1956), and that both are closely related to *T. radix* is suspected (Ruthven, 1908; Wright and Wright, 1957). In this respect it is interesting that male *T. butleri* tested by Ford (1982a) apparently showed no preference for female pheromone trails of their species over those of *T. radix*.

THAMNOPHIS RADIX

Plains Garter Snake

THAMNOPHIS RADIX (Baird and Girard, 1853)
Plains Garter Snake

Recognition: This garter snake (to 101.6 cm) has lateral light stripes on the 3rd and 4th scale rows, two rows of black spots between the lateral and dorsal stripes, and black bars on the lips. Another row of black spots is located between the lateral stripe and the ventral scutes, and there may also be a row of dark spots along the sides of the venter. A pair of parietal light spots is usually present. The ground color is dark brown or black, the dorsal stripe yellow or orange, and some reddish pigment may be present along the sides of the body. The pitless body scales are keeled, and occur in 19–21 rows anteriorly but usually only 17 rows near the anus. The anal plate is undivided. The head scalation is like that of other eastern *Thamnophis*, except that there are usually 7 (rarely 8) supralabials and 9 (rarely 10) infralabials. The eye occurs above supralabials 4 and 5. There are 135–175 ventrals with no sexual dimorphism. The hemipenis contains an unbranched sulcus spermaticus, several large basal spines, small spines above these, but no spines or calyces on the apex. Each maxilla has 20–21 recurved teeth; the posterior-most are enlarged.

Males have 67–83 subcaudals; females have 54–74 subcaudals (Smith, 1949). The male tail is somewhat longer, usually 23–25% of total body length, than that of the female, 19–23%. Smith (1946) has reported the presence of tubercles on the chin shields of males.

Karyotype: Each cell has 36 biarmed chromosomes (Baker et al., 1972). The females are heteromorphic ZW, with the Z chromosome submetacentric and the W chromosome acrocentric.

Distribution: *T. radix* ranges from northwestern Indiana westward to the Rocky Mountains, and from southeastern Alberta south to northeastern New Mexico. There are also isolated populations in central Ohio, southwestern Illinois, southcentral Missouri, and southwestern Arkansas.

Geographic Variation: Two subspecies are recognized, but only one, *Thamnophis radix radix* (Baird and Girard, 1853), the eastern plains garter snake, occurs in eastern North America.

Confusing Species: No other eastern *Thamnophis* with the lateral stripe on rows 3–4 has black bars on the lips.

Habitat: *T. radix* inhabits open areas such as prairies and meadows, with access to nearby water in ponds, brooks or sloughs. It is often common in the vacant lots of cities.

Ernst has observed that in Minnesota where it occurred sympatrically with the common garter snake, *T. sirtalis*, the latter occupied more moist microhabitats, such as sloughs, ditches, or the banks of lakes, while *T. radix* was more commonly found in open, less moist areas. Hart (1979) reported a similar partitioning of the habitat in Manitoba.

Behavior: In Kansas, *T. radix* is active from March to November (Collins, 1974), but in the north it is more restricted in annual activity. In Minnesota, Ernst only found them active from late April through September.

The winter months are spent hibernating in some burrow, although they may emerge occasionally to bask on exceptionally warm days. Hibernacula are often the burrows of mammals, such as pocket gophers, ground squirrels, or voles, but Criddle (1937) found them in ant hills, and Dalrymple and Reichenbach (1981) thought they might hibernate in crayfish holes. Rock crevices, old wells, post holes, and holes under sidewalks may also be occupied during the winter (Pope, 1944).

The plains garter snake is almost exclusively diurnal. Dalrymple and Reichenbach (1984) and Reichenbach and Dalrymple (1986) found them active from 1100–1600 hours in the spring and fall, and from 0800–1700 hrs in the summer (June–August), but less active between 1300–1400 hrs. However, Ernst has on several occasions found them in Minnesota feeding on *Pseudacris triseriata* after dark during that frog's breeding season. Diurnal activity usually consists of foraging or basking.

Activity seems to be controlled by air temperature. Seibert and Hagen (1947) reported that *T. radix* was most frequently observed when air temperatures were 21–29 C, and that the snakes usually disappeared when the temperature fell below 7.2 C. Dalrymple and Reichenbach (1981) reported that the average field body temperature of

THAMNOPHIS RADIX

Plains Garter Snake

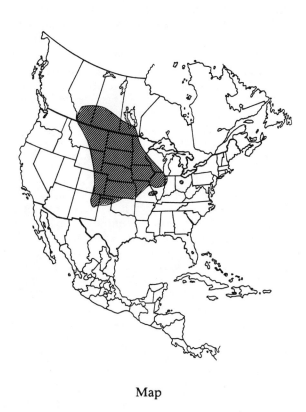

Map

Fig. 64. A juvenile *Thamnophis radix radix* (Carl H. Ernst).

65 Ohio *T radix* was 27.9 C. Hart (1979) found that *T. radix* in Manitoba had significantly higher oral and cloacal temperatures than allopatric *T. sirtalis*; cloacal temperatures depended most upon air temperature, but light intensity and substrate temperature were also important (*T. radix* occurred in a microhabitat of high air but low substrate temperatures). Heckrotte (1962, 1975) studied the effects of light and temperature in the laboratory on the circadian rhythm of *T. radix*, and found that most activity occurred in the light period at low constant temperature, but at a temperature of 31 C most activity shifted to the dark period; the snakes were either diurnal or nocturnal depending on the temperature. Seidel and Lindeborg (1973) reported an apparent lack of change or lag in the metabolic oxygen consumption rate at experimental temperatures between 28 and 34 C, and that *T. radix* had its maximum metabolic rate at 38 C. Lueth (1941) determined the critical thermal maximum and minimum for *T. radix* were 41 and 2 C, but Bailey (1949) reported *T. radix* survived exposure to –2 C for one day.

During their study of population dynamics in Illinois, Seibert and Hagen (1947) observed that most individuals moved less than 2 m per day between captures. One snake, recaptured 4 times, had moved 15 m in two weeks before the first recapture, and 6, 4.5, and 2.7 m in the following three weeks. When last seen on the 5th week, it was only about 11 m from its original location, having traveled a semicircular arc. Apparently *T. radix* has a restricted home range. No territorial behavior was observed during their study.

The plains garter snake does have some homing ability. Thirteen of 32 marked *T. radix* released in foreign territory by Seibert and Hagen (1947) returned to the original area over a 70–day period; 8 wandered 1208 m in one week.

Reproduction: Females apparently attain sexual maturity during their second year (Seibert and Hagen, 1947; Gregory, 1977a). Spermiogenesis occurs in late summer or early autumn and the ovarian cycle is essentially like that of other *Thamnophis* (Cieslak, 1945). Mating usually occurs soon after the snakes have emerged from hibernation in April or May, but Pope (1944) also mentioned the possibility of autumn copulation. A female has been observed mating with several different males, and polygyny may also occur in the wild. Males apparently find females by following their sex pheromone trails (Kubie et al., 1978; Crews, 1980; Ford and Schofield, 1984). These pheromones may be released from the dorsal skin, and shedding (ecdysis) enhances release (Kubie et al., 1978).

One or more males may simultaneously court a female. They crawl along her side poking her with their snouts while nonrhythmic contractions occur along the posterior portions of their bodies. They frequently touch her back with their tongues, and at last one male will successfully position himself to insert his hemipenis. Receptive females remain motionless and raise their tails. After the male releases his sperm, he may place a seminal plug in the female's cloaca which exerts an inhibitory effect on further courtship of that female (Ross and Crews, 1977).

The young are born from late July through September. Litters may number 5–60 young, but most frequently 10–20. Breckenridge (1944) noted a litter of 92 young, but this must either be a mistake, or from an exceptionally large female. Possibly larger litters are produced in more northern populations. Gregory (1977) reported six Manitoba litters to contain 14–54 (x = 29.5) young. There may also be annual variations in litter size due to changes in environmental conditions (Seigel and Fitch, 1985). The young are 175–235 mm at birth. Complete closure of the umbilical scar occurs in 72–110 hours, and the scar lies between the 124th to 150th ventrals in females and the 133rd to 156th in males (Smith, 1947).

Growth And Longevity: In Illinois, *T. radix* grew to lengths of about 45 cm their first year, or 15–20 cm over a period of 112 days or 16 weeks (20 May–9 September); the growth rate was approximately 1.1 cm per week (Seibert and Hagen, 1947). Two–year–olds starting at 40–45 cm probably grew to 55–60 cm at a rate of 0.9 cm per week. Females grew at a faster rate (1.37 and 1.82 cm per week for the first two years, respectively). Gregory (1977a) found similar growth rates in his Manitoba population. Reichenbach and Dalrymple (1986) reported increases of 1.2 mm/day for immature *T. radix* from Ohio, and from 0.17–1.4 mm/day after maturity was reached.

Natural longevity may be longer than the record for captives: 3 years, 7 months, 19 days for a male at the Philadelphia Zoo (Bowler, 1977).

Food And Feeding: The prey of *T. radix* consists almost totally of earthworms, leeches, and small amphibians and their larvae (cricket frogs, chorus frogs, tree frogs, small toads, ranid frogs, and small salamanders). Small fish, rodents and snails are sometimes eaten, and Cebula (1983) reported a wild *T. radix* regurgitated a nestling bird, possibly an eastern meadowlark. The foods eaten in the wild are very similar to those of *T. sirtalis*. Dalrymple and Reichenbach (1984) estimated the ratio of prey biomass to that of *T. radix* in Ohio to range from 40:1 to 91:1; a 1–4 predator/prey biomass ratio is sufficient for maintenance, growth, and reproduction (Reichenbach and Dalrymple, 1986).

Prey trails are followed by olfaction until the animal is seen, then *T. radix* crawls rapidly after it and seizes it in its mouth (Czaplicki, 1975; Secoy, 1979; Kubie and Halpern, 1979; Chiszar et al., 1981).

Predators And Defense: Red–shouldered hawks and other birds of prey, predatory mammals (foxes, coyotes, skunks, minks, domestic cats), and ophiophagous snakes all prey on *T. radix*, but humans with their automobiles, mowers, and habitat destruction may kill more each year than all natural predators combined. Seibert (1950) estimated a natural mortality rate of 20% for his Illinois population.

Plains garter snakes are more mild tempered than *T. sirtalis*, but they will bite if handled. More commonly they secrete musk or defecate on their captor. Arnold and Bennett (1984) have described the variation in antipredator displays in *T. radix*.

Populations: Seibert and Hagen (1947) reported that of 383 snakes marked at an Illinois site, 298 (77.8%) were *T. radix*. Estimation of the population size using the Lincoln Index was 1152 (889 per hectare), and by using the Hayne method was 1093 (845 per hectare) (Seibert, 1950). Reichenbach and Dalyrmple (1986) estimated that 222–531 *T. radix* occurred on their study tract in Ohio; a density of 114–212 per hectare. The estimated biomass over their 3–year study was 3.5–8.6 kg/ha.

Seibert and Hagen (1947) found a sex ratio of 75 males to 100 females in Illinois, but Reichenbach and Dalyrmple (1986) reported a 1:1 sex ratio in Ohio.

Reichenbach and Dalyrmple (1986) found that exploitative competition for food resources between *T. radix* and *T. sirtalis* at their study site in Ohio was unlikely to be a major factor in the population dynamics of either species.

THAMNOPHIS SIRTALIS

Common Garter Snake

THAMNOPHIS SIRTALIS
(Linnaeus, 1758)
Common Garter Snake

Recognition: *Thamnophis sirtalis* is a gray to grayish–brown or black snake (to 124 cm) with a medial and two lateral yellow, green or blue stripes, and dark lip bars. The lateral stripes are always present and are confined to the 2nd and 3rd scale rows, but the medial stripe may be absent, and there may be a double row of black spots between the lateral and medial stripes. The venter is yellow or green with 2 rows of indistinct black spots that are partially hidden by the overlapping of the ventral scutes. Most have 2 small yellow or white spots on top of their heads. The body scales are keeled, lack pits, and usually occur in 19 rows anteriorly and at mid–body, and 17 rows near the anus. The anal plate is undivided. Laterally on the head are a loreal, 1 preocular, 3 (2–4) postoculars, 1 + 2(3) temporals, 7(6–8) supralabials, and 10(8–11) infralabials. Ventrals number 137–178 with no sexual dimorphism; males have 67–84 subcaudals, females 54–80. The hemipenis is simple with an unbranched sulcus spermaticus, 5 large spines at the base, and numerous very small recurved spines in oblique rows on the shaft. Each maxilla has 17(16–18) teeth; the most posterior is slightly longer than those preceding it.

The male's snout–vent length is only about 83% that of the female, and males weigh only about 55% as much as females (Fitch, 1980). The male tail is 21–30% as long as his total length, that of females only 17–22%. Males longer than 475 mm usually have the keels of the dorsal body scales near the vent knobbed, shorter males usually have only weakly developed knobs at best, but usually have no knobs; females of all lengths generally lack knobs (Harrison, 1933).

Karyotype: *T. sirtalis* has 36 chromosomes; 34 macrochromosomes, 2 microchromosomes (Baker et al., 1972).

Fossil Record: *T. sirtalis* is known from the upper Pliocene of Texas (Holman, 1979), and the Pleistocene Irvingtonian of Kansas and South Dakota, and Rancholabrean of Arkansas, Florida, Georgia, Missouri, Pennsylvania, Tennessee and Texas (Holman, 1981; Rogers, 1982).

Distribution: *T. sirtalis* ranges from the Atlantic Coast to the Pacific Coast in North America, and is found farther north in Canada than any other species of snake. It occurs from Prince Edward Island, New Brunswick and Nova Scotia west to the Northwest Territories and southern Alaska thence south through peninsular Florida, to the Gulf Coast from Florida to eastern Texas, northern Utah, and southern California, with isolated populations in the panhandle of Texas, along the Rio Grande River from southern Colorado to western Texas, and in Chihuahua, Mexico.

Geographic Variation: *T. sirtalis* is highly variable; 12 subspecies are currently recognized (Fitch, 1980). However, only four occur in eastern North America. *Thamnophis sirtalis sirtalis* (Linnaeus, 1758), the eastern garter snake, usually has the yellowish vertebral and lateral stripes present and prominent, but in some the dark spots between the stripes dominate the pattern. Some populations about Lake Erie are melanistic, but Sattler and Guttman (1976) conducted an electrophoretic analysis of the melanistic and normally–colored individuals of *T. s. sirtalis* from western Ohio, and found no detectable genetic differences. In Florida, ventral and subcaudal counts are generally higher in the south (Christman, 1980). This subspecies ranges from the southern tip of Hudson Bay southeast through western Quebec, New Hampshire, and Massachusetts to Rhode Island, west to western Ontario, and south, generally east of the Mississippi River, through Florida and to the Gulf Coast as far west as eastern Texas. *T. s. semifasciatus* (Cope, 1892b), the Chicago garter snake, is similar to the nominate race, but differs in having the light lateral stripes interrupted by black bars, and occasionally having black bars also break the dorsal stripe anteriorly. It has a small range around the tip of Lake Michigan in southeastern Wisconsin, northern Illinois and adjacent northwestern Indiana. Smith (1956b) and Benton (1980a, b) discussed the validity and characteristics of this snake. *T. s. pallidula* Allen, 1899, the maritime garter snake, is cinnamon to brown, usually lacks a medial light stripe or, if it is present, the stripe is gray, light brown or pale yellow, and has poorly developed white, gray or light brown lateral stripes. It can be found from Prince Edward Island, Nova Scotia and New Brunswick south to Maine and New Hampshire. The validity of this form has been championed by Bleakney (1959) but questioned by Conant (1975), and we tentatively include it pending additional study. *T. s. similis* Rossman, 1965, the bluestripe garter snake, is brown and has an inconspicuous light brown or gray medial stripe and light blue or bluish–white lateral stripes. It ranges from Wakulla to Pinellas and Hillsborough counties on the Gulf Coast of Florida.

In addition, some individuals from Illinois and Wisconsin have reddish pigment along their sides similar to that found in the red–sided garter snake, *T. s. parietalis* (Say, 1823), but no distinct populations of this subspecies occur east of the Mississippi River.

Dessauer and Fox (1958) have found considerable variation in the electrophoretic plasma protein patterns of *T. sirtalis* from Florida and Louisiana.

Confusing Species: Other eastern species of *Thamnophis* have the lateral stripes at least partially on scale row 4, especially on the neck, except *T. brachystoma* which has a very short head not distinguishable from its neck. *Regina* and *Nerodia* have divided anal plates, and *Tropidoclonion* has a ventral pattern of dark half-moons.

Habitat: We have found this snake in many types of habitats, but most were somewhat moist: deciduous woods, palmetto flats, the banks of drainage ditches, streams, ponds, marshes or swamps, grassy and shrubby fields, quarries, and trash dumps. On the prairies, it is most often found about swales, drainage canals, or streams. It seldom, if ever, enters brackish water (Neill, 1958; Duellman and Schwartz, 1958); but in Washington it has been observed feeding on intertidal fishes (Batts, 1961).

Behavior: The natural history of *T. sirtalis* is better known than that of any other North American snake thanks to the comprehensive studies of Aleksiuk, Burghardt, Carpenter, Crews, Fitch, Gregory, and others.

T. sirtalis is more cold tolerant than many other snakes (Vincent and Secoy, 1978). Its annual cycle of activity over most of the range is from March or April to November, but individuals are often active on warm days during the period from December through February (Wright and Wright, 1957; Fitch, 1965; Franz, 1968; Robinson et al., 1974). Denman and Lapper (1964) reported that *T. sirtalis* in Quebec even work their way through frozen soil and leaves to emerge from hibernation in April. In peninsular Florida and

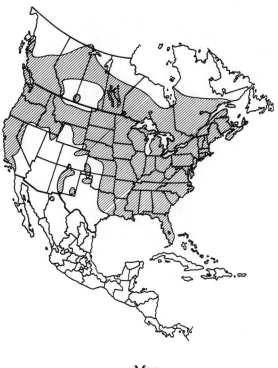

Map

Fig. 65. *Thamnophis sirtalis sirtalis,* blotched phase.

along the Gulf Coast, it may not hibernate during warm winters.

Spring, fall, and winter daily activity is mostly diurnal. Dalrymple and Reichenbach (1981) reported that in the spring 88% of the *T. sirtalis* they caught in Ohio were taken between 1300 and 1500 hours. However, in the spring some crepuscular and nocturnal activity does occur at the time of frog and toad breeding; we have on several occasions found them feeding on frogs after dark. Also, in the summer most activity is either during the morning (0800–1000 hrs) or early evening and at night (1800–2300 hrs). In Quebec, Canada, Bider (1968) reported that these snakes were most active from 2000–2100 hrs in June, 2100–2300 hrs in July, 1400–1500 hrs in August, and 1300–1500 hrs in October. Most annual activity occurred in the fall when the snakes migrated back to hibernacula.

Hibernation may be prolonged in the north or of very short duration in the south. Hibernacula include rock crevices, gravel banks, earth dams, stone causeways, old wells and cisterns, ant mounds, crayfish burrows, mammal burrows, logs and stumps. Almost any site will do, as long as it allows the snake's body temperature to remain slightly above freezing and is moist enough to prevent critical dehydration. Carpenter (1953a) reported cloacal temperatures of 3.4–7.0 C for hibernating Michigan *T. sirtalis*. Often several individuals overwinter together (Aleksiuk, 1977a), and they may share their hibernaculum with other species, such as *T. sauritus*, *T. butleri*, *Storeria dekayi*, *S. occipitomaculata*, *Opheodrys aestivus*, *O. vernalis*, and *Diadophis punctatus*.

Muscle catabolism of glycogen and proteins account for 76–79% of the total winter energy budget which is about 0.45 cal/g/day (Costanzo, 1985). Aleksiuk and Stewart (1971) found that protein and ash, expressed as a percentage of total body weight, remain essentially constant throughout the year. Lipids are low in the spring, increase during the summer, and decrease during the fall and winter. Body water content shows a pattern reverse that of lipids, with the exceptions of a dehydration in the fall and a rehydration in the spring. *T. sirtalis* are near starvation and somewhat dehydrated when they emerge from hibernation.

Brattstrom (1965) reported a minimum voluntary temperature of 9.0 C, a maximum voluntary temperature of 35.0 C, a critical thermal minimum temperature of −2.0 C, and a critical thermal maximum temperature of 38–41 C for 157 *T. sirtalis*. In a thermal gradient, *T. sirtalis* normally selected temperatures of 20–35 C, but after feeding chose 24–34 C, and while undergoing ecdysis,

16–26 C (Kitchell, 1969). Stewart (1965) reported a similar normal range of body temperatures. Most *T. sirtalis* are active within a range of body temperatures of 18–30 C, and seek shelter when their temperature falls below 17 C (Aleksiuk, 1976b). Carpenter (1956) found that about 50% of the cloacal temperatures of active Michigan *T. sirtalis* fell between 25 and 30 C. Moving garter snakes usually have a higher temperature than those of the environment, those undercover about the same temperature, while those basking have cloacal temperatures intermediate between the former activities (Gregory, 1984a). In the spring, a rising body temperature may initiate mating behavior (Morris, 1978).

Gibson and Falls (1979) found that the body temperatures of *T. sirtalis* caught in the field were cooler and more variable early and late in the day, and in the spring and fall. On sunny summer days, females averaged one degree warmer than males. On cloudy days, body temperatures were lower and more variable, and no difference between male and female temperatures existed. Gibson and Falls felt that females were better thermo–regulators than males. They found no indication that gravid females may prefer elevated temperatures, as suggested by Fitch (1965); but did find that melanistic individuals maintained a higher body temperature than striped snakes.

Environmental temperatures may aid in differentiating the niches of sympatric *T. sirtalis* and *T. radix* (Hart, 1979). *T. sirtalis* apparently prefers lower air but higher substrate temperatures than does *T. radix*.

Common garter snakes may travel long distances between summer feeding ranges and hibernacula. Gregory and Stewart (1975) recorded movements as long as 17.7 km in the Interlake Region of Manitoba, and Blanchard and Finster (1933) recovered *T. sirtalis* that had crawled about 3.2 and 2.4 km from the point of first capture. However, most movements are probably shorter distance. Carpenter (1952a), in his study in Michigan, recorded a maximum movement of 300 m, but most were less than 183 m. He thought the average home range was only about 0.8 ha (183 x 48 m). In Kansas, Fitch (1958, 1965) recaptured *T. sirtalis* 0–1158 m from the point of their release; males moved an average distance of 212 m between successive captures, females only 171 m. Fitch (1965) calculated the home ranges to be 14.2 ha for males and 9.2 ha for females. Minton (1972) found marked *T. sirtalis* 457 m from their hibernaculum. In their Ontario study, Freedman and Catling (1979) recorded only short movements of about 10–147 m for males and 10–153 m for females. It appears that the extent of annual and daily movements is largely determined by local environmental conditions. If abundant food and a suitable hibernaculum are present, little movement occurs, while long movements are necessitated if the feeding range and hibernaculum are widely separated.

On a daily basis, Seibert and Hagen (1947) found that Illinois females moved 1.05 m/day and males only 0.72 m. When further differentiated according to age, first-year males moved 0.74 m/day; first-year females, 0.80; second-year males 0.71; and second-year females, 1.58. *T. sirtalis* recovered in May–July averaged longer movements than those in August–October. Radio equipped *T. sirtalis* from Kansas averaged movements of 10 m/day; disregarding shifts of 3 m or less, the typical movement sequence was a shift on each of two days then no movement for 2.6 days (Fitch and Shirer, 1971). The maximum crawling speed increased with higher body temperature and greater body weight; speed increased with increasing length to about 45 cm, but longer snakes showed a speed decrease (Heckrotte, 1967).

T. sirtalis is quite at home in the water, and can often be seen swimming along near the shore of waterbodies (Miller, 1976). They also occasionally climb into trees or low shrubs. Barbour (1950a) once caught one about 1.2 m above the ground under the loosely adhering bark of a dead leaning tree.

Reproduction: Female *T. sirtalis* become sexually mature during their second year when greater than 550 mm in total length (Burt, 1928; Seibert and Hagen, 1947; Carpenter, 1952b; Riches, 1962; Fitch, 1965). Males also mature during their second year at somewhat shorter lengths (Harrison, 1933; Riches, 1962). Harrison (1933) reported that the keels on the dorsal scutes in the anal region are characteristically knobbed in males longer than 475 mm. In males under this length they are usually absent or very poorly developed, and in females of all lengths they are generally absent.

During hibernation and in the early spring after emergence, there is little increase in the size of the ovarian follicles and they lack yolk. Vitellogenesis begins in April or May, the follicles enlarge dramatically, and fertilization may occur from May to July (Crews and Garstka, 1982; Bona–Gallo and Licht, 1983). Iverson (1978) reported that in Florida females contained enlarged follicles on 23 May, nearly full–term fetuses on 11 August, and full–term embryos on 11 October, and that parturition occurred from 19 October to 4 November. Exposure to low temperatures in darkness (hibernation) appears to be required for the induction of sexual receptivity and eventual vitellogenesis, but the relative importance of temperature versus light is unknown (Bona–Gallo and Licht, 1983). In the study by Bona–Gallo and Licht (1983), with few exceptions only females kept in simulated hibernation for at least 16 weeks were sexually receptive, and only those that mated became vitellogenic. Mating causes the level of estrogen to rise, causing enlargement of the follicles and vitellogenesis. The eggs are later fertilized by sperm the female has stored. Then the level of progesterone rises, but its production ceases after birth of the young. An excellent summary of both the female and male reproductive physiology is given by Crews and Garstka (1982).

In the spring the male blood androgen level is low, the testes are small and the vas deferens packed with stored sperm (Fox, 1954; Crews and Garstka, 1982). Plasma testosterone levels are highest in the spring and lowest in summer; testicular testosterone levels are higher in the spring than in the fall but not significantly different in spring than in the summer or in summer than in the fall (Weil, 1985). The androgen level starts to rise about the time the snakes disperse from the hibernaculum. During the summer the testes enlarge and spermatogenesis occurs producing the sperm for the next spring's matings. The testes weight is greatest in early summer (spermatogenesis) with a lesser peak in September (androgenesis). Hawley and Aleksiuk (1976a) found that manipulation of the photoperiod had no effect on the testicular cycle, and that spermatogenesis was more controlled by the onset of higher summer temperatures.

As can be seen from the above discussions on sex cycles, *T. sirtalis* mate at a time when the gonads are small and the blood levels of sex steroid hormones are low (Crews et al., 1984). Male courtship is independent of testicular hormones (Camazine et al., 1980; Garstka et al., 1982; Crews, 1983).

Mating usually occurs after the emergence from hibernation (March–July), but may take place in the fall (Blanchard and Blanchard, 1942; Fitch, 1965). Apparently a period of cold exposure followed by a rapid rise in body temperature is essential for the onset of spring mating behavior in the male (Aleksiuk and Gregory, 1974; Hawley and Aleksiuk, 1975; Vagvolgyi and Halpern, 1983). During the mating period the females release pheromones from their skin which help the males find and identify them (Porter and Czaplicki, 1974a, b; Garstka and Crews, 1981; Crews and Garstka, 1982) These secretions are species specific (Ford, 1978, 1982a; Ford and Schofield, 1984). Surprisingly, some males also release a pheromone that attracts other males. However, Mason and Crews (1985) have shown that in competitive mating trials these "she–

males" mated with females significantly more often than did normal males, demonstrating not only reproductive competency but also a possible selective advantage to males with this female–like pheromone. Ford (1981) reported that male *T. sirtalis* scent trailed best in the spring, presumably in response to pheromones.

The courtship and mating behavior of *T. sirtalis* has been described in detail by Noble (1937), Blanchard and Blanchard (1942), List (1950), and Gillingham and Dickinson (1980). Fitch (l965) has presented the following summary:

> The female was seemingly recognized chiefly by scent. Some females seemed to be more attractive than others to the males. Upon finding a suitable female, the male became animated in his movements, pressed his chin against the female's back and slowly worked his way forward until he was lying extended along her with his cloacal region adjacent to hers. Spasmodic rippling movements passed forward along the male's abdomen and his tail-base was pressed against and beneath that of the female. Two or more males might simultaneously court the same female, but with no evident rivalry. Displacement of one male by another, such as occasionally occurred, appeared not to be purposeful but resulted from the usual vigorous courting movements. The female's role was mainly passive, but copulation could be effected only when she raised her tail (or permitted it to be raised by the male) allowing her cloaca to gape open and thus making possible the insertion of the male's hemipenis. This might be accomplished after courtship as brief as one minute, but typically five to ten minutes were required and sometimes more than an hour. As soon as an attachment had been made, the male's vigorous movements ceased and he slipped off the female. She usually crawled slowly forward, and the male was dragged after her with contact maintained only at the vents. Copulation was typically of 15 to 20 minutes duration. After separation occurred the snakes showed no further interest in each other. The female immediately became intolerant of courtship by other males, whereas the male might soon mate with a second female, or even with several in succession if he had the opportunity to do so.

As can be seen above, females play a passive role in courtship, but a more active role during copulation. The amount of courtship directed at a female and whether or not she is mated both depend on her body length (Hawley and Aleksiuk, 1976b). There seems to be a minimum length for successful copulation. Most matings occur in females greater than 50 cm in snout–vent length, and from 45 to over 60 cm in snout–vent length both the amount of courtship and matings increase.

Several individuals may attempt to copulate with the same female and large, writhing balls of garter snakes may result (Gardner, 1955, 1957).

Mating is not restricted to the ground; Gregory (1975b) observed an aggregation of mating *T. sirtalis* on the top of a bush 1 m off the ground.

At the end of coitus, the male forms a copulatory plug which blocks the oviductal openings in the female's cloaca for a few days. The plug, apparently formed from kidney secretions immediately after insemination, prevents rival males from copulating with that female. Sexually active males do not court recently mated females, thus presenting a competitive advantage to the mated male (Devine, 1975, 1977; Ross and Crews, 1977).

Despite the copulatory plugs, multiple matings by females occur. Gibson and Falls (1975) found that morph frequencies in litters of naturally mated *T. sirtalis* from populations containing a recessive gene for melanism deviated significantly from simple Mendelian estimates. They attributed these deviations to multiple male parentage. Jacobson and Rothman (1961) and Riches (1980) reported double littering by female *T. sirtalis*.

T. sirtalis may store sperm overwinter from spring and fall matings. Such sperm may remain viable for about a year (Fox, 1956); females are known to have produced young after a spring when no mating occurred (Rahn, 1940; Blanchard, 1943). The sperm is stored in specified furrows in the vaginal portion of the oviduct, 3–6 cm anterior to the vent. The epithelial lining sloughs, associates with the sperm and moves anterior to special infundibular storage regions (Halpert et al., 1982). These carrier matrices not only facilitate sperm transport anteriorly, but also function as nutritional stores. Stored sperm are evacuated from storage areas within six hours after spring mating, but new sperm are not evident in the oviduct until 24 hours after mating.

Like other garter snakes, *T. sirtalis* is viviparous, and nourishes its developing young through a placenta (Clark et al., 1955; Hoffman, 1970 a, b). The females usually reproduce annually (Blanchard and Blanchard, 1942; Fitch, 1965). Blanchard and Blanchard (1942) found that in southern Michigan total development (final maturation of ova, ovulation and gestation) required as much as 116 days during cool summers and is little as 87 days in very hot summers.

Litter size ranges from 3–80 (Wright and Wright, 1957; Fitch, 1965), but 11–26 young are probably more common (Fitch, 1985). Larger females produce more offspring. Seigel and Fitch (1985) have also found that the number of young produced varies from year to year in response to environmental conditions.

The young are usually born from late July to early October, and prior to birth the pregnant females may aggregate in secluded places (Gregory,

1975a; Gordon and Cook, 1980; Reichenbach, 1983). Neonate *T. sirtalis* are brightly colored and about 150–220 mm in total length at birth.

A captive male *T. sirtalis* fathered a litter in an interspecific mating with a female *T. butleri* (Steehouder, 1983).

Growth And Longevity: The growth period for *T. sirtalis* is considered to be that annual period in which it is actively feeding. In Michigan, Carpenter (1952b) considered the 153–day duration from May through September as the growth period. In Canada it may be shorter, and in the southern portions of the range more prolonged. The more frequently it feeds, the faster the snake will grow (Myer and Kowell, 1973).

There is a consistent decrease in growth rate as *T. sirtalis* becomes larger. Fitch (1965) calculated that in Kansas young garter snakes 148–426 mm in snout–vent length grew 1–2 mm/day. From 400–449 mm males grew an average of 16–50 mm/month; from 450–499 mm, 7–30 mm/month; from 500–599 mm, 6–13 mm/month; and from 600–699 mm, 5–7.5 mm/month. Females with snout–vent lengths of 500–599 mm grew 23–43.5 mm/month; from 600–699 mm, 10–25 mm/month; from 700–799 mm, 6–9 mm/month; and from 800–899 mm, 6.3 mm/month. The growth rates recorded by Carpenter (1952b) in Michigan were comparable. In Illinois, Seibert and Hagen (1947) calculated that young *T. sirtalis* grew an additional 50–60% in length their first year, males increased 25–37% and females 33–37% the second year, and females 8–15% in the third year. Minton (1972) reported some large increases in length in Indiana *T. sirtalis*; one grew 150 mm between May and November, and another 205 mm in 12 months.

It is not known how long common garter snakes live in the wild, but one individual survived 10 years in captivity (Bowler, 1977).

Food And Feeding: Since *T. sirtalis* has a long annual activity period, it may feed much of the year. Minton (1972) found them with food in their stomachs as early as 20 March and as late as 25 October in Indiana.

Prey taken by this generalist feeder includes frogs (*Rana*), toads (*Bufo*), tree frogs (*Acris, Hyla, Pseudacris*), spadefoots (*Scaphiopus*), narrow–mouthed frogs (*Gastrophryne*), salamanders (*Ambystoma, Desmognathus, Eurycea, Necturus, Notophthalmus, Plethodon*), small snakes (*Agkistrodon, Nerodia, Storeria, Thamnophis*), fish (goldfish, dace, shiners, minnows, mudminnows, sunfish, trout), nestling birds (gulls, terns, goldfinches, juncos, sparrows, robins, thrushes, warblers), mice (*Microtus, Peromyscus, Reithrodontomys*), chipmunks (*Tamias*), shrews (*Blarina,*

Sorex), earthworms, leeches, slugs and snails, sowbugs, crayfish, millipedes, spiders, and various insects (Surface, 1906; Uhler et al., 1939; Pope, 1944; Lagler and Salyer, 1945; Barbour, 1950a; Conant, 1951; Hamilton, 1951b; Carpenter, 1951; 1952a; Fouquette, 1954; Hamilton and Pollack, 1956; Wright and Wright, 1957; Fitch, 1965; Lazell and Nisbet, 1972; Gregory, 1978; Brown 1979a, b; Martin, 1979; Fetterolf, 1979; Allan, 1979; Catling and Freedman, 1980b; Ernst, person. observ.). They may be cannibalistic and eat young of their own species (Hamilton, 1951b), and carrion may also be consumed (Brown, 1979a). One of the strangest reports was that of a captive *T. sirtalis* ingesting its own feces (coprophagy; Peterson, 1980).

Young *T. sirtalis* mostly feed on small frogs, salamanders, worms, slugs, snails, and insects, but older larger snakes are capable of eating full grown frogs, toads, mice, and occasionally nestling birds; however, they are more adept at catching transforming frogs than adult frogs. Amphibians may comprise up to 90% of the adult food (Pope, 1944), but earthworms are also consumed in large quantities (35–57%; Lagler and Salyar, 1945; Hamilton, 1951b). Alpaugh (1980) reported that a male and a female *T. sirtalis* kept in captivity and fed only earthworms for 6 years grew 9 and 13 cm, respectively. The female ate an average of 5.3 earthworms and the male 3.8 per feeding. Reichenbach and Dalrymple (1986) estimated that for a wild population of *T. sirtalis* in Ohio, a 1 to 4 predator/prey biomass ratio was sufficient for maintenance, growth, and reproduction.

Fouquette (1954) reported that *T. sirtalis* in Texas avoid food competition with sympatric *T. proximus* by primarily eating earthworms and secondarily amphibians, while *T. proximus* feeds predominantly on amphibians. Laboratory tests on food preferences have shown innate intraspecific geographic variation (Dix, 1968; Burghardt, 1970, 1975; MacCartney and Gregory, 1981; Kephert, 1982); neonates from some populations preferred fish while others were more interested in amphibians and worms. Possibly this is an adaptation to avoid food competition with other species sympatric of *Thamnophis*.

Common garter snakes are opportunistic feeders, and may shift prey according to annual and seasonal availability (Kephert and Arnold, 1982). Also, the feeding ranges may be separated from hibernacula, requiring long–distance spring migrations before feeding can begin (Gregory and Stewart, 1975). Feeding may occur on land or in water.

Prey is probably found by following scent trails, as olfaction has been shown to be critical to the onset of prey searching behavior (Sheffield et

THAMNOPHIS SIRTALIS

Common Garter Snake

al., 1968; Bughardt, 1971; Burghardt and Pruitt, 1975; Kubie and Halpern, 1975, 1978; Carr and Gregory, 1976; Halpern and Frumin, 1979; Burghardt and Denny, 1983; Gove and Burghardt, 1983). However, when prey is detected, vision supplements olfaction in making the capture, and, when both senses are used, the capture rate is increased (Burghardt, 1969; Drummond, 1983, 1985). When foraging in water, open–mouth searching is common (Drummond, 1983). All prey are seized in the mouth and swallowed as quickly as possible.

There is some evidence that the saliva of *T. sirtalis* has venomous properties. Fitch (1965) reported that in biting, the *T. sirtalis* deeply embeds its long recurved teeth at the rear of the maxilla, piercing the skin of a restraining hand in a way that causes profuse bleeding. Taub (1967) observed that *T. sirtalis* has a serous Duvernoy's gland, and secretions from this gland may be lethal to mice (Rosenberg et al., 1985). Human envenomation has occurred from the bite of other species of *Thamnophis* (McKinistry, 1978); and Ernst has developed a hyperallergic reaction to the saliva of *T. sirtalis*. When bitten, he develops a burning rash at the site. It is strongly possible that the enzymes in the saliva of the common garter snake may help to immobilize active prey, such as frogs, toads or mice, and when the snake bites such prey it often chews before beginning to swallow.

Predators And Defense: Many animals eat *T. sirtalis*. The following is a list of those animals known or suspected to prey on this snake: mammals—badgers, minks, skunks, weasels, raccoons, cats, dogs, foxes, chipmunks, shrews (*Blarina*); birds—hawks, owls, herons, American bitterns, Virginia rails, goldeneye ducks, pheasants, chickens, turkeys, crows, robins, loggerhead shrikes; reptiles—larger garter snakes, coral snakes, copperheads, massasaugas, kingsnakes, milk snakes, racers, box turtles; amphibians —bullfrogs, ambystomid salamanders, fish, larger spiders and crayfish (Gutherie, 1932; Carpenter, 1952a; Fitch, 1965; Davis, 1969; Netting, 1969; Littlefield, 1971; Minton, 1972; Lazell and Nisbet, 1972; Schueler, 1975; Aleksiuk, 1977b; Vogt, 1981). Aleksiuk (1977b) found hibernating *T. sirtalis* with portions of their heads chewed away, probably by rodents, and Swanson (1952) reported that a small common garter snake was found with its head entrapped by a trap–door snail. Weldon (1982) reported newborn *T. sirtalis* recognize the odors of some ophiophagous snakes.

Despite the numerous predators listed above, humans are the biggest threat to *T. sirtalis*. Habitat destruction and the automobile kill thousands each year, and the use of certain pesticides may poison others (Korschgen, 1970).

This species puts up a good fight when captured; flattening the head and body, striking, biting, chewing and spraying musk. Schueler (1975) reported they may even feign death, and some individuals may lose their tails while escaping (Willis et al., 1982). The striped pattern of *Thamnophis* is highly effective for concealing motion.

Populations: *Thamnophis sirtalis* may occur in very large numbers (8000–10000) at some northern hibernacula (Aleksuik and Lavies, 1975; Aleksiuk, 1976a), but populations are less dense on the summer feeding range. Some reported densities per hectare of suitable habitat for typical summer populations are 4 (Ontario; Freedman and Cattling, 1978), 5.4 (Illinois; Seibert, 1950) 7.4–44.5 (Kansas; Fitch, 1965), 18.7 (Illinois; Blaesing, 1979), 24.8 (Michigan; Carpenter, 1952a), and 45–89 (Ohio; Reichenbach and Dalyrmple, 1986). Biomass estimates for the Ohio population studied by Reichenbach and Dalymple (1986) ranged from 2.8 to 5.5 kg/ha.

Adult males were less numerous than adult females, 0.6:1, in Fitch's (1965) study of a Kansas population. Carpenter (1952a) reported a sex ratio at birth of 1:0.91. In Kansas, 2nd year snakes made up 49.7% of the population, 3rd year snakes, 5.2% and those over 5 years of age 5.2%; 85.8% of the females and 93.4% of the males were 4 years old or younger (Fitch, 1965).

THAMNOPHIS PROXIMUS

Western Ribbon Snake

THAMNOPHIS PROXIMUS (Say, 1823)
Western Ribbon Snake

Recognition: This is an elongated (to 76 cm) black to dark brown snake with a narrow orange vertebral stripe, a lateral yellow stripe on scale rows 3 and 4, and a long narrow tail less than 1/3 the length of the body. No dark ventrolateral stripe is present, and the labials and ventrals also lack black markings. The large yellow parietal spots are fused, and the anterior portion of the face and chin are cinnamon–brown or cream. A distinct neck separates the head from the body. The body scales are keeled, pitless, and usually occur in 19 rows anteriorly and at mid–body but only 17 rows near the anus; the anal plate is undivided. Differential head scales include a loreal, 1 preocular, 2–3 postoculars, 2 temporals, usually 8 supralabials (the 4th and 5th enter the orbit), and 6–7 pairs of infralabials. There are 141–181 ventrals and 82–131 subcaudals with no sexual dimorphism. The single hemipenis is short for the genus (usually extending only to the 7th or 8th subcaudals when inverted), and it has a straight sulcus spermaticus which terminates at the apex (Rossman, 1963b). It bears numerous small spines on the distal half, the margins of the sulcus, and the extreme basal area. A pair of enlarged basal hooks occur on each side of the sulcus, and the apical region lacks adornments. Each maxilla bears about 30 teeth.

Males have slightly longer tails (29–31.5% of body length) than do females (28–30.5%) (Rossman, 1962).

See Rossman (1962, 1963b) and Gartside et al. (1977) for discussions of the validity of *T. proximus* as a separate species from *T. sauritus*.

Karyotype: The karyotype consists of 34 macrochromosomes and 2 microchromosomes; females are heteromorphic, ZW (Baker et al., 1972).

Fossils: Pleistocene remains of *T. proximus* have been found at Blancan sites in Kansas, Irvingtonian deposits in Texas, and Rancholabrean deposits in Missouri, Texas, and New Mexico (Holman, 1981).

Distribution: *T. proximus* ranges south from Indiana, Illinois, southern Wisconsin and Iowa to southern Mississippi, Texas and eastern New Mexico in the United States, and south through eastern Mexico to Costa Rica. Populations also occur in Guerrero and Oaxaca on the Pacific coast of Mexico.

Geographic Variation: Six subspecies are recognized, but only two occur east of the Mississippi River. *Thamnophis proximus proximus* (Say, 1823), the western ribbon snake, ranges from Indiana, Illinois and Wisconsin southwest to central Louisiana and Texas. It has a black dorsum and a narrow orange vertebral stripe. *T. p. orarius* Rossman, 1963b, the Gulf Coast ribbon snake, occurs along the Gulf Coast from southern Mississippi westward to southern Texas. It is olive-brown with a broad gold vertebral stripe.

Confusing Species: *T. sauritus* usually has only 7 supralabials; if present, faint, clearly separated parietal spots; and a tail at least 1/3 of the total body length. Other eastern *Thamnophis* with lateral stripes on scale rows 3 and 4 have tails usually less than 1/4 of the total body length.

Habitat: Closely confined to the vicinity of permanent or semipermanent water, either standing (marshes, ponds, sloughs) or running (brooks, creeks, rivers, swamps), where it is most frequently found in the bordering vegetation (grasses, cattails, shrubs). It sometimes enters wet woodlands or prairies, and individuals may climb into weeds or low bushes. Minton (1972) reported that all *T. proximus* he collected in Indiana were in sandy, more open, dry areas than most places where its congener, *T. sauritus* has been found.

Behavior: Over most of the range, active *T. proximus* may be found from April to October, but the annual activity period may be either shorter in the north or extend throughout the year in the extreme southern portions of the range, if the winters are warm (Tinkle, 1957). Clark (1974) reported that in Texas, trapping success during the spring and summer was correlated with rainfall, with fewer snakes captured during dry periods. A lack of precipitation may affect *T. proximus* either through desiccation or by reducing the availability of their amphibian foods.

Tinkle (1957) found a relationship between phenology and the density of *T. proximus* in the

THAMNOPHIS PROXIMUS

Western Ribbon Snake

Map

Fig. 66. *Thamnophis proximus proximus.*

Louisiana population he studied. Early in the year the snakes utilized open areas with maximum exposure to sunlight. When these areas became shaded with the increase in luxuriance of vegetation, the snakes sought other open areas; but when the daily temperatures increased in later months, they moved back to the shaded sites.

Even in the southern states, *T. proximus* may be forced to hibernate if water or air temperatures become too low. In Kentucky, they hibernate in rocky or gravelly banks near water, and in Illinois they have been found hibernating in rock crevices with copperheads and timber rattlesnakes. Other hibernacula include springs, mammal burrows, ant hills, rotten logs and stumps, and behind the bark on trees. We have also found them in pipes draining temporary ponds.

On a daily basis this snake is mostly diurnal, being active in the morning and late afternoon hours, but if the nights are warm it may also prowl. They are very active during light summer rains.

Jacobson and Whitford (1970) reported the mean critical thermal maximum of *T. proximus* acclimated at 15 C was 39 C, while for those acclimated at 30 C it was 42 C. They also observed a leveling off in the oxygen consumption rate between 20–30 C but no lag at 15 C. This was attributed to reduced activity at preferred temperatures, a behavioral adaptation.

Clark (1974) found no significant differences in the mean distances between captures by sex or age. Omitting age distinctions, mean movement for males was 2.5 m/day, and for females, 1.1 m/day. Males moved up to 209 m between captures, and females 97 m. Immature females were much less prone to travel far than were adult females or males. An individual marked by Tinkle (1957) moved almost 100 m in about 5 months.

Reproduction: Tinkle (1957) studied the female reproductive cycle in a Louisiana population. From July through December, the maximum size of ovarian follicles was 5 mm, but most were smaller. Follicles probably remained at this size through January until air temperatures began to warm. In the spring the follicles increased in size until they became greater than 8 mm in April through June, and then were apparently ovulated. The right ovary, which was always longer and more anterior than the left, produced the majority of the eggs. Pregnant females were found as early as April and were present in the population through July.

The smallest sexually mature female examined by Tinkle (1957) was 48.5 cm snout–vent length, and he felt that most females in his population reached sexual maturity at about 50 cm. However, Clark (1974) reported the smallest mature female in his Texas population was 51.5 cm and that none shorter was found pregnant. Females mature in their third year. Brood size averaged 13 in Tinkle's Louisiana population, but only 8.4 in Texas, although the average snout–vent length of the females was similar. Clark postulated that heavier mortality in the Louisiana population had resulted in selection favoring greater per season reproductive effort there. Males mature in 1–2 years at snout–vent lengths of 36.8 cm or longer (Tinkle, 1957; Clark, 1974).

Mating occurs during April and May over most of the range, but earlier farther south. In Kentucky it takes place almost immediately after emergence from hibernation. During this time the males actively pursue the females, probably following pheromone trails (Ford, 1978). Courtship and mating have not been described.

The birth period extends from July to October, but most are born from July to early September. Females may produce two broods in a given year (Conant, 1965). Brood size ranges from 4 (Carpenter, 1958) to 36 (Bowers, 1967), but most broods probably include only 10–15 young. The neonates are about 200 mm long (187–283).

Growth And Longevity: Tinkle (1957) reported that a juvenile with a prominent yolk scar caught in December was 31.5 cm snout–vent length. Its growth represented at least a 50% increase in length since its birth earlier in the year. Clark (1974) presented growth curves for juveniles to 23 months.

Natural longevity is unknown, but a *T. proximus* at the Philadelphia Zoo lived 3 years, 7 months (Bowler, 1977).

Food And Feeding: The diet is chiefly fishes and amphibians, with anurans being more often consumed than salamanders, but this may reflect a lesser availability of salamanders in the microhabitat of *T. proximus* rather than the snake's preference. Fouquette (1954) reported that 82% of its food consisted of amphibians, and Rossman (1963b) presented a table listing 17 anurans, 2 salamanders and 4 fishes as prey species. Clark (1974) found anurans or their tadpoles in 83% of the 24 stomachs he examined containing food; salamanders and fish were found in only 4%, and 8% contained lizards (*Scincella laterale*). Smith (1961) found a large *T. proximus* in Illinois that had eaten two smaller ribbon snakes, and Resetarits (1983) observed a *T. proximus* attempt to swallow the carrion of a road killed toad in Missouri.

If the air is warm, *T. proximus* will forage as readily at night as during the day. We have often seen them prowling among nocturnal choruses of hylid frogs. While hunting cricket frogs, western ribbon snakes often make short thrusting probes with the forepart of their bodies into spots likely to hide prey (Wendelken, 1978). These probes are made with closed mouths, and frequently this behavior involves a rapid sequence of three thrusts directed toward three different areas in a semicircle in front of the snake. When the frogs are disturbed and move, the snake rapidly crawls after them. If it misses, it assumes a motionless posture with its head raised. Wendelken (1978) felt this type of hunting behavior an adaptation to capturing such anurans as cricket frogs which hide and then when disturbed hop away using erratic pathways. Fouquette (in Rossman, 1963b) observed a *T. proximus* stalk a calling Mexican tree frog (*Smilisca baudini*). When the frog's vocal sacs moved, the snake crawled closer, stopping each time the frog stopped calling. Are the above hunting techniques species specific or individual?

Predators And Defense: Large wading birds (such as herons), cranes, hawks, raccoons, foxes, and large ophiophagous snakes (cottonmouths, king snakes, coral snakes) are the chief natural predators of *T. proximus*, but Mulvany (1983) found a tarantula feeding on a juvenile.

T. proximus usually tries to escape when first discovered, and if near water will readily dive in, swim to the bottom, and hide under submerged objects. Occasionally one will hold its ground and give open mouth threats, but they rarely bite.

Populations: Tinkle (1957) found *T. proximus* to be the most common snake at a Louisiana site; 221 were encountered while eight other species of snakes only accounted for 199 individuals. During his study of a Texas population, Clark (1974) found a decline in numbers from an estimated 104 (61/ha) in 1969 to 28 (16/ha) in 1971. The decline was correlated with an unusually dry winter that caused spring soil desiccation resulting in no breeding amphibians; Clark postulated that most died of desiccation while hibernating.

Carpenter (1958) gave the newborn male:female ratio of Oklahoma broods of *T. proximus* as 3:6, 5:7, 4:0, and 7:2 (+ one undetermined). In his Texas study, Clark (1974) reported a 143:114 male to female ratio, but seasonally males were more abundant from March through June and females from August through October. He also found that immature females were recorded twice as often as mature females from March to June.

Clark (1974) calculated a reproductive potential of 373 young for 1969 by assuming that breeding occurred each year, that there was a 1:1 sex ratio, and that there were 38 mature females that had average broods of 9.7 young. This increased the population 4.6 times.

Comments: Habitat disturbance (cultivation, draining and filling of wet areas) is the major threat to the survival of both *T. proximus* and *T. sauritus*, and many populations have disappeared in recent years.

THAMNOPHIS SAURITUS

Eastern Ribbon Snake

THAMNOPHIS SAURITUS
(Linnaeus, 1766)
Eastern Ribbon Snake

Recognition: This is a medium–sized (to 66 cm) snake with the lateral stripes on scale rows 3 and 4 and the dorsal stripe normally yellow, orange, light green or bluish in color. Two rows of black spots are present between the lateral and the dorsal stripe, and below the lateral stripe is a dark (usually brown) ventrolateral stripe involving the 1st and 2nd scale rows and the outer edges of the ventral scutes. The venter is plain yellowish or light green. If present, spots on the parietal scales are usually small, dull, and rarely fused. No dark bars occur on the labials. The keeled, pitless body scales usually occur in 19–19–17 rows. Head scalation is similar to that of *T. proximus*, but there are either 7 or 8 supralabials. The tail is long, about 1/3 the total length of the body. The hemipenis is short, extending only to the 8th subcaudal when inverted, and virtually identical with that of *T. proximus* (Rossman, 1963b). There are 29–32 teeth on each maxilla.

Males have 145–177 ventrals and 98–136 subcaudals; females 143–169 ventrals and 94–131 subcaudals. Tail lengths overlap between the sexes.

Karyotype: Undescribed, but presumably similar to that of *T. proximus*.

Fossil Record: Remains of *T. sauritus* have been found in Pleistocene Rancholabrean deposits at Baker Bluff Cave, Tennessee (Holman, 1981).

Distribution: *T. sauritus* ranges from central Maine and southern Ontario southward east of the Mississippi River to southeastern Louisiana, Mississippi and peninsular Florida. There are also isolated records from Nova Scotia and northeastern Wisconsin.

Geographic Variation: Four subspecies are recognized. *Thamnophis sauritus sauritus* (Linnaeus, 1766), the eastern ribbon snake, ranges from southern Maine, New Hampshire and Vermont west to southern Illinois and southward to Georgia and southeastern Louisiana. It has 7 supralabials, a reddish–brown back, and a golden–yellow vertebral stripe. *T. s. sackeni* (Kennicott, 1859), the peninsula ribbon snake, occurs in southeastern Georgia and peninsular Florida. It has 8 supralabials, a tan to brown back, and a buff or tan–colored dorsal stripe. Christman (1980) reported that ventrals and subcaudals increase clinally to the south on the Florida peninsula. *T. s. septentrionalis* Rossman, 1963b, the northern ribbon snake, ranges from central Maine westward to southern Ontario, Michigan, and northern Illinois. It has 7 supralabials, a black or dark brown back, and a yellow dorsal stripe overlaid with brownish pigment. *T. s. nitae* Rossman, 1963b, the bluestripe ribbon snake, is found only along the Gulf Coast of Florida between Wakula and Pasco counties. It has 8 supralabials, a black back, blue to bluish–white lateral stripes, and an obscure anterior dorsal stripe.

Confusing Species: No other garter snakes are so thin or have such a long tail (1/3 of total body length).

Habitat: *T. sauritus* usually is found on the banks and within the vegetation bordering waterways. Waterbodies with both flowing (brooks, streams, rivers, swamps, marshes) or standing water (bogs, wet meadows, sloughs, ponds) are inhabited. It is not restricted to the ground, but may climb into low vegetation. It also uses animal burrows as retreats; we have seen it emerge from muskrat, (*Ondatra zibethica*) bank burrows, and Birkenholz (in Lee, 1968a) has found them in the lodges of the round–tailed muskrat (*Neofiber alleni*) in Florida.

Minton (1972) reported that it seems to prefer a more moist habitat than does *T. proximus*.

Behavior: Eastern ribbon snakes are predominantly diurnal and are fond of basking but, at least during the frog breeding season, may also forage at night.

T. sauritus has a rather long annual activity cycle. In Florida and at other southern localities, it may be active year round, especially in years with warm winters, but in the north the snake may be forced to hibernate. Conant (1938) found them most active during the spring in Ohio, and Minton (1972) reported collecting them as early as late March and as late as 20 October in southern Indiana. This species requires a moist habitat, and during very hot and dry summers, may estivate for short periods.

It has been found hibernating in ant mounds, vole tunnels and crayfish burrows (Carpenter, 1953a), and we suspect they also utilize muskrat lodges and bank burrows. Body temperatures of 7 hibernating *T. sauritus* were 5.4–5.8 C (Carpenter 1953a); these snakes were buried in a Michigan ant mound at depths to about 50 cm. In Michigan, Carpenter (1952a) found they had a lower winter kill rate than did sympatric *T. sirtalis*.

Carpenter (1956) reported that the maximum and minimum temperature of 123 *T. sauritus* from Michigan were 12.6 and 34.0 C, respectively.

T. sauritus seems to remain within a relatively small home range near its waterway. Carpenter (1952a) reported that the maximum distance moved between captures in Michigan was 278 m, and the greatest width for any movement pattern was 49 m.

Reproduction: Burt (1928) determined that female *T. sauritus sauritus* from Michigan were able to reproduce after attaining a total length of about 60 cm, and later Carpenter (1952a) reported females from southern Michigan attained maturity at 2 to 3 years of age at snout–vent lengths of 42 cm.

Mating occurs in April and May in the north, but earlier in the south. The young are usually born in late July or August in the north, but in July in the southern populations. Rossman (1963b) gives the range of parturition dates as 2 July to 4 October. More than one brood may occur each year (Telford, 1952; Conant, 1965). Brood sizes range from 3 to 26, but 10–12 young are more common. Neonates are 160–239 mm in total length.

Growth And Longevity: Carpenter (1952b) determined the annual growth period in southern Michigan to be 153 days between 1 May and 30 September. He found that there was a consistent decrease in growth rate as *T. sauritus* became larger. Both sexes grew rapidly the first year, but the growth rate of the male slowed more quickly. Carpenter found one female that had grown 26.8 cm in two years.

Natural longevity is unknown, but a *T. sauritus* survived almost 4 years at the Philadelphia Zoo (Bowler, 1977).

Food And Feeding: Eastern ribbon snakes feed mostly on amphibians. Rossman (1963b) presented a table of prey listing 15 species of anurans of the genera *Bufo*, *Acris*, *Pseudacris*, *Hyla*, and *Rana*, 3 species of salamanders of the genera *Notophthalmus*, *Ambystoma*, and *Desmognathus*,

Map

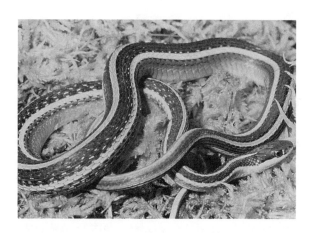

Fig. 67. *Thamnophis sauritus sauritus.*

Fig. 68. *Thamnophis sauritus sackeni* (Carl H. Ernst).

Fig. 69. *Thamnophis sauritus nitae* usually lacks a dorsal stripe.

and 3 fish (*Umbra*, *Gambusia*, and *Heterandria*). Brown (1979b) reported that 21 snakes from Michigan contained only amphibians, of which 93% were anurans, and Carpenter (1952a) found 90% amphibian prey during his Michigan study. Apparently small *T. sauritus* feed on small frogs and toads and their tadpoles, but larger ribbon snakes are capable of swallowing medium-sized to full grown ranid frogs. Other foods eaten include leeches (Carpenter, 1952a), spiders (Hamilton and Pollack, 1956), caterpillars, and other insects (Surface, 1906; Carpenter, 1952a; Linzey and Clifford, 1981). Surface (1906) listed earthworms as food, but both Conant (1951) and Minton (1972) reported captives refused these worms. Duellman (1948) reported a captive female ate her 5 young 3 days after their birth.

Most feeding is done in the morning or early evening, and the snakes actively prowl to find prey. Once discovered they rapidly crawl after it, seize it in their mouths and swallow it. Prey is detected both by olfaction and by vision.

Evans (1942) reported observing an unusual feeding behavior in *T. sauritus*; they fed by swimming with their mouths open and then closed them upon contact with a fish.

Predators And Defense: Many wading birds and small predatory mammals eat this snake, as also do many other serpents. The young are particularly vulnerable, and may be preyed on by fishes, large crayfish, and turtles. Tail loss is frequently an indication of a predator attack, and Willis et al. (1982) found a greater frequency of tail loss in females than in males.

When first disturbed it usually trys to escape, and, if near water, will not hesitate to dive in and swim rapidly away. If handled, they thrash about and spray the captor with musk from anal glands. Occasionally they will coil or flatten out, and may attempt to bite, but biting rarely occurs in these docile snakes.

Populations: Carpenter (1952a) estimated the average total population of *T. sauritus* on his Michigan study plot was 508 (Hayne method) to 755 (Lincoln Index); 244–445 males, 264–310 females.

Remarks: Populations of *T. sauritus* are declining in some areas because of habitat destruction.

Brisbin et al. (1974) collected *T. sauritus* from the vicinity of a nuclear reactor effluent stream at the AEC Savannah River Plant, Aiken, South Carolina. Concentration levels of radiocesium in these snakes averaged 131.5 pCi/g live weight, with a maximum of 1032.6 pCi/g, and represented the highest level of radiocesium ever found in any wild population of vertebrate predator. *T. sauritus* collected elsewhere at the plant had significantly lower levels.

TROPIDOCLONION LINEATUM

Lined Snake

TROPIDOCLONION LINEATUM
(Hallowell, 1857)
Lined Snake

Recognition: This species is the sole representative of this monotypic genus. Its slender body (to 53.3 cm) is olive–brown to gray–brown and bears a grayish–white, cream, yellow, or orange dorsal stripe, and on each side a similarly colored lateral stripe on the 2nd and 3rd scale rows. Bordering the dorsal stripe is a row of black spots, and a similar row of spots occurs dorsal to the two lateral stripes. The small head, scarcely set off from the body, is gray to olive or brown with the scales posterior to the orbits heavily marked with black spots. The pale green to yellowish–green venter bears a double row of dark brown or black half-moon shaped marks that begin as a single row on the neck. Each body scale is keeled and has two small pits near its tip. Most frequently the dorsal scale row count is 17(16–17), 19(17–19), 17(15–17); the greater number of mid–body scale rows is accomplished by the addition of a 4th lateral row which subsequently is dropped posteriorly. The anal plate is undivided. Laterally on the head there are a single (semidivided) nasal scale, a loreal, a preocular, 2 postoculars, 2 temporals (1 + 1), usually 6(5–7, the 3rd and 4th enter the orbit) supralabials, and 7(5–7) infralabials. The mental scale may touch the anterior chin shields. There are 132–156 ventrals with no sexual dimorphism. The unique hemipenis is somewhat bilobed distally with the lateral edges of the lobes extended into long papillae; its single sulcus spermaticus extends directly from the proximal towards the distal end between the lobes, but does not reach the apex (Dowling, 1959a). Four large basal spines and numerous rows of smaller spinules occur toward the distal end. Usually each maxilla has 15 teeth; those most posterior are largest.

Ramsey (1953) reported that the females were slightly longer than the males. Females have 24–40 subcaudals, and shorter tails (usually 11–13.5% of total body length); males have 32–47 subcaudals, and longer tails (usually 15–17% of total body length) (Ramsey, 1953; Clark, 1967a; Quinn, 1979a).

Karyotype: Unknown.

Fossil Record: Pleistocene (Irvingtonian) fossil *Tropidoclonion* have been found in Kansas and Texas (Holman, 1981).

Distribution: *Tropidoclonion lineatum* ranges from central Illinois westward to southeastern South Dakota and eastern Nebraska south to central Texas, with isolated populations occurring in Missouri, eastern Colorado and New Mexico. Populations occurring in Illinois, eastern Iowa, and Missouri are considered relicts (Smith, 1961; Smith and Smith, 1962, 1963).

Geographic Variation: Four subspecies are recognized, but only two occur within the range of this book. *Tropidoclonion lineatum lineatum* (Hallowell, 1857), the northern lined snake, has 143 or fewer ventrals, more than 32 subcaudals in females, and more than 40 subcaudals in males. It ranges from northcentral Illinois westward to southeastern South Dakota and eastern Nebraska, and southward to northern Kansas. *T. l. annectens* Ramsey, 1953, the central lined snake, has more than 143 ventrals, more than 33 subcaudals in females, and more than 40 subcaudals in males. It occurs in isolated colonies in southcentral Illinois and Missouri, and from central Kansas southward to northeastern Texas. Smith and Smith (1962) studied the ten available Illinois specimens and showed that their scale counts fell within an intergrade range between *lineatum* and *annectens*, but were closer to *annectens*. Conant (1975) mapped the northern–most Illinois localities as intergrade *lineatum* x *annectens*, and the southcentral localities as solely *annectens*.

Confusing Species: The garter snakes, *Thamnophis*, usually lack dark ventral spots, which, if present, are not well defined half–moons. The crayfish snakes, *Regina*, all have a divided anal plate.

Habitat: This small snake occurs in habitats ranging from open prairie to oak woodlands with scattered trees, and into suburbs or even inner cities where it hides under leaves, rocks, logs, boards, or other debris. Collins (1974) even found them under dried cow dung in Kansas pastures. All indications are that this species was originally a part of our prairie fauna, but now it is often common in developed areas. In such places, McCoy (1961) collected many from the interiors of the sunken cast–iron boxes housing utility meters.

Behavior: *Tropidoclonion* is secretive and semifossorial.

TROPIDOCLONION LINEATUM

Lined Snake

Map

Fig. 70. Venter of *Tropidoclonion lineatum annectens* (Steve W. Gotte).

Annually, they are active from late February to mid–November (25 February to 13 November, Wright and Wright, 1957). In some areas they are less often found during the hot summer months than in the spring or early fall, but even then they may emerge in numbers following heavy rains.

Most of the winter is spent in hibernation, but Ramsey (1953) reported that lined snakes in Texas emerged during warm spells. Hamilton (1947) found seven hibernating *T. lineatum* in an area of 112 m² in Dallas, Texas. The snakes were buried 75–200 mm in the soil and all were coiled with their head inclined toward the center of the coils. Fitch (1956) found that the minimum and maximum voluntary body temperatures of eleven Kansas *T. lineatum* were 25.5 and 32.4 C, respectively; their mean body temperature was 30.5 C.

Lined snakes are predominantly nocturnal (Force, 1931; Ramsey, 1953), but may be crepuscular during the spring and fall. Ramsey (1953) observed them abroad before sunset and saw a few individuals basking in the early morning sun.

Reproduction: Blanchard and Force (1930) found that dissected spring females from the vicinity of Tulsa, Oklahoma matured sexually at a total body length of 240–350 mm, and that 17 that bore young ranged in size from 270 to 435, or sometimes to 440 mm. A smaller spring size class, 120–200 mm, were still immature, and Blanchard and Force estimated these would reach sexual maturity in the second spring after birth. Mature lined snakes possess knobs on the keels of dorsal body scales near the anal plate, and Force (1936) showed that about 50% of females over 195 mm had these knobs while none under 195 mm had them; knobs develop only in mature females. In contrast, Force (1936) found that juvenile males approaching sexual maturity developed scale knobs; 50% of 125–185 mm males had knobs, while 97% of those over 185 mm (two years old) had developed them. In the genera *Nerodia* and *Thamnophis*, knobbed body scale keels are a male secondary sexual character, but not entirely so in *Tropidoclonion*.

Krohmer and Aldridge (1985a, b) studied the sexual cycles of *Tropidoclonion* from St. Louis, Missouri. They found that testis mass was lowest in early spring and reached a peak in late July. In early spring, seminiferous tubule diameter was smallest and spermatogonia were prevalent. Tubule diameter increased during the summer and reached a maximum size by late July, corresponding to peak spermatogenesis. The most prevalent cell types at this time were spermatids and spermatozoa. Spermiation began in mid–July, with mating in late August. Seminiferous tubule diameter and rate of spermatogenesis decreased significantly by September. Sperm was stored in the vas deferens throughout the winter and early spring, indicating a possibility of spring mating, but by mid–June, sperm was absent from the vas deferens. Males born in August showed advanced spermatogenesis by September with some spermiation in early October. This was considered to be abortive as all males began spermatogenesis in the spring. However, males are probably capable of mating when one year old.

In females, coelomic fat bodies showed a significant reduction in mass corresponding inversely to vitellogenesis prior to ovulation. Coelomic fat mass increased rapidly following parturition and reached a maximum by mid–September. After parturition, follicular growth in adults occurred slowly and follicles attained a maximum length of 5 mm before hibernation. Vitellogenesis began in the spring and the rate of follicular growth increased. Follicles were ovulated in June at a mean length of 14.1 mm. Paturition occurred in mid–August. The number of embryos per clutch was significantly correlated to snout–vent length. The minimum size at which females initiated vitellogenesis was 214 mm snout–vent length. This size was attained by July of their first year, indicating that females would produce a clutch in their second active season. Mating occurred in late summer immediately following parturition. At this time, sperm was abundant in the lower one–third of the oviduct.

Ramsey (1946) observed captives copulating on 1 September, and Curtis (1949) saw a pair mating in October. Ramsey (1953) also reported that a male, captured in October, and immediately caged with a female, began courting her about an hour later, but to no avail.

During the September mating observed by Ramsey (1946) the pair remained coupled for 6.5 hours. The male had only the left hemipenis inserted and the snakes remained calmly lying. The female was caged separately from males thereafter, and finally gave birth the following August (Ramsey, 1953). Fox (1956) reported that sperm from fall matings remains viable over winter, and fertilization occurs at ovulation the next spring.

August seems to be the month of birth in *Tropidoclonion*. Force (1931) gives the following account of the birth process in this snake.

> The last week before parturition the females became very restless and often lay in the open with occasional contortions of the body. During each deposition the female elevated her tail, at first quite erect, but later not so stiffly or so high. While the young were being deposited the females were comparatively quiet, except between the last two. The embryos could be seen moving down the body from the anterior end of the oviduct as the adult moved about the cage. In one instance, after the deposition of the last young snake, the female was quite restless, but extremely weak. As she raised her body on the side of the cage she would fall back.

> At birth the young were folded in three parts in such a manner that the middle of the body emerged first, sometimes the head also protruded. The fine tissue membrane of the enveloping embryonic sac was slightly moist. It was usually immediately burst by the movement of the head of the young snake, although sometimes as much as five minutes elapsed before the complete emergence. The body remained coiled until the head had made its exploration. In a few instances the head was free and actively moving before the posterior part of the body had emerged. No egg tooth was discernible. With the first movements, the tissue slipped off the rest of the body except for the attachment of the cord and blood vessels through the opening of the ventral scale sixth from the anal plate. This soon became severed, but the opening did not completely close for several days, and in many adults the double scale, at this point, was still visible.

> The young were deposited quite rapidly. Extrusion was completed in from ten seconds to three minutes, and the intervals between births varied from less than two to more than forty–five minutes.

Two to 13 young, usually 7 or 8, are born at one time (Force, 1931; Funk and Tucker, 1978). The young are 70–130 mm in total length, and grayish in color with poorly defined dorsal stripes, but well defined ventral spots. The ground color later darkens and the gray, yellow or orange stripes become more prominent. Nine newly born young weighed by Ramsey (1946) had mean weights of 0.45 g while those of a brood of four averaged slightly more than 1 g each. Funk and Tucker (1978) reported the following measurements and weights for 13 young from a 378 mm female: total length, 96–112.5 mm; tail length, 14–19 mm (14–18% of total body length); head length, 6.1–6.9 mm; head width, 3.2–3.8 mm; weight, 0.43–0.67 g. The brood consisted of 7 males and 6 females (two males died within the fetal membranes), and a combined weight of 7.29 g (74% of the post–partum weight of the female). Young *Tropidoclonion* usually shed their skins within a few weeks after birth.

Growth And Longevity: Blanchard and Force (1930) estimated an activity period of seven months for Oklahoma lined snakes (mid–March or early April to mid–October or early November). They thought that the smallest young collected in early May represented those born the previous August. These small snakes averaged 161 mm in total length compared to the average new–born length of 111 mm, and, so, had grown about 50 mm in their first 3.5 active months. Females grew at a rate of 14.3 mm per month, and males at a rate of 14.0 mm. Longevity is unknown.

TROPIDOCLONION LINEATUM

Lined Snake

Food And Feeding: The lined snake feeds almost exclusively on earthworms, although Curtis (1949) found one consuming a sowbug. Ramsey (1947) offered small grasshoppers, crickets, snails, sowbugs, and several types of insect larvae to captives, but all were refused. However, when smeared with the fluid from chopped earthworms, the snakes ate dead grasshoppers, grubs, and raw beef. Apparently they use smell and taste to locate and identify their prey. The small size of the head and mouth of *Tropidoclonion* probably limits it to small softbodied animals, such as earthworms, and its nocturnal habits bring it out when earthworms are most active on the surface.

Predators And Defense: Almost any larger carnivorous vertebrate is a potential predator. Coral snakes, kingsnakes, and massasaugas are known to eat lined snakes, and skunks, weasels, raccoons and various birds also take them. Wright and Wright (1957) related the story of a spider capturing a small snake, presumably *T. lineatum.*

When captured they seldom attempt to bite, but frequently void anal gland secretions, urine and feces on their handler.

Remarks: *Tropidoclonion* is a member of the natricine complex (Dessauer, 1967), and seems most like *Thamnophis* and *Nerodia* with which it shares apical scale pits and knobs on those scales near the anal plate. However, its apical pits are very small when compared to the other genera, and the knobs on the dorsal body scales are not restricted to males. *Tropidoclonion* has in the past been considered a degenerate form probably originating from *Thamnophis*, but present evidence does not show it to be any more closely related to *Thamnophis* than to other North American natricines, so its origins are still obscure. Ramsey (1953) thought pattern resemblances a case of parallel evolution.

A glance at the references listed above quickly reveals little new information on this snake has been published since the 1960's; a thorough ecological study is needed.

VIRGINIA STRIATULA

Rough Earth Snake

VIRGINIA STRIATULA
(Linnaeus, 1766)
Rough Earth Snake

Recognition: This is a small (to 32.4 cm) gray-brown to reddish–brown snake with a pointed snout and keeled scales. An obscure light band may cross the back of the head, especially in juveniles, and the venter is plain cream to pink. The head is a peculiar cone–shape, much narrower at the pointed snout and becoming increasingly broader toward the rear, making the neck indistinct. The labial scales are gray to cream. The body scales occur in 17 rows, and the anal plate is usually divided. Lateral head scalation consists of 2 nasals, a long horizontal loreal which touches the orbit (there are no pre– or subocular scales), 1–3 postoculars, 1 + 1 temporals, 5 supralabial scales (the 3rd and 4th touch the orbit), and 6(5–7) infralabials. Clark (1964a) described the spiny hemipenis as asymmetrically bilobed and subcylindrical with a simple sulcus spermaticus that terminates distally between the lobes. On the proximal 1/2 to 2/3 of the hemipenis are laterally compressed, sharply pointed, recurved spines set in fleshy lobes, and proximally on the posterior surface, is a large basal spine with a smaller, slightly distad spine associated with it. The spines become larger and less numerous distally. Sixteen to 20 grooveless teeth occur on each maxilla.

Males are shorter (to 148 mm), have 112–132 ventrals, 26–50 subcaudals, and tails 18.5–23% as long as the total body length. Females (to 324 mm) have 120–139 ventrals, 29–45 subcaudals, and tails only 14–19.5% as long as the total body length.

Karyotype: Hardy (1971) has reported the diploid chromosome number to be 36.

Fossil Record: Pleistocene (Rancholabrean) remains of *V. striatula* have been found at Clear Creek, Denton County, Texas (Holman, 1963); and other fossils assigned to the genus *Virginia* sp. have been found in Irvingtonian deposits in Florida (Meylan, 1982) and at a Rancholabrean site in Virginia (Guilday, 1962).

Distribution: *V. striatula* ranges from southeastern Virginia southward to northern Florida (Alachua County), and westward to Iowa, southeastern Nebraska, eastern Oklahoma and eastern Texas.

Geographic Variation: Unknown.

Confusing Species: *Virginia valeriae* has 6 supralabials, 2 internasals, and smooth or only weakly keeled scales. *Diadophis, Carphophis,* and *Rhadinaea* have smooth scales. *Storeria* has no loreal scale.

Habitat: *V. striatula* occurs in a variety of habitats; pine woods, hardwood forests, wiregrass flatwoods, mesic hammocks, and swamp borders, where it is found under logs and stones, or behind the bark of dead trees or stumps. It also occurs in many cities and towns where it hides beneath urban debris. Clark (1964b) remarked that during the hot summer months (July–August) it prefers heavy objects closely depressed to the ground. Studies of the skin and scale structure of *V. striatula* by Jackson and Reno (1975) prompted them to question the burrowing ability of this snake, especially its keeled scales and protruding eyes. They also found the structure of the ventral and adjacent lateral scales perhaps better to facilitate terrestrial or surface locomotion than burrowing. Jackson (1977) found touch corpuscles densely distributed within the rostral and anterior supralabial scales and less abundant within other head scales.

Behavior: In Texas, Clark (1964b) collected *V. striatula* in every month except August; however, they were decidedly more active in March and April, and again in September and December. He felt that excessive heat and lack of moisture during the summer were more limiting to activity than the cold of winter. Clark found no significant differences in the seasonal activity cycles of the two sexes, but did report more activity in males in the springs of 1962 and 1963. Although this difference was not statistically significant, Clark thought this might be due to males searching for females.

On a daily basis, most activity is nocturnal or crepuscular; however, some may be active during the daylight hours, especially in the spring or fall. Clark (1964b) found only 5 individuals during the day that were not concealed beneath some object; all were found before noon.

Clark and Fleet (1976) observed that movements of this snake were positively correlated with cumulative rainfall for that month plus the two

VIRGINIA STRIATULA

Rough Earth Snake

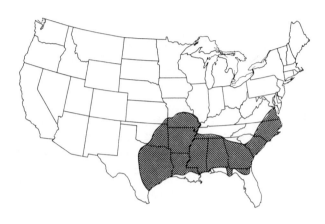

Map

preceding months. Adults moved greater distances than juveniles; mean movement for males was 0.24 m/day, and for females 0.13 m/day. Mean home range estimates using a circle–radius method for tantalum tagged snakes were 81.7 m and 21.2 m for males and females, respectively, and 76.0 m and 100.1 m, respectively, for a polygon method.

Hibernation underground or within logs or stumps occurs in the more northern portions of the range. This may possibly occur in groups; Cook (1954) reported that clusters of 6–10 snakes of varying sizes have been ploughed up in Mississippi in early spring.

Reproduction: In Texas, Clark (1964b) found that 96% of male *V. striatula* were mature at a snout–vent length of 142 mm, and that females with enlarged ovarian follicles were over 182 mm. Females mature during the second fall of their lives and probably mate for the first time the next spring, while some males may mate their first spring at an age of 7–9 months (Clark and Fleet, 1976). The smallest gravid female from Virginia was 175 mm in snout–vent length (Blem and Blem, 1985).

Gehlbach et al. (1972) reported that *V. striatula* follow trails left by their own species, indicating pheromones may play a role in mate attraction. Mating occurs in March and April in

Texas, but ovulation does not occur until at least May or June (Clark, 1964b; Blem and Blem, 1985). Four females contained sperm from 31 May to 14 June, but the amount of sperm was not as great as in the seminal fluid of males, and Clark and Fleet (1976) thought mating had occurred days or weeks before. Since mating precedes ovulation, sperm storage by females is suggested, but Clark (1964b) could not find any seminal receptacles in the oviducts of two females he dissected. However, he thought his histological technique was to blame.

Counts of mature ovarian follicles, oviductal eggs and embryos, and young born in the laboratory ranged from 3–8 (x = 4.9) per female (Clark, 1964b), and broods of 2–13 have been reported in the literature (Wright and Wright, 1957; Anderson, 1965). Females in central Virginia produce about 6 young/litter and reproduce annually (Blem and Blem, 1985). There is a positive correlation between female length and brood size (Clark, 1964b; Mitchell, 1976).

Parturition in this ovoviviparous snake occurs from July to September; the gestation period is about 10 weeks. Clark (1964b) described the birth of a brood of 7 on 12 July which took a total of 226 minutes.

Newborn young are 74–111 mm long, and have a distinct whitish transverse mark on the back of their heads.

Food And Feeding: Clark (1964b), Clark and Fleet (1976), and Brown (1979a) found only earthworms in the *V. striatula* they examined, but they also have been reported to eat insects, sowbugs, slugs, snails, small frogs, and young lizards (Wright and Wright, 1957; Anderson, 1965; Collins, 1974). Ashton and Ashton (1981) collected several *V. striatula* at the edge of ant colonies, near the pupae and larvae, and thought that these may be taken for food.

Gehlbach et al. (1972) reported that *V. striatula* readily follows earthworm trails, so olfaction may play a major role in prey detection.

Predators And Defense: Predaceous snakes and carnivorous mammals probably take their share of *V. striatula*. This species has several defensive mechanisms it employs when disturbed. It does not bite, but will writhe violently and void the contents of its cloacal glands. Kirk (1969) observed an individual being swallowed tail first by a larger unidentified snake turn its head sideways and clamp its jaws over the larger snake's glottis causing it to eventually regurgitate the smaller snake. *V. striatula* is also known to "play dead," becoming rigid with open mouth and protruding tongue (Thomas and Hendricks, 1976).

Populations: The population size estimates, excluding young–of–the–year, for the Texas population studied by Clark and Fleet (1976) ranged from 390 individuals (229/ha) in 1971 to 591 (348/ha) in 1969; the overall sex ratio was 281 males to 260 females, about 1:1. Blem and Blem (1985) reported a ratio of only 26 males to 46 females in their study, a 0.56:1 ratio.

Remarks: This species and *V. valeriae* are sometimes referred to the genus *Haldea*, but Zillig (1958) has shown that *Virginia* is the valid generic name.

Ferguson (1963) reported the apparent death by heptachlor poisoning of a *V. striatula* following application of this insecticide to a Mississippi field for fire ant control.

VIRGINIA VALERIAE

Smooth Earth Snake

VIRGINIA VALERIAE (Baird and Girard, 1853)
Smooth Earth Snake

Recognition: *Virginia valeriae* (to 39.3 cm) is gray to reddish–brown with a pointed snout, and mostly smooth scales (some dorsal to the anal vent may be weakly keeled). An inconspicuous light dorsal stripe may be present, as often are 4 longitudinal rows of small black dots. The unmarked venter is cream to light gray. The pointed head is cone–shaped, and about as wide as the neck. The light labial scales have some dark mottling. The body scales occur in 15–17 rows, and the anal plate is divided. Laterally on the head are 2 nasals, a long horizontal loreal which touches the orbit (there are no pre– or subocular scales), 2(1–3) postoculars, 1 + 1 temporals, 6 supralabials (the 3rd and 4th touch the orbit), and 6 infralabials. The hemipenis is asymmetrically bilobed, and subcylindrical with a simple sulcus spermaticus that terminates distally between the lobes (Clark, 1964a). On the proximal one–half to two–thirds of the hemipenis are laterally compressed, sharply pointed, recurved, stiff spines set in fleshy lobes. Proximally, on the posterior surface, is a large basal spine with a second, smaller spine slightly distad. The spines become larger as they proceed from the base, reaching maximum size about 1/5 to 1/4 along the hemipenis. Near the middle of the hemipenis the recurved spines become smaller, straight and peg–like, losing the fleshy base. These spines become larger distally, reach their maximum size near the apex, but diminish in numbers. There are 19–20 grooveless maxillary teeth.

Males have 109–126 ventrals, 29–45 subcaudals, and their tail length is 12–22% of the total body length; females have 112–134 ventrals, 22–36 subcaudals, and tails 12–24% as long as the total body length.

Karyotype: Hardy (1921) reported the karyotype to be 2n = 36 macrochromosomes; sex determination is ZZ/ZW.

Fossil Record: Unknown

Distribution: *V. valeriae* ranges from central New Jersey and western Pennsylvania south to northern Florida, and west to Iowa, Kansas, Oklahoma, and Texas.

Geographic Variation: There are three subspecies. *Virginia valeriae valeriae* Baird and Girard, 1853, the eastern earth snake, ranges from central New Jersey and southeastern Pennsylvania to western Maryland, south to northern Florida, and west and north to Alabama, southern Ohio and western West Virginia. It is gray to light brown and has 15 rows of mostly smooth body scales, with only faintly keeled dorsal scales near the anal vent. *V. v. elegans* Kennicott, 1859, the western earth snake, ranges from southern Iowa and southwestern Illinois south to western Alabama and Mississippi, and west to eastern Kansas, Oklahoma, and Texas. It is greenish to reddish–brown, and has weakly keeled body scales in 17 rows. *V. v. pulchra* Richmond, 1954b, the mountain earth snake, has a restricted range from western Pennsylvania southward through extreme western Maryland to northern West Virginia. This pretty little snake is dark gray to a rich reddish–brown dorsally, and has weakly keeled scales in 15 rows anteriorly but 17 rows at mid–body and posteriorly.

Confusing Species: *Virginia striatula* has 5 supralabials, an internasal, and distinctly keeled body scales. *Diadophis punctatus* has a distinct neck ring. The worm snakes, *Carphophis*, have 13 mid–body scale rows, small heads, and tiny eyes. *Storeria* has strongly keeled dorsal scales, and no loreal scale.

Habitat: *Virginia valeriae* is mostly a woodland inhabitant, although it has also been taken in fields near woods. We have collected it in both dry and moist soil conditions, with most found hiding under leaf litter, rocks or logs. Occasionally *V. valeriae* may occur in large numbers within city suburbs, where they use the debris of civilization for retreats.

Behavior: The annual cycle in Kentucky is from about 1 April to late September (Barbour, 1971), but *V. valeriae* has been taken in late October in Indiana (Minton, 1972), and in Florida they may be active most of the winter. Collins (1974) reported that in winter they crawl deep into crevices on rocky hillsides to hibernate, and Grizzell (1949) found a hibernating individual buried 26 cm in the soil. Neill (1948a) listed logs, rubbish piles, and dead grass in areas of moist soil as hibernacula. An individual from Georgia collected on 13 October had notable visceral fat (Hamilton and Pollack, 1956).

Fitch (1956) found that two active *V. valeriae* had body temperatures of 23.5 and 31.0 C when the air temperatures were 21.7 and 24.2 C. Fitch also reported *V. valeriae* was more cold resistant than *Diadophis punctatus*; two ring–necked snakes kept with a *V. valeriae* died when the water froze in the container in which all three were hiding, but the *Virginia* survived.

Although thought to be primarily nocturnal, Minton (1972) has taken active *V. valeriae* in full daylight. Heavy rains may also stimulate movement of these snakes.

Little is known of the home range of *V. valeriae*. Stickel and Cope (1947) reported a marked individual moved only 6 m in 4 days.

Reproduction: *V. valeriae* may mate in the spring after emergence from hibernation, but also in the fall (Collins, 1974). The smallest gravid female from Virginia was 185 mm in snout–vent length (Blem and Blem, 1985). Courtship has not been described. The young are born alive from late July to September after a 11–14 week gestation period. Reported litter sizes range from 2 (Anderson, 1965) to 14 (Groves, 1961), but Sinclair (1951) reported a female with 18 ovarian eggs, and Martoff (1955) reported a female that gave birth to 4 young and then 6 days later to 3 more. The mean litter size in Virginia was 6.6 young (Blem and Blem, 1985). The young are 82–111 mm in total length and may be darker in color than adults (Myers, 1963).

Food And Feeding: Earthworms are the primary food (Hamilton and Pollack, 1956; Collins, 1974; Brown, 1979a), but slugs, snails and insects have also been listed as prey (Wright and Wright, 1957; Barbour, 1971; Ashton and Ashton, 1981). Our captives have eaten only earthworms.

Predators And Defense: Predatory birds, mammals and snakes feed upon *V. valeriae*. When first handled they usually do not bite, but often curl up their lips, and eject the contents of their cloacal glands. Yeatman (1983) observed one form a loop knot with its body which prevented it from being swallowed by a black racer, *Coluber constrictor*. A female *V. v. pulchra* collected in Pennsylvania by Ernst and his students pretended to be dead. It rolled onto its back, but bent its neck in such a way as to be able to watch its handler. When placed on its stomach, it quickly rolled over to once again lie belly up.

Populations: Bothner and Moore (1964) reported a ratio of 5 adult males to 18 adult females in a series of *V. valeriae* collected 6 July in northwestern Pennsylvania. Nine of the females were gravid and these produced 61 young; 25 males, 36 females. Male:female ratios of other broods reported in the literature were: 6:19 (Richmond, 1954b); 3:1 (Cooper, 1958), and 8:6 (Pisani, 1971).

Map

Fig. 71. *Virginia valeriae valeriae.*

ELAPIDAE

Elapid Snakes

ELAPIDAE
Elapid Snakes

The approximately 220 species of advanced snakes in this family have extremely dangerous neurotoxic venom, and include the coral snakes, cobras, mambas and sea snakes. The family is well represented in Australia, Southeast Asia, Africa, and South America; fewer species occur in North America, and only two, *Micruroides euryxanthus* and *Micrurus fulvius*, occur in the United States. Elapids are closely related to colubrids, which are probably ancestral. They differ, however, in having a pair of short, permanently erect, hollow (proteroglyphous) fangs near the front of the shortened maxillae. These fangs fit into a pocket on the outside of the mandibular gums (Bogert, 1943). The venom duct is not attached directly to the fang, but enters a small cavity in the gum above the entrance lumen of the tooth. Other shorter teeth may occur behind the fangs on the maxillae, and also on the pterygoids, palatines, and dentaries. Postfrontal coronoid and pelvic bones are absent. The hyoid is Y- or U-shaped with two superficially placed, parallel arms. The body vertebrae have short, recurved hypapophyses. Only the right lung is present, and the spiny hemipenis has a bifurcate centripetal sulcus spermaticus. Dorsally, the head is covered with enlarged plates, but there is no loreal scale; body scales are usually smooth and the ventral scutes are well developed. Reproduction is oviparous or ovoviviparous. There are four subfamilies, but only one, the Micrurinae, occurs in the United States, and only one species, *Micrurus fulvius*, is found east of the Mississippi River.

MICRURUS FULVIUS (Linnaeus, 1766)
Eastern Coral Snake

Recognition: *Micrurus fulvius* is a banded red, yellow and black snake (to 130 cm) on which the red and yellow bands lie beside each other, and the snout is black. The bands continue onto the venter, and there may be some black spots on the red bands. A bright yellow band occurs on the occiput, separating the black neck band from the parietal scales. The body scales are smooth and occur in 15 rows throughout; the anal plate is divided. Head scalation usually consists dorsally of a rostral, 2 internasals, 2 prefrontals, a frontal, 2 supraoculars, and 2 parietals; laterally there are 2 nasals, a preocular, 2 postoculars, 1 + 1 temporals and 7 supralabials; there are no loreal or subocular scales. On the lower jaw are a mental, which does not touch the chin shields, usually 7 pairs of infralabials (the first 4 pairs touch the anterior chin shields) and two pairs of chin shields (the posterior pair being the larger). Roze and Tilger (1983) describe the hemipenis as "12–14 subcaudals in length, bifurcated at the 8th subcaudal; the sulcus spermaticus also bifurcated, running from the base to nearly the apex of each fork, with each fork tapering gradually toward the apex. The base of the organ naked for 2 subcaudals after which small spines and scattered spinules cover it up to the bifurcation where large spines begin. Lip of the sulcus naked for its entire length but covered on both sides with small spines. Large spines begin 1–2 subcaudals before the bifurcation of the organ and gradually diminish in size towards the apex; the area of bifurcation is without spines. Each fork of the hemipenis ends in a spinelike papilla. A large longitudinal naked fold begins almost at the base of the organ and runs approximately parallel to the sulcus, ending shortly before the bifurcation where the large spines begin." No other teeth occur on the maxilla behind the fang.

Males have 185–217 ventrals and 36–47 pairs of subcaudals; females have 205–232 ventrals and 26–38 pairs of subcaudals (Roze and Tilger, 1983). Also, females attain larger snout–vent lengths, while males have longer tails (Jackson and Franz, 1981); tail lengths averaged 13.8% of snout–vent length in males and 9.3% in females.

Karyotype: Graham (1977) reported that the diploid chromosome number of the western subspecies *M. f. tenere* was 32 (16 macrochromosomes and 16 microchromosomes). All chromosome pairs were homomorphic except pair 6, which is hetermorphic (ZW) in females.

Fossil Record: Pleistocene fossil remains of *M. fulvius* have been found at a Florida Irvingtonian site (Meylan, 1982), and in Rancholabrean deposits in Florida and Texas (Holman, 1981).

Distribution: As presented under **Geographic Variation.**

Geographic Variation: Five subspecies are recognized (Roze and Tilger, 1983), but only one, *Micrurus fulvius fulvius* (Linnaeus, 1766), the eastern coral snake, described above, occurs east of the Mississippi River. *M. f. fulvius* occurs from southeastern North Carolina southward through peninsular Florida, and westward to southeastern Louisiana. The other four races range from western Louisiana southwestward through southern Texas to eastern and central Mexico.

The southern Florida coral snakes were designated *M. f. barbouri* by Schmidt (1928) on the basis of a few specimens lacking black spots on their red bands. Subsequently, Duellman and Schwartz (1958) reviewed this character and reported that *Micrurus* from southern Florida often have black spotting on their red bands and that Schmidt's designation was invalid.

Confusing Species: Several subspecies of *Lampropeltis triangulum* and the species *Cemophora coccinea* also have red, yellow and black bands crossing their bodies, but their red and yellow bands are separated by black bands, and their snouts are red instead of black. Also, *Cemophora* has no bands crossing its white or cream–colored venter.

Habitat: *Micurus f. fulvius* uses a variety of habitats. It seems to prefer dry, open or brushy areas, and has been taken in xerophytic rosemary scrub, seasonally flooded pine flatwoods, xerophytic and mesophytic hardwood hammocks, and occasionally in marshy areas (Neill, 1957; Jackson and Franz, 1981), where it spends most of the time buried in the soil, leaf litter, logs, or stumps. They also hide in gopher tortoise burrows where the two reptiles are sympatric.

Behavior: In Florida, active eastern coral snakes have been collected in every month, but there is a distinct bimodal activity pattern with more activity from March to May and, again, from August to November (Jackson and Franz, 1981). The winter months, December–February, are the period of least activity in Florida. North of Florida *M. fulvius* are forced to hibernate, usually underground.

There is a misconception that coral snakes are nocturnal, but Neill (1957) reported that only one of 121 active *M. fulvius* was taken at night. He also summarized the few literature records for nocturnal captures, and concluded that this snake is largely diurnal in Georgia and Florida, prowling in the early morning shortly after sunrise to about 0900 hr. It is most often seen on bright, sunny mornings, but occasionally they also prowl in the late afternoon or early evening. Jackson and Franz (1981) reported that in Florida during April to August, *M. fulvius* is surface active from 0700–0900 hr, remains under cover for much of the day, and resumes activity during the late afternoon, 1600–1730 hr. In March and again in September–November, they appear in mid– or late morning (0900–1000 hr), and with the exception of a mid–afternoon quiescent period (1330–1600 hr), remain active most of the day.

Map

Reproduction: Females mature at a snout–vent length of about 55 cm in 21–27 months (Quinn, 1979b; Jackson and Franz, 1981). The smallest male undergoing spermiogenesis found by Quinn (1979b) was 40.2 cm snout–vent length, and Jackson and Franz (1981) reported that most males that were 45 cm or longer contained sperm, whereas smaller ones did not. This size is reached in 11–21 months. In Texas, ovary weights of *M. f. tenere* increased from March through April, declined slightly in May, and then more rapidly in June; follicle lengths showed the same pattern (Quinn, 1979b). In Florida, vitellogenesis occurs in late winter and early spring (March–May), with follicles reaching preovulatory size by early June (Jackson and Franz, 1981).

Quinn (1979b) found that in male *M. f. tenere* from Texas there was complete regression with spermatogonia and Sertoli cells in May through August, with a peak in June. Early recrudescence with spermatogonial divisions and primary spermatocytes was found in specimens examined from June through October, with a peak in July. In August and September, males had late recrudescense with secondary spermatocytes and undifferentiated spermatids. Active spermiogenesis with mature sperm in the lumen occurred from August to April. Seminiferous tubule diameter was greatest from November to March, and testes weight was greatest from December to February. Quinn found sperm in the ductus deferens from February to December, and in the epididymis from April to December. The male sexual cycle in Florida is essentially the same (Jackson and Franz, 1981).

Mating occurs in the spring, and possibly in the fall. Quinn (1979b) described courtship behavior:

> The male immediately crawled to the female and flicked his tongue several times on her back at mid body. He then raised his head and neck at about a 45° angle and, leaving his neck at that angle, tilted his head down and touched his nose to the female's back. In this position he quickly and smoothly ran his nose along the dorsum of the female to about five cm behind her head. No tongue flicks from the male were seen during this advance, but during this time he aligned his body over hers. He dipped his body and tail at his vent region laterally on the female's right side beside her vent. Immediately anterior to the vent the male's body was at the female's dorsum and immediately posterior to the vent his tail projected upward at about a 30° angle, not touching the female's tail. Her tail rested flat on the substrate. Several vent thrusts were made by the male in an attempt to copulate and his hemipenes occasionally partially everted. The female did not gape her vent and darted away. The male pursued the female and the sequence was repeated. This occurred five times in 40 min, after which the snakes were separated. Sixty % of the time the male moved along the female's dorsum from rear to front. Forty % of the time he went the other direction, and when he reached the area of the female's vent he quickly turned anteriorly without removing his nose from her body and progressed toward her head... after the male had unsuccessfully attempted intromission, he moved his entire body back and forth at about 2.5 cm strokes on the female's dorsum. He completed five of these strokes in about five sec, with the sequence ending in several rapid strokes of his nose only. His nose strokes were about 1.25 cm and were made at a speed of about two per sec.

Although both Zegel (1975) and Quinn (1979b) described the courtship behavior of this species, neither witnessed copulation. Vaeth (1984) described a successful mating between a male *M. f. tenere* and a female *M. f. fulvius*.

> The male stopped moving when his head had approached within 2 cm of the female's head and his vent was in apposition to the left side of the female's vent. He then elevated his tail and tried to wrap it under and around the tail of the female. She responded by slightly elevating her tail and gaping her cloaca. Intromission was accomplished rapidly with the right hemipenis. The elapsed time between introduction and intromission was about 25 minutes.

> There was no attempt to completely entwine tails nor was there any cloacal rubbing prior to intromission as has been observed in snake species that possess supra-anal knobs or keels for cloacal alignment ... It is not known what sensory modalities are used for the appropriate precoital positioning in those species lacking supra-anal knobs.

> Shortly after intromission, the male moved the anterior third of his body off the female. After approximately 10 minutes of coital activity, localized rhythmic contractions were noted in the cloacal region of the male. These contractions continued intermittently for 12 minutes. In this particular mating, ejaculation was not completely efficient since a pool of seminal fluid was observed accumulating under the two snakes soon after the contractions were observed. Presumably, this seminal fluid was leaking from the exposed part of the sulcus on the basal portion of the hemipenis. There were no other body movements exhibited by either snake during the copulation period. Only an occasional tongue flick was seen, and these may have been in response to my movements.

> After 61 minutes of copulation, the male withdrew his hemipenis and crawled away from the female.

The eggs are laid during May to July. Tryon and McCrystal (1982) reported a period of 37 days between copulation and oviposition. Two to 13 eggs may be laid, although 4–7 are more common. The eggs are very elongate (20–47 x 6–14 mm, 3–6 g), and are probably laid underground or beneath leaf litter. Ernst and his students found 4 eggs in a hollow depression beneath an old wooden tie on an abandoned railroad embankment in Collier County, Florida.

The young hatch in August and September after an incubation period of about 70–90 days; they are about 177–205 mm in total body length. Campbell (1973) reported hatchlings emerged from slits in the egg shell about 10 mm long, and that the total time needed for emergence is approximately 4 hours.

Growth And Longevity: *Micrurus* doubles its size in less than 2 years, and by 3 years may grow to nearly 60 cm snout–vent length (Quinn, 1979b; Jackson and Franz, 1981). Natural longevity is unknown, but an individual lived almost 7 years at the Brookfield Zoo in Chicago (Bowler, 1977).

Food And Feeding: Prey lists presented by Jackson and Franz (1981) and Greene (1984) show *Micrurus fulvius* fed almost entirely on reptiles: amphisbaenids (*Rhineura floridana*), lizards (*Ophisaurus, Cnemidophorus, Eumeces, Neoseps, Sceloporus, Scincella*), and snakes (*Leptotyphlops*, 28 species of colubrids, *Agkistrodon*, and other *M. fulvius*). Greene (1984) also reported that anurans and rodents are occasionally eaten. Although these snakes may feed nearly year round in Florida, feeding activity was found to be most intense in September–November with a lesser peak in April–May. They use stereotyped head poking movements and chemical cues to search for prey and to follow prey trails (Greene, 1984). Visual and chemical stimuli elicit attack, and prey is held until immobilized by venom. Prey is almost always swallowed head first.

Fangs of five adult *M. fulvius* (65–83 cm) measured by Ernst were 2.0–2.5 mm in length.

The venom of *M. fulvius*, unlike that of the other venomous snakes in eastern North America, attacks the nervous system, primarily the respiratory center, resulting in difficulty in breathing and death in extreme cases. Pain, sometimes severe, usually occurs at the bite site, and, if the bite is on a limb, may slowly extend up that extremity. Dowling (1975:224) reported that the LD-50 (mg/kg) for a mouse was 1.0, that the lethal amount for a human was 4, and that the normal venom yield for *M. fulvius* was 4 mg. However, Fix and Minton (1976) reported that 8 of 14 adult *M. fulvius* from which they extracted venom gave dry yields in excess of 6 mg, and that 4 gave dry yields of 12 or more mg. There was also a distinct positive correlation (r = 0.87) with the longer snakes giving greater venom yields. Eastern coral snakes can deliver serious, and, in some cases, fatal bites. Fortunately, the percentage of human fatalities (about 20%) is not extremely high; especially if the bite is treated with antivenin (Neill, 1957).

Micrurus hunt their reptilian prey with random head thrusts into leaf litter and debris, they then seize it and vigorously chew in their venom. Since eastern coral snakes have relatively short fangs, the chance of a human receiving a bite in the wild when not handling one is slim. Carr (1940) has reported instances of larger *M. fulvius* actually striking, but such behavior must be rare, and stout shoes or boots, and thick trousers should be sufficient protection for the hiker.

Predators And Defense: Jackson and Franz (1981) summarized observations of predation on *M. fulvius*. They mention instances of diurnal predaceous birds, such as the kestrel, red-shouldered hawk, and loggerhead shrike, attacking eastern coral snakes, and their list of prey items found in the stomachs of *M. fulvius* show it eats members of its own species. Minton (1949b) reported that a large bullfrog had eaten a small *M. fulvius*.

When approached, *M. fulvius* will often tuck its head under its coils, ball up its tail and wave it about, thus drawing the predator's attention away from the head. When pinned down, however, they will strike and chew on the restraining implement.

Populations: Being secretive burrowers, *M. fulvius* are not readily observable, and can live in urban areas without being detected. This gives a false impression of rarity, when these snakes may be quite common. For instance, Beck (in Shaw, 1971) reported that in a 39-month period 1958 eastern coral snakes were turned in for bounties in Pinellas County, Florida.

Remarks: Cadle and Sarich (1981) showed, through immunological assessment of serum albumins, that the American coral snakes (*Micrurus* and *Micruroides*) are close allies with other elapids instead of derivatives of South American colubrids. They suggested a late Oligocene—early Miocene separation between the New and Old World elapid lineages.

The question of whether or not coral snakes and other red, yellow and black banded snakes form a mimicry complex has been discussed for years. Grobman (1978) suggested that similar color patterns have arisen independently of natural selection in unrelated sympatric species occupying similar habitats (pseudomimicry), while Wickler (1968) suggested that the dangerously venomous coral snakes are the mimics of mildly venomous colubrid snakes, not the models for these species. In a recent summary of the problem, Greene and McDiarmid (1981) concluded that field observations and experimental evidence refute previous objections to the coral snake serving as the Batesian model in the mimicry hypothesis, and that their bright colors serve as warning signals to predators. Smith (1975) showed that the naive young of some tropical reptile-eating birds instinctively avoid the red-yellow-black banded pattern of coral snakes. Similarly colored and patterned harmless snakes (*Cemophora coccinea*, *Lampropeltis triangulum elapsoides*) or mildly venomous snakes would also gain protection by their resemblance to the coral snakes. Past objections to the mimicry theory have been based largely on the supposition that once bitten by a coral snake a predator will die from the bite; however, the poorly developed venom delivery system of coral snakes precludes that all bites will be fatal. It has also been supposed that coral snakes are nocturnal, and that their bright colors would be meaningless at night, but recent reports (Neill, 1957; Jackson and Franz, 1981) have shown *M. fulvius* to be largely diurnal. Studies of concordant geographic pattern variation by Greene and McDiarmid (1981) strongly suggested that some colubrid species of *Atractus*, *Erythrolamprus*, *Lampropeltis*, and *Pliocerus* are involved in mimicry systems with local coral snakes.

Parent birds may respond to the sight of a nearby snake by actions that will reveal the location of their nest. If bright, ringed snake patterns elicit this behavior more than do cryptic patterns, then ringed snakes that eat eggs or nestling birds should have a hunting advantage over cryptic snakes. Smith and Mostrom (1985) examined this theory in field tests with American robins and a red, yellow and black ringed coral snake model. The model elicited no more response than did a plain brown snake model. So, based on current evidence, the most likely advantage of bright, ringed patterns to snakes is to confer protection against predators, either by camouflage or as warning coloration in mimicry systems.

Krempels (1984) demonstrated that coral snakes appear to exhibit near infrared reflectance that renders the snake extremely visible against a leaf litter substrate, and this may advertise a warning to potential avian predators.

VIPERIDAE

Viperid Snakes

VIPERIDAE
Viperid Snakes

The vipers are venomous snakes that evolved from colubrid ancestors different from those which eventually gave rise to the elapids. The family consists of about 200 species occurring in Asia, Europe, Africa, and the Americas.

Vipers have evolved an advanced venom injecting apparatus. Their maxillae have become shortened horizontally while becoming deep vertically and are capable of movement on the prefrontal and ectopterygoid bones. This allows the elongated hollow fangs on the maxillae to be rotated until they lie against the palate when the mouth is closed. During the strike the maxillae move causing the fangs to rotate downward and forward into stabbing positions. Such movable fangs are termed solenoglyphous. In contrast to the elapids, the viperid maxilla does not contain any other teeth but the fang and its replacement series. Postfrontal, coronoid, and pelvic bones are absent, as also are premaxillary teeth. The prefrontal bone does not contact the nasal bone, and the ectopterygoid is elongated. A scale-like supratemporal bone suspends the quadrate. The hyoid is either Y-shaped or U-shaped with two long superficially placed, parallel arms. All body vertebrae contain elongated hypapophyses. The left lung is absent, and the hemipenis is deeply bilobed or double, with proximal spines and distal calyces, and a bifurcate or semi-centrifugal sulcus spermaticus. Head scalation is essentially like that of colubrids, but some have the dorsal surface covered with small scales instead of enlarged plates. The secretions produced by the venom glands are predominantly hemotoxic, but several species contain neurotoxic components in their venom. Reproduction is either oviparous or ovoviviparous.

The family is comprised of three subfamilies, but only one, the Crotalinae, occurs in the Americas. Members of the Crotalinae are called pit vipers because of the small hole in their face which opens between the eye and nostril. The maxilla is hollowed out to accommodate the pit, and the membrane at the base of the hole is extremely sensitive to infrared radiations, especially those emitted from warm-blooded prey.

Pit vipers are believed to have evolved from Old World vipers (Darlington, 1957; Brattstrom, 1964), but how they reached the Americas is unknown. Today, 17 species in three genera occur in the United States; six species can be found in eastern North America.

AGKISTRODON CONTORTRIX
(Linnaeus, 1766)
Copperhead

Recognition: The copperhead is a pinkish to grayish-brown snake (to 135 cm) with an orange to copper or rust-red, unpatterned head, and a series of brown to reddish-brown, saddle-shaped bands on the body. These dorsal bands are broader along the sides of the body and narrower across the dorsum presenting a dumbbell-like shape, and small dark spots may occur in the light spaces between the bands (see McDuffie, 1963, for a discussion of variation in the banding pattern). The tail lacks a rattle and is yellow, brown or green. Below the eye, the head pigmentation is usually lighter than dorsally, and in some a dark postocular stripe may be present. A pair of small dark spots may occur on the parietal scales. The venter is pink, light brown, or cream colored with dark blotches along the sides of the ventrals. As many as 23–25 scale rows may occur anteriorly, but usually only 21–23 rows occur at mid-body, and 21 before the anal vent. The body scales are keeled and contain apical pits; the anal plate is undivided. Pertinent lateral head scalation includes 2 nasals, a loreal, 2–3 preoculars, 2–3 suboculars, 3 postoculars, several rows of temporals, 8(7–9) supralabials and 10(8–11) infralabials. The eye has an elliptical pupil and there is a heat-sensitive pit located betwen the nostril and eye. There are 140–157 ventrals and 38–52 subcaudals with no sexual differences. The shortened maxilla contains only the elongated fang. The hemipenis, as described by Fitch (1960b), is deeply bifurcate with approximately 35 large spines on the basal third of the two lobes. Most of these are straight but some are slightly hooked. The distal 2/3 of each lobe is covered with small flattened papillae, each ending in a spine, but not arranged in regular rows. No spines occur in the crotch, and the sulcus spermaticus is forked (see Reese, 1947, for the embryological development of the hemipenis).

Males have tails 12–16% of the total body length, while those of females are 11–14% as long as their bodies.

Karyotype: The diploid chromosome number is 36; 16 macrochromosomes (4 metacentric, 8 submetacentric, 2 subtelocentric; sex determination ZZ/ZW) and 20 microchromosomes (Baker et al., 1972; Zimmerman and Kilpatrick, 1973). The W chromosome is acrocentric (Zimmerman and Kilpatrick, 1973).

Fossil Record: Fossil remains of the copperhead have been found in deposits from the lower Pliocene of Nebraska and upper Pliocene of Kansas and Texas (Holman, 1979), and from the Pleistocene: Blancan, Kansas; Rancholabrean, Kansas, Missouri, Pennsylvania, and Texas (Holman, 1981).

Distribution: *A. contortrix* occurs from southwestern New England west to eastern Kansas, Oklahoma, and westcentral Texas, and south to the panhandle of Florida and the Gulf Coast of Alabama, Mississippi, Louisiana and eastern Texas.

Geographic Variation: Five subspecies have been described (Gloyd and Conant, 1943; Gloyd, 1969), but only two occur east of the Mississippi River. *Agkistrodon contortrix contortrix* (Linnaeus, 1766), the southern copperhead, is pale gray to pinkish in ground color, and has the crossbands well marked and very narrow across the back (often they are medially separated). It is found from southeastern Virginia southward along the coastal plain to Gadsden and Liberty counties, Florida, and west to eastern Texas and northward in the Mississippi Valley to southern Missouri and southwestern Illinois. *A. c. mokeson* (Daudin, 1803), the northern copperhead, is more reddish-brown, has a more coppery head and darker, wider cross bands. It ranges from Massachusetts and Connecticut southward on the piedmont and highlands to Georgia, Alabama, and northeastern Mississippi, and west through southern Pennsylvania and the Ohio Valley to Illinois.

Confusing Species: Colubrid snakes (*Elaphe, Lampropeltis, Nerodia, Heterodon*) lack a facial pit, have rounded pupils, and may have patterned heads. Cottonmouths, *A. piscivorus*, have a band through the eye and lack a loreal scale.

Habitat: In the eastern United States, this snake inhabits oak–hickory hillsides containing rock crevices and slides in woodlands, and swamp borders. It ascends from the coastal plain to elevations of almost 1,200 m. *A. contortrix* utilizes relatively open areas with a higher rock density and less surface vegetation than does the sympatric *Crotalus horridus* (Reinert, 1984a).

Behavior: Although it is diurnally active in the spring and fall, *A. contortrix* becomes crepuscular or nocturnal during the hot summer months. Annually, it is active from April to late October in the northern parts of its range, with most being seen from May to September, but farther south

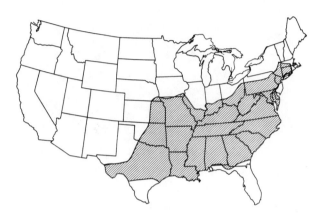

Map

Fig. 72. Juvenile *Agkistrodon contortrix mokeson* (right) and *Agkistrodon piscivorus leucostoma* (left).

Fig. 73. *Agkistrodon contortrix contortrix* (William A. Cox).

the copperhead may remain active until early December.

In the fall they become gregarious and may crawl some distance to a communal hibernaculum, which is sometimes shared with *Crotalus horridus* and *Elaphe obsoleta*. They usually return to this same area each winter (Fitch, 1960b). Weathered outcrops with crevices extending below the frost line are often used, as also are caves, gravel banks, old stone walls and building foundations, animal burrows, hollow logs and stumps, and sawdust piles. Drda (1968) observed several overwintering in a Missouri cave that were quite active most of the winter; of course, air temperatures in the cave were considerably above freezing. Juveniles were found at greater depths than adults. Neill (1948a) reported that on the coastal plain of Georgia copperheads hibernate singly.

Fitch (1956) determined the preferred body temperatures of *A. contortrix* to be 26–28 C. Brattstrom (1965) reported the minimum and maximum voluntary body temperatures for 61 individuals to be 17.5 and 34.5 C, but Fitch (1960b) recorded body temperatures as low as 12.4 C for those under rocks in the early spring. Fitch (1960b) found that gravid females basked more often and seemed to prefer warmer body temperatures. Sanders and Jacob (1981) monitored the body temperatures of 20 copperheads by telemetry. Some basking on clear winter days achieved body temperatures of 10 C or higher. They also found that body temperatures recorded in the summer varied among snakes of different body lengths, and that there was a significant negative correlation between snout–vent length and the critical thermal minimum.

Heart rate and breathing rate increase with rising temperatures (Jacob and Carroll, 1982), but temperature has no effect on heart rate–breathing response over the temperature range at which copperheads are normally active.

Home ranges of *A. contortrix* in Kansas varied between 3.4 hectares for females and 9.8 for males (Fitch, 1958; 1960b). The home range diameter of males averaged 354 m, that of females 210 m. Fitch (1960b) reported movements on the summer range of 1.5–378 m for individuals that remained within their home range, and 442–762 m for those that had apparently shifted their home ranges. He also recorded distances of spring or fall captures at hibernacula from points of capture on the summer range of 232–1183 m. Males travelled longer distances from hibernacula (x = 656 m) than did females (x = 406 m).

Copperheads may climb into low bushes or trees after prey or to bask. Swanson (1952) observed several young resting on laurel bushes 5 cm or more above ground, and Johnson (1948) saw one almost 4 m high in a tree. Fitch (1960b) also reported instances of climbing in *A. contortrix*.

A. contortrix has no special affinity for water, but does favor damp habitats. It will, however, enter waterbodies voluntarily, and has been observed swimming on numerous occasions (Fitch, 1960b; Groves, 1977).

Males occasionally engage in combat dances (Gloyd, 1947; Shaw, 1948; Fitch, 1960b; Collins, 1974; Mitchell, 1981). Typical combat behavior as reported by J. Ackroyd to Gloyd (1947) is as follows:

> Possibly two–thirds of the anterior portions of the snakes' bodies were entwined vertically with the exception of a portion of the neck. The heads were opposite each other and were held horizontally, three or four inches apart. They seemed to gaze hypnotically at each other and there was a slight swaying movement between them. About one turn of coil was wound and unwound, first in a clockwise and then in a counter clockwise direction. At no time did the distance between the heads change during the rhythmic movements, and at no time did the snakes progress along the ground. It seemed as if the posterior ends were definitely anchored.

> On three distinct occasions one of the snakes broke the rhythm of the dance by darting its head rapidly at the other. The visibility was not good but I imagined the movement to be a caress, with contact made somewhere in the region of the chin of the other snake. What

most amazed me was their utter disregard for me. I watched them from a distance of about three feet, engulfed them in the rays of the light for minutes, and yet the dance continued. From the time I first saw them until they were prodded with a stick and moved off into the underbrush, approximately twenty minutes elapsed.

Reproduction: Fitch (1960b) reported that in Kansas at an age of 3 years most, but not all, females are of small adult size (50 cm snout–vent length) and sexually mature. The age and size of maturity in the male copperhead is unknown.

At the time of spring emergence in Kansas, the ova are small (1–9 mm) and occur in several size groups suggesting that they may mature at different times (Fitch, 1960b). In May the ova grow rapidly and ovulation occurs in the latter part of the month. Observations that all females do not breed each season, seem to indicate a biennial female reproductive cycle (Fitch, 1960b; McDuffie, 1961).

Numerous matings have been observed by various biologists and these tend to indicate that, although copulation has taken place from April to October, the prime breeding periods are April and May and September and October. Fitch (1960) found active sperm in the cloaca of a wild caught female on 19 May. On 24 June a second examination showed still abundant motile sperm, but about 75% of the sperm were dead or very slow in their movements. It seems then that copperhead sperm can be stored in the cloaca by the female for only a relatively short time. They apparently survive much longer in the upper end of the oviducts in vascular tissues specialized as seminal receptacles (Fitch, 1960b). Fitch (1960b) found active sperm in the cloaca in April, May, June, and October; other females examined in April, June, July, August, October and November were negative. Twenty–one of 59 sexually mature females obtained by Gloyd (1934) in April and May contained active sperm. He examined the vas deferens of males in April–August and October and found more or less active sperm in all. Schuett (1982) reported that an October copulation resulted in the birth of young on 3 August.

The mating behavior observed by D.W. Sutherland, as reported by Fitch (1960b), is probably typical.

> ...the female copperhead moved from one corner of the cage toward the center, and the male in another part of the cage exhibited immediate excitation. He moved toward her and came in contact with the posterior part of her body. The female's movements ceased when the male made contact. The male then became moderately excited and began to rub his chin along her body in short spasmodic jerks. At first he moved toward the posterior end of her body but corrected his direction and progressed anteriorly, rapidly protruding his tongue, with the points widely spread. When he reached the anterior end of the female, he placed the posterior part of his body alongside and forced it under the female with a rippling movement. When the female began to crawl, the male became extremely active and moved his entire body convulsively, causing the posterior part to disengage and thrash about wildly. The male's head was moved vigorously along the top of the female's head. The posterior portion of his body was again brought alongside the female's body and his tail was twisted encircling hers. The posterior portion of the male's body contracted longitudinally, and forced the female's tail up and forward. The male's head movements increased and his body was in continual movement alongside the body of the female. The female remained impassive during the entire period of courtship.

The young are ovoviviparous (although Dolley, 1939 reported the embryos to be attached to and developing within the oviduct), and are born in August or September, but birthing may be extended to November (Fitch, 1960b). Fitch estimated the gestation period to be 105–110 days, and females may aggregate near the time of parturition (Finneran, 1953). Chenowith (1948) observed the birth process:

> At 6 p.m. on September 4, three small hatchlings were found crawling about in her pen and a fourth one was being born. The mother was lying in a half–moon position with her tail twisted to one side but not raised. The snake was extruded by a series of muscular contractions in the posterior part of the mother's abdomen. Enclosed in its elliptical, membraneous, semi–transparent sac which was about 48 mm. by 35 mm., the fourth little snake did not move at all for about thirty–five minutes. Then it started to break out, struggling five minutes before it was free. Meanwhile the fifth and final one was being ejected. This took approximately ten minutes. When the fifth had wriggled free from its sac, all five juveniles were very lively and struck often when annoyed, vibrating their tails rapidly.

A single brood may contain 1–20 young (Wright and Wright, 1957; White, 1979), but 4–8 are more common. Specific records from published literature and from Fitch's (1960b) Kansas field study indicated a total of 1068 eggs or young from 203 females with an average brood size of 5.26 young. Larger females produced larger broods. Brood size may vary from year to year, apparently due to different environmental conditions (Seigel and Fitch, 1985).

Newborn young are usually 200–250 mm in total length, weigh about 10 g, and are patterned like the adults, but paler in ground color. They have yellow tails. Functional and replacement fangs are present and the young are venomous (Stadelman, 1929b). Hybridization has occurred in captivity with *A. piscivorus* (Mount and Cecil, 1982) and *Crotalus horridus* (Smith and Page, 1972).

Growth And Longevity: Males apparently grow faster than females (Fitch, 1960b). Yearlings in Kansas have snout–vent lengths of 30–40 cm; those 2 years old, 40–57.5 cm; 3 years old, 45–62.5 cm; 4 years old 53–73 cm; 5 years old 55–75 cm (estimated from Fitch, 1960b). In Indiana, Minton (1972) reported yearlings to be 38–43 cm and 2 year olds 53–59 cm.

Bowler (1977) reported the longevity record for *A. contortrix* to be 29 years, 10 months and 6 days.

Food And Feeding: Although containing a heat detecting facial pit, *A. contortrix* is not restricted to warm–blooded prey. It is known to eat various insects (cicadas, mantids, grasshoppers, lepidopteran larvae), small ranid frogs, narrow–mouthed toads (*Gastrophyrne*), turtles (*Sternotherus, Terrapene*), lizards (*Sceloporus, Eumeces, Scincella, Ophiosaurus*), snakes (*Thamnophis, Tantilla*), small birds, shrews (*Sorex, Cryptotis, Blarina*), mice (*Microtus, Peromyscus, Reithrodontomys, Mus, Napaeozapus*), small rats (*Neotoma, Sigmodon*), and juvenile rabbits (*Sylvilagus*) (Hamilton and Pollack, 1955; Wright and Wright, 1957; Fitch, 1960b, Murphy, 1964; Garton and Dimmick, 1969). Smaller individuals eat insects, and lizards; while adults prey more heavily on mammals.

Adults are mostly ambushers, although since they are mainly nocturnal, active hunting behavior may have been missed. Young copperheads actively stalk much of their prey. Neill (1960) has reported that the yellow tail of the newborn may be used to lure small frogs.

Large prey is bitten and released to be tracked later when the venom has taken effect; small prey and birds are retained in the mouth until dead.

Venom And Bites: Snakes of the genus *Agkistrodon* have the same typical solenoglyphous fangs as other vipers (Ernst, 1964, 1965, 1982; Kardong, 1979). Ernst (1965, 1982) found fangs 1.1–7.2 mm in a series of 214 copperheads 17–110 cm in total body length. Fang length increased linearly with growth in body and head length.

A newborn of the *Agistrodon*-complex has fully functional fangs and is capable of injecting venom (Boyer, 1933). These fangs, however, do not remain with the snake throughout its life. Instead they are shed and replaced periodically, an adaptation for replacing broken or loose fangs. A series of five to seven (in less than 3 percent of snakes examined; Ernst, 1982) replacement fangs occur in the gums behind and above the functional fang in alternating sockets on the maxillary bone.

The replacement fangs lie close together and those distal to the functional fang may be only 0.1–0.3 mm apart. In graduated lengths, they may range from a first reserve fang slightly longer than the functional fang (but never more than 0.2 mm longer) to only a short spike about 0.2 mm long in the last of the series. As with rattlesnakes (Klauber, 1939), the graduated reserve fang series shifts forward to occupy an alternate series of sockets on the maxilla. These sockets are divided by a wall of tissue that separates the developing fangs that will enter the outer socket from those that will enter the inner socket. The socket of the first reserve fang is also separated from that of the functional fang by a membrane. Beside the functional fang is a vacant socket into which the first reserve fang migrates just prior to the shedding of the functional fang.

Such a replacement series is even found in the newborn. The fangs do not develop as a complete unit, but rather from the tip (represented by the most distal replacement fang) upward, and the hollow tube–shape is in evidence from the earliest period of development in which shape can be ascertained. Ernst (1982) found that approximately 19 percent of the time, one or both fangs were in the process of replacement. The mean replacement rate for the genus *Agkistrodon* was 21.1 percent. Fitch (1960b) found 19.7 percent of the *A. contortrix* fangs he examined were being replaced, and reported a 33–day fang shedding cycle.

The venom is highly hemolytic, and mice or rats dissected an hour or two after having been bitten show massive hemorraging. The total yield increases with size (Jones and Burchfield, 1971), and a large copperhead may produce up to 0.29 ml of venom. Twenty–five to 75% of the contents of the venom glands may be discharged in one bite (Fitch, 1960b), and Minton (1967) has determined that juveniles are as toxic as their parents.

Symptoms of copperhead bites recorded by Hutchison (1929) were pain and swelling, weakness, giddiness, breathing difficulty, hemorrhage, either an increased or a weakened pulse, nausea and vomiting, gangrene, ecchymosis, unconsciousness or stupor, fever, sweating, headache, and intestinal discomfort. While *A. contortrix* is responsible for many bites each year, mortality from these bites is almost nonexistent. Although other fatal cases may be on record, the only record of a fatal bite we could find was reported by do Amaral (1927) of a 14–year–old boy bitten on the finger and treated too late with antivenin. Probably only the very young or old need worry about this snake. Case histories of bites are given by Boyer (1933), McCauley (1945), Fitch (1960b), and Diener (1961).

Predators And Defense: Ophiophagous snakes (indigo, milk and kingsnakes), opossums, coyotes, cats and red–tailed hawks are natural enemies, and Fitch (1960b) reported that in captivity moles readily killed and ate young copperheads. Over much of the range, habitat destruction and the automobile have severely reduced populations.

In our opinion, copperheads are better lovers than fighters. They usually lie motionless in a coil when an intruder is first detected, and this habit, along with their camouflaged pattern, makes them very dangerous. Many bites have resulted from persons unwittingly stepping on, or touching unseen snakes. When touched, they often quickly strike, but at other times just remain quiet or try to crawl away. When handled, they spray musk on their handler. Contrary to the folktale, this musk has its own odor and does smell like cucumbers.

Populations: Copperheads can occur in large populations, especially around hibernacula or sites with a high prey density. In July, 1960, Barbour (1962b) captured 7 adults in less than 15 minutes in an area no larger than 3 by 6 m in Breathitt County, Kentucky. Fitch (1960b) estimated the total population, based on a 10–year census, in his Kansas study area to be approximately 1664 individuals; the density for the 88 hectares was 18.8 per hectare.

In the populations studied by Fitch (1960b) and Vial et al. (1977), individuals of the smaller and younger size and age classes were more numerous. Snakes older than 8 years represented only 5% of the population, while those no older than 2 years comprised 55%. Vial et al. (1977) constructed life tables for *A. contortrix* based on data in Fitch (1960b). They estimated a skewed sex ratio of 74% males to 26% females at birth, but calculated a greater mortality rate in the males, and predicted the sex ratio would reach unity by the eighth year. This is interesting since the sex ratios of litters are usually much closer to 1:1. Gloyd (1934) reported that in a total of 69 young in 16 litters, 29 (42%) were females and 40 (58%) were males.

Remarks: In a study of the immunoelectrophoretic patterns of venom within the genus *Agkistrodon*, Tu and Adams (1968) showed the American species to be closely related to the Japanese species *A. halys*. Jones (1976) compared the venom of the three New World species of *Agkistrodon* and found both geographical differences between and within the species. Differences were present in the venom of the various

subspecies of *A. contortrix*. His work also showed a greater affinity of the neotropical species *A. bilineatus* to *A. contortrix* than to *A. piscivorus*, contrary to former thought (Brattstrom, 1964).

Klauber (1956) has evaluated the use of the names *Agkistrodon* and *Ancistrodon* for this genus, and has presented a convincing argument for the use of the former.

AGKISTRODON PISCIVORUS

Cottonmouth

AGKISTRODON PISCIVORUS
(Lacepede, 1789)
Cottonmouth

Recognition: This is a heavy–bodied, large (to 189.2 cm), olive, dark brown, or black, amphibious pit viper lacking a loreal scale and broad dumbbell–shaped transverse dorsal bands. Juveniles are lighter olive or brown, and individual snakes become progressively darker with age until almost or totally black. Also, the transverse dorsal bands, characteristic of juveniles, fade with age and are almost or totally absent in large adults. The venter is tan to gray and heavily patterned with dark blotches. Some have a light–bordered, dark cheek stripe, and the rostrum with dark bars. The keeled, doubly pitted, body scales occur in 25–27 anterior scale rows, but only 21 rows near the anal vent; the anal plate is undivided. There is a heat sensitive pit between the nostril and eye, and the pupil is elliptical. Dorsally on the head are nine large plates, as in *A. contortrix*; laterally the scalation is similar to that of *A. contortrix*, but no loreal scale is present and there are 2–3 preoculars, 2–4 postoculars, 5 longitudinal rows of temporals, 8(7–9) supralabials, and 10–11(8–12) infralabials. There are 128 ventrals, and 30–56 subcaudals forming an undivided row. Burkett (1966) reported that one female had only 17 subcaudals. The hemipenis is bilobed with a divided sulcus spermaticus. It has recurved spines near the base and calyces near the apex. The fang is the only tooth on the short maxilla.

Males have 128–141 ventrals, 30–54 subcaudals, and tail lengths 12–18% of the total body length; females have 128–138 ventrals, 36–56 subcaudals, and tails 12–16% as long as the total body length.

Karyotype: As reported for *A. contortrix* (Fischman et al., 1972; Baker et al., 1971; Zimmerman and Kilpatrick, 1973), but Zimmerman and Kilpatrick (1973) found that *A. piscivorus* has a submetacentric W chromosome while this chromosome is acrocentric in *A. contortrix*.

Fossil Record: Pleistocene fossils of *A. piscivorus* have been found in Rancholabrean deposits in Florida and Texas (Holman, 1981).

Distribution: *A. piscivorus* ranges from southeastern Virginia south on the Atlantic Coastal Plain to the Florida Keys, and west along the Gulf Coastal Plain, and south through the Mississippi Valley from southwestern Indiana and southern Indiana, Illinois and Missouri to eastern Texas.

Geographic Variation: There are three subspecies (Gloyd, 1969). *Agkistrodon piscivorus piscivorus* (Lacepede, 1789), the eastern cottonmouth, has no pattern on its light brown snout, the transverse dorsal bands strongly contrasting with the relatively lighter body coloration, 39–51 subcaudals in males and 41–50 in females. This race ranges from southeastern Virginia (including the Eastern Shore) along the Atlantic Coastal Plain to east–central Alabama. *A. p. leucostoma* (Troost, 1836), the western cottonmouth, has no pattern on its dark brown to black snout, the transverse dorsal bands lost in the relatively dark body coloration, and 30–54 subcaudals in males and 36–56 in females. It ranges in the Mississippi Valley from southern Indiana (Wilson and Minton, 1983; Forsyth et al, 1985) and southwestern Illinois through southern Missouri to extreme southeastern Kansas, and south to the Gulf Coast from eastern Texas to Mobile Bay. *A. p. conanti* Gloyd, 1969, the Florida cottonmouth, has the rostrum conspicuously marked with a pair of dark vertical bars, the transverse body bands lost in the relatively dark body coloration, and 45–54 subcaudals in males and 41–49 in females. It is found from southern Georgia and southeastern Alabama south through peninsular Florida and to Mobile Bay.

Confusing Species: Water snakes of the genus *Nerodia* have no facial pits, divided anal plates, round pupils, and two rows of subcaudals. Also, when swimming, *A. piscivorus* inflates its lung resulting in much of its body floating on the surface, while the species of *Nerodia* elevate only the head and neck to the surface. Copperheads, *A. contortrix*, are reddish in color, and have dark dumbbell–shaped band across the dorsum.

Habitat: This species lives in almost any type of water body, from brackish coastal marshes to cypress swamps, bayous, ponds, lakes, rivers, and streams. We have seen or collected this snake in such unlikely habitats as clear, gravelly or rocky piedmont streams in Alabama, Arkansas and Missouri. In Florida, it is found on some offshore keys, and Wharton (1969) reported it is very common in the rookeries of wading aquatic birds, such as ibis, anhingas, herons, and egrets. Lee

(1968a) has also found them in the lodges of round–tailed muskrats, *Neofiber alleni*.

During droughts most cottonmouths remain active and aggregate at remaining waterholes. Apparently they can withstand much drying. Dunson and Freda (1985) reported that *A. piscivorus* has a low skin water permeability similar to its more terrestrial relative, *A. contortrix*.

Behavior: With the advent of warm weather in the spring cottonmouths emerge from hibernation and return to their water bodies. This usually occurs in April over most of the range, although they may first appear in March if the daily temperatures rise high enough. In late August and early September the snakes begin a rather leisurely exodus from the water to upland hibernacula, and by October or early November most have disappeared from their aquatic habitats. Exceptions occur, however, and they have been seen in December in Virginia (Linzey and Clifford, 1981), and in southern Florida they may bask in every month.

Neill (1947, 1948a) has reported that *A. piscivorus* is more tolerant of cold than most snakes, and is one of the last to enter hibernation. The winter is spent on shore at some upland site, such as rock crevices on hillsides with a southern exposure (sometimes with *Elaphe obsoleta* and *Crotalus horridus*, Smith, 1961), logs and stumps in woodlands, under the roots of overturned trees, or in palmetto patches (Wharton, 1969). Dundee and Burger (1948) found them in a limestone cliff 0.3 km from and 36 m above the nearest water body. Often several cottonmouths will use the same hibernaculum. Wharton (1969) took the cloacal temperatures of cottonmouths in a subsurface den in Florida. Their body temperatures were 4.2–16.5 C, and within a few degrees of the air temperature. He thought the soil temperatures kept the snake's temperature intermediate between that of the soil and air.

Brattstrom (1965) recorded the cloacal temperature of 11 active *A. piscivorus* from western Texas, 24.6–27.7C (x = 27.0), and Bothner (1973) reported that active cottonmouths in Georgia had cloacal temperatures 21.0–35.0 C (x = 25.7C).

During the spring and fall, activity is mostly diurnal, but in summer cottonmouths are predominately nocturnal. During the day they either bask, especially in the morning, remain undercover, or lie quietly beside logs or among cyprus trees. At these latter sites, they often come in contact with unexpecting humans, making them quite dangerous.

Wharton (1969) reported the home ranges of cottonmouths on Sea Horse Key, Florida were

Map

Fig. 74. Juvenile cottonmouths (shown) and copperheads have yellow tail tips.

Fig. 75. *Agkistrodon piscivorus leucostoma.*

0.04–1.22 ha; males had slightly larger activity ranges (x = 0.17 ha) than females (x = 0.14 ha). Some showed long movements. A 132 cm male crawled 320 m in 27 months, while a 63.5 cm female moved 380 m in 6 months. Two other females traveled 450 and 498 m, respectively; and another left its home range and established a new one on the other side of a mangrove inlet. While crawling, *A. piscivorus* characteristicly keeps its head and neck elevated off the ground.

Like many other pit vipers, male *A. piscivorus* sometimes participate in combat dances (Carr and Carr, 1942; Ramsey, 1948; Wagner, 1962; Burkett, 1966; Perry, 1978, Martin, 1984). A typical "dance" was described by Perry (1978):

> The specimens were each ca. 0.9 m in length, with one slightly larger and heavier-bodied than the other. They faced each other with the upper third of their bodies raised vertically out of the water. The posterior two-third of their bodies extended out behind them on the water, and their heads were cocked parallel to the water. After a few seconds in this raised position, they would start swaying in unison, and would suddenly lunge at each other with mouths closed, entwining a few coils of their bodies. Next, a vigorous struggle to untangle would ensue which usually ended with the heads of both snakes submerging in the water. After untangling they would face each other and begin the 'dance' again.

Reproduction: Burkett (1966) reported that a female *A. p. leucostoma* with a snout–vent length of 45.5 cm was gravid. The smallest mature female *A. p. leucostoma* found in Louisiana by Kofron (1979a) was 55.2 cm in snout–vent length, and Penn (1943) dissected another Louisiana female with a total length of 63 cm that contained 6 embryos. Blem (1981b) found that female *A. p. piscivorus* 70.7–79.1 cm in total length were mature in southeastern Virginia. Arny (in Wharton, 1966) reported that a female *A. p. leucostoma* was mature at a total length of 59.4 cm, and Wharton (1966) thought a length of 80 cm was required for the attainment of sexual maturity in Florida *A. p. conanti* (which reaches a total length of 189.2 cm). Conant (1933) reported that a female raised in captivity produced young at an age of 2 years, 10 months.

The ovarian follicles begin to enlarge in August and September. Kofron (1979a) first observed vitellogenesis in February in Louisiana, and his females ovulated in May. Wharton (1966) also found ovulation occurred in late May and early June in Florida. Although Burkett (1966) and Wharton (1966) reported a biennial female reproductive cycle, Arny (in Kofron, 1979a), Krofron (1979a) and Blem (1981b, 1982) have presented convincing evidence for an annual female reproductive cycle. Burkett (1966) also reported a case of a female producing young in two consecutive years.

Wharton (1966) found that male *A. p. conanti* over 65 cm were sexually mature. Johnson et al. (1982), studied the male sexual cycle in Alabama cottonmouths. Testicular recrudescense occurred in April, spermiogenesis began in June and peaked in July and August, and spermatogenesis ceased in October. Sperm were stored overwinter in the vas efferens, epididymides and vas deferens.

Mating apparently can occur at anytime during the year (Wright and Wright, 1957; Ashton and Ashton, 1981). Actual dates on which copulation has been observed in the wild or in captivity include 10 and 11 March, 31 August, and 19 October (Allen and Swindell, 1948; Wright and Wright, 1957; Anderson, 1965). Burkett (1966) hypothesized that the females could store viable sperm for long periods. An adequate description of cottonmouth courtship and mating behavior has not been published.

The ovoviviparous young are normally born in August or September after a gestation period of about 160 days (Wright and Wright, 1957). Blem (1981b) showed that there is a direct correlation between the number of young and their size and the female body length and weight; larger females produce more young of greater body length. Litters of from 1–20 young have been reported (Wright and Wright, 1957; Clark, 1949), but 5–7 are probably more common. The birth process has been described by Funk (1964).

> One young was found already to have been born when the cage was examined at 2305 on 22 August 1962. It was not in its sac, but was dead and lying in an extended position a few inches from the sac as if it had for some reason died after emerging from the sac.
>
> At 2307 the second young was born. It ruptured its sac at 2313, and left it at 2354. The third young was born at 2310, ruptured its sac at 2315, and emerged at 0032 (23 Aug.); the fourth was born at 2317, ruptured its sac at 2325, and left it at 0209 (23 Aug.); and the fifth and final young was born at 2321, ruptured its sac at 2332, and emerged at 0006 (23 Aug.)...
>
> All four of the young observed alive took their first breaths after rupturing their sacs but before leaving them. Within one minute of rupturing their sacs, while their heads were protruding, they opened their mouths widely from three to seven times, after which the first breath was taken. The first breaths were deep, and 3 (2 young) or 4 (2 young) were taken each minute for the first three hours, after which the rate decreased to 2 (3 young) or 3 (1 young) per minute.

Newborn young of *A. p. leucostoma* are about 260 mm long (Barbour, 1956a), while those of *A. p. piscivorus* measured by Ernst averaged 254 mm in total length. These young are much shorter than the 338 mm young produced by *A. p. conanti* (Wharton, 1966). The young are light brown with darker brown transverse bands and yellow tails.

Growth And Longevity: Barbour (1956a) studied *A. p. leucostoma* in western Kentucky and presented the following notes on size classes: 7–8 months, 260–298 mm (having grown about 25 mm since birth); 19–20 months, 312–337 mm (having grown about 45 mm in the year before capture); and 31–32 months, x = 425 mm (an average length increment of 95 mm over the preceding group); after this growth was too variable to calculate.

Bowler (1977) reported the maximum known longevity for *A. piscivorus* was 18 years, 11 months.

Food And Feeding: From the numerous types of prey listed for *A. piscivorus* in the literature, one forms the idea that this snake does not care what it eats as long as it moves. This is not entirely correct either, since it is known to also consume carrion. Apparently it is an opportunist, taking as prey that animal which is most available at the time it is hungry. It is known to have eaten snails, spiders, insects, various fish (including bullhead catfish), sirens, toads, spadefoots, tree and ranid frogs, small turtles (*Sternotherus*, *Kinosternon*, *Pseudemys*, *Trachemys*, *Chelydra*), various lizards, snakes (especially *Nerodia*, and occasionally other small cottonmouths), young alligators, the young of aquatic birds, shrews, mice, rats, muskrats, and squirrels. Ernst observed a young cottonmouth swallow a full grown cotton rat (*Sigmodon hispidus*). At times they may gorge themselves; Bothner (1974) saw one swallow 9 fish in 85 minutes. Food studies by Barbour (1956a), Klimstra (1959a), Burkett (1966), and Kofron (1978), have shown that fish and amphibians are eaten most often.

When searching for prey, *A. piscivorus* usually swims with its head elevated above the water. However, Bothner (1974) saw one which explored a pool with its head under water. They may aggregarte at wading bird rookeries, where they eat the young which fall from the nests (Wharton, 1969).

Odor, sight and heat radiation (from birds and mammals) are used to detect prey. If in the water, when prey is identified, they quickly swim to it, seize it, and hold it in their mouths. On land, we have seen them both ambush prey and actively pursue it. If the prey is large and struggles, it is usually held in the mouth until the venom immobilizes it. This can sometimes cause problems; a cottonmouth we had in the laboratory had its tongue and part of its mouth chewed away by a brown rat before the rat died.

Young cottonmouths may wave their yellow tails about to lure frogs and other small prey (Wharton, 1960).

Bothner (1974) observed an apparent dominance of two *A. piscivorus* over a third that arrived late at a feeding pool in Georgia.

Venom And Bites: *A. piscivorus* is a large, sometimes aggressive, dangerous snake. Like other vipers, it has a solenoglyphous venom delivery system with fangs to 11 mm (Ernst, 1964, 1965, 1982; Kardong, 1974). Newborn young have mean fang lengths of 2.67 mm and fully developed venom glands (Ernst, 1982). The fangs are shed periodically, and usually are replaced on one side at a time (Ernst, 1982). Allen and Swindell (1948) reported that the replacement process takes about five days to complete, and that during this time venom is ejected through both the old or the new fang, depending on the stage of development. Ernst has examined several cottonmouths which had four functional fangs at the same time.

Cottonmouth venom is strongly hemolytic, destroying red blood cells and causing coagulation at the site of the bite, and fatalities have occurred (Hutchison, 1929; Allen and Swindell, 1948; Anderson, 1965; Burkett, 1966). They can and will bite underwater. Symptoms of cottonmouth bites include swelling and pain at the site, weakness, giddiness, difficulty in breathing, hemorrhage, weakened pulse or heart failure, lowered blood pressure, nausea and vomiting, occasional paralysis, a drop in body temperature, unconsciousness or stupor, and nervousness (Hutchison, 1929; Essex, 1932; Burkett, 1966). Nasty secondary bacterial infections may also occur, such as tetanus or gas gangrene. Allen and Swindell (1948) reported that 50% of the bites result in crippled fingers or toes due to gangrene. Although a 150 cm cottonmouth once yielded 2.5 ml of venom when "milked" (Allen and Swindell, 1948), most probably release about 0.5 ml per bite. Case histories of bites are given by Hulme (1952) and Burkett (1966).

Predators And Defense: Adults have few enemies other than alligators and humans, but the juveniles are preyed on by a multitude of animals: large fish (gars, bullheads, largemouth bass), snakes (king and indigo snakes), large wading birds, (ibis, egrets) raccoons, otters, dogs, and cats.

The disposition of individual cottonmouths varies greatly. Those we have had ranged from very timid to extremely aggressive, but all would bite if handled. When first disturbed they usually try to escape. If this is not possible, they coil and strike, often repeatedly. The well publicized behavioral trait of gapping open the mouth to show the inner pinkish–white lining does not always occur. In fact, we seldom saw this display while capturing several hundred cottonmouths. When first grasped or pinned down, they thrash about violently, striking at any near object, even biting themselves. Because of their commonness, size, unpredictibility, and violent tempers, cottonmouths are among the most dangerous of our snakes, and should be approached with care.

Populations: Cottonmouths may be the most common reptile in certain habitats. At Murphy's Pond, Hickman County, Kentucky, they formerly occurred in densities of over 700 per hectare (Barbour, 1956a), and Ernst has seen as many as 8 basking on one fallen cyprus tree in Florida. Wharton (1969) reported that during the time water bird rookeries are active, cottonmouths may become very numerous under the nest trees.

Immature individuals made up 32.5% of those snakes examined by Burkett (1966) and about 45% of the Murphy's Pond population (Barbour, 1956a). Fifty–three percent of the adult specimens and in a group of 48 embryos (8 broods) examined by Burkett (1966) were females.

SISTRURUS CATENATUS

Massasauga

SISTRURUS CATENATUS
(Rafinesque, 1818)
Massasauga

Recognition: The massasauga is a small- to medium-sized (to 100.3 cm.) gray to light brown rattlesnake with a row of dark brown to black blotches on the dorsum, and 3 rows of small brown to black spots on each side of the body. Occasional individuals are striped. Its black venter is mottled with yellow, cream, or white marks, and the tail is ringed with alternate dark and light bands. A dark, light-bordered stripe runs backward from the eye, and another dark mid-dorsal, light-bordered stripe extends posteriorly on the back of the head. The pupil is elliptical and a hole (pit) lies between the nostril and the eye. There are usually 25(21-27) rows of keeled scales at mid-body, and the anal plate is undivided. Dorsally on the head are nine enlarged plates: 2 internasals, 2 prefrontals, a large frontal, 2 supraoculars, and 2 parietals. Laterally are 2 nasals, a loreal, 2 preoculars (the upper touches the posterior nasal), 3(2-4) postoculars, 1-2 suboculars, 12(9-14) supralabials, and 12 or 13(10-16) infralabials. The hemipenis is bifurcate with a divided sulcus spermaticus, about 33 recurved spines per lobe, about 23 fringes per lobe, and some spines occurring in the crotch. Only the fang occurs on the short maxilla.

Males have 129-150 ventrals and 24-33 subcaudals; females have 132-157 ventrals and 19-29 subcaudals. Tail length (exclusive of rattle) is 10-12.5% of total length in males, but only 7.5-9.0% in females (Minton, 1972).

Karyotype: The chromosomal complement consists of 16 macrochromosomes (4 metacentric, 6 submetacentric, 4 subtelocentric), and 20 microchromosomes; sex determination is ZZ/ZW (Zimmerman and Kilpatrick, 1973).

Fossil Record: Remains of *S. catenatus* have been found in deposits from the upper Pliocene of Kansas and Texas, and from the Pleistocene (Blancan) of Kansas (Holman, 1979, 1981).

Distribution: *S. catenatus* ranges from southern Ontario, central New York, and northwestern Pennsylvania, west to eastern Iowa, and southwest to western Texas, southern New Mexico and southeastern Arizona. There are also Mexican populations in the Cuatro Cienegas Basin, Coahuila, and near Aramberri, Nuevo Leon (Minton, 1983).

Geographic Variation: Three subspecies are recognized (Minton, 1983), but only one, *Sistrurus catenatus catenatus* (Rafinesque, 1818), the eastern massasauga, occurs in the range of this book. It is found from southern Ontario and central New York, west to Iowa and eastern Missouri.

Confusing Species: The large rattlesnakes (*Crotalus*) have numerous small scales on the crown between the two supraocular scales. In *S. miliarius*, the prefrontal scales are in broad contact with the loreal scale.

Habitat: This pit viper is usually found in moist habitats such as swamps, marshes, bogs, or wet meadows or grasslands.

Behavior: In Ohio, Indiana, and Missouri this species is annually active from April to late October or early November (Conant, 1951; Minton, 1972; Seigel, 1986), but farther south in Texas it may be active by mid-March (Greene and Oliver, 1965).

Most activity is over the period from April to mid-May, and October (Seigel, 1986). Hibernation occurs in rock crevices, rodent and crayfish burrows, old stumps and rotten logs. Maple and Orr (1968) studied the overwintering behavior of *S. catenatus* in northeastern Ohio. By monitoring the temperature of various components of the hibernacula, they concluded that the massasauga is capable of maintaining a cloacal temperature above the ambient temperature for 45 minutes, and that it can survive a freezing body temperature for short periods without harm, but that it usually hibernates in wet crayfish holes at depths below the frost line. During the spring and fall they are more diurnal in their habits and can often be seen basking or crawling in search of food. When the daily temperatures warm in summer, they become mostly nocturnal. Although some activity does occur in the early morning and evening, the heat of mid-day is avoided.

Reinert and Kodrich (1982) equipped 25 *S. catenatus* from western Pennsylvania with radio transmitters and followed their individual movements for up to 50 days. The mean area and length of the home range were 9794 m² and 89 m, respectively, and the mean distance moved per day was 9.1 m. They found no significant differ-

SISTRURUS CATENATUS

Massasauga

Map

Fig. 76. *Sistrurus catenatus catenatus.*

ences between the sexes; however, gravid females had significantly shorter home range lengths than did nongravid females. In the spring and fall, the massasaugas inhabited low, poorly drained areas near the hibernacula, but during the summer habitats with low or sparse vegetation and dry soil were used more frequently, particularly by gravid females.

Massasaugas are accomplished swimmers and readily enter water.

Reproduction: Studies on the reproductive cycles of *S. catenatus* from Wisconsin by Keenlyne (1978) indicated that females became mature in their third year. First summer females showed no follicular growth, those in their second summer had follicles about 7 mm in diameter, and 8 of 16 in their third summer were gravid, and 4 others were post partum. One collected on 31 August had yellow follicles about 25 cm long. Only 2 of 66 fourth-summer females were not gravid or had not already passed their young. Only 7% (6 of 82) third-summer or older females, and only 3% (2 of 66) of fourth-summer females or older were non-reproductive. Keenlyne (1978) thought this strongly suggested an annual female reproductive cycle. However, Reinert (1981) and Seigel (1986) found evidence of a biennial reproductive cycle in western Pennsylvania and Missouri massasaugas. Of 26 females Reinert examined in 1977, 11 were nongravid adults and 3 were juveniles. The percentage of reproductive females in Pennsylvania was only 52%, and varied from 33–71% over 3 years in Missouri. The smallest gravid Pennsylvania specimen was 448 mm in total length. There was a significant size difference between the Pennsylvania and Wisconsin females, those from Wisconsin being larger, and perhaps this helped determine the breeding cycle. Seigel (1986) found a significant positive regression between snout–vent length and brood size in Missouri.

Observations of matings indicate the breeding period extends from May to November (Wright and Wright, 1957; Klauber, 1972; Chiszar et al., 1976; Reinert, 1981).

Chiszar et al., (1976) described the courtship behavior in a captive pair as follows:

> When the courting pair was first observed, they were directly beneath the lamp and remained there for 75 min. after which they moved to a corner which was partially obscured by a rock. Courting continued for at least 2 more hours, and the pair remained together in a quiescent state for about 3 additional hours, during which copulation is presumed to have occurred.
>
> The postures of the male and female followed the general pattern for *Crotalus* and *Sistrurus* ... The male's anterior was balanced atop the female and he frequently rubbed her head and neck with longitundinal strokes of his chin (these chin rubs were accompanied by

flexions of his entire body). Also, the male's tail was looped around the female's tail 5 cm anterior to the base of her rattle ...

The previously unreported feature of this courtship process was the fact that the male massaged the last 5 cm of the female's tail with the loop ... He tightened the loop around her tail and stroked posteriorly until he touched her rattle. Then he reversed the stroke until he arrived back at the site of his original grip. The entire process (i.e., the stroke–cycle) was repeated three times, although occasionally two or four stroke-cycles were observed.

Courtship of the male appeared to consist of a series of chin-rubbing episodes, each of which was bounded at the beginning and end by three stroke-cycles (chin rubbing was discontinued during the stroking). The duration of chin-rubbing episodes was easily timed since they were clearly demarcated. For one hour a stopwatch was activated at the start of every other chin-rubbing episode and stopped when the stroke-cycle began. Also, a hand-held counter was incremented upon every chin rub during the timed episodes. (Only every other episode was timed because the intervening periods were needed to record data and to reset the stopwatch and counter.) Mean duration of 30 chin rubbing episodes was 56.3 s (SD = 19.9; V = 35.3%); the number of chin rubs per episode was 95.4 (SD = 34.1; V = 35.7%); and the mean number of chin rubs/s was 1.68 (SD = 0.18; V = 10.7%). The correlation coefficient between episode duration and number of chin rubs was $r = 0.92$, $p > .01$, indicating that variances of these parameters were strongly associated. Perhaps the simplest way to explain this correlation is to suggest that chin-rubbing rate is relatively constant and that this behavior continues for the entire period of time between successive stroke-cycles. Hence, the longer the duration of the chin-rubbing episode, the greater the number of chin rubs. This view is supported by the fact that episode duration and chin-rubbing rate were uncorrelated ($r = 0.07$, $p > 0.99$).

The young are born from late July to late September. Collins (1974) reported the gestation period for the ovoviviparous young to be 15 to 16 weeks, but Atkinson and Netting (1927) thought it to be about three months. However, if mating occurs in late summer or early autumn and the young are not born until the next summer, either the sperm is stored and not used until the next spring, or the embryos are arrested in development over the winter.

At birth, young *S. c. catenatus* are 181–252 mm in total length and weigh about 9.7 g (Keenlyne and Beer, 1973). As in other rattlesnakes, the newborn's rattle consists only of a scale-like button. Brood size ranges from 3 (Swanson, 1933) to 14 (Wright and Wright, 1957).

Anderson (1965) observed the birth process. From 1–10 minutes occurred between births and the young ruptured the fetal membrane within the first few minutes. Characteristically, the first act after emergence from the membrane was to stretch the jaws as if yawning. The little snakes would shake their tails and strike if annoyed. Conant (1951) related that young only a few days old had venom strong enough to cause the death of bitten mice several hours later.

Bailey (1942) reported a natural hybrid *Sistrurus catenatus* x *Crotalus horridus*.

Growth And Longevity: Wright (1941) reported that yearling Illinois *S. catenatus* were 39–43 cm in total length, and Missouri yearlings had snout-vent lengths of 30–40 cm (Seigel, 1986). Massasaugas with 50–54 cm snout-vent lengths are probably 3–4 years old (Keenlyne, 1978; Seigel, 1986).

The longevity record for this species is 14 years (Bowler, 1977).

Food And Feeding: Reports of the stomach contents of *S. c. catenatus* or of feeding observations in the wild indicate it is rather catholic in its preferences. Klauber (1972) in his review of the foods of this snake listed mice (*Microtus, Peromyscus*), birds, other snakes, and frogs (*Hyla crucifer, Rana pipiens*); Wright and Wright (1957) added insects, crayfish, fish and toads. If foods of the western subspecies are included, lizards (Greene and Oliver, 1965), centipedes (Lardie, 1976), and lark sparrow eggs (Brush and Ferguson, 1986) are added to this list. Ruthven (in Klauber, 1972) thought that the other snakes devoured had probably been found dead. In support of this, Greene and Oliver (1965) found a massasauga in Texas attempting to swallow a recently road killed hognose snake.

Most reports of massasauga foods are based on single observations. The only detailed studies of prey items were conducted by Keenlyne and Beer (1973) in Wisconsin (59 specimens contained 91 food items), and by Seigel (1986) in Missouri (22 of 96 snakes contained food). In Wisconsin, no frogs were found, but nearly 95% of all items were endotherms; 85.7% of the entire diet consisted of *Microtus pennsylvanicus*. Other prey and their percentage of occurrence are as follows: *Peromyscus leucopus*, 4.4; *Thamnophis sirtalis*, 4.4; *Zapus hudsonius*, 2.2; *Agelarus phoeniceus*, 1.1; *Sorex cinereus*, 1.1; and an unidentified snake (probably *Thamnophis*, 1.1). Food items by sex and percentage of snakes containing prey were as follows: males, 83.6; non-gravid females, 55.6; gravid females, 10.4. Stomach items in Missouri fell into two major classes (rodents: *Microtus, Peromyscus*) and snakes (*Storeria, Thamnophis*).

Endothermic prey is probably detected by the heat sensory facial pit, but sight and odors are also important feeding cues (Chiszar et al., 1976, 1979, 1981). Tail luring may also be important for young massasaugas to capture prey; Schuett et al. (1984) observed recently born young wave their tails back and forth over their heads to attract ranid frogs.

The prey is usually struck and then eaten only after it is dead, but frogs may be swallowed alive.

Venom And Bites: Klauber (1939) reported fang lengths of 5.0–5.9 mm for *S. c. catenatus*. The average dry venom yield is 31 mg per adult (Klauber, 1972). The venom is largely hemolytic and causes much ecchymosis as capillary walls are destroyed, but neurotoxins may also be present. Other symptoms of bites include: pain and swelling (although in one case numbness was reported) at the site of the bite, a cold sweat, faintness, nausea, and nervousness (Hutchison, 1929; LaPointe, 1933; Allen, 1956; Klauber, 1972). Fatalities occasionally occur (Lyon and Bishop, 1936).

Predators And Defense: Our knowledge of its natural predators is scanty. Minton (1972) mentions a blue racer preserved in the act of swallowing an adult massasauga, and most likely other species of snakes take the young. Hawks, large wading birds, and carnivorous mammals are also potential predators. However, humans probably kill more of these snakes each year than all natural predators combined.

Although there are reports of this snake being sluggish and mild mannered (Klauber, 1972), they are dangerous. Those we have seen have all been very alert and irritable, rattling their tails and striking if one came too near.

Populations: In Ohio, 27 were once discovered and killed during the harvesting of about 15 hectares of wheat (Conant, 1951), and probably in the past fairly dense populations of these snakes occurred at other suitable sites. However, habitat destruction has destroyed most colonies, and *S. c. catenatus* has been placed on threatened or endangered lists over most of its range (Breisch, 1984; Bushey, 1985; Seigel, 1986). This trend was noted as long ago as 1948 by Loomis, who stated that "cultivation seems to have greatly reduced its numbers." Suitable habitat must be preserved if this interesting species is to remain a part of our fauna.

Of 128 non–hatchling snakes examined in Missouri by Seigel (1986), 42 (33%) were adult females, 36 (28%) were adult males, and 50 (39%) were juveniles; a sex ratio of 0.85:1.

Remarks: Bonilla et al. (1979) found several differences in the chemical properties of the venom of *S. catenatus* and its congener *S. miliarius*. The venom of *S. miliarius* was yellow, that of *S. catenatus* colorless; their electrophoretic patterns were similar, but not identical; and the venom of *S. miliarius* contained a greater percentage of proteins.

SISTRURUS MILIARIUS

Pigmy Rattlesnake

SISTRURUS MILIARIUS (Linnaeus, 1766)
Pigmy Rattlesnake

Recognition: This is a small grayish-colored rattlesnake (to 78.7 cm) with nine enlarged scales on the dorsal surface of the head (see *S. catenatus*), 1–3 rows of lateral dark spots along the body, a series of 23–45 dark brown or black mid-dorsal blotches, and a red to orange mid-dorsal stripe. The ground color usually ranges from gray to tan, but at the northeastern extent of the range in North Carolina, chiefly in Hyde County, reddish-orange to brick red individuals occur (Palmer, 1971). The venter is whitish to cream-colored with a heavy pattern of black or dark brown blotches. A dark black or reddish-brown bar extends backward from the eye to beyond the corner of the mouth. There are also two dark longitudinal stripes on the back of the head. The pupil is elliptical and a hole (pit) is located between the nostril and eye. Nineteen to 25 rows of keeled scales occur at mid-body and 15–19 rows near the anal vent; the anal plate is undivided. There are 2 nasals, 2 preoculars, 3–6 postoculars, 4–5 temporals, 10(8–13) supralabials, and 11(9–14) infralabials on each side of the head, and the loreal scale lies between the postnasal and upper preocular scales. On the venter are 122–148 ventrals and 25–39 subcaudals with no sexual dimorphism. The hemipenis is similar to that described for *S. catenatus*. Only the fang occurs on the maxilla.

Males have tails 10–15% of the total length, while those of females are 9–12% of the total length.

Karyotype: There are 36 chromosomes as described for *S. catenatus* (Zimmerman and Kilpatrick, 1973).

Fossil Record: Fossils have been found at Irvingtonian (Meylan, 1982) and Rancholabrean (Holman, 1981) Pleistocene sites in Florida.

Distribution: *S. miliarius* ranges from Hyde County, North Carolina south to the Florida Keys, and west to eastern Oklahoma and Texas (Palmer, 1978).

Geographic Variation: Three subspecies have been described (Palmer, 1978). *Sistrurus miliarius miliarius* (Linneaus, 1766), the Carolina pigmy rattlesnake, is gray to reddish-brown with 1–2 rows of lateral spots, usually 25 anterior and 23 mid-body scale rows, and the ventral dark spots at least 2 scutes wide. It ranges from Hyde County, North Carolina southwest to central Alabama. *S. m. barbouri* Gloyd, 1935, the dusky pigmy rattlesnake, is dark gray with 3 rows of lateral spots, usually 25 anterior and 23 mid-body scale rows, and a heavily dark spotted venter. This race ranges from extreme southwestern South Carolina south through peninsular Florida and west through southern Georgia, the Florida panhandle, and southern Alabama to southeastern Mississippi. *S. m. streckeri* Gloyd, 1935, the western pigmy rattlesnake, is gray-brown to brown with 1–2 rows of lateral spots, usually 23 anterior and 21 mid-body scale rows, and diffuse ventral blotches about one scale wide. It occurs from "The Land Between the Lakes" in western Kentucky and Tennessee, southern Missouri, and eastern Oklahoma south to the Gulf Coast of Louisiana and eastern Texas.

Christman (1980) found that in Florida the number of ventral and subcaudal scales increases clinally to the south. Also, coastal populations have higher dorsal scale row and blotch counts, and larger, more round dorsal blotches.

Confusing Species: *Crotalus adamanteus* and *C. horridus* have small scales between the supraoculars. *S. catenatus* is much larger and darker in color, and its upper preocular scales touch the postnasal scales. The hognose snakes, *Heterodon*, lack a rattle and facial pit, and have upturned rostral scales.

Habitat: The pigmy rattlesnake lives in a variety of habitats, but none of these are very far from water. Mixed pine-hardwood forest, scrub pine woods, sand hills, and wire grass flatwoods are all occupied. In the Everglades, Duellman and Schwartz (1958) reported that it is seldom encountered in pinewoods or other dry habitats, but that flooding may force it to higher ground such as canal banks and roads. Usually living near water, it is a good swimmer. Where the gopher tortoise is sympatric, this small snake may use its burrow as a retreat, and it is also known to reside in small mammal burrows (Lee, 1968a). Although usually found on the ground, Klauber (1972) related an

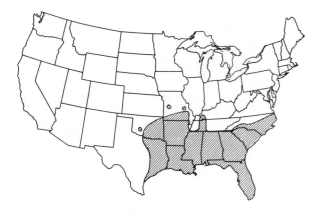

Map

Fig. 77. *Sistrurus miliarius barbouri.*

observation of one on a limb of a tree about 8 meters high.

Behavior: In Florida, southern Georgia and South Carolina, the pigmy rattlesnake may be active in every month (Chamberlain, 1935; Hudnall, 1979), but farther north in North Carolina they are active from March to November (Palmer and Williamson, 1971). During the year, most *S. miliarius* are caught from June–September (Chamberlain, 1935; Palmer and Williamson, 1971).

Little is known of their overwintering behavior. Neill (1948a) found one in February emerging from a probable mammal burrow, and Palmer and Williamson (1971) reported that some *S. miliarius* had apparently hibernated in a small hole in a sawdust pile. Allen (in Klauber, 1972) found them in winter under logs in the dryer portions of swamps. During the warmer portions of the year in Florida this small rattlesnake is active from the late afternoon into the night (Hudnall, 1979). The mornings at this time are spent in basking. From November to February it is active primarily in the afternoon, but most activity is in the form of basking.

Hudnall (1979) studied the movements of marked *S. m. barbouri* in Palm Beach County, Florida. The maximum distance moved from the first capture point of these snakes ranged from 9 to 242 m. A male, recaptured five times, moved an average of 179.6 m between recaptures, while two, recaptured three times, only averaged 81 and 89.5 m between captures. Fleet and Kroll (1978) reported that a gravid *S. m. streckeri* in Texas was never found more than 2 m from its original capture point in 7 observations between 1 July to 3 August, 1976. Apparently this species occupies a rather small home range.

Male combat dances in *S. miliarius* have been reported by Palmer and Williamson (1971) and Lindsey (1979), and are similar to those reported for other rattlesnakes. The essentials as reported by Palmer and Williamson are as follows:

> The two ... males ... were twined about each other with fully half their lengths raised from the cage floor. Several times they appeared to lose balance and fell ... They thrashed and twisted about vigorously and became partially uncoiled. After the falls the combat pose was again resumed. During the entire performance the posterior portions of their bodies were tightly entwined but there was no extrusion of the hemipenes. Their heads occasionally were facing or located one over the other but most often were several inches apart and situated at right angles to one another. The smaller snake initiated the dance after each fall ... At no time did either snake attempt to bite the other ... The dance continued at irregular intervals for at least two or more hours.

Reproduction: The only observation of copulation in nature was by Hamilton and Pollack (1955) who found a mated pair on 18 September, but since most young are born from July–September, spring is probably the mating period.

Iverson (1978) reported that a female collected on 7 January had enlarged ovarian follicles, another had partly developed embryos on 2 July while still another female had nearly full–term fetuses on 16 July, and that three other females gave birth on 15 July, 2 August and 4 October, respectively.

The ovoviparous young are born enclosed in a sheath–like membrane. Fleet and Kroll (1978) reported the following account of birth in this species.

> The female was observed at 1804 hrs. with the first fetal sac partially protruding from her cloaca; it fully emerged one minute later. Young 2, 3, 4, and 5 were born 49, 30, 25 and 80 min. apart, respectively. The female remained coiled during labor and each birth was characterized by a series of from 8–19 undulatory contractions. These peristaltic contractions passed caudad through the posterior two–thirds of the female's body, generally beginning 2–5 min. apart and ending about 10 sec. apart. During contractions, the fetal bulge could be seen to move caudad. Near the end of the undulatory series, there was a series of up to five convulsive cloacal contractions and elevation of the tail. This was followed by emergence of the fetal sac which in three timed instances required 4, 3, and 3 min. Young moved their heads vertically and uncoiled from within the membranes. Subsequently, two young moved their heads from side to side in scraping movements against the female's body which lasted up to 25 sec. and continued at irregular intervals for 16 to 26 min. This behavior may remove mucus and debris from the mouth or loosen the natal skin. The fifth neonate had the shortest time between parturition and shedding and did not exhibit this behavior. Interspersed with the scraping behavior, the young gaped their jaws (1–4 times each) into a yawn–like position.

Litter size varies from 3 (Anderson, 1965) to 32 (Carpenter, 1960), but 7–10 young are most common. Fitch (1985) analyzed available data on litter size and felt a north–south geographic variation was suggested, with northern *S. miliarius* producing fewer young. The young are 126–191 mm in total length at birth and have cream, yellow or orange tails.

Longevity: A male at the Staten Island Zoo lived 15 years, 1 month, 28 days (Bowler, 1977).

Food And Feeding: *S. miliarius* consumes a variety of small prey: insects, spiders, centipedes, frogs, toads, lizards, snakes, nestling birds, and mice (Clark, 1949; Hamilton and Pollack, 1955; Wright and Wright, 1957, Palmer and Williamson, 1971; Klauber, 1972). Chamberlain (1935) and Neill and Allen (1956) questioned insects and centipedes as food for this species, believing instead that these were secondarily ingested in the stomachs of vertebrate prey. However, the high frequency of reports of insects and centipedes in the stomachs of pigmy rattlesnakes makes us feel these are legitimate prey.

Hamilton and Pollack (1955) found food in 12 of 16 *S. miliarius* from Georgia that they examined. Reptiles (5 lizards, 1 snake) were found in 50% of the stomachs, centipedes (*Scolopendra heros*, 50–85 mm) were found in 33%, and mammals (*Peromyscus*, *Microtus*) occurred in 17%.

Some prey may be ambushed, but most are probably actively sought. Many of those we have found seemed to be searching for prey, and Ernst has observed a Florida *S. miliarius* stalk and strike an anole lizard. Neill (1960) felt that juvenile *S. miliarius* may use their yellowish tails as a lure for prey (see *S. catenatus*).

Venom And Bites: The fangs of this small snake are correspondingly short, 5.2–6.3 mm (Klauber, 1939), and the venom yield low, an average of 30 mg for 82 specimens (Allen, in Klauber, 1972); but the venom seems rather virulent to mammals. Small mice bitten by an adult in Ernst's laboratory have died in 30–90 seconds. The venom apparently has little effect on rattlesnakes of the genus *Crotalus*. Munro (1947) reported that a smaller *Crotalus horridus* was bitten by a *S. m. streckeri*, but showed no symptoms of envenomation. However, a *Micrurus fulvius* bitten died in 24 hours (Wright and Wright, 1957).

Hutchison (1929) lists the following symptoms in human bites: swelling, pain, weakness, giddiness, respiratory difficulty, hemorrhage, nausea, ecchymosis, and the passage of bloody urine (for 2 days). The bite is more serious in children than adults, and Guidry (1953) reported that a small child required several weeks of hospitalization when bitten. Case histories of bites are given by Harris (1965) and Klauber (1972).

Predators And Defense: *S. miliarius* is frequently eaten by indigo, king and coral snakes. Opossums, skunks, and domestic dogs and cats may also kill them, and hawks probably prey on them. Most, though, are destroyed by habitat destruction and automobiles.

The pattern and grayish coloration of this species affords it some camouflage. This is especially true of the subspecies *S. m. barbouri* in areas where pine trees have been partially burned and ashes are abundant.

When accosted, this fiery tempered beast quickly coils, bobs its head, and strikes with little warning. Its small rattle can barely be heard.

Populations: In proper habitat, *S. miliarius* is often quite numerous. Bell (in Duellman and Schwartz, 1958) collected 27 individuals in 8 days at one Florida site. The sex ratio of a brood of 32 young was 17 males and 15 females (Carpenter, 1960).

Remarks: *Sistrurus* is thought to be ancestral to *Crotalus*, and to have originated in Mexico and later migrated north to the United States (Klauber, 1972).

CROTALUS ADAMANTEUS

Eastern Diamondback Rattlesnake

CROTALUS ADAMANTEUS
Beauvois, 1799
Eastern Diamondback Rattlesnake

Recognition: This is a large brown rattlesnake (to 244 cm, although most are 100–150 cm in total length) with a dorsal pattern of dark, yellow–bordered, diamond–like (rhomboid) marks, several light stripes on the face, and a ringed brown and white tail. The dorsal diamonds are broader than long. The venter is yellow to cream with some brownish mottling. A dark band extends downward and backward from the eye to the supralabials, and is bordered front and back by a cream to yellow stripe. Several vertical light stripes occur on the rostrum. The pupil is elliptical, and there is a hole (pit) located between the nostril and eye. There are usually 27–29(25–31) midbody rows of keeled scales; the anal plate is undivided. Most dorsal head scales are small, but the rostral, 2 internasals, 4 canthals (between the internasals and supraoculars), and 2 supraoculars are enlarged. Laterally there are 2 nasal scales, several loreals, 2 preoculars, 2(3) postoculars, several suboculars, 14(12–17) supralabials, and 17(15–21) infralabials. The attenuated hemipenis is bifurcate with a divided sulcus spermaticus, and many recurved spines in the basal area. Spines also occur in the crotch between the lobes (see Klauber, 1972:696 for a photograph). As in all North American viperids, only the enlarged, hollow fang occurs on the shortened, rotational maxilla.

Males have 165–176 ventrals, 26–33 subcaudals, and 5–10 rings on the tail; females have 162–187 ventrals, 20–27 subcaudals, and 3–6 rings on the tail.

Karyotype: The karyotype has not been described, but presumably it is like that of other *Crotalus*: 2n = 36, 16 macrochromosomes (4 metacentric, 6 submetacentric, 4 subtelocentric), 20 microchomosomes, sex determination ZZ/ZW) (Zimmerman and Kilpatrick, 1973).

Fossil Record: Pleistocene remains of *C. adamanteus* have been found at Irvingtonian and Rancholabrean sites in Florida (Holman, 1981. Meylan, 1982), and at a Rancholabrean site in Augusta County, Virginia far north of its present range (Guilday, 1962). The fossil forms *C. a. pleistofloridensis* Brattstrom, 1953 and *C. giganteus* Brattstrom, 1953 have been synonymized with *C. adamanteus* (Auffenberg, 1963; Christman, 1975).

Distribution: The eastern diamondback rattlesnake ranges along the coastal plain from southeastern North Carolina to the Florida Keys and southeastern Mississippi, and possibly adjacent Louisiana. However, the Louisiana population has possibly been extirpated (McCranie, 1980b).

Geographic Variation: Christman (1980) reported that *C. adamanteus* from the Florida Keys have higher ventral counts, but no subspecies are recognized.

Confusing Species: No other rattlesnake occurring east of the Mississippi River has the combination of a dorsal diamond–like pattern, light facial stripes, and a ringed tail.

Habitat: *C. adamanteus* is best associated with dry, lowland palmetto or wiregrass flatwoods, pine, or pine–turkey oak woodlands. It usually avoids marshes and swamps, but will swim across streams and narrow bodies of freshwater, and it also occasionally swims or rafts across salt water to offshore islands.

Behavior: In the northern parts of its range, this large snake usually hibernates during the winter in mammal or gopher turtle burrows, hollow logs or stumps, or among the roots of wind–felled trees. Probably, it also uses such retreats to escape severe summer heat, although we have collected active Florida diamondbacks on very hot days. In Florida it may be active all year, but farther north it probably is restricted to an April–October annual cycle.

It is most commonly seen in the evening or early morning when its favorite prey, rabbits are active. Most of those we have caught were found in the morning. However, Ditmars (1936) has reported nocturnal activity in *C. adamanteus*, and many are run over by autos at night. Most daylight hours are spent in hiding, or, if the air is cool, basking.

C. adamanteus occasionally will climb several meters off the ground into trees while pursuing prey (Klauber, 1972).

Wagner (1962) has reported the following combat dance between male *C. adamanteus*.

> On the morning of November 12, 1959, two male Eastern Diamondback Rattlesnakes were observed to be engaged in a combat dance, in the snake pit at the Miami Serpentarium...The classical moves were made,

each snake trying to throw the other off balance. This lasted for almost half an hour. Then the smaller of the two crawled away in apparent defeat.

Shortly, another rattlesnake approached the 'victor' of the previous bout and advanced toward him from the rear. The other snake started to crawl away. Then the challenger caught up with the other and crawled over him, their bodies being parallel. They proceeded to raise the anterior parts of their bodies off the ground, intertwining them while they were raised. When the two heads were about a foot from the ground they started leaning backwards. Soon one or both lost balance and fell to the ground. This time the competition lasted for nearly an hour. At the termination of the dance the same snake that was the victor of the previous bout remained champion.

Reproduction: Kauffeld (1969) stated that in South Carolina *C. adamanteus* has a spring mating season beginning in March, but Meek (in Klauber, 1972) reported they mate in mid–September, and Ashton and Ashton (1981) felt that copulation occurs in both the fall and spring.

The age and size at which sexual maturity is reached is not known, but Murphy and Shadduck (1978) reported that a male and female first attained at total body lengths of about 50 cm did not mate when the male was 135 cm and the female 110 cm, but that a successful copulation finally occurred two years later. Unfortunately their lengths at the time of copulation were not reported. The mating was observed on 30 January at 0800 hr; and the snakes remained joined until 1700 hr. Occasional pulsations near the cloaca of the male were seen, but the female remained passive. On 1 August, after a gestation period of 213 days, 10 young were born.

Mount (1975) reported that female *C. adamanteus* from Alabama seek sheltered places and give birth in late summer or early fall. Judging from the length of gestation in Murphy and Shadduck's (1978) captive female, this would make the mating period late winter or early spring in Alabama. Klauber (1972) gives a range of birth dates from 16 July to 5 October for this species. Most young are born in retreats such as gopher tortoise burrows or hollow logs. It is not known whether female *C. adamanteus* reproduce annually or biennially.

The number of young per brood ranges from 6 (Curran, 1935) to 21 (Klauber, 1972); the mean for 28 litters reported in the literature was 12.8 young. At the time of emergence from the fetal membranes the neonates are 300–380 mm in total length and weigh 35–48.5 g (Murphy and Shadduck, 1978).

Growth And Longevity: Christman (1975) reported measurements which showed that the length of a mid-body vertebrae was directly proportional to the overall length of several species of *Crotalus*. Prange and Christman (1976) studied

Map

Fig. 78. *Crotalus adamanteus.*

CROTALUS ADAMANTEUS

Eastern Diamondback Rattlesnake

this concept further in *C. adamanteus* and calculated correlation coefficients of regression of 0.99 for vertebral length plotted against body length (y = 6.745x − 0.674) and log body weight against log body length (y = 3.108x + 2.766).

C. adamanteus has the potential of a rather long life. One kept by the late Louis Pistoia lived 22 years, 7 months and 3 days (Bowler, 1977).

Food And Feeding: Young *C. adamanteus* feed primarily on mice and rats, while adults seem to prefer rabbits, but will also take cotton rats, squirrels, and birds (see summary in Klauber, 1972). The food need not be fresh; Funderberg (1968) reported that a large female contained a rabbit that was in such a state of decomposition and odor and with numerous broken bones that it had to have been a road kill from a nearby unpaved road.

C. adamanteus may actively seek out prey by following their scent trails, but many animals are caught from ambush. These snakes can often be found lying beside logs or among the roots of fallen trees. In fact, the first eastern diamondback we ever caught was lying between several cotton rat holes under a wind felled tree.

In addition to their odor, endothermic prey emit infrared heat waves which may be detected by the pit on the rattlesnake's face. The membrane at the base of this pit is served by 500–1,500 axons/mm² which eventually lead to the trigeminal nerve (V) (Bullock and Fox, 1957). The transmission spectrum of the fresh membrane shows broad absorption peeks at 3 and 6 microns, and about 50% transmitted in other regions to 16 microns. Strong absorption of the visible spectrum takes place at waves shorter than 490 microns.

Venom And Bites: *C. adamanteus* has a well developed solenoglyphous venom delivery system (Klauber, 1972), with fangs to 27 mm in length (Telford, 1952). Its venom is strongly hemolytic and human deaths from severe untreated bites usually occur in 6–30 hours; the mortality rate may be 40% (Neill, 1957). Total venom yield from a *C. adamanteus* may be as high as 4 cc, producing 0.864 g of dry venom. Venom toxicity varies between individual snakes, even from the same litter (Mebs and Kornalik, 1984).

Hutchison (1929) listed the following symptoms in bites by *C. adamanteus*: swelling, pain, weakness, giddiness, respiratory difficulty, hemorrhage, weak pulse or heart failure (or in some cases an increased pulse rate), enlarged glands, soreness, diarrhea (often bloody), collapse, shock, toxemia and convulsion. Necrosis around the bite and occasionally involving much of the injured limb is fairly common, and sensory disturbances may occur, such as a sensation of yellow vision (Minton, 1974).

Wyeth Laboratories, Inc, Marietta, Pennsylvania produces an antivenin to counteract the venom of *C. adamanteus*, and total doses of 130–170 ml may be needed in severe bites. Case histories of bites by *C. adamanteus* are related by Parrish and Thompson (1958) and Klauber (1972).

Predators And Defense: Adults have little to fear except from humans. The young, however, have many enemies, including hogs (whose thick skin and subcutaneous fat make it difficult for the rattlesnake to effectively bite), carnivorous mammals, raptorial birds, other snakes (especially kingsnakes and the indigo snake), and river frog, *Rana heckscheri* (Neill, 1961). Humans are by far the worst enemy. Most will kill a rattlesnake on sight, and their automobiles and habitat alteration destroy many each year. Recently, commercial rattlesnake roundups have resulted in the death of many *C. adamanteus*. The participants use gasoline to flush hibernating snakes from their retreats. Those snakes which emerge are either collected or killed, while many rattlesnakes and other innocuous animals probably die in the burrows as a result of inhaling the fumes. Rattlesnake meat is tasty, and occasionally they are killed for the gourmet meal.

When disturbed it coils, shakes its tail, and raises the head and neck into a striking position. If further annoyed it does not hesitate to strike, and if picked up will thrash about to deliver a bite. Overall, they are extremely dangerous and should be let alone.

The rattle is a highly diversionary defense mechanism, calling attention to the tail instead of the head. As far as humans are concerned, it is certainly an effective warning device.

Populations: In suitable habitats, *C. adamanteus* can be quite common. Kauffeld (1957) reported that of 280 snakes caught in 74 days of actual hunting over a period of 6 years at Okeetee, South Carolina, 60 were *C. adamanteus*. Stoddard stated that 1000 *C. adamanteus* were killed each year on 7 hunting preserves in the Thomasville–Tallahassee area of Florida where a dollar bounty was being offered for each snake. The late Ross Allen reported that over a period of 28 years he had received 1000–5000 per year at his Florida snake exhibit with a grand total of 50,000 (Klauber, 1972)!

Remarks: Gloyd (1940) felt that *C. adamanteus* was a "climax form" derived from *C. atrox*, the western diamondback rattlesnake, which he thought most close to the ancestral type for the *atrox* group of rattlesnakes. Studies by Meylan (1982) support this theory, but Christman (1980) noted there is no reason to believe *C. adamanteus* arose on the Mexican Plateau and then migrated to Florida. Both Florida and the southwestern United States seem to be refuges where rattlesnakes, like *adamanteus* and *atrox*, evolved more slowly, retaining ancestral characters.

CROTALUS HORRIDUS

Timber Rattlesnake

CROTALUS HORRIDUS
Linnaeus, 1758
Timber Rattlesnake

Recognition: This large rattlesnake grows to 189.2 cm, has transverse chevron–like or v–shaped bands on the body, a gray, dark–brown or black unpatterned tail, and numerous small scales between the supraocular scales on top of the head. The ground color varies from gray to yellow or dark brown, and some individuals (especially in the Northeast) may be totally black. In the South these snakes have a red to reddish–orange mid–dorsal stripe. On the side of the head there may be a dark stripe extending from the eye backward to beyond the corner of the mouth, and some individuals may have round occipital spots. The venter is pink, white, cream or yellow with small, dark, stipple–like marks. The pupil is elliptical and there is a heat sensitive pit located between the nostril and eye. Usually there are 23–24 (21–26) mid–body rows of keeled scales, and the anal plate is undivided. Enlarged scales on the dorsum of the head include a rostral, 2 internasals, 4 canthals, (between the internasals and supraoculars), and 2 supraoculars. Lateral head scalation consists of a prenasal, a postnasal, 1–3 loreals, 2 preoculars, 2–6 postoculars, several suboculars, 13–14(10–17) supralabials, and 14–15 (11–19) infralabials. The bifurcated hemipenis has a divided sulcus spermaticus, over 70 long, thin, recurved spines, and 30 or more fringes per lobe, but no spines in the area between the lobes. Only the fang occurs on the maxilla.

Males grow larger (to 189.2 cm) than females (to 155 cm) (Collins and Knight, 1980). Males have 158–177 ventrals, 20–30 subcaudals, and tail lengths 6–10 percent of the total length. Females have 163–183 ventrals, 13–26 subcaudals, and tails 4–8 percent as long as the total length. Schaeffer (1969) found no significant difference in the frequency of occurrence of dark or light color phases between the sexes of *C. h. horridus*.

Karyotype: The karyotype is 2n = 36; 16 macrochromosomes (4 metacentric, 6 submetacentric, 4 subtelocentric, ZZ or ZW), and 20 microchromosomes (Zimmerman and Kilpatrick, 1973).

Fossil Record: Holman (1981) summarized the Pleistocene fossil record of *C. horridus* as the Irvingtonian of Maryland and the Rancholabrean of Arkansas, Georgia, Missouri, Pennsylvania, Tennessee, and Virginia.

Distribution: *C. horridus* ranges from southern Maine and eastern New Hampshire west through southern Ontario and southern New York to southwestern Wisconsin and adjacent Minnesota and south to northern Florida and eastern Texas.

Geographic Variation: Pisani et al. (1973), after studying variation in *C. horridus*, concluded that no valid subspecies occur, but many of their specimens were from western areas where intergradation between two described subspecies, *C. h. horridus* and *C. h. atricaudatus*, is known to occur. Brown and Ernst (1986) repeated their analyses of morphological characters and added several others relating to adult size and pattern in a study of eastern *C. horridus* where little intergradation is known. They were capable of clearly separating the populations east of the Appalachians into the two subspecies using adult size and pattern differences in conjunction with the number of dorsal scale rows and ventral scales. In view of Brown and Ernst's results, we feel it best to recognize as valid the two described subspecies of *C. horridus*.

Crotalus horridus horridus Linnaeus, 1758, the timber rattlesnake, ranges from southern Maine and New Hampshire to eastern New York and southern Ontario, west to Illinois and southwestern Wisconsin and Minnesota, and south to northern Georgia, northwestern Arkansas and northeastern Texas. It is yellow to gray or black in ground color, lacks a distinct mid–dorsal stripe, and has 23 (21–26) mid–body scale rows. *C. h. atricaudatus* Latreille, 1801, the canebrake rattlesnake, ranges from southeastern Virginia along the Atlantic Coastal Plain to northern Florida, westward to central Texas, and northward in the Mississippi Valley to southern Illinois. It is pinkish brown or gray in ground color, has a distinct reddish–orange mid–dorsal stripe, and 25(21–25) mid–body scale rows.

Confusing Species: The diamondback rattlesnake, *C. adamanteus*, has two white stripes on the side of the face, diamond–like dorsal blotches, and alternating light and dark bands on the tail. The species of *Sistrurus* have nine enlarged plate–like scales on top of the head.

CROTALUS HORRIDUS

Timber Rattlesnake

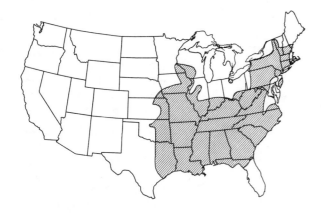

Map

Fig. 79. *Crotalus horridus atricaudatus.*

Habitat: *C. h. horridus* inhabits upland wooded areas, usually with nearby rocky ledges or rockslides. *C. h. atricaudatus* is more at home in lowland thickets, pinewoods, cane thickets, or swamp borders.

Behavior: Annual activity usually occurs in the period from mid–April to late September, but some individuals, especially those in the more southern populations, may emerge from hibernation in March or retreat into hibernacula in October. This usually depends on how warm are the early spring or fall. The early and late records for this species are 5 March (Wright and Wright, 1957) and 26 October (Fitch, 1958). In the spring and fall they are active during the daylight hours, but when the days become hot in summer they shift to a crepuscular or nocturnal activity cycle.

Formerly, *C. horridus* would congregate in large numbers (50–1000 snakes, Wright and Wright, 1957) at suitable hibernacula. Often these were in rock crevices in south facing slopes, but mammal burrows and large hollow logs were probably also used. Timber rattlesnakes from many miles away would crawl over set pathways to reach these sites (Neill, 1948a). While heavily populated dens still exist in remote or protected areas, many *C. horridus* now hibernate individually or in small groups in mammal burrows, old stumps, or shallow rock crevices.

Brattstrom (1965) reported the minimum and maximum voluntary temperatures of five *C. horridus* as 21.2 and 31.7 C, respectively, but Brown et al. (1982), found those of active New York snakes to be 12.5 and 33.3 C. Brown (1982) recorded the body temperatures of hibernating *C. horridus* at a New York den and found a mean temperature of 10.5 C (4.3–15.7) from September through May. The mean rate of body temperature decline was 0.5 C per week through February, in March the temperature stabilized at 4.3 C, and then rose by 0.6 C per week in April and May. Odum (1979) studied timber rattlesnakes in New Jersey and reported the following mean temperatures and percentage relations to activity: hiding completely concealed, 28.4 C (25.0–31.7), 12%; moving (day), 32.0 C, 6%; moving (night), no temperatures, 12%; resting in open shade, 26.2 C (23.0–29.9), 20%; and basking, 30.5 C (24.0–32.8 C), 50%. Snakes studied by Brown et al. (1982), averaged body temperatures of 30.1 C on the surface on clear days but only 27.8 C when on the surface on cloudy days or underground on clear days.

Brown et al. (1982), placed radio transmitters in five adult *C. horridus* and recorded their movements away from the hibernation den and onto their summer ranges. The snakes dispersed a mean 504 m (females 280 m; males 1400 m), and gained a mean 102 m in elevation. One gravid female only moved 39 m between 20 June–5 August. Fitch (1958) and Galligan and Dunsen (1979) also reported little movement in gravid females. Two of the females tracked by Brown et al. (1982) appeared to use the same migratory routes returning to the den in autumn as they had in leaving it in the spring. Studies by Galligan and Dunson (1979) show that *C. horridus* may remain at one spot for a period of time, then move a considerable distance, only to once again settle down for some time. Perhaps this is stimulated by prey availability.

Adult male *C. horridus* are known to occasionally engage in combat dances, and these usually occur in April or May (Sutherland, 1958; Anderson, 1965; Collins, 1974; Klauber, 1972). A description provided to Klauber (1972) by E. A. McIlhenny is as follows:

> As often as 25 times or more, I have seen large specimens of the canebrake rattlesnake (*Crotalus horridus atricaudatus*) fighting, always in the fall of the year, and have watched these fights sometimes for as long as a half-hour or more. Their method of fighting is to face each other, put the sides of the heads together, and gradually rear, still facing each other, with the necks in a half-turn around each other. When the snakes are as high as they can reach into the air, which in a large specimen will be as much as three feet, one will give a lurch upward and then bring its entire weight down across the neck of its opponent, slamming it on the ground with considerable force, evidently to injure the opponent. If the attempted damage fails, the snakes again rise in the same manner, and they will continue thumping each other against the ground until both become weary, whereupon they withdraw in different directions. In the many encounters which I have witnessed, I have never seen a snake injured or run away. The battle has always ended in a draw.

McIlhenny was in error. Often one male dominates the other, who leaves after first having been pinned to the ground.

Reproduction: Gibbons (1972) studied reproduction in *C. h. atricaudatus* from South Carolina, and concluded that females would bear their initial litter in their sixth year at a snout–vent length of over 100 cm and a weight of over 700 g. He also reported that males are mature at 90–100 cm in snout–vent length and probably are mature in their fourth year. Keenlyne (1978) found in Wisconsin that a 67.7 cm (snout to base of rattle) female *C. h. horridus* contained follicles, and that those longer than 89.4 cm produced eggs or contained embryos. Female *C. h. horridus* in Pennsylvania are already mature when they reach a snout–vent length of 77 cm and weigh 430 g (Galligan and Dunson, 1979). *C. h. horridus* is the shorter subspecies, and perhaps this explains their maturing at a smaller size.

Female reproduction is probably biennial (Keenlyne, 1978; Galligan and Dunson, 1979), but Gibbons (1972) thought some from South Carolina were possibly on a triennial cycle. Keenlyne (1978) reported that in Wisconsin both follicular development and vitellogenesis began in late July. In South Carolina, Gibbons (1972) found that follicles were unyolked in the spring (30 April–6 June), and that the females contained a fat content of 4.24%, but in the fall (2–9 October) the follicles were yolked and the female fat content was 5.82% of body weight. Gibbons found embryos in the spring (27 April–6 June) when gravid females contained 3.17% fat, and that after parturition in late summer (24 August–8 September), the fat content was only 0.84%.

It has always been thought that *C. horridus* breeds in the spring, before dispersing from the hibernacula, but this is in error. In Virginia, mating occurs from July to mid–September with the sperm being stored until June of the next year (person. comm., W.H. Martin). Keenlyne (1978) also thought the mating period in Wisconsin to be late summer through the next spring, but Anderson (1965) found a copulating pair on 27 April in Missouri. During courtship the male actively pursues the female and on reaching her repeatedly strokes her neck with his chin (Anderson, 1965). Collins (1974) reported that the male positions himself alongside the female and stimulates her with quick, rapid jerks of his head and body. He then curls his tail beneath hers until the vents touch, and then inserts his hemipenis.

Newborn young can distinguish the scent trail of conspecific young and adult males and females (Brown and MacLean, 1983). It is strongly possible that odor plays an important role in finding and determining the opposite sex, and as a guidance mechanism for newborn young to find a communal hibernaculum.

C. horridus is ovoviviparous, and the young are usually born between late July and September or early October. The birthing process, as observed by Trapido (1939), takes from 5–25 minutes, and the interval between extrusion of the young may be 11 minutes to just less than an hour. Minton (1972) reported that the young are born about 20 minutes apart, and that they may remain in the fetal membranes for 10–60 minutes. Neonates are patterned like the adults, only lighter in hue. They are 271–350 mm in total length and have a button–like scale at the end of the tail. They are dangerous even at this small size, having fangs 2.6–3.8 mm long (Stewart et al., 1960) and a ready supply of venom. Most broods consist of 6–10 young, but broods of 3

CROTALUS HORRIDUS

Timber Rattlesnake

(Wright and Wright, 1957) to 19 (Martof et al., 1980) are known.

Growth And Longevity: Minton (1972) found a 369 mm juvenile on 16 July in Indiana that must have been from a very late brood the previous fall. He estimated that a snake 81 cm in length was almost two years old, and four others were 79 and 95 cm in their second year and 100 and 110 cm in their third year. Gibbons (1972) reported that in his South Carolina population, *C. horridus* were 35–43 cm in snout–vent length shortly after birth, and by the next June had reached 50–60 cm; two–year–olds were 65–75 cm in snout–vent length and three–year–olds 80–90 cm.

The longevity record for this species is 30 years, 2 months and 1 day (Bowler, 1977).

Food And Feeding: Warm–blooded prey are preferred: shrews, moles, bats, mice, rats, chipmunks, young woodchucks, gray and fox squirrels, rabbits, weasels, quail and other birds, and bird eggs (Wright and Wright, 1957; Minton, 1972; Klauber, 1972). However, other prey are also taken: insects, toads, lizards and snakes (Surface, 1906; Hamilton and Pollack, 1955; Myers, 1956; Wright and Wright, 1957; Klauber, 1972). Barbour (1950a) took a snail shell from the stomach of a *C. horridus*, but thought it probably had been secondarily consumed in a chipmunk cheek pouch.

Not all prey is taken alive. Swanson (1952) reported a timber rattlesnake regurgitated a brown rat which, from the smell, had obviously been eaten as carrion. He also noted that a large *C. horridus* once disgorged a half–grown rabbit which contained many maggots.

Uhler et al. (1939), analyzed the stomach contents of 141 Virginia timber rattlesnakes. Mice comprised 38% of the diet, squirrels and chipmunks 25%, rabbits 18%, shrews 5%, and birds (mostly songbirds) 13%. One specimen contained a bat.

The feeding behavior of female *C. horridus* is strongly related to their reproductive condition (Keenlyne, 1972). Gravid females feed very little, if at all, while those with maturing follicles feed more often. *C. horridus* is a "sit and wait" predator, taking up an ambushing position at a site where prey will probably pass (Reinert et al., 1984). The favored ambush position consists of coiling adjacent to a fallen log with the head positioned perpendicular to the log's long axis. Often the chin is rested on the side of the log. However, some prey may be actively sought, as evidenced by the abundant records of this snake climbing into trees, presumably after birds or squirrels. Neill (1960) has suggested the young use their tails as a lure for small prey.

Venom And Bites: Adult *C. horridus* have fangs 8.7–10.4 mm long (Klauber, 1939), and replacement fangs for those lost or broken are already present in the newborn (Barton, 1950).

The venom is strongly hemolytic, and human fatalities have resulted from bites (Hutchison, 1929; Barbour, 1950a; Guidry, 1953). Hutchison (1929) lists the following symptoms in timber rattlesnake bites: swelling, pain, weakness, giddiness, breathing difficulty, hemorrhage, weak pulse or heart failure, nausea and vomiting, ecchymosis, paralysis, unconsciousness or stupor, gastric disturbance, and heart pain. Case histories of bites are given by Parrish and Thompson (1958) and Klauber (1972). Klauber (1972) reported that a typical *C. horridus* contains 139 mg of dried venom, and Minton (1953) reported wet venom volumes of 0.23–0.71 ml/snake. Johnson et al. (1968), published a rather detailed report on the characteristics of venom from *C. horridus*.

Predators And Defense: The young have many predators (predatory birds, carnivorous mammals, ophiophagous snakes), but the adults have few enemies but humans. A few adults are trampled by deer (Minton, 1972), but far more die on our highways or are blown apart by shotguns.

If given a chance, a disturbed *C. horridus* will retreat, but, if prevented from escape, it will form a loose coil with head raised and strike (sometimes with mouth closed) when the intruder gets too close, rattling all the time. Personally, we have found them to be rather mild tempered for rattlesnakes, especially when compared to some of the western *Crotalus*, but they are still extremely dangerous.

Populations: *C. horridus* can occur in large numbers in suitable habitats. Hartwig (1966) has seen up to 17 at one time at a 6 m rock in Pennsylvania. In the ten–year period 1956–1965, he saw 1628 timber rattlesnakes, and also reported that 40–80 newborn may be seen in a September day.

Galligan and Dunson (1979) found the sex ratio of 173 *C. horridus* from Pennsylvania was 111 males to 62 females. Odum (1979) reported the sex ratio at birth for New Jersey litters to be 1:1, but this is in contrast to that reported by other investigators. Edgren (1948) reported a 2:5 male to female ratio in a Minnesota litter, and two Pennsylvania litters examined by Galligan and Dunson (1979) contained 9 males and 5 females. However, Klauber (1972) reported an equal sex ratio for 1491 young of the year.

Remarks: *Crotalus horridus* is a member of the *durissus* subgroup of *Crotalus*, and in North America is most closely related to *C. molossus* (Gloyd, 1940). Recent electrophoretic studies on venom by Foote and MacMahon (1977) have confirmed this.

Glossary Of Scientific Names

abacura (ăb-a-cŭ-rà)—checkered, tesselated

acricus (ă-krē-cŭs)—without a ring

adamanteus (ăd-a-măn-tē-ŭs)—diamond-like

aestivus (ĕs-ti-vŭs)—summer

Agkistrodon (ăg-kĭs-trŏ-dŏn)—hooked tooth

alleni (ăl-ĕn-ī)—a proper name,
Prof. J. A. Allen

amaura (ăm-aŭr-à)—dark, dim

amoenus (ă-mē-nŭs)—pleasing, charming

annectens (ă-nĕk-tĕns)—joining with

arnyi (är-nē-ī)—a proper name, Samuel Arny

atricaudatus (ătri-cău-dā-tŭs)—black tailed

barbouri (bär-bĕr-ī)—a proper name, Thomas
Barbour

blanchardi (blànch-ärd-ī)—a proper name,
Frank N. Blanchard

brachystoma (brăk-ĭ-stō-mà)—short mouth

braminus (brā-mĭ-nus)—belonging to Brahma,
the creator god of the Hindu sacred triad

butleri (bŭt-lĕr-ī)—a proper name, Amos
W. Butler

calligaster (cali-gas-ter)—beautiful belly

carinatus (kăr-ĭ-nāt-us)—keeled

Carphophis (kär-fŏ-fis)—dry twig snake

catenatus (cat-ĕ-nāt-us)—chain, union

Cemophora (cĕ-mŏph-ora)—muzzle bearing

clarki (clàr-kī)—a proper name, John H. Clark

Clonophis (clŏ-nŏ-phĭs)—twig snake

coccinea (cŏx-ĭn-ē-à)—scarlet, crimson

Coluber (cō-lŭb-ĕr)—serpent, harmless snake

compressicauda
(kŏm-prĕs-ĭ-kô-dà)—compressed, flattened tail

conanti (cō-nănt-i)—a proper name, Roger
Conant

confluens (kŏn-flŏo-ĕnz)—confluent

constrictor (kŏn-strĭk-tĕr)—squeezer, hugger

contortrix (kŏn-tôr-trix)—twister

copei (kōp-ī)—a proper name, Edward Drinker
Cope

corais (kŏr-ā-ĭs)—black

coronata (kŏr-ŏ-na-tă)—crowned

couperi (kŏo-păr-ī)—a proper name,
J. Hamilton Couper

Crotalus (crōt-ă-lŭs)—rattle

cyclas (sĭk-lăs)—circle

cyclopion (sīk-clŏ-pē-ŏn)—round eye

deckerti (dĕk-ĕrt-ī)—a proper name,
R. F. Deckert

dekayi (dē-kā-ī)—a proper name, James
Ellsworth DeKay

Diadophis (dī-a-dōph-ĭs)—divided, through,
snake

Drymarchon (drī-măr-chŏn)—wood ruler

edwardsi (ĕd-wärds-ī)—a proper name,
G. Edwards

Elaphe (ĕ-là-fē)—deer-like

elapsoides (ē-lăps-oi-dĕs)—*Elaps*-like

elegans (ĕl-ē-găns)—elegant

emoryi (ĕm-ŏr-ī)—a proper name, Major
William Hensley Emory

erythrogaster (ē-ryth-rō-găs-tĕr)—red belly

erytrogramma (ē-ri-trō-grăm-à)—red-line,
character

extenuatum (ex-ten-ū-ā-tŭm)—extended,
elongated

Farancia (fär-ăn-cĕà)—a coined word,
reference unknown

fasciata (făs-ĭ-ā-tă)—banded

flagellum (flâ-gĕl-lŭm)—whip, flail

flavigaster (flâ-vĭ-găs-tĕr)—yellow belly

flavilata (flâ-vĭ-lātă)—yellow, extensive

floridana (flor-ĭ-dā-nă)—belonging to Florida

foxi (fŏks-ī)—a proper name, Rev. Charles
C. Fox

fulvius (fŭl-vĭ-ŭs)—reddish-yellow, tawny

getulus (get-ū-lŭs)—a proper name, Getulians,
Morocco

gloydi (gloid-ī)—a proper name, Howard
K. Gloyd

gracilis (grăs-ĭ-lĭs)—slender

grahami (grā-ăm-ī)—a proper name, Col. James
Duncan Graham

guttata (gŭ-tāt-à)—spotted

hallowelli (hăll-ŏ-wĕll-ī)—a proper name,
Edward Hallowell

helenae (hĕ-lĕ-naē)—a proper name, Helen
Teunison

helvigularis (hĕl-v̄-gu-lāris)—yellowish throat

Heterodon (hĕt-ĕr-ō-dŏn)—variable teeth

holbrooki (hŏl-brŏŏk-ī)—a proper name, John Edwards Holbrook

horridus (hŏr-rĭd-ŭs)—horrid

insularum (ĭn-sŭ-lăr-ŭm)—of islands

kirtlandi (kûrt-lănd-ī)—a proper name, Jared P. Kirtland

Lampropeltis (lăm-prō-pĕl-tĭs)—shiny shield

latrunculus (lă-trŭn-cŭ-lŭs)—robber, free-booter

leucostoma (leu-cō-stō-mă)—white mouth

limnetes (lĭm-nĕ-tes)—living in marsh, pond

lindheimeri (lĭnd-hī-mĕr-ī)—a proper name, Ferdinand Lindheimer

lineatum (lĭn-ē-ā-tŭm)—bearing lines

lodingi (lō-ding-ī)—a proper name, Henry P. Loding

majalis (măj-ă-lĭs)—sterile, barren

Masticophis (măs-tĕ-cō-phĭs)—whip snake

melanoleucus (mē-lăn-ō-leu-cŭs)—black, white

Micrurus (mī-krŏŏ-rŭs)—small, tail

miliarius (mĭl-ĭ-ā-rĭ-ŭs)—millet

mokeson (mōk-ĕ-sŏn)—mocassin

mugitus (mū-gē-tŭs)—lowing, bellowing

nasicus (nās-ē-cŭs)—nasal

neglecta (nēg-lĕct-ă)—neglected, not recognized

neilli (nēl-ī)—a proper name, Wilfred T. Neill

Nerodia (nĕ-rō-dĕă)—wet-like

niger (nī-gĕr)—black

nitae (nī-tē)—a proper name, Nita J. Rossman

obscura (ŏb-skūr-ă)—dusky, obscure

obsoleta (ŏb-sō-lēt-ă)—dim, obsolete

occipitomaculata (ŏc-cĭp-ĭ-tō-măc-ū-lāt-ă)—occipit, spotted

oolitica (ō-ö-lĭt-ĭ-că)—the Miami, Florida oolite substratum

Opheodrys (ō-fē-ō-drĕs)—snake, oak

orarius (ō-râr-ĭ-ŭs)—belonging to the coast

pallidula (păl-lĭd-u-lă)—pale

paludicola (păl-u-dĭk-ō-lă)—marsh dweller

paludis (pȧ-lū-dĭs)—marsh dweller

pamlica (păm-lē-kă)—the geological Pamlico terrace, Florida

pictiventris (pĭc-tē-vĕn-trĭs)—painted belly

piscivorus (pĭs-cĭ-vōr-ŭs)—fish eating

Pituophis (pĭt-ū-ōphĭs)—pine snake

platyrhinos (plăt-ĭ-rī-nōs)—flat snout

pleuralis (plŏŏr-ră-lĭs)—lateral, on the side

priapus (prē-ā-pŭs)—Greek diety of gardens and reproduction

proximus (prŏx-ĭ-mŭs)—nearest

pulchra (pŭl-kră)—beautiful

punctatus (pŭngk-tāt-ŭs)—dotted

pygaea (py-gaē-ă)—rump

quadrivittata (kwŏd-rē-vĭ-tātă)—four striped

radix (rā-dĭks)—root

Ramphotyphlops (răm-fō-tĭf-lŏps)—beaked, blind

Regina (rē-jĭ-nă)—queen

reinwardti (rīn-wärt-ī)—a proper name, C. G. C. Reinwardt

relicta (rē-lĭkt-ă)—a relic

Rhadinaea (răd-dĭn-ēă)—slender

rhombifera (rŏm-bĭ-fĕr-ȧ)—rhomb-bearing

rhombomaculata (rŏm-bō-măk-u-lātă)—rhomb-spotted

rigida (rĭj-ĭd-ȧ)—rigid, stiff

rossalleni (rŏs-ăl-ĕn-ī)—a proper name, E. Ross Allen

sackeni (săck-ĕn-ī)—a proper name, Baron C. R. Osten-Sacken

sauritus (sō-rē-tŭs)—lizard-like

sayi (sā-ī)—a proper name, Thomas Say

semifasciata (sĕm-ĭ-făsh-ĭ-ā-tȧ)—half banded

Seminatrix (sĕm-ĭ-nāt-rĭx)—half *Natrix*

seminola (sĕm-ĭ-nōl-ȧ)—refers to area of Florida frequented by Seminole Indians

septentrionalis (sĕp-tĕn-trĭ-ō-năl-ĭs)—northern

septemvittata (sĕp-tĕm-vĭ-tā-tȧ)—seven striped

similis (sĭ-mĭl-lĭs)—like, similar to

simus (sī-mŭs)—flat-nosed

sipedon (sĭp-ē-dŏn)—a siren

sirtalis (sĭr-tăl-ĭs)—garter-like

Sistrurus (sĭs-trŭr-ŭs)—rattle tail

spiloides (spĭl-oi-dēs)—spotted, stained

sticticeps (stĭk-tĭ-cĕps)—dotted head

stictogenys (stĭk-tō-gĕ-nēs)—narrow chin shield

Stilosoma (stī-lō-sōmȧ)—pointed body

Storeria (stō-râr-ēȧ)—a proper name, David Humphreys Storer

streckeri (strĕk-ûr-i)—a proper name, John K. Strecker, Jr.

syspila (sĭs-́pĭl-à̇)—completely capped

taeniata (tā-nē-à̆-tà̇)—thin-banded

Tantilla (tăn-tĭl-́à̇)—something small

taxispilota (tăx-́ĭ-spĭl-ō-́tà̇)—regularly patterned stains

texana (tĕx-́ā-nà̇)—belonging to Texas

Thamnophis (thăm-nōf-́ŭs)—bush snake

triangulum (trī-ăng-́gu̇-lŭm)—triangle

Tropidoclonion (trŏp-́ĭ-dŏ-clō-nĭ-ŏn)—keeled twig

valeriae (và̇-lĕr-́ē)—a proper name, Valeria Blaney

vermis (vûr-́mĭs)—worm

vernalis (vûr-năl-́ĭs)—spring

victa (vĭc-́tà̇)—defeated, conquered

Virginia (vĕr-jĭn-́yà̇)—a proper name, the state of Virginia

vulpina (vŭl-pī-́nà̇)—fox-like, after Rev. Charles C. Fox

williamengelsi (wĭl-yăm-ĕn-́gĕl-sī)-́a proper name, William L. Engels

williamsi (wĭl-yăm-sī)-́a proper name, Harold Williams

wrightorum (rīt-ŏr-ŭm)—a proper name, Albert Hazen and Anna Allen Wright

Bibliography

We have attempted to include all of the papers on the ecology, ethology, and systematics of snakes living east of the Mississippi River published between 1 January 1956 and 31 December 1986. Only the more pertinent papers on physiology and morphology have been included, and then only if they are related to the above fields of study. Some important studies published before 1956 are listed, but the reader is referred to Wright and Wright (1957) for other pre-1956 papers. Publications marked with an asterisk (*) are those that contain the original description of a species or subspecies of snake from Eastern North America.

Those who are seriously interested in snake research regularly should consult the following journals: *Copeia*, published by the American Society of Ichthyologists and Herpetologists; *Herpetologica*, published by the Herpetologists' League; and the *Journal of Herpetology*, published by the Society for the Study of Amphibians and Reptiles. Furthermore, anyone with a serious and lasting interest in snakes should join one or more of these societies.

There are also several good state or local amateur herpetological societies for those interested in snakes from a hobby standpoint. Your local zoo or natural history museum can give you more specific information on these societies.

Abercrombie, C. L., III
1973   Life history: *Regina r. rigida*. Hiss News-J. 1:91.

Adams, M. S., and H. F. Clark
1958   A herpetofaunal survey of Long Point, Ontario, Canada. Herpetologica 14:8-10.

Adler, K. K.
1960   On a brood of *Sistrurus* from northern Indiana. Herpetologica 16:38.
1963   An ecological study of the snake *Natrix erthrogaster*, with remarks on its postglacial dispersal. J. Ohio Herpetol. Soc. 4:61-62.

Adler, K. K., and S. G. Tilley
1960   A fish and a snail in the diet of *Natrix septemvittata* (Say). J. Ohio Herpetol. Soc. 2:28-29.

Ahrenfeldt, R. H.
1955   Two British anatomical studies on American reptiles (1650-1750) II. Edward Tyson: comparative anatomy of the timber rattlesnake. Herpetologica 11:49-69.

Albright, R. G., and E. M. Nelson
1959   Cranid kinetics of the generalized colubrid snake, *Elaphe obsoleta quadrivittata*. I. Descriptive morphology. II. Functional morphology. J. Morphol. 105:193-226, 241-282.

Aldrich, J. W., and C. G. Endicott
1984   Black snake predation on giant Canada goose eggs. Wildlife Soc. Bull. 12:263-264.

Aldridge, R. D.
1982   The ovarian cycle of the watersnake *Nerodia sipedon*, and effects of hypo-physectomy and gonadotropin administration. Herpetologica 38:71-79.

Aldridge, R. D., and D. E. Metter
1973   The reproductive cycle of the western worm snake, *Carphophis vermis*, in Missouri. Copeia 1973:472-477.

Aldridge, R. D., and R. D. Semlitsch
1982   The reproductive cycle of the southeastern crowned snake *Tantilla coronata*. Progr. Ann. Jct. Meet. Soc. Stud. Amphib. Rept. & Herpetol. League 1982:56.

Aleksiuk, M.
1971   Temperature dependent shifts in the metabolism of a cool temperate reptile *Thamnophis sirtalis parietalis*. Comp. Biochem. Physiol. 39A:495-503.
1976a   Reptilian hibernation: evidence of adaptive strategies in *Thamnophis sirtalis parietalis*. Copeia 1976:170-178.
1976b   Metabolic and behavioural adjustments to temperature change in the red-sided garter snake (*Thamnophis sirtalis parietalis*): an integrated approach. J. Therm. Biol. 1:153-156.
1977a   Cold-induced aggregative behavior in the red-sided garter snake (*Thamniphis sirtalis parietalis*). Herpetologica 33:98-101.
1977b   Sources of mortality in concentrated garter snake populations. Can. Field-Natur. 91:70-72.

Aleksiuk, M., and P. T. Gregory
1974   Regulation of seasonal mating behavior in *Thamnophis sirtalis parietalis*. Copeia 1974:681–689.

Aleksiuk, M., and B. Lavies
1975   Manitoba's fantastic snake pits. Natl. Geogr. 148:714–723.

Aleksiuk, M., and K. W. Stewart
1971   Seasonal changes in the body composition of the garter snake (*Thamnophis sirtalis parietalis*) at northern latitudes. Ecology 52:485–490.

Allen, B. A., G. M. Burghardt, and D. S. York
1984   Species and sex differences in substrate preference and tongue flick rate in three sympatric species of water species (*Nerodia*). J. Comp. Physiol. 98:358–367.

Allen, E. R.
1939   Habits of *Rhadinaea flavilata*. Copeia 1939:175.

Allen, E. R., and W. T. Neill
1950   The life history of the everglades rat snake, *Elaphe obsoleta rossalleni*. Herpetologica 6:109–112.
1953   The short-tailed snake. Florida Wildl. 6(11):8–9.

Allen, E. R., and D. Swindell
1948   Cottonmouth moccasin of Florida. Herpetologica 4(suppl. 1):1–16.

Allen, G. M.
1899*   Notes on amphibians and reptiles of Intervale, New Hampshire. Proc. Boston Soc. Natur. Hist. 29:63–75.

Allen, M. J.
1932   A survey of the amphibians and reptiles of Harrison County, Mississippi. Amer. Mus. Novitates (542):1–20.

Allen, T. A.
1979   Eastern garter snake predation on dark-eyed junco nests. Jack Pine Warbler 57:168–169.

Allen, W. B., Jr.
1956   The effects of a massasauga bite. Herpetologica 12:151.

Alpaugh, W. C.
1980   Earthworm (*Lumbricus terrestris*) consumption in captive garter snakes (*Thamnophis sirtalis*). Herp Review 11:93.

Anderson, P. K.
1961*   Variation in populations of brown snakes, genus *Storeria*, bordering the Gulf of Mexico. Amer. Midl. Natur. 66:235–249.
1965   The reptiles of Missouri. Univ. Missouri Press, Columbia. 330 pp.

Annandale, N.
1905–
1907   Notes on the fauna of a desert tract in southern India. Part I. —Batrachians and reptiles of the desert region of the North–west Frontier. Mem. Asiatic Soc. Bengal 1:183–202.

Antoinio, F. B.
1984   Random rotation of *Elaphe* eggs during artificial incubation. Bull. Maryland Herpetol. Soc. 20:51–53.

Antoinio, F. B., and J. B. Barker
1983   An inventory of phenotypic aberrancies in the eastern diamondback rattlesnake (*Crotalus adamanteus*). Herp Review 14:108–110.

Arndt, R. G.
1980   A hibernating eastern hognose snake, *Heterodon platyrhinos*. Herp. Review 11:30–32.
1985   Distributional notes on some Delaware snakes, with two first records for the state. Bull. Maryland Herpetol. Soc. 21:67–73.

Arnold, S. J., and A. F. Bennett
1984   Behavioural variation in natural populations. III: Antipredator displays in the garter snake *Thamnophis radix*. Anim. Behav. 32:1108–1118.

Asplund, K. K.
1963   Ecological factors in the distribution of *Thamnophis brachystoma* (Cope). Herpetologica 19:128–132.

Ashton, R. E., Jr., and P. S. Ashton
1981   Handbook of reptiles and amphibians of Florida. Part 1. The snakes. Windward Publ., Inc., Miami, Florida. 176 p.

Atkinson, D. A., and M. G. Netting
1927   The distribution and habits of the massasauga. Bull. Antivenin Inst. America 1(2):40–44.

Auffenberg, W.
1950   A new subspecies of the mud snake, *Liodytes alleni*. Herpetologica 6:13–16.

BIBLIOGRAPHY

1955*   A reconsideration of the racer, *Coluber constrictor*, in eastern United States. Tulane Stud. Zool. 2:89–155.

1963   The fossil snakes of Florida. Tulane Stud. Zool. 10:131–216.

Auffenberg, W., and L. H. Babbitt
1953*   A new subspecies of *Coluber constrictor* from Florida. Copeia 1953:44–45.

Babcock, H. L.
1929   The snakes of New England. Natur. Hist. Guide, Boston Soc. Natur. Hist. (1):1–30.

Babis, W. A.
1949   Notes on the food of the indigo snake. Copeia 1949:147.

Baden, H. P., G. Sazbo, and J. Cohen
1966   Cutaneous melanocyte system of the indigo snake *Drymarchon corais*. Nature 211:1095.

Baeyens, D. A., C. T. McAllister, and L. F. Morgans
1978   Some physiological and morphological adaptations for underwater survival in *Natrix rhombifera* and *Elaphe obsoleta*. Arkansas Acad. Sci. Proc. 32:18–21.

Baeyens, D. A., M. W. Patterson, and C. T. McAllister
1980   A comparative physiological study of diving in three species of *Nerodia* and *Elaphe obsoleta*. J. Hepetol. 14:65–70.

Baeyens, D. A., and R. L. Rountree
1983   A comparative study of evaporative water loss and epidermal permeability in an arboreal snake, *Opheodrys aestivus*, and a semi–aquatic snake, *Nerodia rhombifera*. Comp. Biochem. Physiol. 76A:301–304.

Bagshaw, C., and I. L. Brisbin, Jr.
1984   Long–term declines in radiocesium of two sympatric snake populations. J. Applied Ecol. 21:407–413.

Bailey, R. M.
1942   An intergeneric hybrid rattlesnake. Amer. Natur. 76:376–385.

1948   Winter mortality in the snake, *Storeria dekayi*. Copeia 1948:215.

1949   Temperature toleration of garter–snakes in hibernation. Ecology 30:238–242.

Baird, S. F., and C. Girard
1853*   Catalogue of North American reptiles in the museum of the Smithsonian Institution. Part I.—Serpents. Smithsonian Misc. Coll. 2(5):1–172.

Baker, R. J., J. J. Bull, and G. A. Mengden
1971   Chromosomes of *Elaphe subocularis* (Reptilia:Serpentes), with the description of an in vivo technique for preparation of snake chromosomes. Experientia 27:1228–1229.

Baker, R. J., G. A. Mengden, and J. J. Bull
1972   Karyotypic studies of thirty–eight species of North American snakes. Copeia 1972:57–265.

Barbour, R. W.
1950a   The reptiles of Big Black Mountain, Harlan County, Kentucky. Copeia 1950:100–107.

1950b   The distribution of *Carphophis amoenus* in Kentucky. Copeia 1950:237.

1952   Animal habitats on Big Black Mountain. Trans. Kentucky Acad. Sci. 13:215–220.

1956a   A study of the cottonmouth, *Ancistrodon piscivorus leucostoma*, in Kentucky. Trans. Kentucky Acad. Sci. 17:33–41.

1956b   Poisonous snakes of Kentucky. Kentucky Happy Hunt. Gr. 12(1):18–19, 32.

1960   A study of the worm snake, *Carphophis amoenus* Say, in Kentucky. Trans. Kentucky Acad. Sci. 21:10–16.

1962a   The distribution of *Cemophora coccinea* (Blumenbach) in Kentucky. Copeia 1962:637–638.

1962b   An aggregation of copperheads, *Agkistrodon contortrix*. Copeia 1962:640.

1971   Amphibians and reptiles of Kentucky. Univ. Press Kentucky, Lexington. 334 p.

Barbour, R. W., M. J. Harvey, and J. W. Hardin.
1969   Home range, movements, and activity of the eastern worm snakes, *Carphophis amoenus amoenus*. Ecology 50:470–476.

Barbour, T.
1921*   The Florida pine snake. Proc. New England Zool. Club 7:117–118.

Barbour, T., and A. F. Carr, Jr.
1940   Notes on *Elaphe* and a new species. Occ. Pap. Boston Soc. Natur. Hist. 8:337–342.

Barbour, T., and W. L. Engels
1942*   Two interesting new snakes. Proc. New England Zool. Club 20:101–104.

Barnard, S. M., T. G. Hollinger, and T. A. Romaine
1979   Growth and food consumption in the corn snake, *Elaphe guttata guttata* (Serpentes: Colubridae). Copeia 1979:739–741.

Barr, T. C., Jr., and R. M. Norton
1965   Predation on cave bats by the pilot black snake. J. Mammal. 46:672.

Barten, S. L.
1979   Scarlet kingsnake collecting in North Carolina. Bull. Chicago Herpetol. Soc. 14:94–96.
1980   The consumption of turtle eggs by a western hognose snake, *Heterodon nasicus*: a field observation. Bull. Chicago Herpetol. Soc. 15:97–98.
1981   Reproduction of *Lampropeltis triangulum elapsoides* from Onslow County, North Carolina. Herp Review 12:62.

Barton, A. J.
1950   Replacement fangs in newborn timber rattlesnakes. Copeia 1950:235–236.
1956   A statistical study of *Thamnophis brachystoma* (Cope) with comments on the kinship of *T. butleri* (Cope). Proc. Biol. Soc. Washington 69:71–82.

Batts, B. S.
1961   Intertidal fishes as food of the common garter snake. Copeia 1961:350–351.

Bauman, M. A., and D. E. Metter
1975   Economics, feeding, and population structure of *Natrix s. sipedon* in a goldfish hatchery. Progr. Fish–Cult. 37:197–201.
1977   Reproductive cycle of the northern watersnake, *Natrix s. sipedon* (Reptilia, Serpentes, Colubridae). J. Herpetol. 11:51–59.

Beardsley, H., and S. Barten
1983   A note on reproduction in a captive born indigo snake, *Drymarchon corais couperi*. Bull. Chicago Herpetol. Soc. 18:15–18.

Beatson, R. R.
1976   Environmental and genetical correlates of disruptive coloration in the water snake, *Natrix s. sipedon*. Evolution 30:241–252.

Beauvois, P. de.
1799*   Memoir on amphibia. Serpents. Trans. American Philos. Soc. 4:362–381.

Becak, W., and M. L. Becak
1969   Cytotaxonomy and chromosomal evolution in Serpentes. Cytogenetics 8:247–262.

Becak, M. L., W. Becak, F. L. Roberts, R. N. Shaffner, and E. P. Volpe
1973   *Drymarchon corais corais* (Boie). Chromosome Atlas: fish, amphibians, reptiles, birds. Vol. 2.

Bechtel, E.
1980   Geographic distribution of two color mutants of the corn snake, *Elaphe guttata guttata*. Herp Review 11:39–40.

Bechtel, H. B.
1978   Color and pattern in snakes (Reptilia; Serpentes). J. Herpetol. 12:521–532.

Bechtel, H. B., and E. Bechtel
1958   Reproduction in captive corn snakes, *Elaphe guttata guttata*. Copeia 1958:148–149.
1978   Heredity of pattern mutation in the corn snake, *Elaphe g. guttata*, demonstrated in captive breedings. Copeia 1978:719–721.
1985   Genetics of color mutations in the snake, *Elaphe obsoleta*. J. Heredity 76:7–11.

Bechtel, H. B., and J. Mountain
1960   Interspecific hybridization between two snakes of the genus *Elaphe*. Copeia 1960:151–153.

Belkin, D. A.
1968   Anaerobic brain function: effects of stagnant and anoxic anoxia on persistence of breathing in reptiles. Science 162:1017–1018.

BIBLIOGRAPHY

Bell, E. L.
1957   The food habits of the pilot black snake *Elaphe o. obsoleta* with observations on a captive specimen. Mengel Natur. (2):19–22.

Bennett, A. F., and P. Licht
1975   Evaporative water loss in scaleless snakes. Comp. Biochem. Physiol. 52A:213–215.

Benton, M. J.
1980a   Geographic variation in the garter snakes (*Thamnophis sirtalis*) of the north–central United States, a multivariate study. Zool. J. Linn. Soc. 68:307–323.
1980b   Geographic variation and the validity of the subspecies names for the eastern garter snake, *Thamnophis sirtalis*. Bull. Chicago Herpetol. Soc. 15:57–69.

Bertke, E. M., D. D. Watt, and T. Tu
1966   Electrophoretic patterns of venoms from species of Crotalidae and Elapidae snakes. Toxicon 4:73–76.

Betz, T. W.
1963a   Neonatal *Natrix cyclopion floridana*. Copeia 1963:575–576.
1963b   The gross ovarian morphology of the diamond–backed water snake, *Natrix rhombifera*, during the reproductive cycle. Copeia 1963:692–697.
1963c   The ovarian histology of the diamond–backed water snake, *Natrix rhombifera*, during the reproductive cycle. J. Morphol. 133:245–260.
1966   The ovarian cycle of *Natrix rhombifera* an apparently generalized cycle of snakes of temperate latitudes. Mem. Inst. Butantan. 33:115–120.

Bider, J. R.
1968   Animal activity in uncontrolled terrestrial communities as determined by a sand transect technique. Ecol. Monogr. 38:269–308.

Birchard, G. F., C. P. Black, G. W. Schuett, and V. Blacks
1984   Influence of pregnancy on oxygen consumption, heart rate and hematology in the garter snake: implications for the "cost of reproduction" in live bearing reptiles. Comp. Biochem. Physiol. 77A:519–523.

Black, J. H.
1983a   Northern watersnakes eaten by a channel catfish. Bull. Oklahoma Herpetol. Soc. 8:55–56.
1983b   Red–tailed hawk captures prairie kingsnake. Bull. Oklahoma Herpetol. Soc. 8:63–65.

Blaesing, M. E.
1979   Some aspects of the ecology of the eastern garter snake, *Thamnophis sirtalis sirtalis* (Reptilia, Serpentes, Colubridae), in a semi–disturbed habitat in west–central Illinois. J. Herpetol. 13:177–181.

Blair, C. L., and F. Schitoskey, Jr.
1982   Breeding biology and diet of the ferruginous hawk in South Dakota. Wilson Bull. 94:46–54.

Blanchard, F. C.
1943   A test of fecundity of the garter snake *Thamnophis sirtalis sirtalis* (Linnaeus) in the year following the year of insemination. Pap. Michigan Acad. Sci., Arts, Lett. 28:313–316.

Blanchard, F. N.
1919*   Two new snakes of the genus *Lampropeltis*. Occ. Pap. Mus. Zool. Univ. Michigan (70):1–12.
1921   A revision of the king snakes: genus *Lampropeltis*. Bull. U. S. Natl. Mus. (114):1–260.
1923a* A new North American snake of the genus *Natrix*. Occ. Pap. Mus. Zool. Univ. Michigan (140):1–6.
1923b   The snakes of the genus *Virginia*. Pap. Michigan Acad. Sci., Arts, Lett. 3:343–365.
1924a   The forms of *Carphophis*. Pap. Michigan Acad. Sci., Arts, Lett. 4:527–530.
1924b* A name for the black *Pituophis* from Alabama. Pap. Michigan Acad. Sci., Arts, Lett. 4:531–532.
1926   Eggs and young of the eastern ringneck snake, *Diadophis punctatus edwardsii*. Pap. Michigan Acad. Sci., Arts, Lett. 7:279–292.
1931   Secondary sex characters of certain snakes. Bull. Antivenin Inst. America 4:95–104.
1932   Eggs and young of the smooth green snake, *Liopeltis vernalis* (Harlan). Pap. Michigan Acad. Sci., Arts, Lett. 17:493–508.

1936   Eggs and natural nests of the eastern ringneck snake, *Diadophis punctatus edwardsii*. Pap. Michigan Acad. Sci., Arts, Lett. 22:521–532.

1937   Data on the natural history of the red–bellied snake, *Storeria occipito-maculata* (Storer), in northern Michigan. Copeia 1937:151–162.

1938   Snakes of the genus *Tantilla* in the United States. Zool. Ser. Field Mus. Natur. Hist. 20:369–376.

1942   The ring–neck snakes, genus *Diadophis*. Bull. Chicago Acad. Sci. 7:1–144.

Blanchard, F. N., and F. C. Blanchard
1942   Mating of the garter snake *Thamnophis sirtalis sirtalis* (Linnaeus). Pap. Michigan Acad. Sci., Arts, Lett. 27:215–234.

Blanchard, F. N., and E. B. Finster
1933   A method of marking living snakes for future recognition, with a discussion of some problems and results. Ecology 14:334–347.

Blanchard, F. N., and E. R. Force
1930   The age of attainment of sexual maturity in the lined snake, *Tropidoclonion lineatum* (Hallowell). Bull. Antiv. Inst. Amer. 3:96–98.

Blanchard, F. N., M. R. Gilreath, and F. C. Blanchard
1979   The eastern ringneck snake (*Diadophis punctatus edwardsii*) in Northern Michigan (Reptilia, Serpentes, Colubridae). J. Herpetol. 13:377–402.

Blaney, R. M.
1971   An annotated check list and biogeographic analysis of the insular herpetofauna of the Apalachicola Region, Florida. Herpetologica 27:406–430.

1973   *Lampropeltis*. Catalog. Amer. Amphib. Rept. 150:1–2.

1977   Systematics of the common kingsnake, *Lampropeltis getulus* (Linnaeus). Tulane Stud. Zool. Bot. 19:47–103.

1979a   The status of the Outer Banks kingsnake, *Lampropeltis getulus sticticeps* (Reptilia: Serpentes: Colubridae). Brimleyana (1):125–128.

1979b   *Lampropeltis calligaster*. Catalog. Amer. Amphib. Rept. 229:1–2.

Blaney, R. M., and P. K. Blaney
1979   The *Nerodia sipedon* complex of water snakes in Mississippi and southeastern Louisiana. Herpetologica 35:350–359.

Bleakney, J. S.
1952   The amphibians and reptiles of Nova Scotia. Can. Field–Natur. 66:125–129.

1958a   A zoogeographical study of the amphibians and reptiles of eastern Canada. Bull. Natl. Mus. Canada (155):1–119.

1958b   Variation in a litter of northern water snakes from Ottawa, Ontario. Can. Field–Natur. 72:128–132.

1959   *Thamnophis sirtalis sirtalis* (Linnaeus) in eastern Canada, redescription of *T. s. pallidula* Allen. Copeia 1959:52–56.

Blem, C. R.
1979.   Predation of black rat snakes on a bank swallow colony. Wilson Bull. 91:135–137.

1981a   *Heterodon platyrhinos*. Catalog. Amer. Amphib. Rept. 282:1–2.

1981b   Reproduction of the eastern cottonmouth *Agkistrodon piscivorus piscivorus* (Serpentes: Viperidae) at the northern edge of its range. Brimleyana (5):117–128.

1982   Biennial reproduction in snakes: an alternative hypothesis. Copeia 1982:961–963.

Blem, C. R., and L. B. Blem
1985   Notes on *Virginia* (Reptilia: Colubridae) in Virginia. Brimleyana (11):87–95.

Blem, C. R., and C. Roeding
1983   Intergradation among ringneck snakes, *Diadophis punctatus* (Linnaeus), in Virginia. Virginia J. Sci. 34:207–214.

Bloomer, T. J.
1976   The northern pine snake *Pituophis melanoleucus melanoleucus* in New Jersey. Herp, Bull. New York Herpetol. Soc. 13:33–35.

Blumenbach, J. F.
1788*   Beytrag zur Naturgeschichte der Schlangen. Magazin f. d. Neuste Aug d. Physi u. Naturg. 5:1–13.

Bogert, C. M.
1943   Dentitional phenomena in cobras and other elapids with notes on adaptive modifications of fangs. Bull. Amer. Mus. Natur. Hist. 81:285–360.

Bogert, C. M., and R. B. Cowles
1947   Results of the Archbold Expeditions, No. 58. Moisture loss in relation to habitat selection in some Floridian reptiles. Amer. Mus. Novitates (1358):1–34.

Boie, F.
1827* Bemerkungen uber Merrem's Versuch eines System der Amphibien. Isis 20:508–566.

Bonilla, C. A., W. Seifert, and N. Horner
1971   Comparative biochemistry of *Sistrurus miliarius barbouri* and *Sistrurus catenatus tergeminus* venoms, p. 203–209. *In*: Burcherl, W., and E. E. Buckley (eds.). Venomous vertebrates. Academic Press, New York.

Bono–Gallo, A., and P. Licht
1983   Effects of temperature on sexual receptivity and ovarian recrudescence in the garter snake, *Thamnophis sirtalis parietalis*. Herpetologica 39:173–182.

Bothner, R. C.
1963   A hibernaculum of the short-headed garter snake, *Thamnophis brachystoma* (Cope). Copeia 1963:572–573.
1973   Temperatures of *Agkistrodon p. piscivorus* and *Lampropeltis g. getulus* in Georgia. HISS News–J. 1:24–25.
1974   Some observations on the feeding habits of the cottonmouth in southeastern Georgia. J. Herpetol. 8:257–258.
1976   *Thamnophis brachystoma*. Catalog. Amer. Amphib. Rept. 190:1–2.

Bothner, R. C., and T. R. Moore
1964   A collection of *Haldea valeriae pulchra* from western Pennsylvania, with notes on some litters of their young. Copeia 1964:709–710.

Boulenger, G. A.
1893–
1896   Catalogue of the snakes in the British Museum (Natural History). 3 volumes. London.

Bowers, J. H.
1966   Food habits of the diamond–backed water snake, *Natrix rhombifera rhombifera*, in Bowie and Red River counties, Texas. Herpetologica 22:225–229.
1967   A record litter of *Thamnophis sirtalis proximus* (Say). Southwest. Natur. 12(2):200.

Bowler, J. K.
1977   Longevity of reptiles and amphibians in North American collections. Soc. Stud. Amphib. Rept. Misc. Publ. Herpetol. Circ. (6):1–32.

Boyd, C. E., S. B. Vinson, and D. E. Ferguson
1963   Possible DDT resistance in two species of frog. Copeia 1963:426–429.

Boyer, D. A.
1933   A case report on the potency of the bite of a young copperhead. Copeia 1933:97.

Brady, M. K.
1932   A new snake from Florida. Proc. Biol. Soc. Washington 45:5–8.

Bragdon, D. E.
1953   A histochemical study of the lipids of the corpus luteum of pregnancy in the water snake, *Natrix sipedon sipedon*. Virginia J. Sci. 4:273.

Bragg, A. N.
1960   Is *Heterodon* venomous? Herpetologica 16:121–123.

Brandner, R. L.
1981   *Cemophora coccinea copei* (northern scarlet snake). Reproduction. Herp. Review 12:79.

Branson, B. A., and E. C. Baker
1973   Sexual dimorphism in Kentucky queen snakes (*Regina septemvittata*) based on scute counts. Trans. Kentucky Acad. Sci. 34:57–58.
1974   An ecological study of the queen snake, *Regina septemvittata* (Say) in Kentucky. Tulane Stud. Zool. Bot. 18:153–171.

Braswell, A. L., and W. M. Palmer
1984   *Cemophora coccinea copei* (northern scarlet snake). Reproduction. Herp Review 15:49.

Brattstrom, B. H.
1953   Records of Pleistocene reptiles and amphibians from Florida. Quart. J. Florida Acad. Sci. 16:243–248.

1964 Evolution of the pit vipers. Trans. San Diego Soc. Natur. Hist. 13:185–268.

1965 Body temperatures of reptiles. Amer. Midl. Natur. 73:376–422.

1967 A succession of Pliocene and Pleistocene snake faunas from the High Plains of the United States. Copeia 1967:188–202.

Breckenridge, W. J.
1944 Reptiles and amphibians of Minnesota. Univ. Minnesota Press, Minneapolis. 202 p.

Breen, J. F.
1973 Rhode Island's declining rattlers. Massachusetts Audubon 23:866–868.

Breisch, A. R.
1984 Just hanging in there: the eastern massasauga in danger of extinction. Conservationist, New York 39(3):35.

Brimley, C. S.
1941–
1942 The amphibians and reptiles of North Carolina: the snakes. Carolina Tips 4–5(19–26).

Brisbin, I. L., Jr.
1968 Evidence for the use of postanal musk as an alarm device in the kingsnake, *Lampropeltis getulus*. Herpetologica 24:169–170.

Brisbin, I. L., Jr., M. A. Staton, J. E. Pinder, III, and R. A. Geiger
1974 Radiocesium concentrations of snakes from contaminated and non-contaminated habitats of the AEC Savannah River Plant. Copeia 1974:501–506.

Brock, O. G., and S. N. Myers
1979 Responses of ingestively naive *Lampropeltis getulus* (Reptilia, Serpentes, Colubridae) to prey extracts. J. Herpetol. 13:209–212.

Brode, W. E.
1958 The occurrence of the pickerel frog, three salamanders and two snakes in Mississippi caves. Copeia 1958:47–48.

Brode, W. E., and P. Allison
1958 Burrowing snakes of the panhandle counties of Mississippi. Herpetologica 14:37–40.

Broer, W.
1978 Bastarde bei zwei *Elaphe*-Arten (Reptilia: Serpentes: Colubridae). Salamandra 14:63–68.

Brown, A. E.
1890 On a new genus of Colubridae from Florida. Proc. Acad. Natur. Sci. Philadelphia 42:199–200.

Brown, C. W., and C. H. Ernst
1986 A study of variation in eastern timber rattlesnakes, *Crotalus horridus* Linnae (Serpentes: Viperidae). Brimleyana (12):57–74.

Brown, E. E.
1958 Feeding habits of the northern water snake *Natrix sipedon sipedon* Linnaeus. Zoologica 43:55–71.

1978 A note on food and young in *Natrix rigida*. Bull. Maryland Herpetol. Soc. 14:91–92.

1979a Some snake food records from the Carolinas. Brimleyana (1):113–124.

1979b Stray food records from New York and Michigan snakes. Amer. Midl. Natur. 102:200–203.

Brown, L. E., and J. R. Brown
1975 Evidence of climbing ability by western fox snakes (*Elaphe vulpina vulpina*). Bull. Maryland Herpetol. Soc. 11:179.

Brown, W. S.
1982 Overwintering body temperatures of timber rattlesnakes (*Crotalus horridus*) in northeastern New York. J. Herpetol. 16:145–150.

Brown, W. S., and F. M. MacLean
1983 Conspecific scent–trailing by newborn timber rattlesnakes, *Crotalus horridus*. Herpetologica 39:430–436.

Brown, W. S., D. W. Pyle, K. R. Greene, and J. B. Friedlaender
1982 Movements and temperature relationships of timber rattlesnakes (*Crotalus horridus*) in northeastern New York. J. Herpetol. 16:151–161.

Browning, M. J. S.
1967 *Natrix erythrogaster erythrogaster* in the piedmont region of South Carolina. Herpetologica 23:59.

Browning, M. R.
1973 Brown thrasher encounter with snake. Chat 37:107.

Brush, S. W., and G. W. Ferguson
1986 Predation of lark sparrow eggs by a massasauga rattlesnake. Southwest. Natur. 31:260–261.

Buck, D. H.
1946   Food of *Farancia abacura* in Texas. Herpetologica 3:111.

Buikema, A. L., Jr., and K. B. Armitage
1969   The effect of temperature on the metabolism of the prairie ringneck snake, *Diadophis punctatus arnyi* Kennicott. Herpetologica 25:194–206.

Bullock, R. E.
1981   Tree climbing bullsnakes. Blue Jay 39:139–140.

Bullock, T. H., and R. B. Cowles
1952   Physiology of an infrared receptor: the facial pit of pit vipers. Science 115:541–543.

Bullock, T. H., and W. Fox
1957   The anatomy of the infra–red sense organ in the facial pit of pit vipers. Quart. J. Micro. Sci. 98: 219–234.

Burger, J., and R. T. Zappalorti
1986   Nest site selection by pine snakes, *Pituophis melanoleucus*, in the New Jersey Pine Barrens. Copeia 1986:116–121.

Burger, J. W.
1934   The hibernation habits of the rattlesnake of the New Jersey pine barrens. Copeia 1934:142.

Burghardt, G. M.
1967   Chemical–cue preferences of inexperienced snakes: comparative aspects. Science 157:718–721.
1968   Chemical preference studies on newborn snakes of three sympatric species of *Natrix*. Copeia 1968:732–737.
1969   Comparative prey–attack studies in newborn snakes of the genus *Thamnophis*. Behaviour 33:77–113.
1970   Intraspecific geographical variation in chemical food cue preferences of newborn garter snakes (*Thamnophis sirtalis*). Behaviour 36:246–257.
1971   Chemical–cue preferences of newborn snakes: influence of prenatal maternal experience. Science 171:921–923.
1975   Chemical prey preference polymorphism in newborn garter snakes *Thamnophis sirtalis*. Behaviour 52:202–225.
1983   Aggregation and species discrimination in newborn snakes. Z. Tierpsychol. 61:89–101.

Burghardt, G. M., and D. Denny
1983   Effects of prey movement and prey odor on feeding in garter snakes. Z. Tierpsychol. 62:329–347.

Burghardt, G. M., and C. H. Pruitt
1975   Role of the tongue and senses in feeding of naive and experienced garter snakes. Physiol. Behav. 14:185–194.

Burkett, R. D.
1966   Natural history of cottonmouth moccasin, *Agkistrodon piscivorus* (Reptilia). Univ. Kansas Publ. Mus. Natur. Hist. 17:435–491.

Burnley, J. M.
1971a   Early date records of amphibians and reptiles on Long Island. Engelhardtia 4(1):1–7.
1971b   Late date records of amphibians and reptiles on Long Island. Engelhardtia 4(3):17–22.

Burt, C.H., and W. L. Hoyle
1935   Additional records of the reptiles of the central prairie region of the United States. Trans. Kansas Acad. Sci. 37:193–216.

Burt, M. D.
1928   The relation of size to maturity in the garter snakes, *Thamnophis sirtalis sirtalis* (L.) and *T. sauritus sauritus* (L.). Copeia 166:8–12.

Bury, R. B., F. Gress, and G. C. Gorman
1970   Karyotypic survey of some colubrid snakes from western North America. Herpetologica 26:461–466.

Busack, S. D.
1960   Ophiophagy in *Sceloporus*. Herpetologica 16:44.

Bush, F. M.
1959   Foods of some Kentucky herptiles. Herpetologica 15:73–77.

Bushey, C. L.
1985   Man's effect upon a colony of *Sistrurus c. catenatus* (Raf.) in northeastern Illinois (1834–1975). Bull. Chicago Herpetol. Soc. 20:1–12.

Cadle, J. E.
1984   Molecular systematics of Neotropical xenodontine snakes. III. Overview of xenodontine phylogeny and the history of New World snakes. Copeia 1984:641–652.

Cadle, J. E., and V. M. Sarich
1981 An immunological assessment of the phylogenetic position of New World coral snakes. J. Zoology, London 195:157–167.

Cagle, F. R.
1937 Notes on *Natrix rhombifera* as observed at Reelfoot Lake. J. Tennessee Acad. Sci. 12:179–185.
1942 Herpetological fauna of Jackson and Union counties, Illinois. Amer. Midl. Natur. 28:164–200.
1946 *Typhlops braminus* in the Marianas Islands. Copeia 1946:101.

Cale, W. G., Jr., and J. W. Gibbons
1972 Relationships between body size, size of the fat bodies, and total lipid content in the canebrake rattlesnake (*Crotalus horridus*) and the black racer (*Coluber constrictor*). Herpetologica 28:51–53.

Callard, I. P., and J. H. Leathem
1967 Some aspects of oviduct biochemistry in the snakes *Natrix sipedon pictiventris*, *Coluber c. constrictor* and *Elaphe q. quadrivittata*. Proc. Pennsylvania Acad. Sci. 40:59–62.

Camazine, B., W. Garstka, and D. Crews
1981 Techniques for gonadectomizing snakes (*Thamnophis*). Copeia 1981:884–886.

Camazine, B., W. Garstka, R. Tokarz, and D. Crews
1980 Effects of castration and androgen replacement on male courtship behavior in the red–sided garter snake, *Thamnophis sirtalis parietalis*. Horm. Behav. 14:358–372.

Camin, J. H., and P. R. Ehrlich
1958 Natural selection in water snakes (*Natrix sipedon* L.) on islands in Lake Erie. Evolution 12:504–511.

Camin, J. H., C. Tripplehorn, and H. Walter
1954 Some indications of survival value in type "A" pattern of the island water snakes in Lake Erie. Natur. Hist. Misc. (13):1–3.

Camp, C. D., W. D. Sprewell, and V. N. Powders
1980 Feeding habits of *Nerodia taxispilota* with comparative notes on the foods of sympatric congeners in Georgia. J. Herpetol. 14:301–304.

Campbell, G. R., and W. H. Stickel
1939 Notes on the yellow–lipped snake. Copeia 1939:105.

Campbell, H. W.
1970 Prey selection in naive *Elaphe obsoleta* (Squamata: Serpentes)—a reappraisal. Psychon. Sci. 21:300–301.

Campbell, H. W., and S. P. Christman
1982 The herpetological components of Florida sandhill and sand pine scrub associations, pp. 163–171. *In*: N.J. Scott, Jr. (ed.). Herpetological Communities. U. S. Fish Wildl. Serv. Wildl. Res. Rept. (13).

Campbell, J. A.
1973 A captive hatching of *Micrurus fulvius tenere*. (Serpentes, Elapidae). J. Herpetol. 7:312–315.

Carl, G.
1978 Notes on worm–eating in the prairie ringneck snake, *Diadophis punctatus arnyi*. Bull. Maryland Herpetol. Soc. 14:95–97.

Carpenter, C. C.
1947 Copulation of the fox snake. Copeia 1947:275.
1951 Young goldfinches eaten by garter snake. Wilson Bull. 63:117–118.
1952a Comparative ecology of the common garter snake (*Thamnophis s. sirtalis*), the ribbon snake (*Thamnophis s. sauritus*) and Butler's garter snake (*Thamnophis butleri*) in mixed populations. Ecol. Monogr. 23:235–258.
1952b Growth and maturity of the three species of *Thamnophis* in Michigan. Copeia 1952:237–243.
1953a A study of hibernacula and hibernating associations of snakes and amphibians in Michigan. Ecology 34:74–80.
1953b Weight–length relationship of Michigan garter snakes. Pap. Michigan Acad. Sci., Arts, Lett. 1952. 38:147–150.
1956 Body temperatures of three species of *Thamnophis*. Ecology 37:732–735.
1958 Reproduction, young, eggs and food of Oklahoma snakes. Herpetologica 14:113–115.
1960 A large brood of western pigmy rattlesnakes. Herpetologica 16:142–143.
1982 The bullsnake as an excavator. J. Herpetol. 16:394–401.

1985   *Lampropeltis calligaster calligaster* (Prairie Kingsnake). Reproduction. Herp Review 16:81.

Carpenter, C. C., and G. W. Ferguson
1977   Variation and evolution of stereotyped behavior in reptiles, pp. 335–554. *In*: Gans, C. and D. W. Tinkle (eds.). Biology of the Reptilia, volume 7. Academic Press, London.

Carpenter, C. C., and J. C. Gillingham
1975   Postural response to kingsnakes by crotaline snakes. Herpetologica 31:293–302.
1977   A combat ritual between two male speckled kingsnakes (*Lampropeltis getulus holbrooki*: Colubridae, Serpentes) with indications of dominance. Southwest. Natur. 22:517–524.

Carr, A. F., Jr.
1934   Notes on the habits of the short-tailed snake. Copeia 1934:138–139.
1940   A contribution to the herpetology of Florida. Univ. Florida Publ. Biol. Ser. 3(1):1–118.

Carr, A. F., Jr., and M. H. Carr
1942   Notes on the courtship of the cottonmouth moccasin. Proc. New England Zool. Club 20:1–6.

Carr, A., and C. J. Goin
1955   Guide to the reptiles, amphibians, and freshwater fishes of Florida. Univ. Florida Press, Gainesville. 341 p.

Carr, C. M., and P. T. Gregory
1976   Can tongue flicks be used to measure niche sizes? Can. J. Zool. 54:1389–1394.

Carson, H. L.
1945   Delayed fertilization in a captive indigo snake with notes on feeding and shedding. Copeia 1945:222–225.

Cary, D. L., R. L. Clawson, and D. Grimes
1981   An observation on snake predation on a bat. Trans. Kansas Acad.Sci. 84:223–224.

Catling, P. M., and B. Freedman
1980a   Variation in distribution and abundance of four sympatric species of snakes at Amherstburg, Ontario. Can. Field–Natur. 94:19–27.

1980b   Food and feeding behavior of sympatric snakes at Amherstburg, Ontario. Can. Field–Natur. 94:28–33.

Cebula, J. J.
1983   A note on the food choices of a plains garter snake. Bull. Chicago Herpetol. Soc. 18:46.

Chamberlain, E. B.
1935   Notes on the pygmy rattlesnake, *Sistrurus miliarius* Linnaeus, in South Carolina. Copeia 1935:146–147.

Chance, B.
1970   A note on the feeding habits of *Micurus fulvius fulvius*. Bull. Maryland Herpetol. Soc. 6:56.

Chang, P., J. Balling, and R. Lister
1971   Karyotype of the pilot black snake, *Elaphe obsoleta obsoleta* (Say). Mammal Chromosome Newsl. 12:9.

Chenowith, W. L.
1948   Birth and behavior of young copperheads. Herpetologica 4:162.

Chermock, R. L.
1952   A key to the amphibians and reptiles of Alabama. Univ. Alabama Mus. Pap. (33):1–88.

Chiasson, R. B.
1982   The apical pits of *Agkistrodon* (Reptilia: Serpentes). J. Arizona Nevada Acad. Sci. 16:69–73.

Chiodini, R. J., J. P. Sundberg, and J. A. Czikowsky
1982   Gross anatomy of snakes. Veterin. Med. Sm. Anim. Clin. 77:413–419.

Chiszar, D., V. Lipetz, K. Scudder, and E. Pasenello
1980   Rate of tongue flicking by bull snakes and pine snakes (*Pituophis melanoleucus*) during exposure to food and non–food odors. Herpetologica 36:225–231.

Chiszar, D., C. Radcliffe, R. Boyd, A. Radcliffe, H. Yun, H. M. Smith, T. Boyer, B. Atkins, and F. Feiler
1986   Trailing behavior in cottonmouths (*Agkistodon piscivorus*). J. Herpetol. 20:269–272.

Chiszar, D., C. W. Radcliffe, R. Overstreet, T. Pade, and T. Byers
1985   Duration of strike–induced chemosensory searching in cottonmouths (*Agkistrodon piscivorus*) and a test of the hypothesis that striking prey creates a specific search image. Can. J. Zool. 63:1057–1061.

Chiszar, D., K. Scudder, and L. Knight
1976   Rate of tongue flicking by garter snakes (*Thamnophis radix haydeni*) and rattlesnakes (*Crotalus v. viridis, Sistrurus catenatus tergeminus,* and *Sistrurus catenatus edwardsii*) during prolonged exposure to food odors. Behavior. Biol. 18:273–283.

Chiszar, D., K. M. Scudder, and H. M. Smith
1979   Chemosensory investigation of fish mucus odor. Bull. Maryland Herpetol. Soc. 15:31–36.

Chiszar, D., L. Sminsen, C. Radcliffe, and H. M. Smith
1979   Rate of tongue flicking by cottonmouths (*Agkistrodon piscivorus*) during prolonged exposure to various odors, and strike induced chemosensory searching by the cantil (*Agkistrodon bilineatus*). Trans. Kansas Acad. Sci. 82:49–54.

Chiszar, D., K. Scudder, H. M. Smith, and C. W. Radcliffe
1976   Observations of courtship behavior in the western massasauga (*Sistrurus catenatus tergeminus*). Herpetologica 32:337–338.

Chiszar, D., S. V. Taylor, C. W. Radcliffe, H. M. Smith, and B. O'Connell
1981   Effects of chemical and visual stimuli upon chemosensory searching by garter snakes and rattlesnakes. J. Herpetol. 15:415–423.

Chiu, K. W., and W. G. Lynn
1972   Observation on thyroidal control of sloughing in the garter snake, *Thamnophis sirtalis*. Copeia 1972:158–163.

Christman, S. P.
1975   The status of the extinct rattlesnake, *Crotalus giganteus*. Copeia 1975:43–47.
1980   Patterns of geographic variation in Florida snakes. Bull. Florida St. Mus. Biol. Sci. 25:157–256.

1982   *Storeria dekayi*. Catalog. Amer. Amphib. Rept. 306:1–4.

Cieslak, E. S.
1945   Relations between the reproductive cycle and pituitary gland in the snake *Thamnophis radix*. Physiol. Zool. 18:299–329.

Cink, C. L.
1977   Snake predation on Bell's vireo nestlings. Wilson Bull. 89:349–350.

Clark, D. R., Jr.
1963   Variation and sexual dimorphism in a brood of the western pigmy rattlesnake (*Sistrurus*). Copeia 1963:157–159.
1964a   The structure of the hemipenis as systematic characters in the genus *Virginia* Baird and Girard. Herpetologica 20:33–37.
1964b   Reproduction and sexual dimorphism in a population of the rough earth snake, *Virginia striatula* (Linneaeus). Texas J. Sci. 16:265–295.
1967a   Notes on sexual dimorphism in tail-length in American snakes. Trans. Kansas Acad. Sci. 69:227–232.
1967b   Experiments into selection of soil type, soil moisture level, and temperature by five species of small snakes. Trans. Kansas Acad. Sci. 70:490–496.
1968   A proposal of specific status for the western worm snake, *Carphophis amoenus vermis* (Kennicott). Herpetologica 24:104–112.
1970a   Ecological study of the worm snake *Carphophis vermis* (Kennicott). Univ. Kansas Publ. Mus. Natur. Hist. 19:85–194.
1970b   Age specific "reproductive effort" in the worm snake *Carphophis vermis* (Kennicott). Trans. Kansas Acad. Sci. 73:20–24.
1970c   Loss of the left oviduct in the colubrid snake genus *Tantilla*. Herpetologica 26:130–133.
1974   The western ribbon snake (*Thamnophis proximus*): ecology of a Texas population. Herpetologica 30:372–379.

Clark, D. R., Jr., and G. L. Callison
1967   Vertebral and scute anomalies in a racer, *Coluber constrictor*. Copeia 1967:862–864.

Clark, D. R., Jr., and R. R. Fleet
1976   The rough earth snake (*Virginia striatula*): ecology of a Texas population. Southwest. Natur. 20:467–478.

Clark, H.
1944   The anatomy and embryology of the hemipenis of *Lampropeltis*, *Diadophis* and *Thamnophis* and their value as criteria of relationship in the family Colubridae. Proc. Iowa Acad. Sci. 51:411–445.
1952a   Note on the egg–laying habits of *Heterodon platyrhinos* (L.). Herpetologica 8:28–29.
1952b   A preliminary ovimetric study on *Heterodon platyrhinos* (L.). Herpetologica 8:29–32.
1953   Eggs, egg laying and incubation of the snake *Elaphe emoryi* (Baird and Girard). Copeia 1953:90–92.

Clark, H., B. Florio, and R. Hurowitz
1955   Embryonic growth of *Thamnophis s. sirtalis* in relation to fertilization date and placental function. Copeia 1955:9–13.

Clark, R. F.
1949   Snakes of the hill parishes of Louisiana. J. Tennessee Acad. Sci. 24:244–261.
1954   Eggs and egg–laying of *Lampropeltis c. calligaster* (Harlan). Herpetologica 10:15–16.

Clausen, H. J.
1936a   The effect of aggregation on the respiratory metabolism of the brown snake, *Storeria dekayi*. J. Cell. Comp. Physiol. 8:367–386.
1936b   Observations on the brown snake, *Storeria dekayi* (Holbrook), with especial reference to the habits and birth of the young. Copeia 1936:98–102.

Clay, W. M.
1938   A synopsis of the North American water snakes of the genus *Natrix*. Copeia 1938:173–182.

Clench, W. J.
1925   A possible manner of snake distribution. Copeia (142):40.

Cliburn, J. W.
1956   The taxonomic relations of the water snakes *Natrix taxispilota* and *rhombifera*. Herpetologica 12:198–200.

1957a   Behavior of a captive black pine snake. Herpetologica 13:66.
1957b   Some southern races of the common water snake, *Natrix sipedon*. Herpetologica 13:193–202.
1958   Notes on some snakes from Mississippi. Amer. Midl. Natur. 60:196–201.
1961a   The taxonomic position of *Natrix sipedon insularum* Conant and Clay. Herpetologica 17:166–168.
1961b   The ribbon snakes of southern Mississippi. Herpetologica 17:211–212.
1962   Further notes on the behavior of a captive black pine snake (*Pituophis melanoleucus lodingi* Blanchard. Herpetologica 18:34–37.
1975   The hemipenis of *Pituophis melanoleucus*. J. Herpetol. 9:254–255.
1977   *Elaphe obsoleta spiloides* (Grey rat snake) in aquatic habitats. J. Mississippi Acad. Sci. 22:94–96.

Cochran, D. M., and C. J. Goin
1970   The new field book of reptiles and amphibians. Putnam, New York. 359 p.

Cochran, P. A.
1986   Feeding an eastern hognose snake in a college laboratory setting. Bull. Chicago Herpetol. Soc. 21:96–97.

Cohen, E.
1948a   Emergence of *Coluber c. constrictor* from hibernation. Copeia 1948:137–138.
1948b   Delayed parturition of *Storeria occipitomaculata* (Storer) in captivity. Herpetologica 4:227.

Cohen, H. J.
1978   An observation of double clutch production by *Elaphe obsoleta* in captivity. Herp. Review 9:140–141.

Cole, C. J., and L. M. Hardy
1981   Systematics of North American colubrid snakes related to *Tantilla planiceps* (Blainville). Bull. Amer. Mus. Natur. Hist. 171:199–284.

Collins, J. T.
1964   A preliminary review of the snakes of Kentucky. J. Ohio Herpetol. Soc. 4:69–77.
1970   The corn snake, *Elaphe guttata guttata* (Linnaeus) in Kentucky. Trans. Kentucky Acad. Sci. 31:49–50.
1974   Amphibians and reptiles in Kansas. Univ. Kansas Publ. Mus. Natur. Hist. Publ. Ed. Ser. (1):1–283.

Collins, J. T., R. Conant, J. E. Huheey,
J. L. Knight, E. M. Rundquist, and H. M.
Smith
1982   Standard common and current sci-
entific names for North American
amphibians and reptiles. 2nd. ed.
Soc. Stud. Amphib. Rept. Herpetol.
Circ. (12):1–28.

Collins, J. T., and C. J. Hirschfeld
1963   *Lampropeltis doliata doliata* (Linnaeus) in Kentucky. Herpetologica
19:292–293.
1971   A second record of the eastern
coachwhip snake, *Masticophis flagellum flagellum* (Shaw), from Kentucky. J. Herpetol. 5:193.

Collins, J. T., and J. L. Knight
1980   *Crotalus horridus.* Catalog. Amer.
Amphib. Rept. 253:1–2.

Collins, R. F.
1980   Stomach contents of some snakes
from eastern and central North
Carolina. Brimleyana (4):157–159.

Collins, R. F., and C. C. Carpenter
1970   Organ position–ventral scute relationship in the water moccasin (*Agkistrodon piscivorus leucostoma*),
with notes on food habits and distribution. Proc. Oklahoma Acad. Sci.
49:15–18.

Conant, R.
1933   Three generations of cottonmouths,
Agkistrodon piscivorus (Lacepede).
Copeia 193:43.
1938   On the seasonal occurrence of reptiles in Lucas County, Ohio. Herpetologica 1:137–144.
1940*   A new subspecies of the fox snake,
Elaphe vulpina Baird and Girard.
Herpetologica 2:1–14.
1943a   *Natrix erythrogaster erythrogaster* in
the northeastern part of its range.
Herpetologica 2:83–86.
1943b   Studies on North American water
snakes—I: *Natrix kirtlandii* (Kennicott). Amer. Midl. Natur.
29:313–341.
1945   An annotated check list of the amphibians and reptiles of the Del-
Mar-Va Peninsula. Soc. Natur. Hist.
Delaware, Wilmington. 8 p.
1949*   Two new races of *Natrix erythrogaster.* Copeia 1949:1–15.
1950   On the taxonomic status of *Thamnophis butleri* (Cope). Bull. Chicago
Acad. Sci. 9:71–77.

1951   The reptiles of Ohio, 2nd ed. Notre
Dame Press, Notre Dame, Indiana.
284 p.
1956   A review of two rare pine snakes
from the Gulf Coastal Plain. Amer.
Mus. Novitates (1781):1–31.
1957   Reptiles and amphibians of the
northeastern states, 3rd ed. Zool.
Soc. Philadelphia. 40 p.
1960   The queen snake, *Natrix septemvittata*, in the interior highlands of Arkansas and Missouri, with comments
upon similar disjunct distributions.
Acad. Natur. Sci. Philadelphia
112:25–40.
1963   Evidence for the specific status of
the water snake *Natrix fasciata.*
Amer. Mus. Novitates (2122):1–38.
1965   Notes on reproduction in two
Natricine snakes from Mexico. Herpetologica 21:140–144.
1969   Some rambling notes on rattlesnakes. Arch. Environ. Health
19:768–769.
1975   A field guide to reptiles and amphibians of eastern and central
North America. 2nd ed. Houghton
Mifflin Co., Boston. 429 p.

Conant, R., and R. M. Bailey
1936   Some herpetological records from
Monmouth and Ocean counties,
New Jersey. Occ. Pap. Mus. Zool.
Univ. Michigan (328):1–10.

Conant, R., and W. Bridges
1939   What snake is that? Appleton Cen-
tury, New York. 163 p.

Conant, R., and W. M. Clay
1937*   A new subspecies of water snake
from islands in Lake Erie. Occ.
Pap. Mus. Zool. Univ. Michigan
(346):1–9.
1963   A reassessment of the taxonomic
status of the Lake Erie water snake.
Herpetologica 19:179–184.

Conant, R., and A. Downs, Jr.
1940   Miscellaneous notes on the eggs and
young of reptiles. Zoologica
25:33–48.

Conant, R., and J. D. Lazell, Jr.
1973*   The Carolina salt marsh snake: a
distinct form of *Natrix sipedon.*
Breviora (400):1–13.

Conant, R., E. S. Thomas, and R. L. Rausch
1945   The plains garter snake, *Thamnophis
radix*, in Ohio. Copeia 1945:61–68.

Conway, C. H., and W. R. Fleming
1960   Placental transmission of 22 131 Na and I in *Natrix*. Copeia 1960:53–55.

Cook, D. G., and F. J. Aldridge
1984   *Coluber constrictor priapus* (Southern Black Racer). Food. Herp. Rev. 15:49.

Cook, F. A.
1945   Integradation of *Lampropeltis calligaster* and *L. rhombomaculata* in Mississippi. Copeia 1945:47–48.
1954   Snakes of Mississippi. Mississippi Game Fish Comm., Jackson. 40 p.
1964   Communal egg–laying in the smooth green snake. Herpetologica 24:206.
1967   An analysis of the herpetofauna of Prince Edward Island. Bull. Natl. Mus. Canada (212):1–60.
1984   Introduction to Canadian amphibians and reptiles. Nat. Mus. Canada, Ottawa. 200 p.

Cooper, J. E.
1958   The snake *Haldea valeriae pulchra* in Maryland. Herpetologica 14:121–122.
1961   The distribution of the mole snake in Maryland. Herpetologica 17:141.
1969   A red–bellied water snake from Maryland's western Coastal plain. J. Herpetol. 3:185–186.

Cooper, J. E., and F. Groves
1959   The rattlesnake, *Crotalus horridus*, in the Maryland Piedmont. Herpetologica 15:33–34.

Cooper, W. E.
1977   *Natrix cyclopion cyclopion* X *floridana* (Green water snake). Herp Review 8(1):13.

Coote, J.
1977   Temperature requirements for *Lampropeltis* and *Elaphe*. Herptile 2:4–6.

Cope, E. D.
1860*   Catalogue of the Colubridae in the Museum of the Academy of Natural Sciences of Philadelphia, with notes and descriptions of new species. Part 2. Proc. Acad. Nat. Sci. Philadelphia 12:241–266.
1871*   Ninth contribution to the herpetology of tropical America. Proc. Acad. Natur. Sci. Philadelphia 23:200–224.

1888*   On the snakes of Florida. Proc. U. S. Natl. Mus. 11:381–384.
1889*   On the Entaeniae of southeastern Indiana. Proc. U. S. Natl. Mus. 11:399–401.
1892a* A new species of *Eutaenia* from western Pennsylvania. Amer. Natur. 26:964–965.
1892b* A critical review of the characters and variations of the snakes of North America. Proc. U. S. Natl. Mus. 14:589–694.
1893   The color variation of the milk snake. Amer. Natur. 27:1066–1071.
1895*   On some new North American snakes. Amer. Natur. 29:676–680.
1900   The crocodilians, lizards, and snakes of North America. Report U. S. Natl. Mus. 1898:153–1294.

Costanzo, J. P.
1985   The bioenergetics of hibernation in the eastern garter snake, *Thamnophis sirtalis sirtalis*. Physiol. Zool. 58:682–692.

Cowles, R. B.
1941   Observations on the winter activities of desert reptiles. Ecology 22:124–140.

Cox, D. L., T. J. Koob, R. P. Mecham, and O. J. Sexton
1984   External incubation alters the composition of squamate eggshells. Comp. Biochem. Physiol. 79B:481–487.

Cox, T. M.
1986   More on the bird–eating activities of the black rat snake, *Elaphe obsoleta obsoleta* (Say). Notes From NOAH 14:18–19.

Crews, D.
1976   Hormonal control of male and female sexual behavior in the garter snake *Thamnophis sirtalis sirtalis*. Horm. Behav. 7:451–460.
1980   Studies in squamate sexuality. BioScience 30:835–838.
1983   Alternative reproductive tactics in reptiles. BioScience 33:562–566.

Crews, D., B. Camazine, M. Diamond, R. Mason, R. R. Tokarz, and W. R. Garstka
1984   Hormonal independence of courtship behavior in the male garter snake. Horm. Behav. 18:29–41.

Crews, D., and W. R. Garstka
1982   The ecological physiology of a garter snake. Sci. Amer. 247(5):159–168.

Criddle, S.
1937   Snakes from an ant hill. Copeia 1937:142.

Cundall, D.
1981   Cranial osteology of the colubrid snake genus *Opheodrys*. Copeia 1981:353–371.

Cundall, D., and C. Gans
1979   Feeding in water snakes: an electromyographic study. J. Exp. Zool. 209:189–208.

Cundall, D., and D. A. Rossman
1984   Quantitative comparisons of skull form in the colubrid snake genera *Farancia* and *Pseudoeryx*. Herpetologica 40:388–405.

Curran, C. H.
1935   Rattlesnakes. Natur. Hist. 36:331–340.

Curran, C. H., and C. Kauffeld.
1937   Snakes and their ways. Harper & Bros., New York. 285 p.

Curtis, L.
1949   The snakes of Dallas County, Texas. Field & Lab. 17:1–13.
1950   A case of twin hatching in the rough green snake. Copeia 1950:232.
1952   Cannibalism in the Texas Coral snake. Herpetologica 8:27.

Czaplicki, J.
1975   Habituation of the chemically elicited prey–attack response in the diamond–backed water snake, *Natrix rhombifera rhombifera*. Herpetologica 31:403–409.

Czaplicki, J. A., and R. H. Porter
1974   Visual cues mediating the selection of goldfish (*Carassius auratus*) by two species of *Natrix*. J. Herpetol. 8:129–134.

DaLie, D. A.
1953   Poisonous snakes of America. J. Forestry 51:243–248.

Dalrymple, G. H., and N. G. Reichenbach
1981   Interactions between the prairie garter snake (*Thamnophis radix*) and the common garter snake (*T. sirtalis*) in Killdeer Plains, Wyandot County, Ohio. Biol. Notes Ohio Biol. Surv. (14):244–250.
1984   Management of an endangered species of snake in Ohio, U. S. A. Biol. Conserv. 30:195–200.

Daniel, J. C.
1983   The book of Indian reptiles. Bombay Natur. Hist. Soc. 141 pp.

Darlington, P. J., Jr.
1957   Zoogeography: the geographical distribution of animals. John Wiley & Sons, Inc., New York. 675 p.

Daudin, F. M.
1801*–
1803   Historie naturelle, generale et particuliere des reptiles. 7 vols. F. Dufart, Paris.

Davis, D. D.
1946   Observations on the burrowing behavior of the hog–nosed snake. Copeia 1946:75–78.
1948   Flash display of aposematic colors in *Farancia* and other snakes. Copeia 1948:208–211.

Davis, R. A.
1980a   A large egg clutch from an eastern hognose snake, *Heterodon platyrhinos*. Herp Review 11:91.
1980b   Vipers among us. Cincinnati Mus. Natur. Hist. Quart. 17(2):8–12.

Davis, W. F.
1969   Robin Kills snake. Wilson Bull. 81:470–471.

Deckert, R. F.
1918   A list of reptiles from Jacksonville, Florida. Copeia (54):30–33.

DeGraaf, R. M., and D. D. Rudis
1981   Forest habitat for reptiles & amphibians of the Northeast. Forest Serv., U. S. Dept. Agric., Washington, D. C. 239 p.
1983   Amphibians and reptiles of New England: habitats and natural history. Univ. Massachusets Press, Amherst. 112 p.

Denman, N. S., and I. S. Lapper
1964   The herpetology of Mont St. Hilaire, Rouville County, Quebec, Canada. Herpetologica 20:25–30.

deQueiroz, A.
1984   Effects of prey type on the prey–handling behavior of the bullsnake, *Pituophis melanoleucus*. J. Herpetol. 18:333–336.

Dermid, J.
1961   *Opheodrys aestivus*. Turtox News
        39:79.

Dessauer, H. C.
1967   Molecular approach to the taxon-
        omy of colubrid snakes. Her-
        petologica 23:148–155.

Dessauer, H. C., and W. Fox
1958   Geographic variation in plasma pro-
        tein patterns of snakes. Proc. Soc.
        Exp. Biol. Med. 98:101–105.

Dessauer, H. C., W. Fox, and N. L. Gilbert
1956   Plasma calcium, magnesium and
        protein of viviparous colubrid snakes
        during estrous cycle. Proc. Soc.
        Exp. Biol. Med. 92:299–301.

Dessauer, H. C., and F. H. Pough
1975   Geographic variation of blood pro-
        teins and the systematics of
        kingsnakes (*Lampropeltis getulus*).
        Comp. Biochem. Physiol. 50B:9–12.

Devine, M. C.
1975   Copulatory plugs in snakes: enforced
        chastity. Science 187:844–845.
1977   Copulatory plugs, restricted mating
        opportunities and reproductive com-
        petition among male garter snakes.
        Nature 267:345–346.

deWit, C. A.
1982   Yield of venom from the Osage cop-
        perhead, *Agkistrodon contortrix
        phaeogaster*. Toxicon 20:525–527.

Dial, B.
1961   Incubation of *Opheodrys* eggs. Bull.
        Philadelphia Herpetol. Soc. 9(6):18.

Dickinson, W. E.
1949   Field guide to the lizards and snakes
        of Wisconsin. Milwaukee Publ.
        Mus., Pop. Sci. Handb. Ser.
        (2):1–70.

Dickson, J. D.
1948   Observations on the feeding habits
        of the scarlet snake. Copeia
        1948:216–217.

Diemer, J. E., and D. W. Speake
1983   The distribution of the eastern in-
        digo snake, *Drymarchon corais
        couperi*, in Georgia. J. Herpetol.
        17:256–264.

Diener, R. A.
1957a   A western hognose snake eats a col-
        lard lizard. Herpetologica 13:122.

1957b   An ecological study of the plain-
        bellied water snake. Herpetologica
        13:203–211.
1961   Notes on a bite of the broad-
        banded copperhead, *Ancistrodon
        contortrix laticinctus* Gloyd and
        Conant. Herpetologica 17:143–144.

Dietrich, S. E.
1960   Record clutch of *Lampropeltis* eggs.
        Herpetologica 16:47.

Dihondt, K., and P. Cherlet.
1984   *Lampropeltis getulus floridana*, de
        Florida kettingslang in het terrarium.
        Lacerta 42:146–149.

Dill, C. D.
1972   Reptilian core temperatures: vari-
        ation within individuals. Copeia
        1972:577–579.

Ditmars, R. L.
1931a   The reptile book. Doubleday Doran
        & Co., Garden City, New York. 472
        p.
1931b   Snakes of the World. McMillan,
        New York. 207 p.
1936   The reptiles of North America.
        Doubleday, Doran & Co., Garden
        City, New York. 476 p.
1939   A field book of North American
        snakes. Doubleday, Doran & Co.,
        Inc., New York. 305 p.

Dix, M. W.
1968   Snake food preference: innate in-
        traspecific geographic variation. Sci-
        ence 159:1478–1479.

Dloogatch, M.
1978   Eggs and hatchlings of the worm
        snake, *Carphophis vermis* (Ken-
        nicott). Bull. Chicago Herpetol. Soc.
        13:99–100.

do Amaral, A.
1927   The anti-snake-bite campaign in
        Texas and in the sub-tropical
        United States. Bull. Antivenin Inst.
        Amer. 1:77–85.

Dolley, J. S.
1939   An anomalous pregnancy in the
        copperhead. Copeia 1939:170.

Dove, L. B., D. A. Baeyens, and M. V. Plummer
1982   Evaporative water loss in *Opheodrys
        aestivus* (Colubridae). Southwest.
        Natur. 27:228–230.

Dowling, H. G.

1950*   Studies of the black swamp snake, *Seminatrix pygaea* (Cope), with descriptions of two new subspecies. Misc. Publ. Mus. Zool., Univ. Michigan (76):1–38.

1951a   A proposed method of expressing scale reductions in snakes. Copeia 1951:131–134.

1951b   A proposed standard system of counting ventrals in snakes. British J. Herpetol. 1:97–99.

1952   A taxonomic study of the ratsnakes, genus *Elaphe* Fitzinger IV. A check list of the American forms. Occ. Pap. Mus. Zool. Univ. Michigan (541):1–12.

1957   A review of the amphibians and reptiles of Arkansas. Occas. Paps. Univ. Arkansas Mus. (3):1–51.

1959a   Apical papillae on the hemipenes of two colubrid snakes. Amer. Mus. Novitates (1948):1–7.

1959b   Classification of the Serpentes: a critical review. Copeia 1959:38–52.

Dowling, H. G. (ed.)

1975   Yearbook of herpetology. H. I. S. S. New York, New York. 256 p.

Dowling, H. G., and J. M. Savage.

1960   A guide to the snake hemipenis: a survey of basic structure and systematic characteristics. Zoologica 45:17–28.

Drda, W. J.

1968   A study of snakes wintering in a small cave. J. Herpetol. 1:64–70.

Drummond, H.

1979   Stimulus control of amphibious predation in the northern water snake (*Nerodia s. sipedon*). Zeit. Tierpsychol. 50:18–44.

1983   Aquatic foraging in garter snakes: a comparison of specialists and generalists. Behaviour 86:1–30.

1985   The role of vision in the predatory behaviour of natricine snakes. Anim. Behav. 33:206–215.

Duellman, W. E.

1948   *Thamnophis s. sauritus* eats own young. Herpetologica 4:210.

1949   An unusual habitat for the keeled green snake. Herpetologica 5:144.

Duellman, W. E., and A. Schwartz

1958   Amphibians and reptiles of southern Florida. Bull. Florida St. Mus. Biol. Sci. 3:181–324.

Dumeril, A. M. C., G. Bibron, and A. H. A. Dumeril

1854*   Erpetologie generale ou histoire naturelle complete des reptiles. Vol. 7. Libr. Encyclop. de Roret, Paris.

Dunbar, G. L.

1979   Effects of early feeding experience on chemical preference of the northern water snake, *Natrix s. sipedon* (Reptilia, Serpentes, Colubridae). J. Herpetol. 13:165–169.

Dundee, H. A., and W. L. Burger, Jr.

1948   A denning aggregation of the western cottonmouth. Natur. Hist. Misc. (21):1–2.

Dundee, H. A., and M. C. Miller

1968   Aggregative behavior and habitat conditioning by the prairie ringneck snake, *Diadophis punctatus arnyi*. Tulane Stud. Zool. Bot. 15:41–58.

Dunn, E. R.

1915   The variations of a brood of watersnakes. Proc. Biol. Soc. Washington 28:61–68.

Dunn, E. R., and G. C. Wood

1939*   Notes on eastern snakes of the genus *Coluber*. Notulae Natur. (5):1–4.

Dunson, W. A.

1980   The relation of sodium and water balance to survival in sea water of estuarine and freshwater races of the snakes *Nerodia fasciata*, *N. sipedon* and *N. valida*. Copeia 1980:268–280.

1978   Role of skin in sodium and water exchange of aquatic snakes placed in seawater. Amer. J. Physiol. 235:R151–R159.

1979   Occurrence of partially striped forms of the mangrove snake *Nerodia fasciata compressicauda* Kennicott and comments on the status of *N. f. taeniata* Cope. Florida Sci. 49:94–102.

1982   Salinity relations of crocodiles in Florida Bay. Copeia 1982:374–385.

Dunson, W. A., and J. Freda
1985   Water permeability of the skin of the amphibious snake, *Agkistrodon piscivorus*. J. Herpetol. 19:93–98.

Dymond, J. R., and F. E. J. Fry
1932   Notes on the breeding habits of the green snake (*Liopeltis vernalis*). Copeia 1932:102.

Dyrkacz, S.
1977   The natural history of the eastern milk snake (Reptilia, Serpentes, Colubridae) in a disturbed environment. J. Herpetol. 11:155–159.

Dyrkacz, S., and M. J. Corn
1974   Response of naive, neonate bullsnakes to water extracts of potential prey items. Herp Review 5:74.

Easterla, D. A.
1967   Black rat snake preys upon gray *Myotis* and winter observations of red bats. Amer. Midl. Natur. 77:527–528.

Eberle, W. G.
1972   Comparative chromosomal morphology of the New World natricine snake genera *Natrix* and *Regina*. Herpetologica 28:98–105.

Edgren, R. A., Jr.
1948   Notes on a litter of young timber rattlesnakes. Copeia 1948:132.

Edgren, R. A.
1951   The umbilical scar, a sexually dimorphic character in *Heterodon platyrhinos*. Natur. Hist. Misc. (83):1–2.
1952*   A synopsis of the snakes of the genus *Heterodon*, with the diagnosis of a new race of *Heterodon nasicus* Baird and Girard. Natur. Hist. Misc. (112):1–4.
1953a   Copulatory adjustment in snakes and its evolutionary implication. Copeia 1953:162–164.
1953b   On the chromosomes of the hog-nosed snake, *Heterodon platyrhinos* Linnaeus. Evolution 7:88.
1955   The natural history of the hog-nosed snakes, genus *Heterodon*: a review. Herpetologica 11:105–117.
1957   Melanism in hog-nosed snakes. Herpetologica 13:131–135.

1958   Umbilical scar position and sexual dimorphism in hog–nosed snakes, genus *Heterodon*. Natur. Hist. Misc. (163):1–6.
1961   A simplified method for analysis of clines; geographic variation in the hognose snake *Heterodon platyrhinos* Latreille. Copeia 1961:125–132.

Edgren, R. A., and M. K. Edgren
1955   Experiments on bluffing and death-feigning in the hognose snake *Heterodon platyrhinos*. Copeia 1955:2–4.

Edmund, A. G.
1960   Tooth replacement phenomena in the lower vertebrates. Royal Ontario Mus. Life Sci. Contrib. 52:1–190.

Ehrlich, P. R., and J. H. Camin
1960   Natural selection in Middle Island water snakes (*Natrix sipedon* L.). Evolution 14:136.

Ehrsam, U.
1968   Hautung der Zungenspitzen bei einer Indigonatter (*Drymarchon corais couperi*). Salamandra 4:45–46.

Elick, G. E., and J. A. Sealander
1972   Comparative water loss in relation to habitat selection in small colubrid snakes. Amer. Midl. Natur. 88:429–439.

Engelmann, W. E.
1984   Zum Eiablageverhalten der Kulken-natter (*Elaphe obsoleta quadrivittata*). Zool. Garten (Jena) 54:209–210.

Engelman, W., and F. J. Obst
1981   Snakes: biology, behavior and relationships to man. Exeter Books, New York. 222 p.

Ernst, C. H.
1964   A study of sexual dimorphism in American *Agkistrodon* fang lengths. Herpetologica 20:214.
1965   Fang length comparisons of American *Agkistrodon*. Trans. Kentucky Acad. Sci. 26:12–18.
1974   Taxonomic status of the red–bellied snake, *Storeria occipitomaculata*, in Minnesota. J. Herpetol. 8:347–350.
1982   A study of the fangs of snakes belonging to the *Agkistrodon*-complex. J. Herpetol. 16:72–80.

Ernst, C. H., and S. W. Gotte
1986 Notes on the reproduction of the shorthead garter snake, *Thamnophis brachystoma*. Bull. Maryland Herpetol. Soc. 22:6–9.

Ernst, C. H., S. W. Gotte, and J. E. Lovich
1985 Reproduction in the mole kingsnake, *Lampropeltis calligaster rhombomaculata*. Bull. Maryland Herpetol. Soc. 21:16–22.

Ernst, S. G.
1962 Notes on the life history of the eastern ringneck snake. Turtox News 40:266–267.

Essex, H. E.
1932 The physiologic action of the venom of the water moccasin (*Agkistrodon piscivorus*). Bull. Antiv. Inst. Amer. 5:81.

Estes, R.
1965 Pleistocene snakes from the Seymour Formation of Texas. Copeia 1965:102–104.

Evans, H. E., and R. M. Roecker
1951 Notes on the herpetology of Ontario, Canada. Herpetologica 7:69–71.

Evans, P. D.
1942 A method of fishing used by water snakes. Chicago Natur. 5(3):53–55.

Evans, P. D., and H. K. Gloyd
1948 The subspecies of the massasauga, *Sistrurus catenatus*, in Missouri. Bull. Chicago Acad. Sci. 8:225–232.

Feaver, P. E.
1976 A population study of the northern watersnake, *Natrix sipedon*, in southeastern Michigan. Herp Review 7:81.

Fendley, T. T.
1980 Incubating woodduck and hooded merganser hens killed by black rat snakes. Wilson Bull. 92:526–527.

Ferguson, D. E.
1961 The herpetofauna of Tishomingo County, Mississippi, with comments on its zoogeographic affinities. Copeia 1961:391–396.
1963 Notes concerning the effects of heptachlor on certain poikilotherms. Copeia 1963:441–443.

Ferguson, D. E., and H. R. Bancroft
1957 Distribution of *Carphophis amoenus* in Mississippi. Herpetologica 13:245.

Ferguson J. H., and R. M. Thornton
1984 Oxygen storage capacity and tolerance of submergence of a nonaquatic reptile and an aquatic reptile. Comp. Biochem. Physiol. 774:183–187.

Fetterolf, P. M.
1979 Common garter snake predation on ring-billed gull chicks. Can. Field-Natur. 93:317–318.

Fever, R. C.
1959 Variation in three broods of *Storeria dekayi* from Louisiana. Copeia 1959:261–163.

Finch, D. M.
1981 Nest predation of Abert's towhees by coachwhips and roadrunners. Condor 83:389.

Finneran, L. C.
1949 A sexual aggregation of the garter snake *Thamnophis butleri* (Cope). Copeia 1949:141–144.
1953 Aggregation behavior of the female copperhead, *Agkistrodon contortrix mokeson*, during gestation. Copeia 1953:61–62.

Fischman, H. K., J. Mitra, and H. Dowling
1968 Chromosome analyses of three members of the genus *Elaphe* (Serpentes). Genetics 6:177.
1972 Chromosome characteristcs of 13 species in the Order Serpentes. Mammal Chromosomes Newsl. 13:72–73.

Fisher, C. B.
1973 Status of the flat-headed snake, *Tantilla gracilis* Baird and Girard, in Louisiana. J. Herpetol. 7:136–137.

Fitch, H. S.
1956 Temperature responses in free-living amphibians and reptiles in northeastern Kansas. Univ. Kansas Publ. Mus. Natur. Hist. 8:417–476.
1958 Home ranges, territories, and seasonal movements of vertebrates of the Natural History Reservation. Univ. Kansas Publ. Mus. Natur. Hist. 11:63–326.
1960a Criteria for determining sex and breeding maturity in snakes. Herpetologica 16:49–51.

1960b Autecology of the copperhead. Univ. Kansas Publ. Mus. Natur. Hist. 13:85–288.

1963a Natural history of the racer *Coluber constrictor*. Univ. Kansas Publ. Mus. Natur. Hist. 15:351–468.

1963b Natural history of the black rat snake (*Elaphe o. obsoleta*) in Kansas. Copeia 1963:649–658.

1965 An ecological study of the garter snake *Thamnophis sirtalis*. Univ. Kansas Publ. Mus. Natur. Hist. 15:493–564.

1970 Reproductive cycles in lizards and snakes. Univ. Kansas Mus. Natur. Hist., Misc. Publ. (52):1–247.

1975 A demographic study of the ringsnake snake (*Diadophis punctatus*) in Kansas. Univ. Kansas Mus. Natur. Hist. Misc. Publ. (62):1–53.

1977 Partitioning of food resources in snakes of the University of Kansas Natural History Reservation. Herp Review 8(3) suppl.:8.

1978 A field study of the prairie kingsnake (*Lampropeltis calligaster*). Trans. Kansas Acad. Sci. 81:354–362.

1980 *Thamnophis sirtalis*. Catalog. Amer. Amphib. Rept. 270:1–4.

1985 Variation in clutch and litter size in New World reptiles. Univ. Kansas Mus. Natur. Hist., Misc. Publ. (76):1–76.

Fitch, H. S., and A. V. Fitch
1967 Preliminary experiments on physical tolerances of the eggs of lizards and snakes. Ecology 48:160–165.

Fitch, H. S., and R. R. Fleet
1970 Natural history of the milk snake (*Lampropeltis triangulum*) in northeastern Kansas. Herpetologica 26:387–396.

Fitch, H. S., and H. W. Shirer
1971 A radiotelemetric study of spatial relationships in some common snakes. Copeia 1971:118–128.

Fix, J. D., and S. A. Minton, Jr.
1976 Venom extraction and yields from the North American coral snake, *Micrurus fulvius*. Toxicon 14:143–145.

Flanigan, A. B.
1971 Predation on snakes by eastern bluebird and brown thrasher. Wilson Bull. 83:441.

Fleet, R. R., and J. C. Kroll
1978 Litter size and parturition behavior in *Sistrurus miliarius streckeri*. Herp Review 9:11.

Foley, G. W.
1971 Perennial communal nesting in the black racer (*Coluber constrictor*). Herp Review 3:41.

Foote, R., and J. A. MacMahon
1977 Electrophoretic studies on rattlesnake (*Crotalus & Sistrurus*) venom: taxonomic implications. J. Biochem. Physiol. 57B:235–241.

Force, E. R.
1931 Habits and birth of young of the lined snake, *Tropidoclonion lineatum* (Hallowell). Copeia 1931:51–53.

1935 A local study of the opisthoglyph snake *Tantilla gracilis* Baird and Girard. Pap. Michigan Acad. Sci., Arts, Lett. (1934) 20:645–659.

1936 The relation of the knobbed anal keels to age and sex in the lined snake *Tropidoclonion lineatum* (Hallowell). Pap. Michigan Acad. Sci. Arts, Lett. 21:613–617.

Ford, N. B.
1974 Growth and food consumption in the yellow rat snake, *Elaphe obsoleta quadrivittata*. Herpetologica 30:102–104.

1978 Evidence for species specificity of pheromone trails in two sympatric garter snakes, *Thamnophis*. Herp Review 9:10.

1981 Seasonality of pheromone trailing behavior in two species of garter snake, *Thamnophis* (Colubridae). Southwest. Natur. 26:385–388.

1982a Species specificity of sex pheromone trails of sympatric and allopatric garter snakes (*Thamnophis*). Copeia 1982:10–13.

1982b Courtship behavior of the queen snake, *Regina septemvittata*. Herp Review 13:72.

Ford, N. B., and D. W. Killebrew
1983 Reproductive tactics and female body size in Butler's garter snake. J. Herpetol. 17:271–275.

Ford, N. B., and C. W. Schofield
1984   Species specificity of sex pheromone trails in the plains garter snake, *Thamnophis radix*. Herpetologica 40:51–55.

Forks, T.
1979   Kingsnake "lays turtle eggs." Bull. Chicago Herpetol. Soc. 14:119.

Forster, J. R.
1771*   In Bossu: Travels through that part of North America formerly called Louisiana 1:vii + 407 p.

Forsyth, B. J., C. D. Baker, T. Wiles, and C. Weilbaker
1985   Cottonmouth, *Agkistrodon piscivorus*, records from the Blue River and Potato Run in Harrison County, Indiana (Ohio River Drainage, U. S. A.). Proc. Indiana Acad. Sci. 94:633–634.

Fouquette, M. J., Jr.
1954   Food competition among four sympatric species of garter snakes, genus *Thamnophis*. Texas J. Sci. 6:172–188.

Fowler, J. A.
1966   A communal nesting site for the smooth green snake in Michigan. Herpetologica 22:231.

Fox, W.
1954   Genetic and environmental variation in the timing of reproductive cycles of male garter snakes. J. Morph. 95:415–450.
1956   Seminal receptacles of snakes. Anat. Rec. 124:519–540.

Fraker, M. A.
1970   Home range and homing in the watersnake, *Natrix sipedon sipedon*. Copeia 1970:665–673.

Franz, R.
1968   Early appearance of the eastern garter snake, *Thamnophis sirtalis sirtalis*, in Maryland. Bull. Maryland Herpetol. Soc. 4:81.
1977   Observations on the food, feeding behavior, and parasites of the striped swamp snake, *Regina alleni*. Herpetologica 33:91–94.

Freda, J.
1977   Fighting a losing battle. The story of a timber rattlesnake. Herp, Bull. New York Herpetol. Soc. 13:35–38.

Freedman, W., and P. M. Catling
1978   Population size and structure of four sympatric species of snakes at Amherstburg, Ontario. Can. Field–Natur. 92:167–173.
1979   Movements of sympatric species of snakes at Amherstburg, Ontario. Can. Field–Natur. 93:399–404.

Freeman, J. R., and C. C. Freeman
1982   *Diadophis punctatus edwardsi* (Northern Ringneck Snake). Size. Herp Review 13:96.

Froom, B.
1965   The habits of a captive smooth green snake. Ontario Field Biol. 19:15–17.
1972   The snakes of Canada. McCelland and Stewart, Toronto. 128 p.

Fuller, T. C.
1959   Five new records of *Pituophis* in Kentucky. Herpetologica 15:94.

Fuller, T. C., and R. W. Barbour
1962   The distribution of *Cemophora coccinea* (Blumenbach) in Kentucky. Copeia 1962:637–638.

Funderburg, J. B.
1958   The yellow–lipped snake, *Rhadinaea flavilata* Cope, in North Carolina. J. Elisha Mitchell Sci. Soc. 74:135–136.
1968   Eastern diamondback rattlesnake feeding on carrion. J. Herpetol. 2:161–162.

Funderburg, J. B., and D. S. Lee
1968   The amphibian and reptile fauna of pocket gopher (*Geomys*) mounds in central Florida. J. Herpetol. 1:99–100.

Funk, R. S.
1962   On the reproduction of *Elaphe g. guttata* (Linnaeus). Herpetologica 18:66.
1964   Birth of a brood of western cottonmouths, *Agkistrodon piscivorus leucostoma*. Trans. Kansas Acad. Sci. 67:199.

Funk, R. S., and J. K. Tucker
1978   Variation in a large brood of lined snakes, *Tropidoclonion lineatum* (Reptilia, Serpentes, Colubridae). J. Herpetol. 12:115–117.

Galligan, J. H., and W. A. Dunson
1979   Biology and status of timber rattle-snake (*Crotalus horridus*) populations in Pennsylvania. Biol. Conserv. 15:13–58.

Gardner, J. B.
1955   A ball of gartersnakes. Copeia 1955:310.
1957   A garter snake "ball." Copeia 1957:48.

Garman, S. W.
1874*   Description of a new species of North American serpent. Proc. Boston Soc. Natur. Hist. 17:92–94.

Garnett, P. J.
1979   Electrophoretic analysis of blood serum proteins in three species of water snakes (genus *Nerodia*). Proc. Arkansas Acad. Sci. 33:32–34.

Garstka, W. R., B. Camazine, and D. Crews
1982   Interactions of behavior and physiology during the annual reproductive cycle of the red–sided garter snake (*Thamnophis sirtalis parietalis*). Herpetologica 38:104–123.

Garstka, W. R., and D. Crews
1981   Female sex pheromone in the skin and circulation of a garter snake. Science 214:681–683.
1985   Mate preference in garter snakes. Herpetologica 41:9–19.

Gartside, D. F., J. S. Rogers, and H. C. Dessauer
1977   Speciation with little genic and morphologic differentiation in the ribbon snakes *Thamnophis proximus* and *T. sauritus* (Colubridae). Copeia 1977:697–705.

Garton, J. S., and R. W. Dimmick
1969   Food habits of the copperhead in middle Tennessee. J. Tennessee Acad. Sci. 44:113–117.

Garton, J. S., E. W. Harris, and R. A. Brandon
1970   Descriptive and ecological notes on *Natrix cyclopion* in Illinois. Herpetologica 26:454–461.

Gee, P. A.
1971   Sex chromatin in vertebrates with possible female heterogamety. Acta Anat. 80:127–135.

Gehlbach, F. R.
1970   Death–feigning and erratic behavior in leptotyphlopid, colubrid, and elapid snakes. Herpetologica 26:24–34.
1972   Coral snake mimicry reconsidered: the strategy of self–mimicry. Forma et Functio 5:311–320.
1974   Evolutionary relations of southwestern ringneck snakes (*Diadophis punctatus*). Herpetologica 3:140–148.

Gehlbach, F. R., and B. B. Collette
1959   Distributional and biological notes on the Nebraska herpetofauna. Herpetologica 15:141–143.

Gehlbach, F. R., J. F. Watkins, II, and J. C. Kroll
1972   Pheromone trail–following studies of typhlopid, leptotyphlopid, and colubrid snakes. Behaviour 40:282–294.

George, D. W., and H. C. Dessaur
1970   Immunological correspondence of transferrins and the relationships of colubrid snakes. Comp. Biochem. Physiol. 33:617–627.

Gibbons, J. W.
1972   Reproduction, growth, and sexual dimorphism in the canebrake rattlesnake (*Crotalus horridus atricaudatus*). Copeia 1972:222–226.
1977   Snakes of the Savannah River Plant with information about snakebite prevention and treatment. ERDA's Savannah River Nat. Environ. Res. Park. SRO–NERP–1. 26 pp.

Gibbons, J. W., J. W. Coker, and T. M. Murphy, Jr.
1977   Selected aspects of the life history of the rainbow snake (*Farancia erytrogramma*). Herpetologica 33:276–281.

Gibson, A. R., and J. B. Falls
1975   Evidence for multiple insemination in the common garter snake, *Thamnophis sirtalis*. Can. J. Zool. 53:1362–1368.
1979   Thermal biology of the common garter snake *Thamnophis sirtalis* (L.). I. Temporal variation, environmental effects and sex differences. II. The effects of melanism. Oecologia (Berlin) 43:79–109.

Gilhen, J.
1969   An unusually large, gravid ring-
necked snake, *Diadophis punctatus
edwardsi* (Merrem) with eight eggs
from Nova Scotia. Can. Field-
Natur. 83:277.

1970   An unusual Nova Scotian population
of the northern ringneck snake,
Diadophis punctatus edwardsi (Merrem). Occ. Pap. Nova Scotia Mus.
(9):1-12.

1984   Amphibians and reptiles of Nova
Scotia. Nova Scotia Mus., Halifax,
Nova Scotia. 162 p.

Gillingham, J. C.
1974   Reproductive behavior of the western fox snake, *Elaphe v. vulpina*
(Baird and Girard). Herpetologica
30:309-313.

1976   Early egg deposition by the southern
black racer, *Coluber constrictor
priapus*. Herp Review 7:115.

1979   Reproductive behavior of the rat
snakes of eastern North America,
genus *Elaphe*. Copeia
1979:319-331.

1980   Communication and combat behavior in the black rat snake (*Elaphe
obsoleta*). Herpetologica
36:120-127.

Gillingham, J. C., and C. C. Carpenter
1978   Snake hibernation: construction of
and observations on a man-made
hibernaculum (Reptilia, Serpentes).
J. Herpetol. 12:495-498.

**Gillingham, J. C., C. C. Carpenter, B. J.
Brecke, and J. B. Murphy**
1977   Courtship and copulatory behavior
of the Mexican milk snake,
Lampropeltis triangulum sinaloae
(Colubridae). Southwest. Natur.
22:187-194.

Gillingham, J. C., and J. A. Chambers
1980   Observations on the reproductive behaviour of the eastern indigo snake,
Drymarchon corais couperi, in captivity. British J. Herpetol. 6:99-100.

Gillingham, J. C., and D. L. Clark
1981   Snake tongue-flicking: transfer me-
chanics to Jacobson's organ. Can. J.
Zool. 59:1651-1657.

Gillingham, J. C., and J. A. Dickinson
1980   Postural orientation during courtship
in the eastern garter snake, *Thamnophis s. sirtalis*. Behav. Neur. Biol.
28:211-217.

Gillingham, J. C., and T. Rush
1974   Notes on the fishing behavior of
water snakes. J. Herpetol.
8:384-385.

Gilmore, C. W.
1938   Fossil snakes of North America.
Geol. Soc. Amer. Spec. Publ.
(9):1-96.

Gloyd, H. K.
1928   The amphibians and reptiles of
Franklin County, Kansas. Trans.
Kansas Acad. Sci. 31:115-141.

1934   Studies on the breeding habits and
young of the copperhead, *Agkistrodon mokasen* Beauvois. Pap.
Michigan Acad. Sci., Arts, Lett.
19:587-604.

1935* The subspecies of *Sistrurus
miliarius*. Occ. Pap. Mus. Zool.
Univ. Michigan (322):1-7.

1938   A case of poisoning from the bite of
a black coral snake. Herpetologica
1:121-124.

1940   The rattlesnakes, genera *Sistrurus*
and *Crotalus*. Chicago Acad. Sci.
Spl. Publ. (4):1-266.

1947   Notes on the courtship and mating
behavior of certain snakes. Natur.
Hist. Misc. (12):1-4.

1969* Two additional subspecies of North
American snakes, genus *Agkistrodon*. Proc. Biol. Soc. Washington
82:219-232.

Gloyd, H. K., and R. Conant
1943   A synopsis of the American forms
of *Agkistrodon* (copperheads and
moccasins). Bull. Chicago Acad.
Sci. 7:147-170.

Godley, J. S.
1980   Foraging ecology of the striped
swamp snake, *Regina alleni*, in
southern Florida. Ecol. Monogr.
50:411-436.

1982   Predation and defensive behavior of
the striped swamp snake (*Regina alleni*). Florida Field Natur. 10:31-36.

**Godley, J. S., R. W. McDiarmid, and N. N.
Rojas**
1984   Estimating prey size and number in
crayfish-eating snakes, genus
Regina. Herpetologica 40:82-88.

Goff, C.C.
1936*   Distribution and variation of a new subspecies of water snake, *Natrix cyclopion floridana*, with a discussion of its relationships. Occ. Pap. Mus. Zool., Univ. Michigan (327):1–9.

Goin, C. J.
1943   The lower vertebrate fauna of the water hyacinth community in northern Florida. Proc. Florida Acad. Sci. 6:143–154.
1947   A note on the food of *Heterodon simus*. Copeia 1947:275.

Goin, C. J., O. B. Goin, and G. R. Zug
1978   Introduction to herpetology. 3rd Ed. Freeman, San Francisco. 378 p.

Goldberg, S. R., and W. S. Parker
1975   Seasonal testicular histology of the colubrid snakes, *Masticophis taeniatus* and *Pituophis melanoleucus*. Herpetologica 31:317–322.

Golder, F.
1981   Anomalien bei der Fortpflanzung von *Elaphe g. guttata*. Salamandra 17:71–77.

Goldman, P.
1972   Herring gull predation on common water snake in Lake Erie. Wilson Bull. 83:196–197.

Goldsmith, S. K.
1984   Aspects of the natural history of the rough green snake, *Opheodrys aestivus* (Colubridae). Southwest. Natur. 29:445–452.
1986   Feeding behavior of an arboreal, insectivorous snake (*Opheodrys aestivus*) (Colubridae). Southwest. Natur. 31:246–249.

Goldstein, R. C.
1941   Notes on the mud snake in Florida. Copeia 1941:49–50.

Goodman, J. D.
1958   Material ingested by the cottonmouth, *Agkistrodon piscivorus*, at Reelfoot Lake, Tennessee. Copeia 1958:149.

Gordon, D. M., and F. R. Cook
1980   An aggregation of gravid snakes in the Quebec Laurentians. Can. Field–Natur. 456–457.

Gorham, S. W.
1970   The amphibians and reptiles of New Brunswick. New Brunswick Mus., St. John. 30 p.

Gove, D., and G. M. Burghardt
1975   Responses of ecologically dissimilar populations of the water snake *Natrix s. sipedon* to chemical cues from prey. J. Chem. Ecol. 1:25–40.
1983   Context–correlated parameters of snake and lizard tongue–flicking. Anim. Behav. 31:718–723.

Graham, G. L.
1977   The karyotype of the Texas coral snake, *Micrurus fulvius tenere*. Herpetologica 33:345–348.

Graham, T. E.
1982   Unusual brood and body size in a northern water snake, *Nerodia sipedon sipedon*, from Worcester County, Massachusetts. Massachusetts Herpetol. Soc. Rev. 10:6.

Grass, A.
1972   Robin attacks garter snake. Can. Field–Natur. 86:292.

Gratz, R. K., and V. H. Hutchison
1977   Energetics for activity in the diamondback water snake, *Natrix rhombifera*. Physiol. Zool. 50:99–114.

Greding, E. J., Jr.
1964   Food of *Ancistrodon c. contortrix* in Houston and Trinity counties, Texas. Southwest. Natur. 9:105

Green, N. B.
1954   The amphibians and reptiles of West Virginia, their identification, habits and distribution. Marshall College, Huntington. 35 p.

Greene, H. W.
1976   Scale overlap, a directional sign stimulus for prey ingestion by ophiophagous snakes. Z. Tierpsychol. 41:113–120.
1983   Dietary correlates of the origin and radiation of snakes. Amer. Zool. 23:431–441.
1984   Feeding behavior and diet of the eastern coral snake, *Micrurus fulvius*. Univ. Kansas Mus. Natur. Hist. Spl. Publ. (10):147–162.

Greene, H. W., and G. M. Burghardt
1978   Behavior and phylogeny: constriction in ancient and modern snakes. Science 200:74–77.

Greene, H. W., and R. W. McDiarmid
1981   Coral snake mimicry: does it occur? Science 213:1207–1212.

Greene, H. W., and G. V. Oliver, Jr.
1965   Notes on the natural history of the western massasauga. Herpetologica 21:225–228.

Greenwald, O. E., and M. E. Kenter
1976   The effects of temperature and behavioral thermoregulation on digestive efficiency and rate in corn snakes (*Elaphe guttata guttata*). Physiol. Zool. 53:398–408.

Greenwell, M. G., M. Hall, and O. J. Sexton
1984   Phenotypic basis for a feeding change in an insular population of garter snake. Develop. Pychol. 17:457–463.

Gregory, P. T.
1974   Patterns of spring emergence of the red–sided garter snake (*Thamnophis sirtalis parietalis*) in the Interlake region of Manitoba
1975a   Aggregations of gravid snakes in Manitoba, Canada. Copeia 1975:185–186.
1975b   Arboreal mating behavior in the red–sided garter snake. Can. Field–Natur. 89:461–462.
1977a   Life history observations of three species of snakes in Manitoba. Can. Field–Natur. 91:19–27.
1977b   Life–history parameters of the red–sided garter snake (*Thamnophis sirtalis parietalis*) in one extreme environment, the Interlake Region of Manitoba. Publ. Zool. Nat. Mus. Natur–Sci. Canada (13):1–44.
1978   Feeding habits and diet overlap of three species of garter snakes (*Thamnophis*) on Vancouver Island. Can. J. Zool. 56:1967–1974.
1983   Habitat, diet, and composition of assemblages of garter snakes (*Thamnophis*) at eight sites on Vancouver Island. Can. J. Zool. 2013–2022.
1984a   Correlations between body temperature and environmental factors and their variations with activity in garter snakes (*Thamnophis*). Can. J. Zool. 62:2244–2249.

1984b   Communal denning in snakes. Univ. Kansas Publ. Mus. Natur. Hist. Spl. Publ. (10):57–75.

Gregory, P. T., and K. W. Stewart
1975   Long–distance dispersal and feeding strategy of the red–sided garter snake (*Thamnophis sirtalis parietalis*) in the Interlake of Manitoba. Can. J. Zool. 53:238–245.

Grimpe, R. D., and G. E. Benefield
1981   *Lampropeltis g. holbrooki* (Speckled Kingsnake). Reproduction. Herp Review 12:80.

Grizzell, R. A., Jr.
1949   The hibernation site of three snakes and a salamander. Copeia 1949:231–232.

Grobman, A. B.
1941*   A contribution to the knowledge of variation in *Opheodrys vernalis* (Harlan), with the description of a new subspecies. Misc. Publ. Mus. Zool., Univ. Michigan (50):1–38.
1978   An alternative solution to the coral snake mimic problem (Reptilia, Serpentes, Elapidae). J. Herpetol. 12:1–11.
1984*   Scutellation variation in *Opheodrys aestivus*. Bull. Florida St. Mus. Biol. Sci. 29:153–170.

Grogan, W. L., Jr.
1971   Notes on hatchling mole snakes, *Lampropeltis calligaster rhombomaculata* Holbrook, in Maryland. Bull. Maryland Herpetol. Soc. 7:42.
1974a   Effects of accidental envenomation from the saliva of the eastern hognose snake, *Heterodon platyrhinos*. Herpetologica 30:248–249.
1974b   Notes on *Lampropeltis calligaster rhombomaculata* and *Rana virgatipes*. Bull. Maryland Herpetol. Soc. 10:33–34.
1975   A Maryland hibernaculum of northern brown snakes, *Storeria d. dekayi*. Bull. Maryland Herpetol. Soc. 11:27.

Groves, F.
1957   Eggs and young of the corn snake in Maryland. Herpetologica 13:79–80.
1960   The eggs and young of *Drymarchon corais couperi*. Copeia 1960:51–53.
1961   Notes in two large broods of *Haldea v. valeriae*. (Baird & Girard). Herpetologica 17:71.

BIBLIOGRAPHY

1969   Some reptile breeding records at Baltimore Zoo. Intern. Zoo Yrbk. 9:17–20.

1978   A case of twinning in the ringneck snake, *Diadophis punctatus edwardsi*. Bull. Maryland Herpetol. Soc. 14:48–49.

Groves, J. D.

1967   Notes on albinism in *Elaphe g. guttata*. Bull. Maryland Herpetol. Soc. 3:26–28.

1970   A record size for the northern brown snake, *Storeria dekayi dekayi*. Bull. Maryland Herpetol. Soc. 6:56.

1976   A note on the eggs and young of the smooth green snake, *Opheodrys vernalis* in Maryland. Bull. Maryland Herpetol. Soc. 12:131–132.

1977   Aquatic behavior in the northern copperhead, *Agkistron contortrix mokasen*. Bull. Maryland Herpetol. Soc. 13:114–115.

Groves, J. D., and R. J. Assetto

1976   *Lampropeltis triangulum elapsoides*. Herp Review 7:114.

Groves, J. D., and P. S. Sachs

1973   Eggs and young of the scarlet king snake, *Lampropeltis triangulum elapsoides*. J. Herpetol. 7:389–390.

Guidry, E. V.

1953   Herpetological notes from southeastern Texas. Herpetologica 9:49–56.

Guilday, J. E.

1962   The Pleistocene local fauna of the Natural Chimneys, Augusta County, Virginia. Ann. Carnegie Mus. 36:87–122.

Guillette, L. J., Jr., and W. P. Sullivan

1983   *Coluber constrictor flaviventris* (Eastern Yellowbelly Racer). Reproduction. Herp Review 14:19.

Gunther, A.

1858   Catalogue of colubrine snakes in the collection of the British Museum. London. 281 p.

Guthrie, J. E.

1930   Color dimorphism in Graham's watersnake, *Natrix grahamii* (Baird and Girard). Copeia 1930:39.

1932   Snakes versus birds; birds versus snakes. Wilson Bull. 44:88–101.

Gutzke, W. H. N., G. L. Paukstis and L. L. McDaniel

1985   Skewed sex ratios for adult and hatchling bullsnakes, *Pituophis melanoleucus*, in Nebraska. Copeia 1985:649–652.

Haast, W. E., and R. Anderson

1981   Complete guide to snakes of Florida. Phoenix Publ. Co., Inc., Miami, Florida. 139 p.

Haggerty, T.

1981   Rat snake preys on nestlings of rough–winged swallow and common grackle. Chat 45:77.

Hahn, D. E., and L. D. Wilson

1966   Variation in two broods of *Farancia abacura reinwardti* Schlegel (Serpentes: Colubridae) from Louisiana. J. Ohio Herpetol. Soc. 5:159–160.

Hall, R. J.

1969   Ecological observations on Graham's watersnake (*Regina grahami* Baird and Girard). Amer. Midl. Natur. 81:156–163.

Haller, R.

1971   The diamondback rattlesnakes. Herpetology 3(3):1–34.

Hallowell, E.

1852*   Descriptions of new species of reptiles inhabiting North America. Proc. Acad. Natur. Sci. Philadelphia 6:177–182.

1857*   Notice of a collection of reptiles from Kansas and Nebraska, presented to the Academy of Natural Sciences by Dr. Hammond, U. S. A. Proc. Acad. Natur. Sci. Philadelphia, 1856:241.

Halpern, M., and N. Frumin

1979   Roles of the vomeronasal and olfactory systems in prey attack and feeding in adult garter snakes. Physiol. Behav. 22:1183–1189.

Halpert, A. P., W. R. Garstka, and D. Crews

1982   Sperm transport and storage and its relation to the annual sexual cycle of the female red–sided garter snake, *Thamnophis sirtalis parietalis*. J. Morph. 174:149–159.

Halpin, Z. T.

1983   Naturally occurring encounters between black–tailed prairie dogs (*Cynomys ludovicianus*) and snakes. Amer. Midl. Natur. 109:50–54.

Haluska, F., and P. Alberch
1983   The cranial development of *Elaphe obsoleta* (Ophidia, Colubridae). J. Morph. 178:37–55.

Hamilton, W. J., Jr.
1947   Hibernation of the lined snake. Copeia 1947:209–210.
1951a   Notes on the food and reproduction of the Pelee Island water snake, *Natrix sipedon insularum* Conant and Clay. Can. Field–Natur. 65:64–65.
1951b   The food and feeding behavior of the garter snake in New York State. Amer. Midl. Natur. 46:385–390.

Hamilton, W. J., Jr., and J. A. Pollack
1955   The food of some crotalid snakes from Fort Benning, Georgia. Natur. Hist. Misc. (140):1–4.
1956   The food of some colubrid snakes from Fort Benning, Georgia. Ecology 37:519–526.

Hanebrink, E., and W. Byrd
1986   Species composition and diversity of water snake (*Nerodia* sp.) populations in northeastern Arkansas. Bull. Chicago Herpetol. Soc. 21:72–78.

Harclerode, J., N. A. Underwood, and H. Vallowe
1971   Effect of temperature on the thyroid physiology of the watersnake, *Natrix rhombifera*. Proc. Pennsylvania Acad. Sci. 45:93–97.

Hardy, L. M.
1971   A comparison of karyotypes of the snake genera *Virginia* Baird and Girard and *Storeria* Baird and Girard from northeastern Louisiana. SWANEWS 971:12.

Hardy, L. M., and C. J. Cole
1968   Morphological variation in a population of the snake *Tantilla gracilis* Baird and Girard. Univ. Kansas Publ. Mus. Natur. Hist. 17:613–629.

Harlan, R.
1827*   Genera of North American Reptilia and a synopsis of the species. J. Acad. Natur. Sci. Philadelphia (1) 5:317–372.

Harris, H. H., Jr.
1965   Case reports of two dusky pigmy rattlesnake bites (*Sistrurus miliarius barbouri*). Bull. Maryland Herpetol. Soc. 2:8–10.

Harris, H. S., Jr., and R. S. Simmons
1978   A preliminary account of the rattlesnakes with the descriptions of four new subspecies. Bull. Maryland Herpetol. Soc. 14:105–211.

Harrison, H. H.
1949–
1950   Pennsylvania reptiles and amphibians. Pennsylvania Fish. Comm., Harrisburg. 23 p.
1971   The world of the snake. Lippincott, New York. 160 p.

Harrison, M. B.
1933   The significance of knobbed anal keels in the garter snake, *Thamnophis sirtalis sirtalis* (Linnaeus). Copeia 1933:1–3.

Hart, D. R.
1979   Niche relationships of *Thamnophis radix haydeni* and *Thamnophis sirtalis parietalis* in the Interlake District of Manitoba. Tulane Stud. Zool. Bot. 21:125–140.

Hartwig, S. H.
1966   Rattlesnakes are where and when you find them. J. Ohio Herpetol. Soc. 5:163.

Hawley, A. W. L., and M. Aleksiuk
1975   Thermal regulation of spring mating behavior, in the red–sided garter snake (*Thamnophis sirtalis parietalis*). Can. J. Zool. 53:768–776.
1976a   The influence of photoperiod and temperature on seasonal testicular recrudescence in the red–sided garter snake (*Thamnophis sirtalis parietalis*). Comp. Biochem. Physiol. 53A:215–221.
1976b   Sexual receptivity in the female red–sided garter snake (*Thamnophis sirtalis parietalis*). Copeia 1976:401–404.

Hay, O. P.
1892*   Descriptions of a supposed new species of *Storeria* from Florida, *Storeria victa*. Science 19:199.
1917   Vertebrates mostly from stratus No. 3 at Vero, Florida; together with the descriptions of a new species. Ann. Rep. Florida Geol. Surv. 9:43–68.

Hayes, M. P.
1985   *Coluber constrictor priapus* (Southern Black Racer). Food. Herp Review 16:78.

Haywood, C. A., and R. W. Harris
1972   Fight between rock squirrel and bullsnake. Texas J. Sci. 22:427.

Heatwole, H., and L. L. Getz
1960   Studies on the amphibians and reptiles of Mud Lake Bog in southern Michigan. Jack–Pine Warbler 38:107–112.

Hebrard, J. J., and R. C. Lee
1981   A large collection of brackish water snakes from the central Atlantic Coast of Florida. Copeia 1981:886–889.

Hebrard, J. J., and H. R. Mushinsky
1978   Habitat use by five sympatric water snakes in a Louisiana swamp. Herpetologica 34:306–311.

Heckrotte, C.
1962   The effect of the environmental factors in the locomotory activity of the plains garter snake (*Thamnophis radix radix*). Anim. Behav. 10:193–207.
1967   Relations of body temperature, size, and crawling speed of the common garter snake, *Thamnophis s. sirtalis*. Copeia 1967:759–763.
1975   Temperature and light effects on the circadean rhythm and locomotory activity of the plains garter snake (*Thamnophis radix haydeni*). J. Interdiscipl. Cycle Res. 6:279–290.

Hedges, S. B.
1977   The presence of the scarlet kingsnake, *Lampropeltis triangulum elapsoides* Holbrook (Reptilia, Serpentes, Colubridae), in the Florida Keys. Herp Review 8:125–126.

Hegeman, G.
1961   Enzymatic constitution of *Alsophis* saliva and its biological implications. Breviora (134):1–8.

Heinrich, M. L., and H. E. Klaassen
1985   Side dominance in constricting snakes. J. Herpetol. 19:531–533.

Heller, S. B., and M. Halpern
1981   Laboratory observations on conspecific and congeneric scent trailing in garter snakes (*Thamnophis*). Behav. Neur. Biol. 33:372–377.
1982a   Laboratory observations of aggregative behavior of garter snakes, *Thamnophis sirtalis*. J. Comp. Physiol. Psychol. 96:967–983.
1982b   Laboratory observations of aggregative behavior of garter snakes, *Thamnophis sirtalis*: roles of the visual, olfactory, and vomeronasal senses. J. Comp. Physiol. Psychol. 96:984–999.

Hellman, R. E., and S. R. Telford, Jr.
1956   Notes on a large number of red-bellied mudsnakes, *Farancia a. abacura*, from Northcentral Florida. Copeia 1956:257–258.

Henderson, R. W.
1970   Feeding behavior, digestion and water requirements of *Diadophis punctatus arnyi* Kennicott. Herpetologica 26:520–526.

Henderson, R. W., M. H. Binder, R. A. Sajdak, and J. A. Buday
1980   Aggregating behavior and exploitation of subterranean habitat by gravid eastern milksnakes (*Lampropeltis t. triangulum*). Milwaukee Publ. Mus. Contrib. Biol. Geol. (32):1–9.

Hensley, M.
1962   Another snake recorded in the diet of the bullfrog. Herpetologica 18:141.

Herald, E. S.
1949   Effects of DDT–oil solutions upon amphibians and reptiles. Herpetologica 5:117–120.

Herman, D. W.
1979   Captive reproduction in the scarlet kingsnake, *Lampropeltis triangulum elapsoides* (Holbrook). Herp Review 10:115.
1983   *Cemophora coccinea copei* (northern scarlet snake). Coloration and reproduction. Herp Review 14:119.

Herreid, C. F., II
1961   Snakes as predators of bats. Herpetologica 17:271–272.

Herrington, R. E.
1974   Notes on a brood of *Coluber constrictor helvigularis* Auffenberg. Herp Review 5:38–39.

Hess, J. B., and W. D. Klimstra
1975   Summer foods of the diamond-backed water snake (*Natrix rhombifera*), from Reelfoot Lake, Tennessee. Trans. Illinois St. Acad. Sci. 68:285–288.

Hibbard, C. W., and W. W. Dalquest
1967   Fossils from the Seymour Formation of Knox and Baylor counties, Texas, and their bearing on the late Kansas climate of the region. Contr. Mus. Paleont., Univ. Michigan 21:1–66.

Highton, R.
1956   Systematics and variation of the endemic Florida snake genus *Stilosoma*. Bull. Florida St. Mus. Biol. Sci. 1:73–96.
1976   *Stilosoma, S. extenuatum*. Catalog. Amer. Amphib. Rept. 183:1–2.

Hisaw, F. L., and H. K. Gloyd
1926   The bull snake as a natural enemy of injurious rodents. J. Mammal. 7:200–205.

Hoff, J. G.
1975   Clapper rail feeding on water snake. Wilson Bull. 87:112.

Hoffman, L. H.
1970a   Placentation in the garter snake *Thamnophis sirtalis*. J. Morph. 131:57–88.
1970b   Observations on gestation in the garter snake, *Thamnophis sirtalis sirtalis*. Copeia 1970:779–780.

Hoffman, L. H., and W. A. Wimsatt
1972   Histochemical and electron microscope observations on the sperm receptacles in the garter snake oviduct. Amer. J. Anat. 134:71–95.

Holbrook, J. E.
1836*–
1842   North American herpetology; or, a description of the reptiles inhabiting the United States. Vol. 1–3. J. Dobson, Philadelphia.

Holman, J. A.
1958a   Notes on reptiles and amphibians from Florida caves. Herpetologica 14:179–180.
1958b   The Pleistocene herpetofauna of Saber-tooth Cave, Citrus County, Florida. Copeia 1958:276–280.
1959   Amphibians and reptiles from the Pleistocene (Illinoian) of Williston, Florida. Copeia 1959:96–102.
1960a   Physiographic provinces and distribution of some reptiles and amphibians in Johnson County, Indiana. Copeia 1960:56–58.

1960b   Reproduction in a pair of corn snakes, *Elaphe guttata guttata*. Copeia 1960:239.
1962   A Texas Pleistocene herpetofauna. Copeia 1962:255–261.
1963   Late Pleistocene amphibians and reptiles of the Clear Creek and Ben Franklin Local Faunas of Texas. J. Grad. Res. Center 31:152–167.
1969   The Pleistocene amphibians and reptiles of Texas. Publ. Michigan St. Univ. Mus. (Biol.). 4:163–192.
1977   The Pleistocene (Kansan) herpetofauna of Cumberland Cave, Maryland. Ann. Carnegie Mus. Natur. Hist. 46:157–172.
1979   A review of North American tertiary snakes. Publ. Mus. Michigan St. Univ., Paleontol. Ser 1:201–260.
1981   A review of North American Pleistocene snakes. Publ. Mus. Michigan St. Univ., Paleontol. Ser. 1:261–306.
1982   A fossil snake (*Elaphe vulpina*) from a Pliocene ash bed in Nebraska. Trans. Nebraska Acad. Sci. 10:37–42.
1986   Butler Spring herpetofauna of Kansas (Pleistocene: Illinoian) and its climatic significance. J. Herpetol. 20:568–570.

Holman, J. A., and W. H. Hill
1961   A mass unidirectional movement of *Natrix sipedon pictiventris*. Copeia 1961:498–499.

Holman, J. A., and R. L. Richards
1981   Late Pleistocene occurrence in southern Indiana of the smooth green snake, *Opheodrys vernalis*. J. Herpetol. 15:123–124.

Holt, E. G.
1919   Coluber swallowing a stone. Copeia (76):99–100.

Horton, R. T.
1968   *Seminatrix pygaea* in Alabama. J. Herpetol. 1:94–95.

House, J. H.
1970   Two possible instances of premature hibernation. Bull. Philadelphia Herpetol. Soc. 18:47.

Hudnall, J. A.
1979   Surface activity and horizontal movements in a marked population of *Sistrurus miliarius barbouri*. Bull. Maryland Herpetol. Soc. 15:134–138.

Hudson, R. G.
1947   Ophiophagous young black snakes. Herpetologica 3:178.

Huheey, J. E.
1958   Some feeding habits of the eastern hog-nosed snake. Herpetologica 14:68.
1959*   Distribution and variation in the glossy water snake, *Natrix rigida* (Say). Copeia 1959:303–311.
1970   Behavioral notes on mockingbirds and black rat snake. Chat 34:23.

Huheey, J. E., and W. M. Palmer
1962   The eastern glossy watersnake, *Regina rigida rigida*, in North Carolina. Herpetologica 18:140–141.

Huheey, J. E., and A. Stupka
1967   Amphibians and reptiles of Great Smoky Mountains National Park. Univ. Tennessee Press, Knoxville. 98 p.

Hulme, J. H.
1952   Observation of a snake bite by a cottonmouth moccasin. Herpetologica 8:51.

Hutchison, R. H.
1929   On the incidence of snake bite poisioning in the United States and the results of the newer methods of treatment. Bull. Antivenin Inst. Amer. 3:43–57.

Imler, R. H.
1945   Bullsnakes and their control on a Nebraska wildlife refuge. J. Wildl. Mgt. 9:265–273.

Ippoliti, S.
1980   Cannibalism in a corn snake hatchling (*Elaphe guttata*). Bull. Philadelphia Herpetol. Soc. 28:14.

Irvine, A. B., and H. D. Prange
1976   Dive and breathhold metabolism of the brown water snake, *Natrix taxispilota*. Comp. Biochem. Physiol. 55A: 61–67.

Irvine, F. R.
1954   Snakes as food for man. British J. Herpetol. 1:183–189.

Iverson, J. B.
1975   Notes on Nebraska reptiles. Trans. Kansas Acad. Sci. 78:51–62.
1978   Reproductive notes on Florida snakes. Florida Sci. 41:201–207.

Jackson, D. L., and R. Franz
1981   Ecology of the eastern coral snake (*Micrurus fulvius*) in northern peninsular Florida. Herpetologica 37:213–228.

Jackson, J. A.
1970   Predation of a black rat snake on yellow-shafted flicker nestlings. Wilson Bull. 82:329–330.
1974   Gray rat snakes vs. red cockaded woodpecker: predator-prey adaptation. Auk 91:342–347.
1976   Relative climbing tendencies of gray (*Elaphe obsoleta spiloides*) and black rat snakes (*E. o. obsoleta*). Herpetologica 32:359–361.
1977   Notes on the behavior of the grey rat snake (*Elaphe obsoleta spiloides*). J. Mississippi Acad. Sci. 22:94–96.

Jackson, J. A., and O. H. Dakin
1982   An encounter between a nesting barn owl and a gray rat snake. Raptor Res. 16:60–61.

Jackson, J. F.
1961   Simultaneous constriction habit in *Elaphe obsoleta spiloides*. Herpetologica 17:67–68.
1971   Intraspecific predation in *Coluber constrictor*. J. Herpetol. 5:196.

Jackson, J. F., W. Ingram, III, and H. W. Campbell
1976   The dorsal pigmentation pattern of snakes as an antipredator strategy: a multivariate approach. Amer. Natur. 110:1029–1053.

Jackson, J. F., and D. L. Martin
1980   Caudal luring in the dusky pygmy rattlesnake, *Sistrurus miliarius barbouri*. Copeia 1980:926–927.

Jackson, J. J.
1983   Snakes of the Southeastern United States. Publ. Sect., Georgia Extension Serv. 112 p.

Jackson, M. K.
1977   Histology and distribution of cutaneous touch corpuscles in some leptotyphlopid and colubrid snakes (Reptilia, Serpentes). J. Herpetol. 11:7–15.

Jackson, M. K., and H. W. Reno
1975   Comparative skin structure of some fossorial and subfossorial leptotyphlopid and colubrid snakes. Herpetologica 31:350–359.

Jacob, J. S.
1981   Population density and ecological requirements of the western pygmy rattlesnake in Tennessee. U. S. Fish Wildl. Serv., Denver. 45 p.

Jacob, J. S., and S. L. Carroll
1982   Effect of temperature on the heart rate–ventilatory response in the copperhead, *Agkistrodon contortrix*, (Reptilia: Viperidae). J. Therm. Biol. 7:117–120.

Jacobs, J. S., and H. S. McDonald
1975   Temperature preference and electrocardiography of *Elaphe obsoleta* (Serpentes). Comp. Biochem. Physiol. 52A:591–594.
1976   Diving bradycardia in four species of North American aquatic snakes. Comp. Biochem. Physiol. 53A:69–72.

Jacobson, E. R., and W. G. Whitford
1970   The effect of acclimation on physiological responses to temperature in the snakes *Thamnophis proximus* and *Natrix rhombifera*. Comp. Biochem. Physiol. 35:439–449.

Jacobson, J. C., and N. Rothman
1961   A case of second parity in the eastern garter snake. Bull. Philadelphia Herpetol. Soc. 9(4):19.

Jan, G.
1862   Enumerazione sistematica delle specie d'ofidi del grupo Calamaridae. Archiv. Zool., Anat. Fisiol. 2(1):1–76.
1863*   Enumerazione sistematica degli ofidi appartenenti al gruppo Coronellidae. Arch. Zool. Anat. Fisiol. 2:213–330.

Jayne, B. C.
1985   Swimming in constricting (*Elaphe g. guttata*) and nonconstricting (*Nerodia fasciata pictiventris*) colubrid snakes. Copeia 1985:195–208.
1986   Kinematics of terrestrial snake locomotion. Copeia 1986:915–927.

Jenner, J. V., and H. G. Dowling
1985   Taxonomy of American xenodontine snakes: the tribe Pseudoboini. Herpetologica 41:161–172.

Johnson, B. D., J. Hoppe, R. Rogers, and H. L. Stahnke
1968   Characteristics of venom from the rattlesnake *Crotalus horridus atricaudatus*. J. Herpetol. 2:107–112.

Johnson, J. E., Jr.
1948   Copperhead in a tree. Herpetologica 4:214.

Johnson, L. F., J. S. Jacob, and P. Torrence
1982   Annual testicular and androgenic cycles of the cottonmouth (*Agkistrodon piscivorus*) in Alabama. Herpetologica 38:16–25.

Johnson, R. G.
1955   The adaptive and phylogenetic significance of vertebral form in snakes. Evolution 9:367–388.

Johnson, R. M.
1950   Mating activities between two subspecies of *Elaphe obsoleta*. Herpetologica 6:42–44.

Johnson, R. M., and J. F. Webb
1964   Intergradation in the ringneck snake, *Diadophis punctatus* Linnaeus, in northeastern Tennessee. J. Tennessee Acad. Sci. 39:99–102.

Jones, J. M.
1976   Variations of venom proteins in *Agkistrodon* snakes from North America. Copeia 1976:558–562.

Jones, J. M., and P. M. Burchfield
1971   Relationship of specimen size to venom extracted from the copperhead, *Agkistrodon contortrix*. Copeia 1971:162–163.

Jones, L.
1976a   Field data on *Heterodon p. platyrhinos* in Prince George's County, Maryland. Bull. Maryland Herpetol. Soc. 12:29–32.
1976b   A large brood for a Maryland *Storeria dekayi dekayi*. Bull. Maryland Herpetol. Soc. 12:102.

Jordon, D. R.
1967   The occurrence of *Thamnophis sirtalis* and *T. radix* in the prairie–forest ecotone west of Itasca State Park, Minnesota. Herpetologica 23:304–308.

Jordon, R., Jr.
1970   Death–feigning in a captive red-bellied snake, *Storeria occipitomacu–lata* (Storer). Herpetologica 26:466–468.

BIBLIOGRAPHY

Judd, W. W.

1955   Observations on the habitat and food of the queen snake, *Natrix septemvittata*, at London, Ontario. Can. Field–Natur. 69:167–168.

1960   Observations on the habitat, food, reproductive state and intestinal parasites of the smooth green snake at London, Ontario. Can. Field–Natur. 74:100–106.

Kamb, A. H.

1978   Unusual feeding behavior of the red milk snake, *Lampropeltis triangulum syspila* (Lacepede). Trans. Kansas Acad. Sci. 81:273.

Kapus, E. J.

1964   Anatomical evidence for *Heterodon* being poisonous. Herpetologica 20:137–138.

Kardong, K. V.

1974   Kinesis of the jaw apparatus during the strike in the cottonmouth snake, *Agkistrodon piscivorus*. Forma Functio 7:327–354.

1977   Kinesis of the jaw apparatus during swallowing in the cottonmouth snake, *Agkistrodon piscivorus*. Copeia 1977:338–348.

1979   "Protovipers" and the evolution of snake fangs. Evolution 33:433–443.

1982a   The evolution of the venom apparatus in snakes from colubrids to viperids and elapids. Mem. Inst. Butantan 46:105–118.

1982b   Comparative study of changes in prey capture behavior of the cottonmouth (*Agkistrodon piscivorus*) and Egyptian cobra (*Naja haje*). Copeia 1982:337–343.

Kats, L. B.

1986   *Nerodia sipedon* (Northern water snake). Feeding. Herp Review 17:61, 64.

Kauffeld, C.

1957   Snakes and snake hunting. Hanover House, Garden City, New York. 266 p.

1961   Massasauga Land. Bull. Philadelphia Herpetol. Soc. 9(3):7–13.

1969   Snakes: the keeper and the kept. Doubleday, New York. 248 p.

Kaufman, G. A., and J. W. Gibbons

1975   Weight–length relationships in thirteen species of snakes in the Southeastern United States. Herpetologica 31:31–37.

Keegan, H. L.

1944   Indigo snakes feeding upon poisonous snakes. Copeia 1944:59.

Keenlyne, K. D.

1972   Sexual differences in feeding habits of *Crotalus horridus horridus*. J. Herpetol. 6:234–237.

1978   Reproductive cycles in two species of rattlesnakes. Amer. Midl. Natur. 100:368–375.

Keenlyne, K. D., and J. R. Beer

1973   Food habits of *Sistrurus catenatus catenatus*. J. Herpetol. 7:382–384.

Keiser, E. D., Jr.

1958   The green water snake in Illinois. Herpetologica 13:260.

1970   Sexual dimorphism and ontogenetic variation in the haemapophyses of ophidian postcloacal vertebrae. Herpetologica 26:331–334.

1971   The poisonous snakes of Louisiana and the emergency treatment of their bites. Louisiana Wildlife Fish. Comm. 16 p.

Keiser, E. D., Jr., and L. D. Wilson

1979   Checklist and key to the herpetofauna of Louisiana, 2nd ed. Lafayette Natur. Hist. Mus. Tech. Bull. (1):1–49.

Keith, J., R. Lee, and D. Chiszar

1985   Spatial orientation by cottonmouths (*Agkistrodon piscivorus*) after detecting prey. Bull. Maryland Herpetol. Soc. 21:145–149.

Kelly, H. A., A. W. Davis, and H. C. Robertson

1936   Snakes of Maryland Natur. Hist. Soc. Maryland, Baltimore. 103 p.

Kennedy, J. L.

1978   Field observations on courtship and copulation in the eastern king snake and the four-lined rat snake. Herpetologica 34:51–52.

Kennedy, J. P.

1959   A minimum egg complement for the western mud snake, *Farancia abacura reinwardti*. Copeia 1959:71.

1961   Eggs of the eastern hognose snake, *Heterodon platyrhinos*. Texas J. Sci. 13:416–422.

1964   Natural history notes on some snakes of eastern Texas. Texas J. Sci. 16:210–215.

Kennicott, R.
1856*   Description of a new snake from Illinois. Proc. Acad. Natur. Sci. Philadelphia 8:95–96.
1859*   Notes on *Coluber calligaster* of Say, and a description of a new species of serpents in the collection of the North Western University of Evanston, Ill. Proc. Acad. Natur. Sci. Philadelphia 11:98–100.
1860*   Descriptions of new species of North American serpents in the museum of the Smithsonian Institution, Washington. Proc. Acad. Natur. Sci. Philadelphia 12:328–338.

Kephart, D. G.
1982   Microgeographic variation in the diets of garter snakes. Oecologia (Berlin) 52:287–291.

Kephart, D. G., and S. J. Arnold
1982   Garter snake diets in a fluctuating environment: a seven year study. Ecology 63:1232–1236.

Kerfoot, W. C.
1969   Selection of an appropriate index for the study of variability of lizard and snake body scale counts. Systematic Zool. 18:53–62.

Kieve, R. J.
1979   Growth rate of a black rat snake (*Elaphe o. obsoleta*). Bull. Philadelphia Herpetol. Soc. 27:8.

Kilbourne, C. R.
1957   Rough green snake (*Opheodrys aestivus*). Nature Mag. 50:317–318.

Kilpatrick, C. W., and E. G. Zimmerman
1973   Karyology of North American natricine snakes (Family Colubridae) of the genera *Natrix* and *Regina*. Can. J. Genet. Cytol. 15:355–361.

King, R. B.
1986   Population ecology of the Lake Erie water snake, *Nerodia sipedon insularum*. Copeia 1986:757–772.

Kirk, V. M.
1969   An observation of a predator-escape technique practiced by a worm snake *Potamophis striatulus* (L.). Turtox News 47:44.

Kirn, A. J., W. L. Burger, and H. M. Smith
1949   The subspecies of *Tantilla gracilis*. Amer. Midl. Natur. 42:238–251.

Kitchell, J. F.
1969   Thermophilic and thermophobic responses of snakes in a thermal gradient. Copeia 1969:189–191.

Klauber, L. M.
1936–
1940   A statistical study of the rattlesnakes. Parts I–VII. Trans. San Diego Soc. Natur. Hist. nos. 1–6.
1943   Tail-length differences in snakes with notes on sexual dimorphism and the coefficient of divergence. Bull. Zool. Soc. San Diego 18:1–60.
1956   *Agkistrodon* or *Ancistrodon*? Copeia 1956:258–259.
1972   Rattlesnakes: their habits, life histories, and influence on mankind, 2nd ed. Univ. California Press, Berkeley. 1533 p.

Klimstra, W. D.
1958   Some observations on snake activities and populations. Ecology 39:232–239.
1959a   Food habits of the cottonmouth in southern Illinois. Natur. Hist. Misc. (168):1–8.
1959b   Food habits of the yellow-bellied king snake in southern Illinois. Herpetologica 15:1–5.
1959c   Foods of the racer, *Coluber constrictor*, in southern Illinois. Copeia 1959:210–214.

Klingener, D.
1957   A marking study of the short-headed garter snake in Pennsylvania. Herpetologica 13:100.

Klynstra, F. B.
1957   *Thamnophis sirtalis* Linne. Lacerta 15:26–27.
1959   Pas op met "Ongevaarlijke" slangen. Lacerta 17:31.

Knable, A. E.
1970   Food habits of red fox (*Vulpes fulva*) in Union County, Illinois. Trans. Illinois St. Acad. Sci. 63:359–365.

Knapik, P. G., and J. R. Hodgson.
1986   *Storeria occipitomculata* (redbelly snake). Predation. Herp Review 17:22.

Knepton, J. C., Jr.
1951   Reproduction by a king snake *Lampropeltis getulus getulus* Linnaeus. Herpetologica 7:85–89.

Knight, J. L.
1986   Variation in snout morphology in the North American snake *Pituophis melanoleucus* (Serpentes: Colubridae). J. Herpetol. 20:77–79.

Knight, J. L., and R. K. Loraine
1986   Notes on turtle egg predation by *Lampropeltis getulus* (Linnaeus) (Reptilia: Colubridae) on the Savannah River Plant, South Carolina. Brimleyana (12):1–4.

Kobel, H. R.
1967   Morphometrische kuryotypunalyse einger Schlangenarten. Genetica 38:1–31.

Kochva, E., and C. Gans
1966   Histology and histochemistry of venom glands of some crotaline snakes. Copeia 1966:506–515.

Kofron, C. P.
1978   Foods and habitats of aquatic snakes (Reptilia, Serpentes) in a Louisiana swamp. J. Herpetol. 12:543–554.
1979a   Reproduction of aquatic snakes in south-central Louisana. Herpetologica 35:44–50.
1979b   Female reproductive biology of the brown snake, *Storeria dekayi*, in Louisiana. Copeia 1979: 463–466.
1980   Sperm of the coachwhip *Masticophis flagellum* (Serpentes: Colubridae), and a method of preparation for scanning electron microsopy of vertebrate spermatozoa. Southwest. Natur. 25:118–120.

Kofron, C. P., and J. R. Nixon
1980   Observations on aquatic colubrid snakes in Texas. Southwest. Natur. 25:107–109.

Korschgen, L. J.
1970   Soil–food–chain–pesticide wildlife relationships in aldrin–treated fields. J. Wildl. Mgt. 34:186–199.

Krans, F., and G. W. Schuett
1982   A herpetofaunal study of the coastal zone of northwestern Ohio. Kirtlandia 36:21–54.

Krempels, D. M.
1984   Near infrared reflectance by coral snakes: aposematic coloration? Progr. 6th Ann. Meet. Amer. Soc. Ichthyol. Herpetol. :142.

Krohmer, R. W., and R. D. Aldridge
1985a   Male reproductive cycle of the lined snake (*Tropidoclonion lineatum*). Herpetologica 41:33–38.
1985b   Female reproductive cycle of the lined snake (*Tropidoclonion lineatum*). Herpetologica 41:39–44.

Kroll, J. C.
1976   Feeding adaptations of hognose snakes. Southwest. Natur. 20:537–557.
1977   Self–wounding while death feigning by western hognose snakes (*Heterodon nasicus*). Copeia 1977:372–373.

Kroll, J. C., D. G. Zahradnik, and R. Ford
1973   Thermogenic cycles in *Opheodrys vernalis* and *Elaphe obsoleta* (Serpentes: Colubridae). Proc. West Virginia Acad. Sci. 45:77–81.

Kubie, J. L., J. Cohen, and M. Halpern
1978   Shedding enhances the sexual attractiveness of oestrodiol treated garter snakes and their untreated penmates. Anim. Behav. 26:562–570.

Kubie, J. L., and M. Halpern
1975   Laboratory observations of trailing behavior in garter snakes. J. Comp. Physiol. Psychol. 89:667–674.
1978   Garter snake trailing behavior: effects of varying prey–extract concentration and mode of prey–extract presentation. J. Comp. Physiol. Psychol. 92:362–373.
1979   Chemical senses involved in garter snake prey trailing. J. Comp. Physiol. Psychol. 93:648–667.

Kubie, J. L., A. Vagvolgyi, and M. Halpern
1978   Roles of the vomeronasal and olfactory systems in courtship behavior of male garter snakes. J. Comp. Physiol. Psychol. 92:627–641.

Lacepede, B. G. E.
1788*–
1789   Histoire naturelle des serpens. 2 vols. Paris.

Lachner, E. A.
1942   An aggregation of snakes and salamanders during hibernation. Copeia 1942:262–263.

Lagler, K. R., and J. C. Salyer, II
1945   Influence of availability on the feeding habits of the common garter snake. Copeia 1945:159–162.

Lamson, G. H.
1935   The reptiles of Connecticut. Connecticut St. Geol. Natur. Hist. Surv. Bull. (54):1–35.

Landreth, H. F.
1972   Physiological responses of *Elaphe obsoleta* and *Pituophis melanoleucus* to lowered ambient temperatures. Herpetologica 28:376–380.

Lang, J. W.
1969   Hibernation and movements of *Storeria occipitomaculata* in northern Minnesota. J. Herpetol. 3:196–197.

Langlois, T. H.
1924   Notes on some Michigan snakes. Pap. Michigan Acad. Sci. Arts Let. 4:605–610.
1964   Amphibians and reptiles of the Erie Islands. Ohio J. Sci. 64:11–25.

LaPointe, J.
1953   Case report of a bite from the massasauga, *Sistrurus catenatus catenatus*. Copeia 1953:128–129.

Laposha, N. A., J. S. Parmerlee, Jr., R. Powell, and D. D. Smith
1985   *Nerodia erythrogaster transversa* (blotched water snake). Reproduction. Herp Review 16:81.

Lardie, R. L.
1976   Large centipede eaten by a western massasauga. Bull. Oklahoma Herpetol. Soc. 1:40.
1978   Longevity record for the eastern hognose snake. Bull. Oklahoma Herpetol. Soc. 3:57.

Latreille, P. A.
1801*   *In* C. S. Sonnini and P. A. Latreillle, Histoire naturelle des reptiles.... Vol. 3. Deterville, Paris. 335 p.

Laughlin, H. E.
1959   Stomach contents of some aquatic snakes from Lake McAlester, Pittsburgh County, Oklahoma. Texas J. Sci. 11:83–85.

Lawler, H. E.
1977   The status of *Drymarchon corais couperi* (Holbrook), the eastern indigo snake, in the southeastern United States. Herp Review 8:76–79.

Lawson, R.
1982   Biochemical systematics of the Thamnophiini: the genera *Nerodia* and *Regina*. Prgr. Jt. Meet. Soc. Stud. Amphib. Rept., Herpetologists' League, Raleigh, North Carolina:84.
1985   *Opheodrys vernalis* (smooth green snake). Reproduction. Herp Review 14:20.

Layne, J. N., and T. M. Steiner
1984   Sexual dimorphism in occurrence of keeled dorsal scales in the eastern indigo snake (*Drymarchon corais couperi*). Copeia 1984:776–778.

Layne, J. N., T. J. Walsh, and P. Meylan
1986   New records for the mole snake, *Lampropeltis calligaster*, in Peninsular Florida. Florida Sci. 49:171–175.

Lazell, J.
1971   Black pine snake. Massachusetts Audubon 56:32–35.

Lazell, J. D. Jr., and J. A. Musick
1973   The kingsnake, *Lampropeltis getulus sticticeps*, and the ecology of the Outer Banks of North Carolina. Copeia 1973:497–503.
1981   Status of the Outer Banks kingsnake, *Lampropeltis getulus sticticeps*. Herp Review 12:7.

Lazell, J. D., Jr., and J. C. T. Nisbet
1972   Snake–eating terns. Man Nature 1972(June):27–29.

LeBuff, C. R., Jr.
1951   The habits of young smooth green snakes (*Opheodrys vernalis*) in captivity. Herpetologica 7:80.
1953   Observations on the eggs and young of *Drymarchon corais couperi*. Herpetologica 9:166.

Lederer, G.
1950   Ein Bastard von *Elaphe guttata* (Linne) male X *Elaphe q. quadrivittata* (Holbrook) female und dessen Ruckdreuzung mit der mutenlicken Ausgansart. Zool. Garten, (Leipzig) 17:235–242.

Lee, D. S.
1967   Eggs and hatchlings of the Florida pine snake, *Pituophis melanoleucus mugitus*. Herpetologica 23:241–142.
1968a   Herpetofauna associated with Central Florida mammals. Herpetologica 24:83–84.
1968b   Springs as hibernation sites for Maryland's herpetofauna. Bull. Maryland Herpetol. Soc. 4:82–83.

Leviton, A. E.
1972   Reptiles and amphibians of North America. Doubleday, New York. 250 p.

Lewke, R. E.
1979   Neck–biting and other aspects of reproductive biology of the Yuma kingsnake (*Lampropeltis getulus*). Herpetologica 35:154–157.

Lillywhite, H. B.
1985   Trailing movements and sexual behavior in *Coluber constrictor*. J. Herpetol. 19:306–308.

Lillywhite, H. B., and R. A. Ackerman
1984   Hydrostatic pressure, shell compliance and permeability to water vapor in flexible–shelled eggs of the colubrid snake *Elaphe obsoleta*. Persp. Vert. Sci. 3:121–135.

Lindsey, P.
1979   Combat behavior in the dusky pygmy rattlesnake, *Sistrurus miliarius barbouri*, in captivity. Herp Review 10:93.

Lindstedt, K. J.
1971   Chemical control of feeding behavior. Comp. Biochem. Physiol. 39A:553–581.

Liner, E. A.
1954   The herpetofauna of Lafayette, Terrebonne and Vermilion parishes, Louisiana. Proc. Louisiana Acad. Sci. 17:65–85.
1977   Letisimulation in *Storeria dekayi limnetes* Anderson. Trans. Kansas Acad. Sci. 80:81–82.

Linnaeus, C.
1758*   Systema naturae...10th Ed. Vol. 1. Stockholm, Sweden. 826 p.
1766*   Systema naturae...12th Ed. Stockholm, Sweden. 532 p.

Linzey, D. W.
1979   Snakes of Alabama. Strode Publ., Inc., Huntsville, Alabama. 136 p.

Linzey, D. W., and M. J. Clifford
1981   Snakes of Virginia. Univ. Press Virginia, Charlottesville. 159 p.

List, J. C., Jr.
1950   Observation on the courtship behavior of *Thamnophis sirtalis sirtalis*. Herpetologica 6:71–74.

List, J. C.
1958   Notes on the skeleton of the blind snake, *Typhlops braminus*. Spolia Zeylan. 28:169–174.

Littlefield, C. D.
1971   An unusual encounter between an American bittern and common garter snake. Murrelet 52:27–28.

Lockwood, R. A.
1954   Food habits of the mole snake. Herpetologica 10:110.

Logier, E. B. S.
1939   The reptiles of Ontario. Royal Ontario Mus. Handbk. (4):1–63.
1958   The snakes of Ontario. Univ. Toronto Press, Toronto. 94 p.

Logier, E. B. S., and G. C. Toner
1961   Check list of amphibians and reptiles of Canada and Alaska. Contrib. Royal Ontario Mus. Zool. Palaeon. (53)1–92.

Lohoefener, R., and R. Altig
1983   Mississippi herpetology. Mississippi St. Univ. Res. Cent. Nat. Space Tech. Lab. Bull. (1):1–66.

Lohrer, F. E.
1980   Eastern coachwhip predation on nestling blue jays. Florida Field Natur. 8:28–29.

Loomis, R. B.
1948   Notes on the herpetology of Adams County, Iowa. Herpetologica 4:121–122.

Lord, J.
1982   Artful dodger. Natur. Canada 11(3):13–16.

Love, W. B.
1978   Observations on the herpetofauna of Key West, Florida, with special emphasis on the rosy rat snake. Bull. Georgia Herpetol. Soc. 4:3–8.

Loveridge, A.
1938   Food of *Micrurus fulvius fulvius*. Copeia 1938:201–202.

Lueth, F. X.
1941   Effects of temperature on snakes. Copeia 1941:125–132.

Lynch, J. D.
1966   Communal egg laying in the pilot blacksnake, *Elaphe obsoleta obsoleta*. Herpetologica 22:305.

Lynch, W.
1978   Death–feigning in the eastern yellow–bellied racer. Blue Jay 36:92–93.
1983   Great balls of snakes. Natur. Hist. 92:64–69.

Lyon, M. W., and C. Bishop
1936   Bite of the prairie rattlesnake *Sistrurus catenatus* Raf. Proc. Indiana Acad. Sci. 45:253–256.

Lysenko, S., and J. E. Gillis
1980   The effect of ingestive status on the thermoregulatory behavior of *Thamnophis sirtalis sirtalis* and *Thamnophis sirtalis parietalis*. J. Herpetol. 14:155–159.

MacCartney, J. M., and P. T. Gregory
1981   Differential susceptibility of sympatric garter snake species to amphibian skin secretions. Amer. Midl. Natur. 106:271–281.

MacMahon, J. A.
1957   Observation on mating in the corn snake, *Elaphe guttata guttata*. Copeia 1957:232.

Mahan, H. D.
1956   Nocturnal predation on song sparrow eggs by milksnake. Wilson Bull. 68:245.

Malnate, E.
1939   A study of the yellow–lipped snake, *Rhadinaea flavilata* (Cope). Zoologica 24:359–366.

Malnate, E. V.
1960   Systematic division and evolution of the colubrid snake genus *Natrix*, with comments on the subfamily Natricinae. Proc. Acad. Natur. Sci. Philadelphia 112:41–71.

Mansueti, R.
1946   Mating of the pilot blacksnake. Herpetologica 3:98–100.

Maple, W. T., and L. P. Orr
1968   Overwintering adaptations of *Sistrurus catenatus* in northeastern Ohio. J. Herpetol. 2:179–180.

Marchisin, A.
1978   Observations on an audiovisual "warning" signal in the pigmy rattlesnake, *Sistrurus miliarius* (Reptilia, Serpentes, Crotalidae). Herp Review 9:92–93.

Marion, K. R.
1980   One–egg twins in a snake, *Elaphe guttata guttata*. Trans. Kansas Acad. Sci. 83:98–100.

Markel, R. G.
1979   The kingsnakes: an annotated checklist. Bull. Chicago Herpetol. Soc. 14:101–116.

Markezich, A.
1962   Ophiophagy in western fox snakes, *Elaphe v. vulpina*. Bull. Philadelphia Herpetol. Soc. 10(4):5.

Martin, D. L.
1984   An instance of sexual defense in the cottonmouth, *Agkistrodon piscivorus*. Copeia 1984:772–774.

Martin, K.
1979   Common garter snake predation on robin nestlings. Can. Field–Natur. 93:70–71.

Martin, W. F., and R. B. Huey
1971   The function of the epiglottis in sound production (hissing) of *Pituophis melanoleucus*. Copeia 1971:752–754.

Martin, W. H.
1981   The timber rattlesnake in the Northeast; its range, past and present. HERP: Bull. New York Herpetol. Soc. 17:15–20.

Martof, B.
1954   Variation in a large litter of gartersnakes, *Thamnophis sirtalis sirtalis*. Copeia 1954:100–105.
1955   Some records of reptiles in Georgia. Copeia 1955:302–305.

Martof, B. S.
1956   Amphibians and reptiles of Georgia, a guide. Univ. Georgia Press, Athens. 94 p.

Martof, B. S., W. M. Palmer, J. R. Bailey, J. R. Harrison III, and J. Dermid
1980   Amphibians and reptiles of the Carolinas and Virginia. Univ. North Carolina Press, Chapel Hill. 264 p.

Marvel, B.
1972   A feeding observation on the yellow-bellied water snake, *Natrix erythrogaster flavigaster*. Bull. Maryland Herpetol. Soc. 8:52.

Marx, H., and G. B. Rabb
1972   Phyletic analysis of fifty characters of advanced snakes. Fieldiana: Zool. 63:1–321.

Mason, R. T., and D. Crews
1985   Female mimicry in garter snakes. Nature 316:59–60.

Mattison, C.
1986   Snakes of the world. Facts on File Publ., New York. 190 p.

Mattlin, R. H.
1946   Snake devours its own slough. Herpetologica 3:122.
1948   Observations on the eggs and young of the eastern fox snake. Herpetologica 4:115–116.

McAllister, C. T.
1985   *Nerodia rhombifera*. Catalog. Amer. Amphib. Rept. 376:1–4.

McAllister, W. H.
1963   Evidence of mild toxicity in the saliva of the hognose snake (*Heterodon*). Herpetologica 19:132–137.

McCauley, R. H., Jr.
1945   The reptiles of Maryland and the District of Columbia. Privately Publ., Hagerstown, Md. 194 p.

McComb, W. C., and R. E. Noble
1981   Herpetofaunal use of natural tree cavities and nest boxes. Wildlife Soc. Bull. 9:261–267.

McCoy, C. J., Jr.
1961   A technique for collecting in urban areas. J. Ohio Herpetol. Soc. 3:4.

McCoy, C. J.
1975   Cave-associated snakes, *Elaphe guttata*, in Oklahoma. Natl. Speleol. Soc. Bull. 37:41.

1980   Identification guide to Pennsylvania snakes. Carnegie Mus. Natur. Hist. Educ. Bull. (1):1–12.
1982   Amphibians and reptiles in Pennsylvania. Carnegie Mus. Natur. Hist. (6):1–91.

McCranie, J. R.
1980a   *Drymarchon, D. corais*. Catalog. Amer. Amphib. Rept. 267:1–4.
1980b   *Crotalus adamanteus*. Catalog. Amer. Amphib. Rept. 252:1–2.
1983   *Nerodia taxispilota*. Catalog. Amer. Amphib. Rept. 331:1–2.

McCrea, R., G. McCrea, and B. Hiserote
1963   Excavation habits of the bullsnake, *Pituophis melanoleucus sayi*. Bull. Philadelphia Herpetol. Soc. 11:12.

McDaniel, R. C., W. A. Grunow, J. J. Daly, and M. V. Plummer
1984   Serum chemistry of the diamondback watersnake (*Nerodia rhombifera rhombifera*) in Arkansas. J. Wildl. Dis. 20:44–46.

McDaniel, V. R., and J. P. Karges
1983   *Farancia abacura*. Catalog. Amer. Amphib. Rept. 314:1–2.

McDiarmid, R. W. (Ed.)
1978   Rare and endangered biota of Florida. Vol. 3. Amphibians and reptiles. Univ. Press Florida, Gainesville. 74 p.

McDonald, H. S.
1959   Respiratory functions of the ophidian air sac. Herpetologica 15:193–198.
1960   Nasal obstruction during the premolt period in *Natrix*. Herpetologica 16:115–119.
1974   Bradycardia during death-feigning of *Heterodon platyrhinos* Latreille (Serpentes). J. Herpetol. 8:157–164.

McDowell, A.
1951   Bull snake active in December. Herpetologica 7:142.

McDowell, S. B.
1974   A catalogue of the snakes of New Guinea and the Solomons, with special reference to those in the Bernice P. Bishop Museum, Part 1. Scolecophidia. J. Herpetol. 8:1–57.

McDuffie, G. T.
1961   Notes on the ecology of the copperhead in Ohio. J. Ohio Herpetol. Soc. 3:26–27.

1963   Studies on the size, pattern and coloration of the northern copperhead (*Agkistrodon contortrix mokeson* Daudin) in Ohio. J. Ohio Herpetol. Soc. 4:15–22.

McKay, F., and J. Deco
1957   Garter snakes eating minnows. Blue Jay 15:178–180.

McKinistry, D. M.
1978   Evidence of toxic saliva in some colubrid snakes of the United States. Toxicon 16:523–534.
1983   Morphologic evidence of toxic saliva in colubrid snakes: a checklist of world genera. Herp Review 14:12–14.

Meade, G. P.
1934a   Some observations on captive snakes. Copeia 1934:4–5.
1934b   Feeding *Farancia abacura* in captivity. Copeia 1934:91–92.
1935a   Hibernation of *Farancia abacura* in captivity. Copeia 1935:99.
1935b   The egg–laying of *Farancia abacura*. Copeia 1935:190–191.
1937   Breeding habits of *Farancia abacura* in captivity. Copeia 1937:12–15.
1940   Maternal care of eggs of *Farancia*. Herpetologica 2:15–20.
1945   Further observations on Louisiana captive snakes. Copeia 1945:73–75.

Mebs, D., and F. Kornalik
1984   Intraspecific variation in content of a basic toxin in eastern diamondback rattlesnake (*Crotalus adamanteus*) venom. Toxicon 22:831–833.

Mehrtens, J. M.
1952   Notes on the eggs and young of *Pituophis melanoleucus sayi*. Herpetologica 8:69–70.

Mengden, G. A., and A. D. Stock
1980   Chromosomal evolution in Serpentes; a comparison of G and C chromosome banding patterns of some colubrid and boid genera. Chromosoma (Berlin) 79:53–64.

Merrem, B.
1820*   Tentamen systematis amphibiorum. Johann Christian Krieger, Marburg. 191 p.

Mertens, R.
1950   Uber Reptilien–bastarde. Senckenbergiana 31:127–144.

Messler, R. M., and D. B. Webster
1968   Histochemistry of the rattlesnake facial pit. Copeia 1968:722–728.

Metrolis, A. P.
1971   A feeding observation on the rainbow snake (*Farancia erytrogramma erytrogramma*). Bull. Maryland Herpetol. Soc. 7:41.

Meylan, P. A.
1982   The squamate reptiles of the Ingles IA Fauna (Irvingtonian: Citrus County, Florida). Bull. Florida St. Mus. Biol. Sci. 27:111–196.
1985   *Heterodon simus*. Catalog Amer. Amphib. Rept. 375:1–2.

Michels, T. J.
1979   Further records of snakes in winter. Bull. Philadelphia Herpetol. Soc. 27:6.

Miller, R.
1976   Aquatic behavior in the eastern garter snake, *Thamnophis s. sirtalis*. Bull. Maryland Herpetol. Soc. 12:122.
1978   Reproductive data on *Lampropeltis triangulum temporalis* from Maryland. Bull. Maryland Herpetol. Soc. 14:36–38.

Minesky, J. J., and R. D. Aldridge
1982   The male reproductive cycle of the queen snake (*Regina septemvittata*) in western Pennsylvania. Progr. Jct. Meet. S. S. A. R. and Herpetol. League 1982:114.

Minton, J. E.
1949   Coral snake preyed upon by a bullfrog. Copeia 1949:288.

Minton, S. A., Jr.
1949   The black–headed snake in southern Indiana. Copeia 1949:146–147.
1953   Variation in venom samples from copperheads (*Agkistrodon contortrix mokeson*) and timber rattlesnakes (*Crotalus horridus horridus*). Copeia 1953:212–215.
1959   Observations on amphibians and reptiles of the Big Bend Region of Texas. Southwest. Natur. 3:28–54.
1966   A contribution to the herpetology of West Pakistan. Bull. Amer. Mus. Natur. Hist. 134:27–184.
1967   Observations on toxicity and antigenic makeup of venoms from juvenile snakes. Toxicon 4:294.

1968   The fate of amphibians and reptiles in a suburban area. J. Herpetol. 2:113–116.

1972   Amphibians and reptiles of Indiana. Indiana Acad. Sci. Mongr. (3):1–346.

1974   Venom diseases. Charles C. Thomas, Publ., Springfield, Illinois. 235 p.

1980   *Thamnophis butleri*. Catalog. Amer. Amphib. Rept. 258:1–2.

1983   *Sistrurus catenatus*. Catalog. Amer. Amphib. Rept. 332:1–2.

Minton, S. A., Jr., and A. B. Bechtel
1958   Another Indiana record of *Cemophora coccinea* and a note on egg eating. Copiea 1958:47.

Minton, S. A., Jr., H. G. Dowling, and F. E. Russell
1968   Poisonous snakes of the world. U. S. Govt. Print. Office, Washington, D. C. 212 p.

Minton, S. A., Jr., and M. R. Minton
1969   Venomous reptiles. Scribner's, New York. 274 p.

Mirarchi, R. E., and R. R. Hitchcock
1982   Radio–instrumented mourning dove preyed upon by a gray rat snake. Auk 99:583.

Mitchell, J. C.
1974   The snakes of Virginia. Virginia Wildlife Feb. & April:1–8.

1976   Notes on reproduction in *Storeria dekayi* and *Virginia striatula* from Virginia and North Carolina. Bull. Maryland Herpetol. Soc. 12:133–135.

1977   Geographic variation of *Elaphe guttata* (Reptilia: Serpentes) in the Atlantic Coastal Plain. Copeia 1977:33–41.

1980   Viper's brood. A guide to identifying some of Virginia's juvenile snakes. Virginia Wildlife 41(9):8–10.

1981   Notes on male combat in two Virginia snakes, *Agkistrodon contortrix* and *Elaphe obsoleta*. Catesbeiana 1:7–9.

1982a   *Farancia*. Catalog. Amer. Amphib. Rept. 292:1–2.

1982b   *Farancia erytrogramma*. Catalog. Amer. Amphib. Rept. 293:1–2.

Mitchell, J. C., and W. H. Martin, III
1981   Where the snakes are. Virginia Wildlife 42(6):8–9.

Mitchell, J. C., C. A. Pague, and D. L. Early
1982   *Elaphe obsoleta* (Black Rat Snake). Autophagy. Herp Review 13:47.

Mitchell, J. C., and G. R. Zug
1984   Spermatogenic cycle of *Nerodia taxispilota* (Serpentes: Colubridae) in southcentral Virginia. Herpetologica 40:200–204.

Moehn, L. D.
1967   A combat dance between two prairie kingsnakes. Copeia 1967:480–481.

Moler, P. E.
1985   Distribution of the eastern indigo snake, *Drymarchon corais couperi*, in Florida. Herp Review 16:37–38.

Moll, E. O.
1962   Recent herpetological records for Illinois. Herpetologica 18:207–209.

Monroe, E. A., and S. E. Monroe
1968   Origin of iridescent colors on the indigo snake. Science 159:97–98.

Morris, M. A.
1974a   Notes on parturition in the midland brown snake, *Storeria dekayi*. Trans. Illinois St. Acad. Sci. 67:3–4.

1974b   Observations on a large litter of the snake *Storeria dekayi*. Trans. Illinois St. Acad. Sci. 67:359–360.

1978   Temperature elevation as a releaser of mating behavior in some North American colubrid snakes. Bull. Chicago Herpetol. Soc. 13:9–12.

1982   Activity, reproduction, and growth of *Opheodrys aestivus* in Illinois (Serpentes: Colubridae). Natur. Hist. Misc. (214):1–10.

1984   *Elaphe obsoleta* (black rat snake). Autophagy. Herp Review 15:19.

1985   Envenomation from the bite of *Heterodon nasicus* (Serpentes: Colubridae). Herpetologica 41:361–163.

Mosauer, W.
1932   On the locomotion of snakes. Science 76:583–585.

Moulis, R.
1976   Autecology of the eastern indigo snake, *Drymarchon corais couperi*. HERP: Bull. New York Herpetol. Soc. 12(3–4):14–23.

Mount, R. H.
1972   Distribution of the worm snake *Corphophis amoenus* (Say) in Alabama. Herpetologica 28:263–266.

1975   Reptiles and amphibians of Alabama. Auburn Univ., Agric. Exp. Stat. 347 p.

Mount, R. H. (Ed.)
1984   Vertebrate wildlife of Alabama. Alabama Agric. Exp. St., Auburn. 44 p.

Mount, R. H., and J. Cecil
1982   *Agkistrodon piscivorus* (cottonmouth). Hybridization. Herp Review 13:95–96.

Mount, R. H., and T. D. Schwaner
1970   Taxonomic and distributional relationships between the water snakes *Natrix taxispilota* (Holbrook) and *Natrix rhombifera* (Hallowell). Herpetologica 26:76–82.

Muir, J. H.
1981   Two unusually large egg clutches from a corn snake, *Elaphe guttata guttata*. Bull. Chicago Herpetol. Soc. 16:42–43.
1982   Notes on the climbing ability of a captive timber ratttlesnake, *Crotalus horridus*. Bull. Chicago Herpetol. Soc. 17:22–23.

Mulvany, P. S.
1983   Tarantula preys on a western ribbon snake with notes on the relationship between narrowmouth toads and tarantulas. Bull. Oklahoma Herpetol. Soc. 8:92–99.

Munro, D. F.
1947   Effect of a bite by *Sistrurus* on *Crotalus*. Herpetologica 4:57.
1948   Mating behavior and seasonal cloacal discharge of female *Thamnophis sirtalis parietalis*. Herpetologica 4:185–188.
1949a   Excreta of a blue racer with reference to diet. Herpetologica 5:74.
1949b   Food of *Heterodon nasicus nasicus*. Herpetologica 5:133.
1949c   Gain in size and weight of *Heterodon* eggs during incubation. Herpetologica 5:133–134.
1949d   Hatching of a clutch of *Heterodon* eggs. Herpetologica 5:134–136.

Munyer, E. A.
1967   Behavior of an eastern hognose snake, *Heterodon platyrhinos*, in water. Copeia 1967:668–670.

Murphy, J. B., and B. L. Armstrong
1978   Maintenance of rattlesnakes in captivity. Univ. Kansas Mus. Natur. Hist. Spl. Publ. (3):1–40.

Murphy, J. B., and J. A. Shadduck
1978   Reproduction in the eastern diamondback rattlesnake, *Crotalus adamanteus*, in captivity, with comments regarding taratoid birth anomaly. British J. Herpetol. 5:727–733.

Murphy, J. C., and M. Dloogatch
1980   An additional note on the egg-eating habits of the western hognose snake in Illinois. Bull. Chicago Herpetol. Soc. 15:98.

Murphy, T. D.
1964   Boxturtle, *Terrapene carolina*, in stomach of copperhead, *Agkistrodon contortrix*. Copeia 1964:221.

Mushinsky, H. R.
1979   Mating behavior of the common water snake, *Nerodia sipedon sipedon*, in eastern Pennsylvania (Reptilia, Serpentes, Colubridae). J. Herpetol. 13:127–129.
1984   Observations of the feeding habits of the short–tailed snake, *Stilosoma extenuatum* in captivity. Herp Review 15:67–68.

Mushinksy, H. R., and J. J. Hebrard
1977a   Food partitioning by five species of water snakes in Louisiana. Herpetologica 33:162–166.
1977b   The use of time by sympatric water snakes. Can. J. Zool. 55:1545–1550.

Mushinksy, H. R., J.J. Hebrard, and D. S. Vodopich
1982   Ontogeny of water snake foraging ecology. Ecology 63:1624–1629.

Mushinsky, H. R., J. J. Hebrard, and M. S. Walley
1980   The role of temperature on the behavioral and ecological associations of sympatric watersnakes. Copeia 1980:744–754.

Mushinsky, H. R., and K. H. Lotz.
1980   Chemoreceptive responses of two sympatric water snakes to extracts of commonly ingested prey species. Ontogenetic and ecological considerations. J. Chem. Ecol. 6:523–535.

Myer, J. S., and A. P. Kowell

1971   Loss and subsequent recovery of body weight in water–deprived snakes (*Elaphe obsoleta obsoleta*). J. Comp. Physiol. Psychol. 75:5–9.

1973   Effects of feeding schedule and food deprivation on the growth of neonatal garter snakes (*Thamnophis sirtalis*). J. Herpetol. 7:225–229.

Myers, C. W.

1956   An unrecorded food item of the timber rattlesnake. Herpetologica 12:326.

1963   Ontogenetic color variation of the snake *Virginia valeriae*. Herpetologica 18:273–274.

1965   Biology of the ringneck snake, *Diadophis punctatus*, in Florida. Bull. Florida St. Mus. Biol. Sci. 10:43–90.

1967   The pine woods snake, *Rhadinaea flavilata* (Cope). Bull. Florida St. Mus. Biol. Sci. 11:47–97.

1974   The systematics of *Rhadinaea* (Colubridae), a genus of New World snakes. Bull. Amer. Mus. Natur. Hist. 153:1–262.

Myers, C. W., and A. A. Arata

1961   Remarks on "defensive" behavior in the hognose snake *Heterodon simus* (Linnaeus). Quart. J. Florida Acad. Sci. 24:108–110.

Nakamura, E. L., and H. Smith

1960   A comparative study of selected characters in certain American species of watersnakes. Trans. Kansas Acad. Sci. 63:102–113.

Neill, W. T.

1947   Size and habits of the cottonmouth moccasin. Herpetologica 3:203–205.

1948a   Hibernation of amphibians and reptiles in Richmond County, Georgia. Herpetologica 4:107–114.

1948b   Spiders preying on reptiles and amphibians. Herpetologica 4:158.

1948c   Unusual behavior of *Storeria dekayi dekayi* in Georgia. Herpetologica 4:163.

1949a   Head bobbing, a widespread habit of snakes. Herpetologica 5:114–115.

1949b* A new subspecies of rat snake (genus *Elaphe*), and notes on related forms. Herpetologica 5(2nd suppl.):12.

1950a   Ontogenetic changes in the coloration of the snake *Cemophora coccinea*. Copeia 1950:62.

1950b   The status of the Florida brown snake, *Storeria victa* Copeia 1950:155–156.

1951   Notes on the natural history of certain North American snakes. Publ. Res. Div. Ross Allen's Rept. Inst. 1:47–60.

1954a   Evidence of venom in snakes of the genera *Alsophis* and *Rhadinaea*. Copeia 1954:59–60.

1957   Some misconceptions regarding the eastern coral snake, *Micrurus fulvius*. Herpetologica 13:111–118.

1958   The occurrence of amphibians and reptiles in saltwater areas, and a bibliography. Bull. Mar. Sci. Gulf Caribbean 8:1–97.

1960   The caudal lure of various juvenile snakes. Quart. J. Florida Acad. Sci. 23:173–200.

1961   River frog swallows eastern diamondback rattlesnake. Bull. Philadelphia Herpetol. Soc. 9(1):19.

1963a   A new subspecies of the queen snake, *Natrix septemvittata* from southern Alabama. Herpetologica 19:1–9.

1963b   Polychromatism in snakes. Quart. J. Florida Acad. Sci. 26:194–216.

1964*   Taxonomy, natural history, and zoogeography of the rainbow snake, *Farancia erytrogramma* (Palisot de Beauvois). Amer. Midl. Natur. 71:257–295.

1965   Notes on aquatic snakes, *Natrix* and *Tretanorhinus* in Cuba. Herpetologica 21:62–67.

Neill, W. T., and E. R. Allen

1954   Algae on turtles: some additional considerations. Ecology 35:581–584.

1956   Secondarily ingested food items in snakes. Herpetologica 12:172–174.

Neill, W. T., and J. M. Boyles

1957   The eggs of the crowned snake, *Tantilla coronata*. Herpetologica 13:77–78.

Nelson, D. H., and J. W. Gibbons

1972   Ecology, abundance, and seasonal activity of the scarlet snake, *Cemophora coccinea*. Copeia 1972:582–584.

Nelson, W. F.
1969   Notes on parturition and brood sizes in *Storeria occipitomaculata*. J. Tennessee Acad. Sci. 44:20–21.

Nero, R. W.
1957   Observations at a garter snake hibernaculum. Blue Jay 15:119–120.

Netting, M. G.
1969   Does the robin eat Dekay's snake? Wilson Bull. 81:470–471.

New, J. G.
1953   The young of the snake *Pituophis melanoleucus melanoleucus*. Copeia 1953:183–184.

Newcomer, R. T., D. H. Taylor, and S. I. Guttman
1974   Celestial orientation in two species of water snakes (*Natrix sipedon* and *Regina septemvittata*). Herpetologica 30:194–200.

Nichols, T. J.
1982   Courtship and copulatory behavior of captive eastern hognose snakes, *Heterodon platyrhinos*. Herp Review 13:16–17.

Noble, G. K.
1937   The sense organs involved in the courtship of *Storeria*, *Thamnophis* and other snakes. Bull. Amer. Mus. Natur. Hist. 73:673–725.

Noble, G. K., and H. J. Clausen
1936   The aggregation behavior of *Storeria dekayi* and other snakes with especial reference to the sense organs involved. Ecol. Monogr. 6:269–316.

Nussbaum, R. A.
1980   The Brahminy blind snake (*Ramphotyphlops braminus*) in the Seychelles Archipelago: distribution, variation, and further evidence of parthenogenesis. Herpetologica 36:215–221.

Odum, R. A.
1979   The distribution and status of the New Jersey timber rattlesnake including an analysis of Pine Barren populations. Herp: Bull. New York Herpetol. Soc. 15:27–35.

Oguma, K., and S. Makino.
1932   A revised check–list of the chromosome number in vertebrata. J. Genetics 26:239–254.

Oldak, P. D.
1976   Comparison of the scent gland secretion lipids of twenty–five snakes: implications for biochemical systematics. Copeia 1976:320–326.

Oliver, J. A.
1955   The natural history of North American amphibians and reptiles. Van Nostrand, Princeton, New Jersey. 359 p.
1958   Snakes in fact and fiction. MacMillan, New York. 199 p.

Oliver, J. A., and J. R. Bailey
1939   Amphibians and reptiles of New Hampshire, p. 195–217. Biol. Surv. Connecticut Watershed, Concord, New Hampshire.

Ortenburger, A. I.
1928   The whip snakes and racers: genera *Masticophis* and *Coluber*. Mem. Univ. Michigan Mus. 1:1–247.

Osgood, D. W.
1970   Thermoregulation in water snakes studied by telemetry. Copeia 1970:568–571.
1978   Effects of temperature on the development of meristic characters in *Natrix fasciata*. Copeia 1978:33–47.

Owens, V.
1949a   An overwintering colony of *Coluber c. constrictor* (Say) and *Elaphe o. obsoleta* (Say). Herpetologica 5:90.
1949b   Snakes eaten by the tarantula, *Eurypelma californica*. Herpetologica 5:148.

Packard, M. J., G. C. Packard, and T. J. Boardman
1982   Structure of eggshells and water relations of reptilian eggs. Herpetologica 38:136–155.

Packard, M. J., G. C. Packard, and W. H. N. Gutzke
1984   Calcium metabolism in embryos of the oviparous snake *Coluber constrictor*. J. Exp. Biol. 110:99–112.

Palmer, W. M.
1961   Notes on eggs and young of the scarlet kingsnake, *Lampropeltis doliata doliata*. Herpetologica 17:65.
1965   Intergradation among the copperheads (*Agkistrodon contortrix* Linnaeus) in the North Carolina coastal plain. Copeia 1965:246–247.

1971   Distribution and variation of the Carolina pigmy rattlesnake, *Sistrurus miliarius miliarius* Linnaeus, in North Carolina. J. Herpetol. 5:39–44.

1974   Poisonous snakes of North Carolina. St. Mus. Natur. Hist. North Carolina, Raleigh. 22 p.

1978   *Sistrurus miliarius*. Catalog. Amer. Amphib. Rept. 220:1–2.

Palmer, W. M., and A. L. Braswell
1976   Communal egg laying and hatchlings of the rough green snake, *Opheodrys aestivus* (Linnaeus) (Reptilia, Serpentes, Colubridae). J. Herpetol. 10:257–259.

Palmer, W. M., and J. R. Paul
1963   The black swamp snake, *Seminatrix pygaea paludis* Dowling, in North Carolina. Herpetologica 19:219–221.

Palmer, W. M., and G. Tregembo
1970   Notes on the natural history of the scarlet snake *Cemophora coccinea copei* Jan in North Carolina. Herpetologica 26:300–302.

Palmer, W. M., and G. M. Williamson
1971   Observations on the natural history of the Carolina pigmy rattlesnake, *Sistrurus miliarius miliarius* Linnaeus. Elisha Mitchell Sci. Soc. J. 87:20–25.

Parks, L. H.
1973   An active bull snake in near–freezing temperature. Trans. Kansas Acad. Sci. 72:266.

Parker, H. W.
1977   Snakes of the world. Dover Publ., Inc. New York. 191 p.

Parrish, H. M., and R. E. Thompson
1958   Human envenomation from bites of recently milked rattlesnakes: a report of three cases. Copeia 1958:83–86.

Paul, J. R.
1967   Intergradation among ring–necked snakes in southeastern United States. Elisha Mitchell Sci. Soc. J. 83:98–102.

Paulson, D. R.
1966*   Variation in some snakes from the Florida Keys. Quart. J. Florida Acad. Sci. 29:295–308.

Pauley, T. K.
1973   The status of the genus *Carphophis* in Ohio and West Virginia. Proc. West Virginia Acad. Sci. 45:64–70.

Peabody, F. E.
1958   A Kansas drought recorded in growth zones of a bullsnake. Copeia 1958:91–94.

1961   Annual growth zones in living and fossil vertebrates. J. Morphol. 108:11–62.

Pendlebury, G. B.
1976   The western hognose snake, *Heterodon nasicus nasicus*, in Alberta. Can. Field–Natur. 90:416–422.

Penn, G. H., Jr.
1943   Herpetological notes from Cameron Parish, Louisiana. Copeia 1943:58–59.

Perkens, C. B.
1950   Frequency of shedding in injured snakes. Herpetologica 6:35–36.

1952   Incubation period of snake eggs. Herpetologica 8:79.

Perry, J.
1978   An observation of "dance" behavior in the western cottonmouth, *Agkistrodon piscivorus leucostoma* (Reptilia, Serpentes, Viperidae). J. Herpetol. 12:428–429.

Peters, J. A.
1964   Dictionary of herpetology. Hafner Publ. Co., New York. 393 p.

Peterson, H. W.
1956   A record of viviparity in a normally oviparous snake. Herpetologica 12:152.

Peterson, K. H.
1980   Coprophagy in *Thamnophis s. sirtalis*. Herp Review 11:9.

Petersen, R. C.
1970   Connecticut's venomous snakes. Connecticut St. Geol. Natur. Hist. Surv. Bull. (103):1–39.

Pettus, D.
1958   Water relationships in *Natrix sipedon*. Copeia 1958:207–211.

1963   Salinity and subspeciation in *Natrix sipedon*. Copeia 1963:499–504.

Pewtress, R.
1981   The brown and red–bellied snakes. Genus: *Storeria*. Herptile 6(2):28–30.

Phelps, T.
1981   Poisonous snakes. Blandford Press, Poole, Dorset. 237 p.

Phillips, C.
1939   The flat tailed water snake. Proc. Florida Acad. Sci. 4:210–211.

Pickering, D.
1982   Notes on the reproduction of the western worm snake, *Carphophis amoenus vermis*. Bull. Oklahoma Herpetol. Soc. 7:86–88.

Pinney, R.
1981   The snake book. Doubleday, Garden City, New York. 248 p.

Pisani, G. R.
1967   Notes on the courtship and mating behavior of *Thamnophis brachystoma* (Cope). Herpetologica 23:112–115.
1971   An unusually large litter of *Virginia valeriae pulchra*. J. Herpetol. 5:207–208.

Pisani, G. R., and R. C. Bothner
1970   The annual reproductive cycle of *Thamnophis brachystoma*. Sci. Stud. St. Bonaventure Univ. 26:15–34.

Pisani, G. R., and J. T. Collins
1971   The smooth earth snake, *Virginia valeriae* (Baird and Girard), in Kentucky. Trans. Kentucky Acad. Sci. 32:16–25.

Pisani, G. R., J. T. Collins, and S. R. Edwards
1973   A re-evaluation of the subspecies of *Crotalus horridus*. Trans. Kansas Acad. Sci. 75:255–263.

Platt, D. R.
1969   Natural history of the hognose snakes *Heterodon platyrhinos* and *Heterodon nasicus*. Univ. Kansas Publ. Mus. Natur. Hist. 18:253–420.
1983   *Heterodon*. Catalog. Amer. Amphib. Rept. 315:1–2.
1984   Growth of bullsnakes (*Pituophis melanoleucus sayi*) on a sand prairie in south central Kansas. Univ. Kansas Publ. Mus. Natur. Hist. Spl. Publ. (10):41–55.
1985   History and spelling of the name *Heterodon platirhinos*. J. Herpetol. 19:417–418.

Plummer, M. V.
1977   Predation of black rat snakes in bank swallow colonies. Southwest. Natur. 22:147–148.
1980   Ventral scute anomalies in a population of *Opheodrys aestivus*. J. Herpetol. 14:199.
1981a Communal nesting of *Opheodrys aestivus* in the laboratory. Copeia 1981:243–246.
1981b Habitat utilization, diet and movements of a temporate arboreal snake (*Opheodrys aestivus*). J. Herpetol. 15:425–432.
1983   Annual variation in stored lipids and reproduction in green snakes (*Opheodrys aestivus*). Copeia 1983:741–745.
1984   Female reproduction in an Arkansas population of rough green snakes (*Opheodrys aestivus*). Univ. Kansas Mus. Natur. Hist. Spl. Publ. (10):105–113.
1985   Demography of green snakes (*Opheodrys aestivus*). Herpetologica 41:373–381.
1987   Geographic variation in body size of green snakes (*Opheodrys aestivus*). Copeia 1987: 483–485.

Plummer, M. V., and J. M. Goy
1984   Ontogenetic dietary shift of water snakes (*Nerodia rhombifera*) in a fish hatchery. Copeia 1984:550–552.

Polis, G. A., and C. A. Myers
1985   A survey of intraspecific predation among reptiles and amphibians. J. Herpetol. 19:99–107.

Pope, C. H.
1937   Snakes alive and how they live. Viking Press, New York. 238 p.
1944   Amphibians and reptiles of the Chicago area. Chicago Natur. Hist. Mus. 275 p.
1946   Snakes of the northeastern United States. New York Zool. Soc. 52 p.
1955   The reptile world. Alfred A. Knopf, New York. 325 p.

Porras, L., and L. D. Wilson
1979   New distributional records for *Tantilla oolitica* Telford (Reptilia, Serpentes, Colubridae) from the Florida Keys. J. Herpetol. 13:218–220.

Porter, K. R.
1972   Herpetology. Saunders, Philadelphia. 524 p.

BIBLIOGRAPHY

Porter, R. H., and J. A. Czaplicki
1974a   Responses of water snakes (*Natrix r. rhombifera*) and garter snakes (*Thamnophis sirtalis*) to chemical cues. Anim. Learn. Behav. 2:129–132.
1974b   Shedding facilitates exposure learning in garter snake (*Thamnophis sirtalis*). Physiol. Behav. 12:75–77.
1977   Evidence for a specific searching image in hunting water snakes (*Natrix sipedon*) (Reptilia, Serpentes, Colubridae). J. Herpetol. 11:213–216.

Posey, C. R.
1973   An observation on the feeding habits of the eastern king snake. Bull. Maryland Herpetol. Soc. 9:105.

Pough, F. H.
1976   Multiple cryptic effects of crossbanded and ringed patterns of snakes. Copeia 1976:834–836.
1978   Ontogentic changes in endurance in water snakes (*Natrix sipedon*): physiological correlates and ecological consequences. Copeia 1978:69–75.

Pough, F. H., and M. B. Pough
1971   How cold are cold snakes? Comments on the reliabililty of low temperature records. Herp Review 3:102.

Powell, R.
1982   *Thamnophis proximus* (western ribbon snake). Reproduction. Herp Review 13:48.

Powers, A.
1973   A review of the purpose of the rattle in crotalids as a defensive diversionary mechanism. Bull. Maryland Herpetol. Soc. 9:30–32.

Prange, H. D., and S. P. Christman
1976   The allometrics of rattlesnake skeletons. Copeia 1976:542–545.

Prange, H. D., and K. Schmidt–Nielsen
1969   Evaporative water loss in snakes. Comp. Biochem. Physiol. 28:973–975.

Price, A. H.
1978   New locality records and range extensions for *Thamnophis brachystoma* (Reptilia: Serpentes) in Pennsylvania. Bull. Maryland Herpetol. Soc. 14:260–263.

Price, R. M.
1982   Dorsal snake scale microdermatoglyphics: ecological indicator or taxonomic tool? J. Herpetol. 16:294–306.

Price, R.
1983   Microdermatoglyphics: the *Liodytes–Regina* problem. J. Herpetol. 17:292–294.

Price, W. H., and L. G. Carr
1943   Eggs of *Heterodon simus*. Copeia 1943:193.

Puckette, B. G.
1962   Ophiophagy in *Hyla versicolor*. Herpetologica 18:143.

Quinn, H. R.
1979a   Sexual dimorphism in tail pattern of Oklahoma snakes. Texas J. Sci. 31:157–160.
1979b   Reproduction and growth of the Texas coral snake *Micrurus fulvius tenere*. Copeia 1979:453–463.

Radj, R. H.
1981   *Opheodrys v. vernalis* (smooth green snake). Reproduction. Herp Review 12:80.

Rafinesque, C. S.
1818*   Further account of discoveries in natural history in the western states. Amer. Month. Mag. Crit. Rev. 4:39–42.

Rage, J. C.
1984   Serpentes. Handbuch der Palaoherpetologie. Part II. Gustav Fischer, Stuttgart. 80 p.

Rahn, H.
1940   Sperm viability in the uterus of the garter snake, *Thamnophis*. Copeia 1940:109–115.

Ramsey, L. W.
1946   Captive specimens of *Tropidoclonion lineatum*. Herpetologica 3:112.
1947   Feeding behavior of *Tropidoclonion lineatum*. Herpetologica 4:15–18.
1948   Combat dance and range extension of *Agkistrodon piscivorus leucostoma*. Herpetologica 4:228.
1953*   The lined snake, *Tropidoclonion lineatum* (Hallowell). Herpetologica 9:7–23.

Raney, E. C., and R. M. Roecker
1947   Food and growth of two species of watersnakes from western New York. Copeia 1947:171–174.

Reese, A. M.
1947   The hemipenes of copperhead embryos. Herpetologica 3:206–208.

Reichenbach, N. G.
1983   An aggregation of female garter snakes under corrugated metal sheets. J. Herpetol. 17:412–413.

Reichenbach, N. G., and G. H. Dalrymple
1986   Energy use, life histories, and the evaluation of potential competition in two species of garter snakes. J. Herpetol. 20:133–153.

Reichling, S.
1982   Reproduction in captive black pine snakes *Pituophis melanoleucus lodingi*. Herp Review 13:41.

Reid, M., and A. Nichols
1970   Predation by reptiles on periodic cicada. Bull. Maryland Herpetol. Soc. 6:57.

Reimer, W. J.
1957   The snake *Farancia abacura*: an attended nest. Herpetologica 13:31–32.

Reinert, H. K.
1975   Another winter record of a snake (*Natrix septemvittata*). Bull. Philadelphia Herpetol. Soc. 23:7.
1981   Reproduction by the massasauga (*Sistrurus catenatus catenatus*). Amer. Midl. Natur. 105:393–395.
1984a   Habitat separation between sympatric snake populations. Ecology 65:478–486.
1984b   Habitat variation within sympatric snake populations. Ecology 65:1673–1682.

Reinert, H. K., D. Cundall, and L. M. Bushar
1984   Foraging behavior of the timber rattlesnake, *Crotalus horridus*. Copeia 1984:976–981.

Reinert, H. K., and W. R. Kodrich
1982   Movements and habitat utilization by the massasauga, *Sisturus catenatus catenatus*. J. Herpetol. 16:162–171.

Resetarits, W. J., Jr.
1983   *Thamnophis proximus proximus* (western ribbon snake). Food. Herp Review 14:75.

Reynolds, F. A., and A. N. Solberg
1942   Notes on the life history of the mud snake. Copeia 1942:25–26.

Riches, R. J.
1962   Notes on the garter snake (*Thamnophis sirtalis*), with particular reference to growth and breeding. British J. Herpetol. 3:31–32.
1980   "Double littering" in *Thamnophis sirtalis similis*. Herptile 5(4):12–13.

Richmond, N. D.
1940   *Natrix rigida* Say in Virginia. Herpetologica 2:21.
1944   How *Natrix taxispilota* eats the channel catfish. Copeia 1944:254.
1945   The habits of the rainbow snake in Virginia. Copeia 1945:28–30.
1952   *Opheodrys aestivus* in aquatic habitats in Virginia. Herpetologica 8:38.
1954a   Variation and sexual dimorphism in hatchlings of the rainbow snake, *Abastor erythrogrammus*. Copeia 1954:87–92.
1954b* The ground snake, *Haldea valeriae*, in Pennsylvania and West Virginia with description of new subspecies. Ann. Carnegie Mus. 33:251–260.
1956   Autumn mating of the rough green snake. Herpetologica 12:325.

Richmond, N. D., and C. J. Goin
1938   Notes on a collection of amphibians and reptiles from New Kent County, Virginia. Ann. Carnegie. Mus. 27:301–310.

Ridlehuber, K. T., and N. J. Silvy
1981   Texas rat snake feeds on Mexican freetail bat and wood duck eggs. Southwest. Natur. 26:70–71.

Rigley, L.
1971   "Combat dance" of the black rat snake, *Elaphe o. obsoleta*. J. Herpetol. 5:65–66.

Roberts, A. R.
1947   *Sistrurus* in Michigan. Herpetologica 4:6.

Robinson, J. M., III, R. S. Brodey, and J. M. Robinson, Sr.
1974   Winter records of garter and black snakes. Bull. Philadelphia Herpetol. Soc. 22:33–34.

Roddy, H. J.
1928   Reptiles of Lancaster County and the state of Pennsylvania. Science Press, Lancaster, Pennsylvania. 53 p.

Rodgers, K. L.
1976   Herpetofauna of the Beck Ranch local fauna (upper Pliocene: Blancan) of Texas. Publ. Mus. Michigan St. Univ. Paleontol. Ser. 1:163–200.

1982   Herpetofaunas of the Courland Canal and Hall Ash local faunas (Pleistocene: early Kansas) of Jewell Co., Kansas. J. Herpetol. 16:174–177.

Rodgers, R. B.
1985   *Heterodon platyrhinos* (eastern hognose snake). Behavior. Herp Review 16:111.

Rosenberg, H. J., A. Bdolah, and E. Kochva
1985   Lethal factors and enzymes in the secretion from Duvernoy's gland of three colubrid snakes. J. Exp. Zool. 233:5–14.

Ross, P., Jr., and D. Crews
1977   Influence of the seminal plug on mating behavior in the garter snake. Nature 267:344–345.

Rossman, C. E.
1980   Ontogenetic changes in skull proportions of the diamondback water snake, *Nerodia rhombifera*. Herpetologica 36:42–46.

Rossman, D. A.
1956   Notes on food of a captive black swamp snake, *Seminatrix pygaea pygaea* (Cope). Herpetologica 12:154–155.

1960   Herpetofaunal survey of the Pine Hills area of southern Illinois. Quart. J. Florida Acad. Sci. 22:207–225.

1962   *Thamnophis proximus* (Say), a valid species of garter snake. Copeia 1962:741–748.

1963a   Relationships and taxonomic status of the North American natricine snake genera *Liodytes*, *Regina*, and *Clonophis*. Occ. Paps. Mus. Zool. Louisiana St. Univ. (29):1–29.

1963b*   The colubrid snake genus *Thamnophis*: a revision of the *sauritus* group. Bull. Florida St. Mus. Biol. Sci. 7:99–178.

1965*   A new subspecies of the common garter snake, *Thamnophis sirtalis*, from the Florida Gulf Coast. Proc. Louisiana Acad. Sci. 27:67–73.

1970a   *Thamnophis proximus*. Catalog. Amer Amphib. Rept. 98:1–3.

1970b   *Thamnophis sauritus*. Catalog Amer. Amphib. Rept. 99:1–2.

1973   Evidence for the conspecificity of *Carphophis amoenus* (Say) and *Carphophis vermis* (Kennicott). J. Herpetol. 7:140–141.

1985   *Liodytes* resurrected, reexamined, and reinterred. J. Herpetol. 19:169–171.

Rossman, D. A., and W. G. Eberle
1977   Partition of the genus *Natrix*, with preliminary observations on evolutionary trends in natricine snakes. Herpetologica 33:34–43.

Rossman, D. A., and R. L. Erwin
1980   Geographic variation in the snake *Storeria occipitomaculata* (Storer) (Serpentes: Colubridae) in southeastern United States. Brimleyana (4):95–102.

Rossman, D. A., and R. Powell
1985   *Clonophis, C. kirtlandii*. Catalog. Amer. Amphib. Rept. 364:1–2.

Rossman, D. A., and L. D. Wilson
1965   Comments on the revival of the colubrid snake subfamily Heterodontinae. Herpetologica 20:284–285.

Rossman, N. J., D. A. Rossman, and N. K. Keith
1982   Comparative visceral topography of the New World snake tribe Thamnophiini (Colubridae, Natricinae). Tulane Stud. Zool. Bot. 23:123–164.

Rothman, N.
1961   Mud, rainbow and black swamp snakes in captivity. Bull. Philadelphia Herpetol. Soc. 9(3):17–20.

Roze, J. A.
1967   A check list of the New World venomous coral snakes (Elapidae), with descriptions of new forms. Amer. Mus. Novitates (2287):1–60.

1982   New World coral snakes (Elapidae): a taxonomic and biological summary. Mem. Inst. Butantan 46:305–338.

Roze, J. A., and G. M. Tilger
1983   *Micrurus fulvius*. Catalog. Amer. Amphib. Rept. 316:1–4.

Ruben, J. A.
1976   Aerobic and anaerobic metabolism during activity in snakes. J. Comp. Physiol. 109:147–157.
1983   Mineralized tissues and exercise physiology of snakes. Amer. Zool. 23:377–381.

Ruben, J. A., and C. Geddes
1983   Some morphological correlates of striking in snakes. Copeia 1983:221–225.

Rundquist, E. M.
1981   Longevity records at the Oklahoma City Zoo. Herp Review 12:87.

Russell, F. E.
1983   Snake venom poisoning. Scholium Intern., Inc., Great Neck, New York. 562 p.

Ruthven, A. G.
1904   Butler's garter snake. Biol. Bull. 7:289–299.
1908   Variations and genetic relationships of the garter-snakes. Bull. U.S. Natl. Mus. (61):1–201.
1912   On the breeding habits of Butler's garter-snake. Biol. Bull. 24:18–20.
1915   The gestation period of *Thamnophis butleri* (Cope). Copeia (15):3–4.

Ruthven, A. G., C. Thompson, and H. T. Gaige
1928   The herpetology of Michigan. Univ. Mus., Univ. Michigan Handb. Ser. (3):1–228.

Sabath, M. D., and L. E. Sabath
1969   Morphological intergradation in Gulf coastal brown snakes, *Storeria dekayi* and *Storeria tropica*. Amer. Midl. Natur. 81:148–155.

Sabath, M., and R. Worthington
1959   Eggs and young of certain Texas reptiles. Herpetologica 15:31–32.

Saiff, E.
1975   Preglottal structures in the snake family Colubridae. Copeia 1975:589–592.

Sajdak, R. A.
1978   *Carphophis amoenis vermis* (Western Worm Snake). U. S. A. Wisconsin. Herp Review 9:62.

Sanders, A. E.
1966   The reptiles of Columbia, S. C. and vicinity. Columbia Sci. Mus. Quart. Summer 1966:1–36.

Sanders, J. S., and J. S. Jacob
1981   Thermal ecology of the copperhead (*Agkistrodon contortrix*). Herpetologica 37:264–270.

Sattler, P. W., and S. I. Guttman
1976   An electrophoretic analysis of *Thamnophis sirtalis* from western Ohio. Copeia 1976:352–356.

Saul, D. W.
1968   An unusual hognose snake from Blount Island, Duval County, Florida. Bull. Maryland Herpetol. Soc. 4:21–22.

Say, T.
1823*   *In* Edwin James Account of an expedition from Pittsburgh to the Rocky Mountains, performed in the years 1819, 1820. Vol. 1. Longman, Hurst, Rees, Ovme, and Brown, London. 344 p.
1825*   Descriptions of three new species of *Coluber* inhabiting the United States. J. Acad. Natur. Sci. Philadelphia (1)4:237–241.

Schaefer, N.
1976   The mechanism of venom transfer from the venom duct to the fang in snakes. Herpetologica 32:71–76.

Schaefer, W. H.
1934   Diagnosis of sex in snakes. Copeia 1934:181.

Schaeffer, G. C.
1969   Sex independent ground color in the timber rattlesnake, *Crotalus horridus horridus*. Herpetologica 25:65–66.

Schatti, B., and L. D. Wilson
1986   *Coluber*. Catalog. Amer. Amphib. Rept. 399:1–4.

Schlauch, F. C.
1967   The snakes of Long Island. HERP: Bull. New York Herpetol. Soc. 3(2):28–30.
1970   A brood of eastern garter snakes from a specimen collected at the Montauk region of Long Island. Engelhardtia 3(1):11.
1975   Agonistic behavior in a suburban Long Island population of the smooth green snake, *Opheodrys vernalis*. Engelhardtia 6:25–26.

Schlegel, H.
1837*   Essai sur la physionomie des serpens. Kips and Van Stockum, La Hagae. Partie generale. 314 p., Partie descriptive. 606 p.

Schmidt, K. P.
1928   Notes on American coral snakes. Bull. Antivenin Inst. Amer. 2(3):63–64.
1932   Stomach contents of some American coral snakes, with the description of a new species of *Geophis*. Copeia 1932:6–9.
1953   A check list of North American amphibians and reptiles, 6th ed. Amer. Soc. Ichthyol. Herpetol., Chicago. 280 p.

Schmidt, K. P., and D. D. Davis
1941   Field book of snakes of the United States and Canada. Putnam, New York. 322 p.

Schmidt, K. P., and R. F. Inger
1957   Living reptiles of the world. Hanover House, Garden City, New York. 287 p.

Schroder, R. C.
1950   Hibernation of blue racers and bull snakes in western Illinois. Natur. Hist. Misc. (75):1–2.

Schueler, F. W.
1975   Notes on garter snake (*Thamnophis sirtalis*) spring mortality and behaviour at Long Point, Ontario. Ontario Field Biol. 29:45–49.

Schuett, G. W.
1982   A copperhead (*Agkistrodon contortrix*) brood produced from autumn copulations. Copeia 1982:700–702.

Schuett, G. W., D. L. Clark, and F. Kraus
1984   Feeding mimicry in the rattlesnake *Sistrurus catenatus*, with comments on the evolution of the rattle. Anim. Behav. 32:625–626.

Schwaner, T. D., and H. C. Dessauer
1982   Comparative immunodiffusion survey of snake transferrins focused on the relationships of the natricines. Copeia 1982:541–549.

Schwaner, T. D., and R. H. Mount
1976   Systematic and ecological relationships of the water snakes *Natrix sipedon* and *N. fasciata* in Alabama and the Florida Panhandle. Occ. Pap. Mus. Natur. Hist. Univ. Kansas (45):1–44.

Schwartz, A.
1953   A new subspecies of crowned snake (*Tantilla coronata*) from the southern Appalachian Mountains. Herpetologica 9:153–157.

Scott, D.
1986   Notes on the eastern hognose snake, *Heterodon platyrhinos* Latreille (Squamata: Colubridae), on a Virginia barrier island. Brimleyana (12):51–55.

Scott, N. J., Jr. (Ed.)
1982   Herpetological communities. U. S. Dept. Int., Fish Wildl. Serv. Wildlife Res. Rept. (13):1–239.

Scudder, K. M., N. J. Stewart, and H. M. Smith
1980   Response of neonate water snakes (*Nerodia sipedon sipedon*) to conspecific chemical cues. J. Herpetol. 14:196–198.

Scudder, R. M., and G. M. Burghardt
1983   A comparative study of defensive behavior in three sympatric species of water snakes (*Nerodia*). Z. Tierpsychol. 63:17–26.

Scudder, S.
1972   Observations on snakes in the burrows of mole crickets. Bull. Maryland Herpetol. Soc. 8:95.

Secor, S. M.
1983   *Lampropeltis getulus holbrooki* (speckled kingsnake). Reproduction. Herp Review 14:20.

Secoy, D. M.
1979   Investigatory behaviour of plains garter snakes, *Thamnophis radix* (Reptilia: Colubridae), in tests of repellant chemicals. Can. J. Zool. 57:691–693.

Seibert, H. C.
1950   Population density of snakes in an area near Chicago. Copeia 1950:229–230.
1965   A snake hibernaculum uncovered in midwinter. J. Ohio Herpetol. Soc. 5:29.

Seibert, H. C., and C. W. Hagen
1947　Studies on a population of snakes in Illinois. Copeia 1947:6–22.

Seidel, M. E., and R. G. Lindeborg
1973　Lags in metabolic response to temperature of two garter snakes, *Thamnophis elegans* and *Thamnophis radix*. Herpetologica 29:358–360.

Seigel, R. A.
1986　Ecology and conservation of an endangered rattlesnake, *Sistrurus catenatus*, in Missouri, U. S. A. Biol. Conserv. 35:333–346.

Seigel, R. A., and H. S. Fitch
1984　Ecological patterns of relative clutch mass in snakes. Oecologia (Berlin) 61:293–301.
1985　Annual variation in reproduction in snakes in a fluctuating environment. J. Anim. Ecol. 54:497–505.

Seigel, R. A., H. S. Fitch, and N. B. Ford
1986　Variation in relative clutch mass in snakes among and within species. Herpetologica 42:179–185.

Semlitsch, R. D.
1979　The influence of temperature in ecdysis rates in snakes (genus *Natrix*) (Reptilia, Serpentes, Colubridae). J. Herpetol. 13:212–214.

Semlitsch, R. D., K. L. Brown, and J. P. Caldwell
1981　Habitat utilization, seasonal activity, and population size structure of the southeastern crowned snake *Tantilla coronata*. Herpetologica 37:40–46.

Semlitsch, R. D., and J. W. Gibbons
1978　Reproductive allocations in the brown water snake, *Natrix taxispilota*. Copeia 1978:721–723.
1982　Body size dimorphism and sexual selection in two species of water snakes. Copeia 1982:974–976.

Semlitsch, R. D., and G. B. Moran
1984　Ecology of the redbelly snake (*Storeria occipitomaculata*) using mesic habitats in South Carolina. Amer. Midl. Natur. 111:33–40.

Sexton, O. J.
1979　Remarks on defensive behavior of hognose snakes, *Heterodon*. Herp Review 10:86–87.

Sexton, O. J., and L. Claypool
1978　Nest sites of a northern population of an oviparous snake, *Opheodrys vernalis* (Serpentes, Colubridae). J. Natur. Hist. 12:365–370.

Sexton, O. J., and S. R. Hunt
1980　Temperature relationships and movements of snakes (*Elaphe obsoleta, Coluber constrictor*) in a cave hibernaculum. Herpetologica 36:20–26.

Sexton, O. J., N. Shannon, and S. Shannon
1976　Late season hatching success of *Elaphe o. obsoleta*. Herp Review 7:171.

Shaw, C. E.
1948　The male combat "dance" of some crotalid snakes. Herpetologica 4:137–145.
1951　Male combat in American colubrid snakes with remarks on combat in other colubrid and elapid snakes. Herpetologica 7:149–168.
1971　The coral snakes, genera *Micrurus* and *Micruroides* of the United States and northern Mexico, p. 157–172. *In* W. Buecherl and E. E. Buckley (Eds.) Venomous animals and their venoms. Vol. 2. Venomous vertebrates. Academic Press, New York.

Shaw, C. E., and S. Campbell
1974　Snakes of the American West. Alfred A. Knopf, New York. 332 p.

Shaw, G.
1802*　General zoology or systematic natural history. London. 3(2):1–615.

Sheffield, L. P., J. H. Law, and G. M. Burghardt
1968　On the nature of chemical food sign stimuli for new born snakes. Comm. Behav. Biol. A 2:7–12.

Shields, F. B.
1929　Note on the young of *Storeria dekayi*. Copeia (171):52–54.

Shoop, R.
1957　Eggs and young of the prairie king snake, *Lampropeltis c. calligaster*. Copeia 1957:48–49.

Shuette, B.
1978　Two black rat snakes from one egg. Herp Review 9:92.

Simmons, R. S., and C. J. Stine
1961　Ankylosis and xanthism in the eastern worm snake. Herpetologica 17:206–208.

Simonson, W. E.
1951   Courtship and mating of the foxsnake, *Elaphe vulpina vulpina*. Copeia 1951:309.

Sinclair, R. M.
1951   Notes on Tennessee snakes of the genus *Haldea*. Herpetologica 7:145.

Sinclair, R., W. Hon, and R. B. Ferguson
1965   Amphibians and reptiles of Tennessee. Tennessee Game Fish Comm., Nashville. 29 p.

Sisk, M. E., and C. J. McCoy
1963   Stomach contents of *Natrix r. rhombifera* (Reptiles: Serpentes) from an Oklahoma lake. Proc. Oklahoma Acad. Sci. 44:68–71.

Slevin, J. R.
1951   A high birth rate for *Natrix sipedon sipedon* (Linne). Herpetologica 7:132.

Skehan, P., Jr.
1960   Feeding notes on captive reptiles. Herpetologica 16:32.

Smith, A. G.
1945   The status of *Thamnophis butleri* Cope, and a redescription of *Thamnophis brachystoma* (Cope). Proc. Biol. Soc. Washington 58:147–154.
1946   Notes on the secondary sex characters of *Thamnophis ruthveni*. Copeia 1946:106.
1947   Navel closure time and age in the young of *Thamnophis radix*. Herpetologica 3:153–154.
1948   Intergradation in worm snakes (*Carphophis*) from Kentucky. Natur. Hist. Misc. (18);1–3.
1949   The subspecies of the plains garter snake, *Thamnophis radix*. Bull. Chicago Acad. Sci. 8:285–300.

Smith, A. K.
1975   Incidence of tail coiling in a population of ringneck snakes (*Diadophis punctatus*). Trans. Kansas Acad. Sci. 77:237–238.

Smith, C. R.
1977   Food resource partitioning of burrowing sand–pine scrub reptiles. Herp Review 8(3)suppl.:17.

Smith, D. D.
1975   Death feigning by the western coachwhip snake. Herp Review 6:126.

Smith, G. C.
1976   Ecological energetics of three species of ectothermic vertebrates. Ecology 57:252–264.

Smith, G. C., and D. Watson
1972   Selection patterns of corn snakes, *Elaphe guttata*, of different phenotypes of the house mouse, *Mus musculus*. Copeia 1972:529–532.

Smith, H. M.
1938   A review of the snake genus *Farancia*. Copeia 1938:110–117.
1952   A revised arrangement of maxillary fangs of snakes. Turtox News 30:214–218.
1956   Handbook of amphibians and reptiles of Kansas. Univ. Kansas. Mus. Natur. Hist. Misc. Publ. 2nd ed. (9):1–356.

Smith, H. M., and D. Chiszar
1981   An observation on winter emergence of a garter snake, *Thamnophis radix*. Bull. Maryland Herpetol. Soc. 17:107–109.

Smith, H. M., and H. K. Gloyd
1963   Nomenclatural notes on the snake names *Scytale*, *Boa scytale*, and *Agkistrodon mokasen*. Herpetologica 19:280–282.

Smith, H. M., and J. E. Huheey
1960   The watersnake genus *Regina*. Trans. Kansas Acad. Sci. 63:156–164.

Smith, H. M., and F. N. White
1955   Adrenal enlargement and its significance in the hognose snakes (*Heterodon*). Herpetologica 11:137–144.

Smith, P. W.
1956a   The geographical distribution and constancy of the *semifasciata* pattern in the eastern garter snake. Herpetologica 12:81–84.
1956b   A blotch–count gradient in snakes. Herpetologica 12:156–160.
1961   The amphibians and reptiles of Illinois. Illinois Natur. Hist. Surv. Bull. 28:1–298.

Smith, P. W., and L. M. Page
1972   Repeated mating of a copperhead and timber rattlesnake. Herp Review 4:196.

Smith, P. W., and H. M. Smith
1962   The systematic and biogeographic status of two Illinois snakes. Occ. Pap. C. C. Adams Cent. Ecol. Stud. (5):1–10.

1963   The systematic status of the lined snakes of Iowa. Proc. Biol. Soc. Washington 76:297–304.

1975   Innate recognition of coral snake pattern by a possible avian predator. Science 4178:759–760.

Smith, S. M., and A. M. Mostrom
1985   "Coral snake" rings: are they helpful in foraging? Copeia 1985:384–387.

Snellings, E. Jr.
1982   The pigmy rattlesnake: petite but not passive. Florida Natur. 55(2)12–13.

Snyder, D. H.
1972   Amphibians and reptiles of Land Between the Lakes. Tennessee Valley Auth. 90 p.

Snyder, D. H., D. F. Burchfield, and R. W. Nall
1967   First records of the pigmy rattlesnake in Kentucky. Herpetologica 23:240–241.

Sonnini de Manoncourt, C. N. S., and P. A. Latreille.
1801*   Histoire naturelle des reptiles, avec figures dessinees d'apres nature. Chez Deterville, Paris. Vol. 3, 335 p.

Spangler, J. A., and R. H. Mount
1969   The taxonomic status of the natricine snake *Regina septemvittata mabila* (Neill). Herpetologica 25:113–119.

Spaur, R. C., and H. M. Smith
1971   Adrenal enlargement in the hognosed snake *Heterodon platyrhinos*. J. Herpetol. 5:197–199.

Spencer, R. D.
1915   New color variation of *Storeria occipitomaculata*. Copeia (18):7.

Speake, D. W., J. Diemer, and J. McGlincy
1982   Eastern indigo snake recovery plan. U. S. Fish Wildl. Serv., Atlanta, Georgia. 23 p.

Speake, D. W., and R. H. Mount
1973   Some possible ecological effects of "Rattlesnake Roundups" in the southeastern coastal plain. Proc. 27th Ann. Conf. S. E. Assoc. Game Fish Comm. 1973:267–277.

Stabler, R. M.
1939   Frequency of skin shedding in snakes. Copeia 1939:227–229.

Stadelman, R. E.
1929a   Some venom extraction records. Bull. Antivenin Inst. Amer. 3:29.

1929b   Further notes on the venom of newborn copperheads. Bull. Antivenin Inst. Amer. 3:81.

Stebbins, R. C.
1985   A field guide to western reptiles and amphibians. 2nd ed. Houghton Mifflin Co., Boston. 336 p.

Stechert, R.
1980   Observations on northern snake dens. HERP: Bull. New York Herpetol. Soc. 15:7–14.

1981   Historical depletion of timber rattlesnake colonies in New York state. HERP: Bull. New York Herpetol. Soc. 17:23–24.

Steehouder, A. M.
1983   Breeding results. *Thamnophis radix butleri* x *Thamnophis sirtalis parietalis*. Litteratura Serpentium 3:169–170.

Stejneger, L.
1898   The poisonous snakes of North America. Smithsonian Inst. Report 1898:338–487.

1903a   A new hognose snake from Florida. Proc. Biol. Soc. Washington 16:123–124.

1903b* The reptiles of the Huachua Mountains, Arizona. Proc. U. S. Natl. Mus. 25:149–158.

Stewart, G. R.
1965   Thermal ecology of the garter snakes *Thamnophis sirtalis concinnus* (Hallowell) and *Thamnophis ordinoides* (Baird and Girard). Herpetologica 21:81–102.

Stewart, J. R., and R. E. Castillo
1984   Nutritional provision of the yolk of two species of viviparous reptiles. Physiol. Zool. 57:377–383.

Stewart, M. M.
1961　Biology of the Allegheny Indian Reservation and vicinity. Part 3. The amphibians, reptiles and mammals. Bull. New York St. Mus. (383):63–97.

Stewart, M. M., G. E. Larson, and T. H. Mathews
1960　Morphological variation in a litter of timber rattlesnakes. Copeia 1960:366–367.

Stewart, P. A.
1981　Female wood duck apparently killed by black rat snake. Chat 45:97.

Stickel, L. F., W. H. Stickel, and F. C. Schmid
1980　Ecology of a Maryland population of black rat snakes (*Elaphe o. obsoleta*). Amer. Midl. Natur. 103:1–14.

Stickel, W. H., and J. B. Cope
1947　The home ranges and wanderings of snakes. Copeia 1947:127–136.

Stille, W. T.
1954　Observations on the reproduction and distribution of the green snake, *Opheodrys vernalis* (Harlan). Natur. Hist. Misc. (127):1–11.

Stirnberg, E., and W. Broer
1984　Pflege und Zucht der grossten Nordamerikanischen Schlange: *Drymarchon corais couperi* (Holbrook, 1842) (Serpentes: Colubridae). Salamandra 20:197–204.

Stokes, G. D., and W. A. Dunson
1982　Permeability and chemical structure of reptilian skin. Amer. J. Physiol. 242:F681–F689.

Storer, D. H.
1839*　Reptiles of Massachusetts. Repts. Comm. Zool. Survey Massachusetts: 203–253.

Strecker, J. K.
1926　On the habits of southern snakes. Contrib. Baylor Univ. Mus. 4:1–11.
1927　Observations on the food habits of Texas amphibians and reptiles. Copeia (162):6–9.

Stubbs, T. H.
1979　Moccasin. Florida Natur. 52(4):2–4.

Stull, O. G.
1940　Variations and relationships in the snakes of the genus *Pituophis*. Bull. U. S. Natl. Mus. (175):1–225.

Sullivan, B.
1967　Oxygenation properties of snake hemoglobin. Science 157:1308–1310.

Sullivan, B. K.
1981　Observed differences in body temperature and associated behavior of four snake species. J. Herpetol. 15:245–246.

Surface, H. A.
1906　The serpents of Pennsylvania. Bull. Pennsylvania State Dept. Agric. Div. Zool. (4):133–208.

Sutherland, I. D. W.
1958　The "combat dance" of the timber rattlesnake. Herpetologica 14:23–24.

Swain, T. A., and H. M. Smith
1978　Communal nesting in *Coluber constrictor* in Colorado (Reptilia: Serpentes). Herpetologica 34:175–177.

Swanson, P. L.
1933　The size of *Sistrurus catenatus catenatus* at birth. Copeia 1933:37.
1948　*Natrix sipedon compressicauda* at Key West, Florida. Herpetologica 4:105–106.
1952　The reptiles of Venango County, Pennsylvania. Amer. Midl. Natur. 47:161–182.

Sweet, S. S.
1985　Geographic variation, convergent crypsis and mimicry in gopher snakes (*Pituophis melanoleucus*) and western rattlesnakes (*Crotalus viridis*). J. Herpetol. 19:55–67.

Swenson, L. E.
1950　Food of captive western hog-nosed snakes. J. Colorado–Wyoming Acad. Sci. 4:74–75.

Taub, A. M.
1967　Comparative histological studies of Duvernoy's gland of colubrid snakes. Bull. Amer. Mus. Natur. Hist. 138:1–50.

Taylor, B. M., and P. M. C. Davies
1981　Changes in the weight dependence of metabolism during the sloughing cycle of the snake *Thamnophis sirtalis parietalis*. Comp. Biochem. Physiol. 69A:113–119.

Telford, S. R.
1948   A large litter of *Natrix* in Florida. Herpetologica 4:184.

Telford, S. R., Jr.
1952   A herpetological survey in the vicinity of Lake Shipp, Polk County, Florida. Qt. J. Florida Acad. Sci. 15:175–185.
1955   A description of the eggs of the coral snake *Micrurus f. fulvius*. Copeia 1955:258.
1966*   Variation among the southeastern crowned snakes, genus *Tantilla*. Bull. Florida St. Mus. Biol. Sci. 10:261–304.
1980a   *Tantilla oolitica*. Catalog. Amer. Amphib. Rept. 256:1.
1980b   *Tantilla relicta*. Catalog. Amer. Amphib. Rept. 257:1–2.
1982   *Tantilla coronata*. Catalog. Amer. Amphib. Rept. 308:1–2.

Test, F. H.
1958   Butler's garter snake eats amphibian. Copeia 1958:151.

Thomas, R. A., and J. R. Dixon
1976   Scale row formulae in *Elaphe guttata* (Linnaeus) and notes on their interpretation. Natur. Hist. Misc. (195):1–5.

Thomas, R. A., and F. S. Hendricks
1976   Letisimulation in *Virginia striatula* (Linnaeus). Southwest. Natur. 21:123–124.

Tinkle, D. W.
1951   Peculiar behavior of indigo snakes in captivity. Copeia 1951:77–78.
1957   Ecology, maturation and reproduction of *Thamnophis sauritus proximus*. Ecology 38:69–77.
1959   Observations of reptiles and amphibians in a Louisiana swamp. Amer. Midl. Natur. 62:189–205.
1960   A population of *Opheodrys aestivus* (Reptilia: Squamata). Copeia 1960:29–34.

Tinkle, D. W., and E. A. Liner
1955   Behavior of *Natrix* in aggregations. Field & Lab. 23:84–87.

Todd, R. E., Jr.
1973   The cottonmouth in Kentucky. Kentucky Herpetol. 4(2–4):5–9.

Tomkins, J. R.
1965   Swallow–tailed kite and snake: an unusual encounter. Wilson Bull. 77:294.

Trapido, H.
1937   The snakes of New Jersey: a guide. Newark Mus. 60 p.
1939   Parturition in the timber rattlesnake, *Crotalus horridus horridus* Linne. Copeia 1939:230.
1940   Mating time and sperm viability in *Storeria*. Copeia 1940:107–109.
1944*   The snakes of the genus *Storeria*. Amer. Midl. Natur. 31:1–84.

Trauth, S. E.
1982a   *Cemophora coccinea* (scarlet snake). Reproduction. Herp Review 13:126.
1982b   *Ambystoma maculatum* (Ambystomidae) in the diet of *Heterodon platyrhinos* (Colubridae) from northern Arkansas. Southwest. Natur. 27:230.
1983   *Lampropeltis calligaster* (prairie kingsnake). Predation. Herp Review 14:74.

Treadwell, R. W.
1962   Time and sequence of appearance of certain gross structures in *Pituophis melanoleucus sayi* embryos. Herpetologica 18:120–124.

Trinco, L. A., and H. M. Smith
1971   The karyology of ophidians: a review. Trans. Kansas Acad. Sci. 74:138–146.

Triplehorn, C. A.
1955   Notes on the young of some North American reptiles. Copeia 1955:248–249.

Troost, G.
1836*   On a new genus of serpents, and two new species of the genus *Heterodon*, inhabiting Tennessee. Ann. Lyc. Natur. Hist. New York 3:174–190.

Tryon, B. W.
1984   Additional instances of multiple egg-clutch production in snakes. Trans. Kansas Acad. Sci. 87:98–104.

Tryon, B. W., and G. Carl
1980   Reproduction in the male kingsnake, *Lampropeltis calligaster rhombomaculata* (Serpentes, Colubridae). Trans. Kansas Acad. Sci. 83:66–73.

Tryon, B. W., and H. K. McCrystal
1982   *Micrurus fulvius tenere* reproduction. Herp Review 13:47–48.

Tryon, B. W., and J. B. Murphy
1982   Miscellaneous notes on the reproductive biology of reptiles. 5. Thirteen varieties of the genus *Lampropeltis*, species *mexicana*, *triangulum* and *zonata*. Trans. Kansas Acad. Sci. 85:96–119.

Tschambers, B.
1948   Feeding of the mud snake, *Farancia abacura reinwardtii*, in captivity. Herpetologica 4:210.
1950   Number of young of *Liodytes alleni*. Herpetologica 6:48.

Tsui, H. W., and P. Licht
1974   Pituitary independence of sperm storage in male snakes. Gen. Comp. Endocr. 22:277–279.

Tu, A. T., and B. L. Adams
1968   Phylogenetic relationships among venomous snakes of the genus *Agkistrodon* from Asia and the North American continent. Nature 217:760–762.

Tuck, R. G., Jr., M. K. Klimkiewicz, and K. C. Ferris
1971   Notes on pilot blacksnake (*Elaphe obsoleta obsoleta*) (Serpentes: Colubridae) eggs and hatchlings. Bull. Maryland Herpetol. Soc. 7:96–99.

Tucker, J. K.
1976   Observations on the birth of a brood of Kirtland's water snake, *Clonophis kirtlandi* (Kennicott) (Reptilia, Serpentes, Colubridae). J. Herpetol. 10:53–54.
1977   Notes on the food habits of Kirtland's water snake, *Clonophis kirtlandi*. Bull. Maryland Herpetol. Soc. 13:193–195.

Uhler, F. M., C. Cottam, and T. E. Clarke
1939   Food of snakes of the George Washington National Forest, Virginia. Trans. 4th North American Wildl. Conf.:605–622.

Underwood, G.
1967   A contribution to the classification of snakes. Publ. British Mus. Natur. Hist. (653):1–179.

Vaeth, R. H.
1984   A note on courtship and copulatory behavior in *Micrurus fulvius*. Bull. Chicago Herpetol. Soc. 18:86–88.

Vagvolgyi, A., and M. Halpern
1983   Courtship behavior in garter snakes: effects of artificial hibernation. Can. J. Zool. 61:1171–1174.

Vance, T.
1981   *Heterodon platyrhinos* (eastern hognose snake). U. S. A.: Arkansas. Herp Review 12:14.

Van Duyn, G.
1937   Snakes that "play possum." Nature Mag. 29:215–217.

Van Heerden, J. A.
1978   Een onderzoek naar dominantiegedreg bij slangen aan *Thamnophis sirtalis*. Lacerta 36:143–144.

Van Hyning, O. C.
1931   Reproduction of some Florida snakes. Copeia 1931:59–60.
1932   Food of some Florida snakes. Copeia 1932:37.

Varkey, A.
1979   Comparative cranial myology of North American natricine snakes. Publ. Biol. Geol. Milwaukee Publ. Mus (4):1–70.

Vial, J. L., T. L. Berger, and W. T. McWilliams, Jr.
1977   Quantitative demography of copperheads, *Agkistrodon contortrix* (Serpentes: Viperidae). Res. Popul. Ecol. Kyoto Univ. 18:223–234.

Vincent, T. K., and D. M. Secoy
1978   The effects of annual variation in temperature on cold resistance in a northern population of the red–sided garter snake, *Thamnophis sirtalis parietalis* (Reptilia, Serpentes, Colubridae). J. Herpetol. 12:291–194.

Viosca, P., Jr.
1926   A snake tragedy. Copeia (151):109.

Vogt, R. C.
1981   Natural history of amphibians and reptiles of Wisconsin. Milwaukee Public Mus., Milwaukee, Wisconsin. 205 p.

Voohies, M. R., and R. G. Corner
1977   The hognose snake: a prairie survivor for ten million years. Mus. Notes, Univ. Nebraska St. Mus. (57):1–4.

Vosburgh, K. M., P. S. Brady, and D. E. Ullrey
1982   Ascorbic acid requirements of garter snakes: plains (*Thamnophis radix*) and eastern (*Thamnophis sirtalis*). J. Zoo Anim. Med. 13:38–42.

Wagner, E.
1979   Breeding kingsnakes. Inter. Zoo Yrkb. 19:98–100.
1982   The genetics of pigmentation in the corn snake, *Elaphe guttata*. Herptile 7:23–27.

Wagner, R. T.
1962   Notes on the combat dance in *Crotalus adamanteus*. Bull. Philadelphia Herpetol. Soc. 10(1):7–8.

Waide, R. B., and R. Thomas
1984   Aggression between two *Drymarchon corais melanurus* in Campeche, Mexico. Herp Review 15:10.

Walker, D. J.
1963   Notes on broods of *Virginia v. valeriae* Baird & Girard in Ohio. J. Ohio Herpetol. Soc. 4:54.

Walker, J. M.
1963   Amphibians and reptiles of Jackson Parish, Louisiana. Proc. Louisiana Acad. Sci. 26:91–101.

Wall, F.
1921   Snakes of Ceylon. Gov. Printer, Colombo. 581 p.

Walley, H. D.
1963   The rattlesnake, *Crotalus horridus horridus*, in north–central Illinois. Herpetologica 19:216.

Weatherhead, P. J., and M. B. Charland
1985   Habitat selection in an Ontario population of the snake, *Elaphe obsoleta*. J. Herpetol. 19:12–19.

Weaver, W. G.
1965   The cranial anatomy of the hog-nosed snakes (*Heterodon*). Bull. Florida St. Mus. Biol. Sci. 9:275–304.

Wehekind, L.
1955   Notes on the foods of the Trinidad snakes. British J. Herpetol. 2:9–13.

Weigel, R. D.
1962   Fossil vertebrates of Vero, Florida. Florida Geol. Surv. Spl. Publ. (10):1–59.

Weil, M. R.
1982   Seasonal effects of mammalian gonadotropins (bFSH and bLH) on plasma androgen levels in male water snakes, *Nerodia sipedon*. Comp. Biochem. Physiol. 73A:73–76.
1984   Seasonal histochemistry of the renal sexual segment in male common water snakes, *Nerodia sipedon* (L.). Can. J. Zool. 62:1737–1740.
1985   Comparison of plasma and testicular testosterone levels during the active season in the common garter snake, *Thamnophis sirtalis* (L.). Comp. Biochem. Physiol. 81A:585–587.

Weil, M. R., and R. D. Aldridge
1979   The effect of temperature on the male reproductive system of the common water snake (*Nerodia sipedon*). J. Exp. Zool. 210:327–332.
1981   Seasonal androgenesis in the male water snake, *Nerodia sipedon*. Gen. Comp. Endocr. 44:44–53.

Weldon, P. J.
1982   Responses to ophiophagous snakes by snakes of the genus *Thamnophis*. Copeia 1982:788–794.

Weldon, P. J., and F. M. Schell
1984   Responses of king snakes (*Lampropeltis getulus*) to chemicals from colubrid and crotaline snakes. J. Chem. Ecol. 10:1509–1520.

Wells, K. E., H. M. Smith, and R. C. Spaur
1971   Correlations of certain ophidian sensory modalities with gross brain proportions. J. Herpetol. 5:200–204.

Wellstead, C. F.
1981   Behavioral observations in bullsnakes. Herp Review 12:6.

Wendelken, P. W.
1978   On prey-specific hunting behavior in the western ribbon snake, *Thamnophis proximus*. (Reptilia, Serpentes, Colubridae). J. Herpetol. 12:577–578.

Werler, J. E.
1951   Miscellaneous notes on the eggs and young of Texan and Mexican reptiles. Zoologica 36:37–48.

Werler, J. E., and D. M. Darling
1950   A case of poisoning from the bite of a coral snake, *Micrurus f. tenere* Baird and Girard. Herpetologica 6:197–199.

BIBLIOGRAPHY

Wharton, C. H.
1960   Birth and behavior of a brood of cottonmouths, *Agkistrodon piscivorus piscivorus*, with notes on tail–luring. Herpetologica 16:125–129.

1966   Reproduction and growth in the cottonmouths, *Agkistrodon piscivorus* Lacepede, of Cedar Keys, Florida. Copeia 1966:149–161.

1969   The cottonmouth moccasin on Sea Horse Key, Florida. Bull. Florida St. Mus. Biol. Sci. 14:227–272.

Wheeler, W. E.
1984   Duck egg predation by fox snakes in Wisconsin. Wildlife Soc. Bull. 12:77–78.

White, A. M.
1979   An unusually large brood of northern copperheads (*Agkistrodon contortrix mokeson*) from Ohio. Ohio J. Sci. 79:78.

White, D. R., J. C. Mitchell, and W. S. Woolcott
1982   Reproductive cycle and embryonic development of *Nerodia taxispilota* (Serpentes: Colubridae) at the northwestern edge of its range. Copeia 1982:646–652.

Whitt, A. L., Jr.
1970   Some mechanisms with which *Crotalus horridus horridus* responds to stimuli. Trans. Kentucky Acad. Sci. 31:45–48.

Wickler, W.
1968   Mimicry in plants and animals. McGraw–Hill, New York. 255 p.

Willard, D. E.
1967   Evidence for toxic saliva in *Rhadinaea flavilata* (the yellow lipped snake). Herpetologica 23:238.

Williams, F. R.
1953   Note on the anatomy and feeding habits of a pilot blacksnake. Maryland Natur. 22:23–24.

Williams, K. L.
1978   Systematics and natural history of the American milk snake, *Lampropeltis triangulum*. Milwaukee Public Mus. Publ. Biol. Geol. (2):1–258.

1985   *Cemophora, C. coccinea*. Catalog. Amer. Amphib. Rept. 374:1–4.

Williams, K. L., and L. D. Wilson
1967   A review of the colubrid snake genus *Cemophora* Cope. Tulane Stud. Zool. 13(4):103–124.

Williams, P. R., Jr., and I. L. Brisbin, Jr.
1978   Responses of captive–reared eastern kingsnakes (*Lampropeltis getulus*) to several prey odor stimuli. Herpetologica 34:79–83.

Willard, D. E.
1977   Constricting methods of snakes. Copeia 1977:379–382.

Willis, L., S. T. Threlkeld, and C. C. Carpenter
1982   Tail loss patterns in *Thamnophis* (Reptilia: Colubridae) and the probable fate of injured individuals. Copeia 1982:98–101.

Wilson, A. B., and S. A. Minton
1983   *Agkistrodon piscivorus leucostoma* (western cottonmouth). U. S. A., Indiana. Herp Reveiw 14:84.

Wilson, L. D.
1970a   The coachwhip snake, *Masticophis flagellum* (Shaw): taxonomy and distribution. Tulane Stud. Zool. Bot. 16:31–99.

1970b*   The racer *Coluber constrictor* (Serpentes: Colubridae) in Louisiana and eastern Texas. Texas J. Sci. 22:67–85.

1973a   *Masticophis*. Catalog. Amer. Amphib. Rept. 144:1–2.

1973b   *Masticophis flagellum*. Catalog. Amer. Amphib. Rept. 145:1–4.

1978   *Coluber constrictor*. Catalog. Amer. Amphib. Rept. 218:1–4.

1982   *Tantilla*. Catalog. Amer. Amphib. Rept. 307:1–4.

Wilson, L. D., and L. Porras
1983   The ecological impact of man on the South Florida herpetofauna. Univ. Kansas Mus. Natur. Hist., Spec. Publ. (9):1–89.

Wilson, V.
1951   Some notes on a captive scarlet snake. Herpetologica 7:172.

Wistrand, H. E.
1972   Predation on a snake by *Spermophilus tridecemlineatus*. Amer. Midl. Natur. 88:511–512.

Wittner, D.
1978   A discussion of venomous snakes of North America. HERP.: Bull. New York Herpetol. Soc. 14:12–17.

Wood, J. T.
1944   Fall aggregation of the queen snake. Copeia 1944:253.
1949   Observations on *Natrix septemvittata* (Say) in southwestern Ohio. Amer. Midl. Natur. 42:744–750.

Wood, J. T., and W. E. Duellman
1950   Size and scutellation in *Natrix septemvittata* in southwestern Ohio. Amer. Midl. Natur. 43:173–178.

Woolcott, W. B.
1959   Notes on the eggs and young of the scarlet snake, *Cemophora coccinea* Blumenbach. Copeia 1959:263.

Woolfenden, G. E.
1962   A range extension and subspecific relations of the short–tailed snake, *Stilosoma extenuatum*. Copeia 1962:648–649.

Wozniak, E. M., and R. C. Bothner
1966   Some ecological comparisons between *Thamnophis brachystoma* and *Thamnophis sirtalis sirtalis* on the Allegheny High Plateau. J. Ohio Herpetol. Soc. 5:164–165.

Wright, A. H., and A. A. Wright
1957   Handbook of snakes of the United States and Canada. Comstock Publ. Assoc., Ithaca, New York, Vols. I, II. 1105 p.
1962   Handbook of snakes of the United States and Canada. Vol. III. Bibliography. Edwards Brothers, Inc., Ann Arbor, Michigan. 179 p.

Wright, B. A.
1941   Habit and habitat studies of the massasauga rattlesnake (*Sistrurus catenatus catenatus* Raf.) in northeastern Illinois. Amer. Midl. Natur. 25:659–672.

Wright, R. H.
1965   A king snake dines on a sparrow egg. Natur. Hist. 74(3):50–51.

Wynn, A. H., C. J. Cole, and A. L. Gardner
1987   Apparent triploidy in the unisexual brahminy blind snake, *Ramphotyphlops braminus*. Amer. Mus. Novitates (2868):1–7.

Yarrow, H. C.
1882*   Descriptions of new species of reptiles and amphibians in the United States National Museum. Proc. U. S. Natl. Mus. 5:438–444.

Yeatman, H. C.
1983   *Virginia valeriae* (eastern smooth snake). Defense. Herp Review 14:22.

Young, R. A.
1973   Anthills as hibernating sites for *Opheodrys vernalis blanchardi*. Bull. Chicago Herpetol. Soc. 8:7.
1977   Notes on the Graham's water snake, *Regina grahami* Baird and Girard in DuPage County, Illinois. Bull. Chicago Herpetol. Soc. 8:4–5.

Zappalorti, R. T., and J. Burger
1985   On the importance of disturbed sites to habitat selection by pine snakes in the pine barrens of New Jersey. Environ. Conserv. 12:358–361.

Zappalorti, R. T., E. W. Johnson, and Z. Leszczynski
1983   The ecology of the northern pine snake, *Pituophis melanoleucus melanoleucus* (Daudin) (Reptilia, Serpentes, Colubridae) in southern New Jersey, with special notes on habitat and nesting behavior. Bull. Chicago Herpetol. Soc. 18:57–72.

Zaremba, T.
1978   A fox snake hibernaculum. Bull. Chicago Herpetol. Soc. 13:87–90.

Zegel, J. C.
1975   Notes on collecting and breeding the eastern coral snake, *Micrurus fulvius fulvius*. Bull. Southwest. Herpetol. Soc. 1:9–10.

Zehr, D. R.
1962   Stages in the normal development of the common garter snake, *Thamnophis sirtalis sirtalis*. Copeia 1962:322–329.
1969   Mating, ejaculate, egg laying and hatching of the fox snake, *Elaphe vulpina vulpina*. J. Herpetol. 3:180–181.

Zelnick, G. E.
1966   Midsummer feeding habits of the midland water snake. Southwest. Natur. 11:311–312.

Zillig, L. D.
1958   The status of *Haldea* Baird and Girard and *Virginia* Baird and Girard. Copeia 1958:152.

Zimmerman, A. A., and C. H. Pope
1948   Development and growth of the rattle of rattlesnakes. Fieldiana: Zool.
32:355–413.

Zimmerman, E. G., and C. W. Kilpatrick
1973   Karyology of North American
crotaline snakes (Family Viperidae)
of the genera *Agkistrodon*, *Sistrurus*,
and *Crotalus*. Can. J. Genet. Cytol.
15:389–395.

Zug, D. A., and W. A. Dunson
1979   Salinity preference in fresh water
and estuarine snakes (*Nerodia
sipedon* and *N. fasciata*). Florida
Sci. 42:1–8.

Zweifel, R.
1979   Breeding *Lampropeltis getulus*. Herpetology 10(2):6–7.

Zweifel, R. G., and H. C. Dessauer
1983   Multiple insemination demonstrated
experimentally in the kingsnake
(*Lampropeltis getulus*). Experientia
39:317–319.

Index